EXPLORING Life Science

Anthea Maton
Former NSTA National Coordinator
Project Scope, Sequence, Coordination
Washington, DC

Jean Hopkins
Science Instructor and Department Chairperson
John H. Wood Middle School
San Antonio, Texas

Susan Johnson
Professor of Biology
Ball State University
Muncie, Indiana

David LaHart
Senior Instructor
Florida Solar Energy Center
Cape Canaveral, Florida

Maryanna Quon Warner
Science Instructor
Del Dios Middle School
Escondido, California

Jill D. Wright
Professor of Science Education
Director of International Field Programs
University of Pittsburgh
Pittsburgh, Pennsylvania

 Prentice Hall
Upper Saddle River, New Jersey
Needham, Massachusetts

PRENTICE HALL
EXPLORING
Life Science

Student Text and Teacher's Edition	**Transparency Box**
Teaching Resources	**Computer Test Bank with**
Teacher's Desk Reference	**DIAL-A-TEST™ Service**
Classroom Manager	**Videos/Videodiscs**
Laboratory Manual and	**Level I Videodiscs**
Annotated Teacher's Edition	**Level III Interactive Videodiscs**
Integrated Science Activity Books	**Level III Interactive Videodiscs/CD-ROM**
Product Testing Activities	**Media Guide**

The illustration on the cover, rendered by Joseph Cellini, depicts a panda, which is a member of an endangered species.

Credits begin on page 880.

SECOND EDITION
©1997, 1995 by Prentice-Hall, Inc., a Viacom Company, Upper Saddle River, New Jersey 07458. All rights reserved. No part of this book may be reproduced or transmitted in any form or by any means, electronic or mechanical, including photocopying, recording, or by any information storage and retrieval system, without permission in writing from the publisher. Printed in the United States of America.

ISBN 0-13-418732-6

3 4 5 6 7 8 9 10   99 98 97

PRENTICE HALL
Simon & Schuster Education Group
A VIACOM COMPANY

STAFF CREDITS

Editorial:	Lorraine Smith-Phelan, Maureen Grassi, Joseph Berman, Christine A. Caputo, Matthew C. Hart, Rekha Sheorey, Kathleen Ventura
Design:	AnnMarie Roselli, Laura Bird, Gerry Schrenk
Production:	Suse F. Bell, Christina Burghard, Marianne Peters Riordan, Cathleen Profitko, Gregory Myers, Cleasta Wilburn
Media Resources:	Suzi Myers, Vickie Menanteaux, Martha Conway
Marketing:	Andrew Socha, Arthur C. Germano, Jane Walker Neff, Victoria Willows
Pre-Press Production:	Kathryn Dix, Paula Massenaro, Carol Barbara
Manufacturing:	Rhett Conklin, Loretta Moe
National Science Consultants	Charles Balko, Patricia Cominsky, Jeannie Dennard, Kathy French, Brenda Underwood

CONTENTS

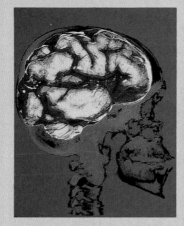

Reference Section

Activities for Exploring Life Science

Discovering

Doing

Calculating

Thinking

Writing

THIS IS A

SMOKE-FREE BUILDING

Reading

Laboratory Investigations

Activity Bank

Features

Problem Solving

Connections

Careers

CONCEPT MAPPING

Throughout your study of science, you will learn a variety of terms, facts, figures, and concepts. Each new topic you encounter will provide its own collection of words and ideas—which, at times, you may think seem endless. But each of the ideas within a particular topic is related in some way to the others. No concept in science is isolated. Thus it will help you to understand the topic if you see the whole picture; that is, the interconnectedness of all the individual terms and ideas. This is a much more effective and satisfying way of learning than memorizing separate facts.

Actually, this should be a rather familiar process for you. Although you may not think about it in this way, you analyze many of the elements in your daily life by looking for relationships or connections. For example, when you look at a collection of flowers, you may divide them into groups: roses, carnations, and daisies. You may then associate colors with these flowers: red, pink, and white. The general topic is flowers. The subtopic is types of flowers. And the colors are specific terms that describe flowers. A topic makes more sense and is more easily understood if you understand how it is broken down into individual ideas and how these ideas are related to one another and to the entire topic.

It is often helpful to organize information visually so that you can see how it all fits together. One technique for describing related ideas is called a **concept map**. In a concept map, an idea is represented by a word or phrase enclosed in a box. There are several ideas in any concept map. A connection between two ideas is made with a line. A word or two that describes the connection is written on or near the line. The general topic is located at the top of the map. That topic is then broken down into subtopics, or more specific ideas, by branching lines. The most specific topics are located at the bottom of the map.

To construct a concept map, first identify the important ideas or key terms in the chapter or section. Do not try to include too much information. Use your judgment as to what is really important. Write the general topic at the top of your map. Let's use an example to help illustrate this process. Suppose you decide that the key terms in a section you are reading are School, Living Things, Language Arts, Subtraction, Grammar, Mathematics, Experiments, Papers, Science, Addition, Novels. The general topic is School. Write and enclose this word in a box at the top of your map.

SCHOOL

Now choose the subtopics—Language Arts, Science, Mathematics. Figure out how they are related to the topic. Add these words to your map. Continue this procedure until you have included all the important ideas and terms. Then use lines to make the appropriate connections between ideas and terms. Don't forget to write a word or two on or near the connecting line to describe the nature of the connection.

Do not be concerned if you have to redraw your map (perhaps several times!) before you show all the important connections clearly. If, for example, you write papers for Science as well as for Language Arts, you may want to place these two subjects next to each other so that the lines do not overlap.

One more thing you should know about concept mapping: Concepts can be correctly mapped in many different ways. In fact, it is unlikely that any two people will draw identical concept maps for a complex topic. Thus there is no one correct concept map for any topic! Even

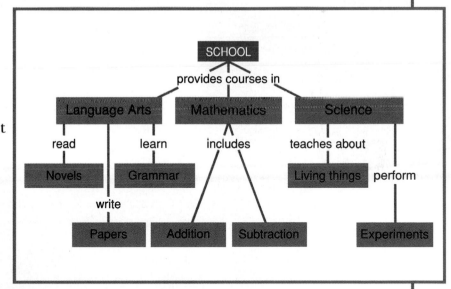

though your concept map may not match those of your classmates, it will be correct as long as it shows the most important concepts and the clear relationships among them. Your concept map will also be correct if it has meaning to you and if it helps you understand the material you are reading. A concept map should be so clear that if some of the terms are erased, the missing terms could easily be filled in by following the logic of the concept map.

U N I T O N E

Characteristics of Living Things

▼ *From the smallest bacteria to the largest whales, the building blocks of all living things are cells.*

What do you think of when you hear the words building blocks? Perhaps your mind drifts back to a younger age when you may have spent a good deal of time playing with wooden or plastic building blocks. (If you are like the author of this textbook, you still enjoy playing with them.) Or perhaps you think of the brick, steel, and wood out of which country houses and modern skyscrapers are constructed. If you enjoy the physical sciences, you might even think of atoms—the building blocks of matter.

In this unit, you are going to explore very special building blocks—the building

blocks of life! What are the building blocks of life? You can probably guess from your knowledge of science that they are cells. All living things—from the tiniest bacteria to the largest blue whales—are made of microscopic building blocks called cells. Cells are the framework upon which living things are constructed. Why are cells so special? Unlike all other kinds of building blocks, cells are alive!

What exactly are cells? How do they perform the activities necessary for life? Are all cells the same or do they vary from organism to organism? These are just a few of the questions you will be able to answer when you have finished your exploration of one of nature's greatest accomplishments—the living cell.

▲ *Like these children in a tug of war, your cells must work together as a team to keep your body running smoothly.*

Discovery *Activity*

How Long Is Long? How Small Is Small?

As you read this unit, you will encounter some rather large numbers and some rather small numbers. For example, you will discover that the history of the Earth and the evolution of cells is a story that began about 4.5 billion years ago. A billion is a 1 followed by 9 zeros! You will also discover that the smallest cells measure about 0.2 micrometer in height. A micrometer is a millionth of a meter, or a fraction with 1 as the numerator and 1 million as the denominator (1/1,000,000).

1. Construct a time line starting with the formation of the Earth and ending with the present day. Include any historical dates you feel are important. As you read this textbook, add new dates to your time line.

2. The average student is about 1.5 meters tall. If you began stacking up the smallest cells, how many would you have to add before your stack reached 1.5 meters?

   ■ Do you now have a better idea of how long is long and how small is small?

Exploring Life Science

Guide for Reading

After you read the following sections, you will be able to

1–1 Science—Not Just for Scientists
- Describe the process of science and the branches of life science.

1–2 The Scientific Method—A Way of Problem Solving
- Identify the steps in the scientific method.

1–3 The Metric System
- Identify the metric units used in scientific measurements.

1–4 Tools of a Life Scientist
- Identify some of the tools used by life scientists.

1–5 Safety in the Science Laboratory
- Explain the importance of safety in the laboratory.

Scientists, like most people, love a mystery. Andrew Blaustein, an ecologist at Oregon State University, has been investigating one such mystery: What has been killing the frogs and toads in Oregon's Cascade Range?

Sadly, Oregon is not the only place where frogs and toads are in trouble. From the rain forests of Costa Rica to the lowland heaths of England, amphibians around the world are disappearing. Scientists think that most of the disappearances are probably the result of pollution or habitat destruction. The case of the frogs and toads of Oregon, however, was particularly mysterious—at least until Blaustein and his graduate students began investigating.

In 1994, Blaustein proposed a solution to the mystery: Increased ultraviolet light from the sun, caused by the thinning of the ozone layer, was killing the frogs' eggs. Blaustein then performed a series of experiments which showed that exposure to excess ultraviolet light will kill frog eggs. But are ultraviolet levels in Oregon unusually high? To date, scientists have found no evidence that the ozone layer over Oregon is thinning. In science, the solution to one problem often leads to other unanswered questions.

Journal *Activity*

You and Your World Is this your first science course? Or are you an old hand at science? In either case, in your journal jot down your feelings about taking a science course. It might be interesting to go back to your entry at the end of the year and see if you still feel the same.

Here you see an azure poison dart frog. Scientists are puzzled because some frogs and toads are disappearing from their habitats.

1–1 Science—Not Just for Scientists

Why do the leaves of some trees change color in autumn? How do homing pigeons find their way home? Where do frogs go during the cold winter months? If you have ever asked questions such as these, then you have been on the road to becoming a scientist. Does that surprise you? If it does, it is probably because you do not understand exactly what a scientist does. Whenever you observe the world about you and ask questions, you are acting like a scientist. Does that statement give you a clue to the nature of science and scientists?

Like you, scientists often observe the world about them. So, whenever you make an observation you are acting like a scientist. Of course, scientists do more than just observe. They question what they see. They wonder what makes things the way they are. And they attempt to find answers to their questions. In fact, the word science comes from the Latin *scire*, which means "to know."

No doubt you also question what you see—at least some of the time. After reading this chapter, you will be better prepared to find answers to some of your questions. That is, you will be better able to look at the world the way a scientist does.

Figure 1–1 *Whenever you observe and question natural occurrences, such as the changing colors of leaves in autumn, you are acting as a scientist does.*

The Nature of Science

There are probably many events in the world that you question and seek answers to. Put another way, the universe is really a collection of countless mysteries. It is the job of scientists to try to solve those mysteries. **The goal of science is to understand the world around us.**

Just how do scientists solve such mysteries of nature? That is, how do they achieve their goal? Like any good detective, scientists use special methods to determine truths about nature. These truths are known as facts. Here is an example of a fact: About 65 million years ago, all of the dinosaurs became extinct (died off). Science, of course, is more than a simple listing of facts—just as studying science is more than just memorizing facts. Jules Henri Poincaré, a nineteenth-century scientist and mathematician, put it this way: "Science is built up with facts, as a house is with stones. But a collection of facts is no more a science than a heap of stones is a house."

Clearly, scientists must go beyond making up a list of facts. Actually, facts are but one tool scientists use

Figure 1–2 *The goal of science is to understand events that occur in the world around us—such as where the animals that inhabit this pond go during the cold winter months.*

Figure 1–3 *Although dinosaurs are said to have become extinct some 65 million years ago, scientists now consider birds as living descendants of dinosaurs.*

to solve the larger mysteries of nature. In a way, you can think of facts as clues to scientific mysteries. Facts are not the answers to mysteries, they are merely guideposts that help us find our way toward the answers. An example of a larger mystery is *why* all of the dinosaurs became extinct 65 million years ago.

Once all the relevant facts are gathered, scientists often propose explanations for the events they observe. Whenever possible, they perform experiments to test their explanations. You will learn more about how scientists go about performing experiments and solving nature's mysteries in the next section of this chapter.

After a scientist has made observations, recorded facts, and performed experiments, he or she may develop a **theory.** A theory is the most logical explanation for events that occur in nature. So scientists do not use the word theory as you may. For example, you may have a theory about why your basketball team keeps losing its games. Your theory may or may not make sense. But it is not a scientific theory. A scientific theory is not just a guess or a hunch. It is a powerful, time-tested concept that makes useful and dependable predictions about the natural world.

Once a scientist proposes a theory, that theory must be tested over and over again. If it passes each test, the theory may be accepted by the scientific community. However, theories can be—and often are—wrong. They may have to be discarded or modified based on new observations or experiments. In some cases, if a hypothesis survives many tests, it becomes a **law**. A law summarizes observed experimental facts—it does not explain the facts. The explanation resides in the appropriate theory. Laws, like theories, may change as new information is provided or new experiments are performed. This flexibility points out the spirit at the heart of science: Always allow questions to be asked and new scientific explanations to be considered.

Branches of Life Science

During your study of science, you will discover that the ability to organize things in a logical, orderly way is an important study skill. This type of organizing is called classification. Classification systems are an important part of science. For example, life scientists classify all life on Earth into five broad groups.

The study of science itself can be classified into groups, or in this case, branches, of science. There are many branches of science, each determined by the subject matter being studied. For our purposes, however, we will group science into three main branches: life science, earth science, and physical science. Because this is a life science textbook, let's consider some of the specialized branches of life science.

Life science deals with living things and their relationship to one another and to their environment. Life science can be divided into a number of specialized branches. One branch of life science is **zoology** (zoh-AHL-uh-jee). Zoology is the study of animals. Another branch of life science is **botany** (BAHT-uh-nee), or the study of plants. A third branch of life science is **ecology,** or the study of the relationships between living organisms and their environment.

Figure 1–4 *Life science includes ecology, or the study of the relationships between living organisms and their environment.*

Figure 1–5 *Learning the meanings of these prefixes and suffixes will make learning new science terms easier. What is the meaning of the word* arthropod?

Prefix	Meaning	Prefix	Meaning	Suffix	Meaning
anti-	against	herb-	pertaining to plants	-cyst	pouch
arth-	joint, joined	hetero-	different	-derm	skin, layer
auto-	self	homeo-	same	-gen	producing
bio-	related to life	macro-	large	-itis	inflammation
chloro-	green	micro-	small	-logy	study
cyto-	cell	multi-	consisting of many units	-meter	measurement
di-	double	osteo-	bone	-osis	condition, disease
epi-	above	photo-	pertaining to light	-phase	stage
exo-	outer, external	plasm-	forming substance	-phage	eater
gastro-	stomach	proto-	first	-pod	foot
hemo-	blood	syn-	together	-stasis	stationary condition

Still another branch of life science is **microbiology.** Microbiology is the study of **microorganisms,** or microscopic organisms.

Just like any branch of science, life science has many special terms that may be unfamiliar to you. Figure 1–5 on page 9 gives the meanings of some prefixes and suffixes that are commonly used in science vocabulary. If you learn the meanings of these prefixes and suffixes, learning new science terms will be easier. For example, suppose you are reading a magazine article and you come across the term *osteology.* You know that the prefix *osteo-* means bone and the suffix *-logy* means study. By joining the meanings of the prefix and suffix, you learn that osteology is the study of bones.

It is essential that you remember that the branches of science are a handy way to classify the subject matter scientists study. But it would be a mistake to think that any branch of science works independently of the other branches. To the contrary, the branches of science overlap most of the time. Science does not happen in a vacuum and the great discoveries of science do not usually occur unless scientists from many branches work together.

1–1 Section Review

1. What is the goal of science?
2. What is a law? What is a theory? Give an example of a law and an example of a theory.
3. Describe three specialized branches of life science. Give an example of a question that might be asked by scientists in each branch.
4. Using Figure 1–5, determine what the terms arthritis and hematology mean.

Critical Thinking—*Relating Concepts*
5. An area in your state has been flooded due to heavy rains. How might scientists from the three main branches of science interact in their study of the flood, its effects, and how future flooding might be controlled?

CONNECTIONS

Modern Medicine—Ancient Cure

While preparing bone specimens for microscopic study, a young college student in Detroit made a fascinating discovery. She found that shining ultraviolet light on the bones made them glow yellow-green. The yellow-green color was characteristic of a *modern medicine* called tetracycline used to combat disease. But the bone specimen was over 1600 years old and was part of a skeleton found in the Nubian desert in Africa. How could ancient bones contain a modern medicine?

The answer to the puzzling question lies with bacteria called *Streptomyces*, which produce tetracycline naturally. Species of *Streptomyces* also make up about 60 percent of the bacteria living in Nubian soil. Scientists believe that *Streptomyces* flourished at the bottom of mud bins used to store grain.

Normally, tetracycline leaves a bitter taste in food. So it is unlikely the people of that time ate the contaminated grain at the bottom of the bin—if they could avoid it. However, every few years that region suffered through serious famines and food became very scarce. At such times we would normally expect disease to rise as people's strength was sapped by the lack of food. But it was during such famines that people were willing to eat the contaminated grain. After all, bitter food is better than no food at all. The ancient people in the Nubian desert could not know how fortunate they were. For just when they needed it most, they ate the grain with the life-saving medicine—without ever realizing how a bacterium was protecting them from disease!

Guide for Reading

*Focus on these questions as
you read.*

▶ What are the steps of the
scientific method?

▶ Why are both a control
setup and experimental
setup important in any scientific investigation?

1–2 The Scientific Method— A Way of Problem Solving

Every day of the year there are many problems being investigated by scientists. Sometimes problems are quickly solved. Sometimes they take many years to solve. And sometimes a problem remains unsolved. Whenever scientists try to solve a problem, they search for an answer in an orderly and systematic way called the **scientific method.** The scientific method is a systematic approach to problem solving. **The basic steps in the scientific method are**

> **Stating the problem**
> **Gathering information on the problem**
> **Forming a hypothesis**
> **Performing experiments to test the hypothesis**
> **Recording and analyzing data**
> **Stating a conclusion**
> **Repeating the work**

The following example shows how a life scientist might use the scientific method to solve a problem.

Stating the Problem

Most people know enough to walk the other way if they should run into a rattlesnake. However, if you could safely observe a rattler, you would discover a rather curious kind of behavior.

With fangs flashing and body arching, the deadly rattler strikes. The snake's fangs quickly inject poisonous venom into its victim. Then, in a surprise move, the rattler allows the wounded animal to run away! But the rattlesnake will not miss its intended meal. After waiting for its poison to take effect, the rattler follows the trail of the injured animal.

Although the rattler cannot see well, somehow it manages to find its victim on the dense, dark, forest floor. Clearly, something leads the snake to its prey. What invisible trail does the snake follow in tracking down its bitten prey? This is a problem that scientists recently tried to solve.

Figure 1–6 *Poisonous snakes, such as the rattlesnake, have fangs. What are the fangs used for?*

Gathering Information on the Problem

The first step in solving a scientific problem is to find out or review everything important related to it. For example, the scientists trying to solve the rattlesnake mystery knew that a rattlesnake's eyes are only sensitive to visible light. However, they also knew that a pair of organs located under the animal's eyes detects invisible light in the form of heat. These heat-sensing pits pick up signals from warm-blooded animals. The signals help the snake locate its intended prey. But the heat-sensing pits cannot help the snake find a wounded victim that has run many meters away. Some other process must be responsible for that.

The scientists knew that a rattler's tongue "smells" certain odors in the air. The rattler's tongue picks up these odors on an outward flick. The odors enter the snake's mouth on an inward flick. The scientists also knew that the sight or smell of an unbitten animal did not trigger the rattler's tracking action. Using all this information, the scientists were able to suggest a solution to the problem.

Forming a Hypothesis

A suggested solution is called a **hypothesis** (high-PAH-thuh-sihs). A hypothesis is almost always

Figure 1–7 *The timber rattlesnake was able to track down its wounded prey after the prey had run away. What hypothesis could explain the snake's behavior?*

formed after the information related to the problem has been carefully studied. But sometimes a hypothesis is the result of creative thinking that often involves bold, original guesses about the problem. In this regard, forming a hypothesis is like good detective work, which involves not only logic, but hunches, intuition, and the taking of chances.

To the problem, "What invisible trail does a rattler follow in tracking down its prey?" the scientists suggested a hypothesis. The scientists suggested that after the snake wounds its victim, the snake follows the smell of its own venom to locate the animal.

Performing Experiments to Test the Hypothesis

The scientists next had to test their hypothesis by performing certain activities and recording the results. These activities are called experiments. Whenever scientists test a hypothesis using an experiment, they must make sure that the results of the experiment clearly support or do not support the hypothesis. That is, they must make sure that one, and only one, factor affects the results of the experiment. The factor being tested in an experiment is called the **variable.** In any experiment, only one variable is tested at a time. Otherwise it would not be clear which variable had caused the results of the experiment.

In the rattlesnake experiments, the scientists tested whether the snake's venom formed an invisible trail that the snake followed. The venom was the variable, or single factor, that the scientists wanted to test. The scientists performed the experiment to test this variable.

First, the scientists dragged a dead mouse that had been struck and poisoned by a rattlesnake along a curving path on the bottom of the snake's empty cage. When the snake was placed in its cage, its tongue flicked rapidly, its head moved slowly from side to side, and it followed the exact trail the scientists had laid out. The results seemed clear, but the scientists had one more experiment to perform.

To be sure it was the scent of the venom and no other odor that the snake followed, the scientists ran a **control experiment.** A control experiment is run

Figure 1–8 *Snakes such as the rattlesnake are able to swallow their prey whole.*

in exactly the same way as the experiment with the variable, but the variable is left out. So the scientists dragged an unbitten dead mouse along a path in the cage. The experiment was exactly the same, except this mouse had not been poisoned. This time the snake seemed disinterested. Its tongue flicked very slowly and it did not follow the path.

Recording and Analyzing Data

The rattlesnake experiments were repeated many times, and the scientists carefully recorded the **data** from the experiments. Data include observations such as measurements. Then the scientists analyzed the recorded data.

Stating a Conclusion

After analyzing the recorded data, the scientists came to a conclusion. They concluded that the scent of venom was the only factor that could cause a rattlesnake to follow its bitten victim. Rattlesnake venom is made up of many different substances. Exactly which ones are responsible for the snake's behavior are as yet unknown. As is often the case in science, a solution to one mystery brings to light another mystery. Using scientific methods similar to those described here, scientists hope to follow a path that leads to the solution to this new mystery.

Repeating the Work

While the scientist conducting the experiment you just read about might be satisfied with the conclusion, he or she would repeat the experiment many more times to make sure the data were accurate. Furthermore, before the conclusion would be accepted by the scientific community, other scientists would repeat the experiment and check the results. Therefore, whenever a scientist writes a report on his or her experiment, that report must be detailed enough so that scientists throughout the world can repeat the experiment for themselves. In most cases, it is only when an experiment has been repeated by scientists worldwide that it is considered to be accurate and worthy of being included in new scientific research.

Changing Theories

Albert Einstein once stated that he would consider his work a failure if new and better theories did not replace his own. Using the following words, write an essay describing how new evidence can change an existing theory.

data
variable
hypothesis
scientific method
control
experiment
conclusions

The Scientific Method—Not Always So Orderly

By now you might have decided that science is a straightforward way of studying the world. After all, you state a problem, gather information, form a hypothesis, run an experiment, and come to a conclusion. It certainly sounds rather neat and tidy. Well, sometimes it is—and sometimes it is not.

In the real world, scientists do not always follow the steps in the scientific method as they have been described to you. Nor do the steps always follow the same order. For example, during an experiment a scientist might observe something totally unexpected. The unexpected event might cause the scientist to forget about the original hypothesis being studied and suggest an entirely new one. In this example, the new hypothesis followed the experiment. In another case, a scientist might not even start out with a particular problem to be studied. Let's go back to those unexpected results. Those results might cause the scientist to consider events in nature in a new and different way. They might even suggest new problems that need to be considered. In this case, the problem followed the experiment.

There is another way in which science does not always follow the rules you have just read about. You learned that every experiment must have only one variable. However, in some experiments it is not possible to eliminate all but one variable. Naturally, the data in such experiments are much more difficult to analyze. For example, suppose scientists want to determine the factors that affect the growth of trees in a particular forest. It is not likely that the scientists will be able to eliminate all the variables in the forest except the one they wish to test. So although using a single variable is a good rule—and one you will follow in almost all of the experiments you design or perform—it is not always a practical rule in the real world.

Figure 1–9 *Although scientists prefer to isolate all but one variable in an experiment, it is not always practical. Could scientists isolate a single variable while studying plant growth in this tropical rain forest? Explain.*

PROBLEM Solving

Fact or Fiction?

Perhaps one of the most interesting aspects of life science is the amazing variety of plants and animals living on planet Earth. Some of these organisms are so unusual that it is often difficult to determine if a statement is true or a figment of someone's imagination. Read the following hypothesis to see what we mean.

Hypothesis: Turtle eggs develop into male turtles in cold temperatures and into female turtles in warm temperatures.

Predict whether this hypothesis is fact or fiction. Then design a simple experiment to show if the hypothesis is or is not correct. Make sure your experiment has an experimental setup and a control setup.

1–2 Section Review

1. Describe the steps in the scientific method.
2. Discuss the importance of a control setup in a scientific experiment.

Critical Thinking—*Designing an Experiment*
3. Design an experiment that tests the hypothesis that a green plant needs light to live. Identify the variable and the control in the experiment.

1–3 The Metric System

As part of the process of experimenting and gathering information, scientists must make accurate measurements. The scientists may need to know the size of a cell or the temperature of a bird's body. They must also be able to share their information with other scientists. To do this, scientists must speak the same measurement "language." The common language of measurement in science used all over the world is the **metric system.**

The metric system is the standard system used by all scientists. The metric system is also referred to as the International System of Units, or SI. The metric system is a decimal system. That is, it is based on the number 10 and multiples of 10.

Scientists use metric units to measure length, volume, mass, weight, density, and temperature. Some frequently used metric units and their abbreviations are listed in Figure 1–10.

Length

Figure 1–10 *The metric system is easy to use because it is based on units of ten. How many centimeters are there in 10 meters?*

The **meter** (m) is the basic unit of length in the metric system. One meter is equal to 39.4 inches. Sometimes scientists must measure distances much

COMMON METRIC UNITS	
Length	**Mass**
1 meter (m) = 100 centimeters (cm)	1 kilogram (kg) = 1000 grams (g)
1 meter = 1000 millimeters (mm)	1 gram = 1000 milligrams (mg)
1 meter = 1,000,000 micrometers (μm)	1000 kilograms = 1 metric ton (t)
1 meter = 1,000,000,000 nanometers (nm)	
1 meter = 10,000,000,000 angstroms (Å)	
1000 meters = 1 kilometer (km)	
Volume	**Temperature**
1 liter (L) = 1000 milliliters (mL) or 1000 cubic centimeters (cm^3)	0°C = freezing point of water 100°C = boiling point of water
kilo- = one thousand centi- = one hundredth milli- = one thousandth	micro- = one millionth nano- = one billionth

longer than a meter, such as the distance a bird may fly across a continent. To do this, scientists use a unit called a kilometer (km). The prefix *kilo-* means 1000. So a kilometer is 1000 meters, or about the length of five city blocks.

A hummingbird, on the other hand, is too small to be measured in meters or kilometers. So scientists use the centimeter (cm). The prefix *centi-* means that 100 of these units make a meter. Thus there are 100 centimeters in a meter. The hummingbird is only about 5 centimeters long. For objects even smaller, another division of the meter is used. The millimeter (mm) is one thousandth of a meter. The prefix *milli-* means $\frac{1}{1000}$. One meter equals 1000 millimeters. In bright light, the diameter of the pupil of your eye is about 1 millimeter. Even this unit is too large to use when describing the sizes of the smallest germs, such as the bacteria that cause sore throats. These germs are measured in micrometers, or millionths of a meter, and nanometers, or billionths of a meter.

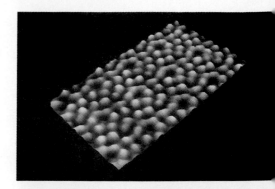

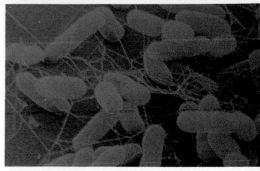

Figure 1–11 *The length of bacteria (bottom) are measured in micrometers or nanometers. What unit of length is used when measuring atoms such as these silicon atoms (top)?*

Volume

The amount of space an object takes up is called its volume. The **liter** (L) is the basic unit of volume in the metric system. The liter is slightly larger than the quart. Here again scientists use divisions of the liter to measure smaller volumes. The milliliter (mL), or cubic centimeter (cm^3), is $\frac{1}{1000}$ of a liter. There are 1000 milliliters, or cubic centimeters, in a liter. The volumes of both liquids and gases are measured in liters and milliliters. For example, a scientist may remove a few milliliters of blood from an animal to study the types of substances the blood contains.

Mass and Weight

The **kilogram** (kg) is the basic unit of mass in the metric system. **Mass** is a measure of the amount of matter in an object. There is more matter in a tree trunk than in a leaf. Therefore, a tree trunk has more mass than a leaf.

Figure 1–12 *To measure the volume of water rushing over Iguazu Falls in Brazil, scientists would use the unit of volume called the liter. What unit of volume would they use to measure the amount of water in a pet's water dish?*

Figure 1–13 *The buffalo is one of the largest land animals on Earth. Harvest field mice are the smallest mice on Earth. Which metric unit would be best for measuring the mass of the buffalo? Of field mice?*

One kilogram is slightly more than two pounds. For smaller units of mass, the gram (g) is used. Remember that the prefix *kilo-* means 1000. There are 1000 grams in a kilogram. One milligram (mg) measures an even smaller mass, $\frac{1}{1000}$ of a gram. How many milligrams are there in one kilogram?

Weight is a measure of the attraction between two objects due to gravity. Gravity is a force of attraction. The strength of the gravitational force between objects depends in part on the distance between these objects. As the distance between objects becomes greater, the gravitational force between the objects decreases. On Earth, your weight is a measure of the Earth's force of gravity on you.

The basic unit of weight in the metric system is the **newton** (N). An object with a mass of 1 kilogram is pulled toward the Earth with a force of 9.8 newtons. So the weight of the object is 9.8 N. What is your weight on Earth?

Because the force of gravity changes with distance, your weight can change depending on your location. For example, you are farther from the center of the Earth when standing atop a tall mountain than when standing at sea level. And although the change may be small, you actually weigh less at the top of the mountain than you do at sea level.

As you just read, the strength of the gravitational force changes with distance. But it also changes depending on mass. An object with a large mass, such as the Earth, exerts a strong gravitational force on other objects. (Which is why you remain rooted to the ground and don't float off into space.) But any object with mass exerts a gravitational force—and that includes you! There is actually a gravitational force of attraction between you and this textbook. But don't worry, the book will not come flying at you as a result of gravity. Why? Your mass is much too small.

We tend to think of the Earth as being extremely large. But as objects in space go, the Earth is not so big. The mass of the planet Jupiter is more than 317 times that of Earth. If you could stand on Jupiter, you would find that your weight would be 317 times greater than your weight on Earth. The mass of the moon is about one eightieth that of the Earth. How would your weight on the moon compare with your weight on Earth?

It should be clear to you by now that mass remains a constant, but weight can change. The amount of matter in an object does not change regardless of where the object is located. But the weight of an object can change due to its location.

Does Air Have Mass and Weight?

1. Blow up two balloons to an equal size.

2. Tape or tie each balloon to one end of a meterstick.

3. Attach a string to the center of the meterstick. Hold the string so that the balloons are balanced. If the balloons are of equal size, the meterstick will be horizontal to the floor.

4. Carefully burst one of the balloons with a pin. What happens?

■ Use the results of your experiment to determine if air has mass, weight, or both.

Density

The measurement of how much mass is contained in a given volume of an object is called its **density.** Density can be defined as the mass per unit volume of a substance. The following formula shows the relationship between density, mass, and volume.

$$\text{Density} = \frac{\text{mass}}{\text{volume}}$$

For example, the mass of 100 cubic centimeters of corn oil is 92.2 grams. The density of corn oil would be

$$\text{Density} = \frac{92.2 \text{ g (mass)}}{100 \text{ cm}^3 \text{ (volume)}} = 0.922 \text{ g/cm}^3$$

Figure 1–14 *Although we speak of astronauts as being "weightless," they are not. However, on Earth this astronaut would never have been able to lift a communications satellite. Explain why.*

Density is an important concept because it allows scientists to identify and compare substances. Each substance has its own characteristic density. For example, the density of water is 1 g/cm³ while that of butterfat is 0.91 g/cm³. An object with a density less than 1 g/cm³ will float on water. Based on this data, will butterfat sink or float in water?

Temperature

Scientists measure temperature according to the **Celsius** scale, in degrees Celsius (°C). The fixed points on the scale are the freezing point of water at sea level, 0°C, and the boiling point of water, 100°C. The range between these points is 100 degrees, and each degree is ¹⁄₁₀₀ of the difference between the freezing point and boiling point of water. Normal human body temperature is 37°C, while some birds maintain a body temperature of 41°C.

Dimensional Analysis

You now know the basic units of measurement in the metric system. But there is still one more thing you must learn—how to go from one unit to another. The skill of converting one unit to another is called **dimensional analysis.** Dimensional analysis involves determining in what units a problem is given, in what

Figure 1–15 *To increase her density so that she can sink to the depths of the sea bottom, this scuba diver wears a belt of lead weights.*

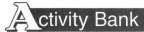

Calculating Density, p. 786

Figure 1–16 *You can see by the way this lizard walks lightly across the hot desert sands that temperature has an effect on almost all living things. Scientists measure temperature in degrees Celsius.*

units the answer should be, and the factor to be used to make the conversion from one unit to another. Keep in mind that you can only convert units that measure the same thing. That is, no matter how hard you try, you cannot convert length in kilometers to temperature in degrees Celsius.

To perform dimensional analysis, you must use a **conversion factor.** A conversion factor is a fraction that *always* equals 1. For example, 1 kilometer equals 1000 meters. So the fraction 1 kilometer/1000 meters equals 1. You can flip the conversion factor and it still equals 1: 1000 meters/1 kilometer equals 1.

In any fraction, the top number is called the numerator. The bottom number is called the denominator. So in a conversion fraction the numerator always equals the denominator and the fraction always equals 1.

This is probably beginning to sound a lot more complicated than it actually is. Let's see how it all works by using an example. Suppose you are told to convert 7500 grams to kilograms. This means that grams are your given unit and you are to convert grams to kilograms. (Your answer must be expressed in kilograms.) The conversion factor you choose must contain the relationship between grams and kilograms that has a value of 1. You have two possible choices:

$$\frac{1000 \text{ grams}}{1 \text{ kilogram}} = 1 \quad \text{or} \quad \frac{1 \text{ kilogram}}{1000 \text{ grams}} = 1$$

To convert one metric unit to another, you must multiply the given quantity times the conversion factor. Remember that multiplying a number by 1 does not change the value of the number. So multiplying by a conversion factor does not change the value of the quantity, only its units.

Now, which conversion factor should you use to change 7500 grams to kilograms? Because you want the given unit to cancel out during multiplication, you should use the conversion factor whose denominator has the same units as the units you wish to convert. Because you are converting grams to kilograms, the denominator of the conversion factor you use must be in grams and the numerator in kilograms.

Using Metric Measurements

Use the appropriate scientific tools and the metric system to measure the following. Construct a chart of your results.

length of the textbook
length of your arm
temperature indoors
temperature outdoors
volume of a glass of water
volume of a bucket of water

The first step in dimensional analysis, then, is to write out the given quantity, the correct conversion factor, and a multiplication symbol between them:

$$7500 \text{ grams} \times \frac{1 \text{ kilogram}}{1000 \text{ grams}}$$

The next step is to cancel out the same units:

$$7500 \text{ grams} \times \frac{1 \text{ kilogram}}{1000 \text{ grams}}$$

The last step is to multiply:

$$7500 \times \frac{1 \text{ kilogram}}{1000} = \frac{7500 \text{ kilograms}}{1000}$$

$$\frac{7500 \text{ kilograms}}{1000} = 7.5 \text{ kilograms}$$

1–3 Section Review

1. What are the basic units of length, volume, mass, weight, and temperature in the metric system?
2. Compare mass and weight.
3. What is dimensional analysis?

Critical Thinking—*Applying Concepts*
4. Without placing an object in water, how can you determine if it will float?

Guide for Reading

Focus on this question as you read.

▶ *What are the various tools used by life scientists?*

1–4 Tools of a Life Scientist

To explore the world around them, life scientists use a variety of tools ranging from simple microscopes to complex computers. The kind of tools scientists use depends on the problems they want to solve. A scientist may use a metric ruler to measure the length of a leaf. At another time, the same scientist may use a computer to analyze large amounts of data concerning hundreds of leaves.

Figure 1–17 *This diagram is of a typical compound light microscope. What is another word for the eyepiece?*

Tools are very important in the advancement of science. In fact, some great discoveries were not made until the appropriate tools were developed. An example is the **microscope,** which is an instrument that produces an enlarged image of an object. Simple microscopes have been used by scientists for many years to study the structure of living things. But it was not until several hundred years after the first microscopes were discovered that scientists were able to see the smallest structures that make up living things!

Microscopes

Have you ever looked at a ladybug through a magnifying glass? If you have, then you used a type of microscope. A magnifying glass is a simple microscope because it has only one lens. A lens is a curved piece of glass. As light rays pass through the glass, they bend. In some kinds of lenses, the bending of the light rays increases the size of an object's image.

THE COMPOUND LIGHT MICROSCOPE **Compound light microscopes** are microscopes that have more than one lens. Like magnifying glasses, compound microscopes use light to make objects appear larger. Magnifying glasses produce an image only a few times larger than the object. But a compound light microscope can make an object appear up to 1000 times larger than it actually is! This amount of magnification allows you to see inside the cells of a leaf. The various parts of a compound light microscope are described in Appendix B on pages 851 to 852.

THE ELECTRON MICROSCOPE Instead of using light to magnify the image of an object, an **electron microscope** uses a beam of tiny particles called electrons. The beam produces pictures, which are focused on photographic film or a television screen. Electron microscopes can magnify objects hundreds of thousands of times. The scanning electron microscope, or SEM, is a type of electron microscope that can produce three-dimensional images. With electron microscopes, scientists can study the smallest parts of plant and animal cells.

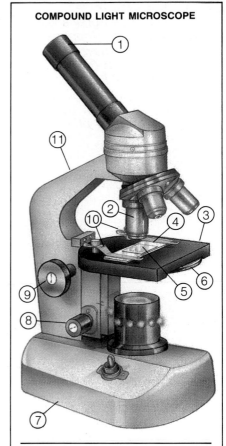

COMPOUND LIGHT MICROSCOPE

1. Ocular lens (eyepiece)
2. Objective lens   3. Stage
4. Glass slide   5. Coverslip
6. Diaphragm
   (regulates light intensity)
7. Base   8. Fine adjustment knob
9. Coarse adjustment knob
10. Stage clips   11. Arm

Activity Bank

Life in a Drop of Water, p. 788

Figure 1-18 *Notice the unmagnified pollen grains visible on the flower (top). Then look at pollen grains that have been magnified 60 times (center). This three-dimensional image of pollen grains (bottom) has been magnified 378 times. What kind of microscope took the photograph at the bottom?*

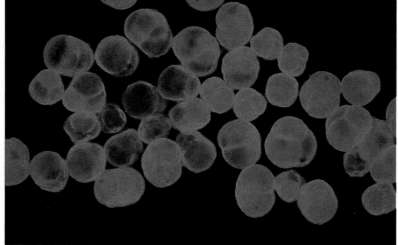

Looking Through Barriers

To learn more about living things, scientists must be able to see the inside of an organism *from the outside*. To do this, scientists use certain tools.

X-RAY   For almost 100 years, scientists have been using invisible radiations known as X-rays. X-rays are blocked by dense materials such as bone, but pass easily through skin and muscle. For this reason, X-rays are often used for taking pictures of bones.

CT SCANS   Computed Tomography, or CT scan, is a new technique that produces cross-sectional pictures of an object. An X-ray machine in a CT-scanner is used to take up to 720 different pictures of an object. Each picture shows a "slice" of the object. A computer analyzes and combines the exposures to construct a picture. Among its many uses, a CT scan can provide detailed pictures of body parts such as the human brain.

MRI   Magnetic resonance imaging, or MRI, is another tool that helps scientists see inside objects. MRI uses magnetism and radio waves to produce images. Scientists can use MRI to study the structure of body cells without harming the living tissue.

ACTIVITY READING

Dutchman's Dilemma

If you enjoy poetry, you may find the humorous poem *The Microscope* by Maxine Kumin a pleasant reading adventure.

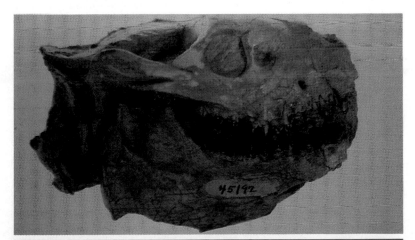

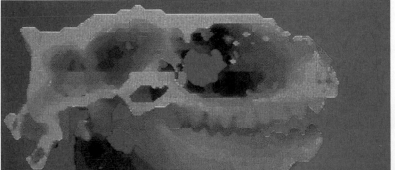

Figure 1–19 *Because this 30-million-year-old skull of a small mammal (top) was a rare find, scientists did not want to break it open. By using a CT scanner, scientists were able to get a three-dimensional view of the inside of the skull (bottom).*

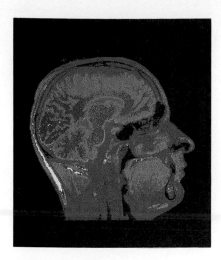

Figure 1–20 *MRI images help scientists study the inside of the body. What important organ can be studied from this MRI?*

Figure 1–21 *Keep in mind that microscopes are but one tool scientists use. Modern science and technology now includes the use of lasers in eye surgery (right) and computer-generated images of disease-causing viruses (left).*

Lasers

Lasers are another tool used by scientists. A laser is an instrument that produces a narrow, intense beam of light. Unlike a microscope, the laser is not used to magnify images. But it can be used as a kind of scalpel. For example, a surgeon may use a laser beam to remove cancer cells from the body. Lasers are also used in certain types of eye surgery.

Computers

A computer is another useful tool for scientists. Computers are electronic devices that collect, analyze, display, and store data. Computers help doctors diagnose diseases and prescribe treatments. In some branches of life science, a computer might be used to help researchers rapidly analyze information about the structure and functions of a living thing.

As you can see, modern life scientists have a variety of tools that they can use in their search for information. And perhaps future scientists will be using even better tools that have yet to be developed. Science, it seems, needs more than keen minds. It needs the kinds of data that very often only special tools can provide.

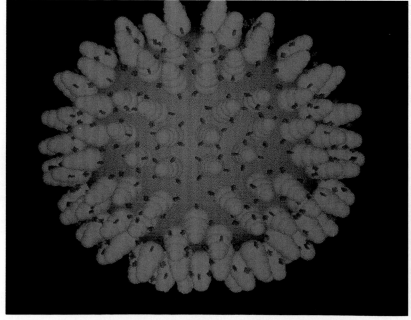

1–4 Section Review

1. List some of the tools used by life scientists and describe the importance of each tool.
2. Explain the difference between the compound light microscope and the electron microscope.
3. What does MRI use to produce an image?
4. Explain why a CT scan might be more useful to a doctor than a simple X-ray.

Connection—*Science and Technology*

5. It has been said that many great discoveries await the tools needed to make them. What does this statement mean to you?

1–5 Safety in the Science Laboratory

Guide for Reading

Focus on this question as you read.

▶ *What important safety rules must you follow when working in the laboratory?*

The scientific laboratory is a place of adventure and discovery. Some of the most exciting events in scientific history have happened in laboratories. The structure of DNA, the blueprint of life, was discovered by scientists in laboratories. The artificial skin that is used to replace skin destroyed by burns was first made by scientists in a laboratory. The list goes on and on.

To better understand the facts and concepts you will read about in life science, you may work in the laboratory this year. If you follow instructions and are as careful as a scientist would be, the laboratory will turn out to be an exciting experience for you.

When working in the laboratory, scientists know that it is very important to follow safety procedures. Therefore, scientists take precautions to protect themselves and their fellow workers.

All of the work you will do in the laboratory this year will include experiments that have been done over and over again. When done properly, the experiments are not only interesting but also perfectly safe. But if they are done improperly, accidents can occur. How can you avoid such problems?

Figure 1–22 *It is important to always point a test tube that is being heated away from yourself and your classmates (right). What two safety precautions is this student taking before picking up a hot beaker (left)?*

The most important safety rule is to always follow your teacher's directions or the directions in your textbook exactly as stated. Never try anything on your own without asking your teacher first. And when you are not sure what you should do, always ask first. As you read the laboratory investigations in the textbook, you will see safety symbols. Look at Figure 1–23 to learn the meanings of these symbols and the important precautions you should take.

In addition to the safety procedures listed in Figure 1–23, there is a more detailed list of safety rules in Appendix C on pages 853 to 854 of this textbook. Before you enter the laboratory for the first time, make sure that you have read each rule carefully. Then read them over again. Make sure that you understand each rule. If you do not understand a rule, ask your teacher to explain it. If you wish, you may even want to suggest further rules that apply to your particular classroom.

1–5 Section Review

1. What is the most important general rule to follow when working in the laboratory?
2. Suppose your teacher asks you to boil some water in a test tube. What precautions should you take to make sure this activity is done safely?

Connection—*You and Your World*
3. How can you apply the safety rules in Figure 1–23 to rules that should be followed when working in a kitchen? In a machine shop?

Glassware Safety

1. Whenever you see this symbol, you will know that you are working with glassware that can easily be broken. Take particular care to handle such glassware safely. And never use broken or chipped glassware.
2. Never heat glassware that is not thoroughly dry. Never pick up any glassware unless you are sure it is not hot. If it is hot, use heat-resistant gloves.
3. Always clean glassware thoroughly before putting it away.

Fire Safety

1. Whenever you see this symbol, you will know that you are working with fire. Never use any source of fire without wearing safety goggles.
2. Never heat anything—particularly chemicals—unless instructed to do so.
3. Never heat anything in a closed container.
4. Never reach across a flame.
5. Always use a clamp, tongs, or heat-resistant gloves to handle hot objects.
6. Always maintain a clean work area, particularly when using a flame.

Heat Safety

Whenever you see this symbol, you will know that you should put on heat-resistant gloves to avoid burning your hands.

Chemical Safety

1. Whenever you see this symbol, you will know that you are working with chemicals that could be hazardous.
2. Never smell any chemical directly from its container. Always use your hand to waft some of the odors from the top of the container toward your nose—and only when instructed to do so.
3. Never mix chemicals unless instructed to do so.
4. Never touch or taste any chemical unless instructed to do so.
5. Keep all lids closed when chemicals are not in use. Dispose of all chemicals as instructed by your teacher.

6. Immediately rinse with water any chemicals, particularly acids, that get on your skin and clothes. Then notify your teacher.

Eye and Face Safety

1. Whenever you see this symbol, you will know that you are performing an experiment in which you must take precautions to protect your eyes and face by wearing safety goggles.
2. When you are heating a test tube or bottle, always point it away from you and others. Chemicals can splash or boil out of a heated test tube.

Sharp Instrument Safety

1. Whenever you see this symbol, you will know that you are working with a sharp instrument.
2. Always use single-edged razors; double-edged razors are too dangerous.
3. Handle any sharp instrument with extreme care. Never cut any material toward you; always cut away from you.
4. Immediately notify your teacher if your skin is cut.

Electrical Safety

1. Whenever you see this symbol, you will know that you are using electricity in the laboratory.
2. Never use long extension cords to plug in any electrical device. Do not plug too many appliances into one socket or you may overload the socket and cause a fire.
3. Never touch an electrical appliance or outlet with wet hands.

Animal Safety

1. Whenever you see this symbol, you will know that you are working with live animals.
2. Do not cause pain, discomfort, or injury to an animal.
3. Follow your teacher's directions when handling animals. Wash your hands thoroughly after handling animals or their cages.

Figure 1–23 *You should become familiar with these safety symbols because you will see them in the laboratory investigations in this textbook.*

Laboratory Investigation

A Moldy Question

Problem

What variables affect the growth of bread mold?

Materials   (per group)

2 jars with lids
2 slices of bread
1 medicine dropper

Procedure 🔬

1. Put half a slice of bread into each jar. Moisten each half slice with ten drops of water. Cap the jars tightly. Keep one jar in sunlight and place the other in a dark closet.

2. Observe the jars every few days for about two weeks. Record your observations. Does light seem to influence mold growth? Include your answer to this question (your conclusion) with your observations.

3. Ask your teacher what scientists know about the effect of light on mold growth. Was your conclusion correct? Think again: What other variables might have affected mold growth? Did you think of temperature? How about moisture? Light, temperature, and moisture are all possible variables in this investigation.

4. Design a second experiment to retest the effect of light on mold growth. Record your procedure, observations, and conclusions.

5. Design another experiment to test one of the other variables. Test only one variable at a time. Work with other groups of students in your class so that each group tests one of the other two variables. Share your results and draw your conclusions together.

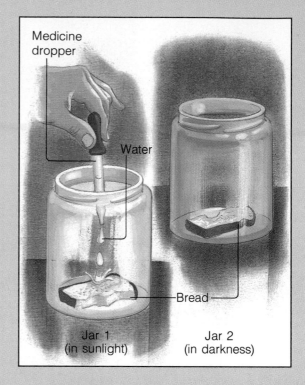

Jar 1
(in sunlight)

Jar 2
(in darkness)

Observations

Study the class data for this experiment. What variables seem to affect mold growth?

Analysis and Conclusions

1. In each of your additional experiments, what variable were you testing? Did you have a control setup for each experiment? If so, describe it.

2. Juanita set up the following experiment: She placed a piece of orange peel in each of two jars. She added 3 milliliters of water to jar 1 and placed it in the refrigerator. She added no water to jar 2 and placed it on a windowsill in the kitchen. At the end of a week, she noticed more mold growth in jar 2. Juanita concluded that light, a warm temperature, and no moisture are ideal conditions for mold growth. Discuss the accuracy of Juanita's conclusion.

Summarizing Key Concepts

1-1 Science—Not Just for Scientists

▲ The goal of science is to understand the world around us.

▲ A theory is the most logical explanation for events that occur in nature.

▲ Life scientists study living things and their parts and actions.

1-2 The Scientific Method—A Way of Problem Solving

▲ The basic steps in the scientific method are stating the problem, gathering information, forming a hypothesis, experimenting, recording and analyzing data, stating a conclusion, and repeating the work.

▲ A hypothesis is a proposed solution to a scientific problem.

1-3 The Metric System

▲ The basic units in the metric system are the kilogram, the liter, the newton, and the degree Celsius.

1-4 Tools of a Life Scientist

▲ Compound light microscopes contain an eyepiece lens and an objective lens.

▲ Electron microscopes use a beam of electrons to magnify an object.

▲ X-rays, CT scans, and MRI scans are some of the tools scientists use to look "inside" an object.

1-5 Safety in the Science Laboratory

▲ When working in the laboratory, it is important to heed all necessary safety precautions.

Reviewing Key Terms

Define each term in a complete sentence.

1-1 Science—Not Just for Scientists
theory
law
zoology
botany
ecology
microbiology
microorganism

1-2 The Scientific Method—A Way of Problem Solving
scientific method
hypothesis
variable
control experiment
data

1-3 The Metric System
metric system
meter
liter
kilogram
mass
weight
newton
density
Celsius
dimensional analysis
conversion factor

1-4 Tools of a Life Scientist
microscope
compound light microscope
electron microscope

Chapter Review

Content Review

Multiple Choice

Choose the letter of the answer that best completes each statement.

1. The most logical explanation for events that occur in nature is known as a
   a. theory.   c. hypothesis.
   b. law.   d. conclusion.

2. The branch of science that deals with the study of plants is
   a. microbiology.   c. botany.
   b. ecology.   d. zoology.

3. An orderly, systematic approach to problem solving is called the
   a. experiment.   c. hypothesis.
   b. conclusion.   d. scientific method.

4. The most important safety rule in the laboratory is to
   a. have a partner.
   b. wear a lab coat.
   c. wear safety goggles.
   d. always follow directions.

5. The factor being tested in an experiment is the
   a. hypothesis.   c. control.
   b. variable.   d. problem.

6. The basic unit of length in the metric system is the
   a. kilometer.   c. liter.
   b. meter.   d. Celsius.

7. In dimensional analysis, the conversion factor must be equal to
   a. the numerator.   c. 1.
   b. the denominator. d. 10.

8. Which tool would a scientist use to observe the structure of leaf cells?
   a. X-ray   c. CT scan
   b. MRI   d. SEM

True or False

If the statement is true, write "true." If it is false, change the underlined word or words to make the statement true.

1. Recorded observations that often involve measurements are called <u>conclusions.</u>
2. The part of the experiment with the variable is called the <u>experimental</u> setup.
3. Most experiments must have <u>two</u> variables to be accurate.
4. The symbol of a <u>razor blade</u> means you are working with a sharp instrument.
5. The <u>liter</u> is the basic unit of volume in the metric system.
6. The amount of space an object takes up is called its <u>mass.</u>
7. One type of <u>compound light</u> microscope is the SEM.
8. The force of attraction between objects is called <u>gravity.</u>

Concept Mapping

Complete the following concept map for Section 1–1. Then construct a concept map for the entire chapter.

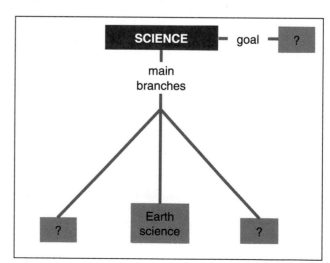

34

Concept Mastery

Discuss each of the following in a brief paragraph.

1. Discuss the uses and limitations of a compound light microscope and an SEM.
2. Describe the importance of a standard system of measurement.
3. Explain why mass is constant whereas weight can change.
4. Discuss the different metric units of length and explain when you might use each .
5. Your friend wants you to convert kilograms to meters. Explain why that is not possible.
6. List and describe at least three examples of how you act like a scientist.
7. Describe the steps of the scientific method.
8. Describe three science questions you would like to have answered.

Critical Thinking and Problem Solving

Use the skills you have developed in this chapter to answer each of the following.

1. **Making calculations** Use dimensional analysis to convert each of the following.
   a. A blue whale is about 33 meters in length. How many centimeters is this?
   b. The Statue of Liberty is about 45 meters tall. How tall is the statue in millimeters?
   c. Mount Everest is about 8.8 kilometers high. How high is it in meters?
   d. A Ping-Pong ball has a mass of about 2.4 grams. What is its mass in milligrams?
   e. An elephant is about 6300 kilograms in mass. What is its mass in grams?
2. **Relating concepts** Explain why every substance has a characteristic density, but not a characteristic mass.
3. **Following safety rules** Explain the potential danger in each of the following situations. Describe the safety precautions that should be used to avoid injury to you or your classmates.
   a. Pushing a rubber stopper far down into a test tube.
   b. Tasting a white powder to see if it is salty.
   c. Deciding on your own to mix two chemicals together.

4. **Applying concepts** Explain how the scientific method could be used by a mechanic to determine why a car won't start on a cold morning.
5. **Designing an experiment** Design an experiment to determine the best place to grow flowers in your classroom. With your teacher's permission, conduct the experiment and draw a conclusion.
6. **Using the writing process** Although Congress legalized the use of the metric system in 1866, its use is not required by the United States. Write a letter to the editor of your newspaper in which you explain why the United States should or should not convert to the metric system.

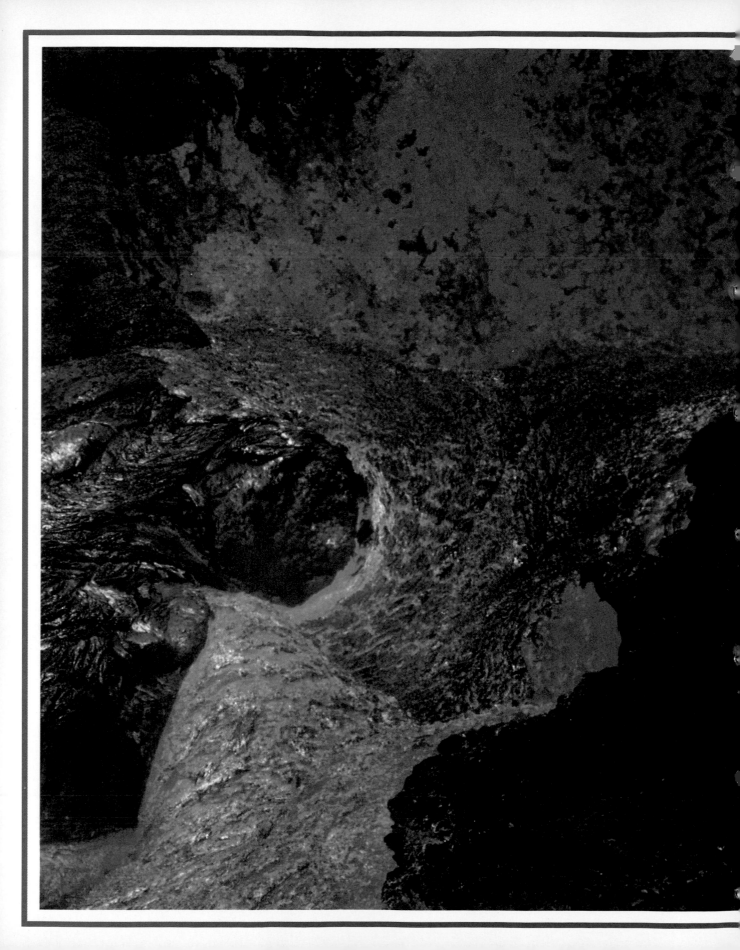

The Nature of Life

2

Guide for Reading

After you read the following sections, you will be able to

2–1 The Origin of Life
■ Describe the formation of Earth.
■ Discuss several theories about how life formed on Earth.

2–2 Characteristics of Living Things
■ Identify the basic characteristics of living things.
■ Describe metabolism.

2–3 Needs of Living Things
■ Identify the basic needs of living things.
■ Define homeostasis.

2–4 Chemistry of Living Things
■ Distinguish between elements and compounds.
■ Describe the organic compounds that are the building blocks of life.

A huge cloud of swirling dust and hot gases glows in the eerie darkness of space. Over many billions of years, gravity begins to pull the dust and gas toward the center of the cloud. In time, the cloud condenses into a giant sphere of matter. A planet has formed.

Half a billion years pass. The planet has begun to cool, and solid rocks dot its surface. Volcanoes spring up everywhere, shaking the planet with their constant eruptions. A poisonous atmosphere begins to form.

Another 200 million years pass. The planet is now cool enough to allow liquid water to flow on its surface. Thunderstorms begin to drench the planet with rain—year after year after year. In time, planet-wide oceans form. Although it will take another 300 million years, eventually living things will call these oceans home. Slowly but surely, these living things become more complex and begin to change, or evolve. Over the next 3.5 billion years, many living things will come and go on this planet as it floats in space. But one day very special living things will arise—living things that can pick up this textbook and discover what life is all about. Try it!

Journal *Activity*

On Your Own   When you read about the origin of Earth and the beginning of life, you read about events occurring over millions, even billions, of years. To help you get a better sense of time relationships, in your journal begin your time line with the major events discussed in this chapter. You may add any other events you desire—perhaps your birthday.

◄ *About 4 billion years ago, spectacular volcanic eruptions on Earth were a common occurrence.*

2–1 The Origin of Life

Slowly, the scientist fills the clear glass flask. First he pours in three colorless gases. The odor is awful, stinging the scientist's nose and bringing tears to his eyes. Then the scientist adds another gas. Nothing seems to happen. The flask looks empty. But if everything goes right, the gases it contains may be changed into something very special!

The mixture needs a spark to produce the necessary change. The scientist sends a surge of electricity through the flask again and again. At the same time, he shines ultraviolet light at the flask. Suddenly, a sticky brown coating begins to form on the walls of the flask. The mixture of gases inside is changing—turning into substances that may help to solve the key mystery of life.

Magic? It may seem to be, and at times the scientist may seem to be a magician. But his exciting experiment was actually performed, and its results are being used by scientists today as they attempt to study the "stuff of life."

In 1953, the American scientist Stanley Miller mixed together three gases: hydrogen, methane, and ammonia. To this mixture he added gaseous water. Then he passed an electric current to simulate lightning through the colorless mixture. Soon a brown tarlike substance streaked the sides of the container. Dr. Miller analyzed the tarlike substance and found that it contained several of the same substances that make up all living things. From nonliving chemicals, Stanley Miller had made some of the building blocks of life!

How can lifeless chemicals change into the matter that makes up life? To answer that question, we must go back to the formation of Earth.

Figure 2–1 *In 1953, Stanley Miller demonstrated that some of the chemicals that make up living things could have formed on ancient Earth.*

The Early Earth

You have read about the formation of Earth at the beginning of this chapter. Naturally, no one was there to see Earth form and to record exactly how it happened. Although we lack direct evidence about early Earth, we can make some basic generalizations about it. But keep in mind that much is still unclear

Figure 2–2 *You can see from this illustration of ancient Earth that most modern living things would not easily survive those rugged conditions.*

and that the complete picture has not yet been achieved.

Planet Earth formed about 4.6 billion years ago. (A billion is a 1 followed by 9 zeros!) But it would be more than half a billion years before the planet cooled and a rocky surface was created. And, as you have read, hundreds of millions of years more would pass before the oceans formed.

If you could turn back time and visit ancient Earth, you would be in for quite a surprise. The atmosphere was quite poisonous and could not support life as we know it. Scientists do not know the exact composition of that early atmosphere. Most agree that it contained some water vapor (gaseous water), carbon monoxide and carbon dioxide, nitrogen, hydrogen sulfide, methane, and hydrogen cyanide. Did the atmosphere contain any oxygen, so necessary for life on Earth today? The answer is unclear. Many scientists believe there was little or no oxygen in the early atmosphere. But recent evidence indicates such theories may have to be adjusted; the early atmosphere may have contained oxygen. In either case, you would not have been able to breathe the air and survive.

ACTIVITY
READING

Strange New Worlds

If you like science fiction and enjoy reading about new worlds, you might like to read *Last and First Men* by Olaf Stapledon. In his journey into the far future, Stapledon writes of the evolution of people and the many worlds they conquer.

The Molecules of Life Form

The experiment performed by Stanley Miller showed that compounds necessary for life can be produced from nonliving substances. Miller's experiment opened the door to the exploration of how life formed on Earth. Today we know that the gases Miller placed in the flask probably did not match the atmosphere of early Earth. So we cannot say that life began in a manner similar to Miller's experiment. But we can say that the chemicals that make up living things could have been produced on early Earth. The exact process that would have made this possible is another question scientists have not as yet answered.

A batch of chemicals is a long way from a living thing. And just as scientists cannot say with certainty how the chemicals of life formed, they also cannot say how these chemicals came together to form the first living things. But based on current evidence, they can develop theories.

One theory begins with the notion that the early oceans began somehow to fill with the chemicals that make up living things. We can think of these oceans as a kind of "soup" containing the substances needed for life. Using solid evidence about the behavior of matter, scientists do have ideas about how some chemicals in the soup may have come together to form the beginning of life. For example, we now know that under the right conditions amino acids will link together on their own to form small chains. This is significant because a chain of amino acids is called a protein and proteins are among the basic building blocks of living things. Other chemicals, which scientists believe might have been in that original soup, have also been observed to link together on their own to produce carbohydrates, alcohols, and fatty substances called lipids. (You will learn more about proteins, carbohydrates, lipids, and other chemicals of life later in this chapter.) So

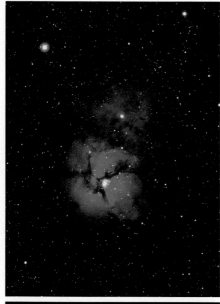

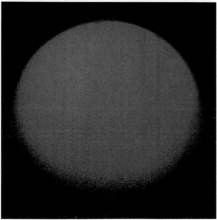

Figure 2–3 *Analysis of distant nebulae has shown that some chemicals of life form spontaneously in the dust and gas of outer space (top). Many scientists feel that conditions in the atmosphere of Titan, Saturn's largest moon, may be similar to conditions on primitive Earth (bottom). Some scientists suggest that microscopic living things may have evolved on Titan.*

Figure 2–4 *One theory proposes that much of the water on Earth was carried to the primitive planet as frozen ice in meteors and asteroids.*

although we cannot say exactly how it happened, we can say with some certainty that it was possible for chemicals in the soup to produce some of the building blocks of life.

How Cells Formed

Later in this chapter you will discover that one of the basic characteristics of living things is that they are made of cells. So it is safe to assume that life on Earth began when the first cells formed. How did that process occur? Again, there are no clear answers—only theories based on current evidence.

One theory states that the first cells arose in shallow pools containing the early soup of chemicals. These cells formed as the chemicals in the soup collected into droplets. The droplets were surrounded by a wall, or barrier, that kept the chemicals inside and the soup outside. Over time, the substances necessary for life developed and the droplets became true cells.

Yet another theory states that the first cells formed in beds of clay on early Earth. The structure of the clay allowed the chemicals necessary for life to become concentrated, or trapped in the clay. As time went on, these chemicals grouped together to produce the first living cells.

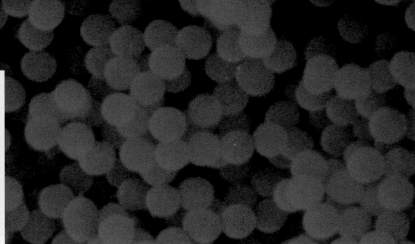

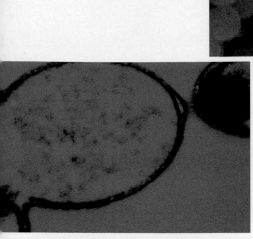

Figure 2–5 *These droplets, magnified 3000 times, were created in the laboratory of Sidney Fox. Although the droplets are not alive, they can perform some of the basic life functions. Some droplets can actually reproduce by dividing into two separate droplets.*

There are other theories regarding the origin of the first true cells. At this time, however, no one can say whether any one theory is right or wrong. What can be said is that somehow, through some process, the chemicals that make up living things did group together and form the first cells. Once these first cells formed, the parade of life on Earth began—a parade that continues to this day.

The First True Cells

Scientists have discovered fossils (remains of living things) that indicate that the first true cells evolved and inhabited Earth as far back as 3.5 billion years ago. The origin of these first true cells is still unknown. But no matter how they formed, some generalizations about them can be made.

The first true cells were doubtless organisms that did not require oxygen. Remember, the early atmosphere probably contained little or no oxygen. So it is safe to assume that early cells did not require oxygen. It is also safe to assume that these early cells were consumers, or organisms that did not produce their own food. The soup in which these early forms of life floated was their source of food. And indeed, the early cells had plenty of food to feed upon. But as you might expect, over time the food in the soup gradually began to dwindle. In order for life to have continued, cells capable of producing their own food must have evolved. These cells used chemicals from their environment to produce food and energy. Thus, living things began to change from consumers to producers.

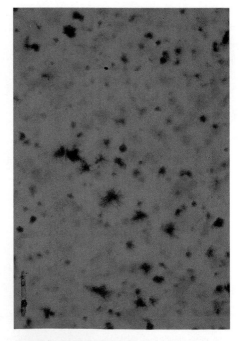

Figure 2–6 *You can see 2-billion-year-old fossils of bacteria cells in this thin slice of rock. When do scientists estimate the first true cells formed?*

Photosynthesis

Earth today is filled with both consumers and producers. You, for example, are a consumer. You must eat food in order to obtain energy and important nutrients. Green plants, on the other hand, are producers. They use chemicals in their environment and the energy of sunlight to produce their own food. Green plants produce food in a process called photosynthesis. (You will learn much more about photosynthesis in Chapter 9.)

Scientists theorize that at some point certain early cells were able to perform photosynthesis. This is an extremely important event in the history of Earth. Do you know why? One of the waste materials plants produce during photosynthesis is a gas called oxygen. As early cells began to perform photosynthesis, they also began to change the atmosphere of Earth. Over millions of years, Earth's poisonous atmosphere was changed to one that contains about one fifth part oxygen. The stage was now set for organisms that use oxygen to evolve.

Modern Cells Form

The production of oxygen by early cells transformed Earth and gave rise to cells that use oxygen for many of the chemical reactions that take place within them. Cells that use oxygen are much more efficient in their production of energy than cells that do not use oxygen. With greater energy efficiency, cells were free to evolve in a wide variety of ways.

The history of cell evolution is a fascinating topic and one that is hotly debated. How did cells that use oxygen first evolve? How were the cells we find in living things today produced? These questions are as yet unanswered. Perhaps they never will be. But one thing is certain: Along with photosynthesis and cells that use oxygen came other evolutionary advances.

One advance was the appearance of multicellular organisms, or organisms that contain many cells. The jump from single-celled (unicellular) organisms to multicellular organisms was an important leap in the development of living things. In time, cells in multicellular organisms began to specialize and perform

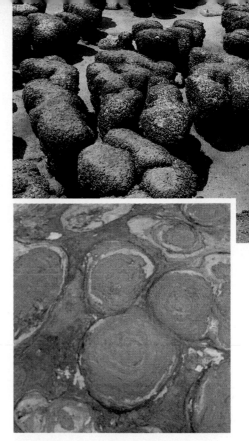

Figure 2–7 *The first photosynthetic organisms grew in layered mats called stromatolites. Shark Bay, Australia, is one of the few places where living stromatolites still exist. Fossils of stromatolites can be found throughout the world.*

ACTIVITY

DISCOVERING

A Different Light

1. Plant several of the same type of seeds in five different containers.

2. When the seedlings are about 2.5 cm above the soil, cover each top of the container with one of the following cellophane sheets: red, green, yellow, blue and clear.

■ How do the different sheets of cellophane affect plant growth?

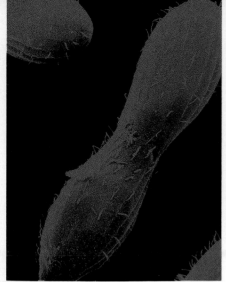

Figure 2–8 *In asexual reproduction, such as the division of a protozoan, each new cell is an exact copy of the original cell. In sexual reproduction, however, offspring inherit traits from two parents, increasing variation in the species.*

specific functions. A new form of reproduction developed as well. Early cells reproduced by splitting into two cells. And in time a type of reproduction called sexual reproduction developed. During sexual reproduction, sex cells from two different parents join together to form a new organism. With the development of multicellular organisms and sexual reproduction, all the facets that make up life had arisen. All that was left was to wait and see what evolved—a process we are still exploring today.

2–1 Section Review

1. What is the age of Earth?
2. How do we know that the first living things did not require oxygen?
3. Are you unicellular or multicellular? Explain.

Critical Thinking—*Drawing Conclusions*
4. Could the events that led to the first true cells recur on Earth today? Explain your answer.

Guide for Reading

Focus on this question as you read.

▶ *What are the characteristics of living things?*

2–2 Characteristics of Living Things

Take a short walk in the city or the country and you will see an enormous variety of living things. In fact, scientists estimate that there are up to 10 million different types of organisms on Earth, ranging in size from single-celled bacteria to huge blue whales. Yet all these living things are composed mainly of the same basic elements: carbon, hydrogen, nitrogen, and oxygen. These elements make up the gases Stanley Miller placed in his flask. And often, along with iron, calcium, phosphorus, and sulfur, these four elements link together in chains, rings, and loops to form the stuff of life.

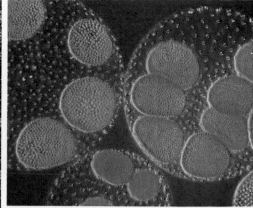
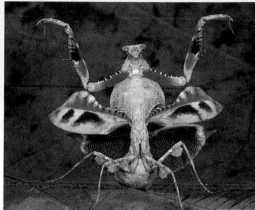

Figure 2–9 *The walrus (left), bottle tree (center), Volvox (top right), and dead-leaf mantis (bottom right) are among the great variety of living things that inhabit planet Earth. Yet despite their diversity, all living things are made of the same basic elements.*

Well-known chemical rules govern the way these elements combine and interact. But less well understood is what gives this collection of chemicals a very special property—the property of life.

Spontaneous Generation

People did not always understand that living matter is so special. Until the 1600s, most people believed in **spontaneous generation.** According to this theory, life could spring from nonliving matter. For example, people believed that mice came from straw and that frogs and turtles developed from rotting wood and mud at the bottom of a pond.

In 1668, an Italian doctor named Francesco Redi disproved the spontaneous-generation theory. Here is how he did it. In those days, maggots (a wormlike stage in the life cycle of a fly) often appeared on decaying (rotting) meat. People believed that the rotten meat had actually turned into maggots. This could only mean that flies (adult maggots) formed from dead animals (meat)—or that nonliving things could give rise to living things. In a series of

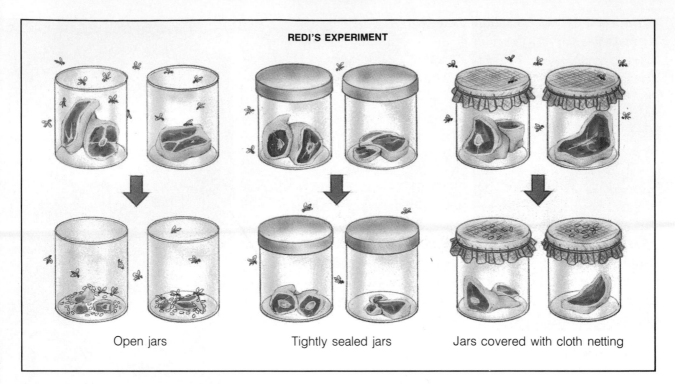

REDI'S EXPERIMENT

Open jars

Tightly sealed jars

Jars covered with cloth netting

Figure 2–10 *In Redi's experiment, no maggots were found on the meat in jars covered with netting or in those tightly sealed. Maggots appeared on the meat only when flies were able to enter the jars and lay eggs.*

ACTIVITY

WRITING

Life From Life

Using reference materials in the library, find out about each of these scientists:

John Needham
Lazzaro Spallanzani
Louis Pasteur

In a written report, describe how each scientist used the scientific method to prove or disprove the theory of spontaneous generation.

experiments, which are illustrated in Figure 2–10, Redi proved that the maggots hatched from eggs laid by flies.

Redi's experiment was quite simple. He placed rotting meat in several jars. He left two jars open and sealed two others. He covered the third set of jars with a cloth netting. The netting let in air but did not allow flies to land on the meat. In a few days, Redi observed flies on and above the meat in the open jars. There were no flies in the sealed jars or in the jars covered with netting. When people attempted to discredit Redi's results by claiming no flies were created in the meat in the sealed jars because the jars kept out air, Redi pointed out that air could enter the jars covered with netting. In a simple but elegant experiment, Redi had proved that spontaneous generation does not occur. Today there is no doubt that living things can arise only from other living things.

At this chapter's beginning you read about the origin of life. Now you have read about spontaneous generation and how it is an incorrect theory. Is this double talk? Could life have arisen from nonliving things on early Earth, even though it does not occur on Earth today? The answer is yes. The conditions on early Earth were such that living things could arise from the soup of chemicals that formed on the Earth. Today that soup no longer exists. The formation of life as it occurred on early Earth cannot occur on its own again—at least not on Earth. On other planets—who knows!

Now that we have explored a bit about how life began (and why those processes cannot recur), it is time to examine just what makes living things so special. That is, what distinguishes even the smallest organism from a lifeless streak of brown tar on a laboratory flask?

There are certain characteristics that all forms of life share. Living things are made of cells and most are able to move. They perform complex chemical activities, grow and develop, respond to a stimulus, and reproduce.

Living Things Are Made of Cells

All living things are made of small units called cells. That is, cells are the basic building blocks of living things just as atoms are the basic building blocks of matter. Each cell contains living material surrounded by a border, or barrier, that separates the cell from its environment.

As Francesco Redi showed, cells are never formed by nonliving things. Cells come only from other cells. Nonliving matter may contain the remains of once-living cells, however. For example, firewood is made largely of cells that were once part of living trees.

Figure 2–11 *If you had no knowledge of trees, could you tell by a walk through a winter forest if these trees were living or nonliving?*

Figure 2–12 *All life on Earth is cellular. Some living things, such as these spherical bacteria, are unicellular. Other living things, such as the rhinoceros and her young, are multicellular.*

Some living things contain only a single cell. Single-celled, or unicellular, organisms include microscopic bacteria. (The Latin prefix *uni-* means one, so unicellular means single-celled.) The single cell in a unicellular organism can perform all the functions necessary for life. Most of the living things you are familiar with, such as cats and flowering plants, contain many cells, or are multicellular. What do you think the prefix *multi-* means in Latin?

Multicellular organisms may contain hundreds, thousands, or even trillions of cells. It has been estimated that humans contain about 6 trillion cells. Although the cells of multicellular organisms perform the basic functions of life, they are often specialized to perform a specific function in the organism. You will learn more about cells in Chapter 3. For now, all you need to remember is that the cell is the basic building block of living things.

Living Things Can Move

The ability to move through the environment is an important characteristic of many living things. Why? Animals must be able to move in order to find food and shelter. In times of danger, swift movement can be the difference between safety and death. Of course, animals move in a great many ways. Fins enable fish such as salmon to swim hundreds of kilometers in search of a place to mate. The kangaroo uses its entire body as a giant pogo stick to bounce along the Australian plains looking for scarce patches of grass upon which to graze. You have to move to turn the page and continue reading this chapter.

Figure 2–13 *In order to find food and shelter, most animals must be able to move. The arctic tern holds the long-distance record for birds in flight, as it covers nearly 32,000 kilometers in its yearly migration from the Arctic to the Antarctic and back. The kangaroo uses its body as a pogo stick as it bounces along the Australian plains. The larval crab gets around by hitching a ride on a jellyfish.*

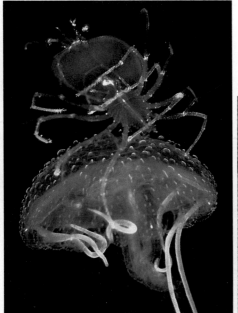

Most plants do not move in the same way animals do. Only parts of the plants move. The stems of many plants, for example, bend toward sunlight so the leaves on the plants can catch the sun's rays.

Living Things Perform Complex Chemical Activities

Building up and breaking down is a good way to describe the chemical activities that are essential to life. During some of these activities, simple substances combine to form complex substances. These substances are needed by an organism to grow, store energy, and repair or replace cells and other body parts. During other activities, complex substances are broken down, releasing energy and usable food substances. Together, these chemical activities are called **metabolism** (muh-TAB-uh-lih-zuhm). Metabolism is another characteristic of living things.

Metabolism is the sum total of all the chemical reactions that occur in a living thing. But before metabolism can begin, most organisms must perform a physical activity—taking in food.

INGESTION All living things must either take in food or produce their own food. For most animals, **ingestion,** or eating, is as simple as putting food into their mouths.

Green plants do not have to ingest food. Green plants are able to make their own food. Using their roots, green plants absorb water and minerals from the soil. Tiny openings in the underside of their

Stimulus-Response Reactions

1. Hold your hands close to a friend's face. Quickly clap your hands while observing your friend's eyes.

2. While standing in front of a mirror, cover one of your eyes with your hand for a minute. Remove your hand and immediately look into the mirror and note any changes in your eye.

3. With a knife, cut a slice of lemon. **Caution**: *Be careful when using a knife.* Bring the lemon slice close to your mouth or put it in your mouth.

In a data table, describe the stimulus and the response for each of these activities.

Figure 2–14 *Green plants can make their own food, but animals must eat food. The grasshopper is feeding on a sunflower plant. The gecko, however, prefers a meatier dinner.*

leaves allow carbon dioxide to enter. The green plants use the water and carbon dioxide, along with energy from the sun, to make food in the process called photosynthesis.

DIGESTION   Getting food into the body is a first step. Now the process of metabolism can begin. But there is a lot more to metabolism than just eating. The food must be digested in order to be used. **Digestion** is the process by which food is broken down into simpler substances. Later some of these simpler substances are reassembled into more complex materials for use in the growth and repair of the living thing. Other simple substances store energy that the organism will use for its many activities.

RESPIRATION   All living things require energy to survive. To obtain energy, living things combine oxygen with the products of digestion (in animals) or the products of photosynthesis (in green plants). The energy is used to do the work of the organism. The process by which living things take in oxygen and use it to produce energy is called **respiration**. You get the energy you need by combining the foods you eat with the oxygen you breathe.

EXCRETION   Not all the products of digestion and respiration can be used by an organism. Some products are waste materials that must be released. The process of getting rid of waste materials is called **excretion.** Like ingestion, excretion is a physical process. Without excretion, the waste products of digestion and respiration will build up in the body and eventually poison the organism.

Living Things Grow and Develop

The concept that living things grow is certainly not new to you. In fact, at this moment you are in the process of growth yourself. (How many times have you been told "When you grow up you can . . ."?)

When you think of growth, you probably think of something getting bigger. And that is certainly one part of growth. But growth can mean more than just an increase in size. Living things also become more complex, or develop, during the growth process. Sometimes this development results in dramatic changes. A tadpole, for example, swims for weeks in

Figure 2–15 *The gazelle obtains the energy it needs to run away from a predator by combining oxygen with food in a process called respiration. Although the killer whale spends most of its time under water, it must return to the surface to take in the oxygen it requires for respiration. Where do fish obtain the oxygen they require?*

Figure 2–16 *All living things grow and develop. Usually growth means simply getting larger, not changing form. But that is not always the case. This caterpillar will grow and develop into an adult lime butterfly.*

a summer pond. Then one day that tadpole becomes the frog that sits near the water's edge. And surely the caterpillar creeping through a garden gives little hint of the beautiful butterfly it will soon become. So both growth and development must be added to the list of characteristics of living things.

One of the important aspects of growth and development is **life span**. Life span is the maximum length of time a particular organism can be expected to live. Life span varies greatly from one type of organism to another. For example, an Indian elephant may live to be 70 years old. A bristlecone pine tree may live to be 5500 years old!

Living Things Respond to Their Environment

Scientists call each of the signals to which an organism reacts a **stimulus** (plural: stimuli). A stimulus is any change in the environment, or surroundings, of an organism that produces a **response** by that organism. A response is some action, movement, or change in behavior of the organism.

Figure 2–17 *In certain organisms, growth and development take up most of the life span. The mayfly spends two years in lakes, growing and developing into an adult. The adult, however, lives for only one day, during which it finds a mate, reproduces, and then dies. The life span of the bristlecone pine, on the other hand, can last up to 5500 years.*

Figure 2–18 *Living things respond to stimuli from their environment. What stimuli is the bat responding to? What will be the response of the frog?*

ACTIVITY
DOING

The Great Redi Experiment

1. Obtain 3 wide-mouthed jars. In each jar, place a piece of raw meat about the size of a half dollar.

2. Cover one jar with plastic wrap and another with two thicknesses of cheesecloth. Use rubber bands to hold the plastic wrap and cheesecloth in place. Leave the third jar uncovered.

3. Put the jars in a warm sunny place outdoors where they will remain undisturbed for 3 days. *Do not merely place the jars on a windowsill.*

4. After 3 days, examine the meat in each jar.

In which jar did you find maggots (young flies that resemble worms)? Did you find eggs in or on any of the jars? What does this activity tell you about spontaneous generation?

Some stimuli come from outside an organism's body. For example, smells and noises are stimuli to which you respond. So is tickling. Light and water are stimuli to which plants respond. Other stimuli come from inside an organism's body. A lack of oxygen in your body is a stimulus that often causes you to yawn.

Some plants have special responses that protect them. For example, when a gypsy moth caterpillar chews on a leaf of an oak tree, the tree responds by producing bad-tasting chemicals in its other leaves. The chemicals discourage all but the hungriest caterpillars from eating these leaves. Can you think of responses that help you protect yourself?

Living Things Reproduce

You probably know that dinosaurs lived millions of years ago and are now extinct. Yet crocodiles, which appeared on Earth before the dinosaurs, still exist today. An organism becomes extinct when it no longer produces other organisms of the same kind. In other words, all living things of a given kind would become extinct if they did not reproduce.

The process by which living things give rise to the same type of living thing is called reproduction. Crocodiles, for example, do not produce dinosaurs; crocodiles produce only more crocodiles. You are a human—not a water buffalo, duck, or tomato plant—because your parents are humans. An easy way to remember this is *like produces like.*

There are two different types of reproduction: **sexual reproduction** and **asexual reproduction**. Sexual reproduction usually requires two parents. Most

multicellular forms of plants and animals reproduce sexually.

Some living things reproduce from only one parent. This is asexual reproduction. When an organism divides into two parts, it is reproducing asexually. Bacteria reproduce this way. Yeast forms growths called buds, which break off and then form new yeast plants. Geraniums and African violets grow new plants from part of a stem, root, or leaf of the parent plant. All these examples illustrate asexual reproduction.

Sexual and asexual reproduction have an important function in common. In each case, the offspring receive a set of special chemical "blueprints," or plans. These blueprints determine the characteristics of that living thing and are passed from one generation to the next.

2–2 Section Review

1. List and describe the characteristics of living things. Which of these characteristics is not necessary for the survival of an organism?
2. Describe Redi's experiment on the spontaneous-generation theory.
3. Define metabolism. What are the main parts of metabolism?
4. Compare sexual and asexual reproduction.

Critical Thinking—*Applying Concepts*
5. A snowball rolling over fresh snow will grow larger. Explain why a rolling snowball is not a living thing.

ACTIVITY
DISCOVERING

Living or Nonliving?

1. Obtain 6 mL of gelatin solution and 4 mL of gum arabic solution from your teacher. Add these solutions together in a test tube.

2. Stopper the test tube. Gently turn it upside down several times to mix the two solutions. **Note:** *Do not shake the test tube.*

3. Remove the stopper from the test tube and add 3 drops of weak hydrochloric acid. **CAUTION:** *Be careful when using acid.*

4. Dip a glass rod into the mixture. Touch a drop of the mixture onto a piece of pH paper. Compare the color of your pH paper to the color scale on the package of pH paper. Repeat steps 3 and 4 until the mixture reaches a pH of 4.

5. Place 2 drops of the mixture on a glass slide. Cover the slide with a coverslip and examine it under low power. Record your observations.

■ In what ways do the droplets seem to be living? In what ways do they seem to be nonliving?

PROBLEM Solving

Helpful Hints

You have been selected the new editor for your school newspaper. Your first assignment is the Helpful Hints column. Answer the following questions submitted by your fellow students. Your answers should relate to the fact that stimulus-response reactions are a method of protection against potentially harmful situations.

Relating Cause and Effect

1. Why do I squint in bright sunlight?

2. Why do birds migrate south in the winter?

3. When dirt gets in my eye, my eye blinks and produces tears. Why?

4. My dog pants heavily after a long run. Is she ill?

2–3 Needs of Living Things

Living things interact with one another as well as with their environment. These interactions are as varied as the living things themselves. Birds, for example, use dead twigs to build nests, but they eat live worms and insects. Crayfish build their homes in the sand or mud of streams and swamps. They absorb a chemical called lime from these waters and use it to build a hard body covering. Crayfish rely, however, on living snails and tadpoles for their food. And some people rely on crayfish for a tasty meal!

Figure 2–20 *All living things interact with their environment, as this hermit crab demonstrates. It crawls slowly up a tree while wearing the discarded shell of a snail.*

Clearly, living things depend on both the living and nonliving parts of their environment. **In order for a living organism to survive, it needs energy, food, water, oxygen, living space, and the ability to maintain a fairly constant body temperature.**

Energy

All living things need energy. The energy can be used in different ways depending on the organism. A lion uses energy to chase and capture its prey. The electric eel defends itself by shocking its attackers with electric energy.

What is the source of energy so necessary to living things? The primary source of energy for most living things is the sun. Does that surprise you? Plants use the sun's light energy to make food. Some animals feed on plants and in that way obtain the energy stored in the plants. Other animals then eat the plant eaters. In this way, the energy from the sun is passed on from one living thing to another. So next time you are eating a delicious meal— whether tacos, spaghetti, or bean-sprout salad—give silent thanks to the sun.

Food and Water

Food is a need of all living things. It is a source of energy as well as a supplier of the raw materials needed for growth, development, and repair of body parts.

ACTIVITY

DISCOVERING

Love That Light

Obtain two coleus plants of equal size. Using the two plants and a sunny window, design and perform an experiment that will show if plants move in response to light. *Hint:* You are using two plants for a reason.

■ What conclusions can you draw about the movement of plants in response to light?

Figure 2–21 *Plants, which make their own food through photosynthesis, are producers. Animals cannot make their own food. What term is given to organisms that cannot make their own food?*

55

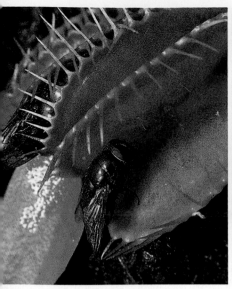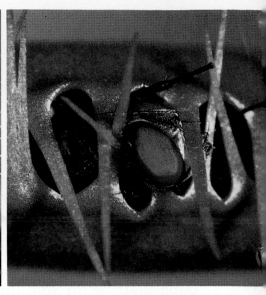

Figure 2–22 *Not all plants rely only on photosynthesis for food. When a fly touches the tiny hairs lining a leaf of a Venus' flytrap plant, the leaf responds by closing and trapping the fly. The plant will then digest the unlucky fly.*

FOOD The kind of foods organisms eat varies considerably. You would probably not want to eat eucalyptus leaves, yet that is the only food a koala eats. A diet of wood may not seem tempting, but for the termite it is a source of energy and necessary chemical substances.

WATER Although you would probably not enjoy it, you could live for a week or more without food. But you would die in only a few days without water. It may surprise you to learn that 65 percent or more of your body is water. Other living things are also made up mainly of water.

In addition to making up much of your body, water serves many other purposes. Most substances dissolve in water. In this way, important chemicals can be transported easily throughout an organism. The blood of animals and the sap of trees, for example, are mainly water.

Most chemical reactions in living things cannot take place without water. Metabolism would come to a grinding halt without water. And it is water that carries away many of the metabolic waste products produced by living things. For green plants, water is also a raw material for photosynthesis (the food-making process).

Figure 2–23 *The gazelles and elephants drinking together at an African waterhole illustrate the importance of water to the survival of living things.*

Oxygen

You already know that for most living organisms oxygen is necessary for the process of respiration. Where do organisms get their oxygen? That depends on where they live. Organisms that live on land, whether plant or animal, obtain their oxygen directly from the air. Organisms that live under water either come up to the surface for oxygen (porpoises, for example) or remove the oxygen dissolved in the water (fish or seaweed, for example).

When organisms use oxygen they produce a waste product called carbon dioxide. For example, you breathe in oxygen when you inhale and breathe out carbon dioxide when you exhale. But the carbon dioxide is not wasted. Plants take carbon dioxide from the air and use it as a raw material in the process of photosynthesis. This cycling of oxygen and carbon dioxide is one reason living things have not used up all the available oxygen and carbon dioxide in the air.

Living Space

Do you enjoy the chirping of birds on a lovely spring morning? If you do, you may be surprised to learn that the birds are staking out their territory and warning intruders to stay away.

ACTIVITY CALCULATING

You're All Wet

About 65 percent of your body mass is water.

Determine how many kilograms of water you contain.

Figure 2–24 *Organisms do not compete only for food and water. These elephants are crashing tusks in a power struggle for territory.*

Often there is a limited amount of food, water, and energy in an environment. As a result, only a limited number of the same kind of living thing can survive in a particular location. That is why many animals defend a certain area they consider to be their living space. The male sunfish, for example, defends its territory in ponds by flashing its colorful fins at other sunfish and darting toward any sunfish that comes too close. Coyotes howl at night to mark their territory and to keep other coyotes away. You might think of these behaviors as a kind of competition for living space.

Competition is the struggle among living things to get the proper amount of food, water, and energy. Animals are not the only competitors for these materials in their living space. Plants compete for sunlight and water as well. Smaller, weaker plants often die in the shadow of larger plants.

Proper Temperature

During the summer, temperatures as high as 58°C have been recorded on Earth. Winter temperatures can dip as low as –89°C. Most organisms cannot survive at such temperature extremes because many metabolic activities cannot occur at these temperatures. Without metabolism, an organism dies.

Actually, most organisms would quickly die at far less severe temperature extremes if it were not for **homeostasis** (hoh-mee-oh-STAY-sihs). Homeostasis is

Figure 2–25 *The coldblooded frilled-neck lizard is basking in the sun in order to achieve homeostasis. The warmblooded prairie dog relies on chemical activities in its body to maintain a constant body temperature.*

the ability of an organism to keep conditions inside its body the same, even though conditions in its external environment change. Maintaining a constant body temperature, no matter what the temperature of the surroundings, is part of homeostasis. Birds and certain other animals, such as dogs and horses, produce enough heat to keep themselves warm at low temperatures. When temperatures get too high, many birds make their throats flutter to cool off. Like dogs, some birds also pant to lower their body temperatures. Sweating has a similar effect on horses. Animals that maintain a constant body temperature are called warmblooded animals. Warmblooded animals can be active during both day and night, in hot weather and in cold.

Animals such as amphibians, reptiles, and fishes have body temperatures that can change somewhat with changes in the temperature of the environment. These animals are called coldblooded animals. But that does not mean that their blood is cold. Rather, it means that they must use their behavior to help maintain homeostasis. To keep warm, a coldblooded reptile, such as a crocodile, must spend part of each day lying in the sun. At night, when air temperature drops, so does the crocodile's body temperature. The crocodile becomes lazy and inactive. Coldblooded animals do not move around much at relatively high or low temperatures.

ACTIVITY

CALCULATING

Temperature Range

Calculate the range in temperature between the highest recorded temperature, 58°C and the lowest recorded temperature, –89°C.

What was the change in temperature in your area yesterday?

Find out the record high and low temperatures in your area. What is the difference in temperature?

2–3 Section Review

1. List and describe the basic needs of living things.
2. What is the relationship between the sun and the energy needed by living things?
3. Define homeostasis and explain its importance to living things.

Connection—*Ecology*

4. Thermal (heat) pollution occurs when heated water from factories and power plants is released into lakes and streams. Based on what you know about homeostasis, what problems to wildlife might result from thermal pollution?

A Heated Experiment

The year was 1774. The English doctor Matthew Dobson decided to try a most unusual experiment. Even more unusual, he convinced four of his friends to help out. Dobson and his friends entered a heated room and sealed the door. While the temperature in the room rose higher and higher, the gleeful group continued to feed a fire blazing away in a stove in the room.

Five, ten, then twenty minutes passed. The room grew hotter and hotter. Dobson and his friends took their temperature every few minutes. To their surprise, even as raw eggs left in the room cooked before their eyes, their body temperatures barely rose at all. But they did sweat—oh, did they sweat!

After a while the adventurous group left the room. Once back in a more normal (and comfortable) condition, they began to analyze their observations and draw conclusions. Some of these conclusions may seem obvious to you, but to most people of that time they were significant discoveries. One conclusion was that sweating and the resulting *evaporation* of sweat was actually a way in which the body cooled itself. Of greater importance was the understanding that a healthy body keeps a stable internal temperature despite the outside environment. That is, the five men developed the idea that homeostasis is a basic requirement of life. From that concept came the notion that taking a person's temperature using a thermometer was one way of determining if that person was ill.

2-4 Chemistry of Living Things

What do foil wrap, a light-bulb filament, and a diamond have in common? These objects look very different and certainly have very different uses, but all are examples of **elements.** An element is a pure substance that cannot be broken down into any simpler substances by ordinary means.

When two or more elements are chemically joined together, **compounds** are formed. Water is a compound made of the elements hydrogen and oxygen. Table salt, which you may use to flavor your food, is a compound made of sodium and chlorine. Sand and glass are compounds composed of the elements silicon and oxygen. There are thousands of different compounds all around you. In fact, you are made of many compounds. Scientists classify compounds into two groups.

Inorganic Compounds

Compounds that may or may not contain the element carbon are called inorganic compounds. Most inorganic compounds do not contain carbon. However, carbon dioxide is an exception. Table salt, ammonia, rust, and water are inorganic compounds.

Organic Compounds

Most of the compounds in living things contain carbon, which is usually combined with other elements such as hydrogen and oxygen. These compounds are called **organic compounds.** The term organic refers to life. Because some of these compounds were first discovered in living things, they were appropriately named organic compounds.

Guide for Reading

Focus on these questions as you read.
▶ *What are elements and compounds?*
▶ *What organic compounds are basic to life?*

Figure 2-26 *Nonliving things, such as these amethyst crystals, are made of inorganic compounds. Living things, such as the mushroom and green plants, are made primarily of organic compounds. What element is found in all organic compounds?*

ACTIVITY

A Starchy Question

You can use iodine to find out if a particular food is high in starch. To find out how, place a few drops of iodine on a potato that has been sliced in half. Potatoes are high in starch.

Choose four food samples you think contain starch and four you think do not.

■ Determine if your predictions were true for each sample.

■ Is there a way you can determine whether the amount of starch in a food is high or low? Try it.

Figure 2–27 *A thick layer of fat and a nice fur coat keep this Black bear warm throughout the year.*

There are more than 3 million different organic compounds in living things. **Organic compounds that are basic to life include carbohydrates, fats and oils, proteins, enzymes, and nucleic acids.**

CARBOHYDRATES The main source of energy for living things is **carbohydrates**. Carbohydrates are made of the elements carbon, hydrogen, and oxygen. Sugar and starch are two important carbohydrates. Many fruits are high in sugar content. Potatoes, rice, noodles, and bread are common sources of starch. What are some foods you eat that contain sugars and starches?

Carbohydrates are broken down inside the body into a simple sugar called glucose. The body then uses glucose to produce the energy needed for life activities. If an organism has more sugar than it needs for its energy requirements, it will store the sugar for later use. In plants, sugar is stored as starch. Starch, then, is a stored form of energy.

FATS AND OILS Another group of energy-rich compounds made of carbon, hydrogen, and oxygen are **fats** and **oils.** The more proper scientific term for these compounds is lipids. How can you tell a fat from an oil? Actually, it is quite easy. Fats are solid at room temperature; oils are liquid at room temperature.

PROTEINS Like carbohydrates and fats, **proteins** are organic compounds made up of carbon, hydrogen, and oxygen. But proteins also contain the element nitrogen and sometimes the elements sulfur and phosphorus. Some important sources of proteins are eggs, meat, fish, beans, nuts, and poultry.

The building blocks of proteins are **amino acids.** There are 20 different amino acids. But because amino acids combine in many ways, they form thousands of different proteins.

Proteins perform many jobs for an organism. They are necessary for the growth and repair of body structures. Proteins are used to build body parts such as hair and muscles. Some proteins, such as those in blood, carry oxygen throughout the body. Other proteins fight germs that invade the body. Still other proteins make chemical substances (hormones) that start, stop, and regulate many important body activities.

ENZYMES   A special type of protein that regulates chemical activities within the body is called an **enzyme.** Enzymes act as catalysts. A catalyst is a substance that speeds up or slows down chemical reactions but is not itself changed by the reaction. Without enzymes, the chemical reactions of metabolism could not take place or would occur so slowly that they would be of little help to the organism.

NUCLEIC ACIDS   Do you remember the "blueprints" of life we discussed earlier in this chapter? These blueprints are organic chemicals called **nucleic acids**. Nucleic acids, which are very large compounds, store information that helps the body make the proteins it needs. The nucleic acids control the way the amino acids are put together so that the correct protein is formed. This process is similar to the way a carpenter uses a blueprint to build a house. Can you now understand why nucleic acids are called the blueprints of life?

One nucleic acid is **DNA,** or deoxyribonucleic (dee-ahks-ih-righ-boh-noo-KLEE-ihk) acid. DNA stores the information needed to build a protein. DNA also carries "messages" about an organism that are passed from parent to offspring.

Another nucleic acid is called **RNA**, or ribonucleic (righ-boh-noo-KLEE-ihk) acid. RNA "reads" the message carried by DNA and guides the protein-making process. Together, these two nucleic acids contain the information and carry out the steps that make each organism what it is.

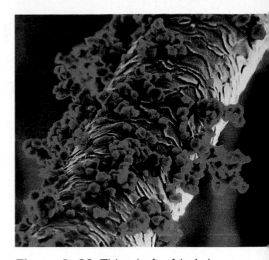

Figure 2–28 *This shaft of hair is composed primarily of proteins. The green droplets are the result of spraying the hair with dry shampoo.*

2–4 Section Review

1. Compare an element and a compound.
2. List and describe the basic organic compounds necessary for life.
3. Why is it important that enzymes are not changed by the reactions they control?

Connection—*Nutrition*

4. Based on your knowledge of the chemistry of living things, explain why it is important to eat a balanced diet.

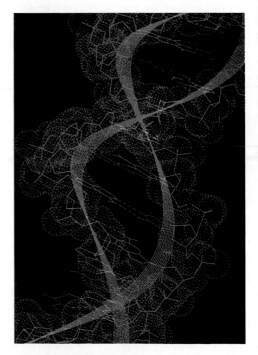

Figure 2–29 *Nucleic acids have been called the blueprints of life. The computer-generated image shows the structure of a DNA molecule, the molecule that controls protein production and heredity.*

Laboratory Investigation

You Are What You Eat

Problem

Does your school lunch menu provide a balanced diet?

Materials *(per group)*

school lunch menu for the current week
pencil
paper
reference book or textbook on nutrition

Procedure

1. Obtain a copy of your school's lunch menu for one week.

2. Make a table similar to the one shown here that lists the five food groups: meat group, vegetable group, fruit group, milk group, bread-cereal group.

3. For each day of the week, place each item from the menu in the appropriate food group in your table. An example has been provided in the sample table.

4. Make a second table similar to the one shown here that lists the three major nutrients: carbohydrates, fats, and proteins. List those foods containing large amounts of these nutrients under the proper heading in your table. An example has been provided.

5. On a third table similar to the one shown here, identify those foods that are plants or plant products and those that are animals or animal products. An example has been provided.

Observations

Study the data you have collected and organized.

Analysis and Conclusions

1. What conclusions can you draw regarding your school's lunch program?

2. According to your data, do the foods represent a balanced diet? Do foods in certain categories appear much more often than foods in other categories?

3. What changes, if any, would you make in the menus?

4. **On Your Own** Do a similar exercise, but this time analyze the dinners you eat for a week.

Meat Group	Vegetable Group	Fruit Group	Milk Group	Bread-Cereal Group
Hamburger				Roll

Carbohydrates	Fats	Proteins
Roll	Hamburger	Hamburger

Plants or Plant Products	Animals or Animal Products
Roll	Hamburger

Summarizing Key Concepts

2–1 The Origin of Life

▲ Scientists have shown that some of the substances that make up living things could have formed on Earth some 4 billion years ago.

▲ The first living things to evolve on Earth were single-celled organisms.

▲ Early cells were consumers, feeding off the soup of chemicals in which they floated. In time, cells that could perform photosynthesis evolved.

▲ Over time, early cells developed the ability to use oxygen in their metabolic pathways.

2–2 Characteristics of Living Things

▲ Living things are cellular; that is, they are made up of one or more cells.

▲ Metabolism is the sum of all chemical activities essential to life.

▲ A living thing reacts to a stimulus, which is a change in the environment, by producing a response.

▲ Reproduction is the process by which organisms produce offspring. Reproduction may be asexual or sexual, depending on the organism.

2–3 Needs of Living Things

▲ Living things need energy for metabolism. The primary source of energy for almost all living things is the sun.

▲ All living things need food and water.

▲ Oxygen in the air or dissolved in water is used by organisms during respiration.

▲ All living things need living space that provides adequate food, water, and energy.

▲ Homeostasis is the ability of an organism to keep conditions constant inside its body when the outside environment changes.

2–4 Chemistry of Living Things

▲ Most inorganic compounds do not contain the element carbon. Organic compounds do contain carbon. The organic compounds important to life are carbohydrates, fats and oils, proteins, enzymes, and nucleic acids.

▲ DNA and RNA are the nucleic acids that carry information that controls the building of proteins. DNA also is considered the "blueprint" for life as it directs the development of an organism's offspring.

Reviewing Key Terms

Define each term in a complete sentence.

2–2 Characteristics of Living Things
spontaneous
 generation
metabolism
ingestion
digestion
respiration
excretion
life span
stimulus

response
sexual reproduction
asexual reproduction

2–3 Needs of Living Things
homeostasis

2–4 Chemistry of Living Things
element

compound
organic compound
carbohydrate
fat
oil
protein
amino acid
enzyme
nucleic acid
DNA
RNA

Chapter Review

Content Review

Multiple Choice

Choose the letter of the answer that best completes each statement.

1. Earth's early atmosphere was changed dramatically by the evolution of
   a. amino acids.
   b. sexual reproduction.
   c. photosynthesis.
   d. asexual reproduction.
2. The theory that life could spring from nonliving matter is called
   a. spontaneous generation.
   b. asexual reproduction.
   c. homeostasis.
   d. stimulus/response.
3. The building up and breaking down of chemical substances necessary for life is called
   a. respiration.   c. digestion.
   b. ingestion.   d. metabolism.
4. The complex compound that carries the information needed to make proteins is
   a. carbohydrate.   c. DNA.
   b. enzyme.   d. lipid.

5. The struggle among living things to obtain the resources needed for survival is called
   a. spontaneous generation.
   b. competition.
   c. homeostasis.
   d. metabolism.
6. Which of these is a substance made of a single element?
   a. table salt   c. diamond
   b. water   d. glass
7. Carbohydrate is to glucose as
   a. fat is to oil.
   b. protein is to amino acid.
   c. DNA is to RNA.
   d. hydrogen is to oxygen.
8. The process of combining oxygen with the products of digestion to produce energy is called
   a. respiration.   c. homeostasis.
   b. excretion.   d. reproduction.

True or False

If the statement is true, write "true." If it is false, change the underlined word or words to make the statement true.

1. Planet Earth is about <u>4.6 million years</u> old.
2. The theory of <u>spontaneous generation</u> states that life can spring from nonliving matter.
3. The process by which an organism puts food into its body is <u>digestion</u>.
4. Green plants produce the waste product <u>carbon dioxide</u> during photosynthesis.
5. The process of getting rid of body wastes is called <u>digestion</u>.
6. Ammonia and water are examples of <u>inorganic compounds</u>.
7. Carbohydrates include <u>sugars</u> and <u>starches</u>.

Concept Mapping

Complete the following concept map for Section 2–2. Then construct a concept map for the entire chapter.

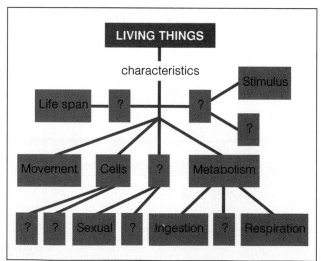

Concept Mastery

Discuss each of the following in a brief paragraph.

1. Describe at least five ways in which you can tell a living thing from a nonliving thing.
2. Your friend insists that plants are not alive because they do not move. Give specific examples to explain why your friend is wrong.
3. Describe four examples of metabolic processes.
4. Defend this statement: All plants and animals get their energy from the sun.

Critical Thinking and Problem Solving

Use the skills you have developed in this chapter to answer each of the following.

1. **Drawing conclusions** Is a peach pit living or nonliving? Explain your answer.
2. **Relating concepts** Why is the study of chemistry important to the understanding of living things?
3. **Relating cause and effect** In the days when people believed in spontaneous generation, one scientist developed the following recipe for producing mice: Place a dirty shirt and a few wheat grains in an open pot; wait three weeks. Suggest a reason why this recipe may have worked. How could you prove that spontaneous generation was not responsible for the appearance of mice?

4. **Applying concepts** Figure 2–10 on page 46 shows three sets of jars that illustrate Redi's experiment. Explain why the second set of jars did not provide enough evidence to disprove the spontaneous-generation theory.
5. **Making comparisons** Compare the growth of a sand dune to the growth of a living organism.
6. **Synthesizing data** Which is more likely to result in increased variety among organisms, sexual reproduction or asexual reproduction?
7. **Designing an experiment** A plant salesperson tells you that plants respond to the stimulus of classical music by growing more quickly. Design an experiment to test the salesperson's claim.
8. **Using the writing process** Develop a poster or an advertising campaign that explains the importance of eating a balanced diet in terms of the needs of living things.

Cells, Tissues, and Organ Systems

Guide for Reading

After you read the following sections, you will be able to

3–1 The Cell Theory

■ Discuss the cell theory.

3–2 Structure and Function of Cells

■ Describe the structures and functions of a typical cell.

■ Compare a plant cell and an animal cell.

3–3 Cell Processes

■ Discuss some of the life processes performed by a cell.

3–4 Cell Growth and Division

■ Describe the events that occur during cell division.

3–5 Cell Specialization

■ Describe the five levels of organization of living things.

When it first appeared on Earth about 3.5 billion years ago, it was a tiny structure made up of tinier parts alive with activity. Over the course of millions of years, it changed a bit here and a bit there. As new parts evolved, it became able to do increasingly different jobs: It could build complex chemicals, it could release bursts of energy, and eventually it could even move by itself.

Today these tiny structures still exist. They are a bridge to the distant past. They are the building blocks of all living things. They are cells!

Cells are fascinating and, in many ways, mysterious objects. Scientists probe the secrets of cells much as explorers journeying through parts of an uncharted world do. Read on and you too will become an explorer as you take a fantastic journey through the microscopic world of the cell.

Journal *Activity*

You and Your World Living things are made of cells. Cells are the building blocks of living things. This textbook is made of atoms. Atoms are the building blocks of matter. In your journal, describe in words or pictures why cells are alive and atoms are not. When you complete this chapter, go back to your journal and make any changes you feel are necessary.

◀ *The round objects in the photograph are white blood cells located in the thymus, an organ in which certain white blood cells are produced. A computer has highlighted the cells, giving them their green appearance.*

3–1 The Cell Theory

The basic units of structure and function of living things are **cells.** Most cells are too small to be seen with the unaided eye. As a result, many of the even smaller structures that make up a cell remained a mystery to scientists for hundreds of years. The structures that make up a cell are called **organelles,** which means tiny organs. The organelles were not revealed until the seventeenth century, when the first microscopes were invented.

In 1663, while looking at a thin slice of cork through a compound microscope, the English scientist Robert Hooke observed tiny roomlike structures. He called these structures cells. But the cells that Hooke saw in the slice of cork were not alive. What Hooke saw were actually the outer walls of dead plant cells.

At about the same time, Anton van Leeuwenhoek (LAY-vuhn-hook), a Dutch fabric merchant and amateur scientist, used a simple microscope to examine materials such as blood, rainwater, and scrapings from his teeth. In each material, van Leeuwenhoek observed living cells. He even found tiny living things in a drop of rainwater. Van Leeuwenhoek called these living things "animalcules." The smallest of the organisms observed by van Leeuwenhoek are today known as bacteria. Bacteria are single-celled organisms. These discoveries made van Leeuwenhoek famous all over the world.

During the next two hundred years, new and better microscopes were developed. Such microscopes made it possible for the German botanist Matthias Schleiden to view different types of plant parts. Schleiden concluded that all the plant parts he examined were made of cells. One year later, the German zoologist Theodor Schwann made similar observations using animal parts. About twenty years later, a German physician named Rudolph Virchow discovered that all living cells come only from other living cells.

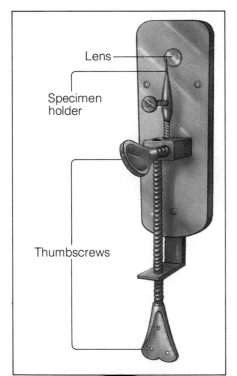

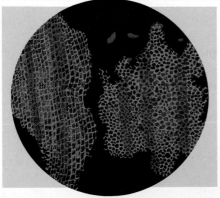

Figure 3–1 *Van Leeuwenhoek's simple microscope (top) could magnify objects a few hundred times. Robert Hooke made this drawing of cork cells (bottom) using a microscope he built. Hooke was not looking at living cells, but rather at the cell walls that surround living cork cells.*

Lens

Specimen holder

Thumbscrews

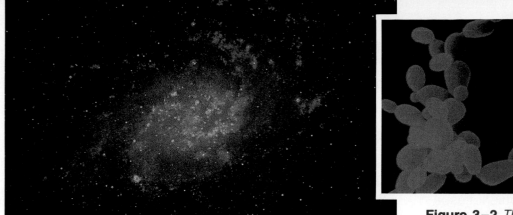

The work of Schleiden, Schwann, Virchow, and other biologists led to the development of the **cell theory,** which is one of the cornerstones of modern biology. **The cell theory states that**

- **All living things are made of cells.**
- **Cells are the basic units of structure and function in living things.**
- **Living cells come only from other living cells.**

3–1 Section Review

1. What is the cell theory?
2. What term is used for the structures that make up a cell?

Connection—*Science and Technology*

3. Discuss the relationship between technology and the development of the cell theory.

3–2 Structure and Function of Cells

You are about to take an imaginary journey. It will be quite an unusual trip because you will be traveling inside a living organism, visiting its tiny cells. On your trip you will be observing some of the typical structures found in plant and animal cells.

All living things are made of one or more cells. As you have just learned, cells are the basic units of structure and function in living things. Most cells are much too small to be seen without the aid of a

Guide for Reading

Focus on this question as you read.

▶ *What structures are found within a typical cell and what function do they serve?*

Plant Cells

1. To view a plant cell, remove a very thin transparent piece of tissue from an onion.

2. Place the onion tissue on a glass slide.

3. Add a drop of iodine stain to the tissue and cover with a coverslip.

4. Observe the onion tissue under low power and under high power of your microscope.

Draw a diagram of an onion cell and label its parts.

Figure 3–3 *The cell wall gives support and protection to plant cells, enabling giant redwoods to grow tall and straight.*

microscope. In fact, most cells are smaller than the period at the end of this sentence. (One exception is the yolk of an egg, which is actually a large single cell.) Within a cell are even smaller structures called organelles. **The structures within a cell function in providing protection and support, forming a barrier between the cell and its environment, building and repairing cell parts, transporting materials, storing and releasing energy, getting rid of waste materials, and increasing in number.**

Whether found in an animal or in a plant, most cells share certain similar characteristics. It is these characteristics that you are going to learn about. So hop aboard your imaginary ship and prepare to enter a typical plant cell. You will begin by sailing up through the trunk of an oak tree. Your destination is that box-shaped structure directly ahead. See Figure 3–4.

Cell Wall: Support and Protection

Entering the cell of an oak tree is a bit difficult. First you must pass through the **cell wall.** Strong and stiff, the cell wall is made of cellulose, a nonliving material. Cellulose is a long chain of sugar molecules that the cell manufactures. (The stringy part of celery is cellulose found in the cell walls of the celery stalk.)

The rigid cell wall is found in plant cells, but not in animal cells. The cell wall helps to protect and support the plant so that it can grow tall. Think for a moment of grasses, trees, and flowers that support themselves upright. No doubt you can appreciate the important role the cell wall plays for the individual cell and for the entire plant.

Although the cell wall is stiff, it does allow water, oxygen, carbon dioxide, and certain dissolved materials to pass into and out of the cell. So sail on through the cell wall and enter the cell.

Cell Membrane: Doorway of the Cell

As you pass through the cell wall, the first structure you encounter is the **cell membrane.** In a plant cell, the cell membrane is just inside the cell wall. In an animal cell (which has no cell wall), the cell membrane forms the outer covering of the cell.

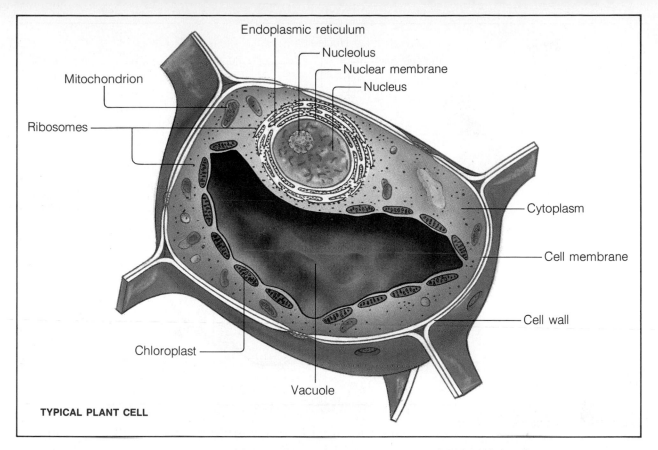

Endoplasmic reticulum

Nucleolus

Nuclear membrane

Nucleus

Mitochondrion

Ribosomes

Cytoplasm

Cell membrane

Cell wall

Chloroplast

Vacuole

TYPICAL PLANT CELL

Figure 3–4 *A typical plant cell contains many different structures, each having a characteristic shape and function. What is the outer barrier surrounding a plant cell called?*

The cell membrane has several important jobs. One of these important jobs is to provide protection and support for the cell. Unlike a plant cell, an animal cell does not have a rigid cell wall. Instead, an animal's cell membrane contains a substance called cholesterol that strengthens the cell membrane. As you might expect, a plant's cell membrane does not contain cholesterol.

As your ship nears the edge of the cell membrane, you notice that there are tiny openings, or pores, in the membrane. You steer toward an opening. Suddenly your ship narrowly misses being struck by a chunk of floating waste material passing out of the cell. You have discovered another job of the cell membrane. This membrane helps to control the movement of materials into and out of the cells. You will learn more about how materials pass through the cell membrane in the next section.

In a sense, the cell membrane is like the walls that surround your house or your apartment. Just as the walls of your home form a barrier between you and the outside world, the cell membrane forms a barrier between the living material inside the cell

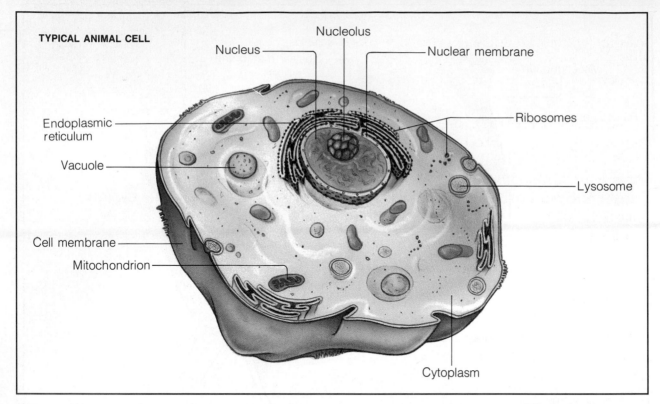

TYPICAL ANIMAL CELL

Nucleolus

Nucleus

Nuclear membrane

Endoplasmic reticulum

Ribosomes

Vacuole

Lysosome

Cell membrane

Mitochondrion

Cytoplasm

Figure 3–5 *An animal cell has many of the same structures as a plant cell. What is the outer barrier surrounding an animal cell called?*

and the outside environment of the cell. No doubt you would be quite unhappy if nothing could get into and out of your home. After all, you need to have food, water, and electricity come into your home. And you need to have waste products removed from your home before they build up. To ensure the survival of the cell, the cell membrane must allow materials to pass into and out of the cell. So you can think of the cell membrane as a barrier with doorways.

Everything the cell needs, from food to oxygen, enters the cell through the cell membrane. And harmful waste products exit through the cell membrane as well. In this way, the cell stays in smooth-running order, keeping conditions inside the cell the same even though conditions outside the cell may change. As you may recall from Chapter 2, the ability to maintain a stable internal environment, or homeostasis, is one of the important needs of all living things. Now sail on through a doorway in the cell membrane and enter a living cell.

Nucleus: Control Center of the Cell

As you sail inside the cell, a large, oval structure comes into view. This structure is the control center of the cell, or the **nucleus** (NOO-klee-uhs). The nucleus acts as the "brain" of the cell, regulating or controlling all the activities of the cell. See Figure 3–7.

NUCLEAR MEMBRANE Like the cell itself, the nucleus is also surrounded by a membrane. As you might expect, it is called the nuclear membrane. This membrane is similar to the cell membrane in that it allows materials to pass into or out of the nucleus. Small openings, or pores, are spaced regularly around the nuclear membrane. Each pore acts as a passageway. So set your sights for that pore just ahead and carefully glide into the nucleus.

CHROMOSOMES Those thick, rodlike objects floating directly ahead in the nucleus are **chromosomes.** Steer carefully to avoid colliding with the delicate chromosomes. For it is the chromosomes that direct all the activities of the cell, including growth and reproduction. In addition, chromosomes are responsible for passing on the traits of the cell to new cells. Chromosomes, for example, make sure that skin cells grow and divide into more skin cells.

The large, complex molecules that make up the chromosomes are compounds called nucleic acids. Nucleic acids store the information that helps a cell make the proteins it requires. And proteins are necessary for life. Some proteins are used to form parts of the cell, such as the cell membrane. Other

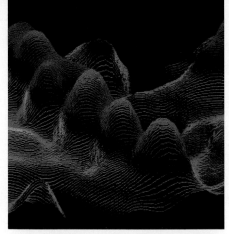

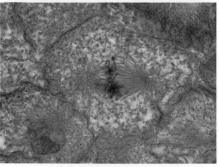

Figure 3–6 *Notice the rodlike chromosomes in the nucleus (bottom). This unusual photograph is an image of DNA in a chromosome, produced by a scanning electron microscope (top). The colors have been added by a computer.*

Figure 3–7 *The nucleus directs all the activities of a cell. Notice the various structures that make up the nucleus and the appearance of the nucleus in a liver cell viewed through an electron microscope.*

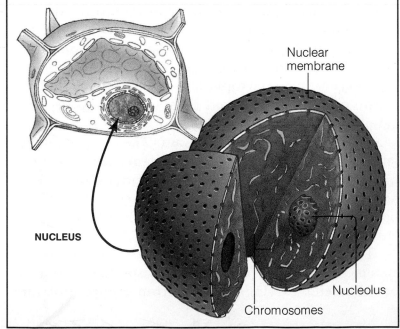

Nuclear membrane

NUCLEUS

Nucleolus

Chromosomes

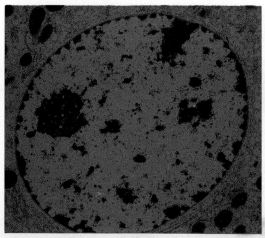

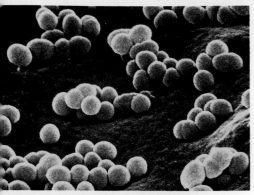

Figure 3–8 *As you read about the structures in a typical cell, keep in mind that organisms do differ in cell structure. Bacteria, members of the kingdom Monera, do not contain a distinct nucleus (top). Fungi, which look similar to plants, have nuclei but do not always have cells separated by a cell wall. For this reason, fungi are placed in the kingdom Fungi (bottom).*

proteins make up different enzymes and hormones used inside and outside the cell. Enzymes and hormones regulate cell activities.

The two nucleic acids found in cells are DNA and RNA. In Chapter 2 we called the nucleic acids the carriers of the blueprints of life. Working together, DNA and RNA store the information and carry out the steps in the protein-making process necessary for life. The DNA remains in the nucleus. But the RNA, carrying its protein-building instructions, leaves the nucleus through pores in the nuclear membrane. So hitch a ride on the RNA leaving the nucleus and continue your exploration of the cell.

NUCLEOLUS As you prepare to leave the nucleus, you spot a small object floating past. It is the nucleolus (noo-KLEE-uh-luhs), or "little nucleus." For many years the function of the nucleolus remained something of a mystery to scientists. Today it is believed that the nucleolus is the site of ribosome production. Ribosomes, as you will soon learn, are involved in the protein-making process in the cell.

Endoplasmic Reticulum: Transportation System of the Cell

As you leave the nucleus, you find yourself floating in a clear, thick, jellylike substance called the **cytoplasm.** The cytoplasm is the term given to the region between the nucleus and the cell membrane. While you are in the cytoplasm your ship needs no propulsion. For the cytoplasm is constantly moving, streaming throughout the cell. Many of the important cell organelles are located within the cytoplasm.

Steering in the cytoplasm is a bit difficult because of the organelles scattered throughout. The first organelle you encounter as you sail out of the nucleus is a maze of tubular passageways. These passageways lead out from the nuclear membrane. Some of the passageways lead to the cell membrane. Others lead to all the other areas of the cell. These clear, tubular passageways form the **endoplasmic reticulum** (en-doh-PLAZ-mihk rih-TIHK-yuh-luhm).

The endoplasmic reticulum is a transportation system. Its network of passageways spreads throughout the cell, carrying proteins from one part of the

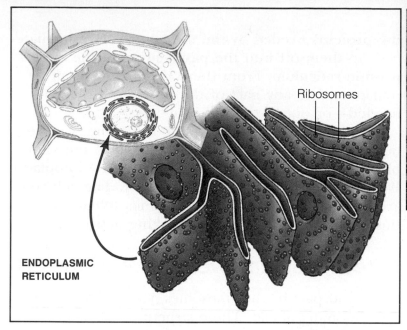

ENDOPLASMIC
RETICULUM

Ribosomes

Figure 3–9 *The endoplasmic reticulum is a canal system that can transport proteins throughout the cell. In this photograph of the endoplasmic reticulum, the dark spots are ribosomes, the sites of protein production.*

cell to another—or from the cell through the cell membrane and out the cell. If you look at Figure 3–9, you will see that the endoplasmic reticulum is well suited for its transportation job.

Ribosomes: Protein Factories of the Cell

Steer your ship directly into the endoplasmic reticulum passageways. From here you can travel anywhere you want in the cell. Before moving on, however, look closely at the inner surface of the endoplasmic passageways. Attached to the surface are grainlike bodies called **ribosomes.** Recall that ribosomes are produced in the nucleolus. From the nucleolus they pass out of the nucleus. Many of them end up attached to the outer lining of the endoplasmic reticulum.

Ribosomes, which are made primarily of the nucleic acid RNA, are the protein-making sites of the cell. The RNA in the ribosomes, along with the RNA sent out from the nucleus, directs the production of proteins. (Keep in mind that the production of RNA is controlled by the DNA in the chromosomes. So the DNA in the chromosomes is the real control center of the cell.)

It is no surprise that many ribosomes are found in the endoplasmic reticulum. This is a perfect location for them. For, once the ribosomes have made

ACTIVITY

DOING

Observing Cells

1. Obtain a thin piece of cork and a few drops of rainwater.

2. Place each sample on a different glass slide and cover with a coverslip.

3. Obtain a prepared slide of human blood.

4. Observe each slide under low power and under high power of your microscope.

5. Make a labeled diagram of what you see on each slide.

Compare how cells appear under low power and under high power.

Using reference books, find diagrams of these materials as seen by Hooke and van Leeuwenhoek. How do your diagrams compare with theirs?

the proteins needed by the cell, they can immediately drop them off into the passageways of the endoplasmic reticulum. From there the proteins can be transported to any part of the cell where they are needed—or out of the cell if necessary.

As you leave the endoplasmic reticulum, you notice that not all ribosomes are attached to the endoplasmic reticulum. Some float freely in the cytoplasm. Watch out! There go a few passing by. The cell you are in seems to have many ribosomes. What might this tell you about its protein-making activity?

Mitochondria: Powerhouses of the Cell

As you pass by the ribosomes, you see other structures looming ahead. These structures are called **mitochondria** (might-oh-KAHN-dree-uh; singular: mitochondrion). Mitochondria supply most of the energy for the cell. Somewhat larger than the ribosomes, these rod-shaped structures are often referred to as the "powerhouses" of the cell. See Figure 3–10.

Inside the mitochondria, simple food substances such as sugars are broken down into water and carbon dioxide gas. Large amounts of energy are released during the breakdown of sugars. The mitochondria gather this energy and store it in special energy-rich molecules. These molecules are convenient energy packages that the cell uses to do

Figure 3–10 *Mitochondria are the powerhouses of the cell. They provide the cell with the energy it needs to survive. Note the structure of the mitochondrion in the diagram and in the electron micrograph.*

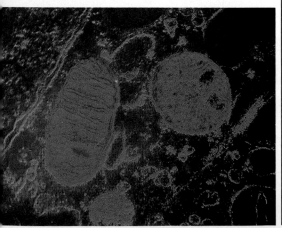

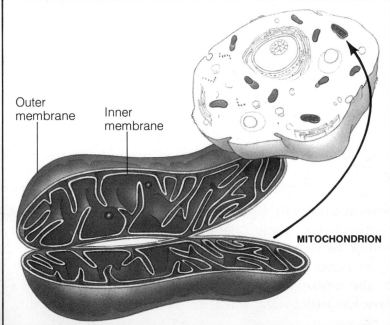

Outer membrane

Inner membrane

MITOCHONDRION

all its work. The more active the cell, the more mitochondria it has. Some cells, such as human liver cells, contain more than 1000 mitochondria. You will read more about mitochondria and energy in Chapter 4.

Because mitochondria have a small amount of their own DNA, scientists hypothesize that mitochondria were once tiny living organisms. These organisms, it is believed, invaded other cells millions of years ago. The DNA molecules in the mitochondria were passed from one generation of cells to the next as less complex organisms evolved into more complex organisms. (Keep in mind that even the smallest cells are still quite complex.) Now all living cells contain mitochondria. No longer invaders, mitochondria are an important part of living cells.

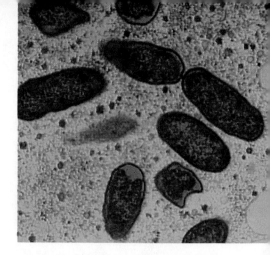

Figure 3–11 *Before they became permanent members of living cells, ancient mitochondria may have been similar in structure to these rickettsia. Mitochondria are no longer outside invaders. The rickettsia shown here, however, cause a serious disease called Rocky Mountain Spotted Fever.*

Vacuoles: Storage Tanks for Cells

Steer past the mitochondria and head for that large, round, water-filled sac floating in the cytoplasm. This sac is called a **vacuole** (VA-kyoo-ohl). Most plant cells and some animal cells have vacuoles. Plant cells often have one very large vacuole. Animal cells, if they contain any vacuoles, generally have a few small ones.

Vacuoles act like storage tanks. Food and other materials needed by the cell are stored inside the vacuoles. Vacuoles can also store waste products. In plant cells, vacuoles are the main water-storage areas. When water vacuoles in plant cells are full, they swell and make the cell plump. This plumpness keeps a plant firm.

Lysosomes: Cleanup Crews for the Cell

If you carefully swing your ship around the vacuole, you may be lucky enough to see a **lysosome** (LIGH-suh-sohm). Lysosomes are common in animal cells but are not often observed in plant cells.

Lysosomes are small, round structures involved with the digestive activities of the cell. See Figure 3–13 on page 80. Lysosomes contain enzymes that break down large food molecules into smaller ones. These smaller food molecules are then passed on to the mitochondria, where they are "burned" to provide energy for the cell.

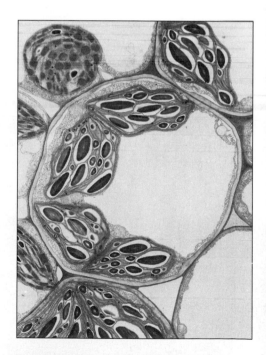

Figure 3–12 *The large, roundish, empty spaces in these plant cells are vacuoles. What materials do vacuoles store?*

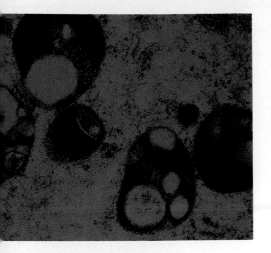

Figure 3–13 *These spherical organelles are lysosomes that have been magnified approximately 95,000 times. Lysosomes contain enzymes that can digest other organelles that have outlived their usefulness.*

Lysosomes are not involved just in digesting food. Many parts of the cell age and outlive their usefulness. One task of lysosomes is to digest old cell parts, releasing the substances in those aging cell parts so that they can be used again to build new parts. In this sense, you can think of lysosomes as the cell's cleanup crew.

Although lysosomes contain powerful digestive enzymes, you need not worry about your ship's safety. The membrane surrounding a lysosome keeps the enzymes from escaping and digesting the entire cell! Lysosomes can, however, digest whole cells when the cells are injured or dead. In an interesting process in the growth and development of a tadpole into a frog, lysosomes in the tadpole's tail cells digest the tail. Then the material is reused to make new body parts for the frog.

Chloroplasts: Energy Producers for the Cell

Your journey through the cell is just about over. But before you leave, look around you once again. Have you noticed any large, irregularly shaped green structures floating in the cytoplasm? If so, you have observed **chloroplasts.** Chloroplasts are green because they contain a green pigment called chlorophyll. Chlorophyll captures the energy of sunlight, which can then be used to help produce food for

Figure 3–14 *Chloroplasts are organelles that use sunlight to produce food in a process called photosynthesis. Would you be likely to find a chloroplast in an animal cell?*

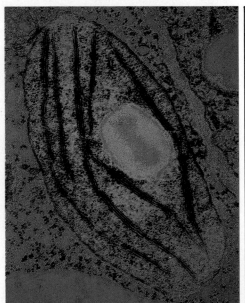

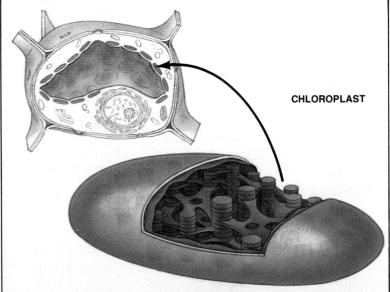

CHLOROPLAST

the plant cell. This process is called photosynthesis. You will read more about chloroplasts and photosynthesis in Chapter 9.

3–2 Section Review

1. List and describe the organelles found in a typical cell.
2. How would you distinguish between a plant cell and an animal cell?

Connection—*You and Your World*
3. Compare each of the cell organelles to a structure in your house or apartment. Give an explanation for each comparison.

3–3 Cell Processes

The cell carries out a variety of processes necessary to life. **Life processes performed by cells include metabolism, respiration, diffusion, osmosis, and active transport.** The cell, which is basic to all forms of life, resembles a miniature factory that produces many kinds of chemicals. Like any factory, a cell must have energy to do work. Working day and night, a cell traps, converts, stores, and uses energy. As you will discover, obtaining and using energy is one of the most important activities of a living cell.

Metabolism

Even while you sleep, you need energy to keep you alive. But where does this energy come from? Cells provide it. Although cells cannot make energy, they can change energy from one form to another. Cells obtain energy from their environment and change it into a usable form.

This energy-conversion process is very complex. It involves many chemical reactions. Some reactions break down molecules. Other reactions build new molecules. In Chapter 2 you learned that the sum of all the building-up and breaking-down activities that occur in a living cell is called metabolism.

Guide for Reading

Focus on these questions as you read.

▶ *What are some life processes performed by the cell?*

▶ *How do diffusion, osmosis, and active transport differ?*

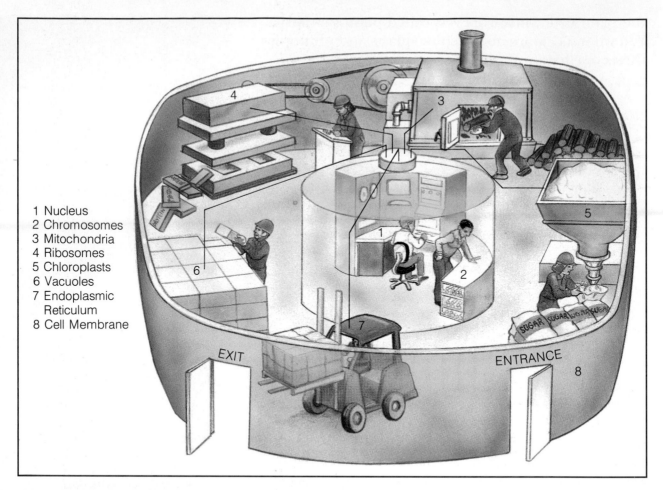

1 Nucleus
2 Chromosomes
3 Mitochondria
4 Ribosomes
5 Chloroplasts
6 Vacuoles
7 Endoplasmic
  Reticulum
8 Cell Membrane

EXIT

ENTRANCE

Figure 3–15 *A cell is like a miniature factory that carries out all the activities necessary to life. Is the diagram a representation of a plant cell or an animal cell?*

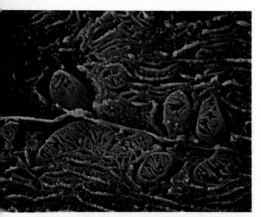

Figure 3–16 *The mitochondria in this thinly sliced human cell appear orange.*

Think for a moment of all the things cells do: grow, repair structures, absorb food, manufacture proteins, get rid of wastes, and reproduce. The energy for these activities is locked up in the molecules in food. As a result of metabolism, the stored energy in food is set free so it can be used to do work necessary for the cells' survival.

Respiration

Earlier you learned that energy is released when simple food substances such as sugars are broken down inside the mitochondria. The process in which simple food substances such as glucose are broken down, and the energy they contain is released is called **respiration.** Because living things need a continuous supply of energy, respiration is performed constantly by all living things.

There are two types of respiration. In aerobic (ehr-OH-bihk) respiration, food enters the mitochondria where it is broken down when it combines with oxygen. During this process, water and carbon dioxide are produced. The energy that is released is stored in an energy-rich molecule called **ATP**. The energy in ATP can then be used directly by the cell to do work when it is needed. Although aerobic respiration occurs in a series of complicated steps, the overall reaction can be shown in the following chemical equation.

$$C_6H_{12}O_6 + 6\ O_2 \longrightarrow 6\ CO_2 + 6\ H_2O + ATP$$

glucose   oxygen   carbon   water   energy
dioxide

How do you get the oxygen needed for respiration? How do you get rid of the carbon dioxide that is produced during respiration?

In anaerobic (an-ehr-OH-bihk) respiration, energy is released and ATP is produced without oxygen. Scientists use the term **fermentation** when they speak of anaerobic respiration. Keep in mind that the amount of energy released during fermentation is much less than the amount of energy released during aerobic respiration. Yeasts, for example, are one type of organism that uses fermentation. In yeast cells, glucose is broken down to carbon dioxide, alcohol, and ATP. During strenuous exercise, your muscle cells may lack oxygen. At this time, the energy that you need is released by anaerobic respiration.

Diffusion

Remember how you sailed through the cell membrane to enter the cell? Well, the substances that get into and out of the cell do the same thing. Food molecules, oxygen, water, and other materials enter and leave the cell through the pores (openings) in the cell membrane.

The driving force behind the movement of many substances into or out of a cell is called **diffusion** (dih-FYOO-zhuhn). Diffusion is the process by which molecules of a substance move from areas of higher concentration of that substance to areas of lower concentration of that substance.

Figure 3–17 *During the production of bread, yeast cells produce carbon dioxide as part of the fermentation process. The carbon dioxide causes the bread to rise and forms the air spaces in the bread. During strenuous exercise, muscles may not get an adequate supply of oxygen. At such times, the muscles use a form of fermentation that produces lactic acid. The buildup of lactic acid causes the painful, burning sensation all athletes have experienced. When the muscles relax, the lactic acid is removed and the pain goes away.*

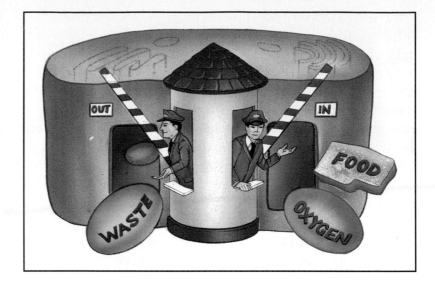

Figure 3–18 *The cell membrane is selective, permitting oxygen and food molecules to enter and waste materials to leave.*

Activity Bank

Coming and Going, p. 791

ACTIVITY

Seeing and Smelling Diffusion

You can see diffusion at work. To observe diffusion, drop some ink into a glass of water and watch what happens. Record and explain your observations.

You can also smell the effects of diffusion. To do so, open a perfume bottle or a bottle of ammonia at one end of a large room. Leaving the container open, move to the other end of the room. How can you tell if diffusion has occurred? Explain your answer.

Why does diffusion occur? Molecules of all substances are in constant motion, colliding continuously with one another. This motion causes the molecules to spread out. The molecules move from an area where there are more of them (higher concentration) to an area where there are fewer of them (lower concentration). See Figure 3–19.

If there are many food molecules outside a cell, for example, some will diffuse through the membrane into the cell. At the same time, waste materials that build up in the cell will diffuse out of the cell.

If substances can move into and out of the cell through the cell membrane, why don't cell organelles and the cytoplasm do likewise? What keeps the ribosomes and mitochondria, for example, from passing out of the cell? And what keeps harmful materials from moving in? The answer is simple but quite elegant. The cell membrane is selectively permeable (PER-mee-uh-buhl). That is, it permits only certain substances—mainly oxygen, water, and food molecules—to diffuse into the cell. Waste products such as carbon dioxide are allowed to diffuse out of the cell.

Osmosis

Water is the most important substance that passes through the cell membrane. In fact, about 80 percent of the cell is made of water. Water passes through the cell membrane by a special type of diffusion called **osmosis** (ahs-MOH-sihs). Osmosis is the diffusion of

Figure 3–19 *Diffusion is the movement of molecules of a substance into a cell (top) or out of a cell (bottom). Substances move from places where they are more concentrated to places where they are less concentrated.*

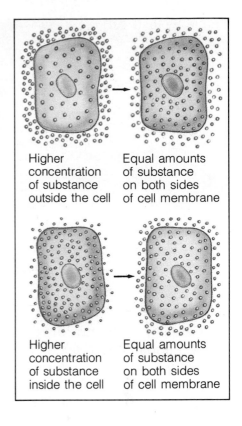

Higher concentration of substance outside the cell

Equal amounts of substance on both sides of cell membrane

Higher concentration of substance inside the cell

Equal amounts of substance on both sides of cell membrane

water into or out of the cell. During osmosis, water molecules move from a place of higher concentration to a place of lower concentration. This movement keeps the cell from drying out.

Suppose you put a cell into a glass of salt water. The concentration of water outside the cell is lower than the concentration of water inside the cell. This is because there are salt molecules taking up space in the salt water, so there are fewer water molecules. Water leaves the cell, and the cell starts to shrink. If too much water leaves the cell, the cell dries up and dies. Using this information, can you now explain why it is not a wise idea for a person to drink salt water—no matter how thirsty that person is?

If a cell is placed into a glass of pure, fresh water instead of salt water, just the opposite occurs. Water enters the cell, and the cell swells. This happens because the concentration of water is lower inside the cell than it is outside the cell. As you might imagine, if too much water enters the cell, the cell bursts. Do you remember reading about the cell organelle called the vacuole? Vacuoles store food and water for the cell. Some of these vacuoles are contractile vacuoles.

Figure 3–20 *Normal red blood cells (left) will shrink (center) if too much water leaves the cells. If too much water enters the cells, the cells will swell (right). By what process does water move into and out of a cell?*

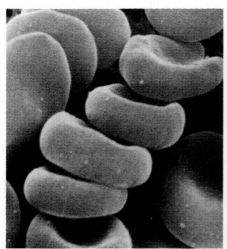
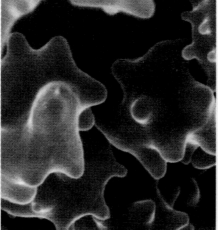
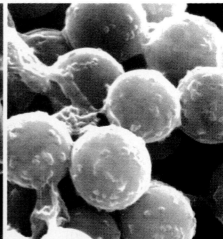

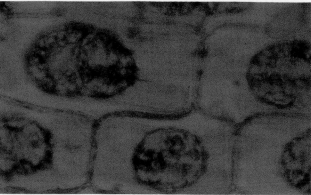

Figure 3–21 *Notice how the organelles fill a normal plant cell (left). When too much water leaves the cell, the cell contents shrink away from the cell wall (right).*

Figure 3–22 *Amebas use a form of active transport in which a large food particle is surrounded by a pocket of the cell membrane. The pocket breaks away from the cell membrane and forms a vacuole within the ameba.*

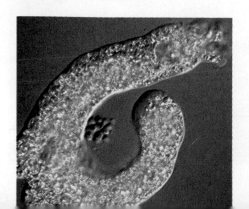

As their name suggests, contractile vacuoles can contract, or become smaller. As contractile vacuoles that store water contract, they force excess water out of the cell through the cell membrane.

One of the neat things about diffusion and osmosis is that they do not require energy. That is, the movement of substances across the cell membrane does not require the cell to use up any of its energy reserves. The movement just happens whenever there are unequal concentrations inside and outside a cell. Sometimes, however, the cell must obtain raw materials that cannot diffuse through the cell membrane. At such times, the cell must use some of its available energy to get the materials it requires.

Active Transport

As you have just learned, the cell membrane is selectively permeable. It can "select" the materials that will pass into or out of the cell. But what if the cell requires substances that cannot simply diffuse through the cell membrane because the membrane is not permeable to those substances? Or what if the cell membrane is permeable, but the concentration of the substances outside the cell is not high enough to cause diffusion to occur? Is the cell out of luck? Not really. In both cases, the cell can use a process called **active transport** to "carry" the substance into the cell. Unlike diffusion and osmosis, however, active transport requires the cell to use some of its energy reserves.

PROBLEM Solving

Shipwrecked!

It had been several days since the Peterson family was marooned on the island. Little did they know that their long-awaited sailing trip would end like this! Things had already been tough, but now they were going to get even tougher. The last of the supplies from their capsized sailboat was almost gone. And they were soon to run out of fresh water.

The Petersons will not last long without water. They need your help. Your job is to find out how they can get the much needed water. But before you tackle that job, see if you can answer these questions.

Can the marooned family simply drink the sea water that they see all around them? Or is there something about sea water that will not quench their thirst? Explain your answer.

Now you are ready to devise a way to provide the Petersons with water. Using any or all of the following items found on the island or taken from the capsized sailboat, try to save the Petersons.

bucket   driftwood
bamboo   coconut
saw   matches
palm leaves

How were you able to save the Peterson family?

There are several methods of active transport available to cells. In the most common method, special transport molecules in the cell membrane actually pick up the substance outside the cell and pull it through the cell membrane. Some substances needed by the cell that are carried in this manner are

ACTIVITY

DISCOVERING

Dissolving Power

Many of the substances that diffuse through the cell membrane are dissolved in the watery fluids surrounding the cell. Do all substances dissolve in water?

■ Using several glass tumblers and common substances found around the home (salt, sugar, starch, flour, baking soda, and so on), determine what substances dissolve in water and what substances do not dissolve in water.

Guide for Reading

Focus on this question as you read.

▶ *What are the phases of cell division that result in the formation of two new daughter cells?*

calcium, potassium, and sodium. Active transport is also used to eliminate substances inside the cell that cannot pass through the cell membrane by diffusion. Regardless of whether materials are passing into or out of the cell, the important thing to remember is that active transport requires energy. Unlike diffusion and osmosis, active transport does not just happen on its own.

3–3 Section Review

1. What are some life processes performed by cells?
2. What is metabolism?
3. Define respiration. What is aerobic respiration? Fermentation?
4. Compare diffusion, osmosis, and active transport.

Connection—*Science and Technology*

5. Waste products in the blood are filtered out by the kidneys. In the past, kidney failure always led to death because of the buildup of poisonous wastes in the blood. Today, however, doctors use dialysis machines to filter wastes out of the blood. Dialysis machines use artificial membranes. Are the membranes in a dialysis machine permeable or selectively permeable? Explain.

3–4 Cell Growth and Division

Growth is usually a fairly obvious characteristic. A human infant, for example, clearly shows growth as it passes through childhood and into adulthood. The growth of a redwood seedling into a tree is also quite apparent.

It might seem that the easiest way for an organism to grow is for its cells to get larger and larger. In the case of our previous example, the cells in an infant might get bigger and bigger as that infant developed into an adult. The fact is, however, that cells do not grow larger and larger in this manner. The cells in a human infant are about the same size as the cells in an adult human—an adult just has a lot more cells than an infant does!

Limits on Cell Growth

Why don't cells get bigger and bigger as an organism grows? The answer involves the transportation of materials into and out of a cell. If a cell continued to grow larger and larger, at some point the cell membrane would not be able to handle the flow of materials passing through it. That is, the amount of raw materials needed by the larger cell would not enter the cell fast enough. The amount of wastes produced by the larger cell could not leave the cell fast enough. The larger cell would then die.

Cell Division

In order for the total number of cells to increase and for an organism to grow, the cells must undergo **cell division.** During cell division, one cell divides into two cells. Each new cell, called a daughter cell, is identical to the other and to the parent cell.

If a parent cell—a skin cell, leaf cell, or bone cell, for example—is to produce two identical daughter cells, then the exact contents of its nucleus must go into the nucleus of each new daughter cell. Recall that the chromosomes, which contain the blueprints of life, are located in the nucleus. If a parent cell simply splits in half, each daughter cell will get only half the contents of the nucleus—only half the chromosomes of the parent cell.

Fortunately, this does not happen. To understand why not, you must know about the process of cell division in more detail. **Cell division occurs in a series of stages, or phases.** Each has a scientific name. It is not important that you memorize the scientific name for each phase. But it is important that you understand the nature of cell division and how a parent cell divides into two daughter cells.

PHASE 1: CHROMOSOMES ARE COPIED During the first phase of cell division, which is called interphase, the cell is performing its life functions, but it is not actually dividing. If you were to observe the nucleus during this phase, you would not be able to see the rodlike chromosomes. Instead, the chromosomes would appear as threadlike coils called **chromatin.** In animal cells, two structures called centrioles (SEHN-tree-ohlz) can be seen outside the nucleus. The centrioles play a part in cell division. Plant cells do not have centrioles.

Figure 3–23 *The adult tiger does not have larger cells than its cub, just more of them. Why can't cells grow larger and larger and larger?*

How Many Cells?

Suppose a cell divides once a day. How many cells will there be in a week? A month? A year?

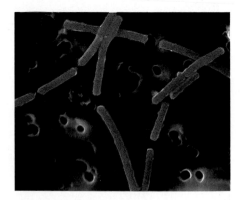

Figure 3–24 *Although bacteria do not contain a nucleus, their chromosomes still must double before the bacterial cells can divide into two identical daughter cells.*

Near the end of phase 1, the process of cell division begins. At this time, all the chromosomes (which still appear as threadlike coils of chromatin) are duplicated. That is, a copy of each chromosome is produced. As a result, the normal chromosome number in the cell doubles. Each chromosome and its sister chromosome (its copy) are attached at an area called the centromere. The sister chromosomes are now called chromatids.

PHASE 2: MITOSIS BEGINS It is during the second phase, which is called prophase, that cell division really gets going. At this point, the process of cell division is called **mitosis** (migh-TOH-sihs). Mitosis is the process by which the nucleus of a cell divides into two nuclei and the formation of two new daughter cells begins.

During phase 2, the threadlike chromatin in the nucleus begins to shorten and form the familiar rodlike chromosomes. Each chromosome is made up of two identical chromatids attached at the centromere. Around this time the two centrioles (in animals cells) begin to move to opposite ends of the cell. In addition, a meshlike spindle begins to develop between the two centrioles, forming a "bridge" between the opposite ends of the cell. (Although plant cells do not contain centrioles, a spindle still forms in the cell at this time.) Near the end of phase 2 of cell division, the nuclear membrane surrounding the nucleus begins to break down, and the nucleolus in the nucleus disappears.

Figure 3–25 *During cell division, one cell divides into two cells. In multicellular organisms, this ensures growth and development and the replacement of dead or injured cells. What is the first stage of cell division called?*

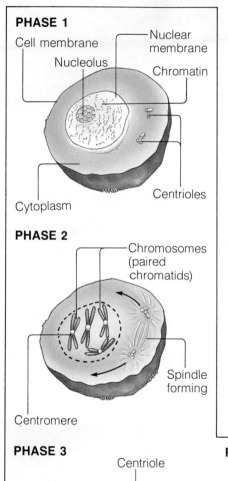

PHASE 1

Cell membrane
Nucleolus
Nuclear membrane
Chromatin
Centrioles
Cytoplasm

PHASE 2

Chromosomes (paired chromatids)
Spindle forming
Centromere

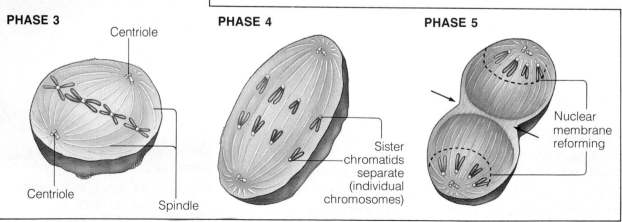

PHASE 3

Centriole
Centriole
Spindle

PHASE 4

Sister chromatids separate (individual chromosomes)

PHASE 5

Nuclear membrane reforming

PHASE 3: CHROMOSOMES ATTACH TO THE SPINDLE During phase 3 of cell division, which is called metaphase, the chromosomes begin to attach to the middle of the meshlike spindle that runs from end to end in the cell. The chromosomes are attached to the spindle by the centromere, which still connects each chromatid to its identical sister chromatid.

PHASE 4: CHROMOSOMES BEGIN TO SEPARATE During phase 4 of cell division, which is called anaphase, the sister chromatids separate from each other. One chromatid from each pair of sister chromatids begins to move toward one end of the cell along the spindle. The other chromatid of the pair begins to move toward the other end. The chromatids are again called chromosomes.

PHASE 5: TWO NEW NUCLEI FORM During phase 5 of cell division, which is called telophase, the chromosomes begin to uncoil and lose their rodlike appearance. The chromosomes again appear as chromatin and a nuclear membrane forms around the chromatin at each end of the cell. In each nucleus, a nucleolus reappears. At this point, the process of mitosis is complete. But cell division still has one more phase to go.

PHASE 6: TWO DAUGHTER CELLS FORM The sixth and final phase of cell division, which is called cytokinesis (sigh-toh-kuh-NEE-suhs), involves the division of the cytoplasm in the cell. The membrane surrounding the cell begins to move inward until the cytoplasm is pinched into two nearly equal parts. Each part contains a nucleus with identical chromosomes. The cell membrane forms and two new daughter cells are produced. In plant cells, a cell wall also forms around each daughter cell.

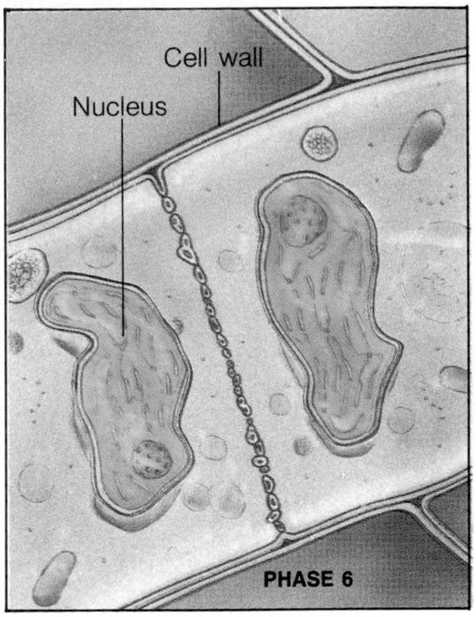

Figure 3–26 *At the same time that telophase is taking place in the nucleus, cytokinesis is taking place in the cytoplasm. Cytokinesis is the division of the cytoplasm and its contents into two individual daughter cells. In plant cells, as shown here, the cytoplasm is divided by a cell plate, which will become the new cell membrane.*

3–4 Section Review

1. Briefly describe the phases of cell division.

Critical Thinking—*Applying Concepts*
2. During sexual reproduction, two sex cells unite to form a single cell that will become the new organism. Would mitosis be an appropriate method for forming sex cells? Explain your answer.

CONNECTIONS

I Feel Dizzy, Oh So Dizzy!

Travel, something we all take for granted in this high-speed age of ours. But think about this. The first Paris to New York nonstop flight in an airplane took 33 hours and 30 minutes, and occurred in 1930. The airplanes that crowd our skies today and that can fly you to Paris in about 4 hours are a comparatively new invention.

What happened before airplanes made transatlantic crossings so popular with millions of travelers? Transatlantic crossings were made by ship. For the very wealthy, these crossings were luxurious and opulent. Fine foods, service, and many changes of clothing each day made life aboard ship pleasurable. For many others—poor immigrants, for example—leaving Europe for a new life in a new land, the unpleasant crossings were made bearable by the hope of a better future.

But for all people, rich and poor alike, one of the most unpleasant factors in an ocean crossing was *seasickness*. Seasickness is caused by the movement of a boat as it plows through the waves. For even though ocean liners are huge and powerful, the ocean is larger and more powerful still. Ocean waves can toss even the largest ship about with abandon. The constant motion of the ocean causes some people to feel nauseated. And after several days trapped on a ship this feeling can be very unpleasant indeed.

Today there is an easy treatment for seasickness, and one that uses a technique you learned about in the chapter—diffusion. Physicians place a small bandagelike patch behind a person's ear. The patch contains a special drug called scopolamine, which enters the body by diffusing through the skin at a constant rate. This method of treatment is successful in most people. This technique is being used to administer other medicines as well. In the future these patches may become even more commonplace as treatments for other diseases are developed.

3–5 Cell Specialization

Earlier in this chapter, you read about the structures found in plant and animal cells. These structures help to keep the cell alive and functioning properly. In unicellular organisms such as bacteria, the single cell performs all the functions necessary for life. But, as you know, many organisms (including yourself) are multicellular. In multicellular organisms, cells are specialized to perform specific tasks for the organism. So it should not surprise you to learn that cells are often organized to better serve the needs of the organism. In other words, within a multicellular organism there is a division of labor. Division of labor means that the work of keeping the organism alive is divided among the different parts of the body. Each part has a specific job to do. And as the part does its specific job, it works in harmony with all the other parts to keep the living thing healthy and alive.

The arrangement of specialized parts within a living thing is sometimes referred to as levels of organization. The five basic levels of organization, arranged from the smallest, least complex structure to the largest, most complex structure are cells, tissues, organs, organ systems, and organisms. Cells, of course, are the first level of organization.

Tissues—Level Two

In any multicellular organism, cells rarely work alone. Cells that are similar in structure and function are usually joined together to form **tissues.** Tissues are the second level of organization. What is the first level of organization?

Like the single cell of the bacterium, each tissue cell must carry on all the activities needed to keep that cell alive. But at the same time, tissues perform one or more specialized functions in an organism's

Guide for Reading

Focus on this question as you read.

▶ *What are the five basic levels of organization in living things?*

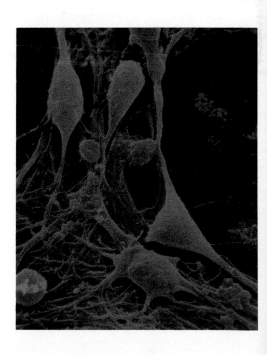

Figure 3–27 *In multicellular organisms, many cells are specialized to perform a specific function for the organism. Here you see nerve cells (neurons) in the part of the brain used for thinking skills such as reading and understanding this textbook.*

body. In other words, tissues work for themselves as well as for the good of the entire living thing.

For example, your bone cells form bone tissue, a strong, solid tissue that gives shape and support to your body. Blood cells in your body are part of blood tissue, a liquid tissue responsible for carrying food, oxygen, and wastes throughout the body. What other types of tissues are found in your body?

Plants have tissues too. The leaves and stems of a plant are covered by a type of tissue called epidermis, which protects the plant and prevents it from losing water. Another type of tissue conducts water and dissolved minerals up through the stems to the leaves. Still another special tissue brings food made in the leaves back down to the stems and roots.

Organs—Level Three

In general, tissues are further organized into **organs,** the third level of organization in living things. Organs are groups of different tissues that work together. Your heart, for example, is an organ made up of muscle tissue, blood tissue, and nerve tissue. You are probably familiar with the names of many of the body organs. The brain, stomach, kidneys, and skin are some examples. Can you name others?

Plants have organs too. Roots, stems, and leaves are common plant organs. Like animal organs, plant organs are made up of groups of tissues performing the same function. For example, various tissues in the leaf help this organ make food for the plant.

Organ Systems—Level Four

Like cells and tissues, organs seldom work alone. They "cooperate" with each other to form specific **organ systems.** Organ systems are the fourth level of organization of living things. An organ system is a group of organs that work together to perform a specific function for the organism.

The organs that make up an organ system vary in number and complexity from one kind of living thing to another. For example, a very simple animal called the hydra has a nervous system that is a simple net of nerves spread throughout the organism. More

Figure 3–28 *Notice how bone cells are organized to form a tissue, an organ, and an organ system.*

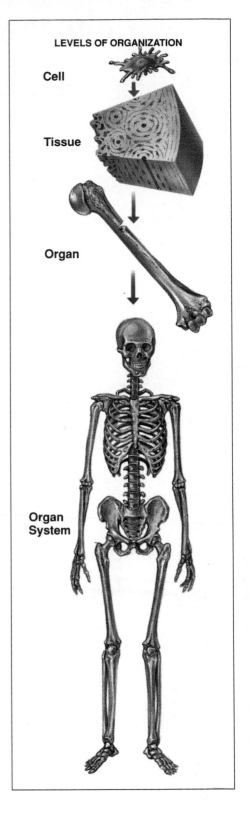

LEVELS OF ORGANIZATION

Cell

Tissue

Organ

Organ System

complex animals, such as the grasshopper, have a more highly organized system of nerves and a primitive brain. The most highly developed animals, people, for example, have nervous systems consisting of a brain, a spinal cord, and nerves.

Figure 3–28 shows the levels of organization in many animals, including yourself. Study this figure until you understand how this organization of cells better serves the needs of an organism.

Organisms—Level Five

You are an **organism.** An organism is an entire living thing that carries out all the basic life functions. A buttercup is an organism, as are an apple tree, a deer, and a dolphin. Even a single-celled bacterium is an organism. The organism is the fifth and highest level of organization of living things.

A complex organism is a combination of organ systems. Each system performs its particular function, but all the systems work together to keep the organism alive. Without the smooth operation of any one of its systems, a living thing could not survive.

Cells, tissues, organs, organ systems, organisms— by now one thing should be clear to you: Each level of organization interacts with every other level. And the smooth functioning of a complex organism is the result of all its various parts working together.

3–5 Section Review

1. List and define the five levels of organization of living things.
2. What is meant by the term "division of labor" in living things?

Critical Thinking—*Making Comparisons*
3. Explain some of the differences between a one-celled organism and one cell in a multicellular organism.

Laboratory Investigation

Using the Microscope

Problem

How do you use the microscope to observe objects?

Materials *(per group)*

small pieces of newspaper print and colorful magazine photographs
microscope slide
medicine dropper
coverslip
microscope

Procedure 🔥

1. Your teacher will instruct you as to the proper use and care of the microscope. Follow all instructions carefully.

2. Obtain a small piece of newspaper print and place it on a clean microscope slide.

3. To make a wet-mount slide, use the medicine dropper to carefully place a drop of water over the newsprint.

4. Carefully lower the coverslip over the newsprint.

5. Place the slide on the stage of the microscope. The newsprint should be facing up and should be in the normal reading position.

6. With the low-power objective in place, focus on a specific letter in the newsprint.

7. Move the slide to the left, then to the right.

8. Looking at the stage and objectives from the side, turn the nosepiece until the high-power objective clicks into place.

9. Using only the fine adjustment knob, bring the letter into focus. Draw what you see.

10. Repeat steps 2 through 9 using magazine samples.

Observations

1. While looking through the microscope, in which direction does the object appear to move when you move the slide to the left? To the right?

2. What is the total magnification of your microscope under low and under high power?

3. What happens to the focus of the objective lens when you switch from low power to high power?

Analysis and Conclusions

1. What conclusion can you draw about the way objects appear when viewed through a microscope?

2. How would you center an object viewed through a microscope when the object is off-center to the left?

3. What is the purpose of the coverslip?

4. **On Your Own** With your teacher's permission, examine samples of hair, various fabrics, and prepared slides through the microscope.

Study Guide

Summarizing Key Concepts

3-1 The Cell Theory

▲ The cell theory states: All living things are made of cells; cells are the basic units of structure and function in living things; and living cells come only from other living cells.

3-2 Structure and Function of Cells

▲ The cell wall gives protection and support to plant cells.

▲ The cell membrane regulates the movement of materials into and out of the cell.

▲ The nucleus is the control center of the cell.

▲ Chromosomes, found in the nucleus, direct the production of proteins and are responsible for cell growth and reproduction.

▲ The endoplasmic reticulum carries proteins from one part of the cell to another.

▲ Ribosomes are the protein-making sites.

▲ Mitochondria, the powerhouses of the cell, provide the energy that cells need to function.

▲ Vacuoles store food, water, and wastes.

▲ Lysosomes contain digestive enzymes.

▲ Chloroplasts capture energy from the sun and use it to make food for plant cells.

3-3 Cell Processes

▲ Some of the life processes performed by cells include metabolism, respiration, diffusion, osmosis, and active transport.

3-4 Cell Growth and Division

▲ The cells of an organism increase in number through cell division, as one cell divides into two daughter cells, each of which is identical to the original parent cell.

▲ Cell division occurs in a series of phases: interphase, prophase, metaphase, anaphase, telophase, and cytokinesis.

3-5 Cell Specialization

▲ The five basic levels of organization, arranged from the smallest, least complex structure to the largest, most complex structure are cells, tissues, organs, organ systems, and organisms.

Reviewing Key Terms

Define each term in a complete sentence.

3-1 The Cell Theory
cell
organelle
cell theory

3-2 Structure and Function of Cells
cell wall
cell membrane
nucleus
chromosome
cytoplasm
endoplasmic reticulum
ribosome
mitochondrion
vacuole
lysosome
chloroplast

3-3 Cell Processes
respiration
ATP
fermentation
diffusion
osmosis
active transport

3-4 Cell Growth and Division
cell division
chromatin
mitosis

3-5 Cell Specialization
tissue
organ
organ system
organism

Chapter Review

Content Review

Multiple Choice

Choose the letter of the answer that best completes each statement.

1. The outer covering of an animal cell is the
   a. cell wall.
   b. organelle.
   c. cell membrane.
   d. mitochondria.
2. The control center of the cell is the
   a. cytoplasm.
   b. nucleus.
   c. mitochondrion.
   d. nucleolus.
3. Food, water, and wastes are stored in
   a. vacuoles.   c. ribosomes.
   b. mitochondria. d. lysosomes.
4. The sum of all the building-up and breaking-down activities that occur in a living cell is called
   a. respiration.   c. osmosis.
   b. diffusion.   d. metabolism.

5. The process in which food is broken down and the energy in the food is released is called
   a. respiration.   c. osmosis.
   b. diffusion.   d. metabolism.
6. The total number of cells in an organism increases as a result of
   a. respiration.   c. osmosis.
   b. cell division. d. diffusion.
7. Chromatids are held together by a
   a. spindle.
   b. centriole.
   c. centromere.
   d. cell membrane.
8. Eyes, kidneys, and skin are examples of
   a. tissues.
   b. cells.
   c. organs.
   d. organ systems.

True or False

If the statement is true, write "true." If it is false, change the underlined word or words to make the statement true.

1. Chromosomes are made up of <u>nucleic acids</u>.
2. <u>Vacuoles</u> are the cell's powerhouses.
3. The <u>endoplasmic reticulum</u> is the "brain" of the cell.
4. Yeasts perform a type of respiration called <u>fermentation</u>.
5. <u>Oxygen</u> and ATP are the end products of respiration.
6. In phase 3 of cell division (metaphase), chromosomes attach to the <u>spindle</u>.
7. The movement of water through a cell membrane is called <u>diffusion</u>.
8. <u>Tissues</u> make up the second level of organization in living things.

Concept Mapping

Complete the following concept map for Section 3–1. Then construct a concept map for the entire chapter.

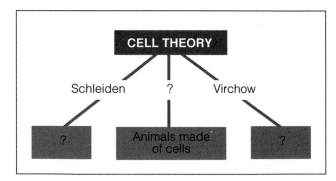

Concept Mastery

Discuss each of the following in a brief paragraph.

1. Based on your knowledge of cells, explain this statement. "Single-celled organisms are often more complex than individual cells of multicellular organisms."
2. What were the contributions of Hooke, van Leeuwenhoek, Schleiden, Schwann, and Virchow to our understanding of the cell?
3. Describe and compare diffusion, osmosis, and active transport.
4. Some people interchange the terms breathing and respiration. Explain why these are not the same in terms of a cell.
5. Describe and compare chromosomes, chromatin, chromatids, and centromeres.
6. Explain the relationship between cells, tissues, organs, and organ systems.

Critical Thinking and Problem Solving

Use the skills you have developed in this chapter to answer each of the following.

1. **Sequencing events**   Prepare a time line that illustrates the events that led to the cell theory.
2. **Interpreting graphs**   Enzymes are substances that control the speed at which certain reactions in a cell take place. Use the graph to answer the following questions: What two factors are described in the graph? How are these two factors related to enzyme activity?

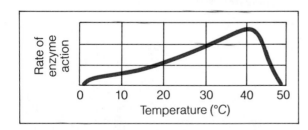

3. **Making inferences**   Why do scientists believe that mitochondria may have been invaders of early cells?
4. **Drawing conclusions**   In a famous science fiction movie called *The Blob,* a giant, amebalike cell terrorizes a community, eating many of its residents. What basic fact about cells did the movie-makers disregard for the sake of drama?
5. **Developing a hypothesis**   Fill one beaker with tap water at room temperature, another beaker with ice water, and a third beaker with hot water. Add equal amounts of food coloring to each beaker. In which beaker does the food coloring diffuse the fastest? The slowest? What is the variable in this experiment? Which beaker is the control? State a hypothesis for this experiment.
6. **Assessing concepts**   Which is better, respiration or fermentation? Explain your answer.
7. **Using the writing process**   Write a short story called "The Day Diffusion Went Backwards."

G:A:Z:E:T:T:E:

Ask Claire Veronica Broome about her work at the Centers for Disease Control in Atlanta, Georgia, and she is apt to break into a grin. "It's very exciting," she says, "because the answers you get are practical." Along with other scientists on her team, Dr. Broome travels to different locations to study outbreaks of disease.

One of the most confusing cases this "disease detective" has ever solved was an outbreak of listeriosis in Halifax, Nova Scotia. Listeriosis is a disease that affects membranes around the brain. This disease is caused by a type of bacterium called *Listeria monocytogenes*. Often the disease affects the

CLAIRE VERONICA BROOME:
DISEASE DETECTIVE

elderly. However, it can infect an infant before it is born. In fact, it was an epidemic of listeriosis in newborn infants that brought this case to Dr. Broome's attention.

Before going to Halifax, Dr. Broome gathered as much data on listeriosis as possible. She discovered that the bacteria that cause listeriosis were identified as a cause of human disease in 1929. At that time, it was learned that the bacteria live in soil and can infect animals. But as late as the 1980s, no one was certain how the bacteria are transmitted to unborn humans.

When Claire Broome and her team of researchers arrived in Halifax, they set to work reviewing hospital records and talking to physicians about past occurrences of listeriosis. Soon, they discovered the hospital in Halifax was experiencing an epidemic.

Dr. Broome compared two groups of people. The mothers of infants born with listeriosis made up one group. Mothers who gave birth to healthy babies made up the second group. People in both groups were interviewed. Dr. Broome collected data that covered several months of the new mothers' lives before they gave birth. Dr. Broome soon noticed a definite trend. The women with sick babies had eaten more cheeses than the women with healthy babies. Could the cheese have been contaminated by the bacteria that made the babies ill?

During her research, Dr. Broome became aware of another case of listeriosis. This case occurred in a Halifax man who had not spent time in a hospital. After examining the contents of the man's refrigerator, Dr. Broome added coleslaw to her list of possible transmitters of listeriosis. She reasoned that coleslaw is made from uncooked cabbage and cabbage grows in soil—a place in which listeria bacteria had already been discovered. Careful chemical analysis revealed that listeria bacteria were present in the coleslaw found in the sick man's refrigerator.

Dr. Broome and her team traced some of the contaminated coleslaw to a cabbage farm.

▲ **In her laboratory, Dr. Broome uses a computer to analyze data about epidemics.**

They found that the farmer used sheep manure to fertilize the cabbage. When the sheep were tested, they were also found to contain the listeria bacteria.

Now it was time for Dr. Broome to interview the mothers of the sick babies again. Not surprisingly, she found that many of them had eaten coleslaw during the time they were carrying their child. Later, Dr. Broome discovered that the bacteria that causes listeriosis can also live in milk and milk products, including cheese.

What made the packaged coleslaw and the milk products a good environment for bacteria to live in? Actually, it was the refrigerator in which these foods were stored that contributed to this disease outbreak. Refrigerators are used to keep foods from spoiling quickly. However, *Listeria monocytogenes* can survive, and even multiply, in cold temperatures. Even under proper storage conditions, the coleslaw and the cheese contained enough bacteria to make people ill.

The mystery of the Halifax listeriosis outbreak was solved. This case was closed. Dr. Broome returned to her office in Atlanta, but she barely had time to unpack before she was off to discover the cause of another "mystery" disease.

UNIT TWO

Monerans, Protists, Fungi, and Plants

The first marchers to appear in the parade of life were monerans, more commonly known as bacteria.

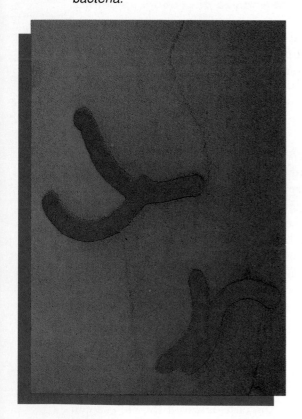

Think about the last time you saw a parade. You may have seen marching bands, beautiful floats, enormous balloons, showers of ticker tape, or waving flags.

At this moment, you are in the middle of the biggest, oldest, most spectacular parade on Earth—the parade of life. This parade began its journey through time more than 3.5 billion years ago, and its marchers are all the living things on Earth—past, present, and future. In this book, you will begin your exploration of the parade of life—an adventure that will take you all over the world.

Two billion years after bacteria started the parade of life, the next group of marchers appeared. This group consists of living things known as protists. Protists, such as wheel-shaped diatoms, are made of a single, complex cell.

C

Flowering plants are newcomers to the parade of life. Many flowers are actually clusters of flowers. Each yellow bump in the center and each "petal" of a painted daisy is a single tiny flower.

Living things that are composed of many cells are relatively recent additions to the parade of life. Many-celled living things include fungi, such as mushrooms, as well as plants.

Discovery *Activity*

Taking a Closer Look

1. Obtain a sample of pond water. What does the pond water look like? Can you see living things in the water?

2. Using a medicine dropper, place a drop of the pond water in the center of a glass microscope slide. Cover the drop with a coverslip.

3. Examine the drop of water with a microscope under low and high powers. What do you observe?

   ■ How do you think the inventor of the microscope felt when he first looked at pond water with his invention?

   ■ What do your observations tell you about some of the living things that march alongside you in the parade of life?

   ■ Why are microscopes necessary tools for studying the parade of life?

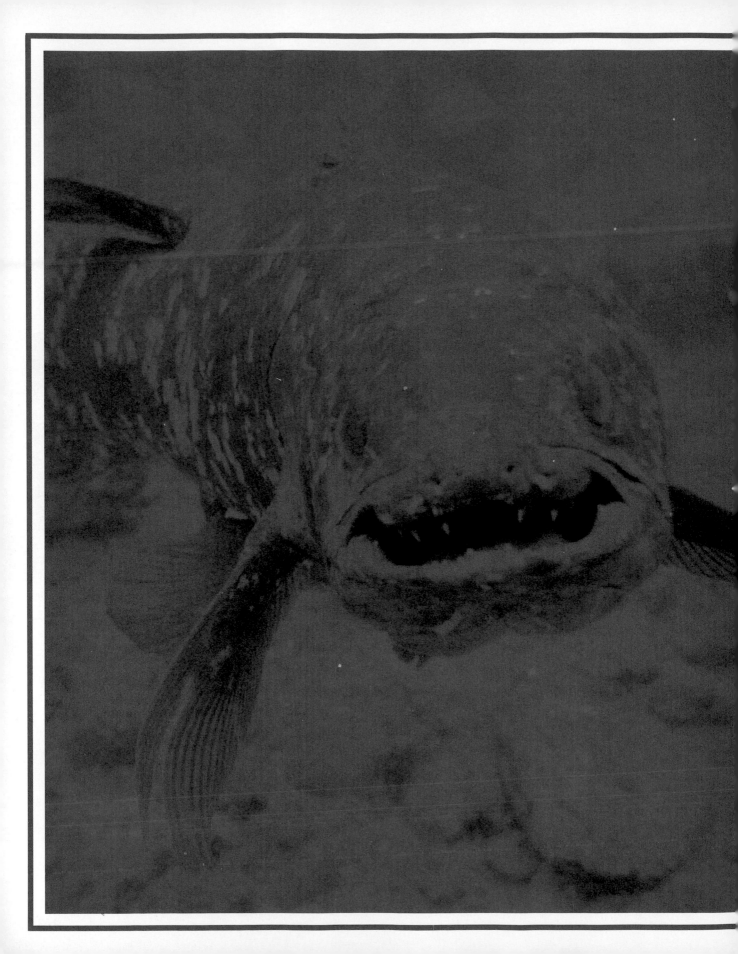

Classification of Living Things

4

Guide for Reading

After you read the following sections, you will be able to

4–1 History of Classification

■ Give examples of the ways classification is used in science and in everyday life.

■ Explain how binomial nomenclature is used to name living things.

4–2 Classification Today

■ Relate biological classification to evolution.

■ List the seven major classification groups.

4–3 The Five Kingdoms

■ Describe some general characteristics of each of the five kingdoms.

Mary Courtnay-Latimer had never seen anything like the creature the crew of a fishing boat had captured near the mouth of the Chalumna River in South Africa. The monstrous fish stretched more than 1.5 meters, or about six times the length of this page. Large spiny steel-blue scales covered its oily body. A powerful jaw hung down from a frightening face. Most peculiar of all, its fins were attached to what appeared to be stubby legs!

After searching through many books but finding no description of the strange fish, Latimer remembered someone she thought might be able to solve the riddle. That someone was Dr. James L. B. Smith, a well-known fish expert at a nearby university.

The scientist was shocked. He later wrote, "I would hardly have been more surprised if I met a dinosaur on the street." Smith was looking at an animal thought to have become extinct more than 60 million years ago. Yet, in a flash, he had been able to identify the fish as a coelacanth (SEE-luh-kanth). Smith gave the coelacanth its scientific name: *Latimeria chalumnae*. To do so, he used biological classification—a special system that helps scientists identify and name organisms. And it is this special system that you will learn about in the pages that follow.

Journal *Activity*

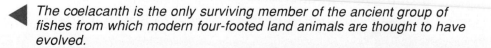

You and Your World You probably know someone who often puts people into categories such as "jocks" or "brains." In your journal, discuss the practice of putting people into categories.

The coelacanth is the only surviving member of the ancient group of fishes from which modern four-footed land animals are thought to have evolved.

4–1 History of Classification

Thousands of years ago, as people made observations about the world around them, they began to recognize that there were different groups of living things. There were animals and there were plants. Of the animals, some had claws and sharp teeth and roamed the land. Others had feathers and beaks and flew in the air. Still others had scales and fins and swam in the water.

Plants too showed a wide range of differences. Not only did they vary in shape, size, and color, but some were good to eat whereas others were poisonous. People soon learned that poisonous plants were best avoided. In a similar way, people learned that some animals, such as those with sharp teeth, were dangerous. Others, such as those with feathers, were relatively harmless.

What these early people were doing is something you often do in your daily life. They were giving order to the world around them by putting things in groups or categories based on certain characteristics. In other words, they were developing simple systems of classification. **Classification is the grouping of things according to similar characteristics.**

Stop and think for a moment about the ways in which you classify things every day. Perhaps you group your clothing by season—lightweight, cool items for summer and heavy, warm items for winter.

Figure 4–1 *When humans first came to North America tens of thousands of years ago, they found a number of unusual animals. How did classifying these animals help humans survive?*

Or perhaps by type—pants, sweaters, skirts, jackets. What are some other things that you sort in a meaningful way?

Classification is important to all fields of science, not just to the subject of biology you are now studying. For example, geologists classify rocks, soils, and fossils. Meteorologists (people who study the weather) classify clouds, winds, and types of storms. And all of the known chemical elements are classified into a system that helps chemists understand their behavior.

Classification is important in subjects other than science. In English, parts of speech are categorized as nouns, verbs, adjectives, and adverbs, to name a few. In mathematics, you work with odd numbers and even numbers, circles, rectangles, and triangles. In history, you group people and events according to time periods or geographic locations. You know that music can be rock-and-roll, rhythm and blues, country and western, or classical.

These are but a few examples of the important role that classification plays in all phases of life. For the people living thousands of years ago, classifying living things according to observable characteristics often helped them to survive. For you, classifying objects probably makes life easier and more meaningful. For scientists, classification systems provide a

ACTIVITY

Classification of Rocks

1. Obtain ten different rocks.

2. Examine the rocks. Notice how they are similar and how they are different.

3. Decide which characteristics of the rocks are most important. Use these characteristics to create a classification system for the rocks.

4. Notice that in this case there is no single correct way to classify your rocks. However, geologists do classify rocks in a particular way. Some characteristics that are important to geologists are the ways rocks are formed, the kind of chemicals that make up the rocks, and the shape of the crystals in the rocks.

Figure 4–2 *Geologists classify minerals according to the chemical compounds that make them up. Malachite (top) and azurite (bottom) are both forms of copper carbonate.*

means of learning more about life on Earth and of discovering the special relationships that exist between different kinds of living things.

But no matter who is doing the classifying or what is being classified, a classification system is always based on observable characteristics a group of things share. Good classification systems are meaningful, easily understood, and readily communicated among people.

Biological classification systems name and organize living things in a logical, meaningful way. To date, scientists have identified more than 2.5 million different types of living things—and their job is not even close to being finished! Some biologists estimate that there may be at least another 7 million different kinds of organisms living in tropical rain forests and in the depths of the Earth's oceans. In order to bring some order to this great diversity of living things, biologists have developed systems of classification.

The science of classification is a branch of biology known as taxonomy (taks-AH-nuh-mee). Scientists

Figure 4–3 *The dizzying variety of corals, fishes, and algae in a coral reef represents only a tiny fraction of the Earth's living things. Why is it necessary for biologists to classify living things?*

Figure 4–4 *The instruments in a marching band can be classified as woodwinds, percussion, and brass. How are some other everyday things classified?*

who work in this field are called taxonomists. Taxonomy has a long history, during which many classification systems were developed, changed to fit new facts and theories, and even rejected and replaced with better systems. This fact should not surprise you if you remember that science is an ongoing process that is often marked by change. This ability to change when new knowledge becomes available is one of science's greatest strengths.

The First Classification Systems

In the fourth century BC, the Greek philosopher Aristotle proposed a system to classify living things. He divided organisms into two groups: plants and animals. He also placed animals into three groups according to the way they moved. One group included all animals that flew, another group included all those that swam, and a third group included all those that walked.

Although this system was useful, it had some problems. Can you see why Aristotle's system for classifying animals is not perfect? It ignores the ways in which animals are similar and different in form. According to Aristotle, both a bird and a bat would be placed in the same group of flying animals. Yet in some basic ways, birds and bats are quite different. For example, birds are covered with feathers, whereas bats are covered with hair.

Figure 4–5 *Although the false vampire bat can fly like a bird, it belongs to the same class as the mouse it is about to eat (left). The egret belongs to a separate class of animals (right). How are the wings and other characteristics of the bat and egret different?*

Although the system devised by Aristotle would not satisfy today's taxonomists, it was one of the first attempts to develop a scientific and orderly system of classification. In fact, Aristotle's classification system was used for almost 2000 years. And until the middle of the twentieth century, scientists continued to use Aristotle's system of classifying living things as either plants or animals.

By the seventeenth century, biologists had started to classify organisms according to similarities in form and structure. They examined the organism's internal anatomy as well as its outward appearance. This helped them to place animals and other organisms into groups that were more meaningful than those Aristotle had created.

The classification system we use today is based on the work of the eighteenth-century Swedish scientist Carolus Linnaeus. Linnaeus built upon the work of previous scientists to develop his new system of classification. Like Aristotle, Linnaeus identified all living things as either plants or animals. Like the seventeenth-century biologists, he grouped plants and animals according to similarities in form. And like almost all other previous taxonomists, he used a system that consisted of groups within larger groups within still larger groups. Linnaeus spent the major part of his life using his classification system to describe all known plants and animals.

Linnaeus also developed a simple system for naming organisms. His system is such a logical and easy way of naming organisms that it is still used today.

Naming Living Things

Before Linnaeus developed his naming system, plants and animals had been identified by a series of Latin words. These words, sometimes numbering as many as 12 for one organism, described the physical features or appearance of the organism. To make things even more confusing, the names of plants and animals were rarely the same from book to book or from place to place.

BINOMIAL NOMENCLATURE The naming system devised by Linnaeus is called **binomial nomenclature** (bigh-NOH-mee-uhl NOH-muhn-klay-cher). In this system, each organism is given two names—which is exactly what the term binomial (consisting of two names) nomenclature (system of naming) means. The two names are a **genus** (plural: genera) name and a **species** name.

To help you understand this method of naming, think of the genus name as your family name. The species name could then be thought of as your first name. Your family name and your first name are the two names that identify you—the two names that most people know you by. They represent the most specific way of identifying you by name.

NAMING ORGANISMS TODAY Each kind of organism is given its very own two-part scientific name. An organism's scientific name is made up of its genus name and species name. The genus name is capitalized, but the species name begins with a small letter. Both names are printed in italics, which will help you recognize scientific names as you do your reading. Here is an example: The genus and species name for a wolf is *Canis lupus*. These two names identify this organism—which, by the way, has become very rare in the wild. Although most scientific names are in Latin, some are in Greek. Now think about the scientific name of the honeybee, *Apis mellifera*. What is the honeybee's genus name? Its species name?

Each organism has only one scientific name. And no two organisms can have the same scientific name. To understand why this is important, consider the following story. In North and South America, a certain large cat is called a mountain lion by some people, a cougar by others, and a puma by still others.

Figure 4–6 *The honeybee was once called* Apis pubescens, thorace subgriseo, abdomine fusco, pedibus posticis glabris utrinque margine ciliatus. *This means "fuzzy bee, light gray middle, brown body, smooth hind legs that have a small bag edged with tiny hairs."* Linnaeus named the honeybee Apis mellifera, *which means "honey-bearing bee."*

ACTIVITY
DOING

All in the Family

Use reference books to learn about the various families in the plant and animal kingdoms. Choose the family that you find most interesting. Make a collage of the family using pictures from old magazines and newspapers. Present the collage to your class.

Figure 4–7 *The wolf and the puma are known by many different common names. However, each organism has its own unique scientific name. What is the scientific name for the wolf? The puma?*

If these people were to talk to one another about this animal, they might get rather confused, thinking they were talking about three different animals. But scientists cannot afford to have such confusion. So scientists throughout the world know this large cat by only one name, *Felis concolor.* This name easily identifies the cat to all scientists, no matter where they live or what language they speak.

Keep in mind that it is not necessary to memorize the scientific names of different organisms. Even biologists know only a few names by heart, and most of these names are of organisms they have studied for years. What is important for you to know is that each organism has a scientific name that is used and understood all over the world, and that this name is related to the way the organism is classified.

4–1 Section Review

1. Describe some ways in which you use classification in everyday life.
2. What is taxonomy?
3. What is binomial nomenclature? How is it used?

Critical Thinking—*Evaluating Systems*
4. Discuss three problems with the classification and naming systems that existed before Linnaeus.

4-2 Classification Today

In the 200 years since Linnaeus developed his classification and naming systems, knowledge of the living world has grown enormously. And as the understanding of organisms improved, it became necessary to adjust the system of biological classification. Two things in particular have had a large effect on biological classification. One of these is Charles Darwin's theory of evolution. The other is advances in technology that have enabled scientists to take a better look at organisms.

Evolution and Classification

As you can see in Figure 4-8, wolves and lions both developed from a meat-eating animal that existed about 60 million years ago. And lions and house cats both developed from a catlike animal that lived about 15 million years ago. During the long history of life on Earth, organisms have changed, or evolved. You can think of evolution as the process in

Guide for Reading

Focus on this question as you read.

▶ *What are the classification groups from largest to smallest?*

Figure 4-8 *Because they evolved from a shared ancestor, lions, cats, wolves, and the catlike animal belong to the same classification group (order Carnivora). Cats and lions also belong to a smaller classification group (family Felidae), which contains all the descendants of the catlike animal. Why aren't wolves placed in the family Felidae?*

Meat-eating animal

Catlike animal

House cat

Wolf

Lion

Time (millions of years ago)

60

45

0

Figure 4–9 *As knowledge of the evolutionary relationships among animals improved, the lesser panda (bottom) and the giant panda (top center) were classified and reclassified. The data now available support a classification scheme in which the giant panda belongs to the same family as other bears, such as the grizzly (top left). The lesser panda is placed in the same family as raccoons (top right).*

which new kinds of organisms develop from previously existing kinds of organisms.

Evolutionary relationships, such as those between the ancient catlike animal and house cats or between wolves and lions, are extremely important to modern taxonomists. Evolutionary relationships are the basis for the modern system of biological classification. Modern taxonomists try to classify living things in such a way that each classification group contains organisms that evolved from the same ancestor.

The knowledge of evolution has changed the nature of biological classification groups. It has also changed the job of taxonomists. Because they did not know about evolution, taxonomists of the past felt free to classify organisms in any manner that made sense to them. They did not classify prehistoric organisms because they did not know about them. And they could choose any characteristics that they thought were important as their basis for classification.

Present-day taxonomists, on the other hand, classify organisms in a way that shows evolutionary relationships. They must consider organisms that existed in the distant past as well as those that exist in the present. And they classify organisms using characteristics that are proven to be good indicators of evolutionary relationships.

Technology and Classification

Today, 200 years after Linnaeus completed his work, scientists consider many factors when classifying organisms. Of course, they still examine the large internal and external structures, but they also rely on other observations. The invention of the microscope has allowed scientists to examine tiny structures hidden within the cells of an organism. It has also allowed them to examine organisms at their earliest stages of development. And special chemical tests have been developed that enable scientists to analyze the chemical building blocks of all living things. All of these techniques are important tools that help scientists group and name organisms.

Classification Groups

At first glance, the modern classification system may seem complicated to you. However, it is really quite simple, especially when you keep in mind its purpose. The system of classification used today does two jobs. First, it gives each organism a unique name that scientists all over the world can use and understand. Second, it groups organisms according to basic characteristics that reflect their evolutionary relationships.

All living things are classified into seven major groups: kingdom, phylum, class, order, family, genus, and species. The largest and most general group is the kingdom. For example, all animals belong to the animal kingdom. The second largest group is the phylum (FIGH-luhm; plural: phyla). A phylum includes a large number of very different organisms. However, these organisms share some important characteristics. A species is the smallest and most specific group in the classification system. Members of the same species share many characteristics and

Figure 4–10 *The male (right) and female (left) grand eclectus parrots look so different that they were once thought to be separate species.*

CLASSIFICATION OF THE LION

Kingdom
Animalia

Phylum
Chordata

Class
Mammalia

Order
Carnivora

Family
Felidae

Genus
Panthera

Species
leo

Figure 4–11 *This chart shows several other organisms that are in the same classification groups as the lion. To what class do lions belong?*

are similar to one another in appearance and behavior. In addition, members of the same species can interbreed and produce offspring. These offspring can in turn produce offspring of their own.

Ideally, the largest classification groups represent the earliest ancestors and the most ancient branches of life's family tree. And the smallest classification groups contain organisms that evolved from shared ancestors that lived in the relatively recent past. But because people do not know everything there is to know about evolution, these categories are not perfect in real life. As scientists learn more and more about evolutionary relationships and about the history of life on Earth, the classification system is changed. Sometimes the changes are tiny. Other times, the changes are quite large. And once in a while, taxonomists choose to keep an old group because it is particularly useful and logical, even if it does not perfectly reflect evolutionary history.

Biologists often think of these classification groups as forming a tree in which the trunk represents the kingdom, the main branches represent the phyla within the kingdom, and the tiny twigs at the tips of the branches represent species. You can also

Figure 4–12 *The relationships among classification groups can be represented as a tree. This classification tree shows the major groups of animals. What animals are in the same phylum as the centipede and the red beetle?*

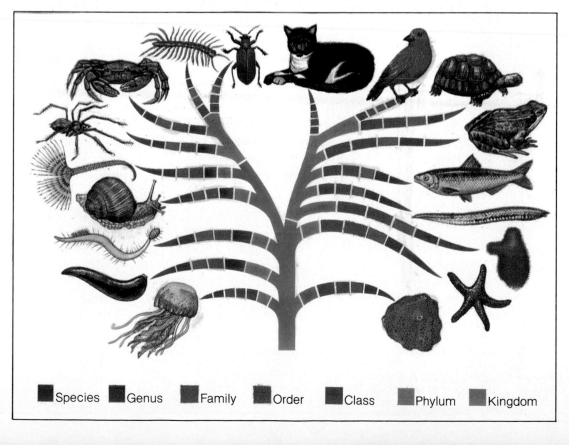

■Species ■Genus ■Family ■Order ■Class ■Phylum ■Kingdom

PROBLEM Solving

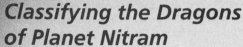

Classifying the Dragons of Planet Nitram

Imagine that you are a famous space explorer and biologist. You have recently arrived on the planet Nitram. Your job is to study the Nitramian animals and develop a system for classifying them.

You decide to begin your work by classifying Nitram's "dragons." You think that this name is not very scientific. However, you must admit that the animals look a lot like the monsters of Earth legends.

You ask the computer to give you a brief summary of all the information it has on Nitramian dragons. The computer produces the following printout.

THE DRAGONS OF NITRAM

Drako: About 5 to 6 meters tall. Four legs. Two batlike wings. Able to fly. Body covered in scales. Lives in mountains. Feeds on large animals.

Quetzalcoatl: About 2 meters long. Two legs. Two birdlike wings. Able to fly. Green and red feathers. Long feathers of many colors on top of head and around neck. Green scales on snakelike tail. Lives in tropical jungles. Eats fruit and small animals.

Sanjorge: About 2 to 5 meters tall. Four legs. Two small batlike wings. Not able to fly. Body has reddish-brown and greenish-brown scales. Lives in mountains. Probably eats animals.

Smaug: Largest known dragon. About 6 to 9 meters tall. Four legs. Two batlike wings. Able to fly. Body red, belly orange. Seems to be covered in scales. Extremely aggressive. Lives in mountains. Feeds on large animals, including humans.

Tailoong: About 4 meters long. Long, thin, snakelike body covered with gold scales. Four legs. Lionlike mane of long, colorful feathers. Lives in forests near lakes. Feeds on flowers and water plants.

Wyvern: About 2 to 3 meters long. Two legs. Two birdlike wings. Able to fly. Head, neck, and tail covered with red, yellow, and brown scales. Long red feathers around base of neck. Wings and body covered with brown feathers. Lives in mountains. Feeds on small animals. May also feed on the remains of dead animals.

Classifying Animals

1. Develop a classification system for the Nitramian dragons. Explain how you devised your classification scheme.

2. Like the animals of Earth, dragons are the result of millions of years of evolution. Which types of dragons seem to be most closely related? Explain.

3. When a sanjorge gets to be about 5 meters tall, its wings begin to grow rapidly. Within a year or two, it can fly. At the same time, its color changes to either red or green. How do these new data affect your classification system?

think of the classification groups as boxes within boxes. For example, you might open a huge kingdom box to discover several large phyla boxes, each of which contains a number of still smaller class boxes. Each time you opened a box, you would find one or more smaller boxes. If you opened the smallest boxes (the species boxes), you would find a number of individuals all of the same type.

By knowing which branches to climb, you can eventually arrive at one particular twig. (Provided, of course, that the branches are strong enough to bear your weight!) If you know which boxes to open in a set of boxes within boxes, you will sooner or later find the one tiny box you are looking for. Similarly, if you go through each level of classification groups, you will finally arrive at one species; that is, one specific kind of organism.

ACTIVITY
DISCOVERING

Classifying Living Things

1. Go for a long walk outside. Take along a pencil and a small notebook.

2. Write down the names of all the living things you see on your walk. (You should notice at least 15 different kinds of organisms.)

■ Develop a classification system for the organisms on your list.

4–2 Section Review

1. List the classification groups from largest to smallest.
2. What is evolution? How does evolution affect the way organisms are classified?

Critical Thinking—*Making Inferences*
3. Explain why knowing the classification of an unfamiliar organism can tell you a lot about that organism.

4–3 The Five Kingdoms

The discoveries of new living things and the changing ideas about the most effective ways of classifying life forms have resulted in the five-kingdom classification system we use now. **Today, the most generally accepted classification system contains five kingdoms: monerans, protists, fungi, plants, and animals.**

As is often the case in science, not all scientists agree on this classification system. And this is an important idea for you to keep in mind. More research may someday show that different systems make more

Guide for Reading

Focus on this question as you read.

▶ *What are the five kingdoms of living things?*

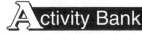
Activity Bank

A Key to the Puzzle, p.793

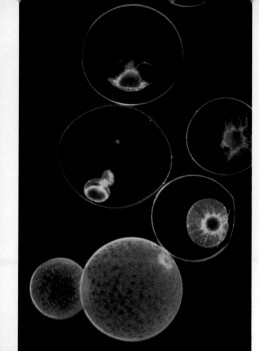

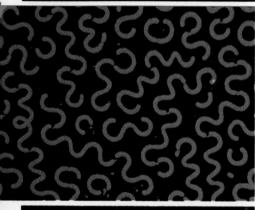

Figure 4–13 *Almost all members of the kingdoms Monera and Protista are microscopic. The blue-green bacterium Anabaena, a moneran, forms squiggly chains of cells. The glow-in-the-dark spheres and foamy starburst are types of protists. What is the main difference between monerans and protists?*

sense and better represent how living things evolved. But for now, this five-kingdom system is a useful tool for studying living things—and that's exactly what taxonomy is all about.

MONERANS Bacteria are placed in the kingdom Monera. Monerans are unicellular organisms, or organisms that consist of only one cell. A moneran's cell does not have its hereditary material enclosed in a nucleus, the structure that in other cells houses this important material. In addition to a nucleus, moneran cells lack many other structures found in other cells. Because of their unique characteristics, monerans are considered to be very distantly related to the other kingdoms.

Like other organisms, monerans can be placed into two categories based on how they obtain energy. Organisms that obtain energy by making their own food are called **autotrophs.** Such a name makes a lot of sense since the prefix *auto-* means self and the root word *-troph* means food. Organisms that cannot make their own food are called **heterotrophs**. The prefix *hetero-* means other. Can you explain why heterotroph is a good name for such organisms? Heterotrophs may eat autotrophs in order to obtain food or they may eat other heterotrophs. But all heterotrophs ultimately rely on autotrophs for food.

Scientists have evidence that monerans were the earliest life forms on Earth. They first appeared about 3.5 billion years ago.

PROTISTS The kingdom Protista includes most of the unicellular (one-celled) organisms that have a nucleus. The nucleus controls the functions of the cell and also contains the cell's hereditary material. In addition, the cell of a protist has special structures that perform specific functions for the cell.

A number of protists are capable of animallike movement but also have some distinctly plantlike characteristics. Specifically, they are green in color and can use the energy of light to make their own food from simple substances. As you can imagine, such organisms are difficult, if not impossible, to classify using a two-kingdom classification system. They are neither plants nor animals. Or perhaps they are both plants and animals! These puzzling organisms are one of the reasons scientists finally decided to abandon the two-kingdom system.

Protists were the first kind of cells that contain a nucleus. Ancient types of protists that lived millions and millions of years ago are probably the ancestors of fungi, plants, animals, and modern protists.

FUNGI   As you might expect, the world's wide variety of fungi make up the kingdom Fungi. Most fungi are multicellular organisms, or organisms that consist of many cells. Although you may not realize it, you may be quite familiar with fungi. Mushrooms are fungi. So are the molds that sometimes grow on leftover foods that have remained too long in the refrigerator. And the mildews that may appear as small black spots in damp basements and bathrooms are also fungi.

Figure 4–14 *The mushroom (left), shelf fungi (top right), and starfish stinkhorn (bottom right) all belong to the kingdom Fungi. The brownish slime on which the flies are feasting contains the stinkhorn's spores. If the spores end up in a favorable place after being deposited in the flies' droppings, they will grow into new stinkhorns.*

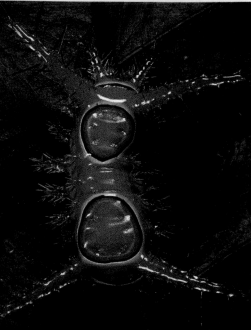

Figure 4–15 *The haired saddleback caterpillar and the pink katydid are both animals that feed on plants. How are animals similar to plants? How are they different?*

For many years, fungi were classified as plants. However, they are quite different from plants in some basic ways. Their cells fit together in a different way. Their cell wall, a tough protective layer that surrounds the cell, is made of a different substance than the cell wall of plants. And most importantly, plants are able to use the energy of light to make their own food from simple substances. Fungi cannot. Like animals, fungi must obtain their food and energy from another source. Are fungi autotrophs or heterotrophs?

PLANTS Plants make up the kingdom Plantae. Most members of the plant kingdom are multicellular (many-celled) autotrophs. You are probably quite familiar with members of this kingdom as it includes all the plants you have come to know by now—flowering plants, mosses, ferns, and certain algae, to name a few.

ANIMALS Animals are multicellular organisms that comprise the kingdom Animalia. Like other multicellular organisms such as plants and certain fungi, animals have specialized tissues, and most have organs and organ systems. Unlike plants, animals are heterotrophs.

4–3 Section Review

1. Name the five kingdoms of living things.
2. List three important characteristics for each of the five kingdoms.
3. How is the way an autotroph gets food different from the way a heterotroph gets food?

Connection—*Classifying Organisms*
4. Suppose that creatures from a distant planet are multicellular heterotrophs whose cells lack cell walls. Which kingdom of the Earth's organisms do these creatures most closely resemble?

CONNECTIONS

What's in a Name?

You may be familiar with the German *fairy tale* "Rumpelstiltskin." In this story, a magical dwarf saves a queen's life by helping her spin straw into gold. To pay the dwarf for his help, the queen must give him her baby—or guess the dwarf's secret name. In the end, she learns the dwarf's name. And everyone (except the dwarf) lives happily ever after.

Tales like this one reflect the ancient idea that names are extremely important. People once believed that knowing something's true name gave you magical power over it.

Knowing the true, or scientific, names of organisms is not going to give you magical power over them. But knowing what the scientific names mean can help give you a different kind of power—the power to figure out unfamiliar words.

As you look over the following examples of scientific names, remember that it is not important to memorize names. And don't let the strangeness of the names scare you. In time, you will become more familiar with scientific names and learn to see—and use—the patterns in them. You will discover that knowing the secrets of scientific names can be informative and even fun.

▲ *Naja melanoleuca* is a black-and-white-lipped cobra, a venomous snake. In India and Southeast Asia, a *naja,* or *naga,* is an imaginary beast that usually takes the form of a giant snake with a human head. A *naga* can also take the form of a human or a snake. (*melano-* means black; *leuca-* means white.)

▲ *Narcissus poeticus* is a sweet-smelling flower. According to a Greek myth, Narcissus was a handsome young man who fell in love with his own reflection. Eventually, the gods transformed Narcissus into a flower. In the spring, narcissus flowers may sometimes be found near a pond or stream. The long stems of the flowers may cause them to lean over the water so that it looks like they are admiring their own reflection. The story of Narcissus has added words other than the name of a flower to the English language. A person who is completely in love with himself (or herself) is called a narcissist. Linnaeus's name for the flower means "narcissus of the poets."

Laboratory Investigation

Whose Shoe Is That?

Problem
How can a group of objects be classified?

Materials *(per group of six)*

students' shoes
pencil and paper

Procedure

1. At your teacher's direction, remove your right shoe and place it on a work table.
2. As a group, think of a characteristic that will divide all six shoes into two kingdoms. For example, you may first divide the shoes by the characteristic of color into the brown shoe kingdom and the nonbrown shoe kingdom.
3. Place the shoes into two separate piles based on the characteristic your group has selected.
4. Working only with those shoes in one kingdom, divide that kingdom into two groups based on a new characteristic. The brown shoe kingdom, for example, may be divided into shoes with rubber soles and shoes without rubber soles.
5. Further divide these groups into subgroups. For example, the shoes in the rubber-soled group may be separated into a shoelace group and a nonshoelace group.

6. Continue to divide the shoes by choosing new characteristics until you have only one shoe left in each group. Identify the person who owns this shoe.
7. Repeat this process working with the nonbrown shoes.
8. Draw a diagram similar to the one shown to represent your classification system.

Observations

1. How many groups are there in your classification system?
2. Was there more than one way to divide the shoes into groups? How did you decide which classification groups to use?

Analysis and Conclusions

1. Was your shoe classification system accurate? Why or why not?
2. If brown and nonbrown shoe groups represent kingdoms, what do each of the other groups in your diagram represent?
3. Compare your classification system to the classification system used by most scientists today.
4. **On Your Own** Follow a similar procedure to classify all the objects in a closet or a drawer in your home.

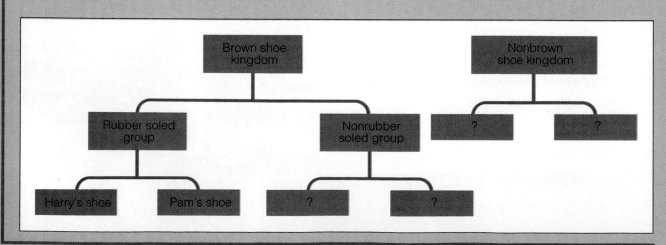

Study Guide

Summarizing Key Concepts

4-1 History of Classification

▲ Classification is the grouping of things according to similar characteristics.

▲Classification is important in all fields of science, in subjects other than science, and in everyday life.

▲ Good classification systems are meaningful, easily understood, and readily communicated among people.

▲ Classification systems organize and name living things in a logical, meaningful way.

▲ The science of biological classification is called taxonomy.

▲ Aristotle invented one of the first systems of biological classification. This system was used for about 2000 years.

▲ The classification and naming systems used today are based on the work of Carolus Linnaeus.

▲ In binomial nomenclature, which was invented by Linnaeus, each kind of organism is given a unique two-part name. This scientific name is used and understood all over the world. The scientific name is also related to the way the organism is classified.

4-2 Classification Today

▲ As our understanding of living things improves, it becomes necessary to revise our system of biological classification.

▲ Evolutionary relationships are the basis for the modern system of biological classification.

▲ Advances in technology have increased our knowledge of living things and thus have had an effect on how organisms are classified.

▲ The classification groups from largest to smallest are: kingdom, phylum, class, order, family, genus, and species. If you go through each level of classification groups, you finally arrive at one specific species.

▲ Each of an organism's classification groups tells you something about its characteristics.

4-3 The Five Kingdoms

▲ Today, the most generally accepted classification system contains five kingdoms: monerans, protists, fungi, plants, and animals.

▲ Autotrophs can make food from simple raw materials. Heterotrophs cannot make their own food.

Reviewing Key Terms

Define each term in a complete sentence.

4-1 History of Classification
binomial nomenclature
genus
species

4-3 The Five Kingdoms
autotroph
heterotroph

Chapter Review

Content Review

Multiple Choice

Choose the letter of the answer that best completes each statement.

1. Which of the following is not a characteristic of a good classification system?
   a. It shows relationships among objects.
   b. It is meaningful.
   c. It is readily communicated among people.
   d. It creates confusion.
2. The branch of biology that deals with naming and classifying organisms is called
   a. exobiology.
   b. taxonomy.
   c. phylum.
   d. binomial nomenclature.
3. The largest classification group is the
   a. species.
   b. order.
   c. phylum.
   d. kingdom.
4. A genus can be divided into
   a. phyla.
   b. orders.
   c. species.
   d. families.

5. Carolus Linnaeus classified plants and animals according to similarities in
   a. color.
   b. habits.
   c. structure.
   d. size.
6. Which organisms have cells that do not contain a nucleus?
   a. monerans
   b. fungi
   c. plants
   d. protists
7. Which of the following statements about animals in the same species is false?
   a. They evolved from a shared ancestor.
   b. They share certain characteristics.
   c. They can interbreed and produce offspring.
   d. They have identical characteristics.
8. Which organism is an autotroph?
   a. frog
   b. mushroom
   c. lion
   d. maple tree

True or False

If the statement is true, write "true." If it is false, change the underlined word or words to make the statement true.

1. In Linnaeus's classification system, the smallest group was the <u>genus</u>.
2. The classification groups from largest to smallest are: <u>kingdom, phylum, class, family, order, species, genus</u>.
3. <u>Multicellular</u> organisms are composed of only one cell.
4. In a five-kingdom classification system, bacteria are classified as <u>plants</u>.
5. Green plants are <u>heterotrophs</u>.
6. <u>Autotrophs</u> are organisms that cannot make their own food.
7. The science of classification is called <u>taxonomy</u>.
8. The first word in a scientific name is the <u>species</u>.

Concept Mapping

Complete the following concept map for Section 4–1. Then construct a concept map for the entire chapter.

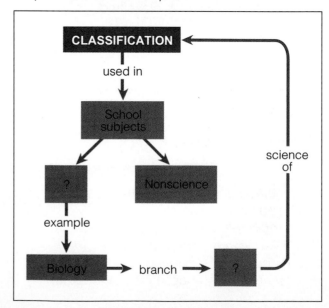

Concept Mastery

Discuss each of the following in a brief paragraph.

1. Why do scientists classify organisms?
2. What type of characteristics did Linnaeus use to develop his classification system of living things?
3. How is the classification system used by scientists today different from the classification system developed by Linnaeus? How is it similar?
4. Describe each of the kingdoms used in the five-kingdom classification system. Give an example of an organism in each kingdom.
5. How do an autotroph and a heterotroph differ? Give an example of each.
6. How did the knowledge of evolution affect the way organisms are classified?
7. What are the two major jobs of the modern classification system? Explain why these jobs are important.

Critical Thinking and Problem Solving

Use the skills you have developed in this chapter to answer each of the following.

1. **Identifying relationships** Which two of the following three unicellular organisms are most closely related: *Entamoeba histolytica, Escherichia coli, Entamoeba coli?* Explain your answer.
2. **Developing a model** Design a classification system for objects that might be found in your closet. Then draw a diagram that illustrates your classification system.
3. **Making comparisons** In what ways were the classification and naming systems developed by Linnaeus an improvement over previous systems?
4. **Applying concepts** Why is it that scientists do not classify animals by what they eat or where they live?
5. **Relating cause and effect** Explain why advances in technology may change the way organisms are classified.
6. **Applying concepts** Suppose you discovered a new single-celled organism. This organism has a nucleus and a long taillike structure that it uses to move itself through the water in which it lives. It also has a large cup-shaped structure that is filled with a green substance. This green substance is involved in making food from simple substances. In what kingdom would you place this organism? What are your reasons?
7. **Using the writing process** Some experts estimate that there are more unknown organisms in the tropical rain forests than there are known organisms in the world. These rain forests may be destroyed before the organisms in them can be studied and classified. It is possible that some of these organisms may be helpful in medicine, farming, and industry. Write a script for a television news program protesting the destruction of rain forests. Offer reasons why rain forests should be protected.

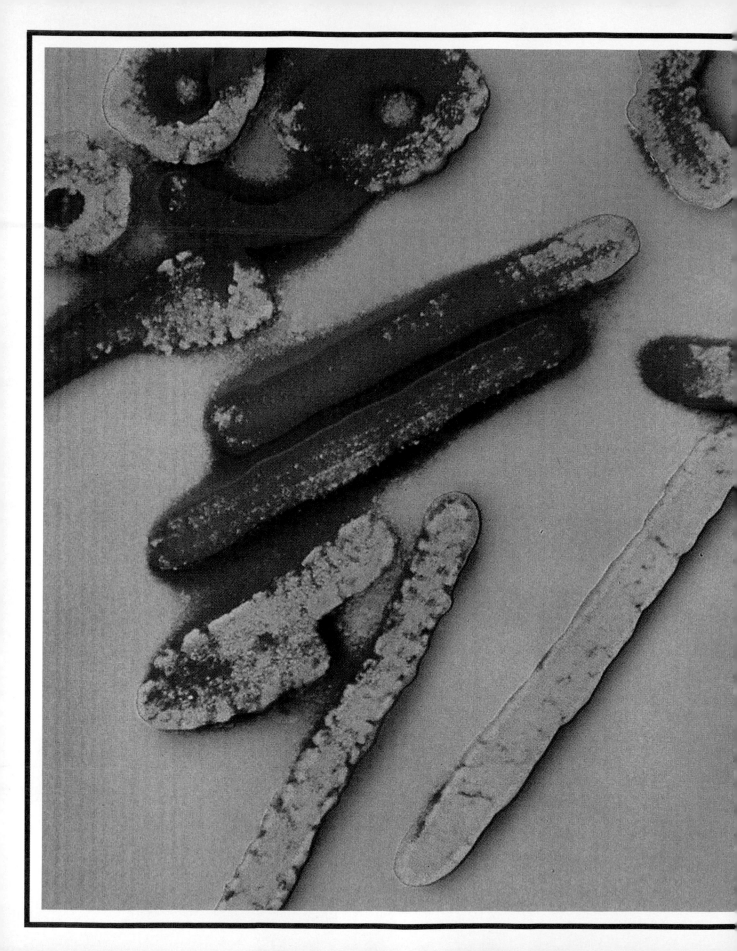

Viruses and Monerans

Guide for Reading

After you read the following sections, you will be able to

5–1 Viruses

- List the parts of a virus.
- Describe how a virus reproduces and causes disease.

5–2 Monerans

- Name and describe the parts of a moneran.
- Compare autotrophic and heterotrophic monerans.
- Discuss the helpful and harmful effects of the monerans.

The story sounds like the screenplay for a Grade B horror movie: In a remote part of Africa, an unseen monster emerges from the rain forest and kills nearly everyone in its path. This elusive killer is not the product of a writer's imagination, however. The "monster" is a virus called the Ebola virus.

The Ebola virus, named after a river in Zaire, causes a deadly disease that is almost always fatal. Symptoms of the disease include a high fever and massive bleeding. The most recent outbreak of the Ebola virus occurred in 1995. The epidemic began in Kikwit, a small town in southwestern Zaire, which was quickly quarantined to prevent further spread of the disease.

Medical researchers have traced at least one strain of Ebola virus to wild chimpanzees. In the case of the Zaire epidemic, both the source of the virus and the cure remain unknown.

As you read this chapter, you will learn a great deal about viruses. You will also find out about tiny one-celled organisms called monerans. So turn the page and begin your journey into a strange world of incredibly small but fascinating living things.

Journal *Activity*

You and Your World In your journal, make a list of ten questions you have about diseases. As you study this chapter, see how many of your questions are answered. Devise a plan for finding out the answers to any questions that remain unanswered.

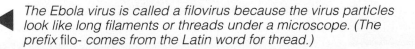

The Ebola virus is called a filovirus because the virus particles look like long filaments or threads under a microscope. (The prefix filo- comes from the Latin word for thread.)

5–1 Viruses

Imagine for a moment that you have been presented with a rather serious problem. A disease is killing one of your country's most important crops. Sick plants develop a pattern of yellow spots on their leaves. Eventually, the leaves wither and fall off, and the plant dies. You must find out what is causing the disease. With this information, it may be possible to save the remaining plants.

You gather some leaves from the sick plants and crush the leaves until they produce a juice. Then you put a few drops of the juice on the leaves of healthy plants. Several days later, you discover yellow spots on the once-healthy leaves. You reason that the cause of the disease can be found in the juice from the sick plants.

You then put the juice through a filter whose holes are so small that not even cells can slip through. You figure that this should take out any disease-causing microorganisms (microscopic organisms) in the juice. In fact, when you use the best light microscope to examine the filtered juice, you find no trace of microorganisms. But to your surprise, the juice still causes the disease in healthy plants! You realize that you must have discovered a germ that is smaller than a cell—too small to be

Figure 5–1 *Viruses come in many shapes. Rabies virus is shaped like a thimble (bottom left). Tobacco mosaic virus is rod-shaped (right). Rubella (German measles) virus is spherical (top left). The viruses that cause chicken pox and related diseases are oval (center) and are the largest viruses—as much as several hundred billionths of a meter long.*

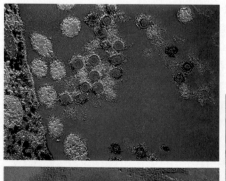

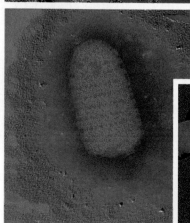

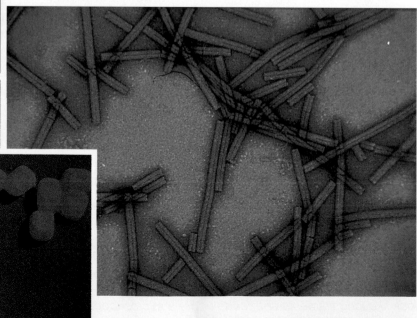

seen even with a microscope. But how could this be, you wonder. Cells are the basic unit of structure and function in living things. All living things are made of cells. There cannot be a living thing smaller than a cell! Or can there?

An additional experiment shows that the disease-causing germ can reproduce in the newly infected plants. This seems to indicate that a living thing is causing the disease. After all, the ability to reproduce is a characteristic of living things. A non-living, sickness-causing substance—a poison, for example—is not able to reproduce itself.

However, the results of other experiments seem to contradict the hypothesis that the disease-causing germ is alive. You discover that the crop-killing germ cannot be grown outside of the plants it infects. This is strange, because all living things can grow by themselves (provided they are given the correct nutrients and environmental conditions, of course). What is going on here, you wonder.

Finally, you decide to use chemical techniques to isolate the germ. After you purify enormous quantities of the juice from the infected plants, you are left with a tiny amount of whitish, needlelike crystals. These crystals show no evidence of being alive. They do not grow, breathe, eat, reproduce, or perform any other life functions. But when you inject the seemingly lifeless crystals into a healthy plant, the plant develops the disease. Clearly the mysterious crystals are the disease-causing germ itself. But what is this germ? And is it alive—or not?

This story is based on real events that started about 100 years ago and unfolded over the next forty years. The disease-causing germ is a **virus.** And whether viruses are alive or not depends on your definition of life. As you read in the story, there are good reasons to think of viruses as living things. And there are equally good reasons to think of viruses as nonliving things.

What Is a Virus?

Viruses are tiny particles that can invade living cells. Because viruses are not cells, they cannot perform all the functions of living cells. For example, they cannot take in food or get rid of wastes. In fact,

Figure 5–2 *Viruses cause a number of diseases in living things. The cherry's leaves are turning yellow and falling off as a result of a virus disease. Why are viruses considered parasites?*

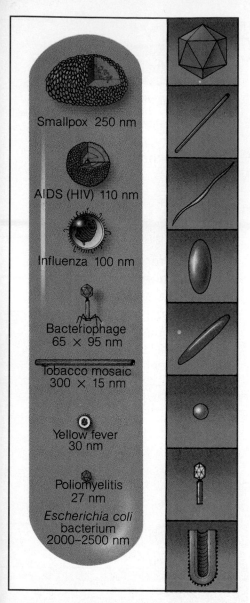

Figure 5–3 *Viruses have a wide variety of shapes and sizes. Viruses are measured in nanometers (nm). A nanometer is one-billionth of a meter. The yellow-green capsule-shaped structure represents a bacterial cell. In general, how do viruses compare to cells in terms of size? In terms of structure?*

Labels in figure:
Smallpox 250 nm
AIDS (HIV) 110 nm
Influenza 100 nm
Bacteriophage 65 × 95 nm
Tobacco mosaic 300 × 15 nm
Yellow fever 30 nm
Poliomyelitis 27 nm
Escherichia coli bacterium 2000–2500 nm

about the only life function that viruses share with cells is reproduction. However, viruses cannot reproduce on their own. They need the help of living cells. The living cells are called **hosts.** Hosts are living things that provide a home and/or food for a **parasite** (PAIR-ah-sight). A parasite is an organism that survives by living on or in a host organism, thus harming it. Because viruses harm their host cells, they are considered to be parasites.

All five kingdoms of living things—plants, animals, fungi, protists, and monerans—are affected by viruses. In fact, experts suspect that all cells are subject to invasion by some kind of virus. It is interesting to note that each type of virus can infect only a few specific kinds of cells. For example, the rabies virus infects only nerve cells in the brain and spinal cord of dogs, humans, and other mammals. So a mammal's skin cells cannot be infected with rabies. And an organism that is not a mammal—such as a frog, plant, mushroom, or protist—cannot get rabies.

The origin of viruses is unknown. Because viruses need living cells in order to reproduce, it is likely that they appeared after the first cells. Many scientists think that viruses evolved from bits of hereditary material that were lost from host cells. This may mean that a virus is more closely related to its host than it is to other viruses. Thus the virus that causes your cold may be more closely related to you than it is to the virus that causes a plant's leaves to fall off!

Structure of Viruses

A virus has two basic parts: a core of hereditary material and an outer coat of protein. The hereditary material controls the production of new viruses. Like a turtle's shell, the protein coat encloses and protects the virus. The protein coat is so protective that some viruses survive after being dried and frozen for years. The protein coat also enables a virus to identify and attach to its host cell.

With the invention of the electron microscope in the 1930s, scientists were able to see and study the shapes and sizes of certain viruses. Some viruses, such as those that cause the common cold, have 20 surfaces. Each surface is in the shape of a triangle that has equal sides. Other viruses look like fine threads. Still others resemble tiny spheres. There are even some that look like miniature spaceships.

Reproduction of Viruses

In order to understand how a virus reproduces and causes disease, it might be helpful to examine the activities of one kind of virus known as a bacteriophage (bak-TEER-ee-oh-fayj). A bacteriophage is a virus that infects bacteria (singular: bacterium). In fact, the word bacteriophage means "bacteria eater." Bacteria are unicellular (one-celled) microorganisms that belong to the kingdom Monera.

In Figure 5–4, you can see how a bacteriophage (virus) attaches its tail to the outside of a bacterium. The bacteriophage quickly injects its hereditary material directly into the living cell. The protein coat is left behind. Once inside the cell, the bacteriophage's hereditary material takes control of all of the bacterium's activities. As a result, the bacterium is no longer in control. The bacterium begins to produce new bacteriophages rather than its own chemicals.

Figure 5–4 *The electron micrograph shows a bacterium under attack by numerous bacteriophages (inset). What stage in the diagram does this represent? What are the events in the life cycle of a bacteriophage?*

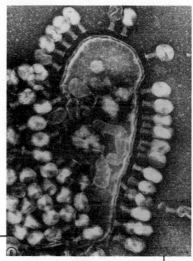

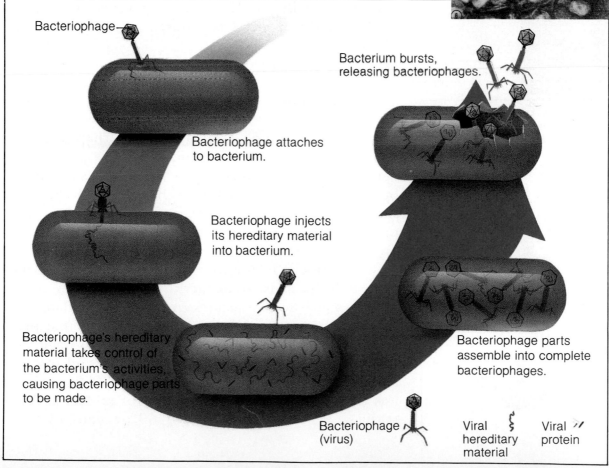

Bacteriophage

Bacteriophage attaches to bacterium.

Bacteriophage injects its hereditary material into bacterium.

Bacteriophage's hereditary material takes control of the bacterium's activities, causing bacteriophage parts to be made.

Bacterium bursts, releasing bacteriophages.

Bacteriophage parts assemble into complete bacteriophages.

Bacteriophage (virus)

Viral hereditary material

Viral protein

Figure 5–5 *Like many animal viruses, influenza viruses escape from their host cell by forming tiny bubbles at its surface.*

Figure 5–6 *A bacteriophage looks like a miniature spaceship. What are the main parts of a bacteriophage? What kind of cell is host to a bacteriophage?*

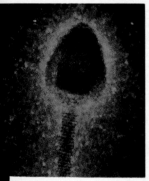

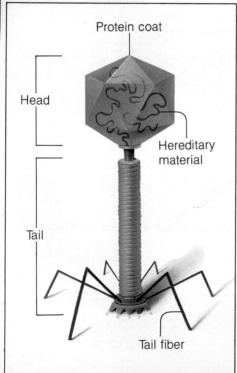

Protein coat

Head

Hereditary material

Tail

Tail fiber

Soon the bacterium fills up with new bacteriophages, perhaps as many as several hundred. Eventually, the bacterium bursts open. The new bacteriophages are released and infect nearby bacteria.

Not all viruses act like a bacteriophage. Some viruses keep their protein coat when they enter their host cell. Others, including some bacteriophages, simply join their hereditary material to that of the host cell and cause no immediate effects. A few cause disease by changing the behavior of their host cell and making it into a cancer cell. And many viruses do not cause their host cell to burst. Instead, a newly made virus particle causes the host cell to produce a tiny bubblelike structure on its edge. As you can see in Figure 5–5, this bubble eventually pinches off the side of the cell, carrying the virus with it.

Although the details of the "life" cycle vary from virus to virus, the basic pattern is the same for all viruses. **First, a virus gets its hereditary material into the host cell. Then the host cell makes more virus particles. Finally, the virus particles leave the original host cell and infect new hosts.**

Viruses and Humans

Viruses cause a large number of human diseases. Some of these diseases—such as colds, fever blisters, and warts—are simply annoying and perhaps a bit painful. Others are serious and can cause permanent damage or even death. Among the diseases caused by viruses are AIDS, measles, influenza, hepatitis, smallpox, polio, encephalitis, mumps, and herpes.

Much of the research on viruses has concentrated on ways of preventing and treating viral diseases. However, researchers have found ways of using viruses to help humans. Weakened or killed viruses are used to make some vaccines. A vaccine stimulates the body to produce antibodies (substances that prevent infection). Viruses can also be used to wage germ warfare on disease-causing bacteria and insects and on other agricultural pests. In the 1950s, a virus was used to control the population of rabbits in Australia. The virus killed about 80 percent of the

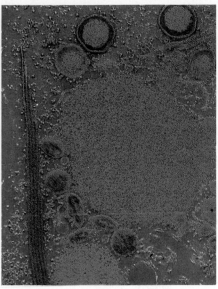

rabbits, enabling people to reclaim land for livestock and wildlife. Why might viruses be a better weapon against pests than poisons?

Recently, researchers have learned to put hereditary material into viruses. They can then use the viruses to put the hereditary material into cells. In the not-too-distant future, scientists may be able to use viruses to replace faulty information in a person's hereditary material. This could cure diseases such as diabetes, cystic fibrosis, sickle cell anemia, and many other hereditary disorders. Scientists may also be able to use viruses to improve crops. For example, corn plants might be "infected" with hereditary material that enables them to make their own fertilizer or resist pests.

Figure 5–7 *The population of rabbits in Australia was brought under control with the help of the virus that causes the rabbit disease myxomatosis. Why are viruses good for controlling pests? Can you think of some situations in which using viruses for pest control might be a bad idea?*

Figure 5–8 *The red circles are herpes viruses inside a human cell. The colors that you see do not actually exist in real life. They are added to photographs to make structures easier to see.*

5–1 Section Review

1. How does a virus reproduce? How does this relate to how the virus causes disease?
2. Would you classify viruses as living or nonliving? Explain.
3. What is a bacteriophage?
4. Describe the structure of a virus.

Connection—*Technology*
5. Why were scientists unable to study the structure of viruses until after the electron microscope was invented?

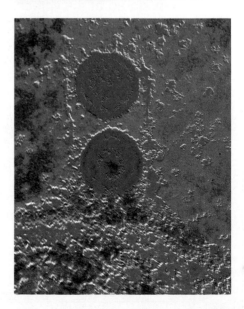

CONNECTIONS

Computer Viruses: An Electronic Epidemic

"Shuttle to mission control. Do you read me?"

"We read you loud and clear. Commence data transmission." The computer screen flickered with changing numbers and words as mission control began to receive astronomical information from the Space Shuttle. Suddenly, the screen went blank.

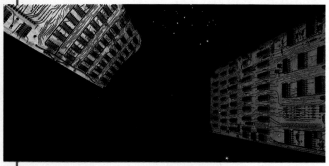

Before the startled technician could adjust the computer's controls, a familiar television character appeared where the data should have been.

"Cookie!" it demanded. The technician stared at the screen, horrified. She then tried to type instructions. But the computer did not respond.

"No cookie, no play. Bye-bye." With these words, the figure on the screen disappeared. And so did all the hard-won information from the Space Shuttle. Within only a few seconds, a computer virus had undone years of work!

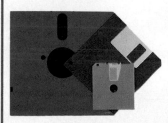

Although all the events in this story are imaginary, they are not impossible. Because many activities of modern life involve computers,

computer viruses are a matter of great concern. A computer virus is not really a virus. It is simply a program, or set of instructions to a computer. Computer viruses do not invade cells or cause diseases. They do not harm living things—at least not directly. They are made by humans and are definitely not alive. And the information they contain is in the form of magnetic or electric signals.

Some computer viruses, such as the one in the story you just read, are carried via telephone wires. Others are transmitted by computer diskettes that are "infected" with the virus program. If such diskettes are used, the virus is stored in the computer. The virus program then causes the computer to copy the computer virus onto every diskette it contacts in the future!

Don't be a victim of a virus! Whether biological or computer, viruses are enough to make you sick. A word to the wise is sufficient: Protect yourself from getting viruses and spreading them!

5-2 Monerans

Monerans are tiny organisms that consist of a single cell. As you learned in Chapter 4, moneran cells are different from all other cells because they lack a nucleus and certain other cell structures. At one time, the term bacteria was used to refer to only certain kinds of monerans. Other monerans were known as blue-green algae. Blue-green algae are now known as cyanobacteria, or blue-green bacteria. (The prefix *cyano-* means blue.) Because all monerans are now considered to be bacteria, the terms bacteria and monerans are used interchangeably. We will usually use the term bacteria in this chapter because it is more familiar and used more often than the term monerans. As you read this chapter, keep in mind that monerans and bacteria are the same thing.

As you may recall from Chapter 4, bacteria are the oldest forms of life on Earth. The first bacteria appeared about 3.5 billion years ago. Bacteria were Earth's only living things for about 2 billion years.

Bacteria are among the most numerous organisms on Earth. Scientists estimate that there are about 2.5 billion bacteria in a gram of garden soil. And the total number of bacteria living in your mouth is greater than the number of people who have ever lived!

As you might expect of such a large, ancient group, bacteria are quite varied. They may be rod-shaped like a medicine capsule, round as a marble, coiled like a stretched spring, round and stalked like a candied apple on a stick, or completely shapeless. They come in colors ranging from reds and yellows

Guide for Reading

Focus on this question as you read.

▶ How do monerans fit into the world?

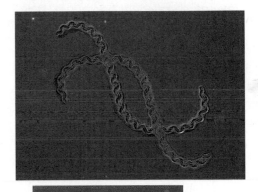

Figure 5–9 *The most common shapes of bacteria are spheres (left), rods (bottom right), and spirals (top right). However, some bacteria—such as Y-shaped Bifidiobacterium (center right)— have unusual shapes that do not fit into any of these categories.*

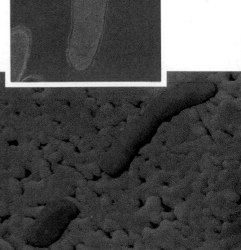

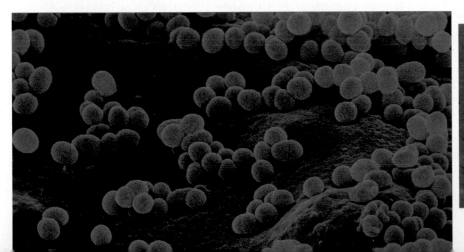

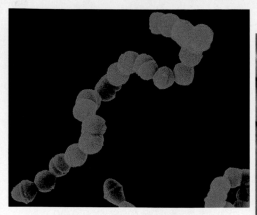

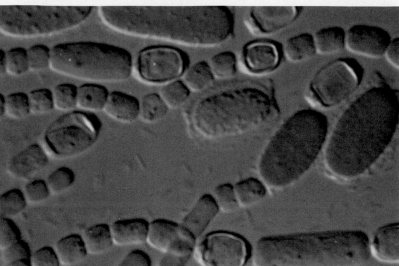

Figure 5–10 *Bacteria, such as many blue-green bacteria (right), may live in groups of cells attached to one another. The name of a bacterium can be a clue to what it looks like. For example, strepto- means chain and -coccus means a spherical bacterium. Why was this bacterium named* Streptococcus *(left)?*

to blues and violets. Some bacteria live alone as single cells. Others live in groups of cells that are attached to one another.

Bacteria are found in water, air, soil, and the bodies of larger organisms. In fact, bacteria live almost everywhere—even in places where other living things cannot survive. For example, some bacteria live in volcanic vents at the bottom of the ocean. The temperature of the water in these vents can be as high as 250°C—two and one-half times the temperature of boiling water.

Bacteria are considered the simplest organisms. However, bacteria are more complex than they may appear. Each bacterial cell performs the same basic functions that more complex organisms, including you, perform.

Structure of Bacteria

One of the most noticeable features of a bacterium is the cell wall. See Figure 5–12. The cell wall is a tough, rigid structure that surrounds, supports, shapes, and protects the cell. Almost all bacteria have a cell wall. In some bacteria, there is a coating on the outside of the cell wall. This coating is called the capsule. How might the capsule provide protection for a bacterium?

Lining the inside of the cell wall is the cell membrane. The cell membrane controls which substances enter and leave the cell. Within the cell membrane

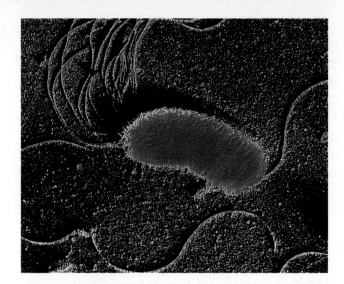

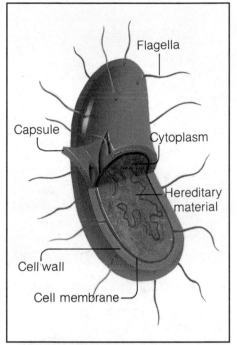

is the cytoplasm. The cytoplasm is a jellylike mixture of substances that makes up most of the cell.

Unlike most other cells, the hereditary material of bacteria is not confined in a nucleus. (A nucleus is a membrane-enclosed structure that can be thought of as the "control center" of a typical cell.) In other words, there is no membrane separating the hereditary material from the rest of the cell in monerans.

Many bacteria are not able to move on their own. They can be carried from one place to another by air and water currents, clothing, and other objects. Other bacteria have special structures that help them move in watery surroundings. One such structure is a flagellum (flah-JEHL-uhm; plural: flagella). A flagellum is a long, thin, whiplike structure that propels a bacterium through its environment. Some bacteria may have many flagella.

Life Functions of Bacteria

Bacteria have more different ways of getting the energy they need to live than any other kingdom of organisms. In fact, bacteria obtain energy in more ways than all of the other kingdoms combined. Like most other organisms, many bacteria need oxygen in order to get energy from food. Other bacteria can thrive without oxygen. And still other kinds of bacteria will die if they are exposed to oxygen.

Many bacteria are heterotrophs. Recall from Chapter 4 that a heterotroph cannot make its own food. A heterotroph gets energy by eating food,

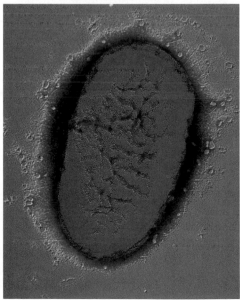

Figure 5–12 *The diagram shows the structure of a typical bacterium. Can you locate the flagella, capsule, cytoplasm, and genetic material on the photograph of the whooping cough bacterium?*

Figure 5–13 *If you could look at this scene with a powerful microscope, you would discover bacteria busily breaking down the remains of the dead tree. Why are some bacteria called decomposers?*

usually other organisms. Some bacteria feed on living organisms. These bacteria are parasites. As you just learned, parasites are organisms that live and feed either inside or attached to the outer surface of a host organism, thus harming the host. Such bacteria cause infections in people, animals, and plants. Other bacteria feed on dead things. These bacteria are **decomposers.** Decomposers break down dead organisms into simpler substances. In the process, they return important materials to the soil and water.

Some bacteria are autotrophs. An autotroph, you will recall, makes its own food. Some food-making bacteria use the energy of sunlight to produce food. Other bacteria use the energy in certain substances that contain sulfur and iron to make food. The nauseating "sulfur" smell of mud flats or rotting food is due to the action of such bacteria.

When food is plentiful and the environment is favorable, bacterial cells grow and then reproduce by dividing into two cells. Under the best conditions, most bacteria reproduce quickly. Some types can double in number every 20 minutes. At this rate, after about 24 hours the offspring of a single bacterium would have a mass greater than 2 million kilograms, or as much as 2000 mid-sized cars! In a few more days, their mass would be greater than that of the Earth. Obviously, this does not happen. Why do you think this is so?

When food is scarce or conditions become unfavorable in other ways, some bacteria form a small internal resting cell called an endospore. As you can see in Figure 5–15, an endospore consists of hereditary material, a small amount of cytoplasm, and a

Figure 5–14 *Bacteria reproduce by splitting into two cells (left). This process increases the number of bacteria. There are also processes that produce new bacteria but do not increase the number. An old bacterium is changed into a new one when genetic material is transferred via a special tube from one bacterium to another (right).*

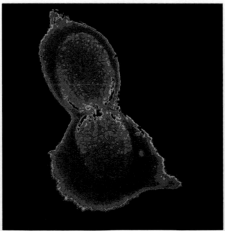
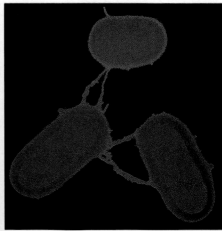

thick protective outer coat. An endospore can survive long periods in which the environment is not suitable for bacterial growth. Some endospores can survive being touched by disinfectant chemicals, blown through the atmosphere, frozen in polar ice, baked in the desert sun, boiled for an hour, and bombarded with powerful radiation. When environmental conditions improve, the endospores burst out of their protective coats and develop into active bacteria. Can you now explain why bacteria are found all over the world—and why some bacteria are extremely hard to kill?

Bacteria in Nature

Most types of bacteria are not harmful and do not cause disease. In fact, many types of bacteria are helpful to other living things and perform important jobs in the natural world.

FOOD AND ENERGY RELATIONSHIPS **Bacteria are an essential part of the food and energy relationships that link all life on Earth.** As you learned earlier, some bacteria (decomposers) break down dead materials to form simpler substances. These simpler substances can be used by autotrophs—such as green plants and blue-green bacteria—to make food. Small heterotrophs (organisms that cannot make their own food) such as certain protists and tiny animals feed on plants and blue-green bacteria. These small heterotrophs are food for large heterotrophs, which are

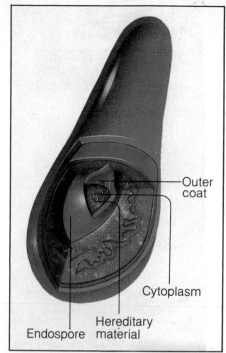

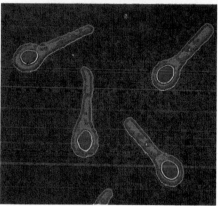

Figure 5–15 *The bacterium that causes the disease tetanus, or lockjaw, forms endospores. The structure of an endospore is shown in the diagram. What is the function of an endospore?*

Outer coat

Cytoplasm

Hereditary material

Endospore

Figure 5–16 *Flamingoes feed on blue-green bacteria and small organisms, which they filter from the water with their beaks. The structure of their filtering beak causes flamingoes to do "headstands" when feeding. Colored substances in the blue-green bacteria give flamingoes their pink color.*

Food Spoilage

1. Obtain two small glass tumblers.

2. Place a small amount of milk in each glass.

3. Place one glass of milk in the refrigerator. Place the other glass of milk in a warm place.

4. After several days, examine both glasses. How are the contents of the glasses different?

■ What caused these changes?

■ How can such changes be prevented?

in turn food for still larger heterotrophs. When heterotrophs and autotrophs die, they become food for decomposers, such as certain bacteria. Thus the cycle continues.

OXYGEN PRODUCTION The food-making process of blue-green bacteria produces oxygen as well as food. Billions of years ago, this resulted in a dramatic change in the composition of the Earth's atmosphere. The percentage of oxygen gas increased from less than 1 percent to about 20 percent. This made it possible for oxygen-using organisms such as protists, plants, animals, and fungi to evolve.

CHANGING ENVIRONMENTS Bacteria continue to change environments in ways that make them suitable for other organisms. For example, bacteria are among the first organisms to grow on the bare rock created by the action of volcanoes. As they grow, the bacteria break down the rock and help create soil. Soon small plants can take root in the developing soil. The bacteria and small plants provide food and homes for tiny animals, fungi, and protists. These new arrivals further change the environment, making it possible for larger organisms to survive. Eventually, a variety of large and small organisms live on what was once bare, lifeless rock.

SYMBIOSES Some bacteria help other organisms by forming a partnership, or **symbiosis** (sihm-bigh-OH-sihs; plural: symbioses). Symbiosis is a relationship in which one organism lives on, near, or even inside another organism and at least one of the organisms benefits. Here is an example. Food-making

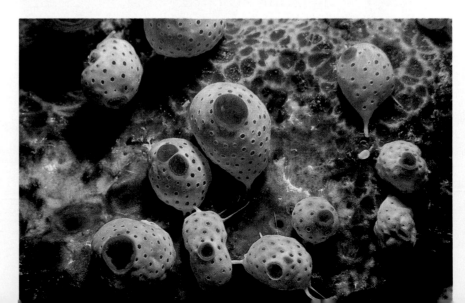

Figure 5–17 *Certain sea squirts are involved in a symbiosis with food-making bacteria. What is symbiosis?*

bacteria live in the bodies of sea squirts and deep-sea tube worms. The bacteria are protected by the body of their host. In return, they provide their host with food. In another example of symbiosis, certain bacteria that live in the intestines of animals such as cows, termites, horses, and humans break down plant cell walls. This enables the host to digest plant materials such as wood, grass, and fruit. Bacteria called nitrogen-fixing bacteria turn nitrogen gas, which plants cannot use, into nitrogen compounds that plants can use to make biologically important substances. Nitrogen-fixing bacteria also help replace the nitrogen compounds in the soil. Without such nitrogen-fixing bacteria, most nitrogen compounds in the soil would be quickly used up and plants could no longer grow. Some nitrogen-fixing bacteria live as individual cells in soil. Others form strandlike colonies in water. Still others live in lumps on the roots of plants such as alfalfa, soybean, and clover. See Figure 5–18.

Bacteria and Humans

Bacteria help humans in many ways. Bacteria are involved in the production of food, fuel, medicines, and other useful products. Some are used in industrial processes. Others help break down pollutants, which are substances such as waste materials or harmful chemicals that dirty the environment.

Although most bacteria are either helpful or harmless, a few can cause trouble for humans. The trouble comes in a number of forms. Some harmful bacteria spoil food or poison water supplies. Others damage property or disrupt manufacturing processes. Still others cause diseases in people, pets, livestock, and food crops.

FOOD Many food products, especially dairy products, are produced with the help of bacteria. Bacteria (and products made by bacteria) are used to make cheeses, buttermilk, yogurt, sour cream, pickles, soy sauce, vinegar, and high-fructose corn syrup. Nitrogen-fixing bacteria provide substances that crops need to grow. In flooded fields such as those used to grow rice, nitrogen-fixing blue-green bacteria fertilize the crops naturally. But bacteria do more

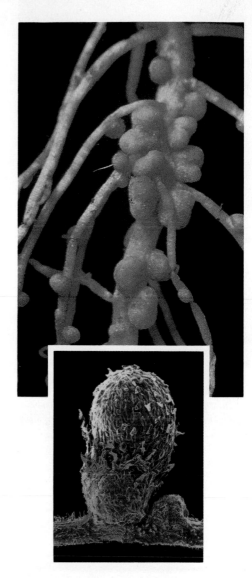

Figure 5–18 *The nodules, or lumps, on the roots of the pea plant are home to symbiotic nitrogen-fixing bacteria (top). If you were to break open a nodule such as this, you would discover the bacteria housed inside (bottom). How does this symbiosis help the pea plant and the bacteria?*

Activity Bank

Yuck! What Are Those Bacteria Doing in My Yogurt? p.794

Figure 5–19 *Some bacteria harm humans and livestock when they grow in and poison water supplies.*

than help to make foods. They can serve as the food itself. Blue-green bacteria, which may grow in water as large masses of strands, have long been used as food. True, blue-green bacteria might not sound very appetizing, but they are quite nutritious. They are about 70 percent protein, rich in vitamins and other nutrients, and easy to digest.

Some helpful bacteria break down food to make tasty or useful products. For example, one kind of helpful bacterium breaks down milk to produce yogurt. Unfortunately, harmful bacteria may also break down food, making smelly, bad-tasting, or even poisonous products. In other words, some harmful bacteria may cause food to spoil.

Food spoilage can be prevented or slowed down by heating, drying, salting, cooling, or smoking foods. Each of these processes prevents or slows down the growth of bacteria. For example, milk is heated to 71°C for 15 seconds before it is placed in containers and shipped to the grocery or supermarket. This process, called pasteurization, destroys most of the bacteria that would cause the milk to spoil quickly. Heating and then canning foods such as vegetables, fruits, meat, and fish are also used to prevent bacterial growth. But if the foods are not sufficiently heated before canning, bacteria can grow inside the can and produce poisons called toxins. Toxin-producing bacteria may also produce a gas

Figure 5–20 *Although the 1990 oil spill in Huntington Beach, California, was not particularly large, it still took a great deal of effort to clean it up. Oil-eating bacteria are now being used on an experimental basis to help clean up such spills.*

that causes the can to bulge. You should never eat food from such a can.

Harmful bacteria can also spoil water supplies. When environmental conditions are changed by pollution or other causes, blue-green bacteria and other bacteria in a body of water may multiply rapidly. The huge numbers of bacteria form an ugly, often smelly, scum and poison the water. Humans and livestock can get very sick from drinking the poisoned water.

FUEL Certain bacteria break down garbage such as fruit rinds, dead plants, manure, and sewage to produce methane. Methane is a natural gas that can be used for cooking and heating. Over millions and millions of years, heat and pressure within the Earth changed the remains of ancient blue-green bacteria, among other organisms, into an oily mixture of chemicals. This mixture of chemicals is called petroleum. Petroleum is the source of heating oil, gasoline, kerosene, and many other useful substances.

ENVIRONMENTAL CLEANUP Bacteria clean up the environment in many ways. Some are used to treat sewage; others cause garbage to decompose, or rot. A few types of bacteria are able to break down the oil in oil spills. Still others break down complex chemicals such as certain pesticides and a few types of plastic.

HEALTH AND MEDICINE Some bacteria help to keep you healthy. For example, bacteria that live inside

ACTIVITY

CALCULATING

Bacterial Growth

If a bacterium reproduces every 20 minutes, how many bacteria would there be after one hour? After two hours? After four hours? After eight hours? (Assume all bacteria survive and reproduce.)

If each bacterium is 0.005 mm long, how many bacteria, laid end to end, would equal 1 mm in length?

Using a metric ruler, determine the length of your thumbnail in millimeters. How many 0.005 mm-long bacteria laid end to end would equal the length of your thumbnail?

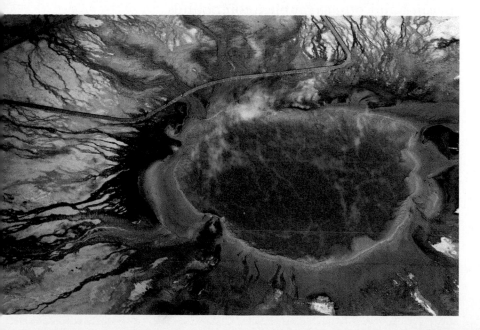

Figure 5–21 *Ancient blue-green bacteria, similar to the modern ones that give the hot springs in Yellowstone National Park their beautiful colors, were the source of the fuel called petroleum.*

the human intestines help you to digest food. They also make vitamins that the body cannot make on its own. And they may help to prevent disease by crowding out harmful bacteria.

Certain helpful bacteria produce substances that are used to fight disease. Some bacteria naturally produce chemicals that have been found to destroy or weaken other bacteria. Such chemicals are known as **antibiotics.** Why would the production of antibiotics be useful to such bacteria? Recently, scientists have developed ways to change the hereditary material in bacteria. By putting new information into the bacteria's hereditary material, scientists cause the bacteria to produce medicines and other useful substances.

Some human diseases caused by bacteria include strep throat, certain kinds of pneumonia, diphtheria, cholera, tetanus, tuberculosis, bubonic plague, and Lyme disease. Bacteria that live in the mouth cause tooth decay and gum disease. Some of these diseases can be prevented by proper hygiene or immunization shots. Others can be treated with antibiotics.

INDUSTRY Helpful bacteria have long been used in the process of tanning leather. Recently, people have begun to use bacteria to extract copper, gold, and other useful and valuable metals from rock. Interestingly, some types of metal-rich rocks, or ores, may have been created by the actions of bacteria that lived millions of years ago. Scientists hope to develop an inexpensive way to use bacteria to make plastics and other complex compounds.

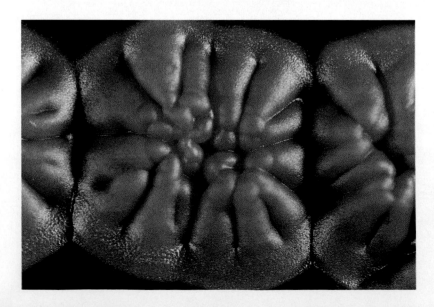

Figure 5–22 *The lumpy growths of* Streptomyces *are made of huge numbers of bacteria growing together.* Streptomyces *is the source of many antibiotics. Why are antibiotics useful to humans?*

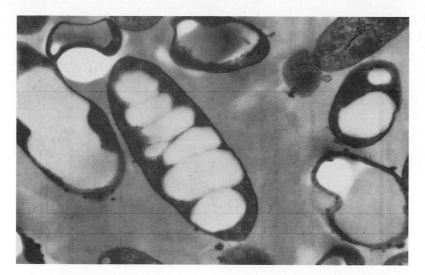

Figure 5-23 *The large, light-colored blobs inside these bacteria are grains of plastic. Someday, most of the plastics you use may come from bacteria!*

Although the time is not yet right for bacterial plastics, other substances made by bacteria are manufactured commercially. These substances are used for many different purposes—coloring food and cosmetics, tenderizing meat, removing stains, processing paper and cloth, and changing one chemical to another, to name a few.

Harmful bacteria can disrupt industrial processes. They damage leather during the tanning process, ruin paper pulp, and turn fruit juice and wine into vinegar. Some harmful bacteria break down asphalt and thus damage roads, parking lots, and other paved surfaces. And bacteria cause millions of dollars of damage each year to oil-drilling machinery, water and gas pipes, and supplies of petroleum.

ACTIVITY

Benefiting From Bacteria

Write a 200-word essay on some of the useful ways bacteria contribute to nature and humankind. Give specific examples.

5-2 Section Review

1. Describe two ways in which bacteria are helpful and two ways in which they are harmful.
2. What is an endospore? How does it help bacteria survive?
3. Describe the structure of a bacterium.

Critical Thinking—*Applying Concepts*

4. Many antibiotics work by damaging a bacterium's cell wall. Explain why such antibiotics are not effective against viruses and certain kinds of bacteria that lack cell walls.

Laboratory Investigation

Examining Bacteria

Problem

Where are bacteria (monerans) found?

Materials (per group)

5 petri dishes with sterile nutrient agar
glass-marking pencil
pencil with eraser
soap and water

Procedure 🧪

1. Turn each petri dish bottom side up on the table. **Note:** *Be careful not to open the petri dish.*

2. With the glass-marking pencil, label the bottom of the petri dishes containing the sterile nutrient agar A, B, C, D, and E. Turn the petri dishes right side up.

3. Remove the lid of dish A and lightly rub a pencil eraser across the agar in the petri dish. Close the dish immediately.

4. Remove the lid of dish B and leave it open to the air until the class period ends. Then close the lid.

5. Remove the lid of dish C and lightly run your index finger over the surface of the agar. Then close the lid immediately.

6. Wash your hands thoroughly. Remove the lid of dish D and lightly rub the same index finger over the surface of the agar. Then close the lid immediately.

7. Do not open dish E.

8. Place all five dishes upside down in a warm, dark place for three or four days.

9. After three or four days, examine each dish. **CAUTION:** *Do not open dishes.*

10. On a sheet of paper, construct a table similar to the one shown here. Fill in the table.

11. Return the petri dishes to your teacher. Your teacher will properly dispose of them.

Observations

1. How many clusters of bacteria appear to be growing on each petri dish? Are there different types of clusters?

2. Which petri dish has the most bacterial growth? Which has the least?

Petri Dish	Source	Description of Bacterial Colonies
A		
B		
C		
D		
E		

Analysis and Conclusions

1. Which petri dish was the control? Explain.

2. Did the dish that you touched with your unwashed finger contain more or less bacteria than the one that you touched with your washed finger? Explain.

3. Explain why the agar was sterilized before the investigation.

4. Design an experiment to show if a particular antibiotic will inhibit bacterial growth in a petri dish.

5. Suggest some methods that might stop the growth of bacteria.

6. What kinds of environmental conditions seem to influence where bacteria are found?

Summarizing Key Concepts

5-1 Viruses

▲ Viruses are tiny noncellular particles that infect living cells.

▲ Viruses are parasites that probably affect all types of cells. Each type of virus can infect only a few specific kinds of cells.

▲ Viruses cannot carry out any life functions unless they are in a host cell. Viruses may have evolved from bits of hereditary material that were lost from host cells.

▲ The development of the electron microscope made it possible to see viruses.

▲ Viruses consist of a core of hereditary material and an outer coat of protein.

▲ The basic "life" cycle is the same for all viruses. First, a virus gets its hereditary material into the host cell. Then the host cell makes more virus particles. Finally, the virus particles infect new hosts.

▲ Viruses cause a number of diseases that range from annoying to serious to fatal.

▲ Viruses cause human diseases such as colds, chicken pox, rabies, polio, and AIDS.

▲ Weakened or killed viruses are used to make some vaccines.

▲ Viruses are used to kill pests. They are also used to change the hereditary material of cells in specific ways.

5-2 Monerans

▲ Monerans are single-celled organisms that lack a nucleus and many other cell structures.

▲ The terms monerans and bacteria are interchangeable.

▲ Bacteria are the oldest forms of life on Earth. They are also among the most numerous and varied.

▲ Some bacteria live in colonies. A colony is a group of organisms that live together in close association. Some members of these colonies may be specialized for specific functions.

▲ Some bacteria are heterotrophs. Some heterotrophic bacteria are parasites. Others are decomposers.

▲ Some bacteria are autotrophs. Some autotrophic bacteria produce oxygen.

▲ Bacteria fit into the world in many ways. They are involved in many food and energy relationships with other organisms. Some change environments in ways that make them suitable for other organisms—by making soil, oxygen, or nitrogen compounds, for example. Others are involved in symbioses with other organisms.

▲ Some bacteria are helpful to humans. Others are harmful.

Reviewing Key Terms

Define each term in a complete sentence.

5-1 Viruses
virus
host
parasite

5-2 Monerans
decomposer
symbiosis
antibiotic

Chapter Review

Content Review

Multiple Choice

Choose the letter of the answer that best completes each statement.

1. An example of a disease caused by a virus is
   a. bubonic plague.   c. strep throat.
   b. measles.   d. tetanus.
2. Which of the following statements is true?
   a. Because they break down wastes and dead organisms, viruses are called decomposers.
   b. Viruses are the only organisms that lack a nucleus.
   c. Viruses consist of a core of protein surrounded by a coat of hereditary material.
   d. To perform their life functions, viruses require a host cell.
3. Almost all bacteria are surrounded and supported by a tough, rigid protective structure called the
   a. cell membrane. c. protein coat.
   b. cell wall.   d. capsule.
4. Which of the following is not found in bacteria?
   a. hereditary material   c. cytoplasm
   b. cell membrane   d. nucleus
5. Viruses are best described as
   a. autotrophs.   c. parasites.
   b. decomposers.   d. lithotrophs.
6. Bacteria cause a number of human diseases, including
   a. tuberculosis.   c. AIDS.
   b. influenza.   d. rabies.
7. Humans use viruses to
   a. make antibiotics.
   b. make fuels such as methane.
   c. break down sewage.
   d. put new hereditary material into cells.
8. Monerans are also known as
   a. bacteria.   c. viruses.
   b. bacteriophages.   d. fungi.

True or False

If the statement is true, write "true." If it is false, change the underlined word or words to make the statement true.

1. Organisms that break down wastes and the remains of dead plants and animals are called producers.
2. Some bacteria use whiplike structures called flagella to propel them through their environment.
3. When conditions become unfavorable, some bacteria produce a small internal resting cell called a capsule.
4. Symbiosis is a relationship in which one organism lives in close association with another organism and at least one of the organisms benefits.
5. Bacteria can be used by scientists to insert hereditary material into cells.

Concept Mapping

Complete the following concept map for Section 5–1. Then construct a concept map for the entire chapter.

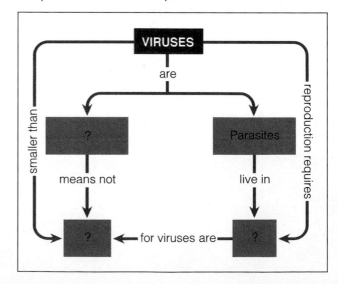

Concept Mastery

Discuss each of the following in a brief paragraph.

1. How are viruses different from cells?
2. Describe how a typical bacteriophage reproduces.
3. Identify three ways in which viruses help people.
4. How do autotrophs and heterotrophs differ in the ways they obtain food?
5. What is symbiosis? Give one example of symbiosis.
6. Briefly describe the structure of a typical bacterial cell. What is the most important structural difference between the cells of bacteria and the cells of organisms in the other four kingdoms?
7. How do bacteria affect food production, food processing, and food storage?
8. Can viruses be grown in the laboratory on synthetic material? Explain.

Critical Thinking and Problem Solving

Use the skills you have developed in this chapter to answer each of the following.

1. **Applying definitions** Why is the relationship between a parasite and a host considered to be a form of symbiosis?
2. **Making inferences** When a cell is placed in water that contains a large quantity of dissolved substances such as sugar or salt, the cell will shrivel up and die. Explain why food can be preserved by putting it into honey or brine (very salty water).
3. **Interpreting a graph** The accompanying graph shows the growth of bacteria. Describe the growth of the bacteria using the numbers given for each growth stage. Why do you think the growth leveled off in stage 3 and then fell in stage 4?

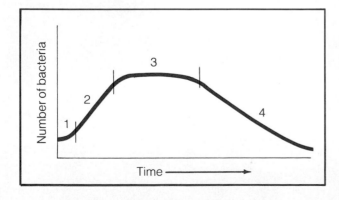

4. **Designing an experiment** Design an experiment to test the effect of temperature on the growth of bacteria. Be sure you have a control and a variable in your experiment. What results do you expect to get in this experiment? How can you apply these results in order to control food spoilage?
5. **Applying concepts** Every few years, a farmer plants a field with alfalfa or clover. At the end of the growing season, the farmer does not harvest these plants. Instead, the alfalfa or clover is plowed under, and the field is replanted with grain. Explain how the actions of bacteria account for the farmer's behavior.
6. **Using the writing process** In *The War of the Worlds,* a wonderful book by H. G. Wells, the Earth is invaded by Martians. Human weapons are useless against the invaders, and the Earth seems doomed. The Earth is saved, however, when the invaders die from diseases they contract here. Many other science-fiction writers have written stories that involve diseases. Now it is your turn. Write a science-fiction story in which a disease plays an important part.

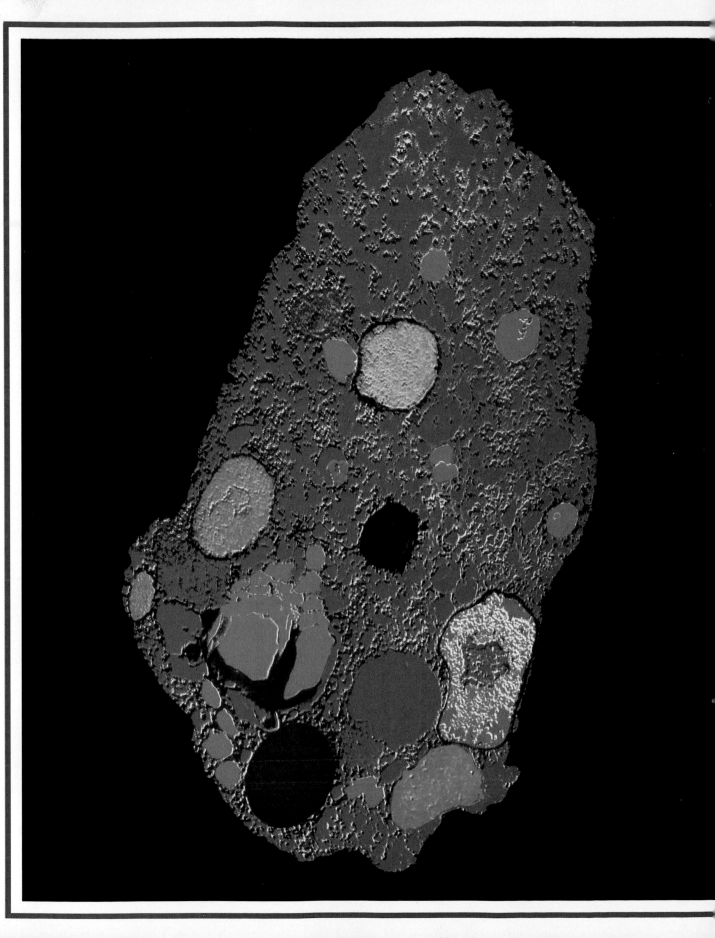

Protists

Guide for Reading

After you read the following sections, you will be able to

6–1 Characteristics of Protists
- Describe the characteristics of protists.

6–2 Animallike Protists
- Identify the four groups of animallike protists.

6–3 Plantlike Protists
- Describe plantlike protists.

6–4 Funguslike Protists
- Compare slime molds to other protists.

Imagine for a moment that you have stepped into a time machine. Your destination: the world of 1.5 billion years ago. You arrive in a strange and barren place. No animals roam the land or swim in the ocean. No birds fly in the air. No trees, shrubs, or grasses grow from the soil. Earth at first seems lifeless.

A closer look at your surroundings reveals a slippery black film on the rocks and greenish threads in the water. Bacteria live here! When you use a microscope to examine the water of early Earth, you discover that a new form of life has come into being. Like the bacteria that came before it, this form of life is unicellular (one-celled). But these cells are much more complex than those of bacteria. You are surprised and delighted to recognize one large structure in the cells—the nucleus.

These first cells with a nucleus are protists. Protists represent the first step in the series of evolutionary events that eventually led to the development of multicellular (many-celled) organisms such as mushrooms, trees, fishes, birds, and humans. In this chapter, you will learn a great deal about protists—complex and fascinating organisms.

Journal *Activity*

You and Your World When did you first find out that you were surrounded by living things too small to see? In your journal, explore the thoughts and feelings you had upon learning about the unseen world around you.

◀ *The numerous structures within this ameba look like tiny jewels. These structures represent an important evolutionary step toward increasing complexity in living things.*

6–1 Characteristics of Protists

The members of the kingdom Protista are known as **protists.** Like bacteria (monerans), protists are unicellular (one-celled) organisms. Also like bacteria, protists were one of the first groups of living things to appear on Earth. Although protists are larger than monerans, most cannot be seen without the aid of a microscope. Protists, however, are quite different from bacteria. The most important difference is that protists have a nucleus and a number of other cell structures that bacteria lack.

Protists can be defined as single-celled organisms that contain a nucleus. However, you will discover in this chapter that there are a few protists that do not fit this definition perfectly. In fact, as scientists develop new techniques for examining the structure and chemistry of cells, the definition of protist continues to change. And as new evidence is obtained, analyzed, and interpreted, scientists revise their ideas about which protists should be classified together—and even about which organisms should be classified as protists!

Figure 6–1 *The major difference between protists and bacteria is that protists have many complex cell structures. The most important of these is the nucleus, which looks like a string of beads in* Stentor *(left), and a thin squiggle in* Vorticella *(center). Protists also have complex external structures, such as the hairlike projections on* Tetrahymena *(right).*

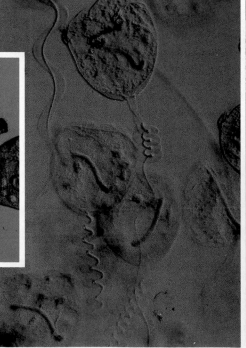
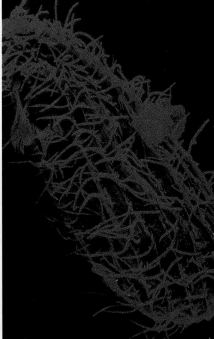

Most protists live in a watery environment. They can be found in the salty ocean and in bodies of fresh water. Some protists live in moist soil. Others live inside larger organisms. Many of these internal protists are parasites. (Parasites, you will recall, are organisms that live on or in a host organism and harm it.) But some of the protists that live inside other organisms help their hosts.

Protists generally live as individual cells. However, many protists live in colonies such as the ones shown in Figure 6–2. A protist colony consists of a number of relatively independent cells of the same species that are attached to one another. Some colonies are foamlike clusters of cells. Others are branching and treelike. A few are rings or chains of cells. And one type of colony consists of an intricate network of slime tunnels. The members of this type of colony move through the tunnels like miniature subway cars.

Evidence from fossils indicates that protists evolved about 1.5 billion years ago—about 2 billion years after bacteria. According to one hypothesis, the first protists were the result of an extremely successful symbiosis among several kinds of bacteria. Recall from Chapter 5 that a symbiosis is a close relationship of two or more organisms in which at least one organism benefits. In this case, some of the bacteria lived inside another bacterial cell. Each kind of bacterium performed activities that helped the "team" survive. Over time, the partners in the symbiosis became more specialized (suited for one particular task) and lost their independence. Traces of this early symbiosis can still be seen in protists and other cells that possess a nucleus. Within these cells are certain structures that are quite similar to bacterial cells. They even contain their own hereditary material.

Protists vary greatly in appearance and in the ways in which they carry out their life functions. For example, some protists are autotrophs. Autotrophs are able to use energy such as sunlight to make their own food from simple raw materials. Other protists are heterotrophs. Heterotrophs get their energy by eating food that has already been made. And a few protists are able to function as either autotrophs or heterotrophs, depending on their surroundings.

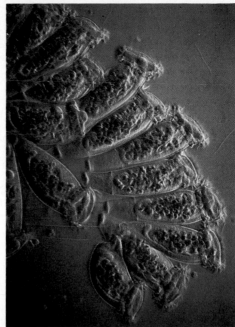

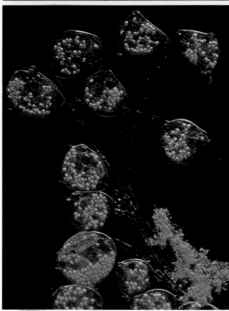

Figure 6–2 *Some protists such as* Epistylis *(top) and* Carchesium *(bottom) live in colonies of attached but relatively independent cells. Colonial protists may have been the first evolutionary step toward true multicellular organisms.*

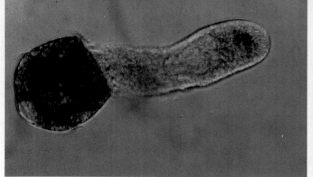

Figure 6–3 *These diatoms growing in fan-shaped colonies are autotrophs. The short, dark, thimble-shaped* Didinium *and the long, oval* Paramecium *it is eating are both heterotrophs. What is the major difference between autotrophs and heterotrophs?*

ACTIVITY

DOING

Protist Models

1. Using modeling clay and/or other appropriate materials, build a model of the protist of your choice. Use the diagrams in your textbook or other reference materials as a guide. You may wish to use different colors of clay or paint the model in order to show the different structures in the protist.

2. Mount the model on a piece of stiff cardboard.

3. Label each of the protist's structures.

4. Share your model and what you learned while making it with your classmates. Compare your model to the ones your classmates have constructed. How are protists different? How are they similar? What are some good characteristics in the protist models?

As you might have guessed of such a large and diverse group of organisms, the kingdom Protista is divided into many phyla. Because there are many different ways to interpret what we know about protists, the classification of protists is a matter of scientific debate. Experts recognize anywhere from about nine to more than two dozen phyla. For the sake of simplicity, protists can also be grouped in three general categories. These categories, which are the ones you will read about here, are: animallike protists, plantlike protists, and funguslike protists.

6–1 Section Review

1. What are the major characteristics of protists?
2. Explain why scientists have not yet agreed on a single classification system for protists.
3. How are protists similar to monerans? How are they different?
4. When did protists first appear on Earth?

Connection—*You and Your World*

5. While standing in line at the supermarket, you notice the following newspaper headline: "Science Shocker: Alien Invaders in Every Cell of Your Body!" Explain why there may be some truth in this headline. (*Hint:* Fungi, plants, and animals evolved from protists that lived millions of years ago.)

6–2 Animallike Protists

Animallike protists are sometimes known as protozoa, which means first animals. Long ago, these organisms were classified as animals because they have several characteristics in common with animals. Their cells contain a nucleus and lack a cell wall. They are heterotrophs. Most of them can move. Animallike protists are no longer placed in a separate kingdom from more plantlike protists. Scientists have discovered that some animallike protists are so similar to certain plantlike protists that it does not make sense to place them in separate kingdoms.

Animallike protists are divided into four main groups. These four groups are the **sarcodines** (SAHR-koh-dighnz), the **ciliates** (SIHL-ee-ihts), the **zooflagellates** (zoh-oh-FLAJ-ehl-ihts), and the **sporozoans** (spohr-oh-ZOH-uhnz).

Sarcodines

Sarcodines are characterized by extensions of the cell membrane and cytoplasm known as pseudopods (SOO-doh-pahdz). The word **pseudopod** comes from the Greek words that mean "false foot" because these footlike extensions are always temporary. Pseudopods are used to capture and engulf particles of food. Some sarcodines also use psuedopods to move from one place to another.

Many sarcodines have shells that support and protect the cell. As you can see in Figure 6–4, these shells come in many forms. The shells of foraminiferans (fuh-ram-ih-NIHF-er-anz) may resemble coins, squiggly worms, the spiral burner coils of an electric stove, clusters of bubbles, and tiny sea shells. The shells of radiolarians (ray-dee-oh-LAIR-ee-uhnz) are studded with long spines and dotted with tiny holes. Because of this, radiolarian shells often look a lot like crystal holiday ornaments. When foraminiferans and radiolarians die, their shells sink to the ocean floor and form thick layers. Over millions of years, these shells are changed to rock. Some rocks that contain ancient protist shells, such as limestone and marble, are used in building. Others are used

Guide for Reading
Focus on these questions as you read.

▶ *How are animallike protists similar? How are they different?*

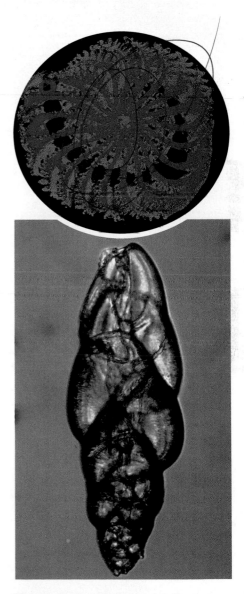

Figure 6–4 *Many foraminiferans have beautiful shells. The shells of ancient foraminiferans help to make up limestone, marble, and chalk.*

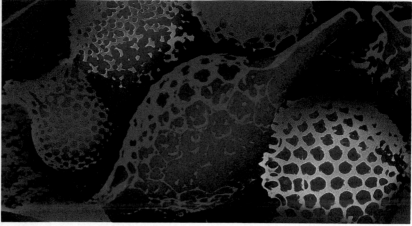

Figure 6–5 *The pores and spines of radiolarian shells make them glitter in the light like tiny glass decorations.*

for writing and drawing—the chalk used by teachers is made of prehistoric foraminiferans!

The most familiar type of sarcodine is the bloblike **ameba** (uh-MEE-bah). Amebas use their pseudopods to move and to obtain food. An ameba first extends a thick, round pseudopod from part of its cell. Then the rest of the cell flows into the pseudopod. As an ameba nears a small piece of food, such as a smaller protist, the ameba extends a pseudopod around the food. Soon the food particle is completely surrounded by the pseudopod. As you can see in Figure 6–8, this process produces a bubblelike structure that contains the food. This structure is called a food vacuole. The food is digested (broken down into simpler materials) inside the food vacuole. The digested food can then be used by the ameba for energy and growth. The waste products of digestion are eliminated when the food vacuole joins with the cell membrane.

Figure 6–6 *This diagram shows the structure of* Amoeba proteus, *a typical ameba. According to Greek mythology, the sea god Proteus had the magical ability to change his shape. How do amebas change their shape?*

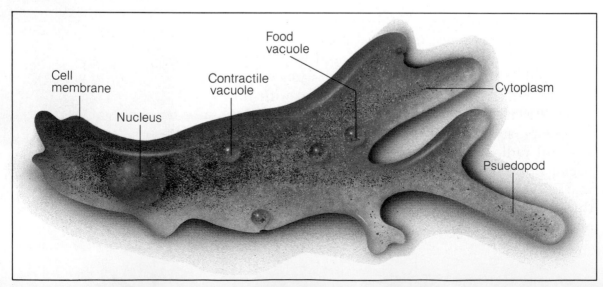

Food vacuole

Cell membrane

Contractile vacuole

Cytoplasm

Nucleus

Psuedopod

The process just described is used to transport "large" particles, such as bits of food or solid wastes, through the cell membrane. Other substances, such as water, oxygen, and carbon dioxide do not need to be carried in and out of the cell this way. These substances simply pass right through the cell membrane.

Protists that live in fresh water, such as many kinds of amebas, must deal with a tricky problem. Water tends to come into the cell from the environment. What do you think might happen to an ameba if excess water was allowed to build up in its cell? Fortunately, protists have a special cell structure that enables them to keep the right amount of water in the cell. This structure is called the contractile vacuole. Excess water collects in the saclike contractile vacuole. When the contractile vacuole is full, it contracts (hence its name) to squirt the water out of the cell.

Amebas reproduce by dividing into two new cells. Because amebas have a nucleus, the process of cell division involves more than simply making a copy of the hereditary material and then splitting in two. (This, you should recall, is the way in which monerans reproduce.) In amebas and all other cells with a nucleus, cell division involves a complex series of events.

Amebas respond in relatively simple ways to changes in their environments. They are sensitive to bright light and move to areas of dim light. Amebas are also sensitive to certain chemicals, moving away from some and toward others. How do you think these behaviors help amebas survive?

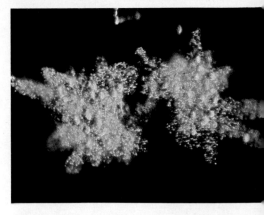

Figure 6–7 *Amebas, like most other protists, reproduce by dividing into two new cells.*

ctivity Bank

Putting the Squeeze On, p.796

Figure 6–8 *Look carefully at these images of a feeding ameba. How does an ameba capture its food?*

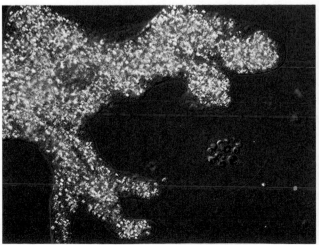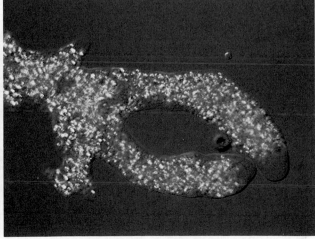

Ciliates

Ciliates have small hairlike projections called cilia (SIHL-ee-uh; singular: cilium) **on the outside of their cells.** The **cilia** act like tiny oars and help these organisms move. The beating of the cilia also helps to sweep food toward the ciliates. In addition, the cilia function as sensors. When the cilia are touched, the ciliate receives information about its environment.

Cilia may cover the entire surface of a ciliate or may be concentrated in certain areas. In some ciliates, the cilia may be fused together to form structures that look like paddles or the tips of paint brushes. A few ciliates possess cilia only when they are young. As adults, they attach to a surface and lose their cilia.

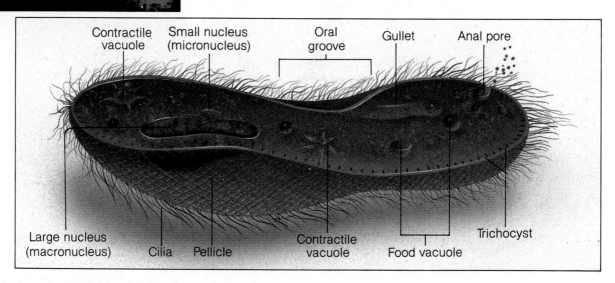

Figure 6–9 *Slipper-shaped* Paramecium *is probably the most familiar ciliate. What structures does a paramecium use in obtaining and digesting food?*

One of the most interesting ciliates is the **paramecium** (par-uh-MEE-see-uhm; plural: paramecia). As you can see in Figure 6–9, a paramecium has a tough outer covering called the pellicle (PEHL-ih-kuhl). The pellicle, which consists of the cell membrane and certain underlying structures, gives the paramecium its slipper shape. The cilia of the paramecium sweep food particles floating in the water into an indentation, or notch, on the side of the paramecium. This indentation, which is called the oral groove, leads to a funnellike structure known as the gullet. At the base of the gullet, food vacuoles form around the incoming food. Then the food vacuoles pinch off into the cytoplasm. As a food vacuole travels through the cytoplasm, the food is digested and the nutrients distributed. When the work of the food vacuole is completed, it joins with an area of the pellicle called the anal pore. The anal pore empties waste materials into the surrounding water.

Paramecia, like other ciliates, have two kinds of nuclei. The large nucleus controls the life functions of the cell. The small nucleus is involved in a complicated process called conjugation. During conjugation, two ciliates temporarily join together and exchange part of their hereditary material.

As you can see in Figure 6–11, paramecia reproduce by splitting in half crosswise. During this process, many cell structures are copied, divided, broken apart, and formed anew. Now take a moment to refer to the diagram of the paramecium in Figure 6–9 on page 160. Imagine that this paramecium is about to divide. Its left half is going to become one new cell, and its right half is going to become another new cell. What structures does the left half require in order to become a fully functional paramecium? What structures does the right half require?

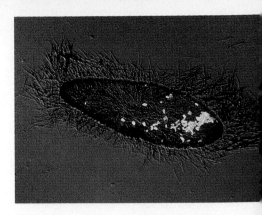

Figure 6–10 *When disturbed, a paramecium may release sharp spines known as trichocysts. How do these structures help the paramecium?*

Figure 6–11 *Paramecia reproduce by dividing in half (left). This increases the number of paramecia. The process of conjugation also produces new paramecia but does not increase the number. The genetic material exchanged during conjugation may help to make one or both of the paramecia better able to deal with a changing environment (right).*

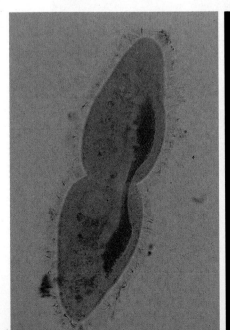
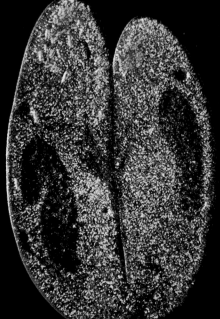

ACTIVITY

Capturing Food

1. Place one drop of a paramecium culture on a microscope slide. Use a depression slide if you have one.

2. Add one drop of *Chlorella*, a green algae, to the slide.

3. Locate a paramecium under the microscope using low power. Then switch to high power. What happened to the *Chlorella*?

4. "Feed" a tiny amount of carmine red granules or India ink to the paramecia. What happens to these inedible (impossible to eat) substances? What do you think will eventually happen to them?

ACTIVITY

How Big Is Big?

Protists range greatly in size. Some tiny flagellates are only 1 or 2 micrometers long. (A micrometer is one-millionth of a meter.) A paramecium is about 300 micrometers long. The fossil foraminiferan *Camerina* had a shell 10 centimeters wide. (A centimeter is one-hundredth of a meter.) Huge slime molds can be as large as 1 meter across.

Using a metric ruler and a calculator when necessary, find the numbers that make the following statements true:

1. I am _____ meters tall, or _____ centimeters tall, or _____ micrometers tall.

2. _____ zooflagellates 2 micrometers long placed end to end would equal 1 meter in length.

3. _____ *Camerina* shells placed end to end would equal 1 meter in length.

4. About _____ paramecia placed end to end could be placed across one *Camerina* shell.

5. _____ copies of this textbook laid end to end would equal 1 meter in length.

Zooflagellates

Flagellates (FLAJ-eh-layts) are protists that move by means of flagella. Recall from Chapter 5 that a **flagellum** is a long whiplike structure that propels a cell through its environment. Flagellates may be animallike, plantlike, or funguslike. Plantlike and funguslike flagellates will be discussed later.

Animallike flagellates are called zooflagellates. (The prefix *zoo-* means animal.) **Zooflagellates usually have one to eight flagella, depending on the species.** However, some types of zooflagellates have thousands of flagella.

Many zooflagellates live inside the bodies of animals. Can you explain why such zooflagellates are said to be symbiotic? Some symbiotic zooflagellates do not have any effect on their host. Others benefit their host and may even be essential to its survival. For example, termites and wood roaches rely on zooflagellates in their intestines to digest the wood that the insects eat. Without the zooflagellates, these wood-eating insects would quickly starve. Still other zooflagellates harm their host. Do you remember what this type of symbiotic relationship is called?

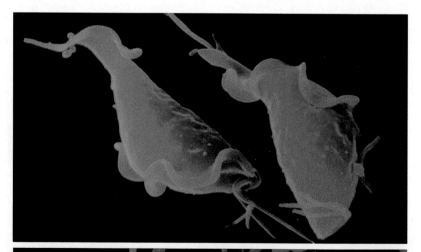

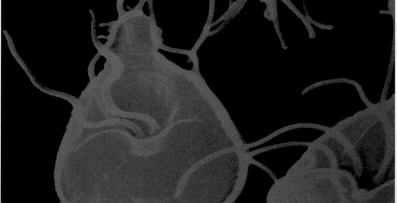

Figure 6–12 *Some zooflagellates cause diseases in humans.* Trichomonas *causes an infection of the female reproductive system (top).* Giardia *causes problems with the digestive system when it attaches to the walls of the small intestine (bottom).*

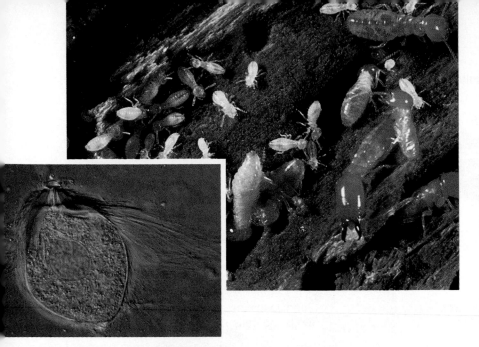

Figure 6–13 *Termites digest the wood they eat with the help of zooflagellates such as* Trichonympha *(inset). Why is the relationship between termites and* Trichonympha *an example of symbiosis?*

Parasitic zooflagellates are responsible for a number of diseases in humans and animals. One parasitic zooflagellate causes African sleeping sickness, which is transmitted from one host to another through the bite of the tsetse fly. Other kinds cause various types of diseases of the intestines.

Sporozoans

All sporozoans are parasites that feed on the cells and body fluids of their host animals. Many sporozoans have complex life cycles that involve more than one kind of host animal. During these life cycles, sporozoans form cells known as spores. The spores enable sporozoans to pass from one host to another. How does this happen? A new host may become infected with the sporozoans if it eats food containing the spores. Or it may become infected if it is bitten by a tick, mosquito, or other animal that has spores in its body.

Perhaps the most famous type of sporozoan is the organism that causes the disease malaria. This organism is *Plasmodium* (plaz-MOH-dee-uhm). *Plasmodium* has two hosts: humans and the *Anopheles* mosquito. Both hosts are necessary for *Plasmodium* to complete its life cycle.

When a mosquito infected with *Plasmodium* bites a human, it injects its saliva. The saliva contains substances that keep blood flowing so that the mosquito

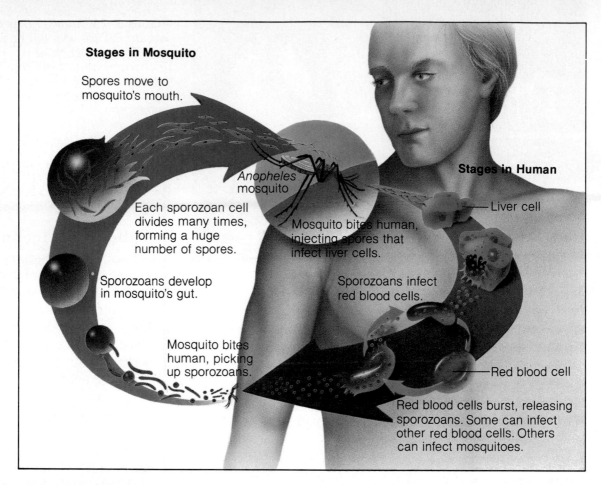

Stages in Mosquito

Spores move to mosquito's mouth.

Anopheles mosquito

Each sporozoan cell divides many times, forming a huge number of spores.

Sporozoans develop in mosquito's gut.

Mosquito bites human, picking up sporozoans.

Stages in Human

Mosquito bites human, injecting spores that infect liver cells.

Liver cell

Sporozoans infect red blood cells.

Red blood cell

Red blood cells burst, releasing sporozoans. Some can infect other red blood cells. Others can infect mosquitoes.

Figure 6–14 *The life cycle of* Plasmodium *is quite complex. Why is* Plasmodium *considered a parasite? What are its hosts?*

can drink its fill. The saliva also contains *Plasmodium* spores. The injected spores are carried by the bloodstream to the person's liver. There the spores divide many times, producing a large number of sporozoan cells. The resulting sporozoans are a form that can infect red blood cells. After several days, these sporozoans burst out of the liver cells and invade red blood cells, where they grow and multiply. Eventually the sporozoans burst out of the red blood cells, destroying them.

Some of the sporozoans released when the red blood cells burst can infect more red blood cells. Others can infect mosquitoes. If the person with malaria is bitten by another *Anopheles* mosquito, the sporozoans along with the blood enter that mosquito. In the mosquito, the sporozoans undergo several stages of development and eventually form spores, which continue *Plasmodium's* life cycle.

The malaria-causing sporozoans inside a patient's body develop in such a way that all the millions of

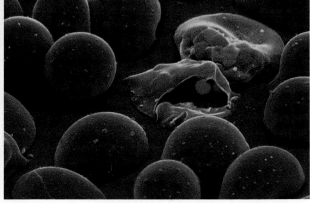

infected red blood cells burst at roughly the same time. Can you see why this is bad news for the patient? Within a few short hours, large amounts of parasites, bits of cells, and other kinds of "garbage" are dumped into the bloodstream. These released materials cause the patient with malaria to develop a high fever (about 41°C, or 105°F). As the patient's temperature climbs, the patient feels very cold and develops "goosebumps" all over. When the patient's temperature begins to return to normal, the patient feels very hot and sweats a great deal. And the disease has only just begun! The chills and fever of malaria occur again and again for weeks. In the most common kind of malaria, the chills and fever occur every 48 hours, last for about 6 to 8 hours each time, and persist for several weeks. Toward the end of that time, the chills and fever become less frequent and less severe. However, all may not be well even if the patient appears to have recovered. Several weeks after it first began, malaria often happens all over again.

Figure 6–15 *Humans contract the disease malaria through the bite of an infected mosquito (left). During the course of the disease, infected red blood cells burst at regular intervals, releasing* Plasmodium *cells that can infect other red blood cells or mosquitoes (right).*

6–2 Section Review

1. Briefly describe the four groups of animallike protists.
2. Compare the ways in which sarcodines, ciliates, and zooflagellates move.
3. Describe three ways in which animallike protists affect other organisms.

Critical Thinking—*Applying Concepts*
4. Explain why destroying the places where mosquitoes breed can help prevent malaria.

ACTIVITY
CALCULATING

Divide and Conquer

The ciliate *Glaucoma* reproduces by dividing into two cells. It reproduces at the fastest rate of all protists, dividing once every three hours under the best conditions. Assuming that conditions are perfect, how many times will *Glaucoma* divide during a day? If you start off with one cell that divides at the very start of the day, how many cells will you have at the end of the day if all of the cells survive?

Revenge of the Protist

Bzzzzzzz! You hear a high-pitched whine, then feel an itch on your arm. You slap at the itch. Thwack! That mosquito is never going to bite anyone again.

Swatting is a great way to get rid of a few mosquitoes. But what do you do if you want to kill lots and lots of mosquitoes? No, bug spray is not a good answer.

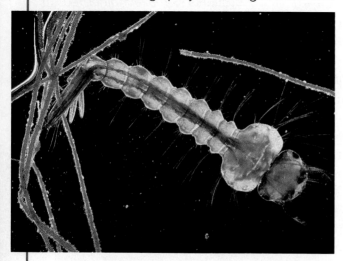

The poisons in bug spray *pollute* the environment, kill helpful insects such as bees and butterflies, and may be hazardous to your health. Although it may sound strange, a better answer is to use protists.

Scientists at the University of California at Berkeley recently discovered that a tiny ciliate called *Lambornella clarki (L. clarki)* can be a formidable foe to young mosquitoes. Young mosquitoes are worm-like, wingless, and legless creatures. They live at the surface of the water in quiet ponds, rain barrels, treeholes, and just about any other place that collects and holds water. The young mosquitoes feed on tiny particles that they filter from the water by using bristly mouthparts. These particles include small protists such as *L. clarki*.

To avoid being eaten, many microorganisms (microscopic organisms) change form. Some that are normally small and round make themselves large and flat. Others develop spines. *L. clarki* does something more amazing—it changes into a parasite that destroys the mosquitoes that feed on it.

Usually, *L. clarki* is a peaceful football-shaped ciliate that lives in treeholes and eats bacteria and other tiny bits of food. But when young mosquitoes are present, *L. clarki* cells become spherical, like a softball. These softball-shaped cells attach to the skin of young mosquitoes and then burrow into the body. The *L. clarki* cells multiply inside the body of their host, doing their deadly work. Eventually, the cells escape from the body of their dead or dying mosquito host. They can then infect other young mosquitoes. In nature, *L. clarki* cells can kill off all the young mosquitoes in a treehole. Having taken their revenge on the protist-devouring mosquitoes, the *L. clarki* cells resume life as peaceful football-shaped ciliates.

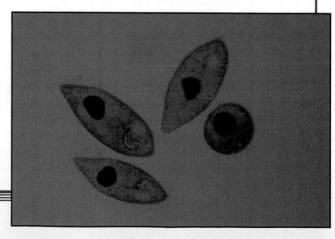

6–3 Plantlike Protists

Like other protists, plantlike protists are unicellular and most of them are capable of movement. **Like plants, plantlike protists are autotrophs that use light energy to make their own food from simple raw materials.** This food-making ability makes plantlike protists a vital part of the natural world. Can you see why? Many organisms rely directly on plantlike protists for food. Some of these organisms, such as animallike protists and tiny water animals, eat the plantlike protists. Others—certain animallike protists, sea anemones, corals, and giant clams, for example—are involved in symbioses with plantlike protists. The plantlike protists live inside their host's body and help to provide it with food. Still other animals rely indirectly on plantlike protists for food. For example, humans eat large fishes that eat smaller fishes that eat tiny animals that eat plantlike protists.

In addition to capturing energy and making it available to other organisms in the form of food, plantlike protists play another important role in the world. They produce oxygen as a byproduct of their food-making process. About 70 percent of the Earth's supply of oxygen is produced by plantlike protists.

Most kinds of plantlike protists are flagellates; that is, they move by means of flagella. To distinguish them from zooflagellates, plantlike flagellates are often called phytoflagellates. (The prefix

Guide for Reading

Focus on this question as you read.

▶ *What are plantlike protists?*

Figure 6–16 *Plantlike protists that do not belong to the three most important groups may still be rather interesting organisms. Some have elegant networks of glassy tubes that make up their skeleton (left). Others are covered with strange scales during their resting stage (top right and bottom right).*

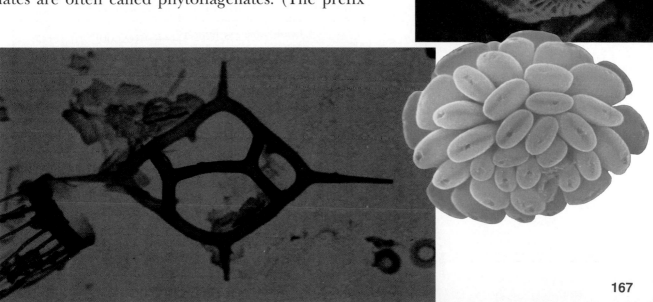

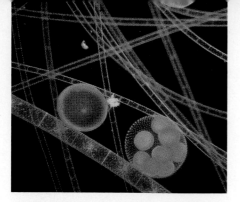

Figure 6–17 *Scientists do not agree where the dividing line between plantlike protists and plants should be placed. We classify long-stranded* Spirogyra *as a protist and spherical* Volvox *as a plant.*

Activity Bank

Shedding a Little Light on Euglena, p.798

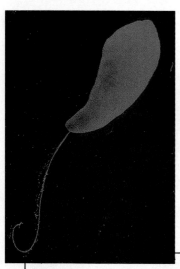

phyto- means plant.) There are many different kinds of plantlike protists. In this section, you will read about three of the more interesting groups: **euglenas** (yoo-GLEE-nahz), **diatoms** (DIGH-ah-tahmz), and **dinoflagellates** (digh-noh-FLAJ-eh-layts).

Euglenas

Euglenas come in a variety of forms. Some are long and oval. Others are shaped like triangles, hearts, or tops. Still others live in branching colonies that look like bushes with oversized leaves. And a few live in cup-shaped "houses." Although euglenas are quite varied, most share three characteristics: a pouch that holds two flagella, a reddish eyespot, and a number of grass-green structures that are used in the food-making process. Scientists call the green food-making structures chloroplasts (KLOHR-oh-plasts).

One kind of euglena is shown in Figure 6–18. Like the paramecium you read about in the previous section, euglenas have a tough outer covering called the pellicle. The pouch on one end of the euglena holds two flagella, one long and one short. The long flagellum is used in movement. In the cytoplasm near the pouch is the reddish eyespot. The eyespot is sensitive to light. Why is it important for a euglena to be able to find light?

Figure 6–18 *The diagram shows the structure of a typical euglena. The pattern of grooves in a euglena's pellicle may be seen with the help of a scanning electron microscope (inset).*

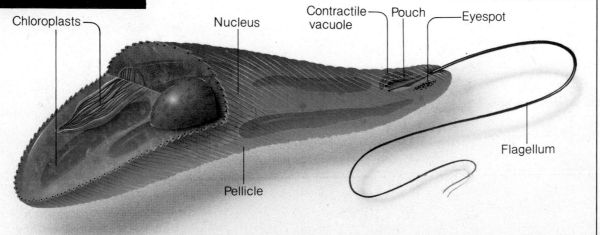

Chloroplasts — Nucleus — Contractile vacuole — Pouch — Eyespot — Flagellum — Pellicle

Diatoms

How would you feel about brushing your teeth with protists? Chances are you might not be too keen on the idea. But like it or not, you are probably doing exactly this every time you brush your teeth. Why? Because a part of many toothpastes is made from plantlike protists called diatoms.

Diatoms are among the most numerous of protists. There are about 10,000 living species of these aquatic (water-dwelling) organisms. And as you can see in Figure 6–19, diatoms are among the most attractive of organisms. Each diatom is enclosed in a two-part glassy shell. The shell looks like a tiny glass box or petri dish, with one side fitting snugly into the other. The two parts of the shell are covered with beautiful patterns of tiny ridges, spines, and/or holes. Imagine how surprised people must have been when they first looked at diatoms through a microscope and discovered lacy designs like those of stained-glass windows on tiny grains of sand!

When diatoms die, their tough glassy shells remain. In time, the shells collect in layers and form deposits of diatomaceous (digh-ah-tuh-MAY-shuhs) earth. Diatomaceous earth is a coarse, powdery

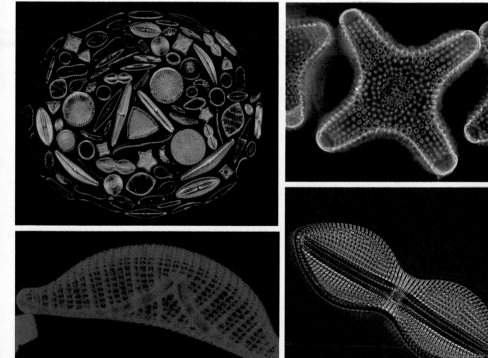

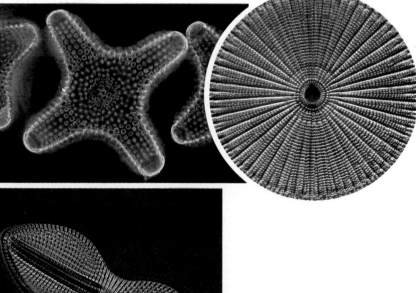

Figure 6–19 *The delicate glassy shells of diatoms are among the most beautiful forms in nature.*

169

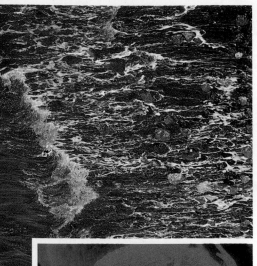

Figure 6–20 *Under certain conditions, dinoflagellates (inset) may form populations so huge that the water takes on their color. What are these population explosions called? What is their effect?*

material. This makes it an excellent polishing agent—and thus an important ingredient in toothpastes and car polish. Because diatomaceous earth reflects light, it is also added to the paint used to mark traffic lanes on roads and highways. Why do you think diatomaceous earth might be added to scouring cleansers?

Dinoflagellates

In August of 1987, the waters off the southwestern coast of Florida suddenly turned yellow and brown. Soon thousands of dead fish washed up on shore. Two months later, the same thing happened along much of the North Carolina coast. Tourism and fishing industries in that state were hard hit by the poisoned, discolored waters of what is called the red tide. A variety of illnesses in at least 41 people was another result. This was not the first time a red tide had struck the United States, or for that matter, other places in the world. Red tides have swept onto beaches in New England, Los Angeles, Taiwan, Guatemala, Korea, and Tasmania, to name a few.

Red tides occur when protists known as dinoflagellates reproduce so rapidly that the water becomes colored by them. Although they are called red tides, such occurrences are not necessarily red in color. This is because dinoflagellates range in color from yellow-green to orange-brown. Red tides can be dangerous because some dinoflagellates produce toxins (poisons) that can injure or even kill living things.

If you observed dinoflagellates through a microscope, you would notice that most have cell walls that look like plates of armor. They also have two flagella that propel them through the water. One flagellum trails from one end like a tail. The other wraps around the middle of the organism like a belt. The movement of this flagellum causes the dinoflagellate to spin like a tiny top.

Some dinoflagellates have a characteristic that has amazed sailors since they first set sail on the world's oceans. On some nights, ocean waves glitter with thousands of tiny sparkles or glow with an eerie bluish light. The twinkling or glowing lights are produced by dinoflagellates. This glow is similar to the glow produced by fireflies, or lightning bugs.

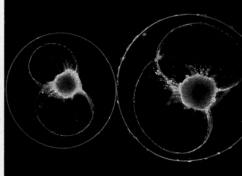

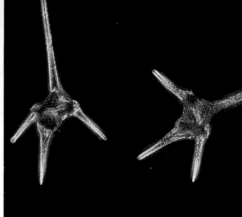

6–3 Section Review

1. Name and briefly describe three groups of plantlike protists.
2. Discuss three ways in which plantlike protists affect other living things.
3. How does a euglena detect light?
4. What is a red tide?
5. Why do experts disagree about how euglenas should be classified?

Connection—*Language Arts*

6. The Greek word *dinos* means to whirl or rotate. Why is dinoflagellate an appropriate name?

Figure 6–21 *A few dinoflagellates, such as* Noctiluca *(top right), glow at night. Most dinoflagellates have elaborate armored cell walls (top left).* Ceratium *(bottom) gets its name from a Greek word meaning horn or antler. Can you see why the name is appropriate?*

6–4 Funguslike Protists

Funguslike protists can have a great effect on human life, as the Great Potato Famine in Ireland illustrates. In 1845 and 1846, one type of funguslike protist destroyed the entire potato crop, creating a famine that caused the deaths of about one third of Ireland's population. Funguslike protists can also attack other crops, such as cabbages, corn, and grapes. Animals get diseases caused by funguslike protists. The fuzzy white growths that sometimes appear on the fins and mouth of aquarium fishes is one such disease.

Guide for Reading

Focus on this question as you read.

▶ How do slime molds differ from other protists?

Figure 6–22 *The fuzzy white growth that covers this dead aquarium fish is the funguslike protist that killed it.*

Although it is clear that funguslike protists are important, it is not clear exactly what they are. But we do know about their characteristics. Funguslike protists are heterotrophs. Most have cell walls, although a few lack a cell wall altogether. Some are almost identical to amebas during certain stages in their life cycles. Many have flagella at some point in their lives. Because of characteristics like these, many experts classify these puzzling organisms as protists.

One of the more interesting types of funguslike protists are the **slime molds.** At one point in their life cycle, these protists are moist, flat, shapeless blobs that ooze slowly over dead trees, piles of fallen leaves, and compost heaps. A few slime molds in this stage of life are shown in Figure 6–23. Can you see why the name slime molds is appropriate for these organisms?

Reproduction in slime molds involves the production of a structure called a fruiting body, which contains spores. Spores are special cells that are encased in a tough protective coating. Each spore can develop into a new organism.

Spores released by a slime mold develop into small amebalike cells. In one phylum of slime molds, each amebalike cell may develop into a single huge cell several centimeters in diameter. This large cell contains many nuclei. Eventually, the large cell settles in one place and produces fruiting bodies.

In the other phylum of slime molds, the small amebalike cells live independently for a while and reproduce rapidly. When the food supply is used up, groups of the amebalike cells gather together to produce a large mass of cells. This mass of cells begins to function as a single organism. Could this have

Figure 6–23 *Unlike most protists, slime molds are visible to the unaided eye at some stages of their life cycle. In one phylum of slime molds, a single amebalike cell may grow into an enormous cell that contains many nuclei (left). In the other phylum, many amebalike cells come together to produce a large mass of cells that behaves like a primitive multicellular organism (right).*

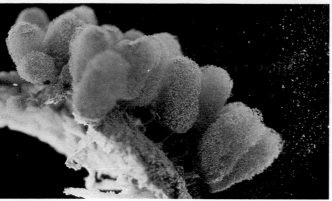

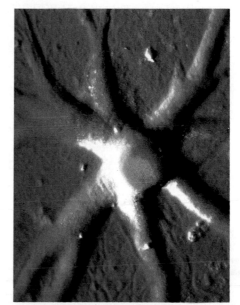

Figure 6–24 *The reproductive structures in slime molds, which are known as fruiting bodies, contain spores. What do the spores become?*

been a way in which many-celled organisms evolved from single-celled ones? Some scientists believe it could. This unusual behavior forces scientists to stretch the definition of protists. Protists are defined as being unicellular—but here is a group of protists acting like a primitive multicellular (many-celled) organism!

The solid mass of cells may travel for several centimeters. It then forms a fruiting body that produces spores. These spores develop into amebalike cells that continue the cycle.

The slime molds that form multicellular structures are interesting to biologists who study how cells communicate. The formation of a complex structure like the fruiting body from what was formerly a group of independent cells is an intriguing process. It has kept biologists busy for decades, and its secrets are still not fully understood.

6–4 Section Review

1. How do slime molds differ from other protists?
2. What are the characteristics of funguslike protists?
3. Draw a flowchart that shows the life cycles of the two types of slime molds.
4. How do funguslike protists affect humans?

Critical Thinking—*Expressing an Opinion*
5. Should slime molds be placed in a kingdom by themselves? Why? What sort of information would you like to have in order to make a better, more informed decision on this matter?

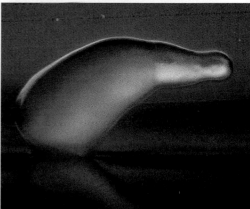

Figure 6–25 *In one phylum of slime molds, small amebalike cells come together (top) to form a mass of cells that behave like a single organism (bottom).*

Laboratory Investigation

Examining a Slime Mold

Problem

What are the characteristics of a slime mold?

Materials *(per group)*

large glass beaker	crushed oatmeal flakes
small glass bowl	
paper towel	medicine dropper
filter paper containing slime mold	magnifying glass
	dissecting needle

Procedure 🔥 ▱

1. Wrap the small glass bowl with a paper towel so that the mouth of the bowl is covered by a smooth flat paper surface.
2. Place the covered bowl in the beaker so that the mouth of the bowl faces up.
3. Partially fill the beaker with water so that the water level is about three fourths of the way up the sides of the bowl.
4. Place the small piece of filter paper containing the slime mold in the center of the paper towel that covers the bowl.
5. Sprinkle a tiny amount of crushed oatmeal flakes next to the piece of filter paper.
6. Using the medicine dropper, add two to three drops of water to the slime mold and oatmeal flakes. Set in a cool, dark place.
7. Examine the beaker each day for three days. Record your observations.
8. After three days, remove the glass bowl from the beaker. Place the bowl on your work surface.
9. Using your magnifying glass, examine the slime mold.
10. With a dissecting needle, puncture a branch of the slime mold. **CAUTION:** *Be careful when using a dissecting needle.* Observe the slime mold for a few minutes.

Observations

1. Describe the changes that took place in the slime mold during the three-day observation period.
2. What activity did you observe in the slime mold when you examined it with the magnifying glass?
3. Describe what happened to the puncture that you made in the slime mold.

Analysis and Conclusions

1. Explain why oatmeal was sprinkled on the paper towel.
2. Is the slime mold a heterotroph or an autotroph? Explain.
3. Based on your observations, describe the characteristics of a slime mold.
4. **On Your Own** Design an experiment to determine the response of the slime mold to substances such as salt or sugar.

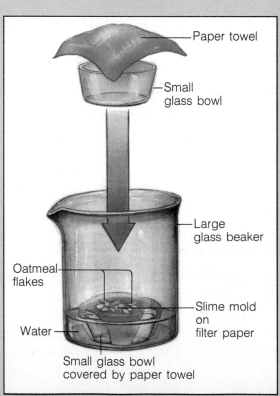

Paper towel

Small glass bowl

Large glass beaker

Oatmeal flakes

Slime mold on filter paper

Water

Small glass bowl covered by paper towel

Summarizing Key Concepts

6–1 Characteristics of Protists

▲ Protists are microscopic, unicellular organisms that have a nucleus and a number of other specialized cell structures.

▲ According to one hypothesis, the first protists were the result of a symbiosis among several types of bacteria.

▲ Although there is much debate about their proper classification, protists can be grouped in three general categories. These are: animallike protists, plantlike protists, and funguslike protists.

6–2 Animallike Protists

▲ Like animals, animallike protists are heterotrophs that can move and that are made up of cells that contain a nucleus and lack a cell wall.

▲ Animallike protists are divided into four main groups: sarcodines, ciliates, zooflagellates, and sporozoans.

▲ Sarcodines have pseudopods.

▲ Ciliates are characterized by cilia.

▲ Flagellates move by means of flagella.

▲ Sporozoans are parasites.

6–3 Plantlike Protists

▲ Plantlike protists are autotrophs that use light energy to make their own food from simple raw materials.

▲ Many organisms rely on plantlike protists for food.

▲ About 70 percent of the Earth's supply of oxygen is produced by plantlike protists.

6–4 Funguslike Protists

▲ Some funguslike protists cause diseases in crops or in animals.

▲ Funguslike protists are heterotrophs.

Reviewing Key Terms

Define each term in a complete sentence.

6–1 Characteristics of Protists
protist

6–2 Animallike Protists
sarcodine
ciliate
zooflagellate
sporozoan
pseudopod
ameba
cilia
paramecium
flagellum

6–3 Plantlike Protists
euglena
diatom
dinoflagellate

6–4 Funguslike Protists
slime mold

Chapter Review

Content Review

Multiple Choice

Choose the letter of the answer that best completes each statement.

1. Which of the following is characteristic of most protists?
   a. They are unable to move on their own.
   b. They can be seen with the unaided eye.
   c. They lack a nucleus and many other cell structures.
   d. They are unicellular.
2. Which structure helps a freshwater protist get rid of excess water?
   a. food vacuole
   c. macronucleus
   b. contractile vacuole
   d. cilium
3. Malaria is caused by a type of
   a. sporozoan.
   c. dinoflagellate.
   b. sarcodine.
   d. zooflagellate.
4. Which of the following uses cilia to move?
   a. euglena
   c. paramecium
   b. ameba
   d. *Plasmodium*
5. Which of the following is considered to be an animallike protist?
   a. slime mold
   c. euglena
   b. ameba
   d. dinoflagellate

6. Animallike protists
   a. have a thick cell wall.
   b. produce about 70 percent of the Earth's supply of oxygen.
   c. are responsible for red tides.
   d. are heterotrophs.
7. Which is not a type of plantlike protist?
   a. zooflagellate
   c. phytoflagellate
   b. dinoflagellate
   d. diatom
8. Radiolarians, foraminiferans, and amebas belong to the group of protists known as
   a. ciliates.
   c. sporozoans.
   b. sarcodines.
   d. euglenas.
9. Slime molds
   a. are always unicellular.
   b. are autotrophs.
   c. are considered to be animallike protists.
   d. form structures called fruiting bodies.

True or False

If the statement is true, write "true." If it is false, change the underlined word or words to make the statement true.

1. <u>Funguslike</u> protists are also known as protozoa.
2. Each euglena contains one or more grass-green <u>macronuclei</u>.
3. A radiolarian captures food by using its <u>pseudopods</u>.
4. African sleeping sickness is caused by <u>ciliates</u>.
5. The first protists probably developed from a <u>symbiosis</u> among several kinds of bacteria.
6. All sporozoans are <u>producers</u>.
7. Paramecia swim using <u>flagella</u>.

Concept Mapping

Complete the following concept map for Section 6–1. Then construct a concept map for the entire chapter.

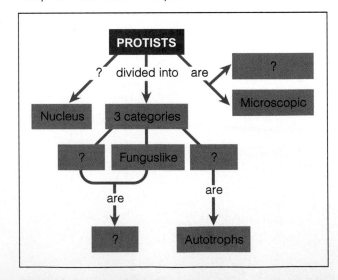

Concept Mastery

Discuss each of the following in a brief paragraph.

1. Name the group of protists that is most closely linked with each of the following:
   a. chalk
   b. diatomaceous earth
   c. red tides
   d. malaria
   e. African sleeping sickness
   f. turning chloroplasts on and off
   g. two kinds of nuclei
   h. fruiting bodies
   i. pseudopods
   j. two-part glassy shell
   k. potato famine
   l. digesting wood
2. How are sarcodines similar to one another? How are they different?
3. Explain how a paramecium catches the bacteria on which it feeds. Then describe the cell structures a captured bacterium would encounter from the time it enters the paramecium cell to the time the digested bacterium is expelled from the cell.
4. What protist causes malaria? How is this protist transmitted from one host to another?
5. Tiny plantlike protists are found in the cells of certain radiolarians. How do these plantlike protists help their host? How might the radiolarian help its "guests"?

Critical Thinking and Problem Solving

Use the skills you have developed in this chapter to answer each of the following.

1. **Relating cause and effect** Certain kinds of chemical wastes cause plants and plantlike organisms to grow at an extremely rapid rate. With this in mind, how might pollution cause red tides?
2. **Applying concepts** Examine the protist in the accompanying photograph. In what group of protists should this organism be placed? Explain. What sort of information would help you to classify this protist?

3. **Making predictions** What would happen if all the plantlike protists were to vanish from the face of the Earth? Explain.
4. **Evaluating theories** When a certain amebalike protist is treated with a bacteria-killing antibiotic, something strange happens. The small rod-shaped structures located around each of its many nuclei disappear, and the protist soon dies. Does this finding support the hypothesis that protists evolved from a symbiosis among several kinds of bacteria? Why or why not? What additional information would you like to have in order to be more sure of your answer?
5. **Using the writing process** Imagine that you are the protist of your choice. Write a letter to a potential pen pal describing yourself, where you live, your hopes and dreams, and whatever else you think is important.

Fungi

Early on a spring morning, a large pampered pig is pushed in its own wheelbarrow into an oak forest near Perigord, France. There its master gently puts the pig on a leash. The pig is now ready for the hunt!

Soon the pig catches a whiff of a wonderful odor—one that is too faint for people to smell. The pig begins to dig, but its master quickly stops it. He does not want the animal to destroy the buried treasure it has found. This "treasure" is not gold or silver. It is an ugly round black fungus known as a truffle. Because of its delicious flavor, this thick-skinned, warty cousin of the mushroom is considered a delicacy. In fact, truffles can sell for more than $1400 a kilogram!

Truffles are just one of the many different kinds of fungi. What are fungi? What do they look like? How do they affect humans and other living things? Read on to discover more about the strange world of the kingdom Fungi.

Journal *Activity*

You and Your World Have you ever eaten a mushroom? What do you remember about the first time you ate a mushroom? Has your opinion of mushrooms changed since your first tasting? In your journal, explore your thoughts and feelings about this edible fungus.

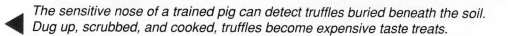

The sensitive nose of a trained pig can detect truffles buried beneath the soil. Dug up, scrubbed, and cooked, truffles become expensive taste treats.

7–1 Characteristics of Fungi

Unnoticed, a speck of dust lands on the back of an ant. But this is no ordinary dust—it is alive! Tiny glistening threads emerge from the dust and begin to grow into the ant's body. As they grow, the threads slowly devour the ant while it is still alive. Chemicals released by the threads dissolve the ant's tissues. The threads absorb the dissolved tissues and use the energy from them to spread further into the ant's body. Within a few days, the ant's body is little more than a hollow shell filled with a tangle of the deadly threads. Then the threads begin to grow up and out of the dead ant, winding together to produce a long stalk with a knobby lump at its tip. The stalked structure releases thousands of dustlike spores, which are carried by the wind to new victims.

The strange ant killer is a **fungus** (FUHN-guhs; plural: fungi, FUHN-jigh). Fungi range in size from tiny unicellular (one-celled) yeasts to huge tree fungi over 140 centimeters long. Fungi may look like wisps of gray cotton, white volleyballs, tiny brightly colored umbrellas, blobs of melted wax, stubby fingers of yellow-green slime, or miniature red bowls. (And there are many that defy description!) Although fungi come in a variety of shapes, sizes, and colors, they share many important characteristics. They are similar in the way they get their food, in their structure, and in the way they reproduce.

Figure 7–1 *When the insect-killing fungus has completed its deadly work, it produces stalked fruiting bodies that grow from the empty husks of its insect victims. What is the function of the fruiting bodies?*

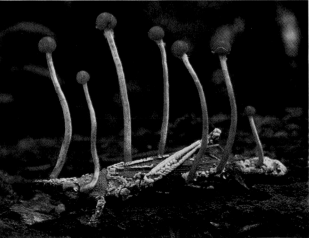

"Feeding" in Fungi

All fungi are heterotrophs (organisms that cannot make their own food). They obtain the energy and chemicals they need by growing on a source of food. **Fungi release chemicals that digest the substance on which they are growing and then they absorb the digested food.** (Animals, on the other hand, first take in—eat—their food and then digest it.)

Some fungi capture small animals for food. Oyster mushrooms, for example, release a chemical that stuns tiny roundworms in the soil. Certain threadlike soil fungi have tiny nooses that they use to snare their roundworm prey. Once a roundworm has been captured, the fungus begins to grow on it. Can you describe what happens after the fungus starts to grow on its prey?

Other fungi obtain their food through symbiotic relationships. (Remember that a close relationship between two kinds of organisms in which at least one of the organisms benefits is known as a symbiosis.) Some symbiotic fungi, like the ant-killing fungus you just read about, are parasites that harm their host. Other symbiotic fungi help their host. Later in this chapter, you will read about some specific examples of harmful and helpful symbiotic fungi.

Many species of fungi get their food from the remains of dead organisms. These fungi are decomposers. Recall from Chapter 5 that decomposers break down dead plant and animal matter. The broken-down products become the foods of other living things. Why can such fungi, along with certain bacteria, be called "the Earth's cleanup crew"?

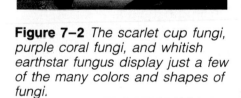

Figure 7–2 *The scarlet cup fungi, purple coral fungi, and whitish earthstar fungus display just a few of the many colors and shapes of fungi.*

Figure 7–3 *An unlucky roundworm struggles in vain as the nooses of a soil fungus tighten around it in this microscopic drama.*

*Making Models
of Multicellular Organisms*

You can get a better idea of how different the structure of fungi is from that of other multicellular organisms by constructing a model. For these models you will need some sugar cubes and thin licorice whips.

1. For your model of a fungus, tangle and twist the licorice whips together to form a compact structure.

2. For your model of a plant or animal, stack the sugar cubes to produce a compact structure that is several cubes in length, height, and depth.

What do the licorice whips represent? What do the sugar cubes represent?

■ How is the basic structure of a fungus different from that of other multicellular organisms?

Structure of Fungi

A few fungi, such as the yeast used by bakers, are unicellular (one-celled). Most fungi, however, are multicellular (many-celled). The fat white toadstools at the base of a tree, the black spots of mildew on a shower curtain, and the fuzzy greenish mold on a piece of old cheese are all examples of multicellular fungi.

Multicellular fungi are made up of threadlike tubes called hyphae (HIGH-fee; singular: hypha). The **hyphae** branch and weave together in various ways to produce many different shapes of fungi. Hyphae can grow quite quickly—certain fungi can produce about 40 meters of hyphae in an hour. This is part of the reason mushrooms seem to pop up in fields and lawns overnight!

Interestingly, fungi are not multicellular in the same way that plants and animals are. All of the cells that make up the bodies of plants and animals are distinct units. Each plant or animal cell contains one nucleus (although there are some exceptions) and is enclosed by a cell membrane that separates it from other cells. The hyphae of fungi, on the other hand, are continuous threads of cytoplasm that contain many nuclei. Now can you explain why substances move more quickly and freely in fungi than in other multicellular organisms?

Figure 7–4 *Fungi are made up of threadlike structures called hyphae (right). A close examination of a bread mold reveals that it is made of white, threadlike hyphae peppered with round black spore cases (left). The thick, heavy plates of shelf fungi are also made up of hyphae (center). In which kind of fungi are the hyphae more closely packed together?*

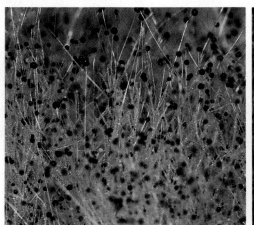

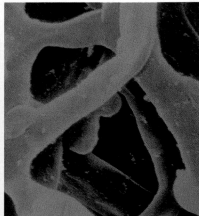

The hyphae of some fungi are divided into compartments by incomplete cross walls. Although these compartments are traditionally referred to as "cells," they are not enclosed by a cell membrane. Nuclei and other cell structures move quite freely through the openings in the cross walls. The only "real" cells are reproductive cells located at the tips of some of the hyphae.

Reproduction in Fungi

Many fungi reproduce by means of spores. Fungal **spores** are tiny reproductive cells that are enclosed in a protective cell wall. Because they are very small and light in weight, spores can be carried great distances by the wind. If a spore lands in a place where growing conditions are right, it can sprout and develop hyphae. How does this fact help to explain why fungi are found just about every place in the world?

Fungi produce spores in a special structure called the fruiting body. Some fungi have simple fruiting bodies that consist of a stalk with a cluster of spores at its tip. Other fungi—mushrooms, cup fungi, and puffballs, for example—have large, complex fruiting bodies made up of many closely packed hyphae. A

Activity Bank

Spreading Spores, p.799

Figure 7–5 *Puffballs release a cloud of spores when touched (right). The girl posing beside the giant puffball (above) would be well advised to avoid touching the fungus! The spores of puffballs are spread by the wind. Some fungi spread their spores in other ways. The lacy stinkhorn produces a fluid that smells like rotting meat (top left). When a fly eats the fluid, it also takes in spores. The spores pass unharmed through the fly's body and are deposited over great distances. Tiny* Pilobolus *can throw its spore cases as much as a meter away (bottom left)! This is roughly equivalent to throwing a baseball the length of several football fields.*

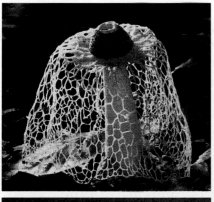

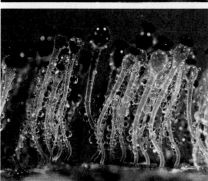

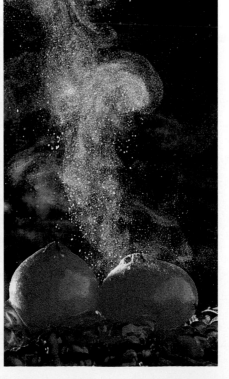

183

single fruiting body such as a large puffball may produce trillions of spores.

So why aren't we surrounded by millions of mushrooms or buried in puffballs? The answer is simple: Very few fungal spores find the proper combination of temperature, moisture, and food that they need to survive. Even fewer young fungi survive long enough to produce spores of their own. Can you now explain why fungi produce huge numbers of spores?

7–1 Section Review

1. Briefly discuss the basic characteristics of fungi.
2. What are hyphae?
3. How do fungi obtain food?
4. Describe how fungi reproduce.

Critical Thinking—*Relating Concepts*
5. Explain why it is important for fungi (and other organisms that cannot move) to produce offspring that can easily travel from one place to another.

Guide for Reading

Focus on these questions as you read.

▶ *How are mushrooms, yeasts, and molds similar? How are they different?*

7–2 Forms of Fungi

Fungi, like other organisms, are classified in a way that best shows the evolutionary relationships among the members of the group. As you might expect for such a strange and diverse group of organisms, the guidelines for classifying fungi are rather complex. As a result, people find it useful to group fungi according to their basic form, or shape. It is important to note that these groupings are not the formal classifications you learned about in Chapter 4. There are three basic forms of fungi: mushrooms, yeasts, and molds. **Mushrooms are shaped like umbrellas. Yeasts consist of single cells. And molds are fuzzy, shapeless, fairly flat fungi that grow on the surface of an object.**

Figure 7–6 *Although a morel looks, smells, and tastes like a mushroom, it is more closely related to baker's yeast than to mushrooms.*

Although these three categories are handy for everyday purposes, they do not make up a perfect organizational system. Why? Some fungi have very unusual shapes and cannot be placed in any of these categories. Others have more than one shape. The fungus that causes the disease known as thrush, for example, occurs both as a yeast and as a mold. Still others appear to have the correct shape for a group but are not placed in that group. Even though the morel shown in Figure 7–6 looks (and tastes) a lot like a true mushroom, it is not a mushroom.

Mushrooms

Have you ever ordered a pizza with all the trimmings? If so you ate fungi known as **mushrooms.** Figure 7–7 shows some mushrooms that might be encountered on a walk through the woods. As you can see, a mushroom has a stemlike structure called a stalk. In many types of mushrooms, the stalk is decorated with a structure called a ring, which looks somewhat like a very short skirt. On top of the stalk is the mushroom's cap. The mushroom's spores are produced on the underside of the cap. The spores are often located on thin sheets of tissue called gills, which extend from the stalk to the outer edge of the cap.

Figure 7–7 *Most familiar mushrooms produce their spores on gills. Some mushrooms, however, produce their spores in tubes and release them through pores. Others bear their spores on tiny flaps known as teeth.*

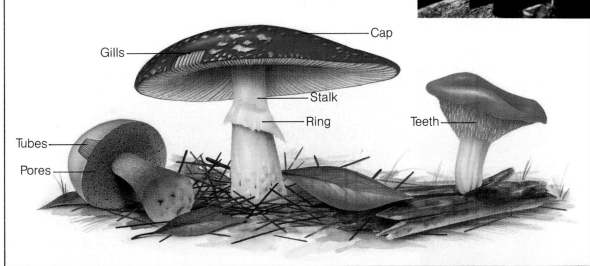

PROBLEM Solving

A Hot Time for Yeast

Yeasts are tiny unicellular fungi. Some yeasts are used to make alcoholic beverages and foods such as bread. The accompanying graph shows the effect of temperature on the level of activity of yeast cells. Use the graph to answer the questions that follow:

Interpreting Graphs

1. How does temperature affect yeast activity?

2. At what temperature is the yeast activity the highest?

3. At what temperature does the yeast activity decrease sharply?

4. Why is yeast dissolved in warm water when it is used to make bread?

5. Explain why bread dough is sometimes placed in a slightly warm oven for an hour or so before it is made into a loaf and baked in a hot oven.

6. Would you expect to find live yeast cells in a slice of bread? Explain.

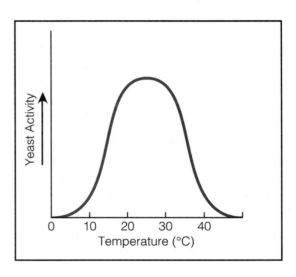

Figure 7–8 *Yeasts are used to produce bread, fuel, vitamins, chemicals, and even medicines such as the vaccine for hepatitis B. Yeasts reproduce by budding. A round scar results when a bud breaks off from its parent cell. How many buds has the larger yeast cell produced?*

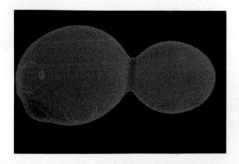

Yeasts

Most people cannot help but stop and take a deep breath when they pass a bakery. There is something about the smell of fresh bread that excites the senses. The next time you pass a bakery you might whisper a soft thank-you to another type of fungi, the **yeasts.**

In order to make soft, fluffy bread, bakers add yeast to the flour, water, sugar, salt, and other ingredients that make up bread dough. The bakers then allow the dough to sit for a while in a warm place. Bread dough is a great environment for yeast—moist, warm, and full of food. As it grows, the yeast produces carbon dioxide gas. The carbon dioxide gas forms millions of tiny bubbles in the dough. You see these bubbles as holes in a slice of bread. What do you think would happen if a baker forgot to put yeast in the bread dough?

Unlike other fungi, yeasts may reproduce by a process known as budding. During budding, a portion of the yeast cell pushes out of the cell wall and forms a tiny bud. In time, the bud breaks away from the parent cell and becomes a new yeast.

Molds

Centuries ago people sometimes treated infections in a rather curious way. They placed decaying breads, cheeses, or fruits on the infection. Although the people did not have a scientific reason for doing this, every once in a while the infection was cured. What these people did not and could not know was that the cure was due to a type of **mold** that grows on certain foods.

In 1928, the Scottish scientist Sir Alexander Fleming found out why this treatment worked. Fleming discovered that a substance produced by the mold *Penicillium* could kill certain bacteria that caused infections. Fleming named the substance penicillin. Since that time penicillin, an antibiotic, has saved millions of lives.

Molds are used to make many foods, such as tofu (bean curd), soy sauce, and cheeses. The blue streaks in blue cheese, for example, are actually

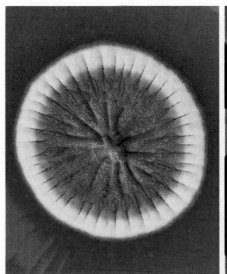
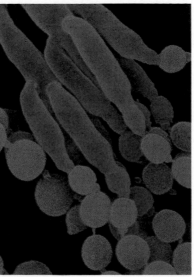

ACTIVITY DOING

Making Spore Prints

1. Place a fresh mushroom cap, gill side down, on a sheet of white paper. Cover with a large glass jar, open end down. **CAUTION:** *If you use a wild mushroom, wash your hands thoroughly after handling it. Do not leave wild mushrooms where small children can reach them. Some wild mushrooms are poisonous.*

2. After several days, carefully remove the jar and lift off the mushroom cap. You should find a spore print on the paper.

3. Very carefully spray the paper with clear varnish or hair spray to make a permanent spore print.

4. Examine the print with a magnifying glass.

5. (Optional) Prepare a spore print using a different kind of mushroom.

What color are the spores in your spore prints? How are your spore prints similar? How are they different? How do your spore prints compare to ones prepared by your fellow classmates?

Figure 7–9 *The mold* Penicillium *(left) produces spores at the tips of tiny branches (right). What important antibiotic comes from* Penicillium?

mold. Of course, not all molds help to make foods or provide valuable medicines. Most molds are just plain, ordinary fungi. So if you discover fuzzy growths of mold on decaying breads, cheeses, or fruits, you should probably just clean out the refrigerator or take out the trash.

7–2 Section Review

1. How is a yeast different from a mushroom?
2. List five different uses for yeasts.
3. Discuss three ways in which molds affect people.

Critical Thinking—*Evaluating Classification Schemes*
4. Explain why fungi are not divided into phyla according to basic shape.

Guide for Reading

Focus on these questions as you read.

▶ How do fungi harm other organisms?
▶ How do fungi help other organisms?

ACTIVITY
READING

A Secret Invasion

What might mushrooms say if they could speak? Are these small umbrella-shaped organisms as innocent as they seem? For one poet's answers to these questions, read the poem "Mushrooms," by Sylvia Plath.

7–3 How Fungi Affect Other Organisms

Fungi interact with other organisms in many different ways. Some fungi harm other organisms. Such fungi are often disease-causing parasites of plants and animals. Other fungi are helpful to other organisms and may even be necessary for their survival.

Fungi and Disease

Have you ever looked closely at an apple and noticed a sprinkling of small, hard brown "scabs" on its skin? Or have you ever seen round black or gray spots on the leaves of a lilac or rose bush? These scabs and spots are the result of plant diseases caused by fungi. And although the apple is still safe to eat, the lilac or rose plant might be in serious trouble.

Scabs and spots are not the only signs of fungal diseases. Some disease-causing fungi make the stem, roots, or fruit of crop plants rot, or decay. Others, such as those that cause Dutch elm disease and

chestnut blight, kill trees that are prized for their beauty and wood. A few change kernels of growing grain into bags of useless fungal spores. Still others damage stored crops such as wheat, corn, oats, peanuts, and rice, making them unfit to eat. Can you now explain why farmers and gardeners spend millions of dollars on fungicides (fungus-killing substances) each year?

In addition to damaging or even completely destroying crops, some fungi that infect plants produce toxins (poisons) that can injure or even kill humans and animals. For example, one fungus that grows on stored grain produces a toxin that is one of the most powerful cancer-causing substances. (Scientists know this toxin as aflatoxin.) In small doses, this toxin can cause liver cancer. In large doses, it is fatal. Like most fungi, the toxin-producing fungus will grow only if there is sufficient moisture. Why is it important to thoroughly dry crops such as peanuts or corn before they are stored?

Another fungus replaces grains of rye with hard spiky poisonous growths known as ergot. People who eat bread or other grain products containing ergot may experience burning or prickling sensations, hallucinations, and convulsions. In extreme cases, the flow of blood to the arms and/or legs may be cut off, resulting in infections and possible loss of the affected limbs.

Ergot poisoning can be fatal—although not necessarily through the direct actions of the toxins. Some historians have suggested that the witchcraft trials in Salem, Massachusetts, may have been due in part to people's terror at the strange symptoms of ergot poisoning. Early in 1692, several girls in Salem

Figure 7–10 *Fungi affect other organisms in many ways. Leafcutter ants grow the fungi they eat on bits of plants they carry to their underground nests (top right). Gypsy moth caterpillars (left), which cause a great deal of damage to trees, can be controlled with the help of a parasitic fungus. Grains of corn are changed into bags of toxic spores by the fungus known as corn smut (bottom right).*

Figure 7–11 *The long, curved spikes on this head of rye are ergot. What is the connection between fungi and the Salem witchcraft trials?*

began suffering from pains and odd behaviors that were thought to be caused by witchcraft. By the end of the year, 19 people had been hanged as witches as a result of the ensuing witch hunt and trials.

Animals, like plants, can become infected by fungal diseases. Fungi cause a number of severe, sometimes fatal, lung diseases in poultry (chickens, ducks, and other kinds of farm birds). They can also produce itchy or painful sores on the skin of pets such as dogs, cats, and birds. While most fungal diseases of animals are troublesome, a few have proven to be useful to humans. Plant-eating pests such as gypsy moth caterpillars, mites, and aphids can be killed by deliberately infecting them with certain fungi. These fungal pesticides are a lot more effective than chemicals—and a lot safer for the environment, too!

Although some human fungal diseases are serious, most are simply annoying. One causes the fingernails or toenails to grow in crooked and/or fall out. The diseases known as ringworm and athlete's foot cause itchy, reddened, and raw patches on the skin.

Fungus-Root Associations

As you have discovered, plants are plagued by a host of fungal diseases. However, plants get help against some of these diseases from—you guessed

ACTIVITY

WRITING

Human Fungal Diseases

Using reference materials in the library, prepare a brief report on one of the following diseases:

athlete's foot
coccidioidomycosis (San Joaquin Valley fever)
farmer's lung
histoplasmosis
ringworm
sporotrichosis (rose-prick fever, rose-gardener's syndrome)
thrush (candidiasis)

In your report, give the name of the fungus that causes the disease. Also include information about the transmission, symptoms, and treatment of the diseases.

Figure 7–12 *Some mycorrhizae send up mushrooms or puffballs. This sometimes produces a "fairy ring" around a tree. Folklore has it that trees surrounded by fairy rings are the favorites of fairies, so chopping down such trees is extremely bad luck.*

it—other fungi. Helpful fungi coat the roots of about 80 percent of the world's plants. Some of these fungi simply cover the surface of the roots. Others actually send hyphae into the roots' cells. Scientists give these fungus-root associations a fancy name: mycorrhizae (migh-koh-RIGH-zee; singular: mycorrhiza), which is Greek for "fungus roots."

The word mycorrhizae is also used to refer to the helpful fungi in fungus-root associations. The hyphae of these helpful fungi spread out into the soil in all directions, increasing their host's ability to gather nutrients by ten times or more. The fungus-root associations protect the plant against drought, cold, acid rain, and root diseases caused by harmful fungi. Currently, Australian researchers are trying to alter the hereditary material of one kind of mycorrhiza so that it produces natural insecticides. This helpful fungus would then be able to help guard its host against harmful insects as well as provide all of its normal benefits.

Lichens

Suppose someone asked you what kind of organism can live in the hot, dry desert as well as the frozen Arctic. What if the person added that this organism can also survive on bare rocks, wooden poles, the sides of trees, and even the tops of mountains? You might reply that no one organism can survive in so many different environments. In a way, your response would be right. For although **lichens** (LIGH-kuhnz) can actually live in all of these

ACTIVITY
WRITING

Taking a "Lichen" to It

Lichens are used in a variety of ways. Some are used to make dyes. Others are a source of food for people and livestock. Go to the library and find out the details about some of the ways lichens are used around the world. Prepare a report on your findings.

Figure 7–13 *Lichens show three basic patterns of growth: flat and crusty, bushy, and leafy. The British soldier lichen is a bushy lichen (right). What growth pattern do these yellow lichens show?*

environments, they are not one organism but two. **A lichen is made up of a fungus and an alga that live together.** An alga (AL-gah; plural: algae, AL-jee) is a simple plantlike autotroph that uses sunlight to produce its food. An alga lacks true roots, stems, and leaves. Blue-green bacteria, certain protists, and a number of simple plants are considered to be algae. Combined, the two organisms (alga and fungus) in a lichen can live in many places that neither could survive in alone.

The fungus part of the lichen provides the alga with water and minerals that the fungus absorbs from whatever the lichen is growing on. The alga part of the lichen uses the minerals and water to make food for the fungus and itself. Why is the relationship between the fungus and alga considered to be one of the best examples of symbiosis?

Lichens are sometimes known as pioneers because they are often one of the first living things to appear in rocky, barren areas. Lichens release acids that break down rock and cause it to crack. Dust and dead lichens fill the cracks, which eventually become fertile places for other organisms to grow. In time, the rocky area may become a lush, green forest.

7–3 Section Review

1. Discuss three ways in which fungi harm humans.
2. How are fungal diseases useful to people?
3. Explain why fungus spores are sometimes mixed into the soil in which young trees are to be grown.
4. What is a lichen?
5. Why do agricultural inspectors check samples of grain with a microscope before permitting the grain to be ground up for food?

Connection—*Ecology*
6. Many lichens are extremely sensitive to pollution. Even when there is very little pollution, these lichens will grow poorly or not at all. How might environmental scientists use this information in their work?

CONNECTIONS

Murderous Mushrooms

To avoid becoming one of the several hundred cases of mushroom poisoning in the United States each year (or worse yet, a "dear departed"), a mushroom hunter must be able to accurately identify mushrooms. The difficulty of this task is particularly well-illustrated by the mushrooms in the genus *Amanita. A. caesarae* was a favorite food of the Caesars, the rulers of ancient Rome. *A. rubescens* is also edible and delicious—but it is poisonous when it is not sufficiently cooked. *A. muscaria* is a poisonous mushroom. In fact, people in northern Europe once soaked *A. muscaria* caps in milk and set them out to attract and kill flies. If accidentally eaten by humans, *A. muscaria* causes hallucinations, sweating, wildly crazy behavior, and deep sleep. *A. verna,* which is known by the common names fool's mushroom and destroying angel, causes cramps, severe abdominal pain, vomiting, diarrhea, liver and kidney failure, and death in over half its victims.

Interestingly, the deadly poisonous *Amanita* mushrooms taste good. (Most poisonous substances are bitter or otherwise unpleasant.) This characteristic has caused these mushrooms to be used by murderers on more than one occasion in *history.* In 54 AD, the emperor Claudius I of Rome was fed poisonous mushrooms by his wife, who wanted her son Nero to become emperor and did not want to wait for Claudius to die of natural causes. Pope Clement VII, who died in 1534, was also a victim of poisonous mushrooms.

Mushrooms in the genus Amanita *include* A. muscaria *(bottom right),* A. caesarea *(top left),* A. rubescens *(bottom left), and* A. verna *(top right).*

Laboratory Investigation

Growing Mold

Problem

How does mold grow?

Materials *(per group)*

large covered container
paper towel
piece of bread
piece of cheese
piece of apple
magnifying glass

Procedure 🧪

1. Line the container with moist paper towels.
2. Place the pieces of food in the container.
3. Allow the container to remain uncovered overnight. Then cover the container.
4. Store the container in a dark place. Examine its contents daily for mold.
5. After the container's contents become moldy, examine the mold with a magnifying glass. **CAUTION:** *Be careful not to accidentally inhale mold spores. Some people are allergic to mold.*
6. Make a drawing of what you observe. Record your observations next to your drawing.
7. Observe and draw the mold every two to three days for a week.

Observations

1. When did mold start to grow?
2. How do the molds appear to the unaided eye? Under a magnifying glass?
3. How do the molds change over time?
4. Did you observe fruiting bodies and spores? What did these look like?

Analysis and Conclusions

1. Do different kinds of mold grow on different kinds of substances? Why do you think this is so?
2. On which substance did the molds grow best? Develop a hypothesis to explain why. How might you test your hypothesis?
3. Why did you leave the container uncovered? What would have happened if you had covered the container immediately?
4. **On Your Own** Design an experiment to find out how light, temperature, moisture, dust, or household disinfectants affect the growth of molds. If you receive the proper permission, you may perform the experiment you have designed.

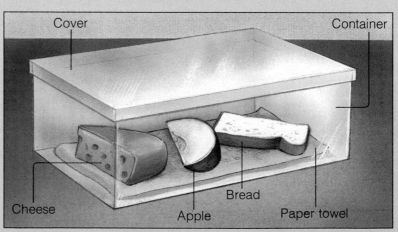

Summarizing Key Concepts

7-1 Characteristics of Fungi

▲ Fungi come in a variety of sizes, shapes, and colors.

▲ Fungi are heterotrophs. They obtain food by releasing chemicals that digest the substance on which they are growing and then by absorbing the digested food.

▲ Some fungi catch and eat tiny animals. Others are decomposers. Still others obtain food through symbiotic relationships. Some symbiotic fungi are parasites. Others help their host.

▲ Some fungi are unicellular. Most fungi are multicellular.

▲ Multicellular fungi are made up of threadlike tubes called hyphae.

▲ Fungi typically reproduce by means of spores, which are produced in structures known as fruiting bodies.

7-2 Forms of Fungi

▲ There are three basic forms of fungi: mushrooms, yeasts, and molds.

▲ Mushrooms are shaped like umbrellas. Some are good to eat. Others are poisonous.

▲ Yeasts are unicellular. They are used by bakers, brewers, industrial chemists, and medical researchers, to name a few.

▲ Molds are fuzzy, shapeless, fairly flat fungi that grow on the surface of an object. Some are used to make foods. A few are the source of important medicines.

7-3 How Fungi Affect Other Organisms

▲ Many diseases of crop and garden plants are caused by fungi.

▲ Some fungi that infect plants produce toxins that are harmful to humans and animals.

▲ Fungi cause a number of diseases in animals and humans. Some of these are simply annoying. Others are serious and even deadly.

▲ Certain fungi form fungus-root associations with most of the Earth's plants. These symbiotic relationships are extremely helpful to the plants.

▲ Lichens are produced by a symbiosis between a fungus and an alga.

Reviewing Key Terms

Define each term in a complete sentence.

7-1 Characteristics of Fungi
fungus
hypha
spore

7-2 Forms of Fungi
mushroom
yeast
mold

7-3 How Fungi Affect Other Organisms
lichen

Chapter Review

Content Review

Multiple Choice

Choose the letter of the answer that best completes each statement.

1. Most fungi reproduce by means of
   a. budding.
   b. spores.
   c. binary fission.
   d. conjugation.
2. Yeasts consist of
   a. many long hyphae that are tightly wound together.
   b. a stemlike stalk that is topped by a cap.
   c. single cells.
   d. cup-shaped fruiting bodies.
3. Fungi that get their food from the remains of dead organisms are known as
   a. decomposers.
   b. producers.
   c. parasites.
   d. symbionts.
4. Fungi produce spores in structures known as
   a. buds.
   b. stalks.
   c. puffballs.
   d. fruiting bodies.
5. Which of the following is not necessary for fungi to grow and survive?
   a. sunlight
   b. proper temperature
   c. moisture
   d. food
6. A lichen is a symbiotic partnership between a
   a. yeast and a mold.
   b. fungus and a plant's roots.
   c. mold and an ant.
   d. fungus and an alga.
7. Which of the following is not a disease caused by fungi?
   a. ringworm
   b. mycorrhiza
   c. chestnut blight
   d. athlete's foot
8. Any close relationship between two organisms in which at least one of the organisms benefits is known as
   a. heterotrophy.
   b. symbiosis.
   c. autotrophy.
   d. parasitism.
9. The month-old leftovers that you discover at the back of the refrigerator are spotted with a velvety blue-green fungus. This fungus is probably a
   a. yeast.
   b. mushroom.
   c. lichen.
   d. mold.

True or False

If the statement is true, write "true." If it is false, change the underlined word or words to make the statement true.

1. Most fungi are made up of threadlike structures known as <u>fruiting bodies</u>.
2. The scientific name for the organisms called <u>lichens</u> is mycorrhizae.
3. Fleming discovered that a certain mold produced an antibiotic that he called <u>cyclosporine</u>.
4. The three basic forms of fungi are <u>mushrooms, molds, and mildews</u>.
5. Fungi are classified according to <u>characteristics that show their evolutionary relationships</u>.

Concept Mapping

Complete the following concept map for Section 7–1. Then construct a concept map for the entire chapter.

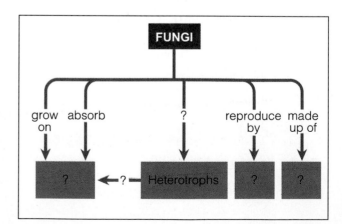

Concept Mastery

Discuss each of the following in a brief paragraph.

1. Explain why fungi are placed in their own kingdom.
2. How do fungi obtain energy and nutrients?
3. How do the alga and the fungus in a lichen help each other?
4. Describe three ways in which molds help humans.
5. Why are yeast cells used in baking bread?
6. Describe the structure of a typical mushroom and explain the function of each structure.
7. Explain how fungi that infect plants can harm humans.

Critical Thinking and Problem Solving

Use the skills you have developed in this chapter to answer each of the following.

1. **Relating concepts** What is the connection between reproduction by spores and the rapid spread of crop diseases caused by fungi?
2. **Designing an experiment** Design a set of experiments to show how light, temperature, and dryness affect the growth of bread mold. Be sure to include a control in each of your experiments—and make sure that each experiment tests only one variable.
3. **Making inferences** As you can see in the accompanying photograph, a sharpei dog looks like its skin is many sizes too large. People who own a sharpei dog must rearrange its loose folds of skin every now and then. This is especially true in areas where there is a lot of moisture in the air. What might happen to a sharpei dog if its owner neglected to rearrange its folds of skin?
4. **Assessing concepts** Fungi are sometimes divided into two groups: yeasts (unicellular fungi) and molds (multicellular fungi). Is this informal classification system useful? Why or why not?
5. **Using the writing process** While looking something up in the local library's new set of encyclopedias, you notice that fungi are defined as "plants that lack chlorophyll (the green substance involved in food-making)." Write a letter to the editors of the encyclopedia explaining why this is not a good description of fungi.
6. **Using the writing process** Imagine that you are the alga in a lichen. Write a letter to an old friend describing your fungal partner.

Plants Without Seeds

The waves lapping around your face are so cold that your skin goes numb. You make a few last-minute adjustments to your wet suit, then raise your gloved hand, forming a circle with your thumb and forefinger—O.K. One of your friends on the boat gives you a thumbs-up. With a practiced movement of your arms, you descend feet first into an alien world.

Once underwater, you find yourself in a strange, dreamlike forest. Thin, vinelike "trees" stretch up toward the silver sky far above your head. Below you, the trees extend so far down into murky darkness that they seem to go on forever. Fishes dart like birds among the swaying ribbonlike leaves of the trees. A curious young harbor seal suddenly appears and stares at you with large dark eyes. Then it does a flip with a half-twist and vanishes like a ghost among the long, thin trees of seaweed.

The trees of this underwater forest are a type of seaweed known as kelp. Kelp forests—found off the coasts of Washington, Oregon, and northern California—are home to slugs, snails, fishes, seals, sea otters, and many other living things.

Kelps are just one kind of plant without seeds. In this chapter, you will read about the strange and ancient world of plants without seeds.

Journal *Activity*

You and Your World In your journal, record your thoughts about studying plants. Do you think this chapter and the one that follows will be easy? Difficult? Interesting? When you have completed Chapters 8 and 9, look back at this entry and see if the chapters were as you expected.

◀ *Long, ropy strands of kelp sway gracefully with the movement of the ocean's waves and currents as a diver explores the mysterious, dimly lit world of the seaweed "forest."*

Guide for Reading

Focus on these questions as you read.

▶ How are red, brown, and green algae similar? How are they different?

8–1 Plants Appear: Multicellular Algae

Have you ever walked along a beach? If so, you may have found flat greenish-brown ribbons, brown ropes, or delicate reddish tangles of seaweed washed up on the sand. You may have discovered bits of yellowish seaweed that contain bubbles which squish with a satisfying pop. Looking into tide pools, you might have seen transparent green veils of sea lettuce, dainty mermaid's cups, or pink coralline algae.

Even if you have never been to a beach, you have probably encountered seaweed in other forms. For example, the edible blackish wrapper on certain kinds of sushi (Japanese rice rolls) is made of dried seaweed. Ground-up seaweed is mixed with water and sprayed on gardens to make plants grow better. And chemicals from seaweed are added to ice cream, jellies, candy, and many other foods to give them a smooth texture.

Seaweeds are some of the most familiar types of multicellular **algae** (AL-jee; singular: alga, AL-gah). As you learned in Chapter 7, the term alga refers to any simple plantlike autotroph that uses sunlight to produce its food. Thus the term algae is used to refer to everything from microscopic unicellular blue-green bacteria to enormous multicellular strands of kelp as long as a football field.

Scientists do not agree about the formal classification of algae. Some scientists think that all algae (except blue-green bacteria) should be classified as protists. Others think that all algae should be classified

Figure 8–1 *Algae come in many forms. Mermaid's cups resemble shallow drinking glasses (top). The bubblelike structures on giant kelp help to keep it afloat in its watery home (bottom right). The delicate branches of coralline algae contain so much limestone that they look and feel as if they were carved out of reddish stone (bottom left).*

as plants. Both of these views have evidence to support them. In this textbook, we have decided to use the following classification system: Blue-green bacteria belong to the kingdom Monera. Most of the other unicellular algae are assigned to the kingdom Protista. Multicellular algae and closely related species of unicellular algae are placed in the kingdom Plantae.

In Chapter 5, you learned about blue-green bacteria. In Chapter 6, you learned about plantlike protists. In this chapter, you will learn about multicellular algae and the unicellular algae that are closely related to them. For convenience and simplicity, from this point on we will refer to multicellular algae and their close relatives as algae.

Algae were the first kinds of plants to appear on Earth. The oldest fossils (preserved remains of ancient organisms) of algae are about 900 million years old. Fossil evidence indicates that land plants evolved from certain types of these ancient algae.

Although algae resemble the land plants that are familiar to you, there are some important differences. **Algae lack the special tubes that transport water and other materials through the bodies of land plants.** This means that algae do not have true roots, stems, or leaves. By definition, roots, stems, and leaves contain these special tubes. **Algae do not have seeds.** Because they lack transporting tubes and seeds, algae must live in or near a source of water in order to survive and reproduce.

Algae are divided into three phyla: **brown algae, red algae,** and **green algae.** The phyla get their names from the **pigments,** or colored chemicals, that are found within the cells of the algae.

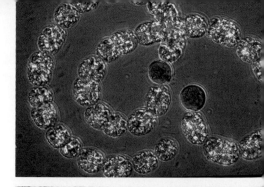

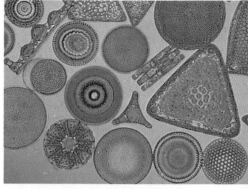

Figure 8–2 *Blue-green bacteria (top) and diatoms (bottom) are both types of algae that do not belong to the plant kingdom.*

Figure 8–3 *Multicellular algae are divided into three phyla according to the pigments they contain. Which of the algae shown here is a red alga? Which is a green alga? Which is a brown alga?*

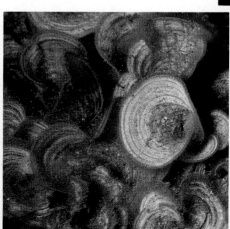

In green algae, the most noticeable pigment is the green chemical chlorophyll. Chlorophyll captures light energy so that it can be used in the food-making process. Red algae and brown algae also contain chlorophyll. However, the green color of the chlorophyll is masked by other kinds of pigments. These pigments, which are known as accessory pigments, absorb light energy and transfer it to chlorophyll for use. The main accessory pigments in red algae are pink, red, reddish purple, and reddish black. What color would you expect the main accessory pigment in brown algae to be?

Brown Algae

For centuries it was the subject of sailors' nightmares—a haunted sea located somewhere in the Atlantic Ocean between the African coast and the islands of the West Indies. The sailors whispered the name of this sea when they dared to say it at all—the Sargasso Sea. According to legend, if a ship was foolish or unlucky enough to sail into this sea, it would encounter seaweed that could cling to the sides of the ship like monster hands. As the ship sailed on, the seaweed would become thicker and thicker, slowing the ship to a crawl, and then to a halt. A ship trapped in the horrible seaweed of the Sargasso Sea would remain there forever, joining a fleet of dead ships guarded by skeletons.

The legends about the ghost ships of the Sargasso Sea are purely imaginary. Although there really is a Sargasso Sea, it is not an obstacle to ships. In the Atlantic Ocean between Africa and Bermuda lies the real Sargasso Sea. It is an area of calm winds and gentle waves that is a perfect home for the brown algae *Sargassum* (sahr-GAS-uhm). *Sargassum* floats on or near the ocean's surface, held up by tiny round air-filled structures that act like inflatable life preservers. These air-filled structures, or air bladders, help to ensure that the *Sargassum* stays close to the surface of the ocean, where it can get plenty of sunlight. Why is sunlight important for *Sargassum*?

In most parts of the ocean, a clump of seaweed would quickly be torn apart by the action of the wind and waves. But there is little wind and wave action in the Sargasso Sea. As a result, *Sargassum* is

ACTIVITY

DOING

That's About the Size of It

1. Using a meterstick, determine the height in meters of each person in your science class (including your teacher). Record your measurements.

2. Using a calculator, add up the heights of all the people in your class (make sure you put the decimal point in the right place!). You have now defined the length of an unofficial unit of measurement known as a bakalian. How many meters long is a bakalian?

3. Giant kelps can be as long as 100 meters. How does the length of a bakalian compare to that of such a kelp plant? How long is a 100-meter kelp plant in bakalians?

able to form enormous floating mats many kilometers long. These mats are home to fishes, crabs, jellyfish, and many other ocean animals. Can you find the crab and the fish hiding among the strands of *Sargassum* in Figure 8–4?

While the Sargasso Sea did not provide an answer to the mysterious disappearance of sailing ships, it did explain a few biological mysteries. One of these mysteries involved the snakelike fishes known as eels. For more than two thousand years, people wondered where eels in the lakes and rivers of Europe came from. No one had ever seen a baby eel. No one had ever seen eels mate or lay eggs. Aristotle, a philosopher and scientist of ancient Greece, thought that eels simply sprang out of the mud. During the eighteenth century, some people thought that eels were formed from the hairs on horses' tails.

It was not until the end of the nineteenth century that the mystery was solved: Adult eels leave the rivers and lakes and travel thousands of kilometers to the Sargasso Sea to mate and lay their eggs. The baby eels, which are leaf-shaped fish that look nothing like adult eels, live for a while among the mats of *Sargassum*. Then, over a period of several years, the baby eels gradually travel back across the ocean to Europe. As they grow, the baby eels slowly change their shape. By the time they reach the mouths of the European rivers and begin swimming upstream, the baby eels have grown up into small adult eels.

Sargassum is not the only kind of brown algae. The kelp that you read about earlier is another type of brown algae. So is the rockweed that grows on rocky coasts. As you can see in Figure 8–6 on page 204, brown algae come in a wide variety of shapes

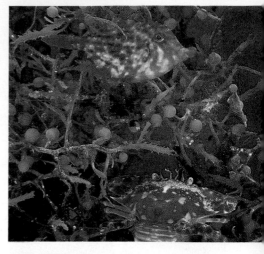

Figure 8–4 *The enormous floating mats of* Sargassum *are home to many animals. The spherical structures on the* Sargassum *are air bladders. What is the function of the air bladders?*

Figure 8–5 *Baby eels spend the first few years of their lives in the Sargasso Sea. Then they travel to the rivers of Europe. On their journey, they take on their adult shape (left) and develop pigments so they are no longer transparent. Silvery-gray adult European eels may wiggle across patches of dry land as they begin their journey back to the Sargasso Sea to breed (right).*

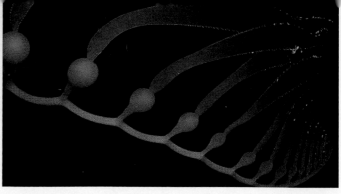

Figure 8–6 *Brown algae come in all shapes and sizes. Can you locate the air bladders on the kelp (top right)?*

and sizes. Most brown algae live in the ocean. Some, like *Sargassum*, float freely. Others, such as kelps and rockweed, are attached to the sea floor.

Brown algae have long been used as food for humans in China, Japan, Canada, Ireland, New Zealand, and many other parts of the world. They can also be used as food for livestock. For example, in some places in Scotland and Ireland, cattle and sheep graze on brown algae at low tide. Chemicals extracted from brown algae (known as algins or alginates) are added to salad dressings and other foods to make them smooth and prevent their ingredients from separating.

Red Algae

Like brown algae, most red algae are multicellular and live in the ocean. Red algae can grow to be several meters long, but they never reach the size of brown algae such as *Sargassum* or giant kelps. The shapes of red algae are just as varied as those of brown algae. Some red algae form clumps of delicate, branching red threads. Others grow in large, rounded, flat sheets. Still others produce hard, stiff branches rich in calcium carbonate (the substance that makes up the shells of foraminifers, corals, snails, and crabs).

Red algae usually grow attached to rocks on the ocean floor. Red algae can be found at depths up to 170 meters—far deeper than other kinds of algae. Very little sunlight penetrates to these extreme depths. Chlorophyll alone cannot absorb enough light energy to allow the food-making process to continue at a life-sustaining level. How, then, do deep-water red algae get the light they need to survive?

The answer involves the accessory pigments that give red algae their characteristic color and their

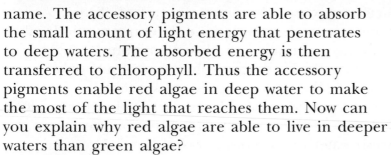

name. The accessory pigments are able to absorb the small amount of light energy that penetrates to deep waters. The absorbed energy is then transferred to chlorophyll. Thus the accessory pigments enable red algae in deep water to make the most of the light that reaches them. Now can you explain why red algae are able to live in deeper waters than green algae?

Red algae are used by humans in a number of ways. Some species are eaten as food. Other species are harvested by the ton and added to soil to make it better for crops. Chemicals extracted from red algae are used to manufacture certain foods. The next time you eat ice cream, use a creamy salad dressing, drink chocolate milk, or frost a cake with ready-made frosting, read the list of ingredients on the package. You may find carrageenan (KAIR-uh-geen-uhn), a substance that comes from red algae, on the list. Another substance derived from red algae is agar (AH-gahr). Agar plays an important role in medical research. It is used to make the jellylike nutrient mixtures on which bacteria and other microorganisms are grown.

Figure 8–7 *Red algae may resemble fingers of transparent red cellophane, dark pink rock formations, or clumps of purplish-black hair.*

ⒶActivity Bank

Seaweed Sweets, p.800

Figure 8–8 *The white streaks on the agar in this petri dish consist of millions of bacteria. Because most microorganisms cannot live on agar alone, nutrients and other substances are added to the agar. In this case, blood has changed the color of the agar from pale yellow to red.*

Green Algae

Deep in space, a silvery ship is in its second year of a four-year journey to study the planets. On board, the astronauts are about to finish dinner. Although they have brought along enough food to last the entire journey, they could not carry enough oxygen to last several years. Are the astronauts doomed to suffocate in space? Of course not.

In a tiny room near the back of the ship sits a tank of water filled with green algae. The green algae use the carbon dioxide exhaled by the astronauts

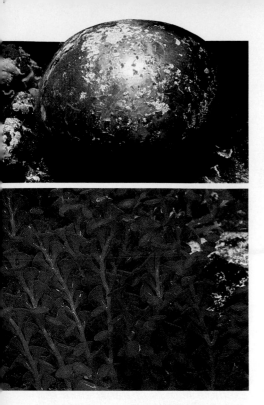

Figure 8–9 *Some green algae look like exotic vines with cone-shaped leaves. Others form enormous green bubbles.*

Figure 8–10 *Hydras are freshwater relatives of jellyfishes and sea anemones. The greenish color of* Chlorohydra *is caused by the hundreds of green algal cells that live within its body. How do the algal cells help their partner?*

to make food. During the food-making process, the algae release oxygen, which the astronauts breathe. If you could look closely at the tank, you would see bubbles of oxygen floating toward the surface. The relationship between the breathing of the astronauts and the food-making process in the algae means that the astronauts and the green algae support each other's lives.

This scene is purely imaginary. However, science fiction may soon become science fact. Today, scientists are hard at work developing methods of growing green algae in closed environments. And someday, future space explorers may rely on algae to maintain the air supply aboard spacecraft.

For now, the only place you can find green algae is here on planet Earth. Most green algae live in fresh water or in moist areas on land. However, some green algae do live in rather unusual places. Several may live in a close partnership with fungi, forming lichens. A few can live in bodies of water many times saltier than the ocean, such as the Great Salt Lake in Utah. And some can live within the bodies of worms, sponges, and protists such as *Paramecium.*

Green algae have life cycles, pigments, and stored food supplies similar to those of complex land plants. These similarities, along with a few others, suggest that land plants evolved from green algae. Of course, modern species of green algae are not the ancestors of land plants. But in the distant past, modern species of land plants and modern species of green algae shared a common ancestor. Because the remains of algae rarely become fossils, it is unlikely that we will ever know exactly what this common ancestor was. But by examining modern species of green algae and using imagination, scientists have developed a pretty good idea of how land plants may have evolved from green algae.

Modern species of green algae that represent important steps in the development of land plants are shown in Figure 8–11. As you can see, the earliest forms of green algae were probably unicellular organisms. Later, colonies consisting of many relatively independent cells developed. The next step on the way to land plants were multicellular green algae that lived in water. After that came multicellular green algae that lived on land. Finally, about 450 to 500 million years ago, algaelike land plants evolved from green algae ancestors. One group of early land plants evolved into mosses and their relatives. Another group evolved into ferns and other more complex land plants.

Figure 8–11 *By studying modern forms of green algae, scientists have been able to reconstruct the basic stages of the evolution of plants. Unicellular algae, such as Chlamydomonas (top left), gave rise to colonial algae such as Volvox (bottom left). Colonial algae gave rise to simple multicellular algae such as Ulva (top right), which in turn gave rise to more complex multicellular forms (bottom right). What was the next big step in the evolution of land plants from algae?*

8–1 Section Review

1. Compare the three phyla of algae.
2. Why can red algae survive in deeper water than other kinds of algae can?
3. Why are brown algae important to humans?
4. How are green algae related to land plants?

Connection—*Social Studies*

5. On his first voyage to the New World, Christopher Columbus had a lot of trouble with sailors who wanted to turn back. Some historians think that the sailors were afraid of falling off the edge of the world. Other historians disagree. Explain how brown algae may have played a part in the near-mutiny of Columbus's sailors.

8–2 Plants Move Onto Land: Mosses, Liverworts, and Hornworts

In the ocean, a kelp plant may stand as tall as a very large tree. Its leaves are held up by the water so that they are exposed to enough light. Kelp absorbs water, carbon dioxide, minerals, and all the other substances it needs from ocean water. It reproduces by releasing egg cells and sperm cells into the water, where the sperm cells can swim to the eggs and fertilize them.

Now imagine that the same kelp plant is taken from the water and planted on land. Can the plant stand upright and hold up its leaves? Can it absorb minerals and water from the new substance (air) that surrounds it? Can its sperm cells swim on dry land? Can the kelp plant survive on land? The answer to all of these questions is no.

As the example of the kelp plant indicates, it is not easy for aquatic organisms to live on dry land. The plants that invaded the land millions of years

Figure 8–12 *The first forests appeared on Earth more than 380 million years ago. Unlike the forests of today, these ancient forests were dominated by plants without seeds. What adaptations did plants require in order to successfully invade the land?*

ago had to evolve in ways that made them better suited to meet the challenges of their new environment. Let's look at some of the tasks that plants need to perform in order to survive on land.

Land plants need to support the leaves and other parts of the body so that they do not collapse. Supporting structures enable land plants to position the parts of their body that make food so that they are exposed to as much sunlight as possible.

Land plants need to obtain water and minerals. In an aquatic environment, plants are surrounded by water and dissolved minerals. On land, however, water and minerals are located in the soil.

Land plants need to transport food, water, minerals, and other materials from one part of the body to another. In general, water and minerals are taken up by the bottom part of a land plant and food is made in the top part. To supply all the cells of the body with the substances they need, water and minerals must be transported to the top part of the plant and food must be transported to the bottom part.

Land plants need to prevent excess water loss to the environment. Because air contains less water

than body cells, the body cells of land organisms tend to lose water. (Have you ever noticed how a puddle of rainwater on a sidewalk gradually shrinks and then disappears? This happens because there is a greater concentration of water in the puddle than in the air, and the water evaporates. The same basic principle applies to living cells.) To avoid drying up, land organisms need ways of minimizing water loss.

Land plants need to get sperm cells and egg cells together so that reproduction can occur. Sperm cells need water in order to swim and to fertilize egg cells.

Now that you know what the necessary tasks are, let's look at the ways in which mosses, liverworts, and hornworts accomplish these tasks. As you read about mosses and their relatives, you may want to refer to Figure 8–13 to see what these plants look like.

Mosses, liverworts, and hornworts are tiny plants that live in moist places. They can be found on wet rocks, damp tree bark, and the muddy banks of ponds and streams. In some places, such as bogs and forests, they may cover the ground like a fuzzy green carpet. Because they are small and live in places where water is plentiful, they have few special adaptations for dealing with the challenges of life on

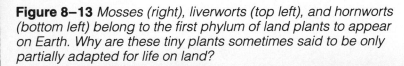

Figure 8–13 *Mosses (right), liverworts (top left), and hornworts (bottom left) belong to the first phylum of land plants to appear on Earth. Why are these tiny plants sometimes said to be only partially adapted for life on land?*

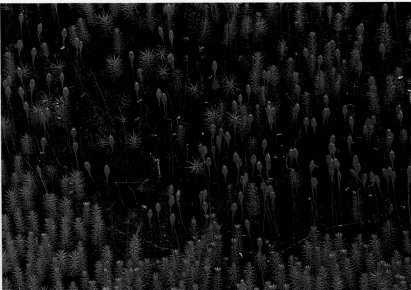

Figure 8–14 *At one stage in their life cycles, mosses produce many dustlike spores. If a spore lands in a place with favorable growing conditions, it will grow into a new leafy green moss plant.*

land. (This is quite different from the more complex plants you will read about later, which have many adaptations for survival on land.) You can think of mosses and their relatives as representing one solution to the problems of living on land: avoiding the most difficult challenges.

Because they are small and low to the ground, these plants do not need sturdy stems or other special supporting structures. The stiff, rigid cell walls that surround their cells provide all the support they need. Their small size also means that they do not need a special system to transport materials throughout their body. They can simply transfer materials from one cell to the next. This method of transport does not allow materials to be carried very far or very efficiently—but it is good enough for a very small plant.

Because the places in which they live are quite moist, mosses, liverworts, and hornworts do not need an adaptation to prevent water loss, such as a waxy covering. However, the reproductive cells that develop into new plants often have a thick, watertight coat. This enables the reproductive cells to survive dry periods. The moist conditions in their environment make it possible for mosses and their relatives to carry out certain life functions as if they lived in water. For example, these plants absorb water and minerals through their entire body surface. And their sperm cells swim to the egg cells when the body of the plant is covered with rainwater or dew.

ACTIVITY

THINKING

Moss-Grown Expressions

Consider these two old sayings:

1. A rolling stone gathers no moss.

2. Moss grows on the north side of a tree.

Do you think there is any truth to either of these sayings? Why or why not?

Figure 8–15 *In Washington State's Olympic National Park, mosses thrive in the cool, extremely damp Hoh Rain Forest. There, the mosses cover the trees like shaggy green coats (top). In most other forests, mosses do not cover the trees but may form a soft carpet on the forest floor (bottom).*

Although mosses are not particularly impressive plants, they are quite useful to humans. Certain Japanese-style gardens feature gently curving mounds of soil covered with a plush layer of emerald green moss. At least one modern artist has created living patchwork quilts of mosses. Dried sphagnum (SFAG-nuhm) moss is added to garden soil to enrich the soil and improve its ability to retain water. Sphagnum moss also changes the chemical balance in the soil so that the soil is better for growing certain plants, such as azaleas and rhododendrons. Ground-up sphagnum moss is added to soil and sprinkled around seedlings to help prevent the growth of certain disease-causing bacteria and fungi. In the past, people have used sphagnum moss to treat burns and bruises and to bandage wounds. Can you explain why sphagnum moss may have been a good substance for covering a wound?

Over the course of hundreds of years, layer after layer of sphagnum moss and other plants may accumulate at the bottom of a bog or swamp. Under the right conditions, the deposits of dead plants form a substance called peat. Peat is used as a soil conditioner. It is also dried and used as fuel. Because the conditions in peat bogs greatly slow the process of decay, scientists who study ancient civilizations have found many interesting things within the deposits of peat—including the lifelike body of a man who was buried about 2000 years ago.

8–2 Section Review

1. List five tasks that plants need to perform in order to live on land.
2. How are mosses and their relatives adapted for life on land?
3. What are three ways in which humans use mosses?

Critical Thinking—*Relating Cause and Effect*
4. Explain why mosses and their relatives never grow very large.

8–3 Vascular Plants Develop: Ferns

Guide for Reading

Focus on this question as you read.

▶ *How are ferns different from other kinds of plants without seeds?*

How would you like to be able to make yourself invisible? Sound like fun? Well, folklore has it that all you have to do is gather fern seed by the light of the moon at midnight on Saint John's Eve. Carrying some fern seed so gathered is guaranteed to make you invisible to human eyes.

But before you go off into the woods on a midsummer night to look for ferns, you should know there is a catch. Like the algae, mosses, liverworts, and hornworts you read about earlier, ferns do not have seeds.

Unlike the other seedless plants you read about in this chapter, however, ferns do have a number of special adaptations to life on land. For example, they have a waxy covering on their leaves that helps to prevent water loss and roots that enable them to gather water and minerals from the soil. The most important adaptations, however, involve a system of tiny tubes that transport food, water, and other materials throughout the body of the fern. These tiny tubes are known as vascular tissue. **Because they have vascular tissue, ferns are said to be vascular plants.** Plants that lack vascular tissue—such as algae and mosses—are known as **nonvascular plants.**

The first **vascular plants,** which appeared about 400 million years ago, represent a major step in plant evolution. Vascular plants, such as ferns, are much better adapted to life on land than nonvascular plants. Vascular tissue allows materials to be

Figure 8–16 *Ferns do not have seeds. The dots or lines visible on the underside of fern leaves are formed by clusters of spore cases (left). As this 200-million-year-old fossil indicates, ferns are among the most ancient types of vascular plants (right).*

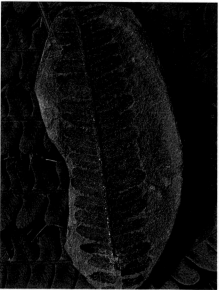

Figure 8–17 *Vascular plants without seeds include horsetails (left) and club mosses such as the peacock "fern" (right). They also include ferns.*

transported quickly and effectively throughout the body of a plant. In addition, the type of vascular tissue that carries water from the roots in the soil to the leaves in the air is made of cells that have extremely thick, strong cell walls. These sturdy cell walls greatly strengthen the stems. Now can you explain why vascular plants can grow much larger than nonvascular plants?

Thanks to their vascular tissue, ferns can grow much taller than mosses and their relatives. In the mainland United States, most ferns range in height from a few centimeters to about a meter. Tree ferns, which grow in rain forests in Hawaii, the Caribbean, and other tropical areas, can be enormous. If laid along the ground, the tallest tree fern would extend from the pitcher to the batter on a baseball diamond, or from the foul line to the pins in a bowling lane.

Figure 8–18 *A close examination of this tree fern leaf reveals that it is divided into smaller leaflike parts, which in turn are divided into still smaller leaflike parts. A few ferns have leaves that are not at all fernlike. For example, the water fern* Marsilea *has rounded leaves that make it look like a four-leaf clover.*

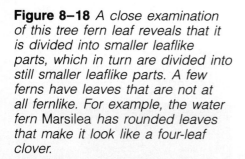

Like other vascular plants, ferns have true leaves, stems, and roots. As you can see in Figure 8–18, the leaf of a fern is often divided into many smaller parts that look like miniature leaves. In many types of ferns, the developing leaves are curled at the top and look much like the top of a violin. Because of their appearance, these developing leaves are called fiddleheads. As they mature, the fiddleheads uncurl until they reach their full size.

People often mistake the sticklike central portion of a fern leaf for a stem. This is quite understandable when you realize that the stems of most ferns are hidden from view. In some ferns, the stems look like fuzzy brown strands of yarn lying on the ground. The stems are hidden by the feathery fern leaves that emerge from them. In other ferns, the stems run below the surface of the soil.

If you were to pull part of a fern's stem from the ground, you would discover clumps of wiry structures growing down from the stem here and there. These structures are the fern's roots. The roots anchor the fern to the ground. They also absorb water and minerals for the plant.

Although ferns are much better adapted to life on land than other nonvascular plants, they are not fully adapted. Take a moment now to look back at the list of tasks that plants need to perform in order to survive on land (pages 209–210). How do ferns accomplish each task? Can you guess for which task ferns require a watery environment? That's right: Ferns need standing water in order for their sperm cells to swim to their egg cells. Like other plants without seeds, they need an abundant supply of water in order to reproduce.

Ferns are useful to humans in a number of ways. Because ferns have lovely, interestingly shaped leaves and thrive in places that have little sunlight, they are popular houseplants. Products from ferns are often used to grow other kinds of houseplants. For example, orchids may be grown on the tangled masses of fern roots or on fibrous chunks of tree-fern stems. Ferns may also assist in the growth of crops. In southeast Asia, farmers grow a small aquatic fern in rice fields. Tiny pockets in the fern's leaves provide a home for special blue-green bacteria that produce a natural fertilizer. Thus the fern and its microscopic

Figure 8–19 *The developing leaves of most ferns are tightly coiled. This makes them look like the scroll at the top of a violin. What are these developing fern leaves called?*

ACTIVITY
READING

The Secret of the Red Fern

What would you expect a book called *Where the Red Fern Grows* to be about? No, this wonderful book by Wilson Rawls is not about ferns and where they can be found. However, the red fern plays a small but important part in this story. What is the meaning of the red fern? Why does the author include it in this story? Read, and find out.

Figure 8–20 *Ferns are valued ornamental plants. The* Dipteris *fern has paired leaves that look like lacy wings (top right). The leaves of maidenhair ferns are divided into many small, dainty leaflike parts (bottom right). A young leaf from a Sri Lankan fern is a beautiful red color when it first uncoils (bottom left). Ferns may also be valued for reasons other than their beauty. For example, the tiny water fern* Azolla *(top left) helps to fertilize rice fields.*

partner help the farmers to grow food. Some ferns are eaten directly as food. During the spring, edible (fit to be eaten) fern fiddleheads may be sold in specialty food shops, supermarkets, and roadside vegetable stands. When properly cooked, fiddleheads make a delicious vegetable dish. However, unless you are absolutely certain which ferns are edible, you should not gather fiddleheads for food.

8–3 Section Review

1. What is the most important difference between ferns and the other plants without seeds that you studied in previous sections?
2. Describe the structure of a typical fern.
3. How are ferns adapted to life on land?

Critical Thinking—*Designing an Experiment*
4. Design a series of experiments to determine the best conditions for growing ferns.

CONNECTIONS

I Scream, You Scream, We All Scream for Ice Cream

You know that *ice cream* is sweet, cold, soft, and creamy—a wonderful treat. But did you know that you can learn a lot about *physical science* by studying ice cream? That's right—ice cream can be the key to understanding many scientific principles.

Consider for a moment the stuff ice cream is made of: milk and cream, sugar, water, a dash of flavoring, and perhaps a pinch of agar or gelatin. Blended together, these ingredients form a syrupy liquid. This liquid mix is transformed into a solid dessert by removing heat energy—that is, by freezing it. And this illustrates an important science concept: The form, or phase, of matter can be changed by adding or taking away energy.

But heat energy does not simply vanish. It has to go somewhere. (Scientists know this principle as the first law of thermodynamics.) In a home ice-cream maker, the heat energy is taken up by a mixture of ice and rock salt. Because nature tends to work to even things out (scientists call this principle the second law of thermodynamics), heat energy is transferred from the ice-cream mix, which has more heat energy,

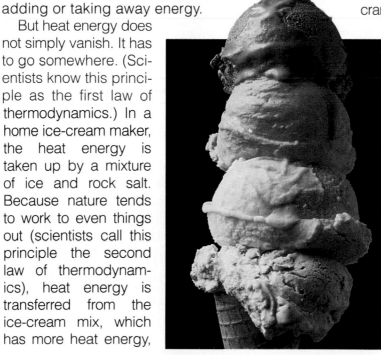

to the mixture of ice and rock salt, which has less heat energy.

Have you ever tried to restore a dish of melted ice cream by putting it into the freezer? If you have, you know that the resulting frozen substance is hard and unappetizing—more like ice than ice cream. Why? One of the most important ingredients of ice cream is air. Turning the crank on a home ice-cream maker stirs air into the mix (as well as helps the mix cool evenly). Tiny bubbles of air about 0.1 mm across make ice cream soft.

Ice cream plants use a similar process, but on a much larger scale. For example, large fanlike blades replace the hand crank. Spinning at high speed, the blades whip an enormous amount of air bubbles into the frozen mix, causing its volume (amount of space an object takes up) to increase. The increase in volume is what makes ice cream soft. If air bubbles were not added to your favorite flavor of ice cream, eating a spoonful of it would be like eating a sweetened ice cube—hardly a wonderful treat!

Laboratory Investigation

Comparing Algae, Mosses, and Ferns

Problem

How are algae, mosses, and ferns similar? How are they different?

Materials *(per group)*

3 glass slides
3 coverslips
medicine dropper
microscope
hand lens
metric ruler
scissors
brown alga plant
moss plant
fern plant

Procedure 🔬 ⬛

1. Examine the brown alga carefully. Use the hand lens to get a closer look at the plant.

2. Draw a diagram of the alga on a sheet of unlined paper. Try to be as neat, accurate, and realistic as you can.

3. Next to your diagram, write down your observations about the color, texture, flexibility, and any other characteristics of the plant that you think interesting or important.

4. Using the metric ruler, measure the length and width of the entire plant. You should also measure any parts of the plant that you think appropriate. Write these measurements on or next to the appropriate part of your diagram.

5. Using the scissors, carefully cut a piece about 5 mm long from the tip of a "leaf" on the plant.

6. Place the plant piece in the center of a glass slide. With the medicine dropper, place a drop of water on the plant piece. Cover with a coverslip.

7. Examine the plant piece under the low- and high-powers of the microscope. Draw a diagram of what you observe.

8. Examine the moss plant using the procedure outlined in steps 1 through 7.

9. Examine the fern plant using the procedure outlined in steps 1 through 7.

Observations

1. What are the dimensions of the alga, moss, and fern?

2. Which land plant grows larger—the moss or the fern?

3. Which plant has vascular tissue? How can you tell?

4. How do the top and bottom surfaces of the fern leaf differ from each other?

Analysis and Conclusions

1. Why is the fern able to grow larger than the moss?

2. What alga structures appear to be adaptations to life in water? Explain.

3. Why is one side of the fern leaf shinier than the other? How is this an adaptation to life on land?

4. How are the plants similar?

5. How are the plants different?

6. **On Your Own** Examine a liverwort, green alga, and/or red alga. How do these plants compare to the ones you examined in this investigation? How are they adapted to the places in which they live?

Study Guide

Summarizing Key Concepts

8–1 Plants Appear: Multicellular Algae

▲ Algae are nonvascular plantlike autotrophs that use sunlight to produce food. Algae do not have true roots, stems, or leaves.

▲ The algae that are classified as plants are divided into three phyla: brown algae, red algae, and green algae.

▲ Algae were the first kinds of plants to appear on Earth.

▲ Algae must live in or near a source of water in order to survive.

▲ Chlorophyll captures light energy so that it can be used in the food-making process.

▲ Accessory pigments absorb light energy and then transfer it to chlorophyll.

▲ Algae are useful to humans in many ways.

▲ Land plants evolved from green algae.

8–2 Plants Move Onto Land: Mosses, Liverworts, and Hornworts

▲ Adaptations of plants for living on land include structures for support, roots, vascular tissue, structures for minimizing water loss, and methods of reproduction that do not require standing water.

▲ Mosses, liverworts, and hornworts are small nonvascular plants that live in moist places. They are not fully adapted for life on land.

8–3 Vascular Plants Develop: Ferns

▲ Vascular plants, such as ferns, are much better adapted to life on land than nonvascular plants.

▲ Vascular tissue, a system of tiny tubes within vascular plants, allows food, water, and other materials to be transported quickly and effectively throughout the body of a plant.

▲ Water-conducting vascular tissue helps to strengthen and support stems.

▲ Vascular plants have true roots, stems, and leaves.

▲ Ferns are one of the earliest types of vascular plants. Although ferns have many adaptations to life on land, they are still dependent on standing water for reproduction.

Reviewing Key Terms

Define each term in a complete sentence.

8–1 Plants Appear: Multicellular Algae
alga
brown alga
red alga
green alga
pigment

8–3 Vascular Plants Develop: Ferns
nonvascular plant
vascular plant

Chapter Review

Content Review

Multiple Choice

Choose the letter of the answer that best completes each statement.

1. Which of these is a vascular plant?
   a. moss   c. *Sargassum*
   b. hornwort   d. fern
2. The most important characteristic in the classification of multicellular algae and their close relatives is the
   a. structure of the leaves.
   b. type of pigments present.
   c. method of producing or obtaining food.
   d. presence or absence of a nucleus.
3. The first kinds of plants to invade the land were probably
   a. algae.   c. mosses.
   b. ferns.   d. liverworts.
4. Ferns have
   a. simple seeds.
   b. no special adaptations for life on land.
   c. true roots, stems, and leaves.
   d. all of these.

5. Most agar comes from
   a. mosses.   c. red algae.
   b. ferns.   d. green algae.
6. If they existed today, the ancestors of land plants would probably be classified as
   a. ferns.   c. brown algae.
   b. red algae.   d. green algae.
7. All ferns, green algae, and mosses
   a. live only in water.
   b. are multicellular.
   c. lack vascular tissue.
   d. contain chlorophyll.
8. Mosses, liverworts, and hornworts
   a. rely on air bladders for support.
   b. can grow as tall as 60 meters.
   c. have true roots, stems, and leaves.
   d. require abundant water for reproduction.

True or False

If the statement is true, write "true." If it is false, change the underlined word or words to make the statement true.

1. *Sargassum* is a type of <u>red algae</u>.
2. Plants without seeds have methods of reproduction that <u>require</u> standing water.
3. In your textbook, <u>all</u> algae are classified as plants.
4. Mosses and their relatives have <u>few</u> special adaptations for life on land.
5. Red and brown algae <u>do not contain</u> chlorophyll.
6. The young leaves of <u>liverworts</u> are known as fiddleheads.
7. In the food-making process, plants <u>take in oxygen and release carbon dioxide</u>.
8. Ferns are <u>nonvascular</u> plants.

Concept Mapping

Complete the following concept map for Section 8–1. Then construct a concept map for the entire chapter.

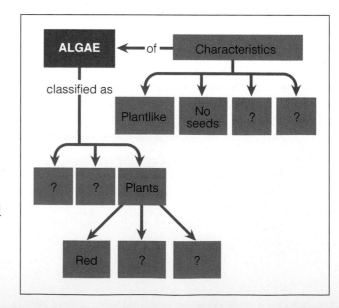

Concept Mastery

Discuss each of the following in a brief paragraph.

1. What are pigments? Why are pigments important to plants?
2. Describe a current or potential use for green algae, red algae, brown algae, mosses, and ferns.
3. How do mosses and their relatives perform the tasks necessary for life on land?
4. How do ferns perform the tasks necessary for life on land?
5. Why can vascular plants grow so much larger than nonvascular plants?
6. What is vascular tissue? Explain why the development of vascular tissue was an important step in the evolution of plants.

Critical Thinking and Problem Solving

Use the skills you have developed in this chapter to answer each of the following.

1. **Making comparisons** How are red, brown, and green algae similar? How are they different?
2. **Applying concepts** A friend tells you that he has seen mosses that were 2 meters tall. Is your friend mistaken? Explain why or why not.
3. **Relating facts** Why do most algae live in shallow water or float on the surface of the water?
4. **Applying concepts** Why can ferns live in drier areas than mosses?
5. **Classifying objects** Examine the accompanying photograph of a plant without seeds. What kind of plant do you think it is? Why? How would you go about confirming your identification?
6. **Using the writing process** Now it's your turn to try being a science teacher. Prepare an outline for a lesson on one of the plants you learned about in this chapter. Your lesson should include an aim, or goal. (For example, the aim of a lesson on classification might be "What are the five kingdoms of living things?") Write a five-question fill-in-the-blank quiz to accompany your lesson and to test whether you have accomplished your aim.

Plants With Seeds

9

Guide for Reading

After you read the following sections, you will be able to

9–1 Structure of Seed Plants
- Describe the structure of roots, stems, and leaves.
- Give the general equation for photosynthesis.

9–2 Reproduction in Seed Plants
- Discuss the events leading up to the formation of a seed.

9–3 Gymnosperms and Angiosperms
- Describe the four phyla of gymnosperms.
- Describe the structure of a typical flower.

9–4 Patterns of Growth
- Classify plants according to how long it takes them to produce flowers and how long they live.
- Describe some basic ways in which plants grow in response to their environment.

Spotted, striped, or solid-colored; double or single; magenta, pink, scarlet, orange, peach, or white—the brightly colored flowers of the impatiens plant are a familiar sight in suburban gardens and in city window boxes and planters.

Look carefully at the impatiens flowers in the photograph. Can you see a tiny green structure in the center of each flower? After the flower fades and its petals fall off, this structure begins to lengthen, swell, and change color from dark green to a pale yellowish green. Eventually, it is round with a tapered tip and has grooves that run along its length.

Touching the fully grown structure has some startling results. The structure pops off the stem, bursts, and sprays tiny brown objects in all directions. These brown objects are the impatiens's seeds.

Impatiens are just one kind of plant with seeds. What are some other plants with seeds? What do they look like? Where are they found? And why are seeds considered such an important development in plant evolution? Read on to find the answers to these and other questions.

Journal *Activity*

You and Your World Do you remember when you first learned that plants grow from seeds? When you were very young, did you ever plant seeds and watch them grow? In your journal, write about one of your earliest experiences with seeds.

◄ *The tiny green structure in the center of impatiens flowers develops into a seed pod. When ripe, the seed pod bursts open and scatters the seeds within it.*

9–1 Structure of Seed Plants

Seed plants are among the most numerous plants on Earth. They are also the plants with which most people are familiar. The tomatoes and watermelons in a garden, the pine and oak trees in a forest, and the cotton and wheat plants in a field are all examples of seed plants. What other seed plants can you name?

Seed plants are vascular plants that produce seeds. Recall from Chapter 8 that vascular plants have vascular tissue. Vascular tissue forms a system of tiny tubes that transport water, food, and other materials throughout the body of a plant. There are two types of vascular tissue: **xylem** (ZIGH-luhm) and **phloem** (FLOH-ehm). Xylem carries water and minerals from the roots up through the plant. Because xylem cells have thick cell walls, they also help to support the plant. Phloem carries food throughout the plant. Unlike xylem cells, which carry water and minerals upward only, phloem cells carry materials both upward and downward.

Like all vascular plants, seed plants have true **roots, stems,** and **leaves.** It might be helpful for you to review the adaptations that plants need to survive on land, which are found on pages 209–210. Keep these basic adaptations in mind as you read about roots, stems, and leaves in seed plants.

Figure 9–1 *Plants with seeds come in a wide variety of shapes and sizes. Grasses, orchids, and Douglas firs are all plants with seeds.*

Roots

Roots anchor a plant in the ground and absorb water and minerals from the soil. Roots also store food for plants.

The root systems of plants follow two basic plans: fibrous roots and taproots. Fibrous roots consist of several main roots that branch repeatedly to form a tangled mass of thin roots. Grass, corn, and most trees have fibrous root systems. Taproot systems consist of a long, thick main root (the taproot) and thin, branching roots that extend out of the taproot. Carrots, cacti, and dandelions are examples of plants with taproots.

Have you ever pulled up weeds? If so, you might have noticed that weeds with fibrous roots, such as crabgrass, tend to take a big chunk of soil with them when they are pulled up. Weeds with taproots, such as dandelions, tend to be difficult to pull out of the ground. How does the structure of root systems cause these two problems in weeding?

Refer to Figure 9–2 on page 226 as you read about the structure of a typical root. The outermost layer of the root is called the epidermis (ehp-ih-DER-mihs). The term epidermis (*epi-* means upon; *dermis* means skin) is used to refer to the outermost cell layer of just about any multicellular living thing, including plants, worms, fishes, and humans.

The outer surfaces of the cells of a root's epidermis have many thin, hairlike extensions. These extensions are known as root hairs. The root hairs greatly increase the surface area through which the plant takes in water and minerals from the soil. The water and minerals that are taken up by the root hairs pass into the next layer of the root, the cortex. In many plants, the cells of the cortex store food. They also carry water and dissolved minerals into the center of the root, which is made of vascular tissue, that is, cells of xylem and phloem.

As you can see in Figure 9–2, the very tip of the root is covered by a structure called the root cap. The root cap protects the tip of the root as it grows through the soil. Just behind the root cap is a region that contains growth tissue. This is where new cells are formed.

ACTIVITY

DISCOVERING

Fit to Be Dyed

1. Fill a medium-sized jar one-fourth full of water. Then add a few drops of food coloring and stir. **Note:** *Be careful when using dyes, as they can stain.*

2. Place a stalk of celery in the jar so that its leaves are at the top and its base is at the bottom. Only the base should be submerged in the colored water.

3. Place the jar where it will not be disturbed. After 24 hours, examine your stalk of celery. What do you observe?

4. Remove the stalk of celery from the jar. Using a knife, cut off the portion of the stalk that was under water. Be very careful when using a knife. Discard this portion.

5. Examine the base of the stalk. What do you observe? Why does this occur?

■ Florists sometimes sell red, white, and blue carnations for the Fourth of July and other celebrations. Carnations do not naturally occur in this color combination. How do florists color the carnations without painting them?

■ Obtain a white carnation and test your hypothesis.

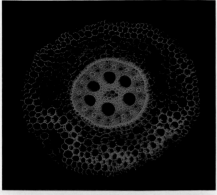

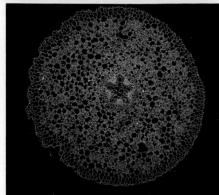

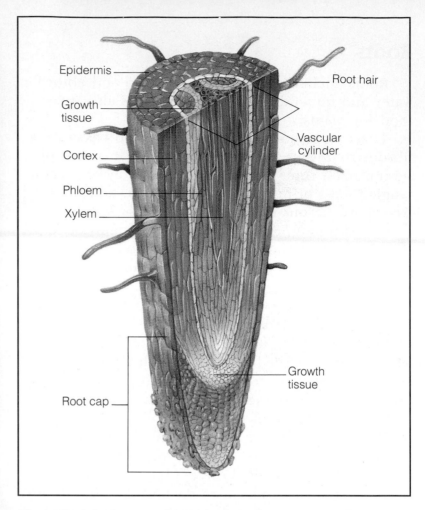

Epidermis

Growth tissue

Cortex

Phloem

Xylem

Root cap

Root hair

Vascular cylinder

Growth tissue

Figure 9–2 *In the root of a buttercup, phloem is located between the arms of a xylem "star" (center left). In the root of a corn plant, yellow circles of xylem alternate with reddish bundles of phloem (top left). Root hairs make this radish sprout look fuzzy (bottom left). What are the functions of the major root structures shown in the diagram?*

For thousands of years, people have used roots in many different ways. Some roots are used for food. Carrots, beets, yams, and turnips are among the many roots that are eaten. The root of the cassava plant is used to make tapioca, which may be familiar to you as the small, starchy lumps in certain kinds of puddings and baby food. Marshmallows were originally candies made from the root of the marsh mallow plant. (Modern marshmallows are made out of sugar, cornstarch, egg white, and gelatin.) Roasted chicory and dandelion roots are used as substitutes for coffee. Some roots—licorice, horseradish, and sassafras, for example—are used as spices. Roots are also used to make substances other than food, such as medicines, dyes, and insecticides.

▶ Roots emerge from the branches of banyans and grow down to the ground. These roots eventually thicken into new trunks, and the banyan continues to spread outward.

▲ Thick, sturdy roots that spread out on the surface of the ground form a stable base for certain giant tropical trees.

◀ Tiny roots that emerge from the stems of philodendrons help these plants to climb walls, tree trunks, and other supporting structures.

▲ The mangrove's spreading roots, which look rather like stilts, trap dead leaves and other debris and help create more soil for the plant.

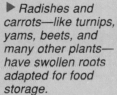

▶ Radishes and carrots—like turnips, yams, beets, and many other plants—have swollen roots adapted for food storage.

Figure 9–3 *Specialized roots*

Stems

Stems provide the means by which water, minerals, and food are transported between the roots and the leaves of a plant. Stems are able to perform this function because they contain xylem and phloem tissue. Stems also hold the leaves of a plant up in the air, thus enabling the leaves to receive sunlight and make food.

Plant stems vary greatly in size and shape. The trunk, branches, and twigs of a tree are all stems. Some plants, such as the strange-looking baobab (BAY-oh-bab) in Figure 9–4 on page 228, have enormous stems that are many meters tall. As you can see, the trunk of the baobab is the most noticeable part of the plant. Other plants, such as the cabbage,

Figure 9–4 *Huge, fat stems and stubby branches make baobab trees look like creatures from another planet. The rectangular patches on the left-hand baobab are places where its bark has been harvested for rope-making.*

Figure 9–5 *Plants bring much color to the world. In spring and summer, flowers such as lupines brighten fields and gardens (bottom). In autumn, the leaves of plants such as the maple turn red and orange (top). Which of these plants is woody? Which is herbaceous?*

have very short stems. The stem of a cabbage is a tough, cone-shaped core that is hidden beneath tightly closed leaves.

Plants may be classified into two groups based on the structure of their stems: herbaceous (her-BAY-shuhs) and woody. Herbaceous plants have stems that are green and soft. Sunflowers, peas, dandelions, grass, and tomatoes are examples of herbaceous plants. As you might expect, woody plants have stems that contain wood. Wood, as de-fined by plant biologists, is a hard substance made of the layers of xylem that form when a stem grows thicker. Unlike herbaceous stems, woody stems are rigid and quite strong. Roses, maples, and firs are woody plants. What other woody plants can you name?

The structure of a woody stem is shown in Figure 9–6. The outermost layer of the stem is the bark. The outer bark, which is tough and water-proof, helps to protect the fragile tissues beneath it. The innermost part of the bark is the phloem. What is the function of phloem?

The next layer of the stem is called the vascular cambium. The vascular cambium is a growth region of a stem, for it is here that xylem and phloem are produced. The center of the stem is called the pith. It contains large, thin-walled cells that store water and food.

If you were to cut through the stem of certain woody plants, a pattern of rings-within-rings that looks somewhat like a target might be visible. See Figure 9–7. These tree rings are made of xylem.

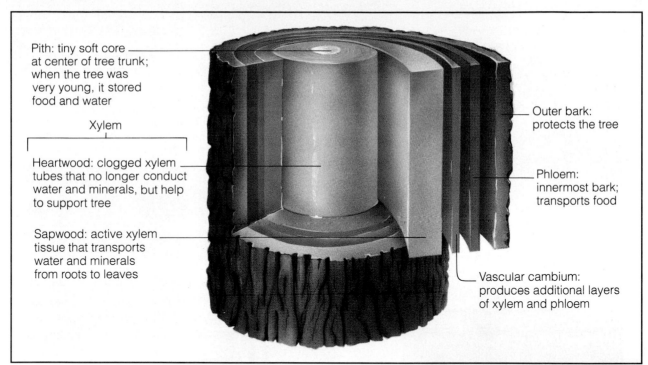

Pith: tiny soft core at center of tree trunk; when the tree was very young, it stored food and water

Xylem

Heartwood: clogged xylem tubes that no longer conduct water and minerals, but help to support tree

Sapwood: active xylem tissue that transports water and minerals from roots to leaves

Outer bark: protects the tree

Phloem: innermost bark; transports food

Vascular cambium: produces additional layers of xylem and phloem

A tree develops rings only if it grows at different rates during the different seasons of the year. For example, many trees in the northern part of the United States grow very little (if at all) in autumn and winter, when the weather is quite cold. They grow rapidly in spring, when it is warm and rainy. And they grow slowly in summer, when it is hot and dry. As a tree grows, a new layer of xylem forms around the old layers. What layer in the stem produces the new xylem cells?

The xylem cells formed in the spring are large and have thin walls. They produce a light brown ring. The xylem cells formed in the summer are small and have thick walls. They produce a dark brown ring. Each pair of light and dark rings represents a year in the life of a tree. How old is a tree with 14 light rings and 14 dark rings?

One of the most important and widely used products of plant stems is wood. Wood is used to

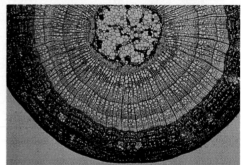

Figure 9–6 *The diagram shows the layers in the stem of a typical tree. The young basswood stem clearly shows its structure. Where is the pith? The vascular cambium? How old is the basswood stem?*

Figure 9–7 *Tree rings can tell you more than just the age of a tree. The spacing and thickness of the rings provide information about weather conditions in the area over time. Thick rings that are far apart indicate years in which conditions were favorable for tree growth—years of much rain. What was the weather like for the first seven years of this larch tree's life? For the last seven years?*

▲ Long stems that run along the surface of the ground allow morning glories to spread into new areas.

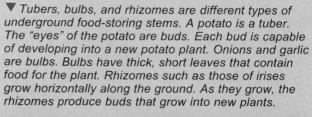

▼ Tubers, bulbs, and rhizomes are different types of underground food-storing stems. A potato is a tuber. The "eyes" of the potato are buds. Each bud is capable of developing into a new potato plant. Onions and garlic are bulbs. Bulbs have thick, short leaves that contain food for the plant. Rhizomes such as those of irises grow horizontally along the ground. As they grow, the rhizomes produce buds that grow into new plants.

▲ The thick green stem of a cactus stores water.

Figure 9–8 *Specialized stems*

make a variety of objects ranging from toothpicks to buildings. Ground-up wood is used to make paper. Can you think of some other uses of wood?

Some stems—such as potatoes, onions, ginger, and sugar cane—are a source of food. Other stems are used to make dyes and medicines. Still others have more uncommon uses. For example, the long, flexible stems of certain trees and vines are woven together to make wicker furniture and baskets. And fibers from the stems of flax plants are used to make linen fabric.

Leaves

Plant leaves vary greatly in shape and size. For example, birch trees have oval leaves with jagged edges. Pines, firs, and balsams have needle-shaped leaves. And maples and oaks have flat, wide leaves. Most leaves have a stalk and a blade. The stalk connects the leaf to the stem; the blade is the thin, flat part of the leaf. The thin, flat shape of most leaves exposes a large amount of surface area to sunlight.

Leaves are classified as either simple or compound, depending on the structure of the blade. A simple leaf has a blade that is in one piece. Maple, oak, and apple trees have simple leaves. A compound leaf has a blade that is divided into a number of separate, leaflike parts. Roses, clover, and palms have compound leaves. Can you name some plants that have simple leaves? Compound leaves?

No matter what their shape, leaves are important structures. For it is in the leaves that the sun's energy is captured and used to produce food.

Up to this point, we have been referring to the process in which light energy is used to make food simply as the food-making process. But this important process has its own special name: **photosynthesis** (foht-oh-SIHN-thuh-sihs). The word photosynthesis comes from the root words *photo*, which means light,

Activity Bank

The Ins and Outs of Photosynthesis, p. 801

Figure 9–9 *An anthurium "flower" actually consists of a stalk of tiny flowers and a large, waxy red leaf (left). The natural holes in the large leaves of the monstera help prevent the plant from being damaged by the wind and heavy rains in its rain-forest home (center left). The leaves of croton (center right) and cassava (top right) plants are beautifully colored. The leaves of the sensitive plant fold up when they are touched (bottom right). Which of these leaves are simple? Which are compound?*

Figure 9–10 *Plants use the energy of sunlight to make food. The process that uses sunlight, water, and carbon dioxide to make food and oxygen is called photosynthesis.*

ACTIVITY

CALCULATING

It Starts to Add Up

Use a calculator to answer the following questions about an apple tree that has 200,000 leaves, each of which has a surface area of 20 cm².

1. What is the total leaf surface area of the tree?

2. The lower surface of each leaf contains 25,000 stomata per cm². How many stomata are on the lower surface of a single leaf? Assuming that the stomata are found only on the lower surface of the leaves, how many stomata are on the tree?

3. In a single summer, each leaf loses about 86 mL of water through transpiration. How much water is transpired by the entire tree?

and *synthesis,* which means to put together. Can you see why this name is appropriate?

Photosynthesis is the process in which food is synthesized using light energy. Photosynthesis is the largest and most important manufacturing process in the world. It is also one of the most complex. Let's take a closer look at this amazing process.

In photosynthesis, the sun's light energy is captured by chlorophyll, which is the green pigment you read about in Chapter 8. Through a complex series of chemical reactions (which will not be discussed here), the light energy is used to combine water from the soil with carbon dioxide from the air. One of the products of the chemical reactions is food, which is generally in the form of a sugar called glucose.

Glucose can be broken down to release energy. Cells need energy to carry out their life functions. Glucose can also be changed into other chemicals. Some of these chemicals are used by a plant for growth and for repair of its parts. Other chemicals are stored in special areas in the roots and stems.

The other product of photosynthesis is oxygen. Oxygen is important to you, and to almost every other living thing on Earth. Do you know why?

An equation can be used to sum up what occurs during photosynthesis. (Do not be alarmed by the appearance of equations! Equations are simply scientific shorthand for describing chemical reactions.) Here is the equation for photosynthesis in words and in chemical notation:

$$\text{carbon dioxide} + \text{water} \xrightarrow[\text{chlorophyll}]{\text{sunlight}} \text{glucose} + \text{oxygen}$$

$$6\ CO_2 + 6\ H_2O \xrightarrow[\text{chlorophyll}]{\text{sunlight}} C_6H_{12}O_6 + 6\ O_2$$

Why does most photosynthesis occur in leaves? To answer this question, you need to know something about the internal structure of a leaf. Refer to Figure 9–11 as you read about the structure and function of a typical leaf.

The outermost layer of a leaf is called the epidermis. The cells of the epidermis are covered with a

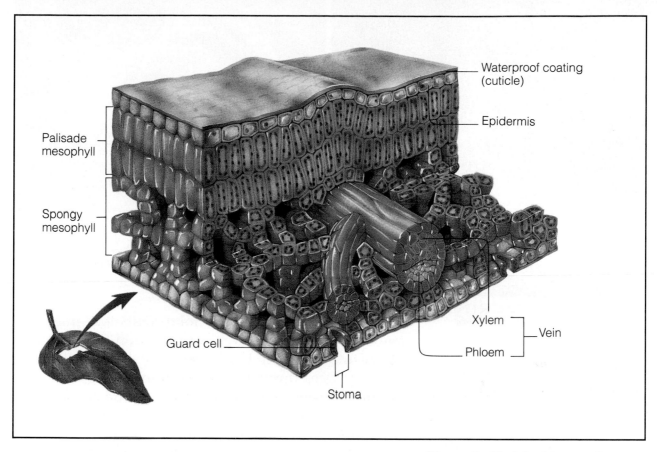

Figure 9–11 *A leaf is a well-designed factory for photosynthesis. How does the structure of each leaf part help the leaf to perform its function?*

Labels in figure:
Waterproof coating (cuticle)
Epidermis
Palisade mesophyll
Spongy mesophyll
Guard cell
Xylem
Phloem
Vein
Stoma

waxy, waterproof coating that helps to prevent excess water loss. This coating makes some real plants look as if they are made of shiny plastic.

Light passes through the epidermis to reach inner cells known collectively as mesophyll. (*Meso-* means middle; *-phyll* means leaf.) The cells of the mesophyll are where almost all photosynthesis occurs. The shape and arrangement of the upper cells maximize the amount of photosynthesis that takes place. The many air spaces between the cells of the lower layer allow carbon dioxide, oxygen, and water vapor (water in the form of a gas) to flow freely.

Carbon dioxide enters the air spaces within a leaf through microscopic openings in the epidermis. These openings are called stomata (STOH-mah-tah; singular: stoma). The Greek word *stoma* means mouth—and stomata do indeed look like tiny mouths!

In addition to permitting carbon dioxide to enter a leaf, stomata allow oxygen and water to exit. The process in which water is lost through a plant's

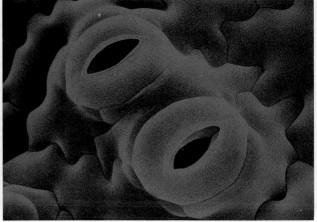

Figure 9–12 *Stomata open to allow carbon dioxide, a raw material of photosynthesis, into the leaf and allow oxygen, a waste product of photosynthesis, out of the leaf. Why do stomata close?*

ACTIVITY

DISCOVERING

Plant-Part Party

Working with a friend or two, make a list of all the foods in your house that come from plants. Remember to include things like ketchup, canned foods, snack foods, and spices. Next to each entry on your list, write the part of the plant from which the food is obtained. If you and your friends cannot identify the source of a food, try to discover its identity using an encyclopedia, cookbook, or botany (plant science) textbook. Compare your list with your classmates'.

■ What foods come from plants?

■ Which plant part was the source of the most foods?

■ One common vegetable looks like stems but is actually the stalks of leaves. What is the name of this vegetable? Were you fooled by these disguised leaves?

leaves is known as transpiration. Plants lose huge amounts of water through transpiration. For example, a full-grown birch tree releases about 17,000 liters of water through transpiration during a single summer season. And the grass on a football field loses almost 3000 liters of water on a summer day.

Although transpiration is necessary for the movement of water through most plants, too much water loss can cause cells to shrivel up and die. One way that plants avoid losing too much water through transpiration is by closing the stomata. Each stoma is formed by two slightly curved epidermal cells called guard cells. When the guard cells swell up with water, they curve away from each other. This opens the stoma. When the water pressure in the guard cells decreases, the guard cells straighten out and come together. This closes the stoma. In general, stomata are open during the day and closed at night. Can you explain why this is so? (*Hint:* When does photosynthesis take place?)

As the cartoon character Popeye tells it, eating spinach is good for you. Popeye is right. In fact, several kinds of leaves are eaten by humans. Spinach, parsley, sage, rosemary, and thyme are just a few examples. What other kinds of leaves are used as food or to season food?

Leaves are also the source of drugs such as digitalis, atropine, and cocaine, of deadly poisons such as strychnine and nicotine, and of dyes such as indigo and henna.

Pitcher plants (left), Venus' flytraps (center), and sundews (right) have leaves that trap insects and other small animals.

▼ The leaves of a kalanchoe are thick and fleshy, allowing the plant to store lots of water. Kalanchoes also produce tiny offspring plants along the edges of their leaves. Eventually, the leaves fall off and the young plants take root.

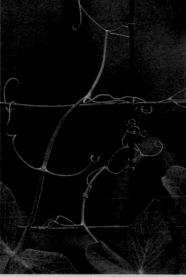

▲ The spines of a cactus are actually leaves, as are the threadlike tendrils of peas.

Figure 9–13 *Specialized leaves*

9–1 Section Review

1. What are seed plants?
2. Describe the structure and importance of roots, stems, and leaves.
3. What is photosynthesis? What is the chemical equation for photosynthesis?

Critical Thinking—*Applying Concepts*

4. Stomata are usually located on the lower surface of leaves. Why do plants with floating leaves, such as water lilies, have stomata on the top surface of their leaves?

CONNECTIONS

Plant Power for Power Plants

Imagine a busy power plant: Workers hurry about, checking gauges and adjusting machinery. The air vibrates with the low roar of the giant wheels that spin to produce electricity. Now imagine a peaceful countryside: A tree lifts its branches to the sun. The wind whispers through the leaves. A bird sings. What do these two scenes have in common?

Not that much—right now. However, power plants and green plants may soon use the same chemical reactions to obtain the *fuel* and food they need to function. Scientists recently reported that they are on the brink of producing artificial versions of the "machinery" of photosynthesis.

The reactions of photosynthesis in plants take place in complex, precisely arranged groups of molecules. Special molecules absorb the energy in light and pass it from one set of molecules to the next. The energy runs the chemical reactions that produce food for the plants—that is, glucose.

By copying the machinery of photosynthesis, scientists will be able to produce fuel using some of the least expensive and most abundant raw materials—sunlight, water, and carbon dioxide. With some slight adjustments, hydrogen gas and methane (natural gas), rather than glucose, will be the end products.

Creating artificial forms of photosynthesis may solve the *energy crisis*. And it may also solve two other serious problems facing us—*global warming* and *air pollution*. Here is why. Global warming is caused by excess carbon dioxide in the air. Photosynthesis—and artificial photosynthesis—uses carbon dioxide. So these processes remove excess carbon dioxide from the air, thus reducing global warming. Much air pollution is caused by burning fuels such as oil and gasoline. Hydrogen, on the other hand, does not pollute when it burns. It simply produces water. As you can see, it makes a lot of sense to use plant power in power plants!

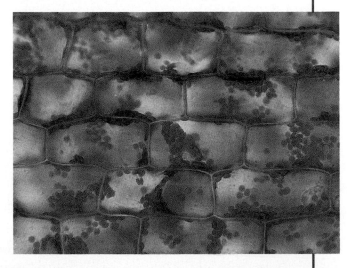

9-2 Reproduction in Seed Plants

Seed plants have made two evolutionary leaps that make them fully adapted for life on land. **Seed plants do not require water to reproduce.** Sperm cells are carried straight to the waiting egg; the sperm cells do not have to swim to the egg. **Young seed plants are encased in a structure that provides food and protection.**

Fertilization in Seed Plants

The reproductive structures of seed plants are known as **cones** and **flowers.** Female cones and flower parts contain structures called **ovules** (AH-vyoolz). Each mature ovule contains an egg cell. Male cones and flower parts produce tiny grains of **pollen** (PAHL-uhn), which you can think of as containing sperm cells. The contents of a pollen grain are enclosed in a tough cell wall. This cell wall may be covered with strange and beautiful patterns of spikes and ridges.

If you have allergies, you may know pollen as an irritating form of dust. However, pollen is nothing to sneeze at! Carried by the wind or by animals, each grain of pollen is capable of delivering a sperm cell to an egg cell. The process by which pollen is carried from male reproductive structures to female reproductive structures is called **pollination.**

If everything goes right, pollination is followed by fertilization. The contents of the pollen grain break

Figure 9–14 *A breeze causes pollen from a cluster of male pine cones to drift away in a dusty yellowish cloud. A few of these pollen grains may eventually reach a female pine cone and fertilize its ovules. Some seed plants, such as the African tulip tree, have flowers rather than cones.*

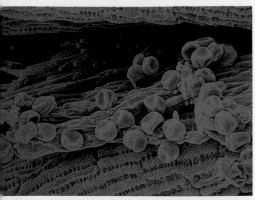

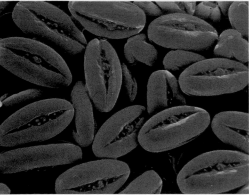

Figure 9–15 *Pollen grains may be spherical or oval, textured or smooth. The pollen grains from a flowering horse chestnut resemble loaves of French bread.*

out of their hard cell wall. They then grow a long tube that delivers the sperm cell to the egg cell in the ovule. The sperm cell joins with the egg cell, fertilizing it. The fertilized egg and the ovule that surrounds it develop into a seed.

In some seed plants, the ovules and the seeds that develop from them are contained within a structure called the ovary (OH-vah-ree). These plants are known as **angiosperms** (AN-jee-oh-sperms). The Greek word *angeion* means vessel; *sperma* means seed. Thus angiosperms are plants whose seeds are contained in a vessel (the ovary).

In other seed plants, the ovules and seeds are not surrounded by an ovary. These plants are known as **gymnosperms** (JIHM-noh-sperms). The Greek word *gymnos* means naked. Thus, gymnosperms are plants whose seeds are naked; that is, not covered by an ovary.

Seeds

Although seeds look quite different from one another, they all have basically the same structure. **A seed consists of a seed coat, a young plant, and stored food.**

The seed coat is a tough, protective covering that develops from the ovule wall. Some familiar seed coats include the "skins" on lima beans, peanuts, and corn kernels. The brown, winglike covering on pine seeds is also a seed coat. So is the fleshy red covering of a yew seed.

Figure 9–16 *Fertilized ovules develop into seeds. The seeds of gymnosperms, such as pines, are not covered by an ovary. Some of the seeds in this pine cone have been removed from their normal position on the top of the woody scales that make up the cone so that they can be clearly seen (top left). The seeds of angiosperms— such as cantaloupes (top right), pomegranates (bottom left), and avocados (bottom right)— are enclosed by an ovary.*

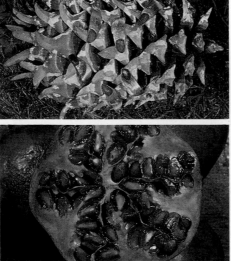

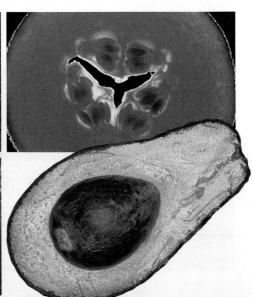

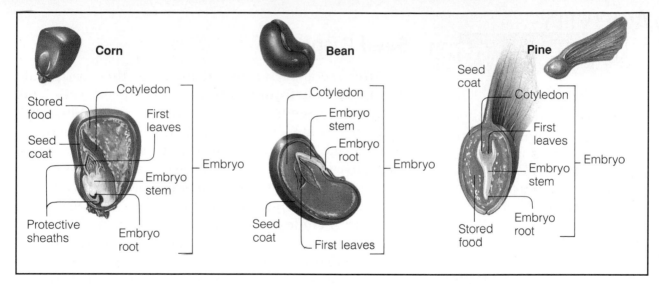

Corn

Cotyledon

Stored food

First leaves

Seed coat

Embryo

Embryo stem

Protective sheaths

Embryo root

Bean

Cotyledon

Embryo stem

Embryo root

Embryo

Seed coat

First leaves

Pine

Seed coat

Cotyledon

First leaves

Embryo

Embryo stem

Stored food

Embryo root

Enclosed within the seed coat is a tiny young plant, or embryo. The embryo develops from the fertilized egg. As you can see in Figure 9–17, the embryo is basically a miniature plant. The top of the embryo eventually gives rise to the leaves and upper stem of the plant. The middle stemlike portion of the embryo becomes the bottom part of the plant's stem. The bottom portion of the embryo becomes the plant's roots.

You probably have noticed that the embryo makes up only a small portion of the seed. In the seeds of most plants, the embryo stops growing when it is quite small and enters a state of "suspended animation." While "sleeping" inside the seed, the embryo can survive long periods of cold, heat, or dryness. When conditions are favorable for growth, the embryo becomes active and the young plant begins to grow once more. Once the young plant begins to grow, it uses the food stored in the seed until it can make its own.

Figure 9–17 *In some seeds, such as those of pines, the embryo is surrounded by stored food. In other seeds, such as corn kernels, some of the food is stored inside a seed leaf, or cotyledon. In still other seeds, such as beans, all of the food is stored inside the cotyledons. Why do most seeds consist mostly of stored food?*

Figure 9–18 *These tropical plants have seeds and fruits that are quite exotic in appearance. Can you identify their seeds and fruits?*

ACTIVITY

Seed Germination

1. Obtain 20 dried beans or unpopped popcorn kernels, 20 test tubes, and some paper towels.

2. Design a two-part experiment that uses these materials to determine whether light and warmth are needed for the seeds to germinate.

3. Write down what you plan to do in your experiment and what results you expect.

4. Soak the seeds in water overnight. Then put together the apparatus for your experiment.

■ What were the results of your experiment? Did the results match your predictions? What were some possible sources of error?

Seed Dispersal

After seeds have finished forming, they are usually scattered far from where they were produced. The scattering of seeds is called seed dispersal (dih-SPER-suhl). Seeds are dispersed in many ways. Have you ever picked a dandelion puff and blown away all its tiny fluffy seeds? If so, you have helped to scatter the seeds. Usually, dandelion seeds are scattered by the wind. Other plants whose seeds are scattered by the wind include maples and certain pines. The winglike structures on these seeds cause them to spin through the air like tiny propellers.

Humans and animals play a part in seed dispersal. For example, burdock seeds have spines that stick to people's clothing or to animal fur. People or animals may pick up the seeds on a walk through a field or forest. At some other place, the seeds may fall off and eventually start a new plant.

The seeds of most water plants are scattered by floating in oceans, rivers, and streams. The coconut, which is the seed of the coconut palm, floats in water. This seed is carried from one piece of land to another by ocean currents.

Other seeds are scattered by a kind of natural explosion, which sends the seeds flying into the air. This is how the impatiens you read about at the beginning of this chapter disperses its seeds.

Figure 9–19 *The seeds of the coconut palm are dispersed by water (center). A tumbleweed is said to disperse its seeds mechanically. The main body of the plant serves as a device for scattering seeds (top right). The seeds of the unicorn plant hitch a ride to new places when spines hook around the hooves (or hiking shoes) of animals that walk by (bottom right). How do you think milkweed seeds are dispersed (left)?*

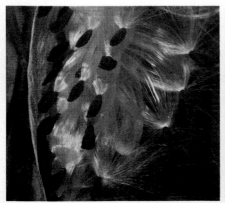

Most seeds remain dormant, or inactive, for a time after being scattered. If there is enough moisture and oxygen, and if the temperature is just right, most seeds go through a process called germination (jer-mih-NAY-shuhn). Germination is the early growth stage of an embryo plant. Some people call this stage "sprouting."

9–2 Section Review

1. Explain how reproduction in seed plants is adapted to life on land.
2. What is a seed? What are the main parts of a seed?
3. How do angiosperms differ from gymnosperms?

Critical Thinking—*Sequencing Events*
4. Put these events in the correct order: germination, fertilization, seed dispersal, release of pollen, seed formation, pollination. Briefly describe each event.

PROBLEM ??? Solving

They Went Thataway!

Seeds are dispersed in many different ways. Seed dispersal is important because it helps plants spread to new areas. It also improves the chances that some of a plant's seeds will grow and survive to produce seeds of their own. Examine the accompanying photographs carefully. Then answer the following questions for each photograph.

Making Inferences
1. How is the seed dispersed? How can you tell?
2. How is the seed or fruit adapted for this method of dispersal?

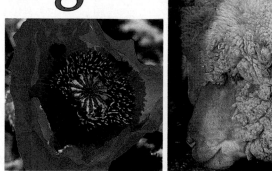

9–3 Gymnosperms and Angiosperms

Gymnosperms are the most ancient group of seed plants. They first appeared about 360 million years ago—about the same time as the first land animals. Throughout the age of the dinosaurs, approximately 65 to 245 million years ago, gymnosperms were the dominant form of plant life on Earth.

Near the end of the age of dinosaurs, about 100 million years ago, a new phylum of plants appeared on the scene. The plants in this new phylum—the angiosperms—soon replaced the gymnosperm phyla as the Earth's dominant form of plant life.

Gymnosperms

Although the reign of gymnosperms has ended, four phyla of gymnosperms have survived to the present day. **The four phyla of gymnosperms are commonly known as cycads, ginkgoes, conifers, and gnetophytes.**

Cycads (SIGH-kadz) are tropical plants that look like palm trees. Some cycads grow up to 15 meters tall, but most grow no taller than a human. The trunk of a cycad is topped by a cluster of feathery leaves. In the center of the leaves of a mature cycad are its cones.

Although ginkgoes (GING-kohz) were fairly common during the age of the dinosaurs, only one species exists today. The ginkgo is sometimes known as the maidenhair tree. Interestingly, the ginkgo does not seem to exist in the wild. The ginkgoes that grow along many city streets in the United States and elsewhere are the descendants of plants from gardens in China. Ginkgo seeds have an incredibly bad odor.

With about 550 species, conifers (KAHN-ih-ferz) make up the largest group of gymnosperms. Most conifers are large trees with needlelike or scalelike leaves. See Figure 9–21. Conifers are found throughout the world, and are the dominant plants in many forests in the Northern Hemisphere. Conifers include the world's tallest trees (coast redwoods) and longest-lived trees (bristlecone pines).

Figure 9–20 *Cycads (top) and ginkgoes (bottom) are gymnosperms that were quite common during the age of the dinosaurs. Unlike a conifer, a cycad or a ginkgo produces either male cones or female cones, not both.*

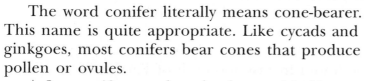

The word conifer literally means cone-bearer. This name is quite appropriate. Like cycads and ginkgoes, most conifers bear cones that produce pollen or ovules.

A few conifers, such as larches and bald cypresses, shed their leaves in autumn. However, most conifers—such as pines, firs, spruces, cedars, and hemlocks—are evergreen. Evergreen plants have leaves year round. Old leaves drop off gradually and are replaced by new ones throughout the life of the plant. The needles or leaves may remain on an evergreen tree for 2 to 12 years.

Conifers are of great importance to people. They are a major source of wood for building and for manufacturing paper. Useful substances such as turpentine, pitch, and rosin are made from the sap of conifers. The seeds of certain pines are rich in protein and are used for cooking and snacking. Juniper seeds are used to flavor food. Recently, scientists discovered that taxol, a substance in the bark of the Pacific yew tree, is showing promise as an effective treatment for certain kinds of cancer.

Gnetophytes (NEE-toh-fights) are a diverse group of plants that share characteristics with both gymnosperms and angiosperms. Gnetophytes include climbing tropical vines with oval leaves, bushes with jointed branches and tiny scalelike leaves, and a peculiar-looking desert plant whose two straplike leaves grow throughout its lifetime.

Figure 9–21 *Some conifers, such as the Port Oxford cedar, have tiny scalelike leaves (left). Others, such as the Douglas fir, have needlelike leaves (center). A few conifers are amazingly large. Why is this giant redwood tree able to live and grow in spite of having a car-sized tunnel cut through it?*

Figure 9–22 Welwitschia mirabilis *is one of the few organisms that can survive in the extremely hot, dry Namib desert of Africa. Although* Welwitschia *has only two leaves, the leaves soon become tattered and torn so that they look like many leaves. To which phylum of gymnosperms does* Welwitschia *belong?*

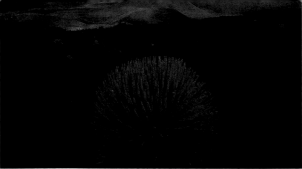

Figure 9–23 *Some flowers, such as sweet alyssum, impatiens, geraniums, and marigolds, are common garden flowers (top left). Others, such as the strange silversword plant of Hawaii, are delightfully uncommon (right). The silversword looks quite different after it develops its enormous stalk of flowers (bottom left). After it produces its seeds, the silversword dies.*

Angiosperms

Angiosperms make up the largest group of plants in the world—there are more than 230,000 known species, with perhaps hundreds of thousands more as yet undiscovered.

Angiosperms vary greatly in size and shape. They can be found in just about all of Earth's environments, including frozen wastelands near the North Pole, steamy tropical jungles, and practically waterless deserts.

Because they produce flowers, angiosperms are also called flowering plants. The flowers of angiosperms fill the Earth with beautiful colors and pleasant smells. But flowers serve a more important purpose. **Flowers are the structures that contain the reproductive organs of angiosperms.**

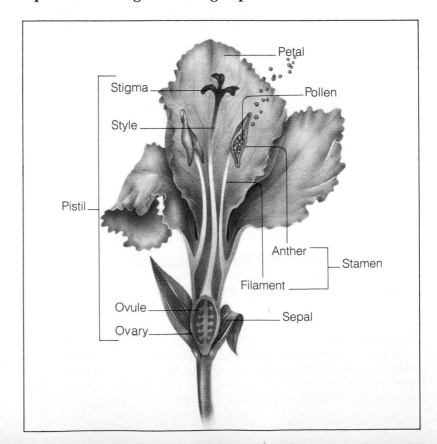

Figure 9–24 *The parts of a flower work together to accomplish the task of reproduction. Which are the male parts of a flower? Which are the female parts?*

Figure 9–25 *Flowers and the animals that pollinate them have evolved in response to one another. How are the hummingbird, bee, and bat adapted to feeding from flowers? Can you tell what kind of animal pollinates the bee orchid, which looks and smells like a female bumblebee (top right)? Plants have also evolved ways that help them to disperse their seeds. How are blackberries adapted for seed dispersal by animals?*

As you can see in Figure 9–23, flowers come in all sorts of sizes, colors, and forms. As you read about the parts of a typical flower, keep in mind that the descriptions do not apply to all flowers. For example, some flowers have only male reproductive parts, and some flowers lack petals.

When a flower is still a bud, it is enclosed by leaflike structures called **sepals** (SEE-puhls). Sepals protect the developing flower. Once the sepals fold back and the flower opens, colorful leaflike structures called **petals** are revealed. The colors, shapes, and odors of the petals attract insects and other animals. These creatures play a vital role in the reproduction of flowering plants.

Within the petals are the flower's reproductive organs. The thin stalks topped by small knobs are the male reproductive organs, or **stamens** (STAY-muhns). The stalklike part of the stamen is called the filament, and the knoblike part is called the anther. The anther produces pollen.

The female reproductive organs, or **pistils** (PIHS-tihls), are found in the center of the flower. Some

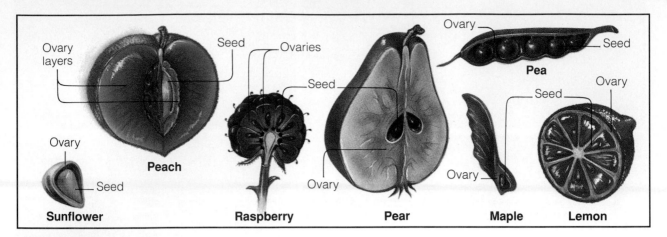

Figure 9–26 *Fruits have evolved in ways that help to disperse seeds. How are maple seeds specialized for being dispersed by the wind? How are peaches, pears, lemons, and raspberries adapted for seed dispersal by animals?*

flowers have two or more pistils; others have only one. The sticky tip of the pistil is called the stigma. A slender tube, called the style, connects the stigma to a hollow structure at the base of the flower. This hollow structure is the ovary, which contains one or more ovules.

A flower is pollinated when a grain of pollen lands on the stigma. (Can you explain why the stigma is sticky?) If the pollen is from the right kind of plant, the wall of the pollen grain breaks open. The contents of the pollen grain then produce a tube that grows down through the style and into an ovule. When the tube has finished growing, a sperm cell emerges from the tube and fertilizes the egg cell in the ovule.

Like gymnosperms, some angiosperms are pollinated by the wind. The flowers of these plants are usually small, unscented, and produce huge amounts of pollen. Most angiosperms, however, are pollinated by insects, birds, and other animals. Flowers that rely on animals for pollination are colorful, scented, and/or full of food. This helps them to attract the animals that pollinate them.

As you have learned, after the egg cell is fertilized, the ovule develops into a seed. As the seed develops, the ovary also undergoes some changes and becomes a fruit. A **fruit** is a ripened ovary that encloses and protects the seed or seeds. Apples and cherries are fruits. So are many of the plant foods you usually think of as vegetables, such as cucumbers and tomatoes. What other kinds of fruits do you eat? The next time you are enjoying a favorite fruit, try to identify the seed, seed coat, and ripened ovary.

ACTIVITY

READING

A World of Fun With Plants

Do you know how to make a shrill whistle with a blade of grass? Learn how to do this and other neat things by reading *Hidden Stories in Plants* by Anne Pellowski.

246

9–3 Section Review

1. What are the four phyla of gymnosperms?
2. What is a flower? How are flowers involved in reproduction in angiosperms?
3. Describe pollination and fertilization in angiosperms.

Connection—*You and Your World*
4. Why are almost all the ginkgoes that are planted male trees?

9–4 Patterns of Growth

Why do some garden plants die and have to be replaced each year? Why do you have to turn a houseplant that is growing on the windowsill every now and then? To answer questions such as these, you have to know something about the patterns of growth in plants.

Annuals, Biennials, and Perennials

Plants are placed into three groups according to how long it takes them to produce flowers and how long they live. The three groups of plants are **annuals, biennials,** and **perennials.**

Some plants grow from a seed, flower, produce seeds, and die all in the course of one growing season. Such plants include marigolds, petunias, and many other common garden flowers. **Plants that complete their life cycle within one growing season are called annuals.** The word annual comes from the Latin word *annus,* which means year. Most annuals have herbaceous (nonwoody) stems. Wheat, rye, and tobacco plants are other examples of annuals.

Plants that complete their life cycle in two years are called biennials. (The Latin word *bi* means two.) Biennials sprout and grow roots, stems, and leaves during their first growing season. Although the stems and leaves may die during the winter, the roots survive. During the second growing season, a

Guide for Reading

Focus on these questions as you read.

▶ *How do annuals, biennials, and perennials differ from one another?*

▶ *How do plants grow in response to their external environment?*

247

Figure 9–27 *Petunias bloom cheerfully throughout the warm months of the year, but die in the winter (top). During its second and final growing season, the foxglove produces a spike of many flowers. The spotted "trail" on a foxglove flower directs bees to the nectar and pollen inside (right). Begonias live for many years, producing flowers each summer (bottom). Which of these plants is a perennial? Which is an annual? Which is a biennial?*

biennial grows new stems and leaves and then produces flowers and seeds. Once the flowers produce seeds, the plant dies. Examples of biennials include sugar beets, carrots, celery, and certain kinds of foxgloves.

Still other plants live for more than two growing seasons. **Plants that live for many years are called perennials.** (The Latin word *per* means through; a perennial lives through the years.) Some perennials, such as most garden peonies, are herbaceous. Their leaves and stems die each winter and are renewed each spring. Most perennials, however, are woody. The long lives of perennials permit them to accumulate lots of layers of woody xylem in their stems. Pine trees and rhododendron bushes are examples of woody perennials. What other plants are woody perennials?

Tropisms

When studying behavior in plants and other living things, it is helpful to be familiar with two terms: stimulus (STIHM-yoo-luhs; plural: stimuli, STIHM-yoo-ligh) and response. A stimulus is something in a

Activity Bank

Lean to the Light, p.803

248

living thing's environment (both its internal and external environment) that causes a reaction, or response.

Plants respond to stimuli in a variety of ways. One way is by adjusting the way they grow. The growth of a plant toward or away from a stimulus is called a **tropism** (TROH-pihz-uhm). If a plant grows toward a stimulus, it is said to have a positive tropism. If it grows away from a stimulus, it is said to have a negative tropism.

There are several kinds of tropisms. The two most important tropisms involve responses to light and to gravity.

All plants exhibit a response to light called phototropism. (Recall that the Greek word *photos* means light.) Think about the houseplant mentioned at the start of this section. If a houseplant is not turned regularly, it soon begins to bend toward the window, the source of its light. Do leaves and stems show positive or negative phototropism?

Plants also show a response to gravity, or gravitropism. Roots show positive gravitropism—they grow downward. Stems, on the other hand, show negative gravitropism—they grow upward, against the pull of gravity.

Figure 9–28 *Because this houseplant was not turned regularly, it started to grow in a crooked way. Why did this happen?*

9–4 Section Review

1. What are annuals, biennials, and perennials?
2. What are tropisms? Describe two tropisms.

Critical Thinking—*Making Predictions*
3. Suppose a tree is knocked over by a storm, but it survives the experience. What will this tree look like a few years after the storm?

ACTIVITY

DISCOVERING

Pick a Plant

In the late winter or early spring, purchase a packet of seeds for an annual plant you would like to grow. You may wish to get together with a classmate or two and split the cost of the seeds. (A packet usually costs $1 to $2.) Following the directions on the seed packet, plant 3 seeds in a clean pint-sized milk carton. Water the seeds and resulting plants every day or two.

■ How long does it take your seeds to sprout? How do your plants change over the course of the year? Make a poster showing the more interesting stages in the life cycle of your plant. The stages shown in your poster should include the seed, the plant when it first begins to sprout, the plant when it has two leaves, the plant when it develops flowers, and the plant when it develops fruits or seeds.

Laboratory Investigation

Gravitropism

Problem

How does gravity affect the growth of a seed?

Materials *(per group)*

4 corn seeds soaked in water for 24 hours	paper towels
	masking tape
petri dish	glass-marking pencil
scissors	clay

Procedure ⚗ ▨

1. Arrange the four seeds in a petri dish. The pointed ends of all the seeds should face the center of the dish. One of the seeds should be at the 12 o'clock position of the circle, and the other seeds at 3, 6, and 9 o'clock.

2. Place a circle of paper towel over the seeds. Then pack the dish with enough pieces of paper towel so that the seeds will be held firmly in place when the other half of the petri dish is put on.

3. Moisten the paper towels with water. Cover the petri dish and seal the two halves together with a strip of masking tape.

4. With the glass-marking pencil, draw an arrow on the lid pointing toward 12 o'clock. Label the lid with your name and the date.

5. With pieces of clay, prop the dish up so that the arrow is pointing up. Place the dish in a completely dark place.

6. Predict what will happen to the seeds. Then observe the seeds each day for about one week. Make a sketch of them each day. Be sure to return the dish and seeds to their original position when you have finished.

Observations

What happened to the corn seeds? In which direction did the roots and the stems grow?

Analysis and Conclusions

1. Which part of the germinating seeds showed positive gravitropism? Which part showed negative gravitropism?

2. What would happen to the corn seeds if the dish were turned so that the arrow was pointed toward the bottom of the dish? If it were turned to the right or the left?

3. Why is it important that the petri dish remain in a stable position throughout the investigation?

4. Explain why the seeds were placed in the dark rather than near a sunny window.

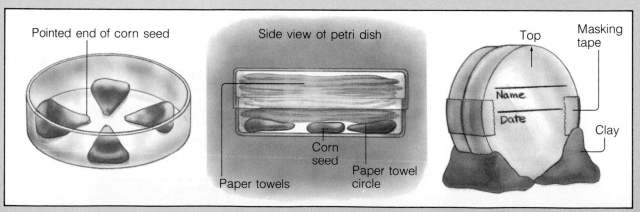

Pointed end of corn seed

Side view of petri dish

Corn seed

Paper towels

Paper towel circle

Top

Masking tape

Name

Date

Clay

Study Guide

Summarizing Key Concepts

9–1 Structure of Seed Plants

▲ There are two types of vascular tissue. Xylem carries water and dissolved minerals. Phloem carries food.

▲ Roots anchor the plant in the ground and absorb water and minerals from the soil.

▲ Stems transport materials between the roots and the leaves and support the leaves.

▲ In most plants, leaves are the structures in which photosynthesis occurs.

▲ Photosynthesis is the process that uses light energy to change carbon dioxide and water into glucose and oxygen.

9–2 Reproduction in Seed Plants

▲ Seed plants do not require standing water to reproduce.

▲ The process in which pollen is carried from male reproductive structures to female reproductive structures is called pollination.

▲ After pollination, the contents of the pollen grain grow a tube into an ovule and release a sperm cell. The sperm cell fuses with the ovule's egg cell to produce a fertilized egg in a process called fertilization.

▲ The ovules and seeds of angiosperms are covered by an ovary; those of gymnosperms are uncovered.

▲ Seeds consist of a seed coat, an embryo, and stored food.

9–3 Gymnosperms and Angiosperms

▲ There are four living phyla of gymnosperms: cycads, ginkgoes, conifers, and gnetophytes.

▲ Because their reproductive structures are contained in flowers, angiosperms are known as flowering plants.

9–4 Patterns of Growth

▲ Plants are classified as annuals, biennials, and perennials according to how long it takes them to produce flowers and how long they live.

▲ The growth of a plant in response to an environmental stimulus is called a tropism.

Reviewing Key Terms

Define each term in a complete sentence.

9–1 Structure of Seed Plants
xylem
phloem
root
stem
leaf
photosynthesis

9–2 Reproduction in Seed Plants
cone
flower
ovule
pollen
pollination
angiosperm
gymnosperm

9–3 Gymnosperms and Angiosperms
sepal
petal
stamen
pistil
fruit

9–4 Patterns of Growth
annual
biennial
perennial
tropism

Chapter Review

Content Review

Multiple Choice

Choose the letter of the answer that best completes each statement.

1. Roots grow away from light. This is an example of
   a. negative gravitropism.
   b. positive gravitropism.
   c. negative phototropism.
   d. positive phototropism.
2. Which phylum has seeds that are enclosed by an ovary?
   a. gnetophytes   c. conifers
   b. angiosperms   d. cycads
3. The movement of gases in and out of the leaf is regulated by the
   a. stomata.   c. cortex.
   b. mesophyll.   d. cambium.
4. Many flowering plants rely on animal partners for
   a. pollination.   c. fertilization.
   b. germination.   d. transpiration.
5. Photosynthesis produces
   a. chlorophyll.   c. water.
   b. carbon dioxide. d. oxygen.

6. The main water-conducting tissue in a plant is
   a. phloem.   c. cambium.
   b. xylem.   d. pith.
7. The functions of anchoring the plant and absorbing water are performed primarily by a plant's
   a. roots.   c. leaves.
   b. stems.   d. anthers.
8. Which structure is not part of a flower's pistil?
   a. style   c. ovary
   b. stigma   d. anther
9. A pine tree is best described as
   a. annual.   c. biennial.
   b. perennial.   d. herbaceous.
10. The union of the sperm cell and the egg cell is known as
    a. pollination.   c. fertilization.
    b. germination.   d. transpiration.

True or False

If the statement is true, write "true." If it is false, change the underlined word or words to make the statement true.

1. Pollen is produced in the <u>anther</u>.
2. The <u>cortex</u> produces new xylem and phloem cells.
3. A four-leafed clover is an example of a <u>simple</u> leaf.
4. Carrots and dandelions have <u>fibrous root</u> systems.
5. The protective outer covering of a seed is called the <u>epidermis</u>.
6. The ovules of a conifer are located in its <u>flowers</u>.
7. The structures that protect a flower bud are called <u>stamens</u>.
8. A <u>fruit</u> is a ripened ovary.

Concept Mapping

Complete the following concept map for Section 9–1. Then construct a concept map for the entire chapter.

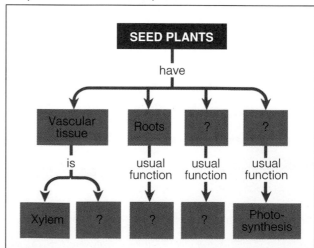

Concept Mastery

Discuss each of the following in a brief paragraph.

1. List the three main parts of a seed and describe their function.
2. Give three examples of ways in which people use conifers.
3. What is seed dispersal? How does it take place? Why is it important?
4. Distinguish between herbaceous and woody plants. Would you expect an annual plant to be woody? Explain.
5. How does the structure of a stem help it to carry out its functions?
6. What is photosynthesis?
7. How are angiosperms and gymnosperms similar? How are they different? Give three examples of each kind of plant.
8. Describe the two most important kinds of tropisms in terms of stimulus and response.
9. Unlike the first plants to appear on Earth, seed plants do not depend on water for reproduction. Explain why.

Critical Thinking and Problem Solving

Use the skills you have developed in this chapter to answer each of the following.

1. **Summarizing information** List the major parts of a typical flower. Briefly describe the function of each part.
2. **Relating concepts** Describe the adaptations in seed plants that help them to avoid excess water loss.
3. **Developing a hypothesis** You observe that hungry deer have eaten the bark on an apple tree as far up as they can reach. At first, the tree seems to remain healthy. However, it eventually dies. Develop a hypothesis to explain your observations. How might you test your hypothesis?
4. **Identifying relationships** When life first appeared on Earth more than 3.5 billion years ago, there was no oxygen gas in the air. But for the past 1.8 billion years or so, the air has been about 20 percent oxygen. How did photosynthesis cause this change in the composition of Earth's air and maintain it? Why is it important to most of Earth's organisms to have so much oxygen in the air?
5. **Making inferences** Pesticides are designed to kill harmful insects. Sometimes, however, they kill helpful insects. What effect could this have on angiosperms?
6. **Designing an experiment** Design an experiment to determine whether or not water is needed for seed germination. Describe your experimental setup. Be sure to include a control.
7. **Using the writing process** Imagine that you are the seed plant of your choice. Describe your life from your earliest memories as a forming seed to the time you produced seeds of your own. (*Hints:* What were seed dispersal and germination like? What changes did you undergo as you grew?)

GAZETTE

Colleen Cavanaugh Explores the Underwater World of

TUBE WORMS

The seabed lies 2500 meters below the ocean's surface. Here, the pressure is nearly 260 times that at the Earth's surface, and the temperature is close to the freezing point. The region is always dark, as sunlight cannot penetrate these ocean depths.

Almost all organisms depend on light as their source of energy in manufacturing food. So scientists had expected to find only the simplest creatures inhabiting this dark area of the Pacific Ocean floor near the Galápagos Islands. To the surprise of a group of scientists from the Woods Hole Oceanographic Institution, however, communities of strange sea animals were found in this forbidding environment.

Among the animals observed by the Woods Hole team are giant clams that measure one-third meter in diameter, oversized mussels, and crabs. But perhaps the most striking organisms are giant tube worms. These worms are so different from anything seen before that scientists have placed them in a new family of the animal kingdom.

Although most of the worms are only 2.5 to 5 centimeters in diameter, they can be as long as 3.5 meters! Like a sausage in a tube, each worm lives inside a tough rigid casing. One end of the tube worm is anchored to the seabed. At the other end, a red plume-like structure made of blood-filled filaments waves in the ocean water.

Internally, the body of the worm is most unusual. Approximately half of its body is made of a colony of densely packed bacteria. These bacteria are the key to a worm's ability to survive in such a harsh environment. But exactly what is the relationship between the bacteria and the tube worms?

Enter Dr. Colleen Cavanaugh, a marine biologist and microbiologist who studies these bacteria and their relationship to the larger life forms they support. She has found

that the bacteria break down hydrogen sulfide, a common sulfur compound, to produce energy. This energy is then used by the tube worms. In this way, the seemingly worthless hydrogen sulfide—which smells like rotten eggs and is poisonous to most organisms—provides the energy for a fascinating aquatic ecosystem.

Hydrogen sulfide is not ordinarily found in sea water. But plenty of hydrogen sulfide is found near hydrothermal vents such as those in the Pacific Ocean areas where the tube worms were first discovered. Hydrothermal vents are openings in the ocean floor that allow ocean water to come into contact with the earth's hot, molten interior. In the vents, ocean water is heated to temperatures as high as 350 degrees Celsius. The hot water is ejected back into the ocean, laced with many different chemical compounds, including hydrogen sulfide. Tube worms and other animals that are able to use sulfur abound in these regions.

Research on tube worms requires interest, dedication, and a broad knowledge of science. So it is not surprising that Colleen Cavanaugh is part of the team at Woods Hole exploring this fascinating underwater world. As a high-school student growing up in Michigan, Colleen Cavanaugh explored many fields of science. She then went on to study general ecology and biology at the University of Michigan. As a graduate student at Harvard University, she developed an interest in microbial ecology. Now she combines these three fields, as well as others such as oceanography, in her work. The work Dr. Cavanaugh has already done on tube worms will be of help in her more general study of the nature of symbiosis, or cooperation, between animals and bacteria. As she points out, the sulfides and sulfide-based ecosystems such as that of the tube worms are not limited just to the ocean depths. They are also found in salt marshes, mud flats, and many other marine environments closer to home. Thus, scientific work in the dark reaches of the sea may shed new light on the nature of life on the surface as well.

▲ Living on the ocean bottom near hydrothermal vents (top), tube worms (center) thrive as a result of a symbiotic relationship with bacteria (bottom).

UNIT THREE

Animals

Everyone loves a friendly animal—the cricket that warms itself by a campfire, the frog that "sings" on a rock in a pond, the first robin to alight on your lawn in the spring, the squirrel that "plants" acorns from your oak tree, or the porpoise that frolics near a boat full of people. These creatures delight us because, unlike most animals, they seem not to be frightened by us.

However, there are animals that scurry away at the mere sound, smell, or sight of humans. Deer, for example, rapidly flee when they hear or smell an intruder. Cottontails use their hind legs to run when their large ears hear approaching danger. When frightened by our presence, an octopus emits an inky cloud to make good its escape!

Other animals—such as termites, flies, rats, mosquitoes, cockroaches, and hookworms—are regarded as pests. These animals cost us millions of dollars annually in damage to property and health. Still other animals are seen as terrifying menaces: the great white sharks, rattlesnakes, lions, tigers, and wolves.

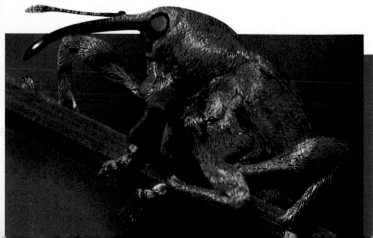

Invertebrates, or animals without backbones, inhabit the Earth's land, sea, and air. The sponge (top) and the insect (right) are two examples of invertebrates.

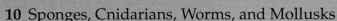

The wolf (left) belongs to a group of vertebrates, or animals with backbones, known as mammals. LIke the wolf, the iguana (bottom) is a vertebrate. It belongs to a group of animals known as reptiles.

Whatever their behavior toward us, each of these animals has a specific role in nature. As you read this textbook, you will discover a great deal about the animals that inhabit the Earth's lands, water, and air. So read on and discover why the Earth is referred to as the living planet.

Discovery *Activity*

Animals, Animals

1. Take a look at a small area near your home. The area can be located in a park, an empty lot, a yard, or on a beach.

2. Make a list of all the animals you observe in the area. Make a sketch of each animal.

   ■ What are the characteristics of the animals you observed?

   ■ Which animals have similar characteristics? Which have different characteristics?

   ■ If you could develop your own system of classification, how would you group each animal on your list?

Sponges, Cnidarians, Worms, and Mollusks

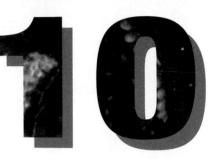

10

No other beast of the sea has been as feared as the octopus. Its very name—devilfish—calls to mind danger and alarm. Yet the truth is that the octopus would be more afraid of you than you should be of it. The octopus, you see, is terrified of anything larger than itself.

Of the hundred or so varieties of octopuses, most grow no larger than one meter across. Some are so tiny that they could sit on your fingernail! In the Mediterranean Sea, where octopuses are common, very few grow tentacles that reach two meters in length. Only in the depths of the Pacific Ocean are there believed to be really tremendous octopuses.

No matter what their actual size, the tales told about octopuses were common among people with vivid imaginations. In such stories, octopuses attacked ships, slung their tentacled arms around the masts, and nearly capsized the vessels. Actually, few scientists believe that octopuses intentionally attack humans.

Octopuses are one of many fascinating animals you will read about in this textbook. In this chapter you will begin to explore this marvelous world by examining sponges, cnidarians, worms, and mollusks.

Journal *Activity*

You and Your World In your journal, write down five common expressions that have to do with animals. Here are two examples: ''At a snail's pace'' and ''It's a fluke.'' Next to each expression, explain its meaning as you understand it. When you have finished reading this textbook, look again at your list. See if you can explain the origin of each expression.

◀ *An octopus resting on its tentacles*

10–1 Introduction to the Animal Kingdom

Think of a fierce lion, a friendly porpoise, a cuddly puppy, a crawling earthworm, an annoying mosquito, and a slimy jellyfish. Now ask yourself what all these organisms have in common. You are correct if you say they are all animals and belong to the kingdom Animalia. As you have learned, animals can be defined as multicellular heterotrophs whose cells lack cell walls.

Animal cells vary greatly in size. Although most cells are too small to be seen without a microscope, some cells are large enough to be seen with the unaided eye. The largest animal cell is the yolk of an

Figure 10–1 *All members of the kingdom Animalia can be grouped into two major divisions: vertebrates and invertebrates. Warthogs (top left) and dusky dolphins (top right) are vertebrates; sea stars (bottom left) and tarantulas (bottom right) are invertebrates. How can you distinguish between a vertebrate and an invertebrate?*

ostrich egg. This yolk, or single cell, is about the size of a baseball. Animal cells also have different shapes. Some are shaped like long rectangles, some like spheres, some like disks. Others are rod shaped or spiral shaped.

In most animals, cells are organized into tissues, tissues into organs, and organs into organ systems. Every kind of cell depends on every other kind of cell for its survival and for the survival of the entire animal.

The animal kingdom can be grouped into two major divisions: **vertebrates** and **invertebrates.** Humans, lions, porpoises, and puppies are all examples of vertebrates. **A vertebrate is an animal that has a backbone, or vertebral** (VER-tuh-bruhl) **column.** Earthworms, mosquitoes, and jellyfishes are all invertebrates. **An invertebrate is an animal that has no backbone.** Invertebrates make up about 95 percent of all animal species.

All animals in the kingdom Animalia are divided into different groups called phyla (FIGH-luh; singular: phylum) according to their body structure. A phylum is the second largest group of organisms after kingdom. As you explore the invertebrate phyla, keep in mind that they share an evolutionary heritage. In other words, the invertebrates (as well as all animals) share a common ancestor. This fact will become evident to you as you move from one animal phylum to another.

Activity Bank

Friends or Foes?, p. 804

ACTIVITY WRITING

Symmetry

The body shapes of invertebrates show either radial symmetry, bilateral symmetry, or asymmetry. Use a science dictionary or science encyclopedia to define each term.

Make a list of the different phyla of invertebrates discussed in this chapter. Indicate what type of symmetry is shown by each phylum.

10–1 Section Review

1. What is an animal?
2. How are vertebrates and invertebrates alike? How are they different?
3. What is a phylum? Would you expect to find more species in a phylum or a kingdom? Explain.

Critical Thinking—*Drawing Conclusions*
4. Why do multicellular organisms need specialized tissues?

10–2 Sponges

The simplest group of invertebrates are the sponges. Sponges are the most ancient of all animals alive today. The first sponges are thought to have appeared on Earth about 580 million years ago.

Although most sponges live in the sea, some can be found in freshwater lakes and streams. Sponges grow attached to one spot and usually stay there for their entire life unless a strong wave or current washes them somewhere else. Because they show little or no movement, sponges were once thought to be plants.

The body of a sponge is covered with many pores, or tiny openings. Sponges belong to the phylum Porifera (poh-RIHF-er-uh). The word porifera means pore-bearers. Moving ocean water carries food and oxygen through the pores into the sponge. The sponge's cells remove food and oxygen from the water. At the same time, the cells release waste products (carbon dioxide and undigested food) into the water. Then, the water leaves through a larger opening.

Figure 10–2 *Sponges are invertebrates and belong to the phylum Porifera. As you can see from the photographs, sponges— such as* Callyspongia *sponges (left), tennis ball sponges (top), red sponges (bottom left), and Caribbean reef sponges (bottom right)—vary in shape, color, and size. What does the word porifera mean?*

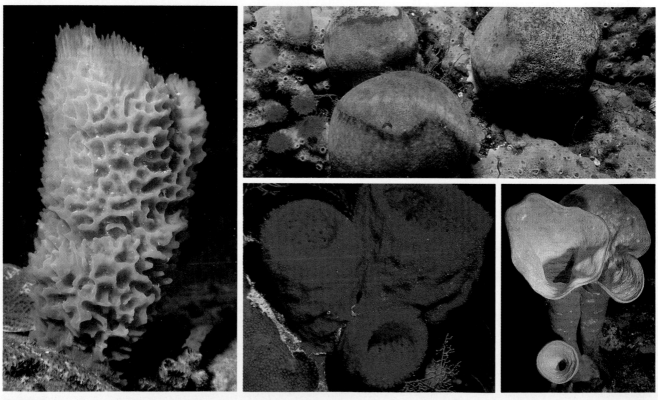

Sponge cells are unusual in that they function on their own, without any coordination with one another. In fact, some people think of sponges as a colony of cells living together. Despite their independent functioning, however, sponge cells have a mysterious attraction to one another. This attraction can be easily demonstrated by passing a sponge through a fine filter so that it breaks into clumps of cells. Within hours, these cells reform into several new sponges. No other animal species shares this amazing ability of sponge cells to reorganize themselves.

Many sponges produce **spicules** (SPIHK-yoolz). Spicules are thin, spiny structures that form the skeleton of many sponges. Spicules are made of either a chalky or a glasslike substance. They interlock to form delicate skeletons, such as the one shown in Figure 10–5 on page 264. Other sponges have skeletons that consist of a softer, fiberlike material. The cleaned and dried skeletons of these sponges are the natural bath sponges that you may have in your home or see in department stores. Still other sponges have skeletons that are made of both spicules and the fiberlike material.

Sponges reproduce sexually and asexually. **Sexual reproduction** is the process by which a new organism forms from the joining of a female cell and a male cell. Reproducing sexually, one sponge produces eggs (female cells); another produces sperm

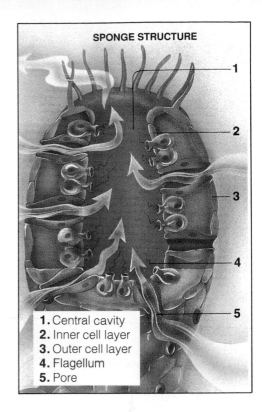

SPONGE STRUCTURE

1. Central cavity
2. Inner cell layer
3. Outer cell layer
4. Flagellum
5. Pore

Figure 10–3 *Notice that the body of a sponge consists of a layer of cells that form a wall around a central cavity. The cells in this layer function independently of one another.*

Figure 10–4 *In some sponges, such as the sponges in the photograph, eggs are squirted into the surrounding water, where they may be fertilized. In others, eggs are fertilized inside the body of the parent sponge.*

ACTIVITY

DISCOVERING

Observing a Sponge

1. Obtain a natural sponge from your teacher.

2. Use a hand lens to examine the surface and the pores. Draw what you see.

3. Remove a small piece of the sponge and place it on a glass microscope slide. Look for the spicules. Draw what you observe.

■ Repeat steps 2 and 3 with a synthetic kitchen sponge. How do a natural sponge and a synthetic sponge compare?

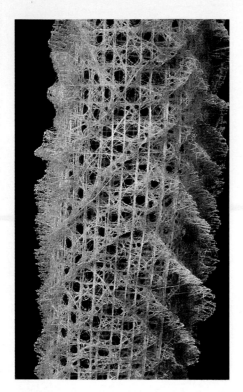

Figure 10–5 *The lacy skeleton of this glass sponge consists of thousands of spicules made of glassy material. What is the function of spicules?*

(male cells). These cells join, and a young sponge develops. **Asexual reproduction** is the process by which a single organism produces a new organism. Sponges reproduce asexually by budding. In budding, part of a sponge simply falls off the parent sponge and begins to grow into a new sponge. During cold winters, some freshwater sponges produce structures that contain groups of cells surrounded by a hard, protective layer. When conditions become favorable again, these structures grow into new sponges.

In addition to being the source of natural sponges, sponges are also an important source of powerful antibiotics that can be used to fight disease-causing bacteria and fungi. Sponges also provide homes and food for certain worms, shrimps, and starfishes.

10–2 Section Review

1. What are the main characteristics of sponges?
2. How do food and oxygen enter a sponge's body?
3. How do sponges reproduce?

Critical Thinking—*Making Predictions*

4. Predict what would happen to a sponge if it lived in water that contained a great deal of floating matter.

Guide for Reading

Focus on this question as you read.

▶ *What are the main characteristics of cnidarians?*

10–3 Cnidarians

The phylum Cnidaria (nigh-DAIR-ee-uh) consists of many invertebrate animals with dazzling colors and strange shapes. The animals that make up this phylum include corals, jellyfishes, hydras, and sea anemones. As you can see in Figure 10–6, cnidarians have two basic body forms: a vase-shaped polyp (PAHL-ihp) and a bowl-shaped medusa (muh-DOO-suh). A polyp usually remains in one place; a medusa can move from place to place.

Cnidarians have a hollow central cavity with only one opening called the mouth. The phylum

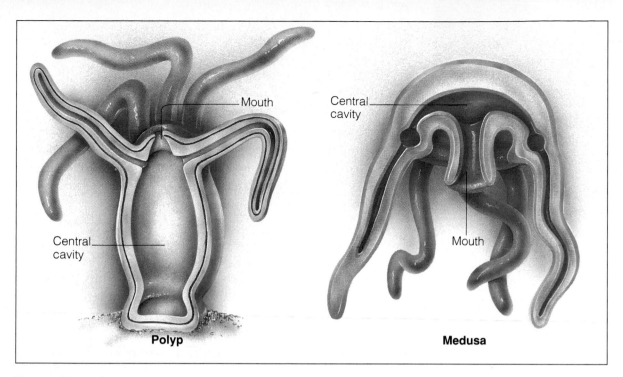

Mouth

Central cavity

Central cavity

Mouth

Polyp

Medusa

Figure 10–6 *Cnidarians have two basic body forms: a vase-shaped polyp and a bowl-shaped medusa. What is the difference between a polyp and a medusa?*

name Cnidaria is taken from the Greek word meaning to sting. All cnidarians have **nematocysts,** which are special stinging structures. Nematocysts are used to stun or kill a cnidarian's prey. It is no surprise then that nematocysts are found on the tentacles surrounding a cnidarian's mouth. After capturing and stunning its prey, a cnidarian pulls the prey into its mouth with the tentacles. Once the food is digested within its central cavity, a cnidarian releases waste products through its only opening, which is its mouth.

Unlike sponges, cnidarians contain groups of cells that perform special functions. In other words, cnidarians have specialized tissues. An example of a specialized tissue is a nerve net, which is a simple nervous system that is concentrated around a cnidarian's mouth but spreads throughout the body. An interesting characteristic of cnidarians can be seen in Figure 10–7. Notice that a cnidarian is symmetrical. If you drew a line through the center of its body, both sides would be the same.

Most cnidarians can reproduce both sexually and asexually. Like sponges, cnidarians reproduce asexually by budding and sexually by producing eggs and sperm.

Figure 10–7 *Jellyfishes have a type of symmetry in which their body parts repeat around an imaginary line drawn through the center of their body. What other invertebrates have this type of symmetry?*

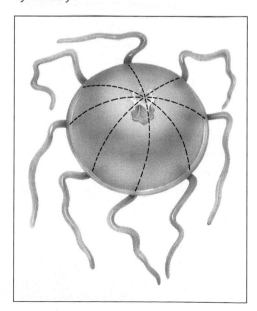

Hydras

Hydras belong to a group of cnidarians that spend their lives as polyps (vase-shaped body forms). Hydras are the only cnidarians that live in fresh water. All other cnidarians live in salty oceans. Unlike most other types of polyps, hydras can move around with a somersaulting movement. They can reproduce either asexually by budding or sexually by producing eggs and sperm.

Figure 10–8 *Unlike most cnidarians, which live in salty oceans, these green hydras live in freshwater lakes and streams. How do hydras reproduce?*

Corals

Like all cnidarians, corals are soft-bodied organisms. However, corals use minerals in the water to build hard, protective coverings of limestone. When a coral dies, the hard outer covering is left behind. Year after year, for many millions of years, generations of corals have lived and died, each generation adding a layer of limestone. In time, a coral reef forms. The Great Barrier Reef off the coast of Australia is an example of a coral reef. The top layer of the reef contains living corals. But underneath this "living stone" are the remains of corals that may have lived millions of years ago when dinosaurs walked the Earth.

Corals are polyps that live together in colonies. These colonies have a wide variety of shapes and

Figure 10–9 *Corals—such as staghorn corals (top left), lettuce corals (top right), grooved brain corals (bottom left), and tube corals (bottom right)—produce skeletons of calcium carbonate, or limestone.*

colors. Some coral colonies look like antlers. Others resemble fans swaying in the water. Still others resemble the structure of a human brain.

At first glance, a coral appears to be little more than a mouth surrounded by stinging tentacles. See Figure 10–9. But there is more to a coral than meets the eye. Living inside a coral's body are simple plant-like autotrophs known as algae. Algae help to make food for the coral. But because algae need sunlight to make food, corals must live in shallow water, where sunlight can reach them. The relationship between a coral animal and an alga plant is among the most unusual in nature.

Activity Bank

To Classify or Not to Classify?, p. 805

CONNECTIONS

No Bones About It

What do coral and bone have in common? Until a few years ago, it was thought they had little in common. Today, however, there are more similarities between coral and bone than meet the eye. And these similarities have made coral an excellent stand-in for bones in repairing serious bone fractures, or breaks.

Because coral resembles bone, doctors have recently begun using it to replace bone. Before the coral is inserted into the body, however, it is heated. The heat changes limestone (calcium carbonate), which is the main substance in coral, into calcium-containing hydroxyapatite, which is the main ingredient in bone. In the process, living coral organisms are killed.

When the coral is placed at the site of the fracture, it blends almost seamlessly with the bone. The maze of channels within the coral provides passageways through which blood vessels from nearby bone can grow. A permanent bond between bone and coral results.

Over time, the coral becomes filled with new bone.

Because coral is made of material naturally found in bones, the body does not treat it as a foreign substance. In other words, coral does not seem to activate the body's immune system (the body's defense against foreign material) nor produce inflammation (a condition that causes redness, pain, and swelling). Thus the coral remains unaffected, and the body remains unharmed as new bone grows.

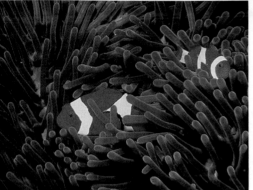

Figure 10–10 *The nematocysts on the tentacles of sea anemones are used to catch food. Although most large sea anemones eat fishes, this clownfish swims undisturbed through the sea anemone's tentacles. How do these two organisms help each other?*

Figure 10–11 *Jellyfishes, such as* Aequorea, *spend most of their life as bowl-shaped medusas.*

Sea Anemones

Can you see the fish swimming through what looks like a plant in Figure 10–10? That plant is actually an animal—a cnidarian known as a sea anemone (uh-NEHM-uh-nee). Sea anemones are polyps that resemble underwater flowers. Their "petals," however, are really tentacles that contain nematocysts (stinging structures). When a fish passes near a sea anemone's tentacles, the nematocysts stun the fish. Then the tentacles pull the fish into the sea anemone, where the stunned prey is digested within the central cavity.

If a fish is lucky enough to be a clownfish, however, it can swim unharmed through a sea anemone's tentacles. This friendly relationship between a sea anemone and a clownfish protects a clownfish from other fishes that might try to attack it. At the same time, a clownfish serves as living bait for a sea anemone. When other fishes see a clownfish swimming among a sea anemone's tentacles, they swim nearer, hoping to make the clownfish their next meal. But before they know it, they are grabbed by the sea anemone's tentacles and become its next meal!

Jellyfishes

If you have ever seen a jellylike cup floating in the ocean near you, you probably knew enough to stay clear of it. This cnidarian, known as a jellyfish, is one that most people recognize immediately.

Although a jellyfish may look harmless, it can deliver a painful poison through its nematocysts, which are located on its tentacles. In fact, even when the nematocysts are broken up into small pieces, they remain active. They can sting a passing swimmer who accidentally bumps into them. The largest jellyfish ever found had tentacles that reached out for more than 30 meters.

Of course, the nematocysts are not there merely to disturb unsuspecting swimmers. Like all cnidarians, jellyfishes use the nematocysts to capture prey. One type of jellyfish, the sea wasp jellyfish, produces a strong nerve poison that has helped scientists to better understand the function of nerves in humans.

10-4 Worms

Most people think of worms as slimy, squiggly creatures. And, in fact, many are. There are, however, many kinds of worms that look nothing like the worms used to bait fishing hooks. You can see examples of such worms in Figure 10–12. Worms are classified into three main phyla based on their shapes. **The three phyla of worms are flatworms, roundworms, and segmented worms.**

If you were to draw an imaginary line down the entire length of a worm's body, you would discover that the right half is almost a mirror image of the left half. See Figure 10–13 on page 270. With the exception of one phylum, this body symmetry

Guide for Reading

Focus on these questions as you read.

▶ *What are the three main groups of worms?*

▶ *What are the characteristics of each group of worms?*

Figure 10–12 *Contrary to popular belief, many worms—such as the feather duster worm (left) and the sea mouse (right)—are neither squiggly nor are they slimy.*

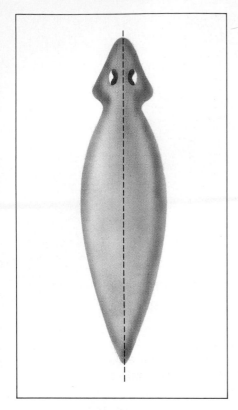

Figure 10–13 *Most of the more complex animals, such as the worms, have bodies in which the left half and the right half are almost mirror images of each other.*

Figure 10–14 *The planarian (right) is an example of a flatworm that is able to regenerate. An injury to this planarian (left) divided its head in half, and then the two halves regenerated their lost parts.*

(sameness of form on either side of a dividing line) is characteristic of all animals you will read about from here on, including worms.

Flatworms

Flatworms, as you might expect, have flat bodies. They are grouped in the phylum Platyhelminthes (plat-ih-hehl-MIHN-theez). The word platyhelminthes comes from two Greek words, *platy-,* meaning flat, and *helminth,* meaning worm. Some scientists believe that flatworms evolved from cnidarians. Other scientists are convinced that flatworms developed independently.

You have probably never seen a flatworm, much less a flatworm like the one in Figure 10–14. This flatworm is called a planarian. Most planarians, which are barely 0.5 centimeter long (a little less than the width of the nail on your pinky), live in ponds and streams—often on the underside of plant leaves or on underwater rocks. Planarians feed on dead plant or animal matter.

When there is little food available, however, some planarians do a rather unusual thing. They digest their own body parts. Later, when food is available once again, the missing parts regrow. Interestingly, if a planarian is cut into pieces, each piece eventually grows into a new planarian! The ability of an organism to regrow lost parts is called **regeneration.**

Some flatworms grow on or in living things and are called **parasites.** Tapeworms, which look like long, flat ribbons, live in the bodies of many animals, including humans. The head of a tapeworm has

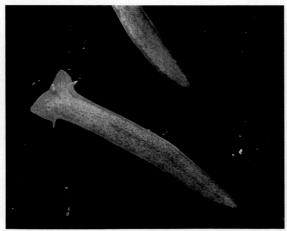
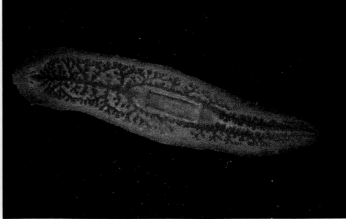

special hooks that are used to attach it to the tissues of a **host,** or the organism in which it lives. The tapeworm causes illness by taking a host's food and water, as well as by producing wastes and blocking the host's intestines.

A tapeworm can grow as long as 6 meters inside its host. However, size is not always a good indicator of danger. The most dangerous human tapeworm is only about 8 millimeters long and enters the body through microscopic eggs in some types of food.

Roundworms

You probably have been told never to eat pork unless it is well cooked. Do you know the reason for this warning? It has to do with a type of roundworm called *Trichinella* (trih-KIGH-nehl-uh), which lives in the muscle tissue of pigs. If a person eats a piece of raw or undercooked pork, *Trichinella* that are still alive in the pork enter the person's body. As many as 3000 roundworms can be contained in a single gram of raw or undercooked pork!

Once inside the body, the roundworms live and reproduce in the intestines of the host. Female roundworms release hundreds of immature round-worms, which are carried in the bloodstream. These immature roundworms then burrow into surrounding tissues and organs. This causes terrible pain for the host. Once inside tissues and organs, *Trichinella* become inactive. The name of this disease is trichi-nosis (trihk-ih-NOH-sihs).

Roundworms resemble strands of spaghetti with pointed ends. They belong to the phylum Nematoda (nehm-uh-TOHD-uh). The word nematode means threadlike. Roundworms live on land or in water. Many roundworms are animal parasites, although some live on plants. One type of roundworm, the hookworm, infects more than 600 million people in the world every year. Hookworms enter the body by burrowing through the skin on the soles of the feet. They eventually end up in the intestines of their hosts, where they live on the blood.

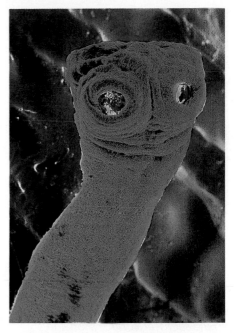

Figure 10–15 *Some flatworms, such as the tapeworm, are parasites. Notice that the head of a tapeworm has suckers and other structures that enable it to attach to the inside of its host's intestines. What is a parasite?*

Figure 10–16 Trichinella *worms, which cause the disease trichinosis, burrow into the muscle tissue of their host (top). These threadworms, tunneling through the tissues of a sheep's small intestine, are parasitic roundworms (bottom).*

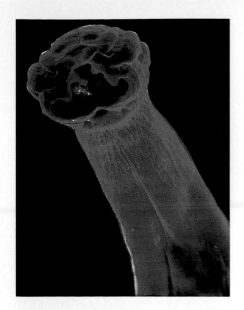

Figure 10–17 *Hookworms use the sharp teeth and hooks on their head end to burrow through their host's skin.*

Like all worms, roundworms have a head and a tail. In fact, worms were the first organisms to evolve with distinct head and tail ends. Roundworms have a tubelike digestive system that has two openings—a mouth and an anus (AY-nuhs). Food enters the digestive system through the mouth (in the head end) and waste products leave the digestive system through the anus (in the tail end). Although the digestive system of roundworms may not seem complex, it is far more advanced than that of cnidarians. As you may recall, cnidarians have one opening for both the intake of food and the elimination of wastes.

Segmented Worms

Segmented worms belong to the phylum Annelida (an-uh-LIHD-uh). The term annelid comes from the Latin word for ringed. This is an appropriate name for these invertebrates because their most obvious feature is a ringed, or segmented, body. These segments are visible on the outside of an annelid's body. Segmented worms live in salty oceans, in freshwater lakes and streams, or in the soil.

The segmented worm you are probably most familiar with is the common earthworm. The body of an earthworm is divided into numerous segments—100 at least. If you have ever touched an earthworm, you know it has a slimy outer layer. This layer, made of a slippery substance called mucus, helps the earthworm to glide through the soil. Tiny setae (SEE-tee; singular: seta), or bristles, on the segments of the earthworm also help it to pull itself along the ground.

As all gardeners know, earthworms are essential to a healthy garden. By burrowing through the soil, earthworms create tiny passageways through which air enters, thus improving the quality of the soil. As earthworms burrow, they feed on dead plant and animal matter. These materials are only partially digested. The undigested portions, or waste products, are eliminated into the surrounding soil, thus fertilizing the soil. The digestive system of an earthworm is shown in Figure 10–19.

Earthworms have a closed circulatory system. A closed circulatory system is one in which all body fluids are contained within small tubes. In an

Figure 10–18 *Many segmented worms, such as the sandworm, use hooklike jaws to capture their prey. To which phylum of invertebrates do sandworms belong?*

earthworm, the fluids are pumped throughout its body by a series of ringed blood vessels found near its head region. Because these blood vessels help to pump fluids through the circulatory system, they are sometimes called hearts.

Earthworms, like most annelids, have no special respiratory organs. Oxygen enters through the skin, and carbon dioxide leaves through the skin. In order for this to happen, the skin must stay moist. If an earthworm's skin dries out—which might happen if the earthworm remains out in the heat of the sun—the earthworm suffocates and dies.

Although earthworms have only a simple nervous system, they are very sensitive to their environment. An earthworm's nervous system consists of a brain found in the head region, two nerves that pass around the intestine, and a nerve cord located on the lower side.

In addition to these structures, an earthworm has a variety of cells that sense changes in its environment. One group of such cells, located on the first few body segments, detects moisture. Recall how important moisture is to an earthworm's survival. If an earthworm emerges from its burrow and encounters a dry spot, it will move from side to side until it finds dampness. If it does not find any moisture, it will retreat into its burrow. An earthworm can also sense danger and warn other earthworms. It does so by releasing a sweatlike material that helps it to glide more easily and to warn others of the nearby danger.

ACTIVITY

DISCOVERING

Worms at Work

1. Put a tall, thin can with the closed end up in a large jar. Fill the large jar with soil to the level of the tin can. Add a thin layer of sand.

2. Put five earthworms in the jar. Add pond water or tap water that has been standing for a day to slightly moisten the soil. Add more water if the soil appears dry.

3. Cover the outside of the jar with black paper and leave the jar undisturbed for a day.

4. Uncover the jar and look for the earthworms. Record your observations.

5. Cover the jar for one more day. Repeat step 4.

■ Have the earthworms been at work? Explain.

Figure 10–19 *The drawing shows the digestive system of the earthworm, a segmented worm. The photograph is of an earthworm moving along the surface of the soil. What structures help the earthworm move?*

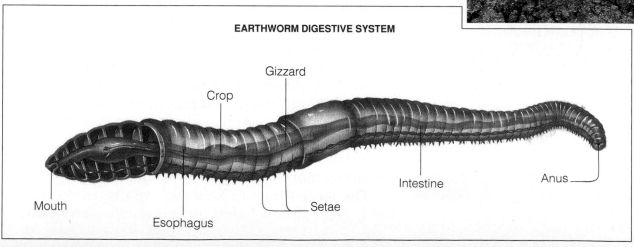

EARTHWORM DIGESTIVE SYSTEM

Gizzard

Crop

Mouth

Esophagus

Setae

Intestine

Anus

Figure 10–20 *An earthworm contains both male and female structures. When two earthworms mate, they exchange only sperm cells.*

10–5 Mollusks

If you enjoy eating a variety of seafood, you are probably already familiar with some members of the phylum Mollusca (muh-LUHS-kuh). Members of this phylum are called mollusks (MAHL-uhsks). Mollusks include clams, oysters, mussels, octopuses, and squids. The word mollusk comes from the Latin word meaning soft. **Mollusks are soft-bodied animals that typically have inner or outer shells.**

Most mollusks also have a thick muscular foot. Some mollusks use this foot to open and close their shell. Other mollusks use it for movement. Still others use the foot to bury themselves in the sand or mud.

The head region of a mollusk generally contains a mouth and sense organs such as eyes. The rest of a mollusk's body contains various organs that are involved in life processes such as reproduction, circulation, excretion, and digestion. A soft mantle covers much of a mollusk's body. The mantle produces the material that makes up the hard shell. As the mollusk grows, the mantle enlarges the shell, providing more room for its occupant.

The more common mollusks are divided into three main groups based on certain characteristics.

These characteristics include the presence of a shell, the type of shell, and the type of foot. **The three main groups of common mollusks are snails, slugs, and their relatives; two-shelled mollusks; and tentacled mollusks.**

Snails, Slugs, and Their Relatives

The largest group of common mollusks are those that have a single shell or no shell at all. The members of this group include snails, slugs, and sea butterflies, to name a few. These mollusks are also known as gastropods (GAS-troh-pahdz). The word gastropod means stomach foot. This name is appropriate because most gastropods move by means of a foot found on the same side of the body as their stomach. Gastropods live in both fresh water and salt water, as well as on land. Those gastropods that live on land, however, still must have a moist environment in order to survive.

Gastropods have an interesting feature called a radula (RAJ-oo-luh) in their mouth. The tongue-shaped radula resembles a file used by carpenters to scrape wood. The radula files off bits of plant matter into small pieces that can easily be swallowed.

The single-shelled gastropod that is probably most familiar to you is a garden snail. Have you ever watched a garden snail as it moves? If so, you might have noticed that it leaves a trail of slippery mucus behind. The mucus enables a snail to slowly glide across different types of surfaces. This is especially helpful when a snail encounters rough surfaces.

Slugs are gastropods that do not have a shell. The absence of a shell may seem to make slugs easy prey for their predators. But slugs are not entirely helpless. Most spend the daylight hours hiding under rocks and logs, thereby staying out of the way of birds and other animals that might eat them. Gastropods such as sea butterflies escape predators by rapidly swimming away. Many sea slugs, or nudibranchs (NOO-dih-brangks), have chemicals in their body that taste bad or are poisonous to unsuspecting predators.

Figure 10–21 *Mollusks—such as garden slugs (top), coquina clams (center), and cuttlefish (bottom)—have soft bodies. Unlike most mollusks, which have internal or external shells, slugs lack shells completely.*

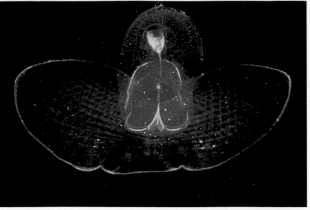

Figure 10–22 *Gastropods, the largest group of common mollusks, have a single shell or no shell at all. The single-shelled gastropod that is probably the most familiar to you is the land snail (left); whereas the sea butterfly (right) is not as common a sight. What are some other examples of gastropods?*

Activity Bank

Moving at a Snail's Pace, p. 806

Figure 10–23 *Scallops can move around by clapping their shells together (left). A scallop is also able to gather information about its surroundings with the help of its eyes, which are located on the mantle and resemble tiny blue dots (right).*

Two-Shelled Mollusks

Clams, oysters, scallops, and mussels are members of the group of common mollusks called bivalves, or two-shelled mollusks. Bivalves have two shells that are held together by powerful muscles. Although most bivalves remain in one place, scallops and a few others can move around rapidly by clapping their shells together. This action forces water out between the shells, thereby propelling the bivalve.

Unlike gastropods, bivalves do not have a radula. Instead, they are filter feeders. This means that as water passes over the body of a bivalve, the bivalve filters out small organisms.

The mantle of a bivalve, like that of most mollusks, contains glands that produce its shell. These glands keep the inside surfaces of the shell smooth. If a foreign object, such as a grain of sand, gets stuck between the mantle and the shell of some types of mollusks, the glands cover it with a shiny secretion. After a few years, the grain of sand becomes completely covered with secretions and is called a pearl.

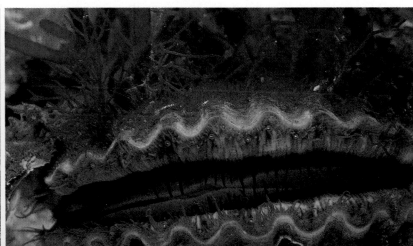

Tentacled Mollusks

The most highly developed mollusks are the tentacled mollusks. The tentacled mollusks are also called cephalopods (SEHF-uh-loh-pahdz). Included in this group are octopuses, squids, and nautiluses. Most cephalopods do not have an outer shell but have some part of a shell within their body. The one exception is the chambered nautilus. The chambered nautilus got its name from the fact that its shell consists of many chambers. These chambers are small when the animal is young but increase in size as the animal grows. As the nautilus grows, it builds a new outer chamber in which it lives.

All cephalopods have tentacles that they use to move themselves and to capture food. But the number and type of tentacles differ from one kind of cephalopod to another. Octopuses, of course, have eight tentacles (the prefix *octo-* means eight); squids have ten.

Even though most cephalopods do not have an outer shell, they do have ways to protect themselves. Most cephalopods can move quickly by either swimming or crawling. Octopuses, squids, and nautiluses can also move by using a form of jet propulsion. Water is drawn into the mantle cavity and then forced out through a tube, propelling the cephalopod backward—away from the danger. In addition, squids and octopuses produce a dark-colored ink when they are frightened. As this ink is released into the water, it helps to hide the mollusk and confuse its predators. The squid or octopus can then escape.

Figure 10–24 *The nautilus (top), squid (center), and octopus (bottom) are examples of cephalopods. What are some characteristics of cephalopods?*

10–5 Section Review

1. What are the main characteristics of mollusks?
2. How are mollusks grouped?
3. List the three main groups of mollusks and give an example of each.
4. What is a mantle? A radula?

Critical Thinking—*Relating Facts*
5. Suppose you found a mollusk with one shell and eyes located on two stalks sticking out of its head. Into which group of mollusks would you place it? Explain.

Laboratory Investigation

Observing Earthworm Responses

Problem

How do earthworms respond to changes in their environment?

Materials *(per group)*

2 live earthworms in a storage container
medicine dropper
paper towels
tray
piece of cardboard
desk lamp

Procedure △ ⫶⫶⊫ 🐀

1. Open the storage container and examine the earthworms. Record your observations of their physical characteristics. Fill the medicine dropper with water and use it to give your earthworms a "bath." **Note:** *Make sure you keep your earthworms moist by giving them frequent baths.*

2. Fold a dry paper towel and place it on one side of your tray. Fold a moistened paper towel and place it on the other side of the tray.

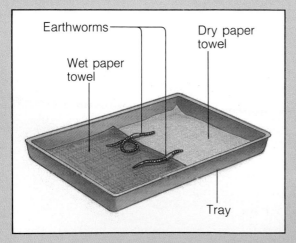

Earthworms
Dry paper towel
Wet paper towel
Tray

3. Place the earthworms in the center of the tray, between the dry paper towel and the moist paper towel. Cover the tray with the piece of cardboard.

4. After 5 minutes, remove the cardboard and observe the location of the earthworms. Record your observations.

5. Return the earthworms to their storage container. Using the dropper, moisten the earthworms with water.

6. Cover the entire bottom of the tray with a moistened paper towel.

7. Place the earthworms in the center of the tray.

8. Cover one half of the tray with the piece of cardboard. Position the lamp above the uncovered side of the tray.

9. After 5 minutes, observe the location of the earthworms. Record your observations.

10. Return the earthworms to their storage container. Using the dropper, moisten the earthworms with water. Cover the container and return it to your teacher.

Observations

Describe the earthworms' color, texture, external features, and other physical characteristics.

Analysis and Conclusions

1. How does an earthworm's response to moisture help it to survive?

2. Does an earthworm's response to light have any protective value? Explain.

3. How is an earthworm's body adapted for movement through the soil?

4. Would you expect to find earthworms in hard soil? Explain.

Study Guide

Summarizing Key Concepts

10-1 Introduction to the Animal Kingdom

▲ Vertebrates are animals with a backbone. Invertebrates are animals without a backbone.

10-2 Sponges

▲ Sponges belong to the phylum Porifera. They are called poriferans because their bodies are covered with many pores.

▲ The cells of sponges remove food and oxygen from ocean water as the water flows through pores. The water flowing out through a larger opening carries away waste products.

▲ Sexual reproduction is the process by which a new organism forms from the joining of a female cell (egg) and a male cell (sperm).

▲ Asexual reproduction is the process by which a single organism produces a new organism.

10-3 Cnidarians

▲ Cnidarians belong to the phylum Cnidaria. They have a hollow central cavity with one opening called the mouth.

▲ Cnidarians have structures called nematocysts on the tentacles around their mouth.

10-4 Worms

▲ The three main groups of worms are flatworms, roundworms, and segmented worms.

▲ Flatworms, members of the phylum Platyhelminthes, have flat bodies and live in ponds and streams.

▲ Organisms that grow on or in other living things are called parasites. The organism upon which a parasite lives is called the host.

▲ Roundworms are members of the phylum Nematoda.

▲ Segmented worms, or annelids, have segmented bodies and live in soil or in salt water or fresh water.

10-5 Mollusks

▲ Mollusks, members of the phylum Mollusca, are animals with soft bodies that typically have inner or outer shells.

▲ Most mollusks have a thick, muscular foot and are covered by a mantle.

Reviewing Key Terms

Define each term in a complete sentence.

10-1 Introduction to the Animal Kingdom
vertebrate
invertebrate

10-2 Sponges
spicule
sexual reproduction
asexual reproduction

10-3 Cnidarians
nematocyst

10-4 Worms
regeneration
parasite
host

Chapter Review

Content Review

Multiple Choice

Choose the letter of the answer that best completes each statement.

1. Which is an animal?
   a. bacterium   c. mushroom
   b. mosquito   d. ameba

2. Organisms that can make their own food are called
   a. protists.   c. fungi.
   b. heterotrophs.   d. autotrophs.

3. Which is an invertebrate?
   a. lion   c. dog
   b. human   d. jellyfish

4. Which animal is a member of the phylum Porifera?
   a. sponge   c. planarian
   b. coral   d. squid

5. Cnidarians have
   a. pores.
   b. a mouth and an anus.
   c. mantles.
   d. nematocysts.

6. Which animal is a flatworm?
   a. hydra   c. planarian
   b. sea anemone   d. jellyfish

7. The animal that causes trichinosis is a
   a. roundworm.
   b. flatworm.
   c. segmented worm.
   d. cnidarian.

8. Tapeworms are
   a. sponges.   c. cnidarians.
   b. flatworms.   d. mollusks.

9. All mollusks have
   a. outer shells.   c. nematocysts.
   b. soft bodies.   d. spicules.

10. Clams are
    a. cnidarians.
    b. mollusks.
    c. flatworms.
    d. roundworms.

True or False

If the statement is true, write "true." If it is false, change the underlined word or words to make the statement true.

1. Animals are multicellular <u>autotrophs</u>.
2. <u>Invertebrates</u> have no backbone.
3. All sponges have <u>pores</u>.
4. Nematocysts are found in <u>mollusks</u>.
5. <u>Flatworms</u> are nematodes.
6. In <u>segmented worms</u>, the mantle produces the shell.
7. An oyster is an example of a <u>tentacled mollusk</u>.
8. The octopus is a <u>cnidarian</u>.

Concept Mapping

Complete the following concept map for Section 10–1. Then construct a concept map for the entire chapter.

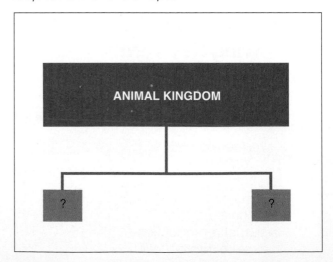

ANIMAL KINGDOM

?   ?

Concept Mastery

Discuss each of the following in a brief paragraph.

1. Why do you think it is important to study animals?
2. List the two groups of animals and give a description of each.
3. Describe the similarities and differences among the three groups of mollusks.
4. List the different methods sponges, cnidarians, worms, and mollusks use to get food.
5. Describe how sponges take in oxygen and give off carbon dioxide.
6. In what ways are sponges useful?
7. Compare a medusa and a polyp.
8. Why are tapeworms parasites?
9. How are mollusks useful?
10. Compare sexual reproduction and asexual reproduction.

Critical Thinking and Problem Solving

Use the skills you have developed in this chapter to answer each of the following.

1. **Making charts** Construct a chart in which you list each phylum of invertebrates discussed in this chapter, the major characteristics of the phylum, and two examples from each phylum.
2. **Applying concepts** Why is it that scientists do not classify animals by what they eat or where they live?
3. **Making generalizations** In what ways are earthworms beneficial to humans?
4. **Designing an experiment** The eyes of a squid are similar in structure to the eyes of a vertebrate. Design an experiment to determine whether or not squids are able to see color. Include a hypothesis, control, and variable.
5. **Relating cause and effect** People with tapeworms eat a lot but still feel hungry and tired. Why?
6. **Making predictions** Would it be safe to eat clams from polluted water? Give a logical reason for your answer.
7. **Relating facts** Explain this statement: In a classification system, an organism is identified by showing what it is not.
8. **Using the writing process** Imagine that you could shrink down to a size small enough to fit inside an earthworm. Describe the adventures you and the earthworm would have in a garden one summer day.

Arthropods and Echinoderms

11

Guide for Reading

After you read the following sections, you will be able to

11–1 Arthropods: The "Joint-Footed" Animals

■ Describe the characteristics of arthropods.

■ Identify the major groups of arthropods.

11–2 Insects: The Most Numerous Arthropods

■ Describe the characteristics of insects.

■ Explain how insects behave.

11–3 Echinoderms: The "Spiny-Skinned" Animals

■ Describe the characteristics of echinoderms.

As darkness falls on a warm summer evening, fireflies light their "lanterns." The temperature has to be warm enough and the late-day light dim enough for them to be seen. If these conditions prevail, the tiny magicians light up the night worldwide.

A firefly's light is one of nature's marvels. It is light with almost no heat—a feat humans have yet to achieve. In fact, a firefly's light is cooler than the warm night air that surrounds it.

The greatest firefly show in the world occurs during summer evenings in Thailand. Male fireflies bunch together on certain trees that line the rivers. Flashing 120 times a minute, the male fireflies soon regulate their flashes so that at one instant there is total blackness, and at the next instant total illumination—over and over again!

Fireflies (which are actually beetles, not flies) belong to a phylum of invertebrates called arthropods. In this chapter you will read about this phylum of fascinating creatures. And you will also be introduced to another phylum of invertebrates, the echinoderms, which includes the lovely yet somewhat dangerous purple sea urchin.

Journal *Activity*

You and Your World Think of a place near your home or school where animals may live. It can be a schoolyard, a backyard, an empty lot, a park, or even an alley. It should have some soil, rocks, green plants, and a source of moisture. Write a detailed description of the area in your journal. Draw a picture of it. Then visit the area and see if your description was accurate. Make any necessary changes in your journal.

◀ *The Thailand night is illuminated by an awesome firefly show.*

11–1 Arthropods: The "Joint-Footed" Animals

The phylum of invertebrates that contains the greatest number of species is the phylum Arthropoda (ahr-THRAHP-uh-duh). Members of this phylum are called arthropods. To date, more than 1 million species of arthropods have been described. Scientists estimate, however, that the total number of arthropod species may be as high as 1 billion billion, or 1,000,000,000,000,000,000! Arthropods live in air, on land, and in water. Wherever you happen to live, you can be sure arthropods live there too. Arthropods are our main competitors for food. In fact, if left alone and unchecked, they could eventually take over the Earth!

Why are there so many arthropods? One reason is that they have been evolving (changing) on Earth for more than 300 million years. During this time, they have developed certain characteristics that allowed them to become so successful. Of these characteristics, three are common to all arthropods. **The three characteristics shared by all arthropods are an exoskeleton, a segmented body, and jointed appendages.**

Figure 11–1 *The spider crab (top left), millipede (top right), daddy longlegs (bottom right), and weevil and ant (bottom left) are members of the largest and most diverse group of invertebrates: the arthropods. What three characteristics are shared by all arthropods?*

The most striking characteristic of arthropods is the **exoskeleton.** An exoskeleton is a rigid outer covering. The exoskeletons of many land-dwelling arthropods are waterproof. Such exoskeletons limit the loss of water from the bodies of arthropods, thus making it possible for them to live in remarkably dry environments such as deserts. In some ways, an exoskeleton is like the armor worn by knights in the Middle Ages as protection in battle. One drawback of an exoskeleton, however, is that it does not grow as the animal grows. So the arthropod's protective suit must be shed and replaced from time to time. This process is called **molting.** While the exoskeleton is replacing itself, the arthropod is more vulnerable to attack from other animals.

Like annelids (segmented worms), arthropods have segmented bodies. This characteristic strongly suggests that annelids and arthropods evolved from a common ancestor. The body of most arthropods, however, is shorter and has fewer segments than an annelid's.

Although the phylum name, Arthropoda, comes from the Greek words meaning jointed legs, it is not just legs that enable arthropods to move. The appendages characteristic of arthropods include antennae, claws, walking legs, and wings as well. See Figure 11–4 on page 286.

An arthropod has an open circulatory system, or one in which the blood is not contained within small tubes. Instead, the blood is pumped by a heart throughout the spaces within the arthropod's body.

Figure 11–2 *In order to increase in size, arthropods must molt, or shed their exoskeletons. This adult cicada is emerging from its exoskeleton, which it has outgrown.*

Figure 11–3 *Some arthropods, such as the Hawaiian lobster and dust mite have hard, tough exoskeletons. Other arthropods, such as the Promethea moth caterpillar, have flexible exoskeletons. What is an exoskeleton?*

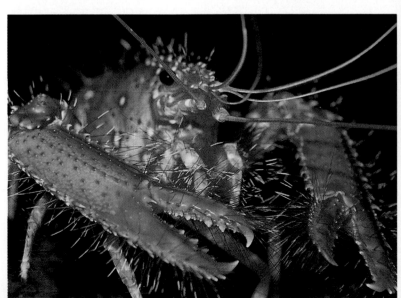

285

Figure 11–4 *Arthropod appendages include the antennae of a harlequin beetle, the claws of a fiddler crab, the legs of a praying mantis, and the wings of a green lacewing fly.*

Ａctivity Bank

Off and Running, p.808

ACTIVITY ─ READING

A Silky Story

You may want to read a wonderful story about an exceptional spider named Charlotte who weaves messages into her web. The book is entitled *Charlotte's Web,* and it was written by E. B. White.

Although an arthropod's blood carries food throughout its body, it does not carry oxygen. Oxygen is carried to all the cells by one (sometimes two) of three basic respiratory (breathing) organs—gills, book lungs, and a system of air tubes.

Arthropods reproduce sexually. That means there are two parents, a male and a female. The male produces sperm, and the female produces eggs. In most arthropods, the sperm and the egg unite inside the body of the female.

Various animals make up this phylum. They include crustaceans (kruhs-TAY-shuhnz), centipedes and millipedes, spiders and their relatives, and insects.

Crustaceans

Do you see the two eyes peering out at you from the shell in Figure 11–5? These eyes belong to an animal known as a hermit crab. A hermit crab is a crustacean that lives in shells discarded by other water-dwelling animals such as mollusks. A crustacean is an arthropod that has a hard exoskeleton, two pairs of antennae, and mouthparts that are used for crushing and grinding food. Crustaceans include crabs, lobsters, barnacles, and shrimp.

The body of a crustacean is divided into segments. A pair of appendages is attached to each segment. The type of appendage varies, depending on the crustacean. Crabs, for example, have claws. The claws of some crabs are so strong that they can be used to open a crab's favorite food, a coconut. Crabs also have walking legs and antennae, which are some other examples of appendages.

Crustaceans such as crabs are able to regenerate (regrow) certain parts of their body. The stone crab, which lives in the waters off the coast of Florida, can grow new claws. This is an important characteristic for a stone crab because its claws are considered particularly tasty by people. When a stone crab is caught, one of its claws is broken off and the stone crab is returned to the water. In about a year's time, the missing claw is regenerated. If a crab is caught again, that claw may once again be removed.

Most crustaceans live in watery environments and obtain oxygen from the water through special respiratory organs called gills. Even the few land-dwelling crustaceans have gills. Such crustaceans, however, must live in damp areas in order to get oxygen.

Figure 11–5 *Water-dwelling crustaceans include the hermit crab and goose neck barnacles.*

Figure 11–6 *The diagram shows some of the internal and external structures of a crayfish.*

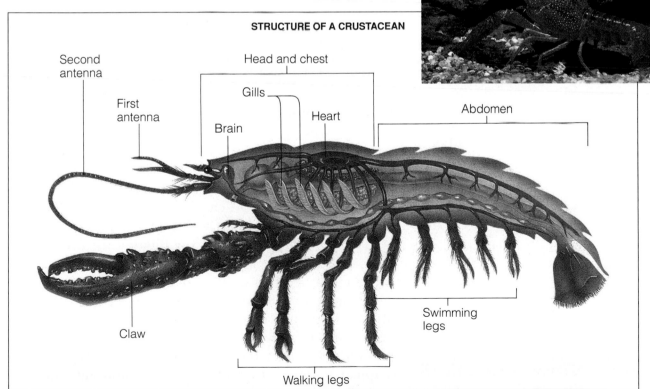

STRUCTURE OF A CRUSTACEAN

Second antenna

First antenna

Head and chest

Gills

Brain

Heart

Abdomen

Claw

Walking legs

Swimming legs

Figure 11–7 *Although a centipede (top) and a millipede (bottom) look very much alike, they do differ in some ways. What are two ways in which centipedes and millipedes differ?*

Centipedes and Millipedes

Centipedes and millipedes are arthropods that have many legs. What distinguishes one from the other is that centipedes have one pair of legs in each segment, whereas millipedes have two pairs of legs in each segment.

If you were an earthworm crawling through the soil, you would certainly be aware of another difference between centipedes and millipedes. Millipedes live on plants and thus would simply pass you by. Millipedes are shy creatures. When disturbed, millipedes may roll up into a ball to protect themselves. Centipedes, on the other hand, are carnivores, or flesh eaters. They are active hunters. To capture you, a centipede would inject poison into your body through its claws. (Another difference between centipedes and millipedes is that centipedes have claws and millipedes do not.)

Unlike many arthropods, the exoskeletons of centipedes and millipedes are not waterproof. To avoid excessive water loss, centipedes and millipedes are usually found in damp places such as under rocks or in soil.

Spiders and Their Relatives

There is a legend in Greek mythology about a young woman named Arachne (uh-RAK-nee) who challenged the goddess Athena to a weaving contest. When Arachne won the contest, Athena tore up Arachne's tapestry. Arachne hanged herself in sorrow. Athena then changed Arachne into a spider and Arachne's tapestry into a spider's web. Today spiders, as well as scorpions, ticks, and mites, are included in a group of arthropods called arachnids (uh-RAK-nihdz). As you can see, the word arachnid comes from the name Arachne.

The body of an arachnid is divided into two parts: a head and chest part and an abdomen part. Although arachnids vary in size and shape, they all have four pairs (8) of walking legs. So if you ever find a small animal you think is a spider, count its legs to make sure.

Spiders usually feed on insects. A few types of tropical spiders, however, can catch and eat small

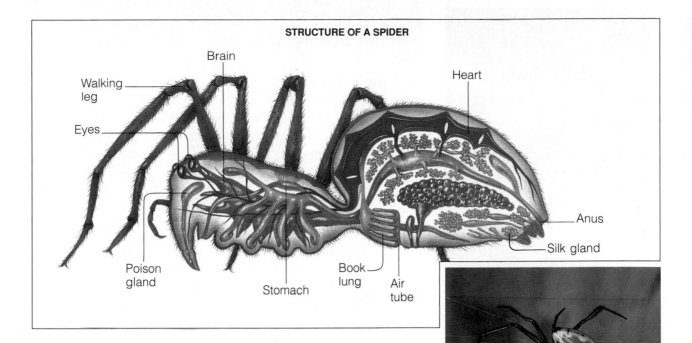

STRUCTURE OF A SPIDER

Walking leg

Brain

Eyes

Heart

Poison gland

Stomach

Book lung

Air tube

Anus

Silk gland

vertebrates such as hummingbirds. Spiders catch their prey in different ways. Many make webs of fine, yet very strong, flexible material called silk. Silk is secreted by special structures located in a spider's abdomen. Many spiders weave a new web every day. At night, the spiders eat the strands of that day's web, recycling the material the following day when they produce a new web. Although many spiders do not spin webs, they all produce silk. The silk that makes up the web is five times stronger than steel!

Some spiders hide from their prey and then suddenly jump out, taking the unsuspecting victim by surprise. For example, the trapdoor spider lives in a hole in the ground covered by a door made of silk. The door itself is hidden by soil and bits of plants. When an unsuspecting insect passes close to the trapdoor, the trapdoor spider jumps out and catches the unlucky victim.

Once a spider catches its prey, it injects venom, or poison, into the prey through a pair of fangs. Sometimes the venom kills the prey immediately. Other times it only paralyzes the prey. In this way, the spider can preserve living creatures trapped in its web for a time when it needs more food.

Most spiders get their oxygen by means of respiratory organs called book lungs. This is an appropriate name for these organs because the several sheets

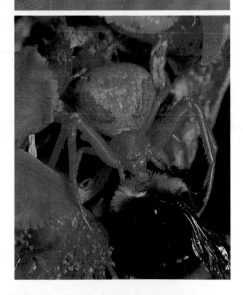

Figure 11–8 *Spiders such as the orchard spider (top) and flower crab spider (bottom) belong to the group of arthropods called arachnids. Compare the structures that you see in the photographs with those shown in the diagram of the spider. How many legs do arachnids have?*

Figure 11–9 *Some spiders, such as the orb weaver spider, build webs to catch their prey. What material makes up the web?*

of tissues that make up the structure resemble pages in a book. As air passes over the book lungs, oxygen is removed. Some spiders, however, have respiratory organs that form a system of air tubes. These air tubes are connected to the outside of the spider's body through small openings in its exoskeleton.

Arachnids live in many environments. Most spiders live on land. One interesting exception is a spider that lives under water inside bubbles of air that it carries down from the surface. When the air bubbles are used up, the spider returns to the water's surface for a fresh supply.

Scorpions are generally found in dry desert areas. Scorpions are active primarily at night. During the day, they hide under logs, stones, or in holes in the ground. People who enjoy camping must be careful

Figure 11–10 *Spiders capture their prey in several ways. The trapdoor spider (left) lies in wait and then leaps out to grab unlucky insects. The wolf spider (bottom right) hides in burrows in the sand waiting for its unsuspecting prey. The tarantula (top right) is large enough to catch and eat small vertebrates.*

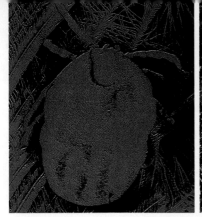

when they put on their shoes or boots in the morning: A scorpion may have mistaken the footwear for a suitable place in which to escape from the heat of the day! When scorpions capture prey, they hold it with their large front claws and, at the same time, inject it with venom through the stingers in their tails.

Ticks and mites live on other organisms. They may live on a plant and stay in one place, or they may live on an animal and travel wherever the animal travels. Like certain flatworms and roundworms, ticks and mites live off the body fluids of plants and animals. Some live by sucking juices from the stems and leaves of plants. Other ticks and mites are very tiny and live on insects. Many ticks suck blood from larger animals. In the process, they may spread disease. For example, Rocky Mountain spotted fever and Lyme disease are spread to people through the bites of ticks.

11–1 Section Review

1. What are the three main characteristics of arthropods?
2. What is an exoskeleton?
3. List four groups of arthropods.
4. What are some ways in which spiders and their relatives catch prey?

Critical Thinking—*Applying Concepts*
5. Blue crabs usually have hard shells. During certain times of the year, however, some blue crabs have thin, papery shells and are called soft-shell crabs. In terms of the life processes of arthropods, explain why these blue crabs have soft shells.

Figure 11–11 *Notice the stinger at the end of the scorpion's tail. The wood tick and the red velvet mites, which are devouring a termite, are arachnids.*

ctivity Bank

Spinning Webs, p.809

Activity

DISCOVERING

The Life of a Mealworm
1. Fill a clean 1-liter jar about one third full of bran cereal.
2. Place four mealworms in the jar.
3. Add a few slices of raw potato to the jar.
4. Shred a newspaper and place it loosely in the jar.
5. Cover the top of the jar with a layer of cheesecloth. Use a rubber band to hold the cheesecloth in place.
6. Observe the jar at least once a week for 4 weeks. Record all changes that take place in the mealworms.

How long was the mealworms' life cycle?

■ Do mealworms undergo complete or incomplete metamorphosis? Explain.

11–2 Insects: The Most Numerous Arthropods

Perhaps you have noticed that one group of arthropods mentioned in the previous section has not yet been discussed. This group, of course, is the insects. It would be hard to overlook insects for long. After all, there are more kinds of insects than there are all other animal species combined. In fact, it has been estimated that there may be as many as 300 million insects for every person on Earth!

Insect Structure

Insects are described as having a body that is divided into three parts—a head, a chest, and an abdomen—and that has three pairs (6) of legs attached to the chest part. In a grasshopper, which is a typical insect, the three pairs of legs are not identical. In order for a grasshopper to jump, one pair of legs must be larger than the other two pairs. Which pair of legs do you think is larger: the front pair or the back pair?

If you look closely at the head of a grasshopper, you will see five eyes peering back at you. Three of these eyes are located on the front of the grasshopper's head and are called simple eyes. Simple eyes can detect only light and dark. The remaining two

Figure 11–12 *Compare this grasshopper with the diagram of the structure of a grasshopper. How many legs does an insect have?*

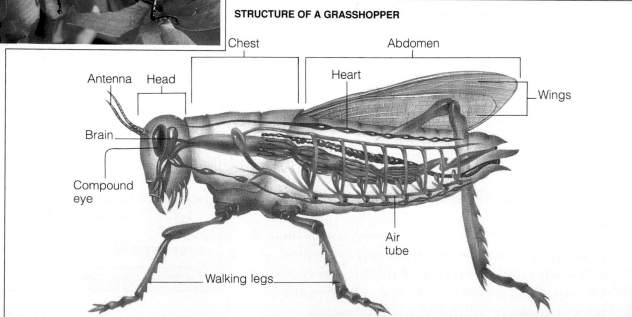

STRUCTURE OF A GRASSHOPPER

Chest

Abdomen

Heart

Antenna Head

Wings

Brain

Compound eye

Air tube

Walking legs

eyes, which are found on each side of the grasshopper's head, are called compound eyes. Compound eyes contain many lenses. Although compound eyes can distinguish some colors, they are best at detecting movement. This ability is important to an animal that is hunted by other animals on a daily basis.

Like most insects, a grasshopper has wings—two pairs of wings, in fact. Although these wings are best suited for short distances, some types of grasshoppers can fly great distances in search of food. Insect flight varies from the gentle fluttering motion of a butterfly to the speedy movement of a hawkmoth, which can fly as fast as 50 kilometers per hour!

Like all insects, a grasshopper does not have a well-developed system for getting oxygen into its body and removing waste gases from its body. What a grasshopper does have is a system of tubes that carries oxygen through the exoskeleton and into its body.

Male grasshoppers produce sperm, and female grasshoppers produce eggs. Like most insects, a male grasshopper deposits sperm inside a female grasshopper during reproduction.

Growth and Development of Insects

Insects spend a great deal of time eating. As a result, they grow rapidly. And like other arthropods, insects must shed their exoskeletons as they grow. During the growth process, insects pass through several stages of development. Some species of insects change their appearance completely as they pass through the different stages. This dramatic change in form is known as **metamorphosis** (meht-uh-MOR-fuh-sihs). The word metamorphosis comes from the Greek words meaning to transform. There are two types of metamorphosis: complete and incomplete.

During complete metamorphosis, insects such as butterflies, beetles, bees, and moths pass through a four-stage process. The first stage produces an egg. When an egg hatches, a **larva** (LAHR-vuh) emerges, completing the second stage. A caterpillar is the larva of an insect that will one day become a butterfly or a moth. Maggots are the larvae of flies, and grubs are the larvae of some types of beetles. A larva spends almost all its time eating.

Figure 11–13 *Insects such as the horsefly have compound eyes. Within the eyes are many lenses that enable the insect to detect the slightest movement of an object.*

Figure 11–14 *Insects, birds, and bats are the only organisms that can fly on their own. Like all insects, the painted beauty butterfly and the drone fly have two pairs of wings.*

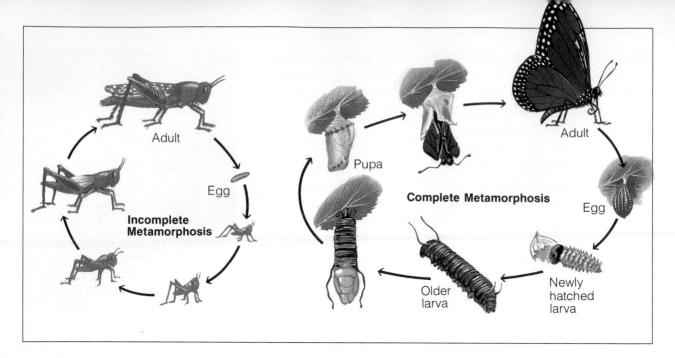

Figure 11–15 *The monarch butterfly (right) undergoes complete metamorphosis, whereas the grasshopper (left) undergoes incomplete metamorphosis. What is another name for the older larva of a monarch butterfly?*

Figure 11–16 *The monarch butterfly begins life as an egg and then becomes a larva, also known as a caterpillar. During the pupa stage, the caterpillar wraps itself into a cocoon called a chrysalis. Finally, the butterfly emerges.*

Eventually, a larva enters the third stage, which produces a **pupa** (PYOO-puh; plural: pupae). Pupae are sometimes wrapped in a covering called a cocoon or chrysalis (KRIHS-uh-lihs). A cocoon is made of silk or other similar material. During this stage, remarkable changes take place, and an adult insect soon emerges. The adult signals the last stage of complete metamorphosis. An adult insect not only looks like a different animal, it also behaves differently.

During incomplete metamorphosis—which occurs in insects such as grasshoppers, termites, and dragonflies—young animals looking very much like the adults hatch from eggs. See Figure 11–15. These young animals do not have the organs of an adult, however, and they often do not have wings either. As the young animals grow, they keep molting (shedding

their exoskeletons) and getting larger until they reach adult size. Along the way, the young animals acquire all the characteristics of an adult animal.

Insect Behavior

Most insects live solitary lives. In this way, they do not compete directly with other members of their species for available food. Male and female insects, however, do interact in order to reproduce. But before they do, they must attract or signal each other. This is done in a variety of ways, depending on the insects. For example, to attract a female, the male cicada (sih-KAY-duh) buzzes by, vibrating a special membrane in its abdomen. A male firefly attracts a female firefly, which in some species is called a glowworm, by turning the light-producing organ in its abdomen on and off. The female gypsy moth attracts a male by releasing extremely powerful chemicals called **pheromones** (FER-uh-mohnz). Pheromones cannot be detected by humans, but only a small amount of pheromones can attract a male gypsy moth from several kilometers downwind.

Other insects, known as social insects, cannot survive alone. These insects form colonies, or hives. Ants, termites, some wasp species, and bees are social insects. They survive as a society of individual insects that perform different jobs. As you can see in Figure 11–18, many of these colonies are highly organized.

One of the most fascinating examples of an insect society is a beehive. A beehive is a marvel of organization. Worker bees, which are all females, perform

Figure 11–17 A male luna moth's feathery antennae can detect pheromones released by a female luna moth several kilometers away. What are pheromones?

Figure 11–18 It may be hard to believe, but this mound was built by termites (left)! Termites, carpenter ants (center), and honeybees (right) are examples of social insects. How do social insects differ from most other insects?

What Kind of Insect Is It?

There are many different kinds, or orders, of insects. Visit the library and look up the following information about insects: name of the order, some characteristics of the order, and two examples of insects found in that order. Arrange this information in the form of a chart.

all the tasks necessary for the survival of the hive. Worker bees supply the other members of the hive with food by making honey and the combs in which the honey is stored. They also feed the queen bee, whose only function is to produce an enormous number of eggs. In addition, worker bees clean and protect the hive. Male bees have only one function: to fertilize a queen's eggs.

Defense Mechanisms of Insects

Insects have many defense mechanisms that enable them to survive. Wasps and bees use stingers to defend themselves against enemies. Other insects are masters of camouflage (KAM-uh-flahj). This means that they can hide from their enemies by blending into their surroundings. For example, insects such as the stick grasshoppers resemble sticks and twigs. These insects survive because their bodies are not easily seen by their predators. See Figure 11–19.

Figure 11–19 *Insects defend themselves in a variety of ways. The tropical walking stick (top right) blends in with its surroundings so that it can hide from its predators. The bombardier beetle (bottom right) sprays a foul-smelling chemical. The peacock moth (bottom left) has eyespots that startle predators. How do you think the thorn bug (top left) defends itself?*

Do You Want to Dance?

How do honeybees communicate information about the type, quality, direction, and distance of a food source to other members of the hive? The answer is that they do a little dance. Actually, they do two basic dances: a round dance and a waggle dance.

In the round dance, the honeybee scout that has found food circles first in one direction and then in the other up the honeycomb, over and over again. This dance tells the other honeybees that food is within 50 meters of the hive.

In the waggle dance, the honeybee scout that has found food runs straight up the honeycomb while waggling her abdomen, circles in one direction, runs straight again, and then circles in the other direction. This dance tells the other honeybees that food is more than 50 meters away from the hive. If food is located toward the sun, the honeybee scout will run straight up the honeycomb in the same direction as the sun. If food is located 30° to the right of the sun, she will make a series of runs to the right of an imaginary vertical line on the honeycomb. If food is located 30° to the left of the sun, the same dance will be performed to the left of the imaginary line.

Use the four diagrams to answer the questions that follow.

1. Where is food located in Diagram C?

2. How far away is food in Diagram B: less than 50 meters or more than 50 meters?

3. Where is food located in Diagram A?

4. How far away is food in Diagram D: less than 50 meters or more than 50 meters?

Applying Facts

■ If you were a honeybee scout, how would you tell your hivemates that food is located more than 50 meters from the hive and 40° to the left of the sun?

■ Do honeybee scouts do waggle dances at night? Explain.

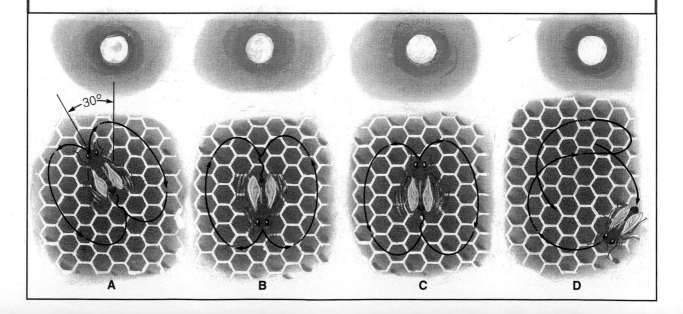

A B C D

Guide for Reading

Focus on this question as you read

▶ What are the characteristics of echinoderms?

Figure 11–20 *Starfishes such as the ochre sea star use their tube feet to open mussels.*

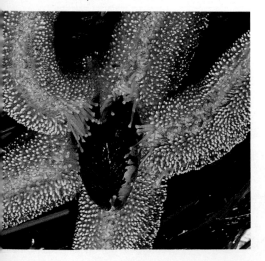

11–3 Echinoderms: The "Spiny-Skinned" Animals

Have you ever seen a starfish? Look at the photograph in Figure 11–21. It shows an interesting example of an invertebrate that belongs to the phylum Echinodermata (ee-kihg-noh-DER-muh-tuh). Members of this phylum are called echinoderms. Echinoderms include starfishes, sea lilies, feather stars, sea cucumbers, sea urchins, and sand dollars—to name just a few. The word echinoderm comes from the Greek words meaning spiny skin. As their name indicates, members of this phylum are spiny-skinned animals.

In addition to having a spiny skin, echinoderms have an internal skeleton, a five-part body, a water vascular system, and structures called tube feet. The internal skeleton of an echinoderm is made of bonylike plates of calcium that are bumpy or spiny. The **water vascular system** is a system of fluid-filled internal tubes that carry food and oxygen, remove wastes, and help echinoderms move. These tubes open to the outside through a strainerlike structure. This structure connects to other tubes, which eventually connect to the suction-cuplike **tube feet.** All echinoderms use their tube feet to "walk." Some echinoderms also use them to get food.

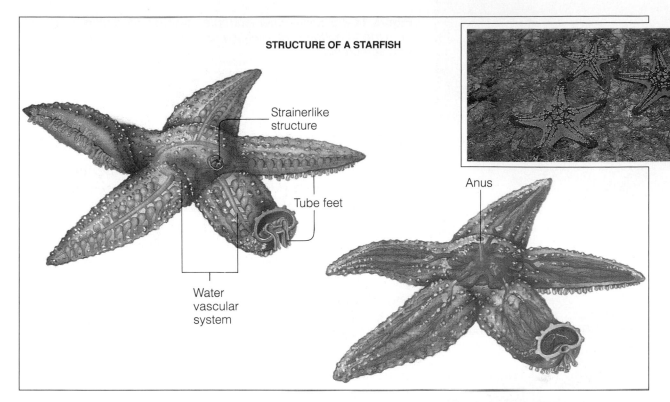

STRUCTURE OF A STARFISH

Strainerlike structure

Tube feet

Water vascular system

Anus

Starfishes

Although starfishes are not fish, most of them are shaped like stars. For this reason, starfishes are also called sea stars. Those that are star shaped have five or more arms, or rays, extending from a central body. On the underside of the arms are hundreds of tube feet that resemble tiny suction cups. These tube feet help the animal to move about and to obtain food. When a starfish passes over a clam, which is one of its favorite foods, the tiny tube feet grasp the clam's shell. The suction action of the hundreds of tube feet creates a tremendous force on the clam's shell. Eventually, the shell opens and the starfish enjoys a tasty meal.

People who harvest clams from the ocean bottom have long been at war with starfish that destroy the clam beds. In the past, starfishes captured near clam beds were cut into pieces and thrown back into the ocean. The people soon learned that, like flatworms and some crustaceans, starfishes have the ability to regenerate. By cutting them up, the people were guaranteeing that there would always be more and more starfishes—exactly the opposite of what they wanted to do.

Figure 11–21 *Echinoderm means spiny skin, which as you can see from this photograph of starfishes is an appropriate name for members of this phylum.*

Figure 11–22 *This sea star regenerated from a single arm.*

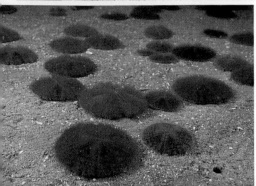

Figure 11–23 *Some other examples of echinoderms include, from top to bottom, sea lilies, sand dollars, sea cucumbers, and sea urchins.*

Other Echinoderms

Members of the other groups of echinoderms vary widely in appearance. Sea lilies and feather stars, which are thought to be the most ancient of the echinoderms, look like flowers and stars with long, feathery arms. These echinoderms spend most of their time attached or clinging to the ocean bottom. They use their long, feathery arms to gather food from the surrounding water.

Sea cucumbers, as their name implies, resemble warty cucumbers, with a mouth at one end and an anus at the other. These animals are usually found lying on the bottom of the ocean. Sea cucumbers move along the ocean bottom by using the five rows of tube feet on their body surface to wiggle back and forth.

Sea urchins and sand dollars are round shaped and rayless. Sand dollars are flat, whereas sea urchins are dome shaped. Many sea urchins have long spines that they use for protection. In some of these sea urchins, poisonous sacs found at the tip of each spine can deliver painful stings.

11–3 Section Review

1. What are the characteristics of echinoderms?
2. List some examples of echinoderms.
3. What are two functions of a starfish's tube feet?
4. Why is cutting up a starfish and throwing it back into the ocean an ineffective way of reducing a population of starfishes?

Critical Thinking—*Making Comparisons*
5. What are some similarities between echinoderms and mollusks? What are some differences? Which group do you think is more complex? Explain.

CONNECTIONS

Insects in Flight

Like a helicopter, a dragonfly can fly straight up or straight down. It can move to the right or to the left. It can glide forward or backward or simply hover in the air. And it can land on a lily pad in a pond without causing even the slightest ripple. It can reach speeds of 40 kilometers per hour and then stop on a dime.

As you can imagine, these amazing insects easily run circles around the best human-designed aircraft. For this reason, one group of researchers has been studying dragonflies to learn some of their secrets of *aerodynamics*. Aerodynamics is the study of the forces acting on an object (an airplane or a dragonfly) as it moves through the air.

One of the first goals of the researchers was to determine the lift that a dragonfly could produce. Lift is the force produced by the motion of a wing through the air. Lift is what gives an airplane the ability to climb into the air and hold itself upright during flight. Using a tiny instrument that detects small forces, researchers measured the lift generated by several species of dragonflies. They discovered that dragonflies produce three times the lift for their mass. (The mass of a dragonfly is only about one seventh the mass of a dime!)

How can dragonflies perform this feat? Researchers discovered that dragonflies twist their wings on the downward stroke. This twisting action creates tiny whirlwinds on the top surfaces of the wings. This action moves air quickly over the wings' upper surfaces, lowering air pressure there and providing incredible lift.

By applying the aerodynamic principles of dragonfly flight to airplanes, scientists may soon be able to design and build more efficient airplanes. Of course, these future airplanes will never be able to bend or flex their wings as a dragonfly does. But they may be able to take off more easily, turn faster, and touch down on tiny landing fields.

Laboratory Investigation

Investigating Isopod Environments

Problem

What type of environment do isopods (pill bugs) prefer?

Materials *(per group)*

collecting jar	aluminum foil
10 isopods	paper towels
shoe box with a lid	masking tape

Procedure 🧪 🐀

1. With the collecting jar, gather some isopods. They are usually found under loose bricks or logs. Observe the characteristics of the isopods.

2. Line the inside of the shoe box with aluminum foil.

3. Place 2 paper towels side by side in the bottom of the shoe box. Tape them down. Place a strip of masking tape between the paper towels.

4. Moisten only the paper towel on the left side of the box.

5. Place 10 isopods on the masking tape. Then place the lid on the shoe box and leave the box undisturbed for 5 minutes.

6. During the 5-minute period, predict whether the isopods will prefer the moist paper towel or the dry paper towel.

7. After 5 minutes, open the lid and quickly count the number of isopods on the dry paper towel, on the moist paper towel, and on the masking tape. Record your observations in a data table.

8. Repeat steps 5 through 7 two more times. Be sure to place the isopods on the masking tape at the start of each trial. Record the results in the data table.

9. After you have completed the three trials, determine the average number of isopods found on the dry paper towel, on the moist paper towel, and on the masking tape. Record this information in the data table. Record your average results in a class data table on the chalkboard.

Observations

1. What characteristics of isopods did you observe?

2. Where were the isopods when you opened the lid of the box? Was your prediction correct?

3. Were there variables in the experiment that could have affected the outcome? If so, what were they?

4. What was the control in this experiment?

5. How did your results compare with the class results?

Analysis and Conclusions

1. Based on your observations of their characteristics, into which phylum of invertebrates would you classify isopods? Into which group within that phylum would you place isopods?

2. From the class results, what conclusions can you draw about the habitats preferred by isopods? Give reasons for your answers.

3. What was the purpose of the masking tape in the investigation?

4. Why did you perform the investigation three times?

5. **On Your Own** Design another investigation in which you test the following hypothesis: Isopods prefer dark environments to light environments. Be sure to include a variable and a control.

Study Guide

Summarizing Key Concepts

11–1 Arthropods: The "Joint-Footed" Animals

▲ Arthropods have an exoskeleton, a segmented body, and jointed appendages. An exoskeleton is a rigid outer covering.

▲ The process by which arthropods shed their exoskeleton as they grow is molting.

▲ Athropods include crustaceans, centipedes and millipedes, arachnids, and insects.

▲ A crustacean has a hard exoskeleton, two pairs of antennae, and mouthparts used for crushing and grinding food.

▲ Centipedes have one pair of legs in each body segment; millipedes have two pairs of legs in each body segment.

▲ The bodies of arachnids are divided into a head and chest part and an abdomen. Arachnids have four pairs of legs.

11–2 Insects: The Most Numerous Arthropods

▲ Insects have three body parts—head, chest, and abdomen—and three pairs of legs.

▲ The dramatic change in form an insect undergoes as it develops is called metamorphosis. There are two types of metamorphosis: complete and incomplete.

▲ During complete metamorphosis, insects go through a four-stage process: egg, larva, pupa, and adult.

▲ During incomplete metamorphosis, young insects looking very much like the adults hatch from eggs.

▲ Some species of insects give off extremely powerful chemicals called pheromones that attract either males or females.

11–3 Echinoderms: The "Spiny-Skinned" Animals

▲ Invertebrates with rough, spiny skin; an internal skeleton; a five-part body; a water vascular system; and tube feet are called echinoderms.

▲ Members of the phylum Echinodermata include starfishes, sea cucumbers, sea lilies, sea urchins, and sand dollars.

Reviewing Key Terms

Define each term in a complete sentence.

11–1 Arthropods: The "Joint-Footed" Animals
exoskeleton
molting

11–2 Insects: The Most Numerous Arthropods
metamorphosis
larva
pupa
pheromone

11–3 Echinoderms: The "Spiny-Skinned" Animals
water vascular system
tube foot

Chapter Review

Content Review

Multiple Choice

Choose the letter of the answer that best completes each statement.

1. Which is a characteristic of all arthropods?
   a. spiny skin   c. gills
   b. exoskeleton   d. backbone
2. Crustaceans obtain oxygen from the water through
   a. book lungs.
   b. water vascular systems.
   c. gills.
   d. air tubes.
3. Which is an example of a crustacean?
   a. sea urchin   c. grasshopper
   b. shrimp   d. scorpion
4. How many pairs of legs do millipedes have per body segment?
   a. 100   c. 1
   b. 2   d. 1000
5. In which stage of metamorphosis is an insect wrapped in a cocoon?
   a. egg   c. pupa
   b. larva   d. adult
6. Which invertebrate produces silk?
   a. lobster   c. mite
   b. spider   d. sand dollar
7. Which group includes animals that can fly?
   a. arachnids   c. crustaceans
   b. echinoderms   d. insects
8. Which is an example of a defense mechanism in insects?
   a. molting
   b. camouflage
   c. pheromone production
   d. metamorphosis
9. Starfishes belong to a group of invertebrates called
   a. crustaceans.   c. arachnids.
   b. arthropods.   d. echinoderms.
10. Which group of invertebrates have tube feet?
   a. echinoderms   c. millipedes
   b. crustaceans   d. arachnids

True or False

If the statement is true, write "true." If it is false, change the underlined word or words to make the statement true.

1. Arthropods have a rigid outer covering called an <u>exoskeleton</u>.
2. <u>Crustacean</u> means joint footed.
3. Crabs have <u>book lungs</u>.
4. Spiders are <u>insects</u>.
5. Mites are <u>arachnids</u>.
6. Insects have <u>three</u> pairs of legs.
7. A caterpillar is an example of a <u>larva</u>.
8. <u>Starfishes</u> have a five-part body.

Concept Mapping

Complete the following concept map for Section 11–1. Then construct a concept map for the entire chapter.

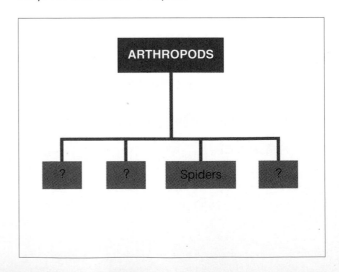

Concept Mastery

Discuss each of the following in a brief paragraph.

1. What are some advantages of having an exoskeleton? What are some disadvantages?
2. Compare complete and incomplete metamorphosis.
3. Describe the different respiratory organs that are used by arthropods.
4. Describe the different types of arthropod appendages.
5. Compare millipedes and centipedes.
6. What is the function of tube feet?
7. How do starfishes move?
8. Why are arthropods the most numerous phylum of animals?
9. What role do pheromones have in the lives of insects?
10. Explain why arthropods undergo molting.
11. Describe the functions that a worker bee, a queen bee, and a male bee have in the hive.

Critical Thinking and Problem Solving

Use the skills you have developed in this chapter to complete each of the following.

1. **Making charts** Construct a chart in which you list the groups in the phyla Arthropoda and Echinodermata, the major characteristics of the group, and three animals from each group.
2. **Classifying objects** Your friend said he found a dead insect with two body parts and eight legs. Is this possible? Explain.
3. **Making generalizations** In what ways are insects beneficial to humans?
4. **Applying concepts** The makers of horror movies invent gigantic insects that terrorize human beings. Why is it impossible for such insects to exist?
5. **Relating concepts** Insects are often described as the most successful group of animals. What characteristics of insects could account for this description?
6. **Applying technology** Pesticides are chemicals used to kill harmful insects. Describe some advantages and disadvantages of pesticide use.
7. **Using the writing process** Observe an insect such as a bee or an ant for 15 minutes. Then write a short story describing what it would be like to be one of these animals.

Fishes and Amphibians

A sea horse is truly an unusual animal. It has the arching neck and head of a horse, the grasping tail of a monkey, and the color-changing power of a chameleon. It has eyes that move independently of each other, so that while one looks under water the other scans the surface. As if all this were not remarkable enough, sea horses have one more interesting feature: male sea horses, not female sea horses, give birth to baby sea horses!

If you look closely at the photograph on the opposite page, you can see the tails of a few baby sea horses sticking out of their father's pouch. A male sea horse bears the young. A female sea horse deposits eggs in a male sea horse's kangaroolike pouch, where they are fertilized and then cared for by the male sea horse. A few weeks later, the first baby sea horse is born, then another and another. The process continues until hundreds of tiny sea horses have emerged.

It may surprise you to learn that sea horses are actually fishes. Yes, fishes—complete with gills and fins. In the pages that follow, you will discover more about other fascinating fishes. You will also learn about the distant relatives of fishes: the amphibians.

Journal *Activity*

You and Your World Visit a supermarket and find out what kinds of fishes are available as food. In your journal, make a list of these fishes. Then choose one fish from your list and find a recipe for preparing it. Copy the recipe into your journal. Then, with the help of an adult, try it out.

◀ *A male sea horse giving birth to live young*

12–1 What Is a Vertebrate?

What do trout, frogs, snakes, turtles, robins, bats, and humans have in common? The answer to this question is that all these animals are **vertebrates. A vertebrate is an animal that has a backbone, or a vertebral column.** The vertebral column of a vertebrate is important because it protects the spinal cord, which runs through the center of the backbone. The spinal cord is the connection between a vertebrate's well-developed brain and the nerves that carry information to and from every part of its body.

The vertebral column makes up part of a vertebrate's endoskeleton, or internal skeleton. (Remember, the prefix *endo-* means inner.) The endoskeleton provides support and helps to give shape to the body of a vertebrate. One important advantage of an endoskeleton is that it is made of living tissue, so it grows as the animal grows. This is quite unlike the exoskeleton of an arthropod, which is made of non-living material and has to be shed as the animal grows.

All vertebrates belong to the phylum Chordata (kor-DAT-uh). Members of the phylum Chordata are known as chordates. **At some time during their lives, all chordates have three important characteristics: a nerve cord, a notochord, and a throat with gill slits.** The nerve cord is a hollow tube located near the animal's back. Just beneath the nerve cord is the notochord. The notochord is a long, flexible supporting rod that runs through part of the animal's body. In most vertebrates, the notochord is replaced by the vertebral column. The gill slits are paired structures located in the throat (or pharynx) region that connect the throat cavity with the outside environment. Water easily flows over the **gills,** allowing oxygen to pass into the blood vessels in the gills and carbon dioxide to pass out into the water. Gills are feathery structures through which water-dwelling animals, such as fishes, breathe.

Figure 12–1 *Vertebrates are animals that have a vertebral column. Examples of vertebrates include the frog and the bat. To what phylum do vertebrates belong?*

Figure 12–2 *In addition to illustrating one hypothesis about the evolutionary relationships among vertebrate groups, this phylogenetic tree also shows approximately when certain characteristics occurred. When did four limbs appear?* ▶

Snakes

Lizards

Turtles

Frogs

Salamanders

Coelacanth

Lungfishes

Ray-finned fishes

Rays and Skates

Sharks

Chimaeras

LAMPREYS

HAGFISHES

Monotremes

Crocodilians

BIRDS

Marsupials

Placentals

MAMMALS

Dinosaurs

Endothermy (?)

REPTILES

Therapsids

Thecodonts

Endothermy

AMPHIBIANS

Amniotic egg   **First Reptiles**

Early Amphibians

4 limbs

BONY FISHES

Early Lobe-fins

Lungs

CARTILAGINOUS
FISHES

Early Jawed Fishes

Paired appendages
Jaws

Early Jawless Fishes
Bone

Invertebrate Chordate
Ancestors

Tertiary

Cretaceous

Jurassic

Triassic

Permian

Carboniferous

Devonian

Silurian

Ordovician

Cambrian

100   200   300   400   500

Millions of years ago

Period

Figure 12–3 *Vertebrates may be either coldblooded or warmblooded. The iguana, which is a reptile, is a coldblooded vertebrate. The polar bear, which is a mammal, is a warmblooded vertebrate.*

There are eight groups of vertebrates within the phylum Chordata. Of the eight groups, six are **coldblooded** and two are **warmblooded.** Coldblooded animals (more correctly called ectotherms), such as fishes, amphibians, and reptiles, do not produce much internal heat. Thus they must rely on their environment for the heat they need. Warmblooded animals (endotherms), such as birds and mammals, maintain their body temperatures internally as a result of all the chemical reactions that occur within their cells. In other words, coldblooded animals have body temperatures that change somewhat with the temperature of their surroundings; warmblooded animals maintain a constant body temperature.

ACTIVITY
DOING

Tunicates

Tunicates are members of the phylum Chordata. Using reference materials in the library, find out about these animals. Present your findings to the class in an oral report. Include a drawing of a tunicate.

Why are these animals classified as chordates?

12–1 Section Review

1. What are the main characteristics of vertebrates?
2. List three characteristics of chordates.
3. Compare a coldblooded animal and a warmblooded animal.
4. What are gills?

Critical Thinking—*Applying Concepts*
5. Are you warmblooded or coldblooded? Explain your answer.

12-2 Fishes

About 540 million years ago the first fishes appeared in the Earth's oceans. These fishes were strange-looking animals, indeed! They had no jaws, and their bodies were covered by bony plates instead of scales. And although they had fins, the fins were not like those of modern-day fishes. But these early fishes were the first animals to have vertebral columns. They were the first vertebrates to have evolved.

Despite these differences, there was something special about these animals—something that would group them with the many kinds of fishes that were to follow millions of years later. **Fishes are water-dwelling vertebrates that are characterized by scales, fins, and throats with gill slits.** It is important to note, however, that not all fishes have all these characteristics. For example, sturgeons, paddlefishes, and sea horses have no scales at all on most of their body. And although most fishes have fins, the fins vary greatly in structure and function. Some fishes have paired fins, whereas others have single fins. Some fishes use their fins to help them remain upright. Other fishes use their fins to help them steer and stop. The side-to-side movement of large tail fins helps most fishes to move through the water. However, all fishes have gill slits.

Guide for Reading

Focus on these questions as you read.

▶ *What are the main characteristics of fishes?*

▶ *What are the main features of the three groups of fishes?*

Figure 12-4 *Early jawless fishes, unlike modern jawless fishes, had bones and their body was often covered with bony armorlike plates. Most early jawed fishes also were covered with bony plates.*

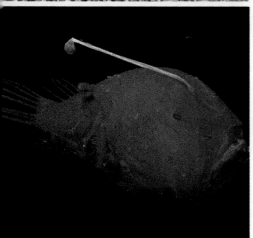

Figure 12–5 *Fishes have developed special structures that enable them to catch or eat a great variety of foods. The parrotfish (top) uses its "beak" to bite off chunks of coral. The oyster toadfish (center) relies on its ability to blend in with its surroundings to catch its prey. The seadevil (bottom) uses its bright lure to attract unsuspecting victims.*

As a group, fishes eat just about everything—from microscopic algae to worms to dead fish. The parrotfish even eats coral! Fishes have developed special structures that enable them to catch or eat the great variety of foods upon which they feed. Swordfishes are thought to slash their way through large groups of fishes and then return to devour the wounded or dead prey. Toadfishes rely on their ability to blend in with their surroundings to catch their prey. And angler fishes have wormlike lures that they dangle in front of their prey.

Like all vertebrates, fishes have a closed circulatory system. A closed circulatory system is one in which the blood is contained within blood vessels. In fishes, the blood travels through the blood vessels in a single loop—from the heart to the gills to the rest of the body and back to the heart. The excretory system of fishes consists of tubelike kidneys that filter nitrogen-containing wastes from the blood. Like many other water-dwelling animals, most fishes get rid of the nitrogen-containing wastes in the form of ammonia.

Fishes have a fairly well-developed nervous system. Almost all fishes have sense organs that collect information about their environment. Most fishes that are active in daylight have eyes with color vision almost as good as yours. Those fishes that are active at night or that live in murky water have large eyes with big pupils. Do you know what this adaptation enables them to do?

Many fishes have keen senses of smell and taste. For example, sharks can detect the presence of one drop of blood in 115 liters of sea water! Although most fishes cannot hear sounds well, they can detect faint currents and vibrations in the water through a "distant-touch" system. As a fish moves, its distant-touch system responds to changes in the movement of the water, thus enabling the fish to detect prey or to avoid objects in its path.

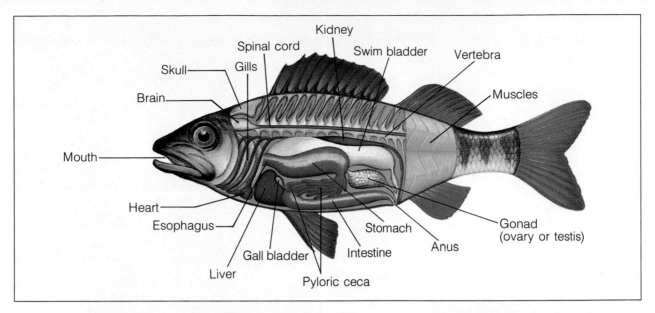

In most species of fishes, males and females are separate individuals. The males produce sperm, and the females produce eggs. There are, however, a number of fish species that are born males but develop into females. Others begin their lives as females and then change into males. Whatever the case, few fishes function as both a male and a female at the same time.

Of the many fishes that lay eggs, most have **external fertilization.** External fertilization is the process in which a sperm joins with an egg outside the body. Certain egg-laying fishes have **internal fertilization.** Internal fertilization is the process in which a sperm joins with an egg inside the body. Of the fishes that have internal fertilization, some—such as sharks and rays—lay fertilized eggs. In other fishes that have internal fertilization, the eggs develop inside the female's body. In this case, each developing fish receives food either directly from the female or indirectly from a yolk sac attached to its body. When all the food in its yolk sac is used up, the young fish is born.

Figure 12–6 *The internal organs of a typical bony fish are shown here. What structures enable fishes to breathe?*

Figure 12–7 *Fishes have well-developed sense organs. For example, the eyes of the four-eyed fish, or quatro ojos, are each divided horizontally into two sections (right). The upper eyes are used to see above the water, whereas the lower eyes are used to see below the water. The "distant touch" system of the rainbow trout, which appears as a series of tiny dots in the pink stripe (left), detects movements in the water.*

Figure 12–8 *Although all sharks have internal fertilization, the young of some sharks, such as the swell shark (left), develop outside the female's body. In grunions (top right), fertilization and development of young occur outside the female's body. In guppies (bottom right), fertilization and development of young occur inside the female's body.*

Many fishes (including some you can keep in an aquarium) have interesting mating behaviors. For example, male guppies dance in front of female guppies to get their attention. The bright red and blue body of a male three-spined stickleback serves to let female sticklebacks know where his nest is, as well as to warn other males to keep away.

The correct scientific classification of fishes is quite complicated. Thus, in this textbook fishes are placed into three main groups. These groups are the jawless fishes, the cartilaginous (KAHRT'l-aj-uh-nuhs) fishes, and the bony fishes.

Jawless Fishes

Jawless fishes are the most primitive of all fishes. They are so primitive, in fact, that in addition to lacking jaws, they also lack scales and paired fins. Something else makes jawless fishes unusual. To find out what it is, hold one of your ears between your fingers and move it back and forth a few times. How are you able to perform this action? The answer is that your ear contains a flexible material called cartilage. The entire skeleton of jawless fishes is made of cartilage. Jawless fishes are vertebrates that have no bone at all. (Later in this section you will read about another group of fishes that also contain no bone.)

The only support the eellike bodies have is a noto-chord. As you might expect, jawless fishes are really flexible.

To see examples of the only two species of jawless fishes still alive—lampreys and hagfishes—look at Figure 12–9. Notice that a lamprey looks like an eel with a suction-cup mouth at one end. This suction-cup mouth, which is surrounded by horny teeth, is extremely efficient. Using its mouth, a lamprey attaches itself to a fish such as a trout (or sometimes a whale or a porpoise) and scrapes away at the fish's skin with its teeth and rough tongue. Then it sucks up the tissues and other fluids of its victim.

The skin of a lamprey is covered with glands that release a slippery, sticky substance called mucus (MYOO-kuhs). This mucus is toxic, or poisonous, and it probably discourages larger fishes from eating lampreys.

The other jawless fishes—the hagfishes—are considered the most primitive vertebrates alive today. The most obvious feature of a hagfish's wormlike body is the four to six short tentacles that surround its nostrils and mouth. The tentacles are used as organs of touch.

A hagfish feeds on dead or dying fishes by tearing out pieces of the fish with a tongue that has teethlike structures. If the fish is large, a hagfish will twist its own body into a knot so that it can thrust itself into the fish with extra power. In no time, the hagfish will be completely inside the prey fish. The ability to twist itself into a knot also enables a hagfish to evade capture, especially when this action is accompanied by the release of a sticky, slimy material from pores located along the sides of its body. A single hagfish can release so much slime that if it is placed in a pail of sea water, it can turn the entire contents of the pail into slime.

Cartilaginous Fishes

When you think of sharks, you probably think of large fast-swimming vicious predators. Although this is true of some sharks, it is not true of most. For the most part, sharks prefer to be left alone.

Sharks—along with rays, skates, and two rare fishes called sawfishes and chimaeras (kigh-MIHR-uhz)—are cartilaginous fishes. Like jawless fishes,

Figure 12–9 *Modern jawless fishes include only two species: the lampreys (top) and the hagfishes (bottom). In addition to being jawless, what are some other characteristics of jawless fishes?*

ACTIVITY

DISCOVERING

The Invasion of the Lamprey

The completion of the St. Lawrence Seaway accidentally introduced lampreys into the Great Lakes. Using reference materials in the library, find out what effects lampreys have had on fishes already living there. Construct a chart that indicates what fishes lived in the Great Lakes before and after the arrival of lampreys.

■ What might have been done to prevent this from happening?

Figure 12–10 *The southern stingray (left), big skate (bottom right), and sawfish (top right) are examples of cartilaginous fishes.*

cartilaginous fishes have skeletons made of cartilage. Most of them also have toothlike scales covering their bodies. The toothlike scales are the reason why the skin of a shark feels as rough as sandpaper. Most of the more than 2000 types of sharks have torpedo-shaped bodies, curved tails, and rounded snouts with a mouth underneath.

The most obvious feature of a shark is its teeth. At any one time, a fish-eating shark will have 3000 very long teeth arranged in six to twenty rows in its mouth. In most sharks, the first one or two rows of teeth are used for feeding. The remaining rows contain replacement teeth, with the newest teeth at the back. As a tooth in the front row breaks or is worn down, it falls out. When this happens, a replacement tooth moves forward in a kind of conveyor-belt system. In its lifetime, a single shark may go through more than 20,000 teeth! Not all sharks, however, have the long teeth characteristic of fish-eating sharks. Sharks that eat mollusks and crustaceans have flattened teeth that help them to crush the shells of their prey.

Unlike sharks, the bodies of skates and rays are as flat as pancakes. For this reason, skates and rays are sometimes called pancake sharks. These cartilaginous fishes have two large, broad fins that stick out from their sides. They beat these fins to move through the water, much as a bird beats its wings to fly through the air. Rays and skates often lie on the ocean bottom, where they hide by using their fins to cover their bodies with sand. When an unsuspecting fish or invertebrate comes near, the hidden skate or ray is ready to attack. Some rays have a poisonous spine at the end of their long, thin tail, which they use for defense rather than for catching prey. Other rays, appropriately called electric rays, have a specialized organ in their head that can discharge about 200 volts of electricity to stun and capture prey. Although 200 volts may not sound like a lot, you only need 120 volts to power almost everything in your home!

Bony Fishes

If you have ever eaten a flounder or a trout, you know why such fishes are called bony fishes. Their skeleton is made of hard bones, many of which are quite small and sharp. Some bony fishes, such as tunas, travel in groups called schools. Because of this schooling behavior, these fishes can be caught in large numbers at one time by people in fishing boats.

Although all bony fishes have paired fins, the shape of the paired fins varies considerably. Most bony fishes have fins supported by a number of long bones called rays. Thus these fishes are called ray-finned fishes. Perches and sea horses are two examples of ray-finned bony fishes. Other fishes have fins with fleshy bases supported by leglike bones. These fishes are known as lobe-finned fishes. Coelacanths (SEE-luh-kanths) are the only living species of lobe-finned bony fishes.

Another characteristic of bony fishes is that they have **swim bladders.** A swim bladder is a gas-filled sac that gives bony fishes buoyancy, or the ability to float in water. By inflating or deflating its swim bladder, a fish can float at different levels in the water.

There are many kinds of bony fishes, some of which have developed remarkable adaptations to life in water. For example, an electric eel can produce jolts of electricity up to 650 volts for use in defending itself or in stunning its prey. A remora uses its sucker to attach itself to sharks or other large fishes, feeding on bits of food they leave behind. Can you see why a remora is sometimes called a shark sucker?

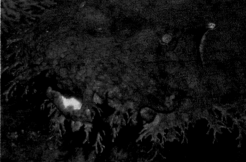

Figure 12–11 The sand tiger shark (top) shows one of the most noticeable characteristics of sharks: enormous numbers of teeth. The flattened body of the wobbegong, or carpet shark (center), and of the blue-spotted stingray (bottom) is an adaptation to life on the bottom of the ocean.

Activity Bank

To Float or Not to Float?, p.811

Figure 12–12 *Bony fishes come in a wide variety of shapes and colors. The queen angelfish (bottom left) has a flattened, highly colorful body. The moray eel (top right) has a narrow, snakelike body. The body of the glass, or ghost, catfish (top left) is almost transparent except for its head and bones. Unlike its ancestors, which lived more than 70 million years ago, the present-day coelacanth (bottom right) still has its paired lobed fins.*

ACTIVITY
READING

A Fish Story

You may want to read a wonderful novel about an old man and his struggle with nature as he pursues a large fish. The novel is entitled *The Old Man and the Sea,* and the author Is Ernest Hemingway.

Another fish that has developed an interesting adaptation to its surroundings is the flounder. All adult flounders are bottom-dwelling fishes. However, a flounder's eggs, which contain oil droplets, float at or near the surface of the water. When a young flounder begins its life, it does so as a normally shaped fish with one eye on each side of its head and a horizontal mouth. But as the young fish develops into an adult, one of its eyes moves to the other side of the head and the mouth twists. Because it does not have a swim bladder, the adult flounder eventually sinks to the ocean's bottom and lies permanently on one side—usually, the blind side. The fact that the flounder has its eyes and mouth on the same side of its body makes it easier for the flounder to see what is going on around it and to take in food. Lying on its side, a flounder is vulnerable to attack from its predators. But another adaptation—the ability to change the color of its body so that it matches the color of the ocean bottom—gives it protection from its predators.

Fishes that live in the depths of the ocean also have developed special adaptations. Lantern fishes, which live at depths of 300 to 700 meters, have light-emitting organs that attract prey. Other deep-sea fishes have huge eyes that help them to see better in the dark depths of the ocean.

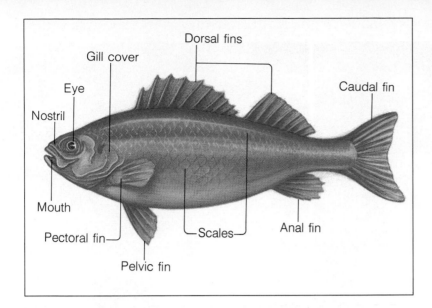

Figure 12–13 *Although this diagram shows the different types of fins that may be present in fishes, not every kind of fish possesses all these fins.*

Dorsal fins

Gill cover

Eye

Nostril

Caudal fin

Mouth

Pectoral fin

Pelvic fin

Scales

Anal fin

Still other fishes have developed adaptations that allow them to come out of water and spend some time on land. For example, mudskippers spend a lot of time using their fins to walk or "skip" on land at low tide. During these periods, a mudskipper can breathe air through its skin, as well as exchange oxygen for carbon dioxide in its mouth and throat. Another type of fish that can live on land for a short time is the African lungfish. When the swamp in which it lives dries up, an African lungfish burrows into the soft mud and becomes inactive until the rains come. When water is again available, the lungfish emerges.

Figure 12–14 *Bony fishes have developed many interesting adaptations to their life in water. The electric eel can discharge small amounts of electricity to protect itself from predators (bottom right). The remora, or sharksucker, has a suctionlike disk that it uses to "hitch a ride" on a shark (top right). The long, graceful rays of the lionfish contain poisonous spines, which help keep its predators away (left).*

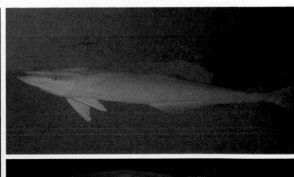

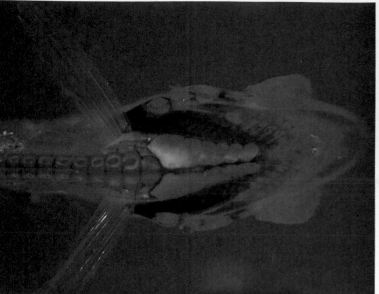

Figure 12–15 *Some bony fishes, such as the lantern fish, have light organs that enable them to live in the dark depths of the ocean. Other bony fishes, such as the African lungfish, have developed adaptations that allow them to live on land for short periods of time.*

12–2 Section Review

1. What are the main characteristics of fishes?
2. List the three groups of fishes and give an example of each.
3. Compare internal and external fertilization.
4. What is the function of a swim bladder?

Connection—*Ecology*
5. How would the Atlantic salmon be affected if its freshwater streams became badly polluted?

Guide for Reading

Focus on these questions as you read.

▶ What are the main characteristics of amphibians?

▶ What are some examples of amphibians?

12–3 Amphibians

The forests of Colombia in South America are home to the Choco Indian tribe. There, the Indians continue a centuries-old tradition of hunting deer, monkeys, and even jaguars with poisoned arrows. In order to do so, the Indians must first capture a number of special kinds of frogs that live in the area. The Indians roast the frogs over a fire so that the poison drips from the skin. The poison is collected in pots and then smeared onto the tips of the arrows. The poison is so powerful that 0.00001 gram is enough to kill a person! So little poison is needed on the tip of an arrow that a 2.5-centimeter frog can produce enough to cover 50 arrows. Appropriately, this frog is known as the arrow-poison frog.

Arrow-poison frogs are members of the second group of coldblooded vertebrates: the amphibians. Amphibians first appeared on Earth about 360 million years ago. They are thought to have evolved from lobe-finned bony fishes that had lungs—fishes similar to a modern coelacanth.

The word amphibian means double life. And most amphibians do live a double life. **Amphibians are vertebrates that are fishlike and that breathe through gills when immature. They live on land and breathe through lungs and moist skin as adults. Their skin also contains many glands, and their bodies lack scales and claws.** Naturally, there are exceptions. Some amphibians spend their entire lives on land. Others live their entire lives in water. But it is safe to say that most amphibians live in water for the first part of their lives and on land in moist areas as adults.

Why must most amphibians live in moist areas? One reason is that their eggs lack hard outer shells. If not deposited in water, such eggs would dry out. Another reason why adult amphibians cannot stray too far from a moist area is that in addition to breathing through lungs, they also breathe through

Figure 12–16 *There are three main groups of amphibians: frogs and toads, salamanders and newts, and legless amphibians. The red-eyed tree frog (left) can climb trees as well as hop. The red-bellied newt (top right) keeps its tail throughout its life. The burrowing caecilian (bottom right) preys on small animals it meets as it tunnels through the ground. What are the main characteristics of all amphibians?*

their skin. And in order to do so, the skin must remain moist. If the skin dries out, most amphibians will suffocate.

The circulatory system of adult amphibians forms a double loop. One loop transports oxygen-poor and oxygen-rich blood back and forth between the heart and the lungs. The other loop transports

Figure 12–17 *The major internal organs of a frog are shown in these two diagrams. Which organs enable the frog to breathe?*

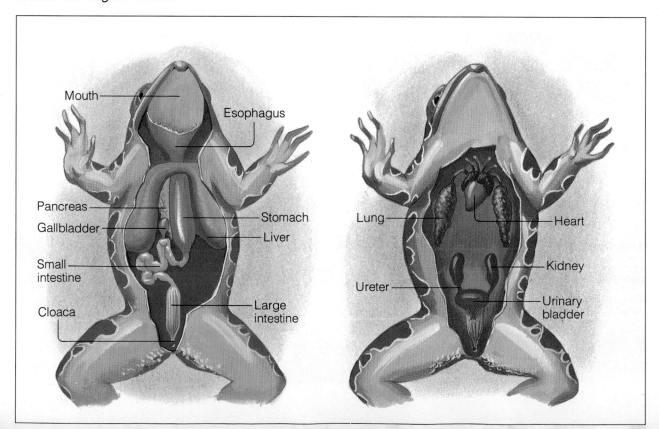

Figure 12–18 *This diagram shows what amphibians may have looked like 270 million years ago. What characteristics do they have in common with modern amphibians?*

oxygen-rich and oxygen-poor blood between the heart and the rest of the body. Tadpoles, or the young of certain amphibians, have a single-loop circulatory system, as do bony fishes. In this type of system, blood travels from the heart to the gills to the rest of the body and back to the heart.

Amphibians have two oval-shaped kidneys that filter wastes from the blood. The nitrogen-containing wastes are in the form of urine, which is then transported by tubes out of the body.

The nervous system and the sense organs are well-developed in amphibians. Large eyes, which bulge out from the sides of the head, provide sharp vision. A transparent membrane protects the eyes from drying out while the animal is on land and from being damaged while the animal is under water.

Many amphibians reproduce by external fertilization. In frogs, for example, a female releases eggs that are then fertilized by a male. After a sticky, transparent jelly forms around the fertilized eggs, the eggs become attached to underwater plants. In a few weeks the eggs hatch into tadpoles, or polliwogs. A tadpole has gills to breathe under water and feeds on plants. Eventually, the process of **metamorphosis** (meht-uh-MOR-fuh-sihs), or the series of dramatic changes in body form in an amphibian's life cycle, begins. During this process, the tadpole undergoes remarkable changes. It loses its tail and develops two

ACTIVITY

DOING

A Frog Jumping Contest

1. Find a flat surface that measures 1.5 m x 1.5 m. Draw four concentric circles with diameters of 30 cm, 60 cm, 90 cm, and 120 cm on the surface.

2. Place a frog in the middle of the innermost circle. Measure how far the frog jumps. Record the distance.

3. Repeat step 2 two more times. Find the average distance your frog jumps.

How far did your frog jump? Which legs do frogs use for jumping—the front legs or the hind legs? To which group of vertebrates do frogs belong? Explain your answer.

pairs of legs. Its gills begin to disappear, and its lungs complete their development. The tadpole is now an adult frog, ready for life on land.

Not all amphibians lay eggs and have external fertilization. Of the many amphibians that have internal fertilization, some lay fertilized eggs. In others, the fertilized eggs develop inside the body of a female, where they receive their food directly from the female or indirectly from a yolk sac. Amphibians have varying ways of caring for their young. Some frogs carry their young in their mouth or in their stomach. Others have special structures on their back in which their young develop.

Figure 12–19 *Like most amphibians, frogs live in water for the first part of their life and on land in moist areas as an adult. Frog eggs are fertilized externally (top right) and generally develop in water (center left). Soon the fertilized eggs develop into young with tails (center right) and then hatch into tadpoles (bottom left). Gradually, the tadpoles grow limbs and begin to lose their tails (bottom right) as they develop into adults. What is this process called?*

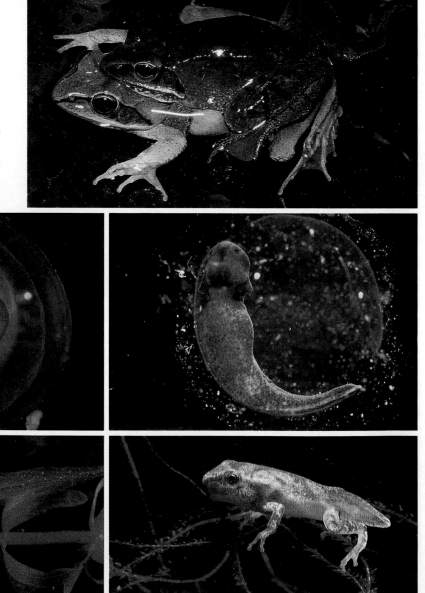

Frogs and Toads

Have you ever wondered what happens to frogs and toads in the winter when the temperature falls? Frogs and toads, like all amphibians, are unable to move to warmer climates. They do, however, survive the cold. Frogs often bury themselves beneath the muddy floor of a lake during the winter. Toads dig through dry ground below the frost line. Then these amphibians go into a winter sleep called hibernation. During hibernation, all body activities slow down so that the animal can live on food stored in its body. The small amount of oxygen needed during hibernation passes through the amphibian's skin as it sleeps. Once warmer weather comes, the frog or toad awakens. If you live in the country, you can usually tell when this happens. The night suddenly becomes filled with the familiar peeps, squeaks, chirps, and grunts that male frogs and toads use to attract female mates.

Although frogs and toads appear similar in shape, you can discover one difference merely by touching

Figure 12–20 *Frogs and toads have developed adaptations that help them escape their predators. The tomato toad (bottom right) has glands behind its eyes that contain poison. The Amazon horned toad (bottom left) is almost invisible as it hides among dead leaves. The European tree frog (top) has long, muscular legs that enable it to quickly leap away from its enemies.*

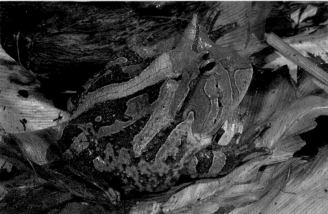

them. Frogs have a smooth, moist skin. Toads have skin that is drier and is usually covered with small wartlike bumps. In many toads, the bumps behind the eyes contain a poisonous liquid, which the toad releases when attacked. A great cane toad can squirt a jet of poison at an attacker almost a meter away. The attacking animal quickly becomes sick and may even die.

If there is one thing most people know about adult frogs and toads, it is that they are excellent jumpers. The main reason for this is that the hind legs of a frog or a toad are much larger than the front legs. It is these powerful hind legs that enable these animals to jump so well and that help them to escape from their enemies.

Salamanders and Newts

Salamanders and newts are amphibians that keep their tails throughout their lives. Like frogs and toads, these animals have two pairs of legs. But their hind legs are not as developed as those of a frog or a toad. Thus salamanders and newts are not able to jump.

Because they are amphibians, salamanders and newts must live in moist areas. One type of salamander, the mud puppy, lives in water all its life even though as an adult it has both lungs and gills. Like frogs and toads, salamanders and newts lay their eggs in water.

Figure 12–21 *Unlike most amphibians, salamanders and newts—such as the mud puppy (left) and red-spotted newt (right)—keep their tail throughout their life.*

12–3 Section Review

1. What are the characteristics of amphibians?
2. List some examples of amphibians.
3. Explain how amphibians live double lives.
4. Compare a tadpole with an adult frog. List at least three differences between them.

Critical Thinking—*Relating Concepts*

5. Amphibians can lay as many as 200 eggs. Why do you think it is necessary for most amphibians to produce so many eggs?

CONNECTIONS

Can Toads Cause Warts?

Have you ever been told that you can get warts by touching a toad? Contrary to superstition, touching the skin of a toad does not cause warts. Although a pair of large glands on the top of a toad's head does give off a poison that can irritate your eyes or make you ill, toads do not produce warts.

Warts—hard, rough growths on the surface of the skin—are actually caused by certain *viruses.* These viruses live in cells on the surface of the skin and do not invade the tissue underneath.

Some warts disappear as mysteriously as they appeared. Perhaps an immunity to the virus develops. An immunity is a resistance to a disease-causing organism or a harmful substance. If a wart does not go away by itself, medical attention should be sought. Under no circumstances should you try to remove a wart without medical help.

So feel free to handle toads all you want. Their wart-producing reputation is simply nonsense!

Laboratory Investigation

Designing an Aquatic Environment

Problem

What type of environment is best for guppies?

Materials *(per group)*

rectangular aquarium (15 to 20 liters)
aquarium light (optional)

gravel	guppies
metric ruler	aquarium cover
water plants	guppy food
aquarium filter	thermometer
snails	dip net

Procedure 🔬 ⚗️ 🛏️

1. Wash the aquarium with lukewarm water and place it on a flat surface in indirect sunlight. Do not use soap when washing the aquarium.

2. Rinse the gravel and use it to cover the bottom of the aquarium to a depth of about 3.5 cm.

3. Fill the aquarium about two-thirds full with tap water.

4. Gently place water plants into the aquarium by pushing their roots into the gravel. If you have a filter, place it in the aquarium and turn it on.

5. Add more water until the water level is about 5 cm from the top of the aquarium. Let the aquarium stand for 2 days.

6. Add the snails and guppies to the aquarium. Use one guppy and one snail for every 4 liters of water.

7. Place the cover on top of the aquarium.

8. Keep the temperature of the aquarium between 23°C and 27°C. Feed the guppies a small amount of food each day. Add tap water that has been left standing for 24 hours to the aquarium as needed. Remove any dead plants or animals.

9. Observe the aquarium every day for 2 weeks. Record your observations.

Observations

1. Do the guppies swim alone or in a school?

2. What do you see when you observe the gills of guppies?

3. Describe the reaction of guppies when food is placed in the aquarium.

4. Describe the method snails use to obtain their food.

5. Was there any growth in the water plants? How do you know?

Analysis and Conclusions

1. To what phylum of animals do snails belong? To what phylum of animals do guppies belong? How do you know?

2. How do fishes obtain oxygen?

3. What is the function of the water plants in the aquarium? The function of snails?

4. Why is it important that you do not overfeed the guppies?

5. Why did you allow the tap water to stand for 24 hours?

6. **On Your Own** Design an experiment to determine how the aquarium would be affected by the following conditions: placing the aquarium in direct sunlight and in darkness and adding guppies.

Study Guide

Summarizing Key Concepts

12-1 What Is a Vertebrate?

▲ A vertebrate is an animal that has a back-bone, or vertebral column. The vertebral column is part of a vertebrate's endoskeleton, or internal skeleton.

▲ All vertebrates belong to the phylum Chordata. At some time during their lives, all chordates have three important characteristics: a nerve cord, a notochord, and a throat with gill slits.

▲ Gills are feathery structures in which the exchange of the gases oxygen and carbon dioxide occurs. Fishes have gills.

▲ Coldblooded animals do not produce much heat. Thus they must rely on their environment for the heat they need.

▲ Warmblooded animals maintain their body temperatures internally as a result of the chemical reactions that occur within their cells.

12-2 Fishes

▲ Fishes are water-dwelling vertebrates that are characterized by scales, fins, and throats with gill slits.

▲ Fertilization in fishes may be external or internal. External fertilization is the process in which a sperm joins with an egg outside the body. Internal fertilization is the process in which a sperm joins with an egg inside the body.

▲ Fishes are placed into three main groups: jawless fishes, cartilaginous fishes, and bony fishes.

▲ Jawless fishes are eellike fishes that lack paired fins, scales, and a backbone.

▲ Cartilaginous fishes have a skeleton of flexible cartilage.

▲ Bony fishes have skeletons of bone. Most have swim bladders, which are gas-filled sacs that give bony fishes their buoyancy.

12-3 Amphibians

▲ Amphibians are vertebrates that are fishlike and that breathe through gills when immature. They live on land and breathe through lungs and moist skin as adults. Their skin also contains many glands, and their bodies lack scales and claws.

▲ Young amphibians have a single-loop circulatory system. Adult amphibians have a double-loop circulatory system.

▲ Fertilization in amphibians may be external or internal.

▲ Metamorphosis is a series of dramatic changes in body form in an amphibian's life cycle.

▲ As adults, frogs and toads develop lungs and legs.

▲ Salamanders and newts are amphibians with tails.

Reviewing Key Terms

Define each term in a complete sentence.

12-1 What Is a Vertebrate?
vertebrate
gill
coldblooded
warmblooded

12-2 Fishes
external fertilization
internal fertilization
swim bladder

12-3 Amphibians
metamorphosis

Chapter Review

Content Review

Multiple Choice

Choose the letter of the answer that best completes each statement.

1. All vertebrates have
   a. bony skeletons.
   b. scales.
   c. vertebral columns.
   d. exoskeletons.
2. Which is not a vertebrate?
   a. snake   c. shark
   b. earthworm   d. lizard
3. Which group of vertebrates are warm-blooded?
   a. mammals   c. amphibians
   b. fishes   d. reptiles
4. Which is best suited for life in water?
   a. toad   c. trout
   b. newt   d. frog
5. Which fish lacks jaws, scales, and paired fins?
   a. paddlefish c. shark
   b. hagfish   d. skate

6. Which is a cartilaginous fish?
   a. electric eel   c. trout
   b. lungfish   d. ray
7. Bony fishes can float at different levels in the water because they have
   a. backbones.   c. fins.
   b. swim bladders. d. gills.
8. Amphibians must lay their eggs
   a. on land.   c. in nests.
   b. in water.   d. in shells.
9. Immature frogs breathe through their
   a. lungs.   c. gills.
   b. skin.   d. mouth.
10. Which is not an amphibian?
    a. frog   c. newt
    b. toad   d. lamprey

True or False

If the statement is true, write "true." If it is false, change the underlined word or words to make the statement true.

1. <u>Vertebrates</u> are members of the phylum Chordata.
2. All vertebrates have an <u>endoskeleton</u>.
3. The <u>cartilaginous</u> fishes are the most primitive group of fishes.
4. The lamprey is a <u>jawless</u> fish.
5. Sharks are <u>bony</u> fishes.
6. The skin of a toad is <u>drier</u> than that of a frog.
7. Adult amphibians obtain most of their oxygen through their <u>lungs</u>.
8. Newts and salamanders are <u>fishes</u> with tails.

Concept Mapping

Complete the following concept map for Section 12–1. Then construct a concept map for the entire chapter.

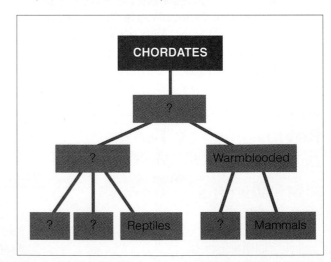

Concept Mastery

Discuss each of the following in a brief paragraph.

1. What adaptations have fishes developed that enable them to live in water?
2. Explain why amphibians must live in a moist environment.
3. Describe the main characteristics of chordates.
4. What adaptations have adult amphibians developed that allow them to live successfully on land?
5. How does a double-loop circulatory system differ from a single-loop circulatory system?
6. What is the "distant touch" system in fishes?
7. How do fishes care for their young?
8. Compare the three groups of fishes.
9. Hypothesize why those vertebrates that reproduce by internal fertilization tend to produce fewer eggs than do those animals that reproduce by external fertilization.
10. Describe metamorphosis in frogs.
11. Explain what happens to frogs and toads when they go into hibernation.

Critical Thinking and Problem Solving

Use the skills you have developed in this chapter to complete each of the following.

1. **Relating facts** Why would you never find frogs living in Antarctica?
2. **Making inferences** People who fish often use a variety of artificial lures. Explain how these lures could attract fishes.
3. **Developing a hypothesis** Some fishes have light colors on their bottom surfaces and dark colors on their top surfaces. Develop a hypothesis to explain how this coloration could be an advantage.
4. **Relating facts** When a raccoon catches a toad, it usually wipes the amphibian along the ground before eating it. Suggest a reason for this strange behavior.
5. **Applying concepts** A female bullfrog can produce as many as 25,000 eggs in a year. Explain why the Earth is not overrun with bullfrogs.
6. **Designing an experiment** Design an experiment in which you determine whether salamanders are able to detect sound. Be sure to include a variable and a control in your experiment.
7. **Using the writing process** Pretend that you received a letter from a friend who lives in another state. She has told you about a small four-legged cold-blooded vertebrate that she found. She wants to know if it is a frog or a salamander. Write a letter telling her how she can determine what her animal is.

Reptiles and Birds

Guide for Reading

After you read the following sections, you will be able to

13–1 Reptiles
- Describe the adaptations that allow reptiles to live their entire lives on land.
- Explain how reptiles carry out their major life functions.

13–2 Birds
- Describe the characteristics of birds.
- Discuss the ways in which birds perform their major life functions.

Imagine that you have just journeyed back in time. You step out of your time machine and enter the world of 150 million years ago.

As you look around at this strange world of the past, it becomes clear to you why this part of Earth's history is sometimes called the Age of Reptiles: Reptiles are the dominant form of life. Long-beaked reptiles soar on narrow wings in the sky above you. Porpoiselike reptiles come to the surface of the ocean for a breath of air, then dive back into the depths with a flick of their fishlike tail. On land, the reptiles known as dinosaurs roam among forests of tree ferns, conifers, and cycads. A rhinoceros-sized dinosaur with huge pointed plates on its back swishes its spike-tipped tail as you approach. Fierce meat-eating dinosaurs as tall as giraffes run swiftly on their two hind legs, pursuing a herd of plant-eating dinosaurs that are, astoundingly, even taller!

Although most of the reptiles of 150 million years ago have died out, some types have survived to the present. What are reptiles? What sorts of reptiles are alive today? Where do reptiles fit in the evolutionary tree of life? Read on and learn about reptiles and birds—living relatives of dinosaurs.

Journal *Activity*

You and Your World In your journal, list ten of the most important facts that you already know about reptiles. Make a similar list for birds. Compare your list with a friend's list and discuss any differences. After you have finished studying this chapter, look over your list. Make any changes you like and briefly note why the changes were made.

◀ *About 150 million years ago, reptiles dominated the Earth.*

13–1 Reptiles

On the barren, windswept shoreline of the Galapagos Islands in the Pacific Ocean, a group of large lizards called marine iguanas (ih-GWAH-nuhz) cling to the rocks. Wave after wave splash against the rocks, but the iguanas do not let go. Suddenly, the iguanas plunge into the cold sea. Their lashing tails and webbed feet propel them through the water as they dive for the seaweed on which they feed. With their bodies chilled by the water, the iguanas soon scramble back onto the rocks to warm up.

Iguanas are just one example of the group of vertebrates known as reptiles. Other reptiles include snakes, turtles, crocodiles, and extinct (no longer living) animals such as dinosaurs and pterodactyls. **Reptiles are vertebrates that have lungs, scaly skin, and a special type of egg.** These characteristics, which you will soon read about in more detail, make it possible for reptiles to spend their entire lives out of water. Another important characteristic

Figure 13–1 *The four living scientific groups of reptiles are represented by the spectacled caiman (top left), Florida red-bellied turtle (top right), tuatara (bottom left), and marine iguana (bottom right).*

Figure 13–2 *The earliest known reptiles resembled a cross between a lizard and a toad. What characteristics make reptiles better suited than amphibians for life on land?*

of living reptiles involves the way they control their body temperature. **All living reptiles are cold-blooded.** Do you recall from Chapter 12 how cold-blooded animals control their body temperature?

Reptiles appeared hundreds of millions of years ago, soon after the first amphibians. As you can see in Figure 13–2, the first reptiles were large, fat, short-legged animals that resembled a cross between a lizard and a toad. Although the first reptiles looked a lot like the ancient amphibians that dominated the Earth at that time, there were several important differences. These differences enabled early reptiles and their descendants (modern reptiles, birds, and mammals) to inhabit all sorts of land environments. As you read about the characteristics of modern reptiles, focus on the ways in which these characteristics make reptiles better suited to life on land than amphibians.

Reptiles have skins that are completely covered by a tough, dry, relatively thick layer of scales. These scales are formed by the outermost layer of the skin. They are made of dead, flattened cells that contain the same hard, tough substance found in your fingernails. The scales form an unbroken waterproof covering that helps to prevent drying out.

Although the waterproof skin helps to prevent excess water loss, it also makes it impossible for a typical reptile to breathe through its skin. A thin, moist membrane is needed to transport oxygen from the environment into the body and carbon dioxide from the body to the environment. Because a typical reptile (unlike a typical amphibian) does not have skin that is thin and moist, it depends entirely on its lungs for gas exchange. Would you expect the lungs of reptiles to be more complex or less complex than those of amphibians? Why?

The waterproof scaly skin is not the only reptilian adaptation for preventing excess water loss. The kidneys of reptiles concentrate nitrogen-containing waste products so that as little water as possible is lost when wastes are eliminated.

Figure 13–3 *As new skin grows in, land vertebrates shed bits of the old, dead, outermost layers of skin. Reptiles such as the chameleon shed their old skin all at once (left). The outermost layer of skin forms a chameleon's horns (center), a rattlesnake's rattle (right), and other structures.*

Reptiles, like adult amphibians, have a double-loop circulatory system. In some reptiles—crocodiles and their relatives, to be exact—the two loops are completely separate. The oxygen-poor blood in one loop never mixes with the oxygen-rich blood in the other loop. Because the bloods never mix, oxygen is delivered more efficiently to the cells of the body. How does this double-loop system differ from the double-loop system in amphibians?

Reptiles have a brain and nervous system quite similar to that of an amphibian, although the brain may be slightly better developed. Most reptile sense organs are well developed, although there are some exceptions. For example, snakes are deaf, and certain burrowing lizards lack eyes.

The scaly skin, improved breathing system, and water-conserving method of waste elimination helped to make early reptiles better suited for life on land than the amphibians that had come before them. But perhaps the reptiles' most important adaptation for living on land was their special egg.

The eggs of fishes and amphibians are delicate sacs that contain stored food and a developing organism. These eggs dry out easily and thus require a watery or extremely damp environment in which to develop. In contrast, the eggs of reptiles can be laid under forest logs, in beach sand, or in cracks in desert rocks. Why is this so?

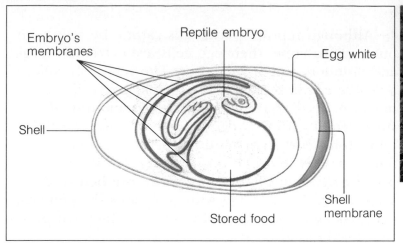

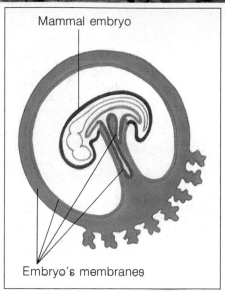

Figure 13–4 *These hognose snakes seem to be pleased by their first glimpse of the world. The membranes that surround reptiles as they develop within the egg are shown in the diagram on the left. These membranes also surround developing mammals, as shown in the diagram on the right.*

Figure 13–4 shows the structures that make it possible for the embryos in reptile eggs to develop on dry land. As you can see, the egg is surrounded by a protective shell that prevents the contents of the egg from drying out. Most reptile eggs have a shell that is tough but a bit flexible—sort of like leather. A few reptile eggs have a hard shell similar to the one on a chicken egg. Although the shell looks solid, it is actually dotted with tiny holes large enough for gases to move in and out but small enough to prevent water from easily escaping. Within the shell are several membranes and a watery fluid, which along with the shell provide further protection for the developing embryo.

The reptilian egg is of great evolutionary importance for two reasons. First, it freed vertebrates from their dependence on water for reproduction and development. Second, it clearly links reptiles to the vertebrates that evolved from them: birds and mammals. Bird eggs have the same basic structure as reptile eggs. And the same membranes that protect and support a reptile or a bird embryo also protect and support mammal embryos.

Fertilization in reptiles is internal. Recall that internal fertilization means that a sperm cell joins with an egg cell inside the parent's body. Why is it necessary for animals with tough, waterproof shells on their eggs to have internal fertilization?

Figure 13–5 *Young reptiles, such as the baby box turtle and newly born copperheads, look like miniature versions of their parents. How does this pattern of development differ from that in most amphibians?*

Although reptile sperm cells cannot be seen without a microscope, their egg cells are extremely large and visible to the unaided eye. The yellowish yolk in a reptile egg is actually the egg cell. Egg cells are immense because they contain huge amounts of stored food. After an egg is fertilized, the female's body builds a shell around it. In some reptiles, the female's body may add a layer of egg white (a thick protein-rich liquid) around the egg cell before the shell is formed. The egg white cushions the embryo, provides extra protein and water, and helps to prevent bacterial infections.

Most reptiles lay their eggs soon after the shells have formed. However, a few reptiles, such as certain snakes and lizards, protect their eggs by retaining them inside the body for part or all of the time it takes for the embryo to reach the stage at which it is ready to be hatched. In almost all reptiles in which the offspring are born alive, the developing young are nourished entirely by the yolk. In a small minority of live bearers, a special connection develops between the embryo's outermost membrane and the body of the female. Through this connection, food and oxygen are delivered from the female's body to her developing offspring. Reptile embryos with this special connection typically have much less yolk than embryos without this connection. Why do you think this is so?

Whether they hatch from eggs or are born alive, young reptiles look like miniature adults. Unlike most amphibians, reptiles do not undergo metamorphosis. Because reptile eggs develop and hatch on land, there is no need for young reptiles to go through an immature water-dwelling stage. They can complete their development inside the safety of the eggshell. How does the more complete development of a reptile relate to the fact that reptile eggs contain a larger amount of yolk than typical amphibian eggs do?

Lizards and Snakes

"Here be dragons" ancient maps sometimes declared about the faraway, poorly known lands at their edges. Of course, as travel to distant places increased, it soon became apparent that there were

no fire-breathing winged reptilian monsters any-where in the world.

But as things turned out, there are dragons—of a sort. In the early part of this century—so the story goes—a pioneering pilot was trying to fly a plane from the islands of Indonesia to Australia. About 1500 kilometers east of Djakarta, the capital of Indonesia, the pilot developed engine trouble and was forced to land on a tiny volcanic island called Komodo. While the pilot tried to repair the engine, the dragons appeared and charged toward him.

The dragons were giant reptiles about 3 meters long and 160 kilograms in mass. They had scaly brownish hides, clawed feet, powerful tails, and short strong legs. Their long, forked tongues flickered in and out of their mouths like thin orange flames. The pilot probably did not wait to see the dragons' teeth before retreating to the safety of the cockpit.

Fortunately, the pilot was able to repair his engine. Although the dragons of Komodo usually hunt animals such as chickens, goats, small deer, and pigs, they are capable of killing large animals such as water buffaloes and humans.

The pilot's tale, along with similar stories from Indonesian pearl divers and fishers, prompted an expedition to obtain scientific specimens of the drag-ons. In 1912, the Komodo dragon was given its sci-entific name and correctly identified as a lizard—the largest (in terms of both length and mass) species of lizard in existence today.

Lizards are reptiles that typically have slender bodies, movable eyelids, long tails, four legs, and

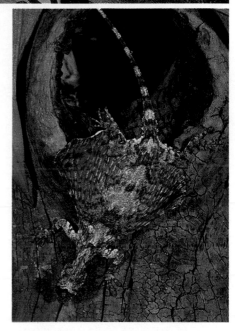

Figure 13–6 *Fire-breathing they are not, but all these lizards are known as dragons. The Komodo dragon (top left), water dragon (top right), and flying dragon (bottom) make their home in Southeast Asia. When fully spread, the reddish flaps of skin and ribs on the flying dragon's sides form "wings," which allow it to glide from tree to tree.*

Figure 13–7 *A basilisk can run across the surface of small ponds and streams (bottom right). Geckos have suction-cuplike toes that enable them to walk up vertical panes of glass and run upside down across ceilings (top right). The horned lizard, which is often called a "horned toad," changes color. This helps it to blend in with its surroundings and to better absorb or reflect heat (left).*

clawed toes. They are placed in the same group of reptiles as snakes. Lizards range in size from tiny geckos 3 centimeters long to tree-dwelling monitor lizards of New Guinea that are more than 4.5 meters long. And as you can see in Figure 13–7, the shapes of lizards also vary.

For the most part, lizards are insect eaters that capture their prey by waiting for it to come nearby. When the prey is within range, the lizard lunges forward and grabs its meal in its jaws. Some lizards have evolved interesting variations on this maneuver. Slow-moving chameleons flick their long sticky tongue out of their mouth and then snap it back inside with a meal attached. The Gila (HEE-lah) monster of the American Southwest subdues its prey by poisoning it. After the Gila monster bites its prey, it hangs onto it tightly. A slow-acting poison made by glands in the lizard's lower jaw flows along grooves in the teeth and into the wounded prey. Contrary to popular stories, Gila monsters do not attack humans unless severely provoked. And although Gila monster bites are not deadly, they are extremely painful.

Figure 13–8 *Zap! A chameleon nabs its dinner with a flick of its long sticky tongue. How does the Gila monster catch and subdue its prey?*

Some lizards have special adaptations that help them to avoid becoming another animal's dinner. Chameleons are one of several kinds of lizards that can change color to match their surroundings. Other lizards have an even stranger way of protecting themselves. If threatened or captured by a predator, these lizards shed their tail. The castoff tail thrashes on the ground, confusing the predator and giving the lizard a chance to escape. Later the lizard grows back the missing tail.

Snakes are basically lizards that have lost their limbs, eyelids, and ears during the course of their evolution into burrowing forms more than 80 million years ago. Surprisingly, these losses did not restrict snakes to being burrowers forever. Snakes are an evolutionary success story—there are many species that live in many different kinds of habitats throughout the world.

A snake moves by wriggling its long, thin, muscular body. The scales on its belly help the animal to grip the surface on which it is moving and push itself forward. Special kinds of wriggling motions enable desert snakes to move across loose desert sand and allow tree-dwelling snakes to creep silently along branches. Many snakes are at home in the water and can swim at the surface or remain submerged. Sea snakes, which spend their entire lives in the ocean, have flattened, paddle-shaped tails that help them to swim swiftly.

Contrary to expressions such as "slimy as a snake," snakes are not at all slimy. They are actually rather pleasant to the touch—cool, dry, and smooth,

Figure 13–9 *In some lizards, the tail is structured in such a way that it can break off cleanly. Look closely and you can see the lizard's lost tail in the foreground. How do breakaway tails help lizards to survive?*

Figure 13–10 *Many snakes, such as the sea snake (top left) and the Siamese cobra (bottom left), have attractive colors and markings. The blue snake is a rare form of the green tree python (right).*

with little grooves around the edges of the scales. A word of warning, however: Snakes should be handled only under the supervision of an expert. Even tame nonpoisonous snakes can inflict painful bites.

Because snakes feed on small animals such as rats and mice, they can be quite helpful to people. But because some snakes are poisonous, people often try to get rid of all the snakes in an area. How would such an action affect the rat and mouse population in that area?

Snakes have a number of interesting adaptations for obtaining food. Although snakes are deaf and have poor eyesight, their other senses make up for these limitations. When a snake flicks its tongue in and out of its mouth, it is actually bringing particles in the air to a special sense organ on the roof of its mouth. This organ "analyzes" chemicals in the air, enabling the snake to find food. Many snakes are able to detect the body heat produced by their prey through special pits on the sides of their head.

Some snakes have glands in their upper jaw that produce a poison that immobilizes their prey. This poison is injected into the prey through special teeth called fangs. Four kinds of poisonous snakes make their home in the United States: rattlesnakes, copperheads, water moccasins, and coral snakes. Other poisonous snakes—such as the king cobra, which is the largest poisonous snake in the world—live on other continents.

Turtles

Turtles are reptiles whose bodies are enclosed in a shell. The shell of a turtle consists of plates of bone covered by shields made of the same substance as scales. Some turtles have extremely strong shells that can support a weight 200 times greater than their own. This is roughly equivalent to your being able to hold two elephants on your back! Not all turtles have hard, bony shells. The leatherback sea turtle, the largest living turtle, has only a few small pieces of bone embedded in the skin of its back.

Turtles do not have teeth. Instead, they have beaks that are similar in structure to the beaks of birds. Many turtles eat plants as well as animals. The alligator snapping turtle has a particularly interesting adaptation for obtaining food. The turtle lies absolutely still on the bottom of a river or pond, looking like a rock or log. The only part of the turtle that moves is a small wormlike structure on the floor of its mouth. When a hungry fish swims into the turtle's mouth to eat the wriggling "worm," the turtle snaps its jaws closed and swallows the fish.

Figure 13–11 *Imagine trying to swallow something as big as your head! This action is impossible for humans, but snakes do it all the time. How do the tongue, teeth, and body muscles of snakes help them to obtain food?*

343

Figure 13–12 *Land-dwelling turtles with domed shells are often called tortoises (top left). The leatherback, the largest living species of turtle, leaves the ocean only to lay its eggs (top right). The desert tortoise uses its beak to nip off tasty bits of plants (bottom left). The matamata of South America spends most of its time hiding among the dead leaves and mud at the bottom of streams (bottom right). It feeds by sucking in water and unwary fishes like a vacuum cleaner.*

Sea turtles known as green turtles are among the most outstanding navigators in the animal kingdom. Soon after hatching, the young turtles head for the ocean. There they wander for many years over thousands of square kilometers. Eventually, the turtles mature and mate. Ready to lay their own eggs, these turtles do something quite amazing. They return to the same beach where they were born!

That beach may be hundreds of kilometers away, across an ocean surface that has no road signs or other markings. Yet the turtles find their way home. How? Recently, scientists have discovered that sea turtles are able to use wave motion and magnetic fields to maintain their direction.

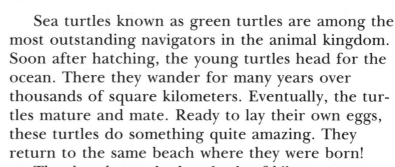

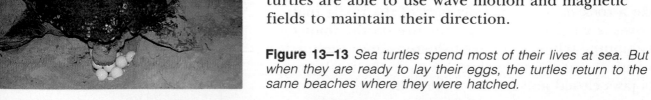

Figure 13–13 *Sea turtles spend most of their lives at sea. But when they are ready to lay their eggs, the turtles return to the same beaches where they were hatched.*

Alligators and Crocodiles

Alligators and crocodiles are large meat-eating lizardlike reptiles that spend much of their time in water. They have long snouts, powerful tails, and thick, armored skin. Although alligators and crocodiles are similar, it is not difficult to tell them apart. Alligators have broad, rounded snouts, whereas crocodiles have narrow, pointed snouts. When an alligator's mouth is closed, only a few of the teeth on its lower jaw are visible. When a crocodile's mouth is closed, most of its teeth are visible. But don't be taken in by the crocodile's welcoming grin. Crocodiles are far more aggressive than alligators, and some species are known to eat humans!

When they are not lying on riverbanks basking in the sun or resting in the shade, alligators and crocodiles spend their time submerged in water. Although these reptiles look lazy and slow, they are capable of moving rapidly, both in water and on land.

Alligators and crocodiles do most of their hunting at night. They eat everything from insects, fishes, and amphibians to birds and large hoofed mammals. (Larger alligators and crocodiles typically hunt larger prey.)

Alligators and crocodiles build nests of mud or plants in which they lay their hard-shelled eggs. In some species, the eggs are abandoned after they are laid. But in other species, the female takes good care of her eggs and offspring.

Figure 13–14 *After her eggs hatch, a female alligator or crocodile will carry her babies in her jaws. The female will continue to care for her young—often with the help of the male.*

Figure 13–15 *Alligators have broad, rounded snouts (bottom left). Crocodiles have narrow, pointed snouts and a distinctive toothy "grin" (bottom right). The gharial of India belongs to the same group of reptiles as alligators and crocodiles (top).*

PROBLEM ??? Solving

Alligator Anxieties

The purely imaginary Gatorville Amateur Conservationist Society (GACS) is faced with a puzzling situation. Three months ago, the Gatorville swamp was drained to make way for a new shopping mall. The adult alligators in the swamp were moved to a wildlife refuge elsewhere in the state. GACS volunteers rescued the newly laid eggs from the alligator nests and placed them in specially designed incubators.

The temperature of all the incubators was set at 30°C. One incubator, however, had a faulty thermostat. The actual temperature in this incubator was 4°C higher than what was indicated on the dials. This problem was not discovered until the eggs had been in the incubators for three weeks.

To everyone's delight, most of the rescued alligator eggs did hatch. But an examination of the baby alligators revealed something strange: All of the

babies from the normal incubators were females, and all the babies from the faulty incubator were males. Why?

Designing an Experiment

1. Develop a hypothesis to explain the results of the alligator-hatching project.

2. Design an experiment to test your hypothesis. What do you expect the results of your experiment to be?

3. If your hypothesis proves to be correct, how might this information affect future conservation efforts?

13–1 Section Review

1. Describe three ways in which reptiles are adapted for life on land.
2. How does the structure of the egg help it to perform its function?
3. Compare the three major groups of reptiles.

Connection—*Wildlife Conservation*
4. Conservationists are concerned, that once sea turtles that nest on a particular beach are killed off, there will never be sea turtles on that beach again. Explain why.

13–2 Birds

People's admiration and affection for birds are reflected in the frequent use of birds as symbols. The eagle shows up on the back of quarters and on postage stamps as the national emblem of the United States. Certain airlines and other businesses feature birds in their emblems. Even sports teams are named after birds. The Toronto Blue Jays, Seattle Seahawks, and Phoenix Cardinals are just three such teams. Can you name others?

Many people think that birds are the most fascinating and colorful animals on Earth. One reason for this is that birds can fly. Along with bats and insects, birds are the only animals with the power of flight, although not all species of birds fly.

Birds are relatively recent additions to the parade of life. Because the skeletons of many small dinosaurs are almost identical to the skeletons of the earliest birds, there is much controversy over which fossils are those of birds and when birds first appeared on Earth. The oldest fossil that is definitely that of a bird is of *Archaeopteryx* (ahr-kee-AHP-ter-ihks). The root word *archaeo-* means ancient, and the root word *-pteryx* means wing. Why is *Archaeopteryx* an appropriate name?

Archaeopteryx lived about 140 million years ago, during a time when dinosaurs and other reptiles ruled the Earth. As you can see in Figure 13–16, this bird did not look much like modern birds. It had a long bony tail and sharp teeth, neither of which is found in modern birds. It had clawed fingers and many other odd features not typical of birds. Despite all the ways in which it was different from modern birds, *Archaeopteryx* was definitely a bird. For around its fossilized bones are the unmistakable impressions of feathers.

Birds are warmblooded egg-laying vertebrates that have feathers. All modern birds—including ostriches, penguins, and other flightless birds—evolved from ancestors that could fly. As you read about birds, focus on the ways in which their characteristics reflect their heritage of flight.

The single most important characteristic of birds is **feathers.** Feathers, like the scales of reptiles, are

Guide for Reading

Focus on these questions as you read.

▶ *What are the major characteristics of birds?*

▶ *How are birds adapted for flying?*

Figure 13–16 *The fossilized remains of* Archaeopteryx *show the shadowy outlines of the feathers that covered the wings and tail. An artist's reconstruction shows how this ancient bird may have appeared when it was alive.*

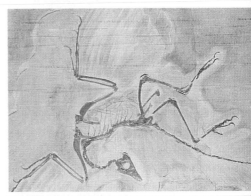

Figure 13–17 *Body feathers help to insulate the mourning dove, and feathers on its wings and tail help it to fly (left). The brightly colored feathers of the rainbow lorikeets help them to communicate (right). Feathers also hide birds from predators. Can you locate the four ptarmigans (center)?*

Activity Bank

Do Oil and Water Mix?, p. 813

ACTIVITY

DISCOVERING

Comparing Feathers

Obtain a few samples of feathers. Try to obtain both down and contour feathers. How are the feathers similar? How are they different?

Gently run your fingers along a contour feather from its tip to its base. What happens? What happens if you rub the feather in the opposite direction?

■ How are feathers put together?

■ How does the structure of a feather help it to perform its functions?

made of dead cells that contain the same material found in your fingernails. Feathers come in many colors, shapes, and sizes. Body feathers help to insulate the body. Feathers on the wings and tail are used in flying. Dull-colored, speckled feathers may help a bird to blend in with its background, hiding it from its natural enemies. Brightly colored feathers help a bird to communicate with other members of its species. For example, the brilliant feathers of male birds such as peacocks advertise their presence to potential mates.

The feathers on the wings and on most of a bird's body are called **contour feathers.** Contour feathers are the largest and most familiar feathers. They give birds their streamlined shape. Other feathers—called **down**—are short, fluffy feathers that act as insulation. Most birds have down feathers on their breasts. As you can see in Figure 13–18, baby birds are often covered with down. As the baby birds grow up, contour feathers grow in and most of the down falls out. Why do you think down from birds such as geese is often used in coats and quilts?

Have you ever heard the expression "eats like a bird"? This phrase, which is used to describe someone who eats very little, was certainly not invented by someone familiar with birds. For birds "eat like pigs." In fact, birds are even bigger eaters than pigs. Because they are warmblooded, birds must expend energy in order to maintain their body temperature. Flying also demands great amounts of energy. In order to meet these energy demands, birds must acquire a lot of energy in the form of food. A pigeon eats about 6.5 percent of its body weight in seeds, crumbs, and other foods every day. A hummingbird eats about twice its weight in nectar (a sugary liquid produced by flowers) daily. How much food would you have to eat every day if you ate like a pigeon? If you ate like a hummingbird?

Birds eat many different kinds of foods, including microscopic blue-green bacteria, fruits and seeds, insects, other birds, mice, monkeys, and the remains of dead animals. The beak of a bird is often remarkably adapted for the type of food it eats. Hawks and owls have sharp, curved beaks used for tearing their prey into pieces small enough to be swallowed. Kiwis and woodcocks have long, thin beaks that are used to probe into the soil for earthworms. Cardinals and sparrows have thick blunt beaks with which they crush the hard shells of seeds.

Bird adaptations for flight are not limited to the outside of the body. Bird bones are hollow and

Figure 13–18 *Birds have fluffy down feathers and leaf-shaped contour feathers. As this young frigate bird grows older, most of its whitish baby down will be replaced by glossy black adult feathers.*

Figure 13–19 *You might think that a toucan's enormous beak would cause the bird to tip over. But the beak is hollow and light for its size (top left). The puffin's tall, flat beak serves as a shovel for digging nesting holes. It is also a handy fish holder (top right). The pelican's pouched beak scoops fishes from the water like a net (bottom).*

Figure 13–20 *Some birds store food. A shrike kills prey and then hangs them on thorns and twigs This shrike looks quite pleased about the striped caterpillar it has caught. How does an acorn woodpecker store food?*

Ⓐctivity Bank

An Eggs-aggeration, p. 814

therefore quite lightweight. Like the bones, the internal organs of birds have evolved in ways that enable birds to fly efficiently. The respiratory system is more advanced in birds than in any other class of vertebrates. How does this relate to the energy needs of birds? (*Hint:* Oxygen is needed to break down food to obtain energy.)

Birds have special structures called air sacs attached to their lungs. The air sacs inflate and deflate in a complex way to ensure that a supply of fresh air is constantly moving in one direction through the lungs. The great efficiency with which birds perform the function of gas exchange is particularly apparent at high altitudes, where the air is thin. Mountain climbers on Mount Everest must carry tanks of oxygen and stop often to rest. Their lungs cannot obtain oxygen efficiently enough to permit long periods of strenuous activity. As the mountain climbers rest, they may observe Himalayan geese flying overhead. The lungs of geese can obtain oxygen efficiently enough to permit the extremely strenuous task of flying. The geese even have spare air—which they use to honk a greeting as they soar past the out-of-breath mountain climbers!

Birds have a double-loop circulatory system in which the two loops are completely separated. This helps to ensure that the oxygen provided by the lungs is delivered effectively to the cells of the body.

Like reptiles and amphibians, birds have two long, oval kidneys that filter nitrogen-containing wastes from the blood. Birds produce the same kind of concentrated nitrogen-containing waste product as land-dwelling reptiles.

Although the term "bird-brained" means stupid, birds are actually quite intelligent. Like the rest of their nervous system, their brain is well developed. The eyesight of many birds—hawks, vultures, and eagles, to name a few—is far keener than that of humans. Some birds have an extraordinarily sharp sense of hearing. The faintest rustle of a mouse as it creeps across the forest floor is all that a hunting owl needs to pinpoint the location of its next meal.

The reproductive organs in birds are often tiny and compact. Only during the breeding season do these organs enlarge to a functional size. All female birds lay eggs. No birds, past or present, bear their young alive. How do these two characteristics of bird reproduction affect flying ability?

Bird eggs, which have the same basic structure as reptile eggs, contain a generous supply of egg white and are covered by a hard shell. Because bird eggs will develop only if they are kept at the proper temperature, almost all are cared for by the parent birds. In some species, only one parent cares for the eggs. In other species, both parents take turns keeping the eggs warm.

In almost all birds, the parents' duties are not finished when the eggs hatch. In some birds, such as chickens and ducks, the young have feathers when they hatch, and they are soon able to run about and feed themselves. However, they still depend on their parents for protection. In other birds, the young are featherless, blind, and helpless when they hatch. Their parents must feed and care for them until they are old enough to fly and take care of themselves.

Bird Behavior

Have you ever heard a bird singing cheerfully on a fine spring day? If you have, you might have wondered what all the excitement was about. Perhaps you might have thought that the bird was happy.

Figure 13–21 Most birds, such as the skimmer, crouch over their eggs to keep them warm (bottom). An Adelie penguin keeps its egg warm by balancing it on its feet (top).

Figure 13–22 Some birds are well-developed when they hatch. The newly hatched Canada geese will soon be waddling through the grass and swimming in the water—with a little encouragement from their parent! Others are featherless, blind, and helpless when they hatch. These newly hatched pelicans will be completely dependent on their parents for quite some time.

Figure 13–23 *Male birds have many ways of attracting a mate. A peacock spreads the long, colorful plumes of his tail and struts about. The male frigate bird puffs up his bright red throat sac. Male weaverbirds demonstrate their skills at nest-building.*

Figure 13–24 *The meadowlark has one of the loveliest songs in nature. Why do birds sing?*

Birds actually sing for rather serious reasons. Early in the breeding season, birds sing to attract a mate and to warn other birds of the same sex to stay away. The song establishes or maintains a **territory.** A territory is an area where an individual bird (or any other animal) lives. Establishing a territory is important because it ensures that fewer birds will compete for food and living space in the same area. Birds may also sing to warn of danger, to threaten an enemy, or to communicate other sorts of information.

Birds communicate with signals that are seen as well as with signals that are heard. The bright feathers of some male birds are used to attract females and to scare off rivals. However, brightly colored feathers also make the bird more noticeable to predators. Can you explain why many birds sport bright colors only during the breeding season?

Some birds attract a mate by doing something unusual. Male bowerbirds build large and colorful constructions of twigs to make females notice them. They may even paint their bowers with berry juice or decorate them with feathers, shells, butterfly wings, and flowers. Male weaverbirds construct a nest that is examined by a prospective mate for soundness and craftsmanship. A male penguin does not construct anything. Instead, he presents his intended mate with a pebble. The pebble indicates that he is ready to breed and to care for a youngster.

Most birds build nests, which are designed to protect the eggs and the young birds as they develop. These nests can be little more than a shallow trench hollowed out in the ground or they can be quite elaborate. Hummingbird nests are tiny cups woven out of spider silk, decorated with bits of plants, and lined with feathers.

Many birds **migrate,** or move to a new environment during the course of a year. Some birds migrate over tremendous distances. For example, the American golden plover flies more than 25,000 kilometers when it migrates. Birds migrate for many reasons, but probably the most important reason is to follow seasonal food supplies. Birds have developed extremely accurate mechanisms for migrating. Scientists have learned that some birds navigate by observing the sun and other stars. Other birds follow coastlines or mountain ranges. Still other birds are believed to have magnetic centers in their brains. These centers act as a compass does to help the bird find its way.

ACTIVITY READING

Rara Aves

This Latin phrase, which literally means rare birds, is used to refer to any type of extraordinary thing. There are a number of works of literature that feature birds in their titles.

A few of these *rara aves* are *The Trumpet of the Swan* by E. B. White; *Jonathan Livingston Seagull* by Richard Bach; *To Kill a Mockingbird* by Harper Lee, and *I Know Why the Caged Bird Sings* by Maya Angelou.

Figure 13–25 *The nests of barn swallows are round clay pots built one beakful of mud at a time. The nests of certain African weaverbirds have several "rooms." The nest mounds built by mallee fowl are up to 4.5 meters high and 10 meters across.*

Types of Birds

There are about 8700 living species of birds. These species are divided among roughly 30 scientific classification groups. As you might imagine, such diversity among birds makes it impossible to discuss all the scientific groups in detail. To simplify matters, birds are often divided into a few broad categories according to one or two significant characteristics. Although these nonscientific categories give no information about evolutionary relationships and also exclude a number of birds, they do provide a glimpse of the enormous diversity among birds.

Most familiar birds are commonly known as songbirds. Cardinals, sparrows, and robins are examples of songbirds. Songbirds range in size from tiny flycatchers 8 centimeters long to birds of paradise whose elegant tail feathers make them more than a meter long. Songbirds have feet that are well adapted for perching on branches, electric wires, and other narrow horizontal structures.

As their name indicates, many songbirds sing beautifully. Nightingales, mockingbirds, warblers, and canaries make some of the loveliest sounds in the natural world. However, some birds with ugly voices—crows and ravens, for example—are also

Figure 13–26 *Songbirds, more correctly known as perching birds, include the scarlet-chested sunbird of Africa (top), the robin of Europe (bottom left), and the Gouldian finch of Australia (bottom right).*

placed in this group. Thus songbirds are more appropriately known as perching birds.

Hunting birds such as hawks, eagles, and owls are known as birds of prey. Birds of prey are superb fliers with keen eyesight. Soaring high in the air, they can spot prey on the ground or in the water far below them. Birds of prey eat fishes, reptiles, mammals, and other birds. Some even eat small monkeys.

Birds of prey are able to fly very fast. The peregrine falcon has been clocked at more than 125 kilometers per hour while diving at its prey. Birds of prey have sharp claws, called talons, on their toes. Talons enable the bird to grasp its prey. Some eagles have talons that are longer than the fangs of a lion. Birds of prey also have strong, curved beaks that are used to tear their prey into pieces small enough to be swallowed.

The birds that swim and dive in lakes and ponds are known as waterfowl. Swans and ducks are typical waterfowl. These birds glide across the surface of the water, propelled by webbed feet that resemble paddles. Occasionally, they duck their head and neck into the water to nibble at water plants with their broad, flat beak.

During the course of evolution, some birds have lost their ability to fly. The wings of these birds are

Figure 13–27 *The king vulture of South America (bottom left), the monkey-eating eagle of the Philippines (bottom right), and the bald eagle of North America (top) are examples of birds of prey.*

Figure 13–28 *Swans (left) and geese (right) are types of waterfowl. What are the main characteristics of waterfowl?*

small compared to the size of their body. Some flightless birds are specialized as runners. Such birds include the ostrich of Africa (the largest bird alive today), the rhea of South America, and the emu and cassowary of Australia. These birds have strong leg muscles that enable them to run quickly and to defend themselves against any enemy foolish enough to challenge them. Penguins are flightless birds that are specialized as swimmers. On land, penguins waddle and hop awkwardly. But in water, they are swift and graceful.

Figure 13–29 *The cassowary of New Guinea (top) and the ostrich of Africa (bottom right) have long, powerful legs that enable them to run swiftly. The comical parade of king penguins shows that penguins cannot move quickly on land (bottom left). However, penguins are remarkably swift swimmers. To what nonscientific category do these three types of birds belong?*

CONNECTIONS

Flights of Fancy

When people talk about the beauty of birds, they usually focus on the spectacular colors of the feathers or the lovely melody of the songs. But it is clear that the beauty of the movement of birds has not been lost on the dancers of the world.

For thousands of years, humans have tried to capture the grace and power of birds in *dance.* The mating dance of the crane—with its spectacular leaps, bows, and flapping of wings—is echoed in some of the dances of the Australian aborigines. The majestic, soaring flight of the eagle is re-created in special Native American ceremonial dances. And the graceful, gliding movement of swans while swimming and while in flight is imitated in ballets such as *Swan Lake.*

13–2 Section Review

1. Describe the major characteristics of birds. Which characteristics are adaptations for flight?
2. What is the difference between down and contour feathers? How are feathers adapted to different functions?
3. How are birds similar to reptiles? How are they different?
4. Name and briefly describe four nonscientific categories of birds.

Critical Thinking—*Making Inferences*
5. The kiwi is a chicken-sized bird that is covered with long brownish hairlike feathers and has no visible wings. It has a very long beak, rather short legs, and feet similar to a chicken's. What do you think this bird eats? What can you infer about the kiwi's behavior, environment, and evolution?

ACTIVITY

THINKING

A Flock of Phrases

Have you ever been accused of being bird-brained? What other common phrases can you think of that have to do with birds? Get together with a friend or two and see how many you can identify. Based on what you know about birds, determine whether they are accurate.

Laboratory Investigation

Owl Pellets

Problem

What does an owl eat?

Materials (per group)

owl pellet	magnifying glass
dissecting needle	small metric ruler

Procedure 🧪 ⚗️

1. Observe the outside of an owl pellet and record your observations.
2. Gently break the pellet into two pieces.
3. Using the dissecting needle, separate any undigested bones and fur from the pellet. Remove all fur from any skulls in the pellet.
4. Group similar bones together in a pile. For example, put all skulls in one group. Observe the skulls. Record the length, number, shape, and color of the teeth.
5. Now try to fit together bones from the different piles to form skeletons.

Observations

1. What does an owl pellet look like? What is it made of?
2. What kinds of bones were the most numerous?
3. What kinds of bones seem to have been missing from the prey?

Analysis and Conclusions

1. What animals were eaten by the owl?
2. Which animals appear to be eaten most frequently by the owl?
3. Why do you think owls cough up pellets?
4. What can you infer about the owl's characteristics from the animals it eats?
5. **On Your Own** Design a study that uses owl pellets to answer a question about the feeding habits of owls. For example, your study might determine whether owls feed on different kinds of prey during different parts of the year.

Shrew	Upper jaw has at least 18 teeth. Skull length is 23 mm or less. Teeth are brown.	
House mouse	Upper jaw has 2 biting teeth. Upper jaw extends past lower jaw. Skull length is 22 mm or less.	
Meadow vole	Upper jaw has 2 biting teeth. Upper jaw does not extend past lower jaw. Molar teeth are flat.	
Mole	Upper jaw has at least 18 teeth. Skull length is 23 mm or more.	
Rat	Upper jaw has 2 biting teeth. Upper jaw extends past lower jaw. Skull length is 22 mm or more.	

Summarizing Key Concepts

13–1 Reptiles

▲ Reptiles are vertebrates that have lungs, scaly skin, and a special type of egg.

▲ All living reptiles are coldblooded.

▲ Reptiles have a number of adaptations that make them well suited for life on land.

▲ Reptiles have a double-loop circulatory system. In most reptiles, the two loops are not completely separated.

▲ Land-dwelling reptiles excrete a concentrated nitrogen-containing waste, which helps them to conserve water.

▲ Reptiles have internal fertilization.

▲ A typical reptile egg has a shell and several membranes that protect the developing embryo.

▲ Most reptiles lay eggs; a few reptiles bear live young.

▲ Some reptiles care for their eggs and young.

▲ One scientific group of reptiles includes lizards and snakes.

▲ One scientific group of reptiles is composed of turtles, which are reptiles whose bodies are enclosed by a two-part shell.

▲ One scientific group of reptiles includes crocodiles and alligators.

13–2 Birds

▲ Birds are warmblooded, egg-laying vertebrates that have feathers.

▲ The bodies of birds are adapted for flight. However, not all species of birds can fly.

▲ Feathers, such as contour feathers and down, have shapes that help them to perform their functions.

▲ Bird beaks and feet show a number of interesting adaptations.

▲ The respiratory system is more advanced in birds than in any other vertebrates. The bird's air sacs enable air to be constantly moved through the lungs in one direction.

▲ Birds have a double-loop circulatory system in which the loops are completely separated.

▲ Almost all birds care for their eggs and young.

▲ Birds have many complex behaviors.

▲ One reason birds sing is to establish and maintain a territory.

▲ Many birds migrate.

▲ Four nonscientific—but useful—categories of birds are songbirds, birds of prey, waterfowl, and flightless birds.

Reviewing Key Terms

Define each term in a complete sentence.

13–2 Birds

feather
contour feather
down
territory
migrate

Chapter Review

Content Review

Multiple Choice

Choose the letter of the answer that best completes each statement.

1. Which of these is a bird of prey?
   a. eagle   c. toucan
   b. pigeon   d. ostrich
2. All living reptiles
   a. lay eggs.
   b. spend their entire lives on land.
   c. undergo metamorphosis.
   d. have lungs.
3. The characteristic that separates birds from all other vertebrates is their
   a. claws.   c. egg-laying.
   b. feathers.   d. flight.
4. Down feathers
   a. are shaped like leaves.
   b. include large flight feathers on wings.
   c. act as insulation.
   d. all of these

5. Birds sing to
   a. establish a territory.
   b. attract a mate.
   c. warn of danger.
   d. all of these
6. A four-legged water-dwelling shelled reptile that lays leathery-shelled eggs is classified as a(an)
   a. alligator.   c. turtle.
   b. crocodile.   d. lizard.
7. To follow seasonal food supplies, birds
   a. perch.   c. build a nest.
   b. migrate.   d. hibernate.
8. All reptile eggs
   a. must be laid in water.
   b. have a leathery shell.
   c. are fertilized externally.
   d. contain protective membranes.

True or False

If the statement is true, write "true." If it is false, change the underlined word or words to make the statement true.

1. Because they can find their way back to the beaches on which they hatched, sea turtles can be said to <u>migrate</u>.
2. The part of a reptile or bird egg that is the egg cell is the <u>egg white</u>.
3. Most <u>birds</u> have a double-loop circulatory system in which the loops are not completely separate.
4. Bird adaptations for flight include <u>hollow bones and egg-laying</u>.
5. <u>Alligators</u> have a narrow triangular snout and a toothy grin.
6. A(An) <u>bower</u> is an area in which an individual <u>animal</u> lives.
7. Snakes use their tongues to <u>sting</u>.
8. Songbirds are more correctly known as <u>birds of prey</u>.

Concept Mapping

Complete the following concept map for Section 13–1. Then construct a concept map for the entire chapter.

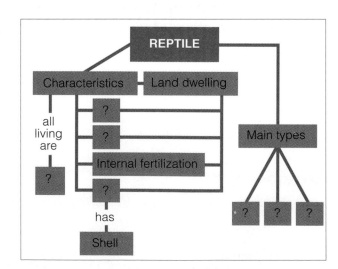

Concept Mastery

Discuss each of the following in a brief paragraph.

1. How are reptiles adapted to life on land?
2. Migration may be described as "animals traveling from where they breed to where they feed." How does this description relate to the behavior of sea turtles and many birds?
3. How is reproduction in birds adapted to the demands of flight?
4. What are the major structures of a typical reptile egg?
5. How do the respiratory and circulatory systems of a bird enable it to maintain a highly active lifestyle?
6. Racing pigeons are driven to a place many kilometers from their home and are then released. Even if they have never been at the starting point before, the birds head straight for home. How do the birds find their way back?
7. Parental care in animals ranges from virtually none to quite a lot. Using specific examples, explain how the behavior of reptiles and birds reflects this wide range of behaviors.
8. What is a territory? Why are territories important?

Critical Thinking and Problem Solving

Use the skills you have developed in this chapter to answer each of the following.

1. **Expressing an opinion** Because the skins of alligators, snakes, and some other reptiles make beautiful leather, many species have been hunted to the point of extinction. Do you think the hunting of reptiles should be allowed to continue? Should it be restricted? Should it be stopped altogether?
2. **Developing a hypothesis** Under what circumstances might a live-bearing bird evolve? Explain your reasoning.
3. **Relating concepts** The poisonous coral snake has alternating bands of black, bright red, and bright yellow. The harmless scarlet king snake has a very similar color pattern. Why is this distinctive pattern an advantage to the king snake?
4. **Evaluating theories** Some scientists say that fossil evidence strongly suggests that dinosaurs (long assumed to be coldblooded and an evolutionary dead end) were warmblooded and were the direct ancestors of birds. What sort of information would you need to better evaluate this two-part theory?

5. **Making inferences** In the spring and summer, male anoles (American chameleons) can be seen throwing their head back and thrusting out a flap of red skin from their throat. What do you think is the purpose of this behavior?
6. **Designing an experiment** A scientist wants to know whether turtles can detect sound. Design an experiment that she can use. Be sure to include a variable and a control in your experiment.
7. **Classifying animals** In the woods, you discover a small four-legged cold-blooded vertebrate. How can you tell whether it is an amphibian or a reptile?
8. **Using the writing process** Imagine that you are the reptile or bird of your choice. Write a short biography describing your life and times.

Mammals

Guide for Reading

After you read the following sections, you will be able to

14–1 What Is a Mammal?
- ■ Describe the main characteristics of mammals.

14–2 Egg-Laying Mammals
- ■ Identify the characteristics of egg-laying mammals.

14–3 Pouched Mammals
- ■ Describe the characteristics of pouched mammals.
- ■ Compare egg-laying and pouched mammals.

14–4 Placental Mammals
- ■ Describe the characteristics of placental mammals.
- ■ Classify ten groups of placental mammals and give an example of each.

A few hundred meters off the coast of California, a small group of animals swim playfully with one another. These whiskered animals are sea otters. A sea otter spends most of its life swimming in the cold waters of the North Pacific Ocean. While floating on its back, a sea otter often balances a rock on its chest. It is against this rock that the sea otter strikes a closed clam shell, cracking open the shell and eating the clam inside.

A sea otter appears to be an intelligent animal. To keep from being swept away by waves, a sea otter wraps itself in strands of giant seaweed growing offshore. It uses the seaweed as giant ropes are used to hold an ocean liner close to a pier.

Although sea otters spend a great deal of time in the water, they are neither fishes nor amphibians. Sea otters belong to the same group of warmblooded vertebrates that you do: the mammals. In addition to swimming in the sea, mammals can be found flying in the air and running along the ground. To learn more about these remarkable creatures, just turn the page.

Journal *Activity*

You and Your World If you have a pet mammal such as a dog, cat, hamster, rat, mouse, gerbil, horse, or guinea pig, observe it for a day. If you do not have a pet, observe one of your friend's pets. In your journal, record all the animal's activities and the time it spends doing each activity. Include a photograph of the animal in your journal.

◀ A sea otter floating on strands of giant seaweed

14–1 What Is a Mammal?

About 200 million years ago, the first mammals appeared on Earth. They evolved from a now-extinct group of reptiles. The first mammals were very small and looked something like the modern-day tree shrew shown in Figure 14–1.

Today there are about 4000 different kinds of mammals living on Earth. In addition to humans and sea otters, mammals include whales, bats, elephants, duckbill platypuses, lions, dogs, kangaroos, and monkeys. Because scientists group together animals with similar characteristics, you might wonder what such different-looking animals have in common.

Mammals have characteristics that set them apart from all other living things. **Mammals are warm-blooded vertebrates that have hair or fur and that feed their young with milk produced in mammary glands.** In fact, the word mammal comes from the term mammary gland. Another special characteristic of mammals is that they provide their young with more care and protection than do other animals.

At one time during their lives, all mammals possess fur or hair. If it is thick enough, the fur or hair acts as insulation and enables mammals such as musk oxen to survive in very cold parts of the world. Musk oxen are the furriest animals alive today. Indeed, the fur of an adult musk ox may be as deep as 15 centimeters! Mammals can also survive in harsh climates because they are warmblooded. Recall from Chapter 12 that warmblooded animals maintain their body temperatures internally as a result of the chemical reactions that occur within their cells. Thus mammals

Figure 14–1 *The first mammals to appear on Earth may have resembled the modern-day tree shrew (top). What characteristics common to all mammals are illustrated by the moose (bottom right) and the musk ox (bottom left)?*

maintain a constant body temperature despite the temperature of their surroundings. What other group of animals can do this?

All mammals, even those that live in the ocean, use their lungs to breathe. The lungs are powered by muscles—a group of muscles that are attached to the ribs and one large muscle that separates the abdomen from the chest.

The circulatory system of mammals consists of a four-chambered heart and an assortment of blood vessels. The heart pumps oxygen-poor blood to the lungs, where the blood exchanges its carbon dioxide for oxygen. After leaving the lungs, the oxygen-rich blood returns to the heart and is pumped to all parts of the body through blood vessels.

Mammals have the most highly developed excretory system of all the vertebrates. Paired kidneys filter nitrogen-containing wastes from the blood in the form of a substance called urea (yoo-REE-uh). Urea combines with water and other wastes to form urine. From the kidneys, urine travels to a urinary bladder, where it is stored until it passes out of the body.

The nervous system of mammals consists of a brain that is the most highly developed of all the animals. The brain makes thinking, learning, and understanding possible; coordinates movement; and regulates body functions. Mammals also have highly

Figure 14–2 *The large, flat, grinding teeth of a white-tailed deer indicate that this mammal eats plants. The sharp, pointed teeth of a gray wolf indicate that this mammal eats the flesh of its prey.*

Figure 14–3 *The brain of a mammal is large compared to that of other animals.*

Figure 14–4 *The 4500 species of mammals can be divided into three main groups. What are the names of the three main groups?*

developed senses that provide them with information about their environment. For example, humans, monkeys, gorillas, and chimpanzees are able to see objects in color. This characteristic is extremely useful because these mammals are most active during the day when their surroundings are bathed in light. Many mammals—cats, dogs, bats, and elephants, for example—are more sensitive to certain sounds than humans are.

Mammals also have more highly developed senses of taste and smell. For example, humans use both their sense of taste and their sense of smell to determine the flavor of food. Dogs and cats, as you might already know, recognize people by identifying specific body odors.

Like reptiles and birds, all mammals have internal fertilization, and males and females are separate individuals. However, the way in which mammals reproduce differs. The differences in reproduction

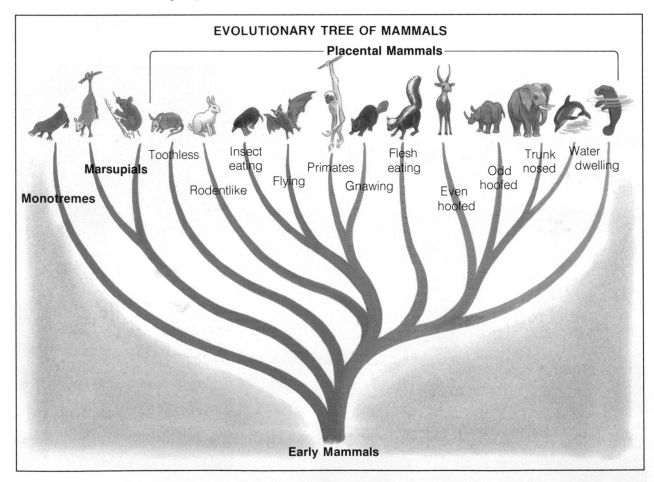

EVOLUTIONARY TREE OF MAMMALS

Placental Mammals

Toothless

Marsupials

Monotremes

Insect eating

Rodentlike

Flying

Primates

Gnawing

Flesh eating

Even hoofed

Odd hoofed

Trunk nosed

Water dwelling

Early Mammals

provide a means of classifying mammals into three main groups. These groups are **egg-laying mammals, pouched mammals,** and **placental** (pluh-SEHN-tuhl) **mammals.** Egg-laying mammals, as their name implies, lay eggs. Pouched mammals give birth to young that are not well developed. Thus the young must spend time in a pouchlike structure in their mother's body. In placental mammals, the young remain inside the mother until their body systems are able to maintain life on their own. At birth, these young are more developed than are those who spend time in their mother's pouch. You will learn more about each group of mammals in the remainder of this chapter.

14–1 Section Review

1. What are the main characteristics of mammals?
2. What is the function of mammary glands?
3. Classify the three groups of mammals.

Critical Thinking—*Relating Concepts*
4. Why does a mammal need more food during cold weather than during warmer weather?

14–2 Egg-Laying Mammals

Guide for Reading

Focus on this question as you read.

▶ *What are egg-laying mammals?*

One of the strangest looking mammals on the Earth today lives in rivers in isolated parts of Australia. It has fur as thick as a sea otter's, feet that are weblike and clawed, and a large flat ducklike beak! What is this strange creature?

If you look at Figure 14–5 on page 368, you will discover what this weird-looking animal is. It is a duckbill platypus. What makes the duckbill platypus stranger still is that although it is a mammal, it lays eggs! **Mammals that lay eggs are called egg-laying mammals, or monotremes** (MAHN-oh-treemz). Because of their ability to lay eggs, egg-laying mammals are sometimes referred to as reptilelike or primitive. The duckbill platypus and the spiny anteaters are the only known monotremes.

Figure 14–5 *The duckbill platypus (top) and the spiny anteater (bottom) are two of the several species of egg-laying mammals that exist today. Egg-laying mammals live in isolated parts of Australia and New Guinea. What is another name for egg-laying mammals?*

When a female duckbill platypus lays her soft marble-sized eggs, which usually number from one to three, she deposits them in a burrow she has dug in the side of a stream bank. The female will keep the eggs warm for the 10 days it takes them to hatch. Once hatched, the young platypuses are not left to find food for themselves (as are the young of reptiles). Instead, the young platypuses feed on milk produced by their mother's mammary glands, which are located on her abdomen. Milk production, as you may recall, is a characteristic of mammals.

Soon after a female spiny anteater lays her eggs, she places them into a pouch on her abdomen. The eggs hatch in 7 to 10 days. Like young platypuses, young spiny anteaters feed on milk produced by their mother's mammary glands.

The unusual body parts of a duckbill platypus help it to gather its food. For example, a duckbill platypus uses its claws to dig for insects, then uses its soft ducklike bill to scoop them up. The bill serves another important purpose: When under water, a platypus closes its eyes and ears. Unable to see as it swims above the riverbed, the platypus feels for snails, mussels, worms, and sometimes small fishes with its bill, which is very sensitive to touch.

Spiny anteaters also have special structures that help them to gather their food: ants and termites. A spiny anteater has a long, thin snout that it uses to probe for food, and it has a sticky, wormlike tongue that it flips out to catch insects. To protect itself, a spiny anteater uses its short powerful legs and curved claws to dig a hole in the ground and cover itself until only its spines are showing. These spines, which are 6 centimeters long, usually discourage almost any enemy.

14–2 Section Review

1. What is a characteristic of egg-laying mammals?
2. Name the two types of egg-laying mammals.

Critical Thinking—*Applying Concepts*
3. Why might egg-laying mammals be considered a link between reptiles and mammals?

14–3 Pouched Mammals

Unlike egg-laying mammals, pouched mammals do not lay eggs. Instead, they give birth to young that are not well developed. Thus the young must spend time in a pouchlike structure in their mother's body. Mammals that have pouches are called **marsupials** (mahr-soo-pee-uhlz).

When most people hear the word marsupial, they think of a kangaroo. Kangaroos, however, are not the only pouched mammals. Pouched mammals also include koalas, opossums, wombats, bandicoots, and gliders. Figure 14–6 shows some of these pouched mammals.

Perhaps the cuddliest and cutest pouched mammal is the koala. See Figure 14–7 on page 370. The koala's ears are big and round and covered with thick fur. Unlike many pouched mammals, a koala has a pouch whose opening faces its hind legs rather than its head. Koalas spend most of their time in trees, munching away on the only food they eat—the

Guide for Reading

Focus on these questions as you read.

▶ *What are pouched mammals?*

▶ *What are the similarities and differences between egg-laying mammals and pouched mammals?*

Figure 14–6 *The hairy-nosed wombat (bottom right), the eastern barred bandicoot (top left), and the sugar glider (bottom left) are examples of pouched mammals.*

leaves of eucalyptus trees. If you have ever smelled cough drops, you are probably familiar with the scent of eucalyptus leaves. The oils of the eucalyptus leaves are put into cough drops. So it is no wonder that koalas smell like cough drops! Because koalas eat only plant material, they, like most marsupials, are called herbivores (HER-buh-vorz).

Kangaroos

"At best it resembles a jumping mouse but it is much larger." These words were spoken in 1770 by the English explorer James Cook. He was describing an animal never before seen by Europeans. He later gave the name "kangaroo" to this strange animal.

Kangaroos live in the forests and grasslands of Australia. They have short front legs but long, muscular hind legs and tails. The tail helps the kangaroo to keep its balance and to push itself forward.

When a kangaroo is born, it is only 2 centimeters long and cannot hear or see. Although only partially developed at birth, it has front legs that enable it to crawl as many as 30 centimeters to its mother's pouch. To get a better idea of just what this feat involves, imagine the following: You are blindfolded, your ears are plugged, and you are placed in the center of a strange room about the size of half a football field. You are then told to find the exit on the first try! Obviously, this task is not easy. In fact, it is almost impossible. But the young kangaroo does it—and successfully, too. The young kangaroo, which is called a joey, stays in its mother's pouch for about 9 months, feeding on its mother's milk.

Figure 14–7 *Pouched mammals, such as the koala, the kangaroo, and the opossum, give birth to young that are not well developed. Thus the young must spend time in a pouchlike structure in their mother's body. Notice the baby kangaroo, called a joey, in its mother's pouch. What is another name for pouched mammals?*

Opossums

Have you ever heard the phrase "playing possum"? Do you know what it means? When in danger, opossums lie perfectly still, pretending to be dead. In some unknown way, this behavior helps to protect the opossum from its predators.

The opossum is the only pouched mammal found in North America. It lives in trees, often hanging onto branches with its long tail. Opossums eat fruits, insects, and other small animals.

Female opossums give birth to many opossums at one time. The females of one species of opossums, for example, give birth to as many as 56 offspring. Unfortunately, most of the newborn opossums do not survive the trip along their mother's abdomen to her pouch. Another species of female opossums produces newborns that are so tiny they have a mass of only 0.14 gram (about the mass of a small nail)!

ACTIVITY
DOING

Endangered Mammals

Endangered species are of concern to almost everyone. Using reference materials in the library, develop an ongoing list of endangered mammals. Be sure to include an illustration of each mammal on your list. Keep your list up to date.

What suggestions can you make to help prevent other mammals from becoming endangered species?

14–3 Section Review

1. What are pouched mammals? Give two examples of these mammals.
2. What is another name for a pouched mammal?
3. What is a herbivore?

Critical Thinking—*Applying Facts*
4. Explain why it is incorrect to refer to the koala as a koala bear.

14–4 Placental Mammals

Placental mammals give birth to young that remain inside the mother's body until their body systems are able to function independently. **Unlike the young of egg-laying and pouched mammals, the young of placental mammals develop more fully within the female.** The name for this group of mammals comes from a structure called a **placenta** (pluh-SEHN-tuh), which develops in females who are pregnant. Through the placenta, food, oxygen, and

Guide for Reading

Focus on these questions as you read.

▶ *What are placental mammals?*

▶ *What are ten major groups of placental mammals?*

Figure 14–8 *Placental mammals, such as the deer mouse, give birth to young that remain inside the mother's body until they can function on their own. What is the placenta?*

wastes are exchanged between the young and their mother. Thus the placenta allows the young to develop for a much longer time inside the mother.

The time the young spend inside the mother is called the **gestation** (jehs-TAY-shuhn) **period.** The gestation period in placental mammals ranges from a few weeks in mice to as long as 18 to 23 months in elephants. In humans, the gestation period is approximately 9 months. After female placental mammals give birth to their young, they supply the young with milk from their mammary glands. You should remember that this is a characteristic of all mammals.

There are many groups of placental mammals, organized here according to how they eat, how they move about, or where they live. Of these groups, 10 are discussed in the sections that follow.

Insect-Eating Mammals

What has a nose with 22 tentacles and spends half its time in water? The answer is a star-nosed mole. As you can see from Figure 14–9, a star-nosed mole gets its name from the ring of 22 tentacles on the end of its nose. No other mammal has this

Figure 14–9 *Insect-eating mammals include the star-nosed mole, the hedgehog, and the pygmy shrew. The star-nosed mole (top right) lives in moist or muddy soil in eastern parts of North America. The hedgehog (bottom right), which is covered by a thick coat of spines, curls into a ball when threatened. The pygmy shrew (bottom left) must eat twice its mass in insects every day to survive.*

structure. Each tentacle has very sensitive feelers, which enable a mole to find insects to eat and to feel its way around while burrowing under ground. Although star-nosed moles have eyes, the eyes are too tiny to see anything. They can only distinguish between light and darkness. A star-nosed mole spends one part of its day burrowing beneath the ground and the other part in the water.

In addition to moles, hedgehogs and shrews are also insect-eating mammals. Because it is covered with spines, a hedgehog looks like a walking cactus. When threatened by a predator, a hedgehog rolls up into a ball with only its spines showing. This action makes a hedgehog's enemy a little less enthusiastic about disturbing the tiny animal.

The pygmy shrew is the smallest mammal on Earth. As an adult, it has a mass of only 1.5 to 2 grams (about the mass of 10 small nails). Because shrews are so active, they must eat large amounts of food to maintain an adequate supply of energy. Shrews can eat twice their mass in insects every day!

ACTIVITY
WRITING

Useful Mammals

Visit your library to find out which mammals have benefited people. On a sheet of paper, make a list of these mammals. Next to each entry indicate the mammal's benefit to people. Discuss with your class whether the benefit listed for each mammal has been harmful, helpful, or neutral to the mammal. Was it necessary for people to use these mammals for their own survival?

Flying Mammals

Bats, which resemble mice, are the only flying mammals. In fact, the German word for bat is *Fledermaus,* which means flying mouse. Bats are able to fly because they have skin stretched over their arms and fingers, forming wings. Other mammals, such as flying squirrels, do not really fly. They simply glide to the ground after leaping from high places.

Although some bats have poor eyesight, all bats have excellent hearing. While flying, a bat gives off high-pitched squeaks that people cannot hear. These squeaks bounce off nearby objects and return to the bat as echoes. By listening to these echoes, a bat knows just where objects are so that it can avoid them. Bats that hunt insects such as moths also use this method to locate their prey.

There are two main types of bats. Fruit-eating bats are found in tropical and desert areas, such as Africa, Australia, India, and the Orient. Insect-eating bats live almost everywhere.

Figure 14–10 *Bats are the only flying mammals. A mouse-eared bat swoops down on its prey—a moth—while the long-tongued bat shows the feature for which it was named.*

The Fastest Runner

The cheetah, the fastest land animal, can run at speeds of up to 100 kilometers per hour. How far can it run in a second? In a minute?

Flesh-Eating Mammals

The frozen ice sheets and freezing waters of the Arctic are home to walruses. They are able to live in this harsh environment because they have a layer of fat, called blubber, under their skin. Blubber keeps body heat in. In addition to their large size, walruses have another noticeable feature: long tusks. These tusks are really special teeth called canines. Walrus canines can grow to 100 centimeters in length!

Walruses do not use their canines (tusks) for tearing and shredding food. Instead, they use their canines to open clams and to defend themselves from their predators: polar bears. Walruses also use their tusks as hooks to help them climb onto ice.

Figure 14–11 *Flesh-eating mammals such as the walrus, the tiger, the coyote, and the grizzly bear are placed in the same group. All these mammals have large pointed teeth that help them tear and shred flesh. What are some other examples of flesh-eating mammals?*

Like a walrus, you too have canines. However, your canines are not as large as a walrus's. You have a total of four canines: two in your upper set of teeth and two in your lower. To find your upper canines, look in a mirror and first locate your eight incisors, or front teeth—four on the bottom and four on top. Incisors are used to bite into food. On either side of your top and bottom incisors is a tooth that comes to a point. These teeth are your canines.

All flesh-eating mammals, including walruses, are known as carnivores (KAHR-nuh-vorz). Some carnivores live on land; others, such as walruses, live in the sea. Land carnivores such as cats, dogs, weasels, lions, wolves, and bears and their relatives have muscular legs that help them to chase other animals. These mammals also have sharp claws on their toes to help them hold their prey.

Like walruses, seals are flesh-eating mammals that live in the sea. The ancestors of these sea carnivores once lived on land but have since returned to the ocean, where they feed on fishes, mollusks (soft-bodied invertebrates that have inner or outer shells), and sea birds. The flipperlike arms and legs of seals, which are so useful in getting around in the water, make moving from place to place on land quite difficult. Regardless of their struggle while on land, seals frequently leave the water.

Toothless Mammals

Although the name of this group indicates that its members do not have any teeth, there are some toothless mammals that actually do have small teeth. They include armadillos and sloths. The mammals in this group that actually have no teeth are the anteaters.

Unlike the spiny anteaters mentioned earlier in this chapter, the anteaters in this group do not lay eggs. As in all placental mammals, the young anteaters remain inside the female until they are more fully developed. However, both types of anteaters have something in common—a long sticky tongue that is used to catch insects. Look at Figures 14–5 and 14–12. Can you see any other similarities or differences between these two anteaters?

CAREERS

Veterinarian Assistant

Working on farms, in kennels, in hospitals, and in laboratories, **veterinarian assistants** are involved in health care for animals. They work under the supervision and instruction of a veterinarian. The duties of a veterinarian assistant include record keeping, specimen collection, laboratory work, and wound dressing. They also help with animals and equipment during surgery.

Patience, compassion, and a willingness to be involved with animal health care are important qualities for those interested in becoming a veterinarian assistant. To receive more information about this career, write to the American Veterinary Medical Association, 1931 North Meacham Road, Schaumburg, IL 60173.

Figure 14–12 *Just as the name of their group implies, the true anteater (right) and the nine-banded armadillo (left) are toothless mammals.*

Armadillos, which live in parts of the southern United States and in Central and South America, eat plants, insects, and small animals. The most striking feature of an armadillo is its protective, armorlike coat. In fact, the word armadillo comes from a Spanish word that means armored. The nine-banded armadillo is the only toothless mammal found as far north as the United States.

Another type of toothless mammal is the sloth. There are two kinds of sloths: the two-toed sloth and the three-toed sloth. Sloths, which feed on leaves and fruits, are extremely slow-moving creatures. They spend most of their lives hanging upside down in trees. You may be amazed to learn that sloths can spend up to 19 hours a day resting in this position.

Trunk-Nosed Mammals

Figure 14–13 *The larger ears of the African elephant (bottom) distinguish it from the Indian elephant (top).*

As the elephant enters the river, it holds its trunk high in the air. Little by little, the water creeps up the elephant's body. Will it drown? The answer comes a few seconds later as the huge animal actually begins to swim!

To an observer on the shore, nothing can be seen of the elephant except its trunk, through which air enters on its way to the lungs. The trunk is the distinguishing feature of all elephants. Elephant trunks are powerful enough to tear large branches from trees. Yet they are agile enough to perform delicate movements, such as picking up a peanut thrown to them by a child at a zoo. These movements are made possible by the action of 40,000 muscles, which are controlled by a highly developed brain.

Elephants are the largest land animals. There are two kinds of elephants: African elephants and Asian elephants. As their names suggest, African elephants live in Africa and Asian elephants in Asia, especially in India and Southeast Asia. Although there are a number of differences between the two kinds of elephants, the most obvious one is ear size. The ears of African elephants are much larger than those of their Asian cousins.

Hoofed Mammals

What do pigs, camels, horses, and rhinoceroses have in common? Not much at first glance. In fact, they could not look more different. Yet if you were to take a closer look at their feet, you would see that they all have thick hoofs.

If you could take an even closer look at several hoofed mammals, you would discover that some have an even number of toes, whereas others have an odd number of toes. Pigs, camels, goats, cows, deer, and giraffes—the tallest of all mammals—have an even number of toes. Horses, rhinoceroses, zebras, hippopotamuses, and tapirs have an odd number of toes.

Hoofed mammals such as pigs, cows, deer, and horses are important to humans and have been so for thousands of years. These hoofed mammals provide humans with food and clothing, as well as with a means of transportation.

ACTIVITY

DISCOVERING

Migration of Mammals

Certain mammals migrate, or move, to places that offer better living conditions. Using posterboard and colored pencils, draw maps that trace the migration patterns of the following mammals: North American bat, African zebra, American elk, and gray whale. Display these maps on a bulletin board at school.

■ Why do you think each type of mammal migrates?

Figure 14–14 *A hippopotamus has an odd number of toes, whereas a giraffe has an even number of toes. Of what importance to people are hoofed mammals?*

Figure 14–15 *The most numerous mammals are the gnawing mammals. Two of the four special incisors that help gnawing mammals chew on hard objects such as wood and nuts can be seen in the photographs of the nutria (center) and the porcupine (bottom). Although the incisors of the chipmunk (top) are concealed by a mouthful of seeds, it too is a gnawing mammal.*

Gnawing Mammals

Hardly a day goes by that people in both the country and the city do not see a gnawing mammal. There are more gnawing mammals than there are any other type of mammal on the Earth. Gnawing mammals are more commonly known as rodents.

Among the rodents are such animals as squirrels, beavers, chipmunks, rats, mice, and porcupines. As you might expect, the characteristic that places these animals in the same group is the way they eat: They gnaw, or nibble. Gnawing mammals have four special incisors. These teeth are chisellike and continue to grow throughout the animal's lifetime. Because rodents gnaw on hard objects such as wood, nuts, and grain, their teeth get worn down as they grow. If this were not the case, a rodent's incisors would become so long that the animal would not be able to open its mouth wide enough to eat.

Some rodents, especially rats and mice, compete with humans for food. They eat the seeds of plants and many other foods used by people. Rodents are responsible for spreading more than 20 diseases, including bubonic plague—which is actually transmitted to people by the bite of a flea that lives on rats. Although it is no longer considered a serious disease, bubonic plague caused the deaths of 25 million people in Europe between the years 1300 and 1600.

Rodentlike Mammals

Rabbits, hares, and pikas (PIGH-kuhz) belong to the group known as rodentlike mammals. Like rodents, these mammals have gnawing teeth. Unlike rodents, however, they have a small pair of grinding teeth behind their gnawing teeth. Rodentlike mammals move their jaws from side to side as they chew their food, whereas rodents move their jaws from front to back.

Rabbits and hares have long hind legs that are used for quick movement and flight from danger. Some larger hares can reach speeds of up to 80 kilometers per hour! In addition, rabbits and hares have large eyes that enable them to remain active during the night.

How are hares and rabbits different? In terms of appearance, hares tend to have longer legs and longer ears than rabbits do. Hares also live on their own on the surface of the ground. Rabbits are born in burrows and are helpless for the first few weeks of their lives.

Pikas, which have large rounded ears and short legs, are not well known because they live high up in the mountains or below ground in burrows. If you are interested in seeing a pika, look at Figure 14–16.

Water-Dwelling Mammals

"Thar she blows!" is the traditional cry of a sailor who spots the fountain of water that a whale sends skyward just before it dives. Although sailors of the past recognized this sign of a whale, they had no idea that this sea animal was a mammal, not a fish.

Whales, porpoises, dolphins, dugongs, and manatees are water-dwelling mammals. Although they live in water most or all of the time, they have lungs and breathe air. They feed their young with milk and have hair at some time in their life.

Whales, dolphins, and porpoises spend their entire lives in the ocean and cannot survive on land. Dugongs and manatees live in shallower water, often in rivers and canals. Because of their large size, it is difficult for dugongs and manatees to move around on land. However, they do so for short periods of time when they become stranded.

Figure 14–16 *The pika (top) and the rabbit (bottom) belong to the group known as the rodentlike mammals.*

Figure 14–17 *Two examples of mammals that live in water are the manatee (left) and the humpback whale (right). What are some other examples of water-dwelling mammals?*

Figure 14–18 *Of all the animals, primates, such as the gibbon (top), the chimpanzee (center), and the orangutan (bottom), have the most highly developed brain and the most complicated behaviors. What are some other characteristics of primates?*

Primates

On a visit to your local zoo, you come upon a crowd of people gathered in front of one of the cages. Hurrying over to see what the excitement is about, you hear strange noises. Carefully you make your way to the front of the crowd, where you see what is causing all the commotion. A family of chimpanzees is entertaining the crowd by running and tumbling about in their cage. The baby chimpanzee comes to the front of the cage and extends its hand to you. You are amazed to see how much like your hand the chimpanzee's hand looks. But it is really no wonder they are similar. After all, the chimpanzee— along with the gibbon (GIHB-uhn), orangutan (oh-RANG-oo-tan), and gorilla—is the closest mammal in structure to humans.

These mammals, along with baboons, monkeys, and humans, belong to the same group—the primates. All primates have eyes that face forward, enabling the animals to see depth. Primates also have five fingers on each hand and five toes on each foot. The fingers are capable of very complicated movements, such as the ability to grasp objects.

Primates also have large brains and are considered the most intelligent mammals. Chimpanzees can be taught to communicate with people by using sign language. Some scientists have reported that chimpanzees can use tools, such as when they use twigs to remove insects from a log. Humans, on the other hand, are the only primates that can make complex tools.

14–4 Section Review

1. What are placental mammals? What is the function of a placenta?
2. What is a gestation period?
3. How do a carnivore and a herbivore differ?
4. List ten groups of placental mammals and give an example of each group.

Connection—*Ecology*

5. Elephants often use their tusks to strip the bark from trees. How might this action harm the environment?

CONNECTIONS

Do You Hear What I Hear?

The question posed in the title is really not so easily answered. If you were a cat, dog, porpoise, or bat—and you could speak—you would have four different answers to this question. Why? Each one of these mammals is capable of hearing sounds other animals cannot!

Sound is a form of energy that is produced when particles vibrate. The number of particle vibrations per second, or the frequency, is an important characteristic of sound. The ear can respond only to certain frequencies. For example, the normal human ear is capable of detecting sounds that have between 20 and 20,000 vibrations per second. Sounds with frequencies higher than 20,000 vibrations per second are called *ultrasonic sounds* (the prefix *ultra*-means beyond). Ultrasonic sounds cannot be heard by the human ear.

Some animals can hear ultrasonic sounds, however. If you have ever used a dog whistle, you know that when you blow on it, your dog comes running even though you cannot hear any sound. Dogs can hear sounds that have frequencies up to 25,000 vibrations per second. Cats can hear sounds with frequencies up to 65,000 vibrations per second. The frequency limit for porpoises is 150,000 vibrations per second. And bats can hear ultrasonic sounds with frequencies up to 200,000 vibrations per second. Bats not only hear ultrasonic sounds, they also produce ultrasonic sounds. They use the echoes to avoid bumping into things and to locate prey such as moths. This process of navigation is called *echolocation.* The echolocation of many bats is so efficient that they can make last-minute swerves in order to intercept a moth that has changed its course!

Laboratory Investigation

Examining Hair

Problem

What are the characteristics of hair?

Materials   *(per student)*

medicine dropper	coverslip
methylene blue	microscope
glass slide	electric light
comb or brush	hand lens
scissors	

Procedure 🧪 ⬛ ⏸ 🔋

1. Using the medicine dropper, put 2 drops of methylene blue in the center of a clean glass slide. **CAUTION:** *Be careful when using methylene blue because it may stain your skin and clothing.*

2. Comb or brush your hair vigorously to remove a few loose hairs.

3. From your comb or brush, select two hairs that each have a root attached. The root is the small bulb-shaped swelling at one end of the hair.

4. Using the scissors, trim the other end of each hair so it will be short enough to fit on the glass slide. Place the trimmed hairs in the drops of methylene blue on the slide. Cover the slide.

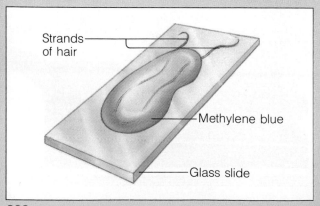

5. Use the low-power objective of the microscope to locate the hairs. Then switch to the high-power objective and focus with the fine adjustment. Make a sketch of the hair strand.

6. Turn the fine adjustment toward you (counterclockwise) to focus on the upper surface of the hair. At one point in your focusing, the hair will appear to be covered by overlapping structures that look like shingles. Draw these structures, which are actually cells.

7. Under bright light, use the hand lens to examine a portion of your skin that does not seem to be covered with hair. (Do not examine the palms of your hands or the soles of your feet.)

Observations

1. Describe the appearance of a strand of hair under the microscope.

2. Describe the appearance of cells covering the strand of hair.

3. What did you observe when you examined the surface of your skin under bright light?

Analysis and Conclusions

1. Based on your observations, what is hair?

2. **On Your Own**   Obtain hair from several of the pets mentioned in the Journal Activity at the beginning of the chapter. Prepare these hair samples as you did your hair sample. Compare the various hair samples. Are they about the same thickness as your hair when observed with the unaided eye? When observed with the microscope? What other similarities or differences do you observe?

Summarizing Key Concepts

14-1 What Is a Mammal?

▲ Mammals are warmblooded vertebrates that have hair or fur and that feed their young with milk produced in mammary glands.

▲ Mammals use their lungs to breathe. Their circulatory system consists of a four-chambered heart and blood vessels. Paired kidneys filter nitrogen-containing wastes from the blood in the form of urea. Urea, water, and other wastes form urine, which is stored in the urinary bladder.

▲ Mammals have well-developed brains and senses, and they have internal fertilization.

▲ Mammals can be placed into three basic groups depending on the way in which they reproduce. These groups are the egg-laying mammals, the pouched mammals, and the placental mammals.

14-2 Egg-Laying Mammals

▲ Mammals that lay eggs are called egg-laying mammals, or monotremes.

▲ The duckbill platypus and the spiny anteater are examples of egg-laying mammals.

14-3 Pouched Mammals

▲ Unlike monotremes, pouched mammals do not lay eggs. Instead, they give birth to young that are not well developed. Thus the young must spend time in a pouchlike structure in their mother's body. Mammals that have pouches are called marsupials.

14-4 Placental Mammals

▲ Placental mammals give birth to young that remain inside the mother's body until their body systems are able to function independently. The placenta is a structure through which food, oxygen, and wastes are exchanged between the young and their mother.

▲ Insect-eating mammals include moles, hedgehogs, and shrews.

▲ Bats are the only flying mammals.

▲ Flesh-eating mammals, or carnivores, include sea-living animals such as walruses and seals. Land-living carnivores include any members of the dog, cat, and bear families.

▲ Toothless mammals include those animals that lack teeth or have small teeth.

▲ The only members of the trunk-nosed mammal group are the elephants.

▲ Hoofed mammals are divided into the group that has an even number of toes on each hoof and the group that has an odd number of toes.

▲ Gnawing mammals, such as beavers, chipmunks, rats, mice, and porcupines, have chisellike incisors for chewing.

▲ Rabbits, hares, and pikas are examples of rodentlike mammals.

▲ Mammals such as whales, dolphins, porpoises, dugongs, and manatees are water-dwelling mammals.

▲ Humans, monkeys, and apes are primates.

Reviewing Key Concepts

Define each term in a complete sentence.

14-1 What Is a Mammal?
egg-laying mammal
pouched mammal
placental mammal

14-4 Placental Mammals
placenta
gestation period

Chapter Review

Content Review

Multiple Choice

Choose the letter of the answer that best completes each statement.

1. All mammals have
   a. pouches.   c. feathers.
   b. hair.   d. fins.
2. The kangaroo is a(n)
   a. pouched mammal.
   b. egg-laying mammal.
   c. placental mammal.
   d. gnawing mammal.
3. The only North American marsupial is the
   a. kangaroo.   c. platypus.
   b. koala.   d. opossum.
4. Young mammals that develop totally within the female belong to the group called
   a. egg-laying mammals.
   b. pouched mammals.
   c. placental mammals.
   d. marsupial mammals.
5. Which is an insect-eating mammal?
   a. whale   c. bear
   b. elephant   d. mole

6. Which teeth are used to tear and shred food?
   a. carnivores   c. incisors
   b. canines   d. herbivores
7. Which is an example of a toothless mammal?
   a. skunk   c. armadillo
   b. mole   d. camel
8. The largest land animal is the
   a. blue whale.   c. elephant.
   b. rhinoceros.   d. giraffe.
9. An example of a water-dwelling mammal is the
   a. spiny anteater.   c. shrew.
   b. dolphin.   d. elephant.
10. To which group of mammals do humans belong?
    a. insect-eating mammals
    b. rodents
    c. primates
    d. carnivores

True or False

If the statement is true, write "true." If it is false, change the underlined word or words to make the statement true.

1. Mammals are <u>invertebrates</u>.
2. Mammals are <u>warmblooded</u> animals.
3. The duckbill platypus is an example of a <u>marsupial</u>.
4. Animals that eat only plants are called <u>herbivores</u>.
5. The <u>gestation period</u> is the time the young of placental mammals spend inside their mother.
6. Rabbits are <u>gnawing</u> mammals.
7. Carnivore means <u>flesh eater</u>.
8. Humans are <u>primates</u>.

Concept Mapping

Complete the following concept map for Section 14–1. Then construct a concept map for the entire chapter.

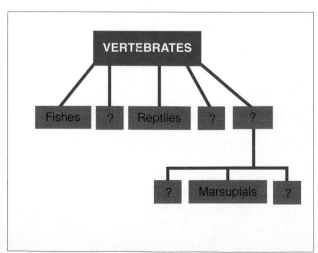

Concept Mastery

Discuss each of the following in a brief paragraph.

1. What are the characteristics of mammals? What are the three groups of mammals? How do they differ from one another?
2. What is the difference between an anteater and a spiny anteater?
3. Name two pouched mammals. Explain how their young develop.
4. What are mammary glands?
5. List ten groups of placental mammals and give an example of each.
6. Why are whales considered mammals and not fishes?
7. What features make carnivores good predators?
8. Why are primates considered the most intelligent mammals?

Critical Thinking and Problem Solving

Use the skills you have developed in the chapter to answer each of the following.

1. **Relating facts** Which group of mammals is most similar to birds? Explain your answer.
2. **Making charts** Prepare a chart with three columns. In the first column, list the ten groups of mammals that you learned about in this chapter. In the second column, list the characteristics of each group. And in the third column, list at least two examples of each group.
3. **Applying concepts** Why do whales usually come to the surface of the ocean several times an hour?
4. **Making inferences** Many species of hoofed mammals feed in large groups, or herds. What advantage could this behavior have for the survival of these mammals?
5. **Making generalizations** What is the relationship between how complex an animal is and the amount of care the animal gives to its young? Provide an example to support your answer.
6. **Designing an experiment** Design an experiment that will test the following hypothesis: Chimpanzees are able to understand the meaning of the spoken words for the numbers 1 through 10.
7. **Using the writing process** Imagine that you are a writer for a wildlife magazine. Your boss tells you that she has decided not to include mammals in the magazine because she finds them dull. Write a memo to change her mind. Include the characteristics that separate mammals from other animals.

GAZETTE

Jack Horner Warms up to Dinosaurs

Paleontologist Jack Horner is not interested in how dinosaurs died. Rather, he is interested in how they lived.

Horner, who teaches at Montana State University and is also curator of paleontology at the Museum of the Rockies in Bozeman, Montana, heads the largest dinosaur research team in the United States. His work focuses on the behavior of dinosaurs, and his research findings are considered quite revolutionary. You see, Horner has discovered that these extinct creatures were not always the enormous, bloodthirsty monsters portrayed in horror movies and popular cartoons. More likely, Horner says, many dinosaurs were social plant-eaters and nurturing parents.

Horner's conclusions are based largely on research he has done in an area called the Willow Creek Anticline in his home state of Montana. He worked there for many years, uncovering fossils that date back to the Cretaceous Period, some 65 to 135 million years ago.

In studying the dinosaurs, Horner is ful-

filling a goal he has had since he discovered his first fossil at age eight. Throughout high school, he knew he wanted to be a paleontologist. But his schoolwork was rather poor and remained so throughout his college experience. (He flunked out of college seven times.) However, he continued taking and excelling in courses in paleontology, eventually earning an assistantship in paleontology at Princeton University. At age 31, while at Princeton, Horner discovered his academic problems were the result of dyslexia. Dyslexia is a condition in which the ability to read is impaired.

While still at Princeton, Horner became particularly fascinated with the study of juvenile dinosaurs—an area of paleontology that had received little or no attention. His fascination took him back to Montana where, quite by accident, he stumbled upon a collection of dinosaur egg fossils. The events leading to this discovery occurred something like this: While traveling through his native state in the late 1970s, Horner and a friend decided to stop for a brief rest at a small shop where rocks were sold. The owner, an amateur fossil collector, asked Horner to identify some bones she had found. Upon close examination, Horner was amazed to see that the collection included some bone fragments from baby hadrosaurs, or duck-bill dinosaurs. No sooner had the shopowner showed Horner where she had found the fossils, than he began to dig.

Working at the Willow Creek Anticline through the 1980s, Horner and his team unearthed many dinosaur eggs and skeletons of young dinosaurs, particularly those of hadrosaurs. The shape and texture of the egg shells, as well as the structure of the baby dinosaur skulls, led Horner to some new and exciting conclusions about the behavior of hadrosaurs. Baby hadrosaurs, Horner says, kept their babylike features—large heads with big eyes and shortened snouts—throughout their lives. These features encouraged adult dinosaurs to nurture them. Adult hadrosaurs, Horner believes, guarded their eggs before they hatched and then fed and protected their young after they were born. He has even given a name to the genus of dinosaur he discovered with these nurturing traits. He calls the genus *Maiasaura*, meaning good mother dinosaur.

Horner brings the past into view of the present and uses the latest techniques of the present to study the past. As curator of paleontology at the Museum of the Rockies, Horner wants his visitors to see how he believes dinosaurs lived during their 140-million-year reign on Earth. For example, he designs his displays to show dinosaurs doing such ordinary actions as scratching their jaws and sitting calmly on the ground. Horner has also coauthored a book on—what else?—dinosaurs. In addition, he is a consultant for a Japanese amusement park that

▲ A duckbilled adult oversees a nest of newly hatched maiasaurs. The hatchlings are tended to for months by adults.

has a huge display—complete with robot models—of the history of Earth.

Horner, the former college dropout, is now well into his forties. The years of struggling with dyslexia have not prevented him from earning the respect of fellow scientists, as well as the prestigious MacArthur Foundation fellowship. Interestingly, this award is also known as the "genius award."

U N I T F O U R

Human Biology

To play soccer, all parts of the bodies of these young soccer players must work together in perfect harmony.

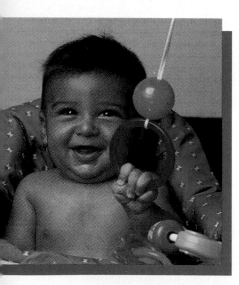

 A smiling child reaching for a toy illustrates how different parts of the body—even a very young body—work together.

The day for the championship soccer game has finally arrived. The stadium is filled to capacity. The game is about to begin. The crowd quiets down as a soccer player on the attacking team prepares to kick off. The defending team members anxiously await the ball on their half of the field so that they can advance the ball into the attacking team's territory. The players on both sides have spent many years of training for this moment.

As the kicker begins to kick off, nerves carry messages to her brain, telling her body exactly what movements it must make. Her muscles move, pulling on her bones so that she kicks the ball out of the center circle. At the same time, chemicals flow through her blood, informing certain parts of her body to speed up and others to slow down.

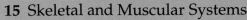

Now comes the kickoff. She moves toward the ball, keeping her nonkicking foot next to the ball, her head down, and her eyes on the ball. Then she swings her kicking leg with the toes pointed downward and kicks the ball squarely with her instep. It's out of the center circle. The game has begun!

To help her team win the championship, all parts of the soccer player's body have to work in perfect harmony. And even though you may never compete in a championship soccer game, your body parts are also working in their own perfect harmony at this very moment. In this unit you will discover how the different parts of your body work and how they all work together as one.

▲ *Exercise, such as running, helps to keep the body in good working condition.*

Discovery *Activity*

Yesterday, Today, and Tomorrow

1. Take a look at your classmates or a group of people who are about your age. Make a mental note of the features that you share with them.

2. Complete the same exercise with a group of adults and a group of young children.

   ■ In what ways are people of all ages the same?

   ■ What changes occur in people as they grow from children to adults?

   ■ Are all changes that occur in people easily observed?

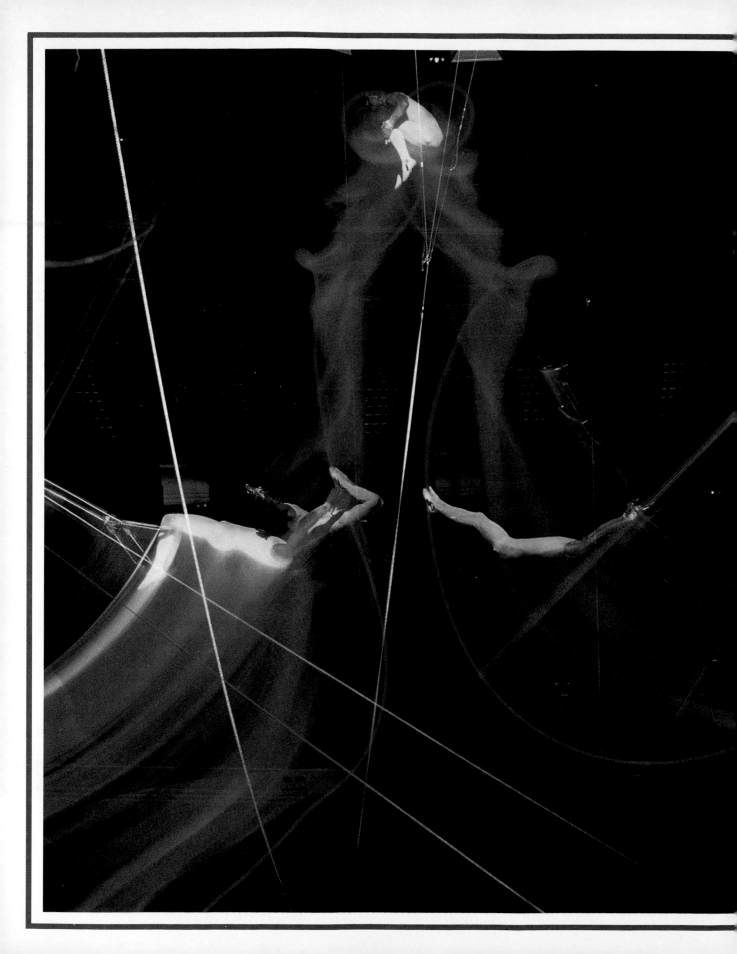

Skeletal and Muscular Systems

Guide for Reading

After you read the following sections, you will be able to

15–1 The Human Body
- Classify the four basic types of tissue in the human body.

15–2 The Skeletal System
- List the functions of each part of the skeletal system.
- Describe the characteristics and structure of bone.
- Describe three types of movable joints.

15–3 The Muscular System
- Classify the three types of muscle tissues.
- Explain how muscles cause movement.

Slowly, the young man climbs up the ladder toward the top of the circus tent. The crowd grows quiet. You feel your heart beginning to beat faster. You tilt your head back. Your eyes follow the man in the glistening costume. As he grabs the trapeze, the muscles in his arms bulge. Suddenly, he leaps and is flying through space. Then he lets go of the trapeze and does a somersault in midair . . . once, twice, three times. You gasp and then gaze in disbelief as, incredibly, the man does another somersault—a quadruple! It has never been done before!

How, you wonder, has the trapeze artist been able to perform such a daring feat? Part of the answer lies in the hundreds of hours he has spent training and practicing. And part of the answer lies in the dedication he has brought to his work. But certainly he could never have performed this spectacular act if it were not for his finely coordinated body. Working together with many of his other organs, the trapeze artist's bones and muscles have made the "impossible" happen. In the pages that follow, you will discover how your skeletal and muscular systems work for you—making the ordinary to the almost impossible possible.

Journal *Activity*

You and Your World   Perform one type of movement with each of the following parts of your body: finger, wrist, arm, and neck. In your journal, describe the motion of each body part. What allows you to move these body parts? How is each motion different?

◀ *A trapeze artist performs a daring feat—a quadruple somersault!*

Activity Bank

A Human Cell vs. an Ameba, p. 815

15–1 The Human Body

Here's a riddle for you: What do you and an ameba have in common? The answer: Both of you are made of cells. Actually, the whole "body" of the ameba is made up of one cell. Your body, however, is made up of many cells. Living things that are composed of only one cell are called unicellular; those that are composed of many cells are called multicellular.

In multicellular living things—humans, birds, trees, turtles, and hamsters, to name just a few—the work of keeping the living things alive is divided among the different parts of their body. Each part has a specific job to do. And as the part does its specific job, it works in harmony with all the other parts to keep the living thing healthy and alive.

The groupings of these specific parts within a living thing are called levels of organization. The levels of organization in a multicellular living thing include cells, tissues, organs, and organ systems.

Figure 15–1 *All living things are made of cells. Bacteria are unicellular, whereas the giraffe is multicellular. Does the giraffe have bigger cells than a bacterium or just more of them?*

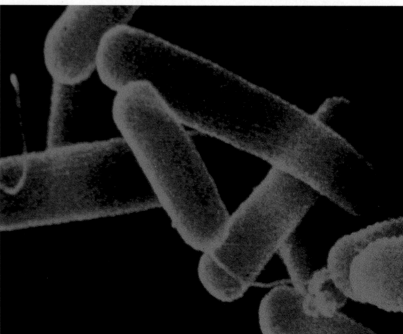

Types of Body Tissue

Your body is made up of trillions of cells, which are organized into **tissues.** As you may recall from Chapter 3, a tissue is a group of similar cells that perform the same function. **There are four basic types of tissue in the human body: muscle, connective, nerve, and epithelial** (ehp-ih-THEE-lee-uhl). Observing these tissues under a microscope, you might be surprised to see how different they are from one another.

MUSCLE TISSUE   The only kind of tissue in your body that has the ability to contract, or shorten, is **muscle tissue.** By contracting and thus pulling on bones, one type of muscle tissue makes your body move. Another type of muscle tissue lines the walls of structures inside your body. This muscle tissue does jobs such as moving food from your mouth to your stomach. A third type of muscle tissue is found only in the heart. This muscle tissue enables the heart to contract and pump blood.

CONNECTIVE TISSUE   The tissue that provides support for your body and connects all its parts is known as **connective tissue.** Bone is an example of connective tissue. Are you surprised to learn that bone is a tissue? Not all tissues need to be soft. Without bone, your body would lack support and definite shape. In other words, without bone you would just be a blob of flesh! Blood is another example of connective tissue. One of the blood's most important jobs is to bring food and oxygen to body cells and carry away wastes. A third kind of connective tissue is fat. Fat keeps the body warm, cushions structures from the shock of a sudden blow, and stores food.

NERVE TISSUE   The third type of tissue is **nerve tissue.** Nerve tissue carries messages back and forth between the brain and spinal cord and every other part of your body. And it does so at incredible speeds. In the fraction of a second it takes for you to feel the cold of an ice cube you are touching, your nerve tissue has carried the message from your finger to your brain. Next time you have a chance to hold an ice cube, think about this.

EPITHELIAL TISSUE   The fourth type of tissue is **epithelial tissue.** Epithelial tissue forms a protective surface on the outside of your body. When you look in a

ACTIVITY

CALCULATING

Fast, Faster, Fastest

Nerve messages travel at incredible speeds. In fact, they can reach speeds of up to 100 meters per second. Nerve messages, however, are not the fastest things on Earth. Sound and light travel at speeds greater than the speed of a nerve impulse. To find out how fast sound and light travel, solve these riddles.

If sound travels 3.3 times faster than a nerve impulse, how fast does sound travel? If light travels 30,000 times faster than a nerve impulse, how fast does light travel? Arrange these speeds from slowest to fastest.

Figure 15–2 *Tissues are groups of similar cells that work together. How do connective tissue (top left), nerve tissue (top right), muscle tissue (bottom right), and epithelial tissue (bottom left) allow for the delicate movements needed to kick a soccer ball?*

mirror, you are looking at a special kind of epithelial tissue, one that makes up your outer covering—your skin! Another kind of epithelial tissue lines the cavities, or hollow spaces, of the mouth, throat, ears, stomach, and other body parts.

Figure 15–3 *Each organ system is made of a group of organs that work together. Which organ system enables the body to move?*

Organs and Organ Systems

Just as cells join together to form tissues, so do the different types of tissue in your body combine to form **organs.** An organ is a group of different tissues that has a specific function. Your heart, stomach, and brain are all organs. The heart is an example of an organ made up of all four kinds of tissue. Although it is mostly muscle, it is covered by epithelial tissue and also contains connective and nerve tissue.

Groups of organs working together are called **organ systems.** Most of the organ systems of the body and their functions are shown in Figure 15–3. Though each system performs a special function for the body, none of them acts alone. Each organ system contributes to the constant teamwork that allows all the parts of the human body to work together in perfect harmony.

15–1 Section Review

1. What are the four basic types of human tissues?
2. List some of the organ systems of the human body.

Connection—*You and Your World*
3. Using a bicycle or any type of machine as an example, explain how each part of the machine works with every other part so that the machine can do its job. Compare this with the way the systems of the body work together.

ORGAN SYSTEMS	
System	**Function**
Skeletal	Protects and supports the body
Muscular	Supports the body and enables it to move
Skin	Protects the body
Digestive	Receives, transports, breaks down, and absorbs food throughout the body
Circulatory	Transports oxygen, wastes, and digested food throughout the body
Respiratory	Permits the exchange of gases in the body
Excretory	Removes liquid and solid wastes from the body
Endocrine	Regulates various body functions
Nervous	Conducts messages throughout the body to aid in coordination of body functions
Reproductive	Produces male and female sex cells

15–2 The Skeletal System

The skeletal system is the body's living framework. This complicated structure contains more than 200 **bones**—actually, about 206—held together by groups of stringy connective tissues called **ligaments.** Another group of connective tissues called **tendons** attach bones to muscles. Together, the bones, ligaments, and tendons make up most of the skeletal system.

Guide for Reading

Focus on these questions as you read.

▶ *What are the five functions of the skeletal system?*

▶ *What is the structure of bone?*

Functions of the Skeletal System

The skeletal system has five important functions: It provides shape and support, allows movement, protects tissues and organs, stores certain materials, and produces blood cells. The first of these important functions—giving shape and support to the body—should be pretty clear to you. Imagine that you did not have a skeletal system. What would you look like? A formless mass? A blob of jelly? The answer is yes to both descriptions! In fact, if the skeletal system did not perform this vital role, it would be meaningless to consider any of its other functions.

The skeletal system helps the body move. Almost all your bones are attached to muscles. As the muscles contract (shorten), they pull on the bones, causing the bones to move. By working together, the actions of the bones and muscles enable you to walk, sit, stand, and do a somersault.

Bones protect the tissues and organs of your body. If you move your fingers along the center of your back, you will feel your backbone, or vertebral column. Your backbone protects your spinal cord, which is the message "cable" between the brain and other body parts. The spinal cord is made up of nerve tissue, which is extremely soft and delicate and, therefore, easily damaged. So you can see why it is important that the spinal cord is protected from injury.

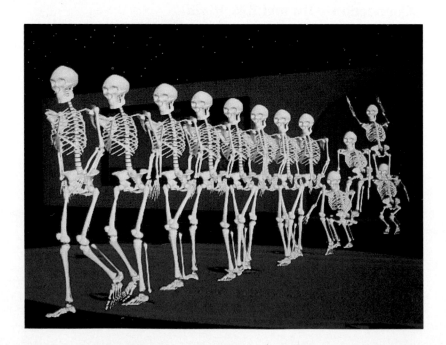

Figure 15–4 *As a result of computer graphics, the jumping and walking movements of a human skeleton take on a ghostly appearance. What type of connective tissue holds the bones of the skeleton together?*

Bones are storage areas for certain substances. Some of these substances give bones their stiffness. Others play a role in blood clotting, nerve function, and muscle activity. If the levels of these substances in the blood should fall below their normal ranges, the body will begin to remove them from where they are stored in the bones.

The long bones in your body (such as those in the arms and legs) produce many blood cells. One type of blood cell carries oxygen. Another type destroys harmful bacteria.

Parts of the Skeleton

Suppose you were asked to make a life-size model of the human skeleton. Where would you start? You might begin by thinking of the human skeleton as consisting of two parts. The first part covers the area that runs from the top of your head and down your body in a straight line to your hips. This part includes the skull, the ribs, the breastbone, and the vertebral column. The vertebral column contains 26 bones, which are called vertebrae (VER-tuh-bray; singular: vertebra, VER-tuh-bruh).

The second part of the skeletal system includes the bones of the arms, legs, hands, feet, hips, and shoulders. There is a total of 126 bones in this part of the skeletal system.

Development of Bones

Many bones are formed from a type of connective tissue called **cartilage** (KAHRT-'l-ihj). Cartilage is a very hard, stiff jellylike material. Although cartilage is strong enough to support weight, it is also flexible enough to be bent and twisted. You can prove this to yourself by moving your nose back and forth and by flapping your ears. The tip of your nose and your ears are made of cartilage.

Many bones in the skeleton of a newborn baby are composed almost entirely of cartilage. The process of replacing cartilage with bone starts about seven months before birth and is not completed until a person reaches the age of about 25 years. At this time, a person "stops growing." However, some forming and reforming of bone still occur even in adulthood, primarily where bone is under a great deal of stress.

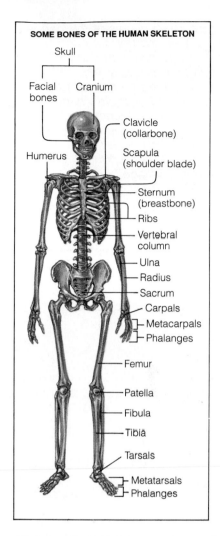

SOME BONES OF THE HUMAN SKELETON

Skull
Facial bones
Cranium
Humerus
Clavicle (collarbone)
Scapula (shoulder blade)
Sternum (breastbone)
Ribs
Vertebral column
Ulna
Radius
Sacrum
Carpals
Metacarpals
Phalanges
Femur
Patella
Fibula
Tibia
Tarsals
Metatarsals
Phalanges

Figure 15–5 *There are approximately 206 bones in the human skeletal system. What is another name for the collarbone?*

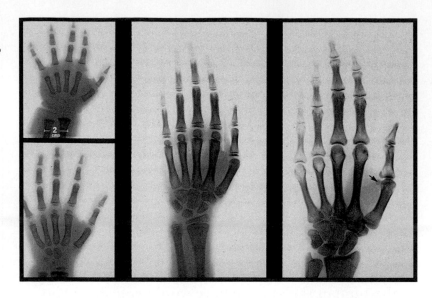

Figure 15–6 *X-rays of the hands of a 2-year-old (top left) and a 3-year-old (bottom left) show that the cartilage in the wrist has not yet been replaced by bone. In the X-ray of a 14-year-old's hand (center), the replacement of cartilage by bone is almost complete, as it is in the hand of a 60-year-old (right). What type of tissue is cartilage?*

Although most of your body's cartilage will eventually be replaced by bone, there are a few areas where the cartilage will remain unchanged, such as in the knee, ankle, and elbow. These areas are usually found where bone meets bone. Here the cartilage has two jobs. One job is to cushion the bones against sudden jolts, such as those that occur when you jump or run. The other job is to provide a slippery surface for the bones so that they can move without rubbing against one another. Because cartilage is three times more slippery than ice, it is ideal for this task.

Structure of Bones

Bone is not only one of the toughest materials in the body; it is also one of the lightest. You may be surprised to learn that the 206 bones of your skeletal system make up barely 14 percent of your body's mass! Because of bone's strength, you may have thought of bone as nonliving. On the contrary, bones are alive. They contain living tissue—nerves, bone-forming cells, and blood vessels.

Bones, however, are similar in some ways to such nonliving things as rocks. Can you think of a few reasons why? Two obvious similarities are hardness and strength. Both bones and rocks owe their hardness and strength to chemical substances called minerals. Rocks contain a wide variety of minerals; bones are made up mainly of mineral compounds that contain the elements calcium and phosphorus. As you may already know, dairy products, such as milk and cheese, are good sources of calcium and phosphorus. So next time someone suggests that you drink lots of milk "to keep your bones strong and healthy," you will know why this suggestion makes sense.

Let's take a close look at the longest bone in the body to see what it (and other bones) is made of. This bone, called the femur (FEE-mer), links your hip to your knee. Probably the most obvious part of this bone is its long shaft, or column. The shaft, which is shaped something like a hollow cylinder, contains compact bone. Compact bone is dense and similar in texture to ivory. Within the shaft of a long bone are hollow cavities, or spaces. Inside these cavities is a soft material called yellow **marrow.** Yellow marrow contains fat and blood vessels. Another type of marrow called red marrow produces the body's blood cells. Red marrow is found in the cavities of such places as the skull, ribs, breastbone, and vertebral column.

Surrounding the shaft of the femur is a tough membrane that contains bone-forming cells and blood vessels. This membrane aids in repairing injuries to the bone and also supplies food and oxygen to the bone's living tissue. Muscles are attached to this membrane's surface. At each end of the shaft is an enlarged knob. The knobs are made of a type of bone called spongy bone. Spongy bone is not soft and spongy, as its name implies, but is actually quite

Figure 15-7 *As the diagram illustrates, the most obvious feature of a long bone is its long shaft, or center, which contains dense, compact bone. Running through compact bone is a system of canals that bring materials to the living bone cells. One such canal is seen in the center of the photograph. What materials are carried through the canals?*

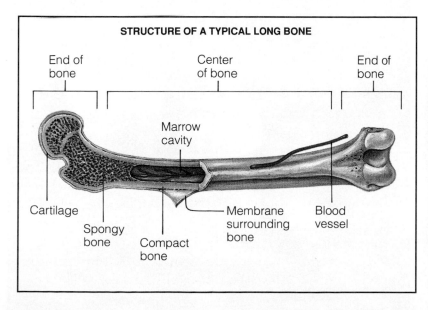

STRUCTURE OF A TYPICAL LONG BONE

End of bone — Center of bone — End of bone

Marrow cavity

Cartilage

Spongy bone

Compact bone

Membrane surrounding bone

Blood vessel

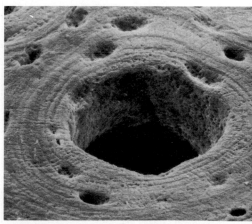

From *Tissues and Organs: A Text-Atlas of Scanning Electron Microscopy.* By Richard G. Kessel and Randy H. Kardon. Copyright © 1979 by W.H. Freeman and Company. Reprinted by permission.

Figure 15–8 *The red marrow of bones such as the skull and ribs produces the body's red blood cells and white blood cells. As seen through an electron microscope, red blood cells are beret shaped and white blood cells are furry looking.*

Figure 15–9 *The actions involved in pitching a ball require the use of many types of joints. What movement does the ball-and-socket joint allow for?*

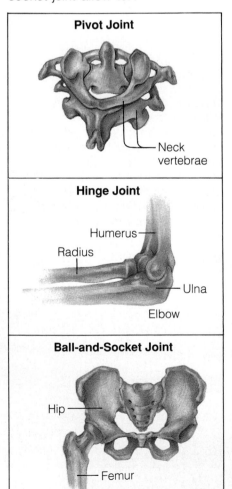

Pivot Joint

Neck
vertebrae

Hinge Joint

Humerus

Radius

Ulna

Elbow

Ball-and-Socket Joint

Hip

Femur

strong. Because spongy bone resembles the supporting girders of a bridge, its presence at the ends of long bones adds strength without adding mass.

Running through the bone is a system of pipelike canals that bring food and oxygen to the living bone cells. These canals also contain nerves. The nerves send messages through the canals to living parts of the bone.

Skeletal Joints

Imagine that you are pitching your first baseball game of the season. The catcher signals you to throw a fast ball. You know that the batter is a powerful hitter, so you shake your head no. The catcher changes the signal to a curve ball. You agree and nod. And then you wind up and send your curve ball sailing over the plate. "Strike one!" the umpire shouts.

You could not make any of these simple movements—shaking and nodding your head or winding up and pitching the ball—if it were not for structures in your skeletal system called **joints.** A joint is any place where two bones come close together. Generally, a joint is responsible for keeping the bones far enough apart so that they do not rub against each other as they move. At the same time, a joint holds the bones in place.

There are several different kinds of joints. Some joints allow the bones they connect to move. Other joints permit little or no movement. Examples of joints

Figure 15–10 *Joints, or places where two bones meet, allow bones to move without damaging each other. The ball-and-socket joint in the shoulder (top) permits the greatest range of movement, whereas the joints in the skull (bottom) do not move at all. What type of joint is found in the elbow?*

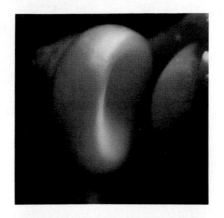

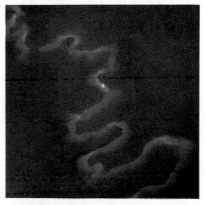

that permit no movement are the joints found in the skull. Although these joints permit no movement, they enable the bones in the skull to fuse (join) as you grow. In the pitching example you just read about, the pivot joint, which is located between the first two vertebrae in your neck, enabled you to shake and nod your head in response to the catcher's signals. A pivot joint allows for rotation of one bone around another.

When you wound up to pitch your curve ball, the ball-and-socket joint of your shoulder allowed you to swing your arm in a circle. Ball-and-socket joints, which provide for the circular motion of bones, consist of a bone with a rounded head that fits into the cuplike pocket of another bone. Can you think of another location in your body where you would find a ball-and-socket joint?

As you moved your arm forward, the bend at your elbow straightened out and you whipped the ball toward the batter. The elbow is a hinge joint. A hinge joint, which is also found at the knee, allows for movement in a forward and backward direction. However, it allows for little movement from side to side. Figure 15–9 shows where the hinge joint and the other joints you just read about are located in the body.

15–2 Section Review

1. What are the five functions of the skeletal system?
2. What is a ligament? A tendon?
3. List three places in the body where cartilage is found.
4. What is marrow?
5. Compare the movements of three types of movable joints.

Critical Thinking—*Relating Facts*

6. Suggest an advantage of having the ribs attached to the breastbone by cartilage.

ACTIVITY

DISCOVERING

Are Joints Necessary?

1. With masking tape, tape the thumb and fingers of the hand that you write with together. Make sure that you cannot move or bend the fingers.

2. Now try these activities with the taped-up hand: button a shirt, tie a shoelace, turn the pages of a book, pick up a pencil, open a door, turn on a radio, and pick up a coin.

■ Explain why it is important to have joints in your fingers.

Turning on Bone Growth

What has *electricity* got to do with the growth of bone? According to researchers Clinton Rubin and Kenneth McLeod at the State University of New York at Stony Brook, low, painless doses of electricity can prevent or treat osteoporosis. Osteoporosis is a disorder that causes a loss and a weakening of bone tissue. Affecting up to half of all women over the age of 45, osteoporosis can lead to spinal deformities and broken hips.

In one study, Rubin and McLeod experimented on turkeys because, like humans, turkeys lose bone tissue as they age. Rubin and McLeod sped up the loss of bone by immobilizing (preventing the movement of) one wing in each of about 40 turkeys. The immobilized bones in these turkeys wasted away significantly within a period of two months. Another group of turkeys wore small electric coils that set up electromagnetic (having to do with electricity and magnetism) fields that produced an electric current that traveled through the wing. The wing bones of these birds showed no wasting away. In fact, they actually showed an increase in

bone mass! In other studies, researchers have shown that cells zapped with electricity absorb greater amounts of calcium, which, as you may recall, is necessary for bone growth.

Although it may seem to you that scientists can turn on bone growth with the flip of a switch, it is not quite as simple as that. To begin with, scientists will have to prove that they are not causing one health problem while fixing another. At present, there is concern about the relationship between electromagnetic fields (which are produced by almost everything from high-power wires to household appliances) and the risk of cancer.

Scientists are now trying to find out just what the relationship and possible dangers are. Meanwhile, the bone researchers point out that they use electromagnetic waves that are different from those generated by power lines and electrical appliances. They also have proof that for the past 20 years, doctors have used currents of electricity to repair bone fractures.

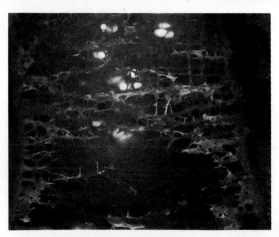

Notice that the bone tissue from an 80-year-old man with osteoporosis (bottom) has larger empty spaces than the bone tissue from a healthy 31-year-old man (top).

15–3 The Muscular System

It is three o'clock in the morning, and you have been asleep for several hours. All day you walked, ran, and played, using your muscles in a variety of ways. Now that you are asleep, all the muscles in your body are also at rest. Or are they?

Without waking you, many of the more than 600 muscles in your body are still working to keep you alive. The muscles in your heart are contracting to pump blood throughout your body. Your chest muscles are working to help move air in and out of your lungs. Perhaps last night's dinner is still being moved through your digestive system by muscles.

Most muscles, or muscle tissue, are composed of muscle fibers that run beside, or parallel to, one another and are held together in bundles of connective tissue. Each muscle fiber is actually a single cylinder-shaped cell. Recall from earlier in this chapter that a tissue is a group of similar cells that work together to perform a specific function. In the case of muscle tissue, that function is to contract, or shorten.

Guide for Reading

Focus on this question as you read.

▶ *What are the three types of muscles?*

Figure 15–11 *Muscle tissue is composed of muscle fibers that run parallel to one another and are held together in bundles of connective tissue. The biceps muscle, which is located in the upper arm, is an example of skeletal muscle tissue. Why is the biceps classified as a skeletal muscle?*

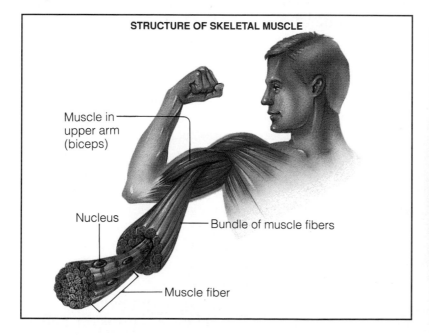

STRUCTURE OF SKELETAL MUSCLE

Muscle in upper arm (biceps)

Nucleus

Bundle of muscle fibers

Muscle fiber

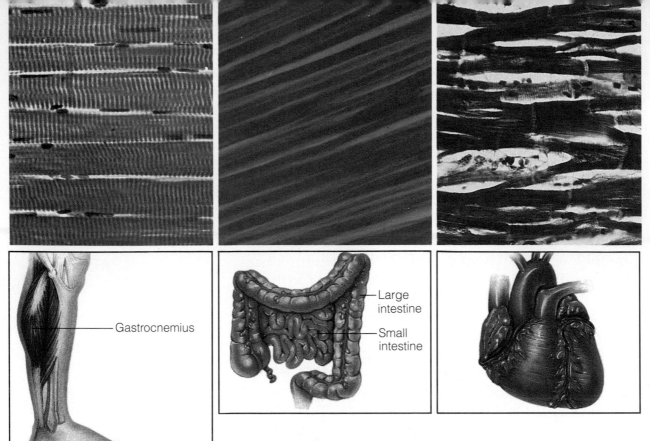

Figure 15–12 *There are three types of muscle tissue: skeletal muscle tissue (left), smooth muscle tissue (center), and cardiac muscle tissue (right). Where in the body are these muscle tissues found?*

Gastrocnemius

Large intestine

Small intestine

Types of Muscles

In the human body, there are three types of muscle tissue: skeletal muscle, smooth muscle, and cardiac muscle. Each type of muscle tissue has a characteristic structure and function. The muscle tissue that attaches to and moves bones is called **skeletal muscle.** This is an appropriate name for this type of muscle tissue because it is associated with the bones of the body, or the skeletal system. By contracting, skeletal muscle causes your arms, legs, head, and other body parts to move.

If you were to look at skeletal muscle under a microscope, you would see that it is striated (STRIGH-ayt-ehd), or banded. For this reason, skeletal muscles are called striated muscles. Figure 15–12 shows the bands associated with skeletal muscle. And because skeletal muscles move only when you want them to, they are also called voluntary muscles.

To appreciate how some of the voluntary (skeletal) muscles in your body work, think of the movements you make in order to write your name on a sheet of paper. The instant you want it to, your arm stretches out to pick up the paper and pencil. You grasp the pencil and lift it. Then you press the pencil down on the paper and move your hand to form the letters in your name. Your eyes move across the page as you write. To do all of this, you have to use more than 100 muscles. Now suppose you did this little task 100 times. Do you think the muscles in your hand would ache? Probably so. For although skeletal muscles react quickly when you want them to, they also tire quickly. You might want to actually try this.

A second type of muscle tissue is called **smooth muscle.** Unlike skeletal muscle, smooth muscle does not have bands. Hence, its name is smooth. In general, smooth muscles can contract without your actively causing them to. Thus, smooth muscles are also called involuntary muscles. The involuntary muscles of the body help to control breathing, blood pressure, and the movements of the digestive system. Unlike skeletal muscles, smooth muscles react slowly and tire slowly. How might this be an advantage for smooth muscles?

A third type of muscle tissue, **cardiac muscle,** is found only in the heart. Branching out in many directions, cardiac muscle fibers weave a complex mesh. The contractions of these muscle fibers make the heart beat. Like smooth muscles, cardiac muscles are involuntary. Heart muscle, as you may have guessed, does not tire.

Action of Skeletal Muscles

As you have learned, muscles do work only by contracting, or shortening. In order for skeletal muscles to bring about any kind of movement, the action of two muscles or two groups of muscles is needed. Put another way, muscles always work in pairs.

For example, if you were to raise your lower arm at the elbow, you would notice that a bulge appears in the front of your upper arm. This bulge is caused by the contraction of a muscle called the biceps. At the same time the biceps contracts, a muscle called the triceps, which is located at the back of your upper arm, relaxes. Now suppose you wanted to straighten your arm. To perform this simple feat, your triceps would have to contract and your biceps would have to relax at the same time. Figure 15–13 on the next page shows how these two muscles work together to help you bend and straighten your arm.

ACTIVITY

DISCOVERING

Muscle Action

1. Obtain a spring-type clothespin.

2. Count how many times you can click the clothespin in two minutes using your right hand. Record the information.

3. Rest for one minute and repeat step 2. Then rest for another minute and repeat step 2 again. Determine the average number of clicks for the right hand.

4. Using your left hand, repeat steps 2 and 3.

Was there a difference in the number of clicks per minute between the right and the left hand? Explain.

■ Why do you think you were able to click the clothespin faster at the beginning of the investigation than you were near the end?

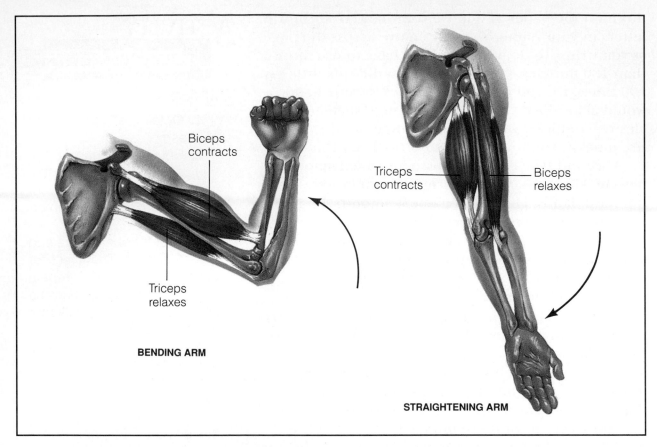

BENDING ARM

Biceps
contracts

Triceps
relaxes

Triceps
contracts

Biceps
relaxes

STRAIGHTENING ARM

Figure 15–13 *When you "make a muscle," the biceps muscle and the triceps muscle work together. Which muscle relaxes when the arm is bent? When the arm is straightened?*

Under Tension, p. 817

The mechanism by which muscles contract is actually a bit more complex than what you have just read. For it is not only muscles that are involved in this action. Nerve tissue is also involved. Skeletal muscles, you see, contract only when they receive a message from a nerve to do so. The nerves carry messages from the brain and spinal cord to the muscles, signaling them to contract.

You may be surprised to learn that there is no such thing as a weak or strong contraction of a muscle fiber. When a fiber receives a message to contract, it contracts completely or not at all. The strength of a muscle contraction is determined by the number of fibers that receive the message to contract at the same time. Strong muscle contractions, such as those that are involved in hitting a ball with a bat, require the contractions of more muscle fibers than would be needed to open a textbook.

PROBLEM Solving

What Kind of Joint Is This?

The pivot, ball-and-socket, and hinge joints that you have read about in the chapter are not the only types of movable joints in the body. There are several other movable joints.

The accompanying drawings illustrate six types of movable joints. Notice the motion that each joint is capable of producing. On a separate sheet of paper, copy the following list of activities.

- Pushing a door open
- Lifting a book from a desk
- Kneeling
- Giving the "thumbs up" signal
- Waving the hand
- Shrugging the shoulders
- Shaking the head from side to side

Applying Concepts

Now compare the motion of each joint with each activity. Determine which type of joint or joints is needed to perform each activity and write the name of the joint next to its appropriate activity.

SIX TYPES OF MOVABLE JOINTS

    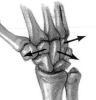 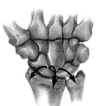

| Shoulder | Elbow | First two neck vertebrae | Base of thumb | Carpals (wrist) | Base of fingers |

| Ball-and-socket joint | Hinge joint | Pivot joint | Saddle joint | Gliding joint | Ellipsoid joint |

15–3 Section Review

1. List the three types of muscle tissue.
2. Compare voluntary and involuntary muscle.
3. Describe how muscles work in pairs.

Critical Thinking—*You and Your World*
4. If your biceps were paralyzed, what movement would you be unable to make?

Laboratory Investigation

Observing Bones and Muscles

Problem

What are the characteristics of bones and muscles?

Materials *(per group)*

2 chicken leg bones	vinegar
tiny piece of raw, lean beef	medicine dropper
	water
2 dissecting needles	2 glass slides
methylene blue	coverslip
2 jars with lids	microscope
knife	paper towel

Procedure ⚗ 🧰 👁 ⚖

Part A

1. Clean all meat off the bones. Place one bone in each of the two jars.

2. Fill one jar with vinegar and the other with water. Cover both jars. Place in refrigerator.

3. After five days, remove the bones from the jars. Rinse each bone with water.

4. With the knife, carefully cut each of the bones in half. **CAUTION:** *Be careful when using a knife.* Examine the inside of each bone.

Part B

1. Place the tiny piece of raw beef on one of the glass slides. With a medicine dropper, place a drop of water on top of the beef.

2. With the dissecting needles, carefully separate, or tease apart, the fibers of the

beef. **CAUTION:** *Be careful when using dissecting needles.*

3. Transfer a few fibers to the second slide. Add a drop of methylene blue. **CAUTION:** *Be careful when using methylene blue because it may stain the skin and clothing.* Cover with a coverslip. Use the paper towel to absorb any excess stain.

4. Examine the slide under the microscope.

Observations

1. How do the two bones differ in texture and flexibility? Describe the appearance of the inside of each bone.

2. Describe the appearance of the beef under a microscope.

Analysis and Conclusions

1. What has happened to the minerals and the marrow within the bone that was put in vinegar? How do you know this?

2. Why was one bone put in a jar with water?

3. What type of muscle tissue did you observe under the microscope?

4. How does the structure of the muscle tissue aid in its function?

5. **On Your Own** Repeat this investigation using substances other than vinegar.

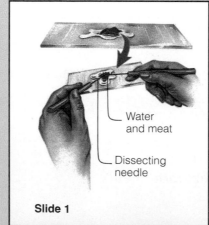

Water and meat

Dissecting needle

Slide 1

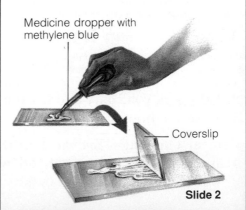

Medicine dropper with methylene blue

Coverslip

Slide 2

Study Guide

Summarizing Key Concepts

15–1 The Human Body

▲ A tissue is a group of similar cells that perform the same function.

▲ The human body contains four types of tissue: muscle, connective, nerve, and epithelial.

▲ An organ is a group of different tissues that performs a specific function.

▲ The human body has organ systems that are made up of groups of organs working together.

15–2 The Skeletal System

▲ Bones are fastened together by connective tissues called ligaments. Tendons are connective tissues that connect muscles to bones.

▲ The skeletal system has five important functions: It provides shape and support, allows movement, protects tissues and organs, produces blood cells, and stores certain materials.

▲ The human skeleton is divided into two parts. One part consists of the skull, the ribs, the breastbone, and the vertebral column. The other part is made up of the bones of the arms, legs, hands, feet, shoulders, and hips.

▲ Cartilage is a flexible connective tissue that supports, acts as a shock absorber, and cushions other skeletal parts.

▲ A joint is a place where two bones come close together.

15–3 The Muscular System

▲ Muscle tissue is made of fibers bundled together by connective tissue. Muscle tissue moves only by contracting, or shortening.

▲ There are three types of muscle tissue: skeletal, smooth, and cardiac. Skeletal muscles permit voluntary movement and are connected to bone. Smooth muscles help control breathing, blood pressure, and movements of the digestive system. Cardiac muscles make the heart beat.

▲ All skeletal muscles work in pairs. When one contracts, the other relaxes.

Reviewing Key Terms

Define each term in a complete sentence.

15–1 The Human Body
tissue
muscle tissue
connective tissue
nerve tissue
epithelial tissue
organ
organ system

15–2 The Skeletal System
bone
ligament
tendon
cartilage
marrow
joint

15–3 The Muscular System
skeletal muscle
smooth muscle
cardiac muscle

Chapter Review

Content Review

Multiple Choice

On a separate sheet of paper, write the letter of the answer that best completes each statement.

1. A tissue that has the ability to contract is
   a. muscle tissue.   c. connective tissue.
   b. nerve tissue.   d. epithelial tissue.
2. Which type of tissue is blood?
   a. muscle tissue.   c. connective tissue.
   b. nerve tissue.   d. epithelial tissue.
3. Bones are held together by stringy connective tissue called
   a. cartilage.   c. ligaments.
   b. joints.   d. tendons.
4. The nose and ears contain a flexible connective tissue called
   a. marrow.   c. muscle.
   b. bone.   d. cartilage.
5. Two minerals that make up the nonliving part of bones are
   a. sodium and chlorine.
   b. calcium and iron.
   c. magnesium and phosphorus.
   d. calcium and phosphorus.
6. A place where two bones come close together is called a
   a. dislocation.   c. tendon.
   b. joint.   d. ligament.
7. The longest bone in the body is the
   a. vertebra.   c. femur.
   b. collarbone.   d. breastbone.
8. An example of a ball-and-socket joint is the
   a. shoulder.   c. elbow.
   b. neck.   d. knee.
9. The elbow is an example of a
   a. ball-and-socket joint.
   b. hinge joint.
   c. pivot joint.
   d. bone.
10. Skeletal muscles are also known as
    a. involuntary muscles.
    b. smooth muscles.
    c. cardiac muscles.
    d. voluntary muscles.

True or False

If the statement is true, write "true." If it is false, change the underlined word or words to make the statement true.

1. Tendons join muscles to bones.
2. Bone is an example of nerve tissue.
3. Cartilage is a flexible muscle tissue.
4. Bones contain the minerals calcium and iron.
5. A joint is a place where two bones come close together.
6. The elbow is an example of a ball-and-socket joint.
7. Skeletal muscle is also called involuntary muscle.
8. Smooth muscle tissue is found only in the heart.

Concept Mapping

Complete the following concept map for Section 15–2. Then construct a concept map for the entire chapter.

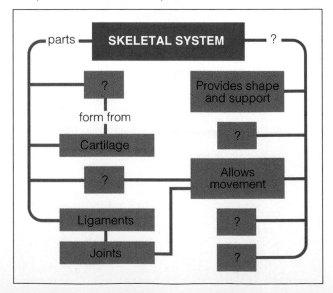

Concept Mastery

Discuss each of the following in a brief paragraph.

1. List and describe each of the four basic types of tissue in the body.
2. Use Figure 15–5 on page 397 to identify the following bones with their scientific names.
   a. thigh
   b. finger
   c. toe
   d. kneecaps
   e. breastbone
   f. shoulder blade
3. Explain the differences among ligaments, tendons, and cartilage.
4. Name the three types of muscle tissue. Discuss their functions.
5. Describe the structure of the femur.
6. List three movable joints. Describe the actions of each joint.
7. Explain how the biceps and triceps enable you to bend and straighten your arm.
8. Compare a voluntary muscle and an involuntary muscle. Give an example of each type of muscle.

Critical Thinking and Problem Solving

Use the skills you have developed in this chapter to answer each of the following.

1. **Relating concepts** What is the advantage of having some joints, such as the knee and elbow, covered by a fluid-filled sac?
2. **Applying concepts** Bones heal faster in children than they do in adults. Why do you think this is so?
3. **Interpreting photographs** Because cartilage does not appear on X-ray film, it is seen as a clear area between the shaft and the knobs of individual bones. Examine the photographs showing the X-rays of two hands. Which hand belongs to the older person? Explain.

4. **Applying concepts** Suggest a reason why there are more joints in the feet and hands than in most other parts of the body.
5. **Relating concepts** What role does good posture play in maintaining healthy muscles and tendons?
6. **Relating facts** Explain why you feel pain when you fracture, or break, a bone.
7. **Sequencing events** Arrange the following terms in order from the most complex to the least complex: cell, organism, tissue, organ system, organ. Give an example of each.
8. **Using the writing process** Choose a five-minute segment out of your day. In a journal, record all the activities that you performed during this time. Then try to identify all the muscles, bones, and joints you used. Use the figures in this chapter to help you, and don't forget those involuntary muscles, too!

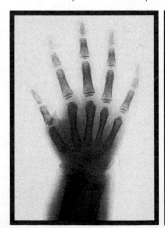 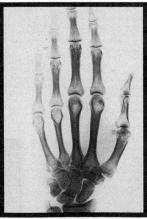

Digestive System

Guide for Reading

After you read the following sections, you will be able to

16–1 The Importance of Food
- Define nutrients.

16–2 Digestion of Food
- Describe how food is digested in the mouth, stomach, and small intestine.
- Compare mechanical digestion and chemical digestion.

16–3 Absorption of Food
- Describe how nutrients are absorbed in the digestive system.

16–4 Maintaining Good Health
- Describe the roles weight control and proper exercise habits play in maintaining good health.

Eating a meal in space is no ordinary event! Mistakes can produce strange and funny scenes. A dropped fork may fall up instead of down. Spilled milk is just as likely to end up on the ceiling as on the floor. And a banana left unattended may float away from an open mouth—or toward one. These "tricks" produced by weightlessness are conditions of space travel to which all astronauts must adjust.

Would you like to live in space? Before you answer, take a moment to consider this: What must it be like to live in a place where every spoonful of pudding is in danger of escaping and lettuce leaves in a salad fly away like butterflies? Perhaps you have never thought seriously about the experience of eating and swallowing food in space. What happens to the food after it is swallowed? Without gravity, will it move up instead of down? And what about food that is already in the stomach? In the pages that follow, you will learn how your body digests and absorbs food—right here on Earth! Then you will be better able to answer the questions about eating in space.

Journal *Activity*

You and Your World What did you have for dinner last night? What did you eat for lunch today? Who was with you, and where did you eat these meals? In your journal, explore the thoughts and feelings you had during these mealtimes.

◄ *Astronauts eating a meal in space*

16-1 The Importance of Food

In a way, you and all human beings are chemical factories. Like any factory, you need raw materials for building new products, repairing old parts, and energy to keep the factory going. These needs are provided by the **nutrients** in the foods you eat. Nutrients are the parts of food your body can use.

To keep your body strong and healthy, you must eat a balanced diet. A balanced diet contains foods from five food groups. These groups are:

- Milk, yogurt, and cheese
- Bread, cereal, rice, and pasta
- Meat, poultry, fish, dry beans, eggs, and nuts
- Fruits
- Vegetables

A balanced diet provides you with the six basic categories of nutrients that your body needs: proteins, carbohydrates, fats and oils, vitamins, minerals, and water.

Figure 16-1 *The Food Guide Pyramid stresses foods from the five major food groups in the three lower sections of the Pyramid. At the top of the Pyramid are the fats, oils, and sweets, which should be used sparingly.*

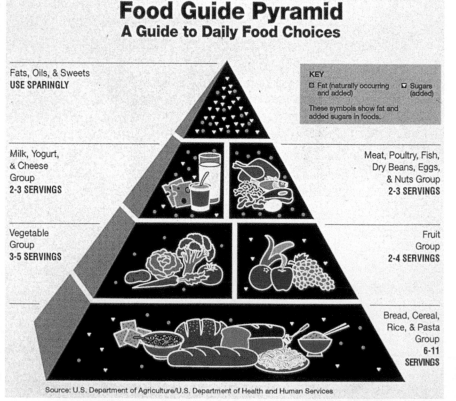

Food Guide Pyramid
A Guide to Daily Food Choices

Fats, Oils, & Sweets
USE SPARINGLY

KEY
▽ Fat (naturally occurring and added)   ▽ Sugars (added)
These symbols show fat and added sugars in foods.

Milk, Yogurt, & Cheese Group
2-3 SERVINGS

Meat, Poultry, Fish, Dry Beans, Eggs, & Nuts Group
2-3 SERVINGS

Vegetable Group
3-5 SERVINGS

Fruit Group
2-4 SERVINGS

Bread, Cereal, Rice, & Pasta Group
6-11 SERVINGS

Source: U.S. Department of Agriculture/U.S. Department of Health and Human Services

THE SIX BASIC NUTRIENTS

Substances	Sources	Needed For
Proteins	Soybeans, milk, eggs, lean meats, fish, beans, peas, cheese	Growth, maintenance, and repair of tissues Manufacture of enzymes, hormones, and antibodies
Carbohydrates	Cereals, breads, fruits, vegetables	Energy source Fiber or bulk in diet
Fats	Nuts, butter, vegetable oils, fatty meats, bacon, cheese	Energy source Insulation
Vitamins	Milk, butter, lean meats, leafy vegetables, fruits	Prevention of deficiency diseases Regulation of body processes Growth Efficient biochemical reactions
Mineral salts Calcium and phosphorus compounds	Whole-grain cereals, meats, milk, green leafy vegetables, vegetables, table salt	Strong bones and teeth Blood and other tissues
Iron compounds	Meats, liver, nuts, cereals	Hemoglobin formation
Iodine	Iodized salt, seafoods	Secretion by thyroid gland
Water	All foods	Dissolving substances Blood Tissue fluid Biochemical reactions

Figure 16–2 *Nutrients are grouped into six categories in this chart. Which nutrient prevents vitamin-deficiency diseases?*

Proteins

Every living part of your body contains **protein.** Proteins are used to build and repair body parts. That is why you need the raw materials used to make proteins—**amino** (uh-MEE-noh) **acids.**

All proteins are made up of chains of amino acids. For this reason amino acids are called the building blocks of proteins. When you eat a protein, your digestive system breaks it up into its amino acid parts.

Most animal proteins, such as meat, fish, poultry, and eggs, contain all the amino acids your body needs. Such proteins are called complete proteins. Other foods, such as rice, cereal, and vegetables, contain only small amounts of one or another amino acid and are known as incomplete proteins.

ACTIVITY

CALCULATING

Determining Your Metabolic Rate

Basal metabolic rate, or BMR, is the energy needed (in Calories) to keep your awake but restful body functioning.

To determine your BMR, multiply 1 Calorie by your weight in kilograms (2.2 lbs = 1 kg). Then multiply this number by 24 hours. You now have your basal metabolic rate in Cal/day. What is your BMR? Would you need more or fewer Calories when you are doing some type of activity? Explain your answer.

Carbohydrates

Carbohydrates supply the body with its main source of energy. Fruits, vegetables, and grain products are good sources of carbohydrates.

The energy value of foods, such as carbohydrates, is measured in units called **Calories.** A Calorie is equal to the amount of heat energy needed to raise the temperature of 1 kilogram of water by 1°C. The number of Calories that a person needs everyday depends on the person's size, body build, occupation, type of activity, and age.

There are two types of carbohydrates—the sugars and the starches. A starch is a long chain of sugars. Sugars can be digested and used for fuel faster than starches. But if you eat more carbohydrates than you need, the excess is stored as starch in your muscles and liver. If these storage places become filled, the carbohydrates are then stored in other places in the body. As a result, a diet with too much carbohydrates can make a person overweight.

Fats and Oils

Like carbohydrates, **fats** and **oils** supply the body with energy. In fact, fats supply the body with twice as much energy as do equal amounts of proteins and carbohydrates. In addition to providing energy, fats help to support and cushion vital organs, protecting them from injury. Fats also insulate the body against loss of heat. Foods that are rich in fats come from both animals and plants. Some sources of fats are nuts, butter, vegetable oils, and cheeses.

Figure 16–3 *Nutrients provide the body with energy for sledding and raking leaves—to name just a few activities. In what unit is the amount of energy obtained from nutrients measured?*

Vitamins and Minerals

In addition to substances that are used for building, repairing, and fueling your body, you also need **vitamins** and **minerals.** Vitamins help regulate growth and the normal functioning of your body. Because you only need them in small amounts, vitamins are sometimes called micronutrients. However, when your body does not get enough of a certain vitamin, you could come down with a vitamin-deficiency disease.

One such disease is scurvy, a painful disease whose victims suffer bleeding gums, loss of teeth, aching muscles, and even death. Scurvy was once

Getting the Iron Out, p. 818

Figure 16–4 *According to this chart, which vitamin is important for proper vision? For blood clotting?*

VITAMINS		
Vitamin	**Source**	**Use**
A (carotene)	Yellow and green vegetables, fish-liver oil, liver, butter, egg yolks	Important for growth of skin cells; important for vision
D (calciferol)	Fish oils, liver, made by body when exposed to sunlight, added to milk	Important for the formation of bones and teeth
E (tocopherol)	Green leafy vegetables, grains, liver	Proper red blood cell structure
K	Green leafy vegetables, made by bacteria that live in human intestine	Needed for normal blood clotting
B_1 (thiamine)	Whole grains, liver, kidney, heart	Normal metabolism of carbohydrates
B_2 (riboflavin)	Milk products, eggs, liver, whole grain cereal	Normal growth
Niacin	Yeast, liver, milk, whole grains	Important in energy metabolism
B_6 (pyridoxine)	Whole grains, meats, poultry, fish, seeds	Important for amino acid metabolism
Pantothenic acid	Many foods, yeast, liver, wheat germ, bran	Needed for energy release
Folic acid	Meats, leafy vegetables	Proper formation of red blood cells
B_{12} (cyanocobalamin)	Liver, meats, fish, made by bacteria in human intestine	Proper formation of red blood cells
C (ascorbic acid)	Citrus fruits, tomatoes, green leafy vegetables	Strength of blood vessels; important in the formation of connective tissue; important for healthy gums

MINERALS

Mineral	Source	Use
Calcium	Milk products, green leafy vegetables	Important component of bones and teeth; needed for normal blood clotting and for normal cell functioning
Chlorine	Table salt, many foods	Important for fluid balance
Magnesium	Milk products, meat, many foods	Needed for normal muscle and nerve functioning; metabolism of proteins and carbohydrates
Potassium	Grains, fruits, many foods	Normal muscle and nerve functioning
Phosphorus	Meats, nuts, whole grains, many foods	Component of DNA, RNA, ATP, and many proteins; part of bone tissue
Sodium	Many foods, table salt	Nerve and muscle functioning; water balance in body
Iron	Liver, red meats, grains, raisins, nuts	Important part of hemoglobin molecule
Fluorine	Water (natural and added)	Part of bones and teeth
Iodine	Seafood, iodized table salt	Part of hormones that regulate rate of metabolism

Figure 16–5 *Minerals help to keep the body functioning normally. Which minerals provide for normal nerve and muscle functioning?*

common among sailors. Many years before the discovery of vitamins, the British naval surgeon James Lind found that a supply of fresh fruit or fresh juice would prevent scurvy. In fact, it was because of the lime juice they had to drink that the British sailors became known as "limeys." Some other vitamin-deficiency diseases are pellagra and rickets. Pellagra is caused by a deficiency in niacin, while rickets is caused by a deficiency in vitamin D.

There are two groups of vitamins. The fat-soluble vitamins are stored in body fat. So high levels of fat-soluble vitamins can be harmful. Water-soluble vitamins are constantly washed out of the body and should be supplied in adequate amounts in the foods you eat each day. See Figure 16–4 on page 417.

Like vitamins, minerals help to maintain the normal functioning of your body. There are 16 essential minerals. Figure 16–5 lists some of these minerals.

Figure 16–6 *Water is essential for our survival. However, if people do not use existing water resources wisely, fertile land may soon become sandy desert.*

Water

Although you can survive many days without eating, several days without water can be fatal. Water is important because all the chemical reactions in the body take place in water. And water carries nutrients and other substances to and from body organs through the bloodstream. Water also helps your body stay at the right temperature, 37°C.

On the average your body is about 50 to 60 percent water. Under normal conditions, you need about 2.4 to 2.8 liters of water daily. You get this water from the fluids you drink and the foods you eat.

16–1 Section Review

1. What are nutrients? Describe the six types of nutrients.
2. What is a Calorie?
3. How do water-soluble and fat-soluble vitamins differ?
4. Why is water important to the body?

Critical Thinking—*Relating Concepts*
5. Explain how it is possible for a person to be overweight and suffer from improper nutrition at the same time.

PROBLEM Solving

Reading Food Labels

Carmen has been asked by her teacher to determine the most nutritious breakfast cereal in her local market. Upon her arrival at the market, Carmen heads for the aisle containing the breakfast cereals and picks up the first cereal box. As a health-conscious and well-informed consumer, Carmen reads the nutrition labeling on the box of cereal. She knows that this information will help her compare similar foods on the basis of their share of nutrients to Calories.

Carmen knows that in order to burn up 1 gram of carbohydrate or protein, her body needs to use 4 Calories. For 1 gram of fat, her body needs to use 9 Calories. She realizes that it takes more than twice the number of Calories to burn up 1 gram of fat than it does to burn up 1 gram of carbohydrate or protein. That is one reason why Carmen tries to limit the amount of fats that she eats.

Carmen also knows that an ideal diet should get no more than 30 percent of its Calories from fats. Of the remaining Calories, 50 to 55 percent should come from carbohydrates and 15 to 20 percent from proteins. The carbohydrates should be in the form of starches rather than sugars.

Take a look at the food label on this page. Notice that the major nutrients are listed both in grams (or milligrams) and as a percentage of the total recommended intake for someone eating 2000 calories a day. For example, the 1 gram of fat in the cereal provides about 2 percent of the suggested daily allowance. The label also provides some general information about nutrition, telling

Nutrition Facts

Serving Size 1 cup (30g)
Servings Per Container About 10

Amount Per Serving	Multi Grain Cereal	with ½ cup Skim milk
Calories	110	150
Calories from Fat	10	15
		% Daily Value**
Total Fat 1g*	2%	2%
Saturated Fat <0.5g	1%	2%
Cholesterol 0mg	0%	1%
Sodium 240mg	10%	13%
Potassium 100mg	3%	9%
Total Carbohydrate 24g	8%	10%
Dietary Fiber 3g	10%	10%
Sugars 6g		
Other Carbohydrate 15g		
Protein 3g		
Vitamin A	25%	30%
Vitamin C	25%	25%
Calcium	4%	20%
Iron	45%	45%
Vitamin D	10%	25%
Thiamin	25%	30%
Riboflavin	25%	35%
Niacin	25%	25%
Vitamin B$_6$	25%	25%
Folic Acid	25%	25%
Phosphorus	10%	20%
Magnesium	6%	10%
Zinc	4%	6%
Copper	4%	4%

*Amount in cereal. A serving of cereal plus milk provides 1.5g fat. <5mg cholesterol, 310mg sodium, 300mg potassium, 30g carbohydrate (12g sugar) and 7g protein.

**Percent Daily Values are based on a 2,000 calorie diet. Your daily values may be higher or lower depending on your calorie needs.

	Calories:	2,000	2,500
Total Fat	Less than	65g	80g
Sat Fat	Less than	20g	25g
Cholesterol	Less than	300mg	300mg
Sodium	Less than	2,400mg	2,400mg
Potassium		3,500mg	3,500mg
Total Carbohydrate		300g	375g
Dietary Fiber		25g	30g

Calories per gram:
Fat 9 • Carbohydrate 4 • Protein 4

you the Daily Values of certain nutrients and the Calories per gram for protein, carbohydrate, and fat.

Now practice your food-label skills on the typical cereal box label shown here. You can use a calculator or computer to help you answer some of the following questions. Keep in mind that in some cases a person's diet may contain nutrients in different amounts from those suggested.

1. How many Calories are in a gram of fat? Of protein? Of carbohydrate?

2. On a 2000-Calorie diet, what is the Daily Value for total fat? For sodium? For fiber?

3. What percentage of the Daily Value of calcium is provided by 1 cup of the cereal? By 1 cup of the cereal with ½ cup skim milk?

4. How many grams of carbohydrate are in a 1-cup serving of the cereal with ½ cup skim milk? What percentage of the Daily Value of a 2000-calorie diet does this represent?

5. What percentages of a 2000-calorie diet's Daily Values are provided by ½ cup of skim milk?

6. In the dry cereal, how many grams of carbohydrates were in the form of starches? In the form of sugars?

16–2 Digestion of Food

Unfortunately, most foods that you eat cannot be used directly by your body. **Food must be broken down into nutrients in a process called digestion. The breaking down of food into simpler substances for use by the body is the work of the digestive system.** Once these simpler substances are broken down, or digested, they are carried to all the cells of the body by the blood. In the following sections, you will follow a mouthful of food through the digestive system.

The Mouth

Close your eyes and imagine your favorite food. Your mouth probably watered. This response occurs because the mouth contains salivary (SAL-uh-vair-ee) glands. Salivary glands produce and release a liquid known as saliva. Seeing, smelling, or even thinking about food can increase the flow of saliva.

Guide for Reading

Focus on these questions as you read.

▶ *What happens to food during the process of digestion?*

▶ *What are the parts of the digestive system?*

Figure 16–7 *The breaking down of food into simpler substances that can be used by the body is the work of the digestive system. The digestive system consists of a number of different organs. Through which organ does food enter the digestive system?*

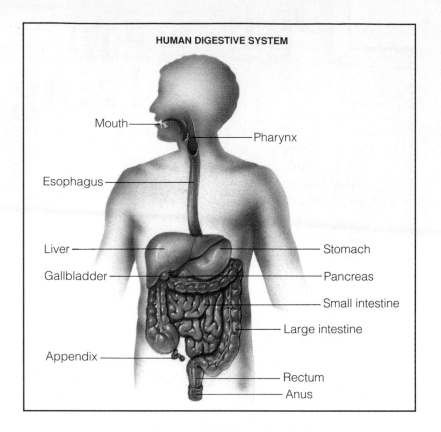

HUMAN DIGESTIVE SYSTEM

Mouth
Pharynx
Esophagus
Liver
Stomach
Gallbladder
Pancreas
Small intestine
Large intestine
Appendix
Rectum
Anus

CHEMICAL DIGESTION Saliva, as you might expect, helps moisten food. It also contains a chemical substance called **ptyalin** (TIGH-uh-lihn). Ptyalin chemically breaks down some of the starches in food into sugars.

Ptyalin is one of many **enzymes** in your body. Enzymes control a wide variety of chemical reactions, including the breaking down of food into simpler substances. The digestion of foods by enzymes is called **chemical digestion.**

Figure 16–8 *The X-ray of the mouth shows the location of the four types of teeth: incisors, canines, premolars, and molars. The brighter areas in the teeth are the fillings. Where are the incisors located?*

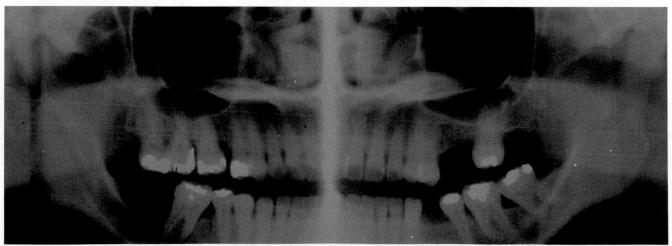

MECHANICAL DIGESTION   You bite into your food with your incisors (ihn-SIGH-zerz), or front teeth. Then you pull the food into your mouth with your lips and use your tongue to push it to the back of your mouth. Here, the flat-headed premolars and molars, or back teeth, grind and crush the food into small pieces. At the same time, the canines (KAY-nighnz), or eyeteeth, tear and shred the food. The physical action of breaking food into smaller parts is called **mechanical digestion.**

TASTE BUDS   The food in your mouth tastes good or bad to you because your tongue has taste buds. See Figure 16–10. There are four types of taste buds. Each reacts to a different group of chemicals in food to produce a taste. The four tastes are sweet, sour, bitter, and salty. But the flavor of food does not come from taste alone. Flavor is a mixture of taste, texture, and odor.

THE EPIGLOTTIS   After you chew your food a few times, you swallow. When you swallow, smooth muscles near the back of your throat begin to force the food downward. At the same time, a small flap of tissue called the epiglottis (ehp-uh-GLAHT-ihs) automatically closes over your windpipe. The windpipe is the tube through which the air you breathe reaches your lungs. When the epiglottis moves over the windpipe, it prevents food or water from moving into the windpipe or "down the wrong pipe." After swallowing, the epiglottis moves back into place to allow air into the windpipe.

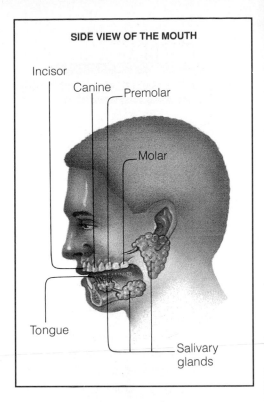

SIDE VIEW OF THE MOUTH

Incisor
Canine
Premolar
Molar
Tongue
Salivary glands

Figure 16–9 *Salivary glands, which are found in the mouth, produce saliva. Saliva contains the enzyme ptyalin. Which nutrient does ptyalin break down?*

Figure 16–10 *Covering the tongue's surface are tiny projections that give it a velvety appearance (left). Located along the sides of these projections are the taste buds (right). The taste buds can detect four different kinds of tastes. What are they?*

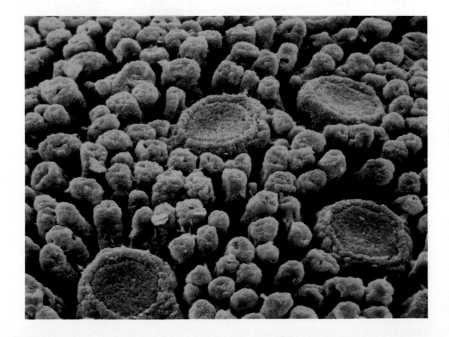

ACTIVITY

How Sweet It Is

1. Obtain two baby-food jars with lids. Label one jar A and the other B.

2. Fill each jar with equal amounts of water.

3. Place a whole sugar cube into jar A and a crushed sugar cube into jar B.

4. Place the lid on each jar and carefully shake each jar about five times.

5. Place the jars on a flat surface where they can remain undisturbed. Observe the rate of solution, or the time it takes for the sugar to dissolve completely, in each jar.

Which jar had the faster rate of solution? Can you think of any other factors that would affect the rate of solution? How would you test for these factors?

■ Relate the results of your investigation to the importance of mechanical digestion.

Figure 16–11 *Peristalsis is the waves of contractions that push food through parts of the digestive system. Use the diagram to identify the parts of the digestive system shown in the X-ray. Notice the vertebral column in the background.*

The Esophagus

After you swallow, smooth muscles force the food into a pipe-shaped tube called the **esophagus** (ih-SAHF-uh-guhs). The word esophagus comes from a Greek word meaning "to carry what is eaten." And that is exactly what this tube does as it transports food down to your **stomach.** The stomach is a J-shaped, muscular organ connected to the esophagus.

The esophagus, like most of your digestive organs, is lined with slippery mucus. This mucus helps food travel through your esophagus to your stomach, which takes about 12 seconds. As soon as food enters the esophagus, powerful waves of muscle contractions push the food downward. This wavelike motion is called **peristalsis** (per-uh-STAHL-sihs).

Digestion in the Stomach

As food enters the stomach, cells in the stomach release gastric juice. This gastric juice contains the enzyme **pepsin,** hydrochloric acid, and thick slippery

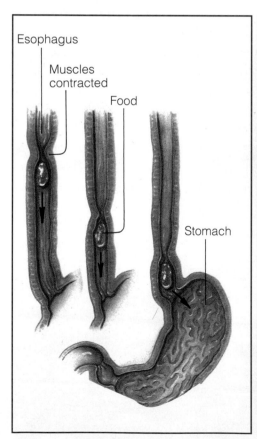

Esophagus

Muscles contracted

Food

Stomach

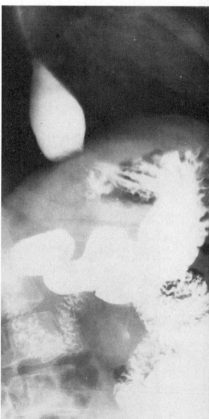

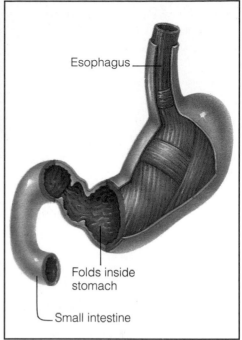

Esophagus

Folds inside
stomach

Small intestine

Figure 16–12 *The stomach wall consists of several layers of smooth muscles (left). When these muscles contract, food and gastric juice within the stomach are mixed together. Notice that the stomach's inner lining contains many folds (right). These folds will smooth out as the organ fills with food. What enzyme does gastric juice contain?*

mucus. The mucus coats and protects the stomach wall. Why do you think such protection is necessary?

With the help of the hydrochloric acid, pepsin breaks down some of the complex proteins in your food into simpler proteins. This is a form of chemical digestion. Food also undergoes a kind of mechanical digestion in the stomach. Muscle contractions mix the food with gastric juice as peristalsis pushes the food toward the stomach's exit.

Digestion in the Small Intestine

Food moving out of your stomach has changed quite a bit since it was first placed in your mouth. After a few hours, muscle contractions and enzymes in your stomach have changed your food into a soft, watery substance. Now it is ready to move slowly from your stomach into another organ of the digestive system—the **small intestine.** Although this organ is only 2.5 centimeters in diameter, it is over 6 meters long. As in the esophagus and the stomach, food moves through the small intestine by peristalsis.

Although some chemical and mechanical digestion has already taken place in the mouth and the

Simulating Peristalsis

1. Obtain a 40-cm piece of clear plastic tubing.

2. Hold the tubing vertically and insert a small bead into the top opening of the tubing. The bead should fit snugly into the tubing.

3. Pinch the tubing above the bead so that the bead is pushed down along the length of the tubing.

How does this action compare with peristalsis?

■ What action would you be simulating if you were to pinch the tubing below the small bead?

Figure 16–13 *According to this chart, which enzymes work on proteins? Which work on fats?*

SOME DIGESTIVE ENZYMES

Digestive Juice	Digestive Enzyme	Works on	Changes It to
Saliva	Ptyalin	Starch	Complex sugars
Gastric	Pepsin	Protein	Simpler proteins
Pancreatic	Amylase Trypsin Lipase	Starch Proteins Fats	Complex sugars Simpler proteins Fatty acids and glycerol
Intestinal	Lactase, maltase, sucrase Peptidase Lipase	Complex sugars Simpler proteins Fats	Simple sugars Amino acids Fatty acids and glycerol

Activity

DOING

Enzymes

Enzymes speed up the rate of certain body reactions that would otherwise occur very slowly. During these reactions, the enzymes are not used up or changed in any way. Using reference materials in the library, look up the meaning of "substrate" and the "lock-and key hypothesis." Using posterboard and colored construction paper, make a labeled diagram of this hypothesis. Present the diagram to the class.

What is the relationship between an enzyme and a substrate?

stomach, most digestion takes place in the small intestine. The cells that line the walls of the small intestine release intestinal juice containing enzymes.

Most chemical digestion that occurs in the small intestine takes place within 0.3 meter of the beginning of the small intestine. Here, intestinal juices help break down food arriving from the stomach. These juices do not work alone. They are helped by juices that are produced by two organs near the small intestine. These organs are the **liver** and the **pancreas** (PAN-kree-uhs). Because no food passes through the liver and the pancreas, they are considered to be digestive helpers.

The Liver

Located to the right of the stomach is the liver, the body's largest and heaviest internal organ. One of its many important functions is to aid digestion by producing a substance called bile. Once the liver produces bile, the bile moves into the **gallbladder.** The gallbladder is an organ that stores bile. As food moves into the small intestine from the stomach, the gallbladder releases bile through a duct, or tube, into the small intestine. Bile breaks up large fat molecules into smaller ones. Which type of digestion is this?

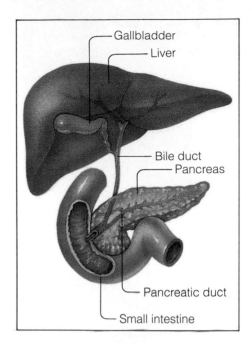

Figure 16–14 *The liver, pancreas, and gallbladder produce and store substances that are released into the small intestine to aid in the digestion of food.*

The Pancreas

The pancreas is a soft, triangular organ located between the stomach and the small intestine. The pancreas produces a substance called pancreatic juice, which is a mixture of several enzymes. These enzymes move into the small intestine at the same time bile does and help break down proteins, starches, and fats.

The pancreas also produces a substance called insulin, which is important in controlling the body's use of sugar. You will read more about the pancreas and insulin in Chapter 19.

16–2 Section Review

1. Describe the process of digestion.
2. Compare mechanical and chemical digestion.
3. What is peristalsis? Why is it important?
4. Where does most of the digestion of food take place?
5. Why are the liver and the pancreas called digestive helpers rather than digestive organs?

Connection—*You and Your World*
6. Why is it important to chew your food thoroughly before swallowing it?

16–3 Absorption of Food

Eventually most of the food in the small intestine is digested. Proteins are broken down into individual amino acids. Carbohydrates are broken down into simple sugar molecules. And fats are broken down into fatty acids and glycerol. However, before these nutrients can be used for energy, they must first pass into the blood through the small intestine walls.

Guide for Reading

Focus on this question as you read.

▶ *What is the process of absorption?*

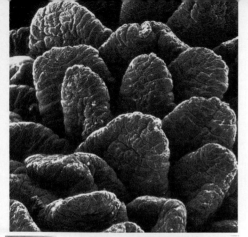

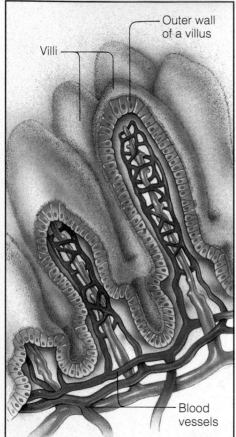

Absorption in the Small Intestine

The small intestine has an inner lining that looks something like wet velvet. This is because the inner walls of the small intestine are covered with millions of tiny fingerlike projections called **villi** (VIHL-igh; singular: villus, VIHL-uhs).

Digested food is absorbed through the villi of the small intestine into a network of blood vessels that carries the nutrients to all parts of the body. If there were no ridges and no villi on the wall of the small intestine, nutrients would move through it too quickly. Nutrients would pass out of the body before they could be absorbed. The ridges and villi increase the surface area of the small intestine. This increased surface allows the maximum amount of nutrients to be absorbed.

Although most of the material in the small intestine is digested, there are some substances in food that cannot be digested. Cellulose, a part of fruits and vegetables, is one such substance.

Absorption in the Large Intestine

After most of the nutrients have been absorbed, undigested food along with water, mucus, bile salts, and scraped-off intestinal cells make their way to the **large intestine.** During the time it takes for these remains to move through the large intestine, most of the water is absorbed. Also, helpful bacteria living in the large intestine feed on the leftovers and make certain vitamins, such as vitamin K and the B complexes, which are absorbed by the body.

The large intestine is shaped like a horseshoe that fits over the coils of the small intestine. It is about 6.5 centimeters in diameter but only 1.5 meters long. Why is it called the large intestine?

Materials that are not absorbed in the large intestine form a solid waste called feces (FEE-seez). At the end of the large intestine is a short tube called the rectum, which stores this waste. The rectum ends at

Villi —

Outer wall of a villus

Blood vessels

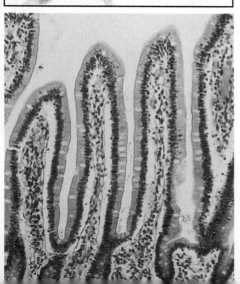

Figure 16–15 *Villi are tiny fingerlike projections that line the inside of the small intestine (top). The blood vessels that are contained inside each villus (center) are covered by a single layer of cells (bottom). What is the function of the villi?*

an opening called the anus, through which feces are eliminated from the body.

The appendix (uh-PEHN-diks) is a worm-shaped organ near the area where the small and large intestines meet. The appendix does nothing and leads nowhere. It sometimes becomes irritated, inflamed, or infected. An infection of the appendix is called appendicitis (uh-pehn-duh-SIGHT-ihs). If treated early, appendicitis usually is not dangerous.

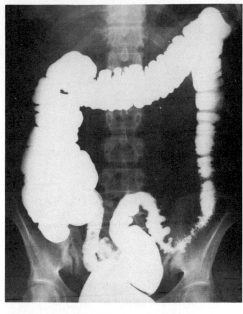

Figure 16–16 *The large intestine forms an upside-down horseshoe that fits over the small intestine.*

16–3 Section Review

1. Describe the process of absorption in the small intestine.
2. What is the function of the villi?
3. Describe the process of absorption in the large intestine.
4. What is the function of the rectum? The anus?

Critical Thinking—*Relating Facts*
5. Gallstones, which are crystals of minerals and salts that form in bile, sometimes block the entrance to the small intestine. What effect would this blockage have on the digestion of food?

16–4 Maintaining Good Health

You already know that by eating a balanced diet you supply your body with the materials it needs for growth, repair, and energy. **By controlling your weight and getting the proper amount of exercise, you can also keep your body healthy and running smoothly for many years.**

Exercise

Activities such as swimming, jogging, bicycling, hiking, calisthenics, or even walking briskly are good ways to exercise. Regular exercise helps to strengthen the heart. Exercise also gives you firmer muscles, better posture, greater strength, more endurance, and an improved sense of balance.

Guide for Reading

Focus on this question as you read.

▶ *What are two important factors in maintaining good health?*

ACTIVITY READING

An Eating Disorder

To gain a better understanding about the eating disorder known as anorexia nervosa, read Steven Levenkron's book *The Best Little Girl in the World.*

Figure 16-17 *In order to maintain good health, most people—including older people—need moderate exercise.*

Weight Control

When the energy in the food you eat exceeds the work your body does, your body stores the excess energy in the form of fat. In order to get rid of this stored fat, you must use up more energy than is provided in the foods you eat. Then your body will break down the fat to release needed energy.

When a person is overweight, all of the organs of the body, including the heart, must work harder. Some people who are overweight may choose to go on a "diet." It is important that the diet chosen is a balanced one containing the proper amounts of nutrients needed by the body. Before starting any weight loss plan, a person should see a doctor. The doctor will give a complete checkup and discuss a sensible diet. Once a person loses the excess weight, he or she can maintain a steady weight by taking in only as many Calories in food as are used up.

16-4 Section Review

1. Explain how exercise and weight control contribute to good health.
2. List four activities that are good forms of exercise.
3. What must be included in any balanced diet?
4. How can you maintain a steady weight?

Connection—*You and Your World*
5. Imagine that you have put on a little weight. Design a balanced diet that will help you lose it.

CONNECTIONS

What's Cooking?

Recall the last time you cooked an egg or boiled some water. Did you use a gas stove or an electric stove? Or did you use a microwave oven? Whichever appliance you used, they had one thing in common: They are all sources of heat. Heat, which is a form of energy, cannot be seen. However, you can see the work that heat does by observing what happens to food when you cook it. In a way, cooking can be defined as the transfer of heat from its source to food. The various cooking methods, such as boiling, frying, and baking, bring about their effects by using different materials—water, oil, air—and different methods of *heat transfer.*

Heat is transferred by three methods: conduction, convection, and radiation. In conduction, heat is transferred through a material without carrying any of the material with it. For example, heat from a gas or an electric burner passes through a pan to the food inside it. In convection, heat is transferred as a liquid or a gas moves from a warm area to a cooler one. In a pan of cold water that has been placed on a hot burner, for example, the water nearer the burner will heat up and move to the top. This will cause the cooler water nearer the top of the pan to

sink. This process will continue until all the water reaches the same temperature.

Unlike the processes of conduction and convection, the process of radiation can occur through a vacuum. In radiation, waves of energy are used to heat materials. This energy is absorbed by the particles in the material, causing them to vibrate. In microwave ovens, for example, the microwaves produced by powerful electromagnetic (electric and magnetic) fields cause the water in food to vibrate. This action releases heat into the food. Because all of the energy is absorbed by the food and not wasted on heating the surrounding air or the oven itself, microwave cooking is quicker and more economical than other types of cooking methods.

Laboratory Investigation

Measuring Calories Used

Problem
How many Calories do you use in 24 hours?

Materials *(per student)*

pencil and paper	scale

Procedure

1. Look over the chart of Calorie rates. It shows how various activities are related to the rates at which you burn Calories. The Calorie rate shown for each activity is actually the number of Calories used per hour for each kilogram of your body mass.

2. Using a scale, note your weight in pounds. Convert your weight into kilograms (2.2 lb = 1 kg). Record this number.

3. Classify all your activities for a given 24-hour period. Record the kind of activity, the Calorie rate, and the number of hours you were involved in that activity.

4. For each of your activities, multiply your weight by the Calorie rate shown in the chart. Then multiply the resulting number by the number of hours or fractions of hours you were involved in that activity. The result is the number of Calories you burned during that period of time. For example, if your weight is 50 kilograms and you exercised strenuously, perhaps by running, for half an hour, the Calories you burned during that activity would be equal to 50 x 10.5 X 0.5 = 262.5 Calories.

5. Add together all the Calories you burned in the entire 24-hour period.

Observations
How many Calories did you use in the 24-hour period?

Analysis and Conclusions

1. Explain why the values for the Calorie rates of various activities are approximate rather than exact.

2. What factors could affect the number of Calories a person used during exercise?

3. Why do young people need to consume more Calories than adults?

4. **On Your Own** Determine the number of Calories you use in a week. In a month.

Activity	Average Calorie Rate
Sleeping	1.1
Awake but at rest (sitting, reading, or eating)	1.5
Very slight exercise (bathing, dressing)	3.1
Slight exercise (walking quickly)	4.4
Strenuous exercise (dancing)	7.5
Very strenuous exercise (running, swimming rapidly)	10.5

Average Caloric Needs Chart		
	Age	Calories
Males	9–12 12–15	2400 3000
Females	9–12 12–15	2200 2500

Study Guide

Summarizing Key Concepts

16–1 The Importance of Food

▲ Nutrients provide the body with raw materials for repair, energy, and building new products. The six categories of nutrients are proteins, carbohydrates, fats and oils, vitamins, minerals, and water.

16–2 Digestion of Food

▲ Digestion is the process of breaking down food into simpler substances.

▲ In the mouth, the salivary glands release saliva, which contains ptyalin. Ptyalin breaks down starches into simple sugars.

▲ The changing of foods into simple substances by enzymes is called chemical digestion.

▲ Mechanical digestion occurs when food is broken down by the chewing of the teeth and the churning movements of the digestive tract.

▲ As food enters the esophagus a wavelike motion called peristalsis pushes the food downward toward the stomach.

▲ Gastric juice contains the enzyme pepsin, which breaks down proteins into amino acids.

▲ After leaving the stomach, food enters the small intestine, where intestinal juice is released, and digests proteins, starches, and fats.

▲ Bile produced by the liver and stored in the gallbladder is carried to the small intestine. There bile aids in the digestion of fats.

▲ Pancreatic juice produced by the pancreas travels to the small intestine and digests proteins, starches, and fats.

16–3 Absorption of Food

▲ Nutrients are absorbed into the bloodstream through villi in the small intestine.

▲ The large intestine absorbs water, as well as forming and absorbing some vitamins that are made by helpful bacteria.

▲ Undigested food substances, or feces, are eliminated out of the body through the anus.

16–4 Maintaining Good Health

▲ By controlling your weight and exercising regularly, you can help keep your body healthy.

Reviewing Key Terms

Define each term in a complete sentence.

16–1 The Importance of Food
nutrient
protein
amino acid
carbohydrate
Calorie
fat
oil
vitamin
mineral

16–2 Digestion of Food
ptyalin
enzyme
chemical digestion
mechanical digestion
esophagus
stomach
peristalsis
pepsin
small intestine
liver
pancreas
gallbladder

16–3 Absorption of Food
villus
large intestine

Chapter Review

Content Review

Multiple Choice

Choose the letter of the answer that best completes each statement.

1. The nutrients that are used to build and repair body parts are
   a. proteins.
   b. minerals.
   c. carbohydrates.
   d. vitamins.

2. Which is not found in the mouth?
   a. pepsin
   b. saliva
   c. ptyalin
   d. taste buds

3. The tube that connects the mouth and the stomach is the
   a. small intestine.
   b. pancreas.
   c. esophagus.
   d. epiglottis.

4. Gastric juice contains the enzyme
   a. bile.
   b. pepsin.
   c. ptyalin.
   d. mucus.

5. The digestion of proteins begins in the
   a. mouth.
   b. liver.
   c. small intestine.
   d. stomach.

6. In the digestive system, proteins are broken down into
   a. fatty acids.
   b. glycerol.
   c. simple sugars.
   d. amino acids.

7. The liver produces
   a. pepsin.
   b. bile.
   c. hydrochloric acid.
   d. ptyalin.

8. The fingerlike structures that form the inner lining of the small intestine are called
   a. cilia.
   b. villi.
   c. enzymes.
   d. nutrients.

9. Water is absorbed in the
   a. small intestine.
   b. pancreas.
   c. large intestine.
   d. liver.

10. Regular exercise helps a person have
    a. good posture.
    b. firm muscles.
    c. a stronger heart.
    d. all of these.

True or False

If the statement is true, write "true." If it is false, change the underlined word or words to make the statement true.

1. The nutrients that supply the greatest amount of energy are the <u>fats</u>.
2. A chemical that breaks down food into simple substances is called an <u>enzyme</u>.
3. Starches and sugars are examples of <u>proteins</u>.
4. Vitamin K is an example of a <u>water-soluble</u> vitamin.
5. <u>Pepsin</u> is the enzyme in saliva.
6. Undigested food substances are stored in the <u>epiglottis</u>.
7. The enzyme pepsin digests <u>proteins</u>.
8. The small, finger-shaped organ located where the small intestine and large intestine meet is the <u>appendix</u>.

Concept Mapping

Complete the following concept map for Section 16–1. Then construct a concept map for the entire chapter.

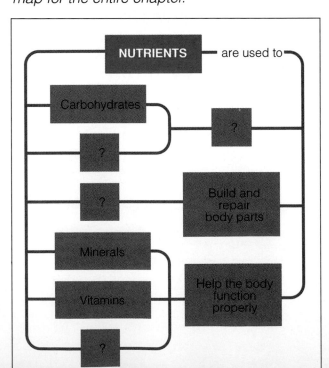

434

Concept Mastery

Discuss each of the following in a brief paragraph.

1. If you were to eat a slice of bread (starch) with butter (fat) and drink a glass of milk (protein), what would happen to each of these foods during digestion?
2. Food does not really enter your body until it is absorbed into the blood. Explain why. *Hint:* Think of the digestive system as a tube passing through your body.
3. Appendicitis is usually treated by removing the appendix. Explain why this treatment does not interfere with the functioning of a person's digestive system.
4. Describe the structure of villi and their role in absorption.
5. Describe the location and function of the epiglottis.
6. Where does mechanical digestion occur? Chemical digestion?
7. Compare absorption in the small intestine with absorption in the large intestine.
8. Why can talking with food in your mouth be a dangerous thing to do?
9. Explain why vomiting can be considered reverse peristalsis.

Critical Thinking and Problem Solving

Use the skills you have developed in this chapter to answer each of the following.

1. **Making inferences** Suppose your doctor prescribed an antibiotic that killed all the bacteria in your body. What effect would this have on your digestive system?
2. **Making comparisons** Compare the human digestive system to an "assembly line in reverse."
3. **Making diagrams** Draw a diagram of the human digestive system and label all the organs. Use a red pencil to color the organs through which food passes. Use a blue pencil to color the organs through which food does not pass.
4. **Applying concepts** Fad diets have become popular in the United States. Some of these diets involve eating only a limited variety of food. Explain why some fad diets may be an unhealthy way to lose weight.
5. **Making comparisons** Compare the process of digestion to the process of absorption.
6. **Relating concepts** Following surgery, most patients are fed a glucose, or simple sugar, solution intravenously. Intravenously means into a vein. Why do you think this is done?
7. **Sequencing events** Trace the path of a piece of hamburger on a bun through the digestive system. Name each digestive organ and describe what happens in each organ.
8. **Using the writing process** Carbohydrate loading is a technique used by athletes to help them reach their peak of efficiency. To find out the benefits and potential problems of this practice, prepare a list of questions that you might ask a doctor and a coach during an interview on this subject.

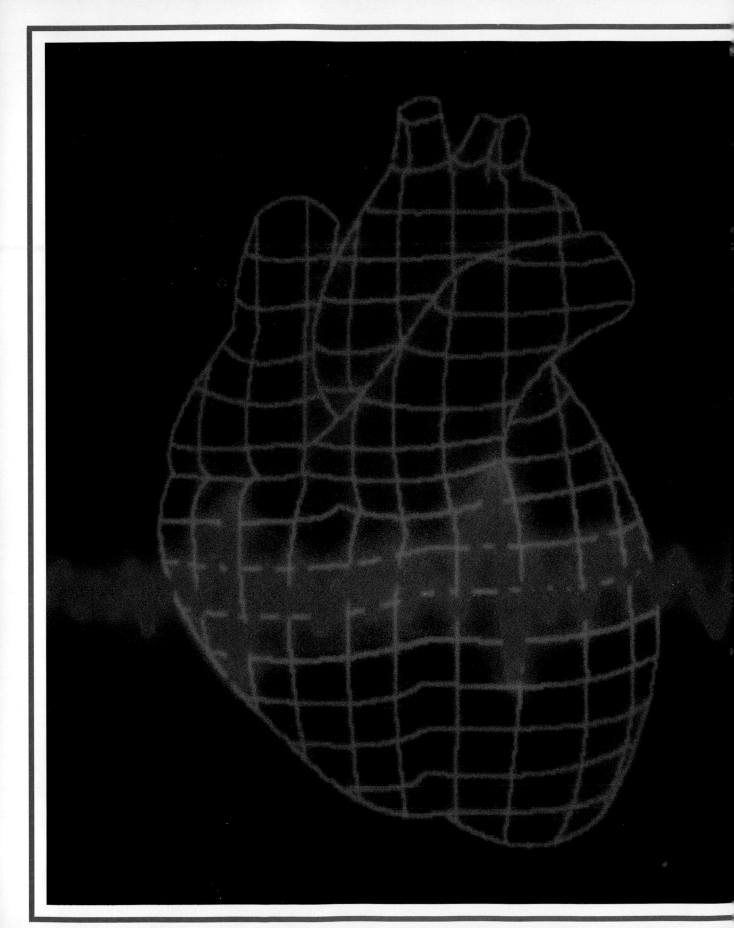

Circulatory System

17

At 6:24 AM, the first call of the day came in. A 73-year-old man who lived 120 kilometers away was having severe chest pains. "Strap yourself in, we're taking off!" shouted the pilot to the chief flight nurse over the roar of the helicopter. The chief flight nurse is one of several highly trained members of Survival Flight, a special medical unit that comes to the aid of people who are having heart attacks.

By 8:12 AM, the nurse had given the patient an injection of a drug that dissolves blockages in the blood vessels near the heart. Such blockages can prevent the heart from receiving an adequate supply of blood. By 8:23 AM, the Survival Flight team was loading the patient onto the helicopter and preparing to rush him to a hospital.

The Survival Flight team's helicopter is equipped with a stretcher, medical instruments, and medicine. But the team's greatest strength is the knowledge possessed by its members. They all know how the heart works and what to do when something goes wrong. By reading the pages that follow, you too will discover some of this special knowledge.

Journal *Activity*

You and Your World In your journal, list all the activities that you do that affect your circulatory system. Then on a new page in your journal, make two columns with the headings Helpful and Harmful. Place the activities from your list in the appropriate column.

◀ *Superimposed on this computer graphic of the heart is a part of an electrocardiogram, or record of the electrical activities of the heart.*

17–1 The Body's Transportation System

The main task of the circulatory system in all organisms is transportation. **The circulatory system delivers food and oxygen to body cells and carries carbon dioxide and other waste products away from body cells.** The power behind this system is the heart. It pumps blood through a network of blood vessels. This network is so large that if it could ever be unraveled, it would wrap around the Earth more than twice!

One of the most important jobs of the circulatory system is delivering oxygen to the cells. As you know, oxygen combines with food inside your body cells to produce usable energy. Without energy, body cells would soon die. The cells that use the most oxygen—and the first to die without oxygen—are brain cells.

When cells combine oxygen and food to produce energy, they also produce a waste product called

Figure 17–1 *The disk-shaped red objects in this photograph are red blood cells. Notice how densely packed the red blood cells are as they squeeze through the tiniest of blood vessels—the capillaries.*

carbon dioxide. Removing carbon dioxide is another important job of the circulatory system.

Still another job of the circulatory system is to transport food to all body cells. At the same time, wastes produced by the cells are carried away by the blood. If the blood did not remove such wastes, the body would poison itself with its own waste products!

Sometimes the body comes under attack from microscopic organisms such as bacteria and viruses. At these times, another transporting function of the circulatory system comes into play—body defense. The blood rushes disease-fighting cells and chemicals to the area under attack.

The circulatory system transports other chemicals as well. These chemicals carry messages sent from one part of the body to another. For example, a chemical messenger from the pancreas is carried by the blood to the liver. Its message is "Too much sugar in the blood. Remove some of the sugar and store it."

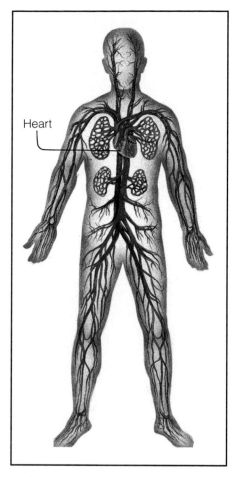

Figure 17–2 *The function of the circulatory system is to deliver food and oxygen to body cells and carry carbon dioxide and other waste products away from body cells. What organ pumps blood throughout the body?*

17–1 Section Review

1. What are the functions of the circulatory system?
2. Why is it important that wastes produced by the cells are carried away by the blood?

Critical Thinking—*Making Calculations*

3. The heart of an average person pumps about 5 liters of blood per minute. How much blood is pumped out of the heart per hour? Per day? Per week?

17–2 Circulation in the Body

In a way, the entire circulatory system is like a vast maze that starts at the heart. Unlike most mazes, however, this one always leads back to the place it began. **In the circulatory system, blood moves from the heart to the lungs and back to the heart. Blood then travels to all the cells of the body and returns again to the heart.** In the next few pages, you will follow the blood

Guide for Reading

Focus on this question as you read.

▶ *What path does blood take through the circulatory system?*

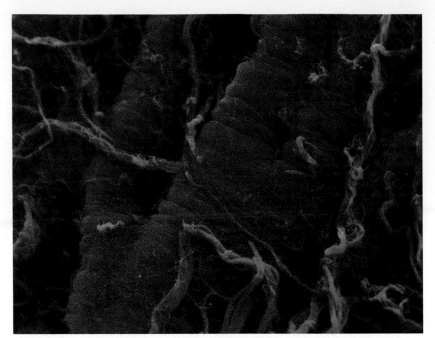

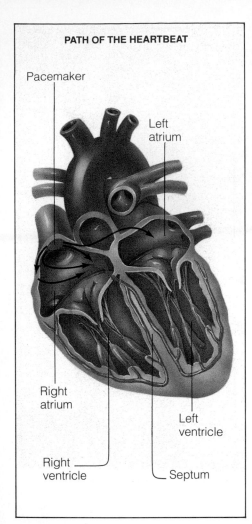

PATH OF THE HEARTBEAT

Pacemaker

Left atrium

Right atrium

Left ventricle

Right ventricle

Septum

Figure 17–3 *The heartbeat is controlled by an area of nerve tissue within the heart called the pacemaker. In the illustration, you can see the path a message from the pacemaker takes as it spreads through the heart. The photograph shows a network of nerves lining a section of a ventricle.*

Activity Bank

You've Got to Have Heart, p. 820

on its journey through the circulatory maze. You will begin, of course, at the heart.

The heart is a muscle that rests only between beats. Even when you are asleep, about 5 liters of blood are pumped through your body every minute. Not much larger than a fist, the heart is located slightly to the left of the center of your chest.

Heartbeat, or the heart's rhythm, is controlled by an area of special tissue in the heart known as the **pacemaker.** Located in the upper right side of the heart, the pacemaker sends out signals to heart muscle that control its contractions. If the body's original pacemaker becomes damaged, it can often be replaced by an artificial pacemaker.

The Right Side of the Heart

The human heart is made up of four hollow chambers. A thick wall of tissue called the **septum** separates the heart into right and left sides, with two chambers on each side. Your journey through the circulatory maze will begin in the right upper chamber, called the right **atrium** (AY-tree-uhm; plural: atria).

Inside the atrium, you find yourself swirling in a dark sea of blood. A great many red blood cells surround you. Red blood cells carry oxygen throughout

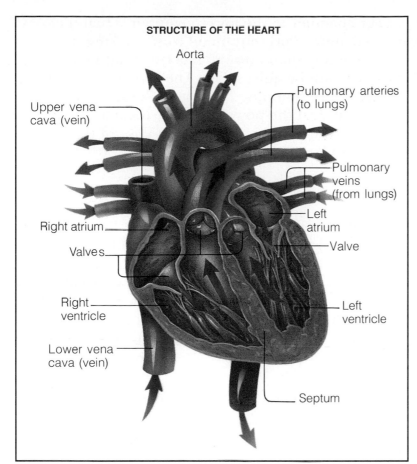

STRUCTURE OF THE HEART

Aorta

Upper vena cava (vein)

Pulmonary arteries (to lungs)

Pulmonary veins (from lungs)

Left atrium

Right atrium

Valve

Valves

Right ventricle

Left ventricle

Lower vena cava (vein)

Septum

Figure 17–4 *The heart is divided into a right side and a left side by a septum, or wall. Each side of the septum contains two chambers: an upper chamber and a lower chamber. The upper chambers are called atria, and the lower chambers are called ventricles. What is the function of the atria?*

the body. When the hemoglobin in a red blood cell hooks up to an oxygen molecule, the blood turns bright red. Such blood is said to be oxygen-rich. However, the blood in which you are swimming in the right atrium is dark red, not bright at all. This can only mean that these red blood cells are not carrying much oxygen. Rather, they are carrying mostly the waste carbon dioxide. This blood, then, is oxygen-poor. And that makes sense. For the right atrium is a collecting chamber for blood returning from its trip through the body. Along the way, the red blood cells have dropped off their oxygen and picked up carbon dioxide.

Suddenly the blood begins to churn, and you feel yourself falling downward. You are about to enter the heart's right lower chamber, called the right **ventricle.** Before you do, you must pass through a small flap of tissue called a heart **valve.** The valve opens to allow blood to go from the

ACTIVITY

DISCOVERING

Catch the Beat

How does temperature affect heartbeat rate? Design an experiment to find the answer to this question by using the following materials:

Daphnia culture
2 glass depression slides
coverslip
microscope
stopwatch
ice cube

As you plan your experiment, keep in mind that it must contain only one variable. Remember to include a control.

■ What effect would warm (not hot) water have on the *Daphnia's* heartbeat rate?

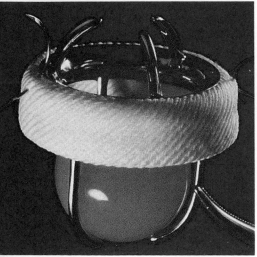

Figure 17–5 *Heart valves control the flow of blood through the heart. A heart valve called the bicuspid valve (top) is found between the left atrium and the left ventricle. Sometimes when a natural heart valve does not work properly, it must be replaced by an artificial heart valve (bottom).*

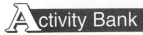

The Squeeze Is On, p. 821

upper chamber to the lower chamber. Then it closes immediately to prevent blood from backing up.

You have fallen into the muscular right ventricle. Your stay will be quite short. The ventricles, unlike the atria, are pumping chambers. Before you know it, you will feel the power of a heartbeat as the ventricle contracts and blood is forced out of the heart through a large blood vessel.

To the Lungs and Back Again

Now your journey has really begun. Since you are surrounded by dark, oxygen-poor blood, your first stop should be obvious. The right ventricle has pumped you toward the lungs. It is a short trip. Soon red blood cells are dropping off the waste carbon dioxide. The carbon dioxide enters the lungs and is immediately exhaled. At the same time, the red blood cells are busy picking up oxygen. What color is the blood at this point?

From the lungs, you might expect the oxygen-rich blood to travel all over the body. But the first stop for the blood after leaving the lungs is the heart. This time you enter the left atrium.

The Left Side of the Heart

The left atrium, like the right atrium, is a collecting chamber for blood returning to the heart. However, the left chamber collects oxygen-rich blood as it returns from the lungs. Once again, the blood quickly flows downward through a valve and enters the left ventricle. The left ventricle has a lot more work to do than the right ventricle. The right ventricle only pumps blood a short distance to the lungs. The left ventricle has to pump blood to every part of the body. In fact, the left side works about six times harder than the right side. That is why you feel your heartbeat on the left side of your chest. And it is also why most heart attacks occur in the left side of the heart.

Arteries: Pipelines From the Heart

As the left ventricle pumps you and the blood you are floating in out of the heart, the blood passes through the largest blood vessel in the body, the

442

aorta (ay-OR-tuh). The aorta is an **artery,** or a pipeline that carries blood away from the heart.

Like all arteries, the aorta is a thick-walled but flexible tube. Much of its flexibility comes from an elastic outer layer. The aorta soon branches into other, smaller arteries. Some return immediately to the heart, feeding heart muscle with food and oxygen. Other arteries branch and branch again, much like the branches of a tree. These branching arteries form a network that connects all parts of the body.

As you pass through the aorta and enter a smaller artery, you notice that the inner wall of the artery is quite smooth. The smooth inner wall allows blood to flow freely.

Outside the smooth layer in the artery is a middle layer that is made up mainly of smooth muscle tissue. When the muscle in the artery expands and contracts, it helps control the flow of blood. In this way, some arteries can expand to send large amounts of blood to one area, while other arteries can contract to lessen the amount of blood flowing somewhere else. Naturally, some blood must go to every part of the body—from the head to the toes.

From the aorta, your path leads you down one of the many branching arteries. Where you go from here depends on many factors. If food has been eaten recently, for example, much of the blood will be directed toward the intestines to pick up food. If the body is exercising, the blood supply to the muscles will probably be increased. If there are a great many wastes in the blood, you may be sent to the liver, where some wastes are changed into substances that are not poisonous to the body. Or you may travel to one of the kidneys, where other wastes are removed from the blood. However, whether it is thinking very hard or not, the brain always gets top priority over any other part of the body.

Capillaries: The Unseen Pipelines

The artery network carries blood all over the body. But arteries cannot drop off or pick up any materials from body cells. Their walls are too thick. Oxygen and food, for example, cannot pass through the artery walls. In order to do its main job—transporting materials—the blood must pass from

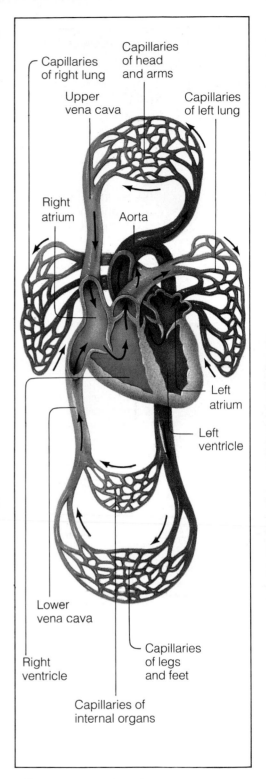

Figure 17–6 *Blood travels through the body in a continuous path. The path of oxygen-rich blood is shown in red, and the path of oxygen-poor blood is shown in blue.*

443

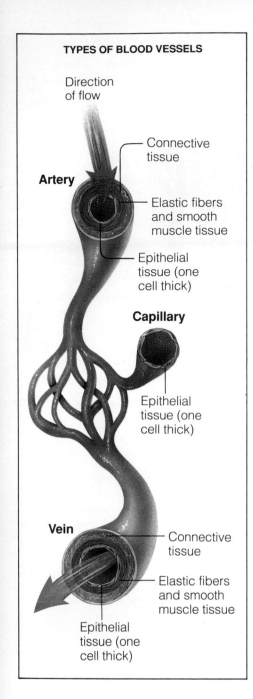

TYPES OF BLOOD VESSELS

Direction of flow

Artery

Connective tissue

Elastic fibers and smooth muscle tissue

Epithelial tissue (one cell thick)

Capillary

Epithelial tissue (one cell thick)

Vein

Connective tissue

Elastic fibers and smooth muscle tissue

Epithelial tissue (one cell thick)

Figure 17–7 *The three types of blood vessels that make up the circulatory system are the arteries, capillaries, and veins. What is the function of each type of blood vessel?*

the thick arteries into very thin-walled blood vessels called **capillaries.**

You will probably have a hard time squeezing through the capillary in which you now find yourself. Don't feel bad. In most capillaries, there is only enough room for red blood cells to pass through in single file. It is here in the capillaries that the basic work of the blood is carried out. Food and oxygen pass through the thin walls and enter the cells. Wastes pass out of the cells and enter the blood. Other materials transported by the blood can leave and enter body cells at this time. What other materials are transported by the blood?

Veins: Pipelines to the Heart

Once the work of giving up oxygen and taking on wastes is completed in the capillaries, your trip through the circulatory maze is just about over. Because the blood has given up its oxygen, it is dark red again. So the blood leaves the capillaries and enters blood vessels called **veins.** Veins carry blood from the body back to the heart.

Figure 17–8 *Capillaries are so tiny that they permit only one red blood cell to squeeze through at a time. What is the function of a red blood cell?*

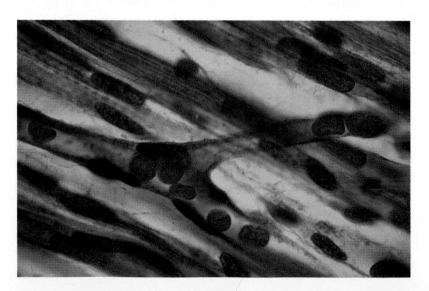

Figure 17-9 *Valves in the walls of veins prevent the backflow of blood and keep it moving in one direction—back to the heart. The contraction of nearby skeletal muscles such as those in the leg help the valves in performing this function.*

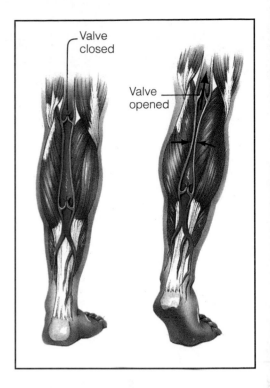

Valve closed

Valve opened

Although veins are much larger than capillaries, their walls are thinner than those of arteries. Unlike arteries, veins have tiny one-way valves. These valves help keep the blood from flowing backward. So blood always flows back to the heart.

17-2 Section Review

1. Trace the path of blood through the circulatory system.
2. List the four chambers of the heart.
3. Describe the three types of blood vessels.
4. Explain why the walls of the ventricles are much thicker than the walls of the atria.

Critical Thinking—*Relating Facts*

5. Why is it important that veins contain valves?

17-3 Blood—The River of Life

In Chapter 15, you learned that blood is a type of connective tissue. That may have been a difficult concept to understand at the time. But now you can see how a fluid tissue—a tissue that does not stay in one place—can connect different parts of the body. Through the blood, the circulatory system transports many different substances. In this sense, blood "connects" all of the body systems.

The liquid portion of the blood is called **plasma.** And the tiny particles floating in the plasma are different types of blood cells and cell fragments—three different types to be exact. **The three different types of floating particles—red blood cells, white blood cells, and platelets—and the plasma in which they float, are the four main components of blood.**

Guide for Reading

Focus on this question as you read.

▶ *What are the four main components of blood?*

ACTIVITY

CALCULATING

Pumping Power

If the heart of an average person pumps about 9000 liters of blood daily, how much blood will be pumped in an hour? In a year?

445

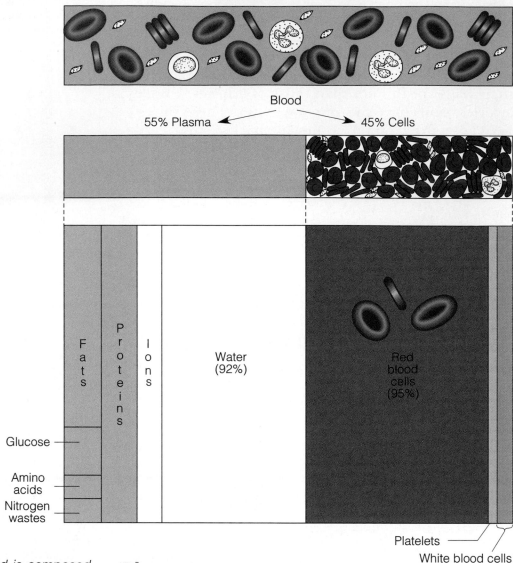

COMPONENTS OF BLOOD

Blood

55% Plasma ← → 45% Cells

Fats

Proteins

Ions

Water (92%)

Red blood cells (95%)

Glucose

Amino acids

Nitrogen wastes

Platelets

White blood cells

Figure 17–10 *Blood is composed of a fluid portion called plasma and three different types of blood particles. Of what substance is plasma mainly composed?*

Plasma

Most people have between 4 and 6 liters of blood. About 55 percent of the blood is a yellowish liquid called plasma. Plasma is 92 percent water and so is easily and quickly replaced by the body. In the plasma, dissolved nutrients, enzymes, wastes, and other materials are transported through the body.

Red Blood Cells

The most numerous of the cells in whole blood are **red blood cells.** Under a microscope, they look like flattened hats with thickened brims and flat centers—almost like tiny berets. The centers of these

Figure 17–11 *These beret-shaped objects are red blood cells as seen through a scanning electron microscope. What is the function of red blood cells?*

Figure 17–12 *White blood cells are larger than red blood cells (top). The main function of white blood cells is to protect the body against attack by invaders such as bacteria, which are the two small rod-shaped structures in this photograph (bottom).*

flexible red disks are so thin that they seem clear. Red blood cells can bend almost in two, a useful trick when trying to squeeze through a narrow capillary.

Have you ever heard people complain they have "iron-poor" blood? That phrase refers to a shortage of an iron-containing protein called **hemoglobin** (hee-muh-GLOH-bihn) that is found in red blood cells. Hemoglobin binds to oxygen in the lungs and carries the oxygen to body cells. Hemoglobin also helps carry carbon dioxide wastes back to the lungs.

Red blood cells are produced in bone marrow. An immature red blood cell, like all living body cells, contains a nucleus. However, as the cell matures, its nucleus grows smaller and smaller until it vanishes. Red blood cells pay a price for life without a nucleus. They are very delicate and have a life span of only 120 days. When a red blood cell becomes old or damaged, it is broken down in the liver and the spleen, an organ just to the left of the stomach. In fact, so many red blood cells are destroyed in the spleen each day that it has been called the "cemetery" of red blood cells.

White Blood Cells

The second kind of cell in whole blood is the **white blood cell.** White blood cells are outnumbered by red blood cells 700 to 1. But what they lack in number they make up for in size and life span. Some white blood cells are twice the size of

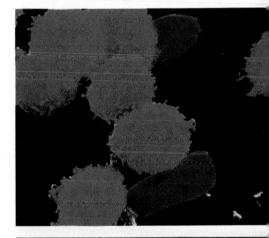

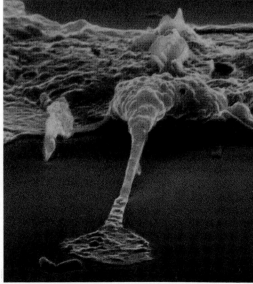

red blood cells. And although certain kinds of white blood cells stay in the circulation for only a few hours, others can last for months or even years!

Like red blood cells, most white blood cells develop in bone marrow. However, white blood cells do not lose their nuclei when they mature. White blood cells are among the most important defense systems of the body. Carried by blood to areas under attack by tiny invaders such as bacteria, some white blood cells surround and digest the invaders. Other kinds of white blood cells produce special chemicals to attack viruses and various other microscopic invaders. You will learn more about white blood cells and body defense in Chapter 21.

Platelets

The third kind of particle in blood is the **platelet** (PLAYT-liht). Actually, platelets are really only bits of cells. They have no nucleus or color. These tiny cell fragments break away from bone marrow and enter the bloodstream. There they last no more than ten days. But in that short time they may save a life!

Have you ever wondered what happens inside a blood vessel when you cut yourself? Why does all your blood not ooze out of your body? As soon as a blood vessel has been cut, platelets begin to collect around the cut. They then release an enzyme that acts on other substances in the blood to create **fibrin** (FIGH-bruhn). Fibrin gets its name from the tiny fibers it weaves across the cut in the blood vessel wall. Blood cells and plasma are trapped by fibrin. See Figure 17–13. The plasma will set and harden and form a

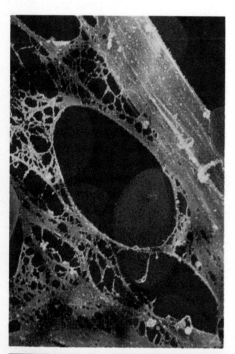

Figure 17–13 *When a blood vessel is punctured (bottom right), blood particles called platelets (bottom left) release chemicals that set off a series of reactions to help stop the flow of blood from the body. One of these reactions produces a threadlike chemical called fibrin that forms a net over the cut to trap blood particles and plasma (top).*

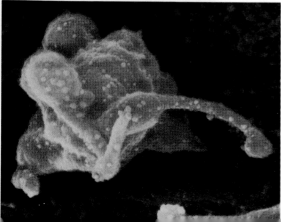

clot. You have probably seen this process of clotting on the surface of your skin when a scab formed over a cut. A scab is a surface blood clot.

The Lymphatic System

As blood moves through the capillaries, some of the plasma leaks out of the blood and through the capillary walls. This fluid, called **lymph** (LIHMF), surrounds and bathes body cells. Eventually the lymph collects in a system of tiny vessels. These vessels make up the lymphatic system.

From the lymph vessels, lymph flows into two veins in the neck. In this way, the lymphatic system transports fluid lost from the blood back into the bloodstream.

On its way through the lymphatic system, lymph passes through masses of tissues called lymph nodes. Special cells in these nodes remove harmful materials, such as bacteria, from the lymph.

Blood Groups

In 1900, Karl Landsteiner, an American scientist, was able to classify human blood into four basic groups, or types: A, B, AB, and O. Everyone is born with a certain type of blood, which stays the same for a lifetime. People with group A blood have an A protein attached to the outer coat of every red blood cell. People with group B blood have a B protein. Group O people have neither protein. What proteins do you think group AB people have?

The process of transferring blood from one body to another is called a transfusion. But there is one problem with transfusions. The problem is that people with group A blood also produce a chemical called anti B. Anti B causes red blood cells with group B protein to clump together. Such a clump in the bloodstream can cause death. In much the same way, people with group B blood produce anti A. Anti A causes red blood cells with group A protein to clump together. Because of the clumping chemicals, blood groups must be carefully matched before a transfusion. In Figure 17–15 on page 450, you can see the four groups of blood and the chemicals that they contain on the red blood cells and in the plasma.

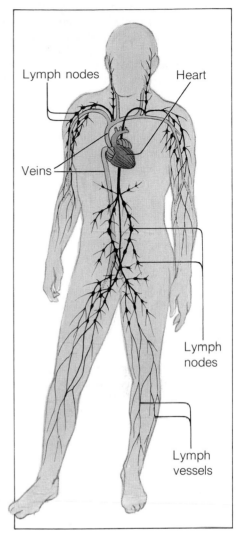

Figure 17–14 *This diagram illustrates the path lymph travels on its way through the lymphatic system. What is lymph?*

Figure 17–15 *Each blood group is characterized by the protein on the red blood cells and the clumping chemical in the plasma. What protein does group AB blood have?*

ABO BLOOD SYSTEM

Blood Group	Proteins on Red Blood Cells	Clumping Chemicals in Plasma	Can Accept Transfusions from Group(s)
A		Anti B	A, O
B		Anti A	B, O
AB		None	A, B, AB, O
O		Anti A Anti B	O

Figure 17–16 *When a person with group B blood receives a transfusion of, for example, group A blood, anti-A chemicals in the group B plasma recognize the group A red cells as foreign. As a result, the red blood cells from the group A blood will clump, or stick together, and possibly clog some of the body's important blood vessels.*

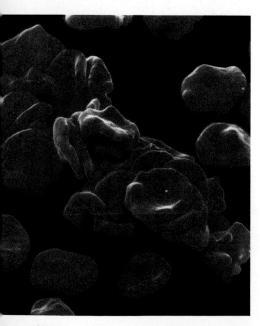

Rh Factor

Several years after the discovery of the ABO blood groupings, Landsteiner and another American scientist, Alexander S. Weiner, discovered another group of about 18 proteins on the surface of human red blood cells. Because Landsteiner and Weiner first found this group of proteins in the rhesus monkey, they named the proteins the Rh blood group. If a person has any one of the 18 proteins, they are said to be Rh positive, or Rh$^+$. Those who do not have any Rh proteins in their blood are Rh negative, or Rh$^-$.

17–3 Section Review

1. List the four main components of whole blood.
2. What is hemoglobin? What is its function?
3. Name, describe, and give the function of each of the three types of blood particles.

Critical Thinking—*Relating Facts*

4. Why do you think group O blood was once called the universal donor?

17–4 Cardiovascular Diseases

People are living longer now than they ever have. And, as people's life expectancy has increased, so has the number of people who suffer from chronic disorders. Usually developing over a long time, chronic disorders also last a long time. Today, cardiovascular (kahr-dee-oh-VAS-kyoo-ler) diseases are the most serious of all chronic disorders, in terms of numbers of people affected. **Cardiovascular diseases, such as atherosclerosis** (ath-er-oh-skluh-ROH-sihs) **and hypertension, affect the heart and blood vessels.**

Atherosclerosis

The most common cause of heart attacks in the United States today is **atherosclerosis.** Atherosclerosis is the thickening of the inner lining of the arteries. This thickening begins when certain fatlike substances in the blood, such as cholesterol, slowly collect on the inner lining of the arteries. Gradually, the inside of the artery becomes narrower and narrower. As a result, the normal circulation of the blood through the arteries is lessened or even blocked. When blood flow is reduced, the cells served by the blood may die. If this occurs in the arteries and the cells of the heart, heart cells begin to die. A heart attack may then occur. A similar blockage can happen

Guide for Reading

Focus on this question as you read.

▶ *What are the effects of atherosclerosis and high blood pressure on the circulatory system?*

ACTIVITY DOING

Simulating a Blood Clot

1. Use a rubber band to hold a 20-cm square of cheesecloth in place over a small beaker.

2. Place some coins and paper clips in another beaker containing water.

3. Carefully pour the contents of the beaker into the middle of the cheesecloth.

What is the relationship between fibrin and the cheesecloth used in this activity? What do the coins and paper clips represent? The water?

Figure 17–17 *A high-fat diet has caused fat droplets, which are the large yellow objects in this photograph, to become deposited on the inside wall of an artery. As more of these fat droplets accumulate inside the artery, it becomes narrower, causing the cardiovascular disease known as atherosclerosis.*

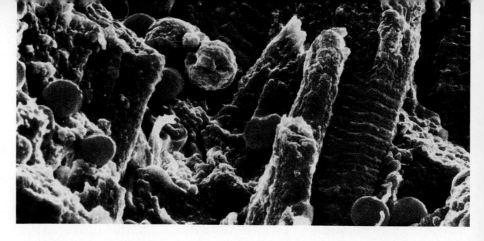

Figure 17–18 *A heart attack occurs when heart cells do not receive enough oxygen. Following a heart attack, dead muscle tissue replaces healthy muscle tissue. In this photograph, the dead muscle tissue appears brown, and the healthy muscle tissue appears red.*

in the brain's arteries, killing some brain cells. This is called a stroke.

Atherosclerosis is normally thought of as a chronic disorder that affects senior citizens. But it is a condition that begins much earlier in life. By the age of 20, in fact, most people have some degree of atherosclerosis, which is often called "hardening of the arteries." For this reason, it is very important to begin proper health habits and care of the heart before atherosclerosis becomes severe.

Many doctors suggest limiting the intake of foods rich in fats and cholesterol. These foods include animal fats, meats, and dairy products. Doctors also suggest a moderate amount of exercise to keep the heart and blood vessels healthy.

Despite all precautions, no one can guarantee that atherosclerosis and the heart problems it can cause can be avoided totally. Fortunately, much research and progress has occurred in the treatment of cardiovascular diseases.

Hypertension

If you have ever used a garden hose, you know that water pressure inside the hose can be increased in two ways. When you turn up the flow of water at the faucet, pressure increases in the hose. The water flows out of it with more force. Another way to increase the water pressure is to narrow the opening of the nozzle with your fingers. So the water pressure in the hose is a result of both the force of the water rushing through the hose and the resistance of the walls of the hose to that flow of water.

Blood pressure can be compared to the pressure of water in a hose. The force of the blood is caused by the pumping of the heart. Blood vessel walls are similar to the walls of a hose. Blood pressure is produced by the force of blood and the resistance of the blood vessel walls. Blood pressure rises each time the heart contracts to pump blood through blood vessels. Blood pressure falls each time the heart relaxes between beats.

Blood pressure can be measured with an instrument called a sphygmomanometer (sfihg-moh-muh-NAHM-uht-er). Measurements of blood pressure are indicated by two numbers. A normal blood pressure reading, for example, is 120/80. The first number is the pressure of the blood when the heart muscle contracts. The second number is the pressure of the blood when the heart relaxes between beats.

Normally blood pressure rises and falls from day to day and hour to hour. Sometimes though, blood pressure goes up and remains above normal. This condition is called **hypertension,** or high blood pressure. The increased pressure can damage blood vessels and make the heart work harder. As a result, hypertension can cause strokes and contribute to heart attacks.

Because people with hypertension often have no obvious symptoms to warn them, hypertension is

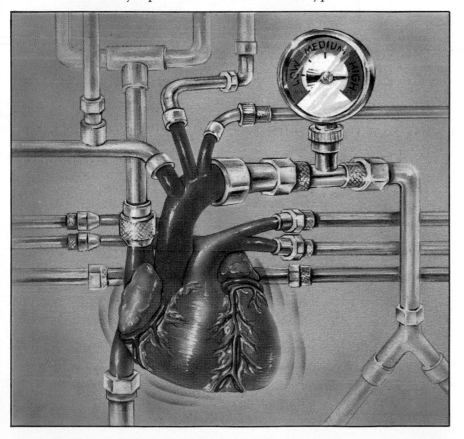

Figure 17–19 *Hypertension occurs when too much pressure builds up in the arteries. If this condition continues and goes untreated, damage to the walls of the arteries, to the heart, and to other organs may occur. What is another name for hypertension?*

453

CONNECTIONS

It's All in a Heartbeat

When you think of *electric currents* (flows of electric charges), electrical appliances and wall outlets probably come to mind. So it may surprise you to learn that your body produces electric currents as well.

The heart, for example, produces electric currents in order to function properly. These electric currents are so powerful that they can be picked up by an instrument called an electrocardiograph. An electrocardiograph is one of a doctor's most important tools in helping to diagnose heart disorders. It translates the electric currents produced by the beating of the heart muscle into wavy lines on paper or a TV-type screen. This record of wavy lines is called an electrocardiogram, and it is often abbreviated as ECG or EKG.

An ECG is made by attaching electrodes (strips of metal that conduct electric currents) to the skin of a patient's chest, arms, and legs. The electrodes pick up the electric currents produced by the heartbeat and send them to an amplifier inside the electrocardiograph. An amplifier is a device that increases the strength of the electric currents. The amplified currents then flow through a fine wire that is suspended in a magnetic field. As the electric currents react with the magnetic field, they move the wire.

The wire's motion is eventually recorded on a moving paper chart in the form of an ECG. A normal heartbeat produces an ECG with a specific pattern of waves; heart disorders change the pattern. By examining the change in pattern, a doctor can identify the type of heart disorder.

often called the "silent killer." That is why it is very important to have blood pressure checked at least once a year.

17–4 Section Review

1. What is cardiovascular disease? Describe two.
2. What is cholesterol?

Connection—*You and Your World*
3. How would a regular exercise program help a person with cardiovascular disease?

PROBLEM Solving

Are Heart Attacks Influenced by the Time of Day?

Whenever blood flow to the arteries of the heart is partially or totally cut off, the heart cells begin to die and a heart attack may occur. Does the time of day have an effect on the frequency of heart attacks? To help answer this question, researchers have interviewed people who have had heart attacks. Some of the data from these interviews are contained in the accompanying graph.

Analyzing Graphs

1. Why do you think the graph was drawn in this particular shape?

2. Approximately how many heart attack patients are represented in this study?

3. At which hour(s) of the day did the greatest number of heart attacks occur? The least number of heart attacks?

4. Did heart attacks tend to occur more often in the morning, afternoon, or evening?

■ Based on the data, do you think there is a relationship between time of day and frequency of heart attacks? Explain your answer.

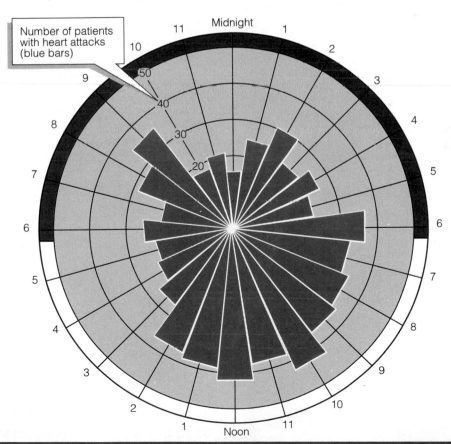

Number of patients with heart attacks (blue bars)

Laboratory Investigation

Measuring Your Pulse Rate

Problem

What are the effects of activity on pulse rate?

Materials *(per group)*

clock or watch with a sweep second
    hand
graph paper

Procedure

1. On a separate sheet of paper, construct a data table similar to the one shown here.

2. To locate your pulse, place the index and middle finger of one hand on your other wrist where it joins the base of your thumb. Move the two fingers slightly until you locate your pulse.

3. To determine your pulse rate, have one member of your group time you for 1 minute. During the 1 minute, count the number of beats in your pulse. Record this number in the data table.

4. Walk in place for 1 minute. Then take your pulse. Record the result.

5. Run in place for 1 minute. Again take your pulse. Record the result.

6. Sit down and rest for 1 minute. Take your pulse. Then take your pulse again after 3 minutes. Record the results in the data table.

7. Use the data to construct a bar graph that compares each activity and the pulse rate you determined.

Observations

1. What pulse rate did you record in step 3 of the Procedure? This is called your pulse rate at rest. How does your pulse rate at rest compare with those of the other members of your group? (Do not be alarmed if your pulse rate is somewhat different from those of other students. Individual pulse rates vary.)

2. What effect did walking have on your pulse rate? Running?

3. What effect did resting after running have on your pulse rate?

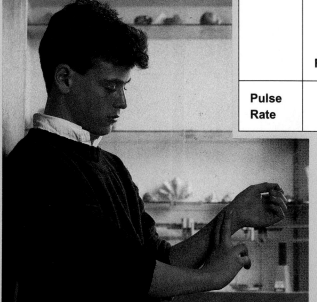

	Resting	Walking	Running	Resting After Exercise (1 min)	Resting After Exercise (3 min)
Pulse Rate					

Analysis and Conclusions

1. What conclusions can you draw from your data?

2. How is pulse rate related to heartbeat?

3. What happens to the blood supply to the muscles during exercise? How is this related to the change in pulse rate?

Summarizing Key Concepts

17–1 The Body's Transportation System

▲ The main task of the circulatory system is to transport materials through the body. Among the materials carried by the circulatory system are oxygen, carbon dioxide, food, wastes, disease-fighting cells, and chemical messengers.

17–2 Circulation in the Body

▲ Blood moves from the heart to the lungs and back to the heart. Then the blood travels to all parts of the body and returns again to the heart.

▲ The two upper collecting chambers of the heart are called atria. The two lower pumping chambers of the heart are called ventricles. Valves between the atria and ventricles keep blood from flowing backward.

▲ Arteries carry blood away from the heart. Veins carry blood back to the heart. Capillaries connect the arteries and veins.

17–3 Blood—The River of Life

▲ The four main components of blood are plasma, red blood cells, white blood cells, and platelets.

▲ Plasma, which is mainly water, is the yellowish fluid portion of blood. Red blood cells, white blood cells, and platelets make up the solid portion of blood.

▲ Red blood cells contain hemoglobin, which binds to oxygen in the lungs and carries oxygen to body cells.

▲ White blood cells are part of the body's defense against invading bacteria, viruses, and other microscopic organisms.

▲ Platelets help form blood clots to stop the flow of blood when a blood vessel is cut.

▲ The two main blood group systems are the ABO blood group and the Rh blood group.

▲ The lymphatic system transports fluid lost from the blood back into the bloodstream.

17–4 Cardiovascular Diseases

▲ Cardiovascular diseases affect the heart and blood vessels.

▲ The thickening of the inner lining of an artery is called atherosclerosis.

▲ Hypertension, or high blood pressure, makes the heart work harder and can cause damage to the blood vessels.

Reviewing Key Terms

Define each term in a complete sentence.

17–2 Circulation in the Body
pacemaker
septum
atrium
ventricle
valve
aorta
artery
capillary
vein

17–3 Blood—The River of Life
plasma
red blood cell
hemoglobin
white blood cell
platelet
fibrin
lymph

17–4 Cardiovascular Diseases
atherosclerosis
hypertension

Chapter Review

Content Review

Multiple Choice

Choose the letter of the answer that best completes each statement.

1. The two upper heart chambers are called
   a. ventricles.   c. septa.
   b. atria.   d. valves.
2. Oxygen-rich blood from the lungs enters the heart through the
   a. left atrium.   c. left ventricle.
   b. right atrium.   d. right ventricle.
3. From the right atrium, blood is pumped to the
   a. brain.   c. right ventricle.
   b. lungs.   d. capillary network.
4. The heart chamber that works hardest is the
   a. right atrium.   c. left atrium.
   b. right ventricle. d. left ventricle.
5. The blood vessels that carry blood back to the heart are the
   a. arteries.   c. capillaries.
   b. veins.   d. ventricles.
6. The cells that contain hemoglobin are the
   a. plasma.   c. white blood cells.
   b. platelets.   d. red blood cells.
7. Red blood cells are produced in the
   a. heart.   c. spleen.
   b. liver.   d. bone marrow.
8. Platelets help the body to
   a. control bleeding. c. carry oxygen.
   b. fight infection.   d. do all of these.
9. People with group AB blood have
   a. both A and B proteins.
   b. neither A nor B proteins.
   c. both anti-A and anti-B clumping chemicals.
   d. none of these.
10. Cholesterol is a fatlike substance associated with
    a. hemoglobin.   c. atherosclerosis.
    b. fibrin.   d. salt.

True or False

If the statement is true, write "true." If it is false, change the underlined word or words to make the statement true.

1. The two lower heart chambers are called <u>ventricles</u>.
2. Oxygen-poor blood enters the heart through the <u>left</u> atrium.
3. The <u>capillaries</u> are the thinnest blood vessels.
4. <u>Veins</u> are blood vessels that contain valves.
5. An iron-containing protein in red blood cells is <u>hemoglobin</u>.
6. The type of blood cell that fights infection is the <u>white blood cell</u>.
7. When you cut yourself, a net of <u>hemoglobin</u> threads forms over the area to stop the blood flow.

Concept Mapping

Complete the following concept map for Section 17–1. Then construct a concept map for the entire chapter.

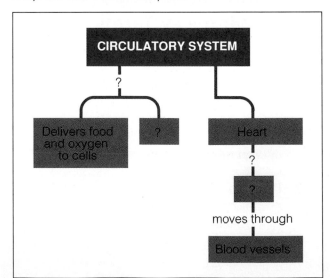

Concept Mastery

Discuss each of the following in a brief paragraph.

1. List and describe the four components of blood.
2. Explain why blood must be matched before a blood transfusion.
3. Explain why red blood cells are the most numerous of the blood cells.
4. What role do platelets have in the body?
5. Describe the path a single red blood cell would take through the heart.
6. Explain why oxygen-rich and oxygen-poor blood never mix in human beings.
7. Do all arteries carry oxygen-rich blood? Do all veins carry oxygen-poor blood? Explain your answer.

Critical Thinking and Problem Solving

Use the skills you have developed in the chapter to answer each of the following.

1. **Sequencing events** Starting at the right atrium, trace the path of the blood through the body.
2. **Relating facts** On a separate sheet of paper, add another column to Figure 17–15. Call it Can Donate Blood to Group(s). Fill in this column.
3. **Making predictions** Explain why chronic disorders are more of a problem today than they were 200 years ago. Predict how great a problem they will be in the future.
4. **Applying concepts** To determine whether a person has an infection, doctors often do blood tests in which they count white blood cells. Explain why such a count is useful.
5. **Making generalizations** To determine whether a person has abnormally high blood pressure, at least three blood-pressure measurements should be taken on three separate days at three different times. Explain why this is so.
6. **Relating cause and effect** How are the structures of an artery, a vein, and a capillary adapted to their functions?
7. **Making inferences** An artificial heart actually replaces only the ventricles of a human heart. Suggest a reason why replacing the atria is not necessary.
8. **Analyzing data** Suppose you are a doctor and have two patients who are in need of a transfusion. Patient 1 has group A blood and Patient 2 has group O blood. Which ABO blood group would you determine safe to give to each of your patients?
9. **Using the writing process** Develop an advertising campaign in favor of the reduction of animal fat in the diet. Make it a full media blitz!

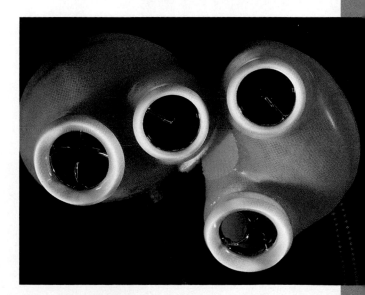

Respiratory and Excretory Systems

Guide for Reading

After you read the following sections, you will be able to

18–1 The Respiratory System

- Describe the structures of the respiratory system and give their functions.
- Explain how the lungs work.

18–2 The Excretory System

- Describe the structures of the excretory system and give their functions.

Watch a bicycle race on an autumn day and what do you see? You see cyclists pedaling hard and fast so that they can be the first to cross the finish line and win the race. What else do you notice about the cyclists? You probably see thin streams of sweat trickling down their faces and bodies. If you are close enough, you may see the quick, deep breaths that some cyclists take as they pedal. You may even see some cyclists drinking water from plastic bottles that are attached to their bicycles.

Why are the cyclists breathing so quickly and deeply? Where do the streams of sweat come from? What is the purpose of the water? In order to supply the cyclists with the energy they need to pedal their bicycles, the cells of their bodies must be provided with an enormous amount of oxygen. The oxygen must enter the cyclists' bodies, and an almost equal amount of wastes must be removed.

These vital functions are the tasks of two body systems: the respiratory system and the excretory system. Turn the page and begin to discover how these two systems perform their remarkable feats.

Journal *Activity*

You and Your World Have you ever had a sore throat or laryngitis? What did you do to make yourself feel better? Draw a sketch of yourself showing how you felt while you had either of these conditions.

◀ *In order to pedal their bicycles hard and fast, these cyclists need an enormous amount of oxygen.*

18–1 The Respiratory System

You cannot see, smell, or taste it. Yet it is as real as land or water. When it moves, you can feel it against your face. You can also see its effect in drifting clouds, quivering leaves, and pounding waves. It can turn windmills and blow sailboats across the sea. What is it?

If your answer is air, you are correct. Air is the mixture of gases that surrounds the Earth. The main gases that make up the air, or atmosphere, are nitrogen and oxygen. In fact, the atmosphere of the Earth is approximately 78 percent nitrogen and 21 percent oxygen. The remaining 1 percent is made of argon, carbon dioxide, water vapor (water in the form of an invisible gas), and trace gases—gases that are present in only very small amounts.

Humans, like all animals, need air to stay alive. You are breathing air right now. Every minute of the day you breathe in about 6 liters of air. Without this frequent intake of air, the cells in your body would soon die. Why? As you have just read, air contains the gas oxygen. It is oxygen that supports the energy-producing process that takes place in your cells. As a result of this process, your cells are able to perform all the various tasks that keep you alive. Try thinking of it this way. You know that a fire burns only if there is enough air—more specifically, enough oxygen in the air. Well, each body cell burns up the food it gets from the blood and releases the energy locked within the food only if it gets enough

Figure 18–1 *Like humans, plants, such as a heliconia, and animals, such as a barred leaf frog on the heliconia plant and a mountain gorilla, use the gases in the Earth's atmosphere to stay alive. What gases make up the Earth's atmosphere?*

oxygen. The energy-releasing process that is fueled by oxygen is called **respiration.** In addition to energy, carbon dioxide and water are produced during respiration.

As you may recall from Chapter 16, the digestive system breaks down food into small particles so that the food can get inside body cells. And as you learned in Chapter 17, the circulatory system transports oxygen and food to body cells via the blood. Now you will discover how oxygen combines with food in the cells to produce the body's much-needed energy and the waste products carbon dioxide and water vapor. **The body system that is responsible for performing the task of getting oxygen into the body and removing carbon dioxide and water from the body is the respiratory system.** Figure 18–2 is a diagram of the respiratory system. You may wish to refer to it as you follow the passage of air from the time it enters the respiratory system to the time it leaves.

The Nose and Throat

All the air that you use to breathe, sing, speak, or shout is usually first taken into the respiratory system through openings in the nose. These openings are called nostrils. If the air is cold, as it may be in winter, it is quickly heated by warm blood that flows through vessels near the inner lining of the nose. Meanwhile, mucus in the nose moistens the air. This keeps the delicate tissues of the respiratory

ACTIVITY

DISCOVERING

What Is in Exhaled Air?

In the presence of carbon dioxide, a chemical called bromthymol blue solution turns green or yellow.

1. Fill two test tubes with 10 mL of water and a few drops of bromthymol blue solution.

2. Label the tubes A and B.

3. Using a straw, gently blow air into the liquid in test tube A.

4. Compare the test tubes. What happened in test tube A? In test tube B? Explain. What was the purpose of test tube B?

■ What characteristic of respiration is illustrated by this activity?

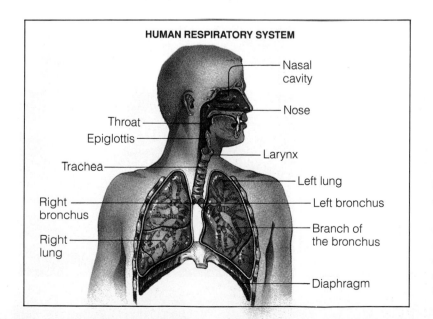

HUMAN RESPIRATORY SYSTEM

Nasal cavity

Nose

Throat

Epiglottis

Larynx

Trachea

Left lung

Right bronchus

Left bronchus

Branch of the bronchus

Right lung

Diaphragm

Figure 18–2 *The human respiratory system is composed of organs that work together to permit the exchange of oxygen and carbon dioxide with the environment. What is the name for the energy-releasing process that is fueled by oxygen?*

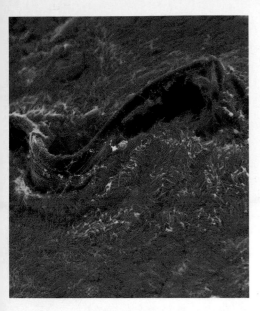

Figure 18–3 *A small piece of dirt that has invaded the body becomes trapped in the mucus and entangled in the cilia that line the bronchus.*

Figure 18–4 *The larynx, which is located at the top of the trachea, contains the vocal cords (left). Notice that the vocal cords are made of two small folds of tissue that are stretched across the larynx (right). What is the function of the vocal cords?*

system from drying out. In addition, large hairs and tiny hairs in the nose trap dust particles and microscopic organisms such as bacteria and keep them from going any farther into the respiratory system. If the nose becomes irritated by these trapped particles, your body responds by producing a little "explosion" to force the particles out. As you may have guessed, this explosion is a sneeze!

Because the nose warms, moistens, and filters the air coming into the body, it is healthier to take in air through the nose than through the mouth. But when the nose is blocked, such as when you have a cold, the mouth acts as a backup organ so that you can continue breathing.

From the nose, the moist, clean air moves into your throat. The air will come to a kind of fork in the road. One path leads to the digestive system. The other path leads deeper into the respiratory system. What directs the air down the respiratory path and objects such as food and water down the digestive path? The "traffic" is routed down the right path by a small flap of tissue called the **epiglottis** (ehp-uh-GLAHT-ihs). The epiglottis cuts off the opening to your windpipe when you swallow and routes all food and water down to your digestive system.

The Trachea

Take a moment to gently run your finger up and down the front of your neck. You will feel alternating bands, or rings, of cartilage and smooth

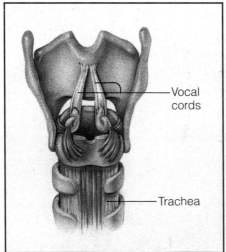

Vocal cords

Trachea

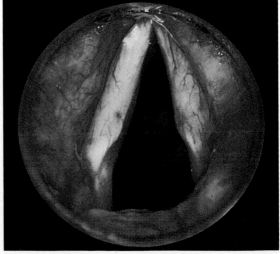

muscle. These rings form the protective wall of your **trachea** (TRAY-kee-uh), or windpipe. If the epiglottis is open, air passes from your throat into the trachea. As the air moves downward, tiny hairs lining the trachea trap dirt particles and bacteria that have managed to get through the nose. Like the nose, the trachea produces tiny explosions in response to irritations. These explosions are called coughs. During a cough, air is sometimes forced out of the trachea at speeds of up to 160 kilometers per hour!

Located at the top of the trachea is the **larynx** (LAR-ihngks), or voice box. The larynx is made of cartilage. Within the lining of the larynx are folds of tissue called **vocal cords.** As air passes out and past the vocal cords, they vibrate. These vibrations, together with the movements of the mouth and tongue, produce sounds.

The Lungs

As you breathe, air passes down the throat and into the trachea. Soon the air reaches a place where the trachea branches into two tubes. Each of these tubes is called a **bronchus** (BRAHNG-kuhs; plural: bronchi). Each bronchus continues to branch into smaller and smaller tubes. The bronchi and their many smaller branches are often described as forming an upside-down tree—the respiratory tree. See Figure 18–5.

The thinnest branches of the respiratory tree lead to grapelike clusters of tiny "balloons" called **alveoli** (al-VEE-uh-ligh; singular: alveolus). The alveoli make up most of the tissue of the **lungs,** the main organs of respiration. It is the alveoli that make the lungs soft and spongy. Because of the hollow alveoli, your lungs are so light that they could float. Each thin-walled alveolus is surrounded by a network of capillaries. It is here that your blood picks up its cargo of oxygen from the air. Oxygen from the alveoli passes into the blood flowing in the capillaries. Afterward, the oxygen-rich blood will be pumped back to the heart and sent through the arteries to all the tissues of the body. Meanwhile, the waste gas carbon dioxide passes from the blood into the alveoli. Within seconds, you breathe out the waste gas carbon dioxide.

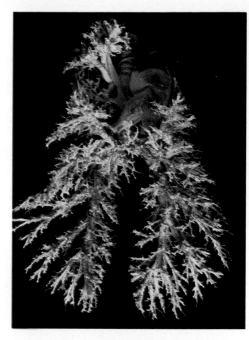

Figure 18–5 *When the spongy lungs are removed, the remaining parts of the respiratory system through which air passes resemble an upside-down tree.*

ACTIVITY DOING

Inhaling and Exhaling

1. After placing a metric tape measure around your chest and directly below your armpits, inhale. Note the size of your chest while inhaling. Record this number.

2. Then exhale and note the size of your chest. Record this number.

How do the sizes compare? What is responsible for the size differences?

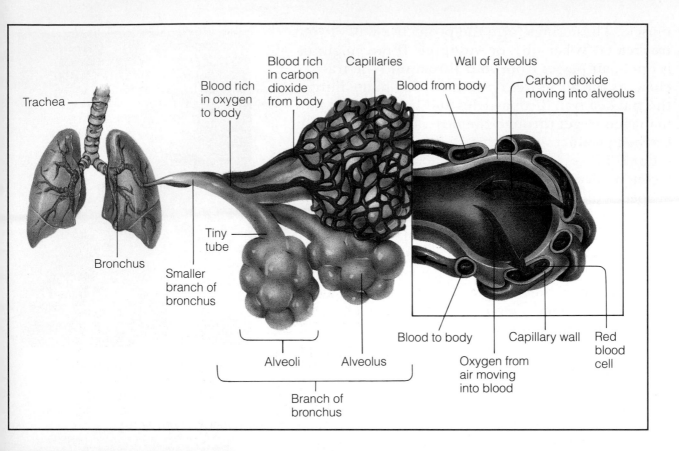

Blood rich in carbon dioxide from body

Capillaries

Wall of alveolus

Blood from body

Carbon dioxide moving into alveolus

Blood rich in oxygen to body

Trachea

Bronchus

Smaller branch of bronchus

Tiny tube

Alveoli

Alveolus

Branch of bronchus

Blood to body

Oxygen from air moving into blood

Capillary wall

Red blood cell

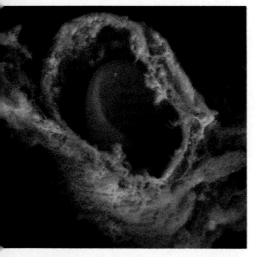

Figure 18–6 *Oxygen and carbon dioxide are exchanged between the blood in the capillaries and the air in the alveoli, or tiny air sacs. In the photograph, a single red blood cell squeezes through a capillary surrounding an alveolus that is less than 0.001 centimeter away.*

Mechanics of Breathing

Look down at your chest as you breathe in and out. What do you see? As you take in a breath, your chest expands. As you let the air out, your chest becomes smaller. Why?

You may be quick to reply that air rushing into your lungs makes your chest expand. And that air rushing out makes your chest shrink. But that is not the way it happens at all. Something else happens first, before the air moves in either direction. That something has to do with some sets of muscles in your chest. Here is how they work.

When you are about to take a breath, muscles attached to your ribs contract and pull upward and outward. At the bottom of your chest, a muscle called the **diaphragm** (DIGH-uh-fram) contracts and pulls down the bottom of your chest. Both of these actions make the chest expand. Suddenly there is more space in it.

When your chest expands, there is more room for air in your lungs. So the same amount of air is in a larger space. This causes the air pressure in

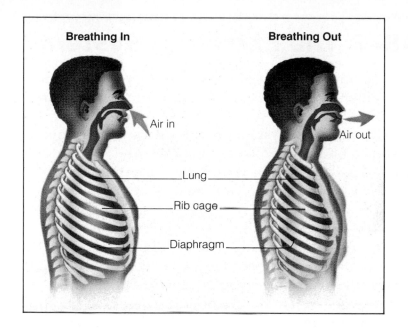

Breathing In   **Breathing Out**

Air in

Air out

Lung

Rib cage

Diaphragm

Figure 18–7 *When you breathe in, the muscles attached to your ribs contract and lift the rib cage up and outward, allowing more room in the lungs for air. When you breathe out, the muscles attached to your ribs relax and lower the rib cage, allowing less room in the lungs for air. What role does the diaphragm have in breathing?*

your lungs to decrease. As a result, the air pressure in your lungs becomes lower than the air pressure outside your body. The difference in pressure forces air to rush into your lungs. That is why your chest must expand before you inhale, or breathe in.

The reverse happens when you breathe out, or exhale. Your chest muscles relax. The space in your chest becomes smaller. The air pressure becomes greater inside than outside. The result? Air rushes out of your lungs as it would out of a squeezed balloon. How many breaths do you take in one minute?

18–1 Section Review

1. What is the function of the respiratory system?
2. What is respiration?
3. What are the structures of the respiratory system? What is the function of each?
4. Explain how the exchange of oxygen and carbon dioxide occurs in the lungs.
5. How do you breathe?

Connection—*You and Your World*

6. When you have laryngitis, or an inflammation of the larynx, you have a hoarse voice, or no voice at all. How might cheering too enthusiastically at a football game cause laryngitis?

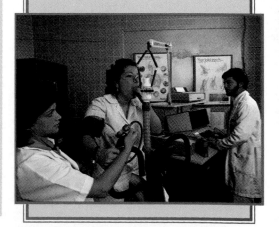

18–2 The Excretory System

The lungs are part of the respiratory system. But did you know that they are also part of the excretory (EHKS-kruh-tor-ee) system?

The excretory system provides a way for various wastes to be removed from the body. The removal process is known as **excretion.** Because the lungs remove carbon dioxide and water, they are considered organs of excretion as well as organs of respiration. Of course, excretion does not refer simply to removing carbon dioxide. Excretion includes the removal of excess water, salts, and certain nitrogen wastes. Nitrogen wastes are produced when excess amino acids, which are the building blocks of proteins, are broken down in the body. Nitrogen wastes, as you might expect, contain the element nitrogen. Excretion also includes the removal of drugs and certain poisons that are taken into the body and absorbed by the blood.

Although you probably do not often think about it, excretion is just as important to your body as breathing and eating. During certain activities, the body produces toxic, or poisonous, wastes. Without excretion, these wastes would build up in the body, possibly leading to illness and death.

The Kidneys

About 60 percent of your body mass is water, over half of which is inside body cells and tissues. The rest of the water bathes all the body's cells. This water is mixed with salts.

The amounts of various salts in body water, particularly in the watery blood tissue, is very important. Too much or too little salt can lead to problems. So it is necessary that the salts in the body be kept at exactly the right concentrations. That task is the job of the two **kidneys.**

Place the palms of your hands over your lowest ribs near your spine. Your palms should now cover the areas in which your kidneys are located inside your body. Each bean-shaped kidney is divided into an inner section and an outer section. The outer section contains millions of microscopic chemical filtering factories called **nephrons** (NEHF-rahnz).

ACTIVITY

DISCOVERING

Close at Hand

1. Using a hand lens, examine the skin on your hand.

2. Identify the epidermis and pores on the ridges of the skin.

3. Place a plastic glove on your hand and remove it after 5 minutes. Look at your hand.

Describe what happened to your hand. If you placed your hand against a chalkboard and then quickly removed it, what would you see?

■ How does this activity illustrate a function of the skin?

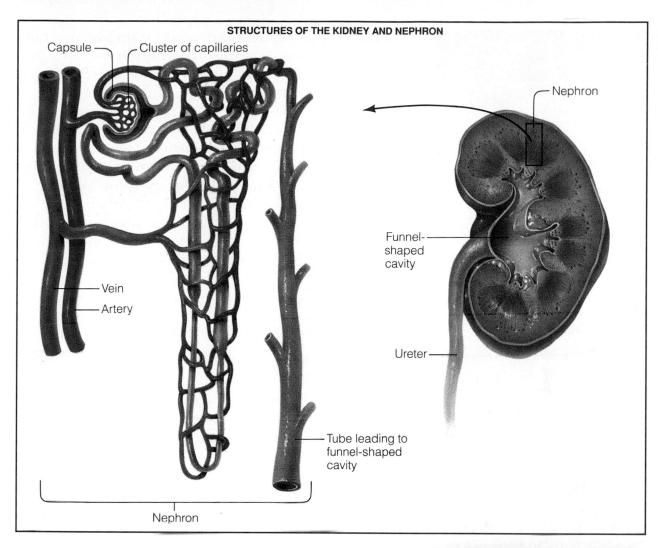

STRUCTURES OF THE KIDNEY AND NEPHRON

Capsule — Cluster of capillaries

Nephron

Vein

Artery

Funnel-shaped cavity

Ureter

Tube leading to funnel-shaped cavity

Nephron

Figure 18–8 *The photograph shows the large number of blood vessels in a kidney. Some of the structures of a kidney as well as the structure of a microscopic nephron are shown in the illustrations.*

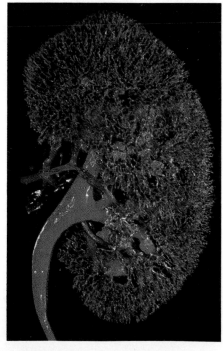

Blood is carried by arteries to the kidneys. Once inside the kidneys, the blood travels through smaller and smaller arteries. Finally, it enters a cluster of capillaries. Various substances in the blood including water, salts, digested food particles, and other materials are filtered out of the blood here. A nitrogen waste called urea (yoo-REE-uh) is also filtered out of the blood. These substances pass into a cup-shaped part of the nephron called the **capsule.** The capsule leads to a tiny twisting tube in the nephron.

As the filtered material moves through the tiny tube in the nephron, much of the water and digested food that was filtered out of the blood is reabsorbed, or taken back, into the bloodstream. If this process

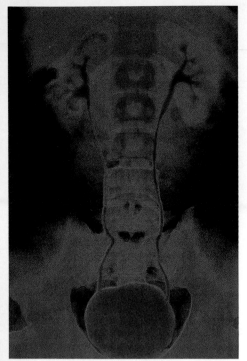

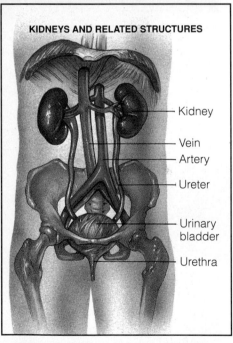

KIDNEYS AND RELATED STRUCTURES

— Kidney

— Vein
— Artery

— Ureter

— Urinary
bladder

— Urethra

Figure 18–9 *The main organs of the excretory system are the two kidneys, which are the green bean shaped organs in this color-enhanced X-ray. Use the illustration to locate the other excretory organs in the X-ray. What is the function of the kidneys?*

did not take place, the body would soon lose most of the fluid and nutrients it needs to survive.

The liquid that is left after reabsorption is called urine. What materials make up urine? In the inner section of the kidney, the urine passes through cone-shaped areas into a funnel-shaped cavity. This cavity is connected to a tube called a **ureter** (yoo-REET-uhr), which conducts the urine to the **urinary bladder.** The urinary bladder is a muscular sac that stores urine. The urinary bladder has the ability to expand as it fills with urine. Eventually the urine passes out of the body through a tube at the bottom of the bladder called the **urethra** (yoo-REE-thruh).

Other Excretory Organs

In addition to the kidneys and the lungs, two other organs of the body play a major role in excretion. These organs are the liver and the skin.

LIVER The **liver** acts as a filter for the blood passing through it. Among other things, the liver removes amino acids not needed by the body. The excess amino acids are broken down to form the urea that is excreted in urine. The liver also changes hemoglobin from worn-out red blood cells into substances that the body can use. In addition, the liver can turn some poisons that have collected in the blood into harmless substances.

SKIN The other excretory organ, the **skin,** is sometimes thought of as the largest organ of the human body. The skin covers an area of 1.5 to 2 square meters in an average person. The skin is about 4 millimeters deep. It is composed of two major layers: the **epidermis** and the **dermis.**

The epidermis is the outer layer of the skin. This layer contains flat cells that are stacked like bricks in a wall. As new cells are produced in the bottom layer of the epidermis, the old cells are pushed upward. Because the cells at the outer layer of the epidermis are far away from a food supply, they soon die. Later, these dead cells are shed and replaced.

The dermis, or inner layer of the skin, is thicker than the epidermis. The dermis is rich in blood vessels and connective tissue. The upper layer of the dermis contains small fingerlike projections similar to the villi in the small intestine. Because the epidermis is built on top of these projections, it has an irregular outline that forms ridges. In turn, these ridges form patterns on the fingertips, on the palms of the hands, and on the soles of the feet. On the fingers, these patterns are known as fingerprints.

The skin also contains hair, nails, and oil and sweat glands. The hair and nails are forms of dead skin cells. The sweat glands are coiled tubes in the dermis that connect to pores, or openings, in the surface of the skin.

Sweat glands help the body get rid of excess water, salts, and wastes such as urea. These materials form a liquid called perspiration, or sweat. When your body perspires, it gets rid of wastes and also regulates its temperature. This happens because, as perspiration evaporates from the skin, the body is cooled.

The oil glands give off oil, which keeps the hair from becoming brittle and dry. The oil also keeps the skin soft.

Activity Bank

How Fast Do Your Nails Grow?, p. 823

Figure 18–10 *The skin, which is the body's largest organ, is made of two main layers. The top layer is called the epidermis, and the bottom layer is called the dermis. In which layer of the skin would you find the blood vessels?*

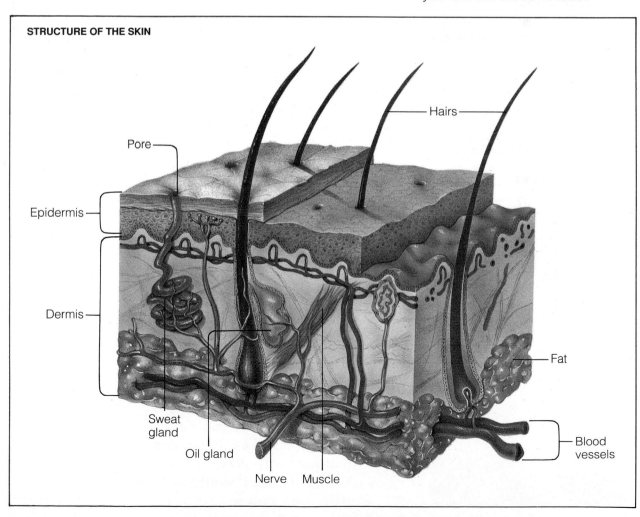

STRUCTURE OF THE SKIN

Hairs

Pore

Epidermis

Dermis

Fat

Sweat gland

Oil gland

Nerve   Muscle

Blood vessels

471

PROBLEM ??? Solving

How Do I Explain This?

From what you have learned about the respiratory and excretory systems, try your hand at developing some explanations for the following situations.

Relating Concepts

1. A humidifier is a device that adds moisture to the surrounding air. A humidifier would be useful to have in a room or building during dry winter weather.

2. A dehumidifier removes moisture from the surrounding air. This device can make a person feel more comfortable during humid summer weather.

3. At higher altitudes, the air is less dense (packed closely together) than it is at lower altitudes. Mountain climbers and athletes who train at higher elevations often have difficulty breathing at these elevations.

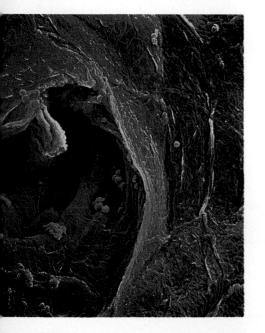

Figure 18–11 *The tiny green round objects inside the sweat gland are bacteria. What is the function of the sweat glands?*

The skin also acts as a sense organ. Nerve endings in the skin make you sensitive to pain, cold, heat, and pressure.

18–2 Section Review

1. What is the function of the excretory system? What structures enable it to perform this function?
2. What is urea? How is it formed?
3. Name and describe the two layers of the skin.
4. Why do you sweat?

Critical Thinking—*Applying Concepts*
5. Suppose that it is a very hot day and you drink a lot of water. Would your urine contain more or less water than it would on a cooler day? Explain your answer.

How a Lie Detector Gives Its Verdict

You have probably seen television courtroom dramas in which the defendant was found guilty solely on the basis of the results of a lie detector test. While being entertained by the television program, you probably never thought that its story line had anything to do with your study of life science. How wrong you were! A lie detector, or polygraph, is an instrument that works on the following idea: People who tell a lie become nervous. Their nervousness increases their blood pressure, pulse and breathing rates, and makes them sweat.

Actually, the lie detector is a combination of three different instruments. The results of each instrument are recorded by a pen that makes ink lines on moving graph paper.

One of the instruments is called the *cardiosphygmometer.* It detects changes in blood pressure (pressure of blood in the arteries) and pulse rate (beating of the arteries caused by the pumping action of the heart). This information is picked up by a cufflike device that is placed over the upper arm. This device is similar to the one your doctor uses when checking your blood pressure.

The second instrument, called the *galvanometer,* monitors the flow of a tiny electric current (flow of charged particles) through the skin. When the skin is moist, as it is with perspiration, it will conduct the electric current better. Small electrodes are taped to the hand to record this activity.

The third instrument is called the *pneumogram,* which records breathing patterns. It consists of a rubber tube that is strapped across the chest. Within the tube are instruments that measure changes in breathing patterns.

One drawback to the use of lie detectors is that some people get so nervous about taking the test that they may appear to lie even though they are telling the truth. And in rare instances, some people may be able to control their emotions so well that they can lie without affecting the results of the test. Although lie detectors are seen in television dramas, their results are generally not considered admissible in real-life courtrooms.

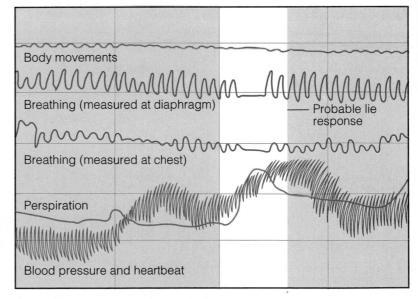

Body movements

Breathing (measured at diaphragm)

Probable lie response

Breathing (measured at chest)

Perspiration

Blood pressure and heartbeat

Laboratory Investigation

Measuring the Volume of Exhaled Air

Problem

What is the volume of exhaled air?

Materials *(per group)*

glass-marking pencil	paper towel
spirometer	graduated cylinder
red vegetable coloring	

Procedure 🔺

1. Obtain a spirometer. A spirometer is an instrument that is used to measure the volume of air that the lungs can hold.
2. Fill the plastic bottle four-fifths full of water. Add several drops of vegetable coloring to the water. With the glass-marking pencil, mark the level of the water.
3. Reattach the rubber tubing as shown in the diagram.
4. Cover the lower part of the shorter length of rubber tubing with the paper towel by wrapping the towel around it. This is the part of the rubber tubing that you will need to place your mouth against. **Note:** *Your mouth should not come in contact with the rubber tubing itself, only with the paper towel.*
5. After inhaling normally, exhale normally into the shorter length of rubber tubing.
6. The exhaled air will cause an equal volume of water to move through the other length of tubing into the graduated cylinder. Record the volume of this water in milliliters in a data table.
7. Pour the colored water from the cylinder back into the plastic bottle.
8. Repeat steps 3 through 7 two more times. Record the results in your data table. Calculate the average of the three readings.

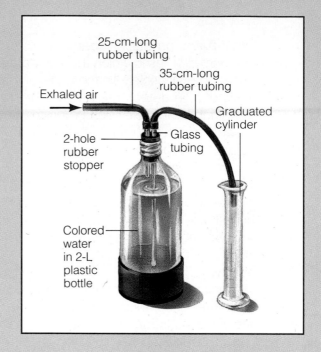

25-cm-long rubber tubing

35-cm-long rubber tubing

Exhaled air

Graduated cylinder

2-hole rubber stopper

Glass tubing

Colored water in 2-L plastic bottle

9. Run in place for 2 minutes and exhale into the rubber tubing. Record the volume of the water in the graduated cylinder.
10. Rest for a few minutes until your breathing returns to normal. Then repeat step 9 two more times and record the results. Calculate the average of the three readings.

Observations

How does your average volume of exhaled air before exercise compare to your average volume of exhaled air after exercise?

Analysis and Conclusions

1. Why is it important to measure the volume of exhaled air three times?
2. Explain how exercise affects the volume of exhaled air.
3. **On Your Own** Describe how you could determine the volume of air you exhale in a minute.

Summarizing Key Concepts

18-1 The Respiratory System

▲ Respiration is the combining of oxygen and food in the body to produce energy and the waste gases carbon dioxide and water vapor.

▲ The main task of the respiratory system is to get oxygen into the body and carbon dioxide out of the body.

▲ The respiratory system consists of the nose, throat, larynx, trachea, bronchi, and lungs. The bronchi divide into smaller tubes, which end inside the lungs in clusters of alveoli.

▲ The larynx, or voice box, contains the vocal cords. These structures are responsible for producing the human voice.

▲ The exchange of oxygen and carbon dioxide occurs in the alveoli, which are surrounded by a network of capillaries.

▲ Breathing consists of inhaling and exhaling. These motions are produced by movements of the diaphragm.

18-2 The Excretory System

▲ The excretory system is responsible for removing various wastes from the body.

▲ Excretion is the process by which wastes are removed.

▲ The principal organs of the excretory system are the kidneys.

▲ Each kidney contains millions of microscopic chemical filtration factories called nephrons.

▲ Within a nephron, substances such as nutrients, water, salt, and urea are filtered out of the blood. These substances pass into the cup-shaped part of the nephron called the capsule. Much of the water and nutrients is reabsorbed into the bloodstream. The liquid that remains in the tubes of the nephron is called urine.

▲ Urine travels from each kidney through a ureter to the urinary bladder. It then passes out of the body through the urethra.

▲ The liver removes excess amino acids from the blood and breaks them down into urea, which makes up urine. The liver also converts hemoglobin from worn-out red blood cells into bile.

▲ The skin has two main layers: the epidermis and the dermis. Sweat glands located in the dermis get rid of excess water, salt, and urea.

Reviewing Key Terms

Define each term in a complete sentence.

18-1 The Respiratory System

respiration
epiglottis
trachea
larynx
vocal cord
bronchus
alveolus
lung
diaphragm

18-2 The Excretory System

excretion
kidney
nephron
capsule
ureter
urinary bladder
urethra
liver
skin
epidermis
dermis

Chapter Review

Content Review

Multiple Choice

Choose the letter of the answer that best completes each statement.

1. In the body cells, food and oxygen combine to produce energy during
   a. digestion.   c. circulation.
   b. respiration.   d. excretion.
2. The lungs, nose, and trachea are all part of the
   a. skeletal system.
   b. digestive system.
   c. respiratory system.
   d. circulatory system.
3. Air enters the body through the
   a. lungs.   c. larynx.
   b. nose.   d. trachea.
4. Another name for the windpipe is the
   a. alveolus.   c. epiglottis.
   b. larynx.   d. trachea.
5. The voice box is also known as the
   a. larynx.   c. trachea.
   b. windpipe.   d. alveolus.

6. The trachea divides into two tubes called
   a. alveoli.   c. bronchi.
   b. air sacs.   d. ureters.
7. The process by which wastes are removed from the body is called
   a. digestion.   c. circulation.
   b. respiration.   d. excretion.
8. The kidneys contain microscopic chemical filtration factories called
   a. alveoli.   c. bronchi.
   b. nephrons.   d. cilia.
9. Urine is stored in the
   a. urinary bladder.   c. alveolus.
   b. urethra.   d. kidneys.
10. The top layer of skin is the
   a. epidermis.   c. alveolus.
   b. dermis.   d. epiglottis.

True or False

If the statement is true, write "true." If it is false, change the underlined word or words to make the statement true.

1. The job of getting oxygen into the body and getting carbon dioxide out is the main task of the <u>respiratory</u> system.
2. Dust particles in the incoming air are filtered by <u>blood vessels</u> in the nose.
3. The flap of tissue that covers the trachea whenever food is swallowed is the <u>larynx</u>.
4. The clusters of air sacs in the lungs are called <u>alveoli</u>.
5. The organs that regulate the amount of liquid in the body are the <u>kidneys</u>.
6. The <u>ureter</u> is the tube through which urine leaves the body.
7. The <u>liver</u> converts hemoglobin into bile.
8. The <u>lungs</u> are excretory organs.

Concept Mapping

Complete the following concept map for Section 18–1. Then construct a concept map for the entire chapter.

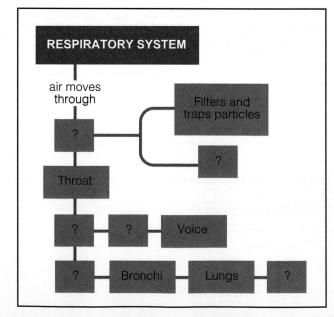

Concept Mastery

Discuss each of the following in a brief paragraph.

1. What is the difference between respiration and breathing?
2. How do the kidneys help to maintain homeostasis?
3. What role do the rib muscles and diaphragm play in breathing?
4. Why are the lungs considered to be both respiratory and excretory organs?
5. Explain the structure and function of a nephron.
6. Why is the skin classified as an excretory organ?
7. How is the kidney similar to a filter?
8. Why is the liver considered to be part of the digestive system as well as part of the excretory system?
9. What changes occur in the lungs when you inhale? What changes occur in the lungs when you exhale?
10. Name and describe four organs of excretion.
11. Trace the path of excess water from the nephrons to the outside of the body.

Critical Thinking and Problem Solving

Use the skills you have developed in this chapter to answer each of the following.

1. **Making comparisons** How are respiration and the burning of fuel similar? How are they different?
2. **Relating concepts** Would urine contain more or less water on a hot day? Explain.
3. **Relating concepts** How do respiration and excretion relate to the process of homeostasis?
4. **Designing an experiment** Design an experiment to show that the lungs excrete water.
5. **Interpreting data** Use your knowledge of the respiratory system to interpret the data table. What are the differences between inhaled air and exhaled air? How do you account for these differences?

6. **Applying concepts** What do you think is the advantage of having two kidneys?
7. **Making comparisons** How are the substances in the capsule of the nephron different from those in the urine that leaves the kidneys?
8. **Relating cause and effect** Emphysema is a disease in which the alveoli are damaged. How would this affect a person's ability to breathe?
9. **Relating cause and effect** Explain what happens to your throat when you sleep with your mouth open, especially when your nose is clogged because of a cold.
10. **Using the writing process** A children's television studio wants to make a movie that explains the process of respiration to young students. You have been asked to write a script that describes the travels of oxygen and carbon dioxide through the human respiratory system. Write a brief outline of your script, including information about what happens in each part of the respiratory system.

	Inhaled Air	Exhaled Air
Nitrogen	79%	79%
Oxygen	21%	16%
Carbon Dioxide	0.04%	4.00%

Nervous and Endocrine Systems

19

Guide for Reading

After you read the following sections, you will be able to

Has this ever happened to you? You wake up from a sound sleep in the middle of the night. Your heart is pounding thunderously in your chest. You are breathing rapidly and your body is covered with perspiration. You've had a bad dream. Even though you know—now that you are fully awake—that it was only a dream, your whole body has responded to the stimulus of your frightening nightmare.

Perhaps you have also had an experience like this: As you wait to take your turn on the balance beam, your palms are sweaty and your heart is pounding. Then you're on the beam. All your nervousness vanishes as you concentrate on making all the right moves while maintaining your balance.

Unknown to you, your nervous system and endocrine system were at work in both these situations. Together, they control your body's activities. Parts of your nervous system—the brain, nerves, and sense organs—obtain information from the outside world. In response to a stimulus, they alert your endocrine system to flood your bloodstream with chemicals. Your nervous system also controls the body movements involved in gymnastics. To find out how the nervous and endocrine systems perform their jobs in any kind of situation, turn the page.

Journal *Activity*

You and Your World Imagine that you have to do without one of your sense organs for a day. Which one would you choose to give up? In your journal, list five everyday tasks you would ordinarily do using this sense organ. Then describe how the absence of this sense organ would affect these tasks.

Coordination between the nervous system and the endocrine system help this gymnast perform her routine on the balance beam.

19-1 The Nervous System

You look up at the clock and realize that you have been working on this one particular math problem for more than half an hour. "Why am I having such a hard time solving this problem?" you ask yourself. Soon your mind begins to wander. Your thoughts turn to the summertime when you will no longer worry about math problems. Suddenly, the solution comes to you! This example, which may sound familiar, shows one of the many remarkable and often mysterious ways in which your nervous system functions. **The nervous system receives and sends out information about activities within the body. It also monitors and responds to changes in the environment.**

The extraordinary amount of information that your body receives at any one time is flashed through your nervous system in the form of millions of messages. These messages bring news about what is happening inside and outside your body—about the itch on your nose, or the funny joke you heard, or the odor of sweet-potato pie. Almost immediately, your nervous system tells other parts of your body what to do—scratch the itch, laugh at the joke, eat the pie.

In the meantime, your nervous system monitors (checks on) your breathing, blood pressure, and body temperature—to name just a few of the processes it takes care of without your awareness. The simple act of noticing that the weather is getting cooler is an example of the way the nervous system

Figure 19–1 *The nervous system controls and monitors all body activities—from the most simple to the most complex.*

Figure 19–2 *A nervous system enables organisms to respond to stimuli, or changes in the environment. In humans, the stimulus could be rain falling during a football game. The response could be opening umbrellas and donning rain gear, leaving the game, or both. In bears, a stimulus could be the sight of a salmon. What could the response be?*

monitors what is happening around you. The way the nervous system responds to this change is to make you feel chilly so you put on warmer clothes.

By performing all its tasks, the nervous system keeps your body working properly despite the constant changes taking place around you. These changes, whether they happen all the time or once in a while, are called **stimuli** (singular: stimulus). To help you better understand what a stimulus is, imagine this situation. An insect zooms toward your eye. You quickly and automatically blink to avoid damage to your eye. In this case, the insect zooming toward you is the stimulus and the blinking of your eye is the response.

Although some responses to stimuli are involuntary (not under your control), such as blinking your eyes and sneezing, many responses of the nervous system are voluntary (under your control). For example, leaving a football game because it begins to rain (stimulus) is a voluntary reaction. It is a conscious choice that involves the feelings of the moment, the memory of what happened the last time you stayed out in the rain, and the ability to reason.

So you can see how important the nervous system is to you. From the instant you are born, the nervous system controls and interprets (makes sense of) all the activities going on within your body. Without your nervous system, you could not move, think, laugh, feel pain, or enjoy the taste of a wonderfully juicy taco.

ACTIVITY

CALCULATING

A Speedy Message

Messages in the nervous system travel at a speed of 120 meters per second. How many seconds would it take a nerve message to travel 900 meters? 1440 meters?

The Neuron—A Message-Carrying Cell

The nervous system is constantly alive with activity. It buzzes with messages that run to and from all parts of the body. Every second, hundreds of these messages make their journey through the body. The messages are carried by strings of one-of-a-kind cells called **neurons,** or nerve cells. Neurons are the basic units of structure and function in the nervous system. Neurons are unique because, unlike most other cells in the body, they can never be replaced. You need not worry about this, however. The number of neurons that you are born with is so large that you will have more than enough to last your entire lifetime.

Although neurons come in all shapes and sizes, they share certain basic characteristics, or features. You can see the features of a typical neuron in Figure 19–3. Notice that the largest part of the neuron is the **cell body.** The cell body contains the nucleus (a large dark structure), which controls all the activities of the cell.

You can think of the cell body as the switchboard of the message-carrying neuron. Running into this switchboard are one or more tiny, branching, thread-like structures called **dendrites.** The dendrites carry messages to the cell body of a neuron. A long tail-like fiber called an **axon** carries messages away from the cell body. Each neuron has only one axon, but the axon can be anywhere from 1 millimeter to more than 1 meter in length!

Figure 19–3 *Use the diagram to identify the basic structures in these neurons from the spinal cord. What is the function of the cell body?*

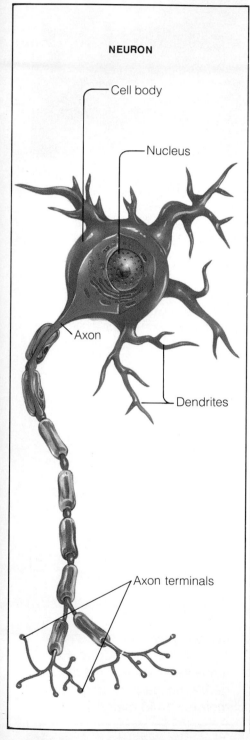

NEURON

Cell body

Nucleus

Axon

Dendrites

Axon terminals

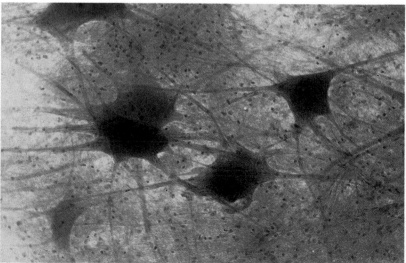

Notice in Figure 19–3 that the axon splits into many featherlike fibers at its far end. These fibers are called axon terminals (ends). Axon terminals pass on messages to the dendrites of other neurons. Axon terminals are usually found some distance from the cell body.

There are three types of neurons in your nervous system—sensory neurons, interneurons, and motor neurons. To find out the function of each neuron, try this activity: Press your finger against the edge of your desk. What happens? You feel the pressure of the desk pushing into your skin. You may even feel some discomfort or pain, if you press hard enough. Eventually, you remove your finger from this position.

How do neurons enable you to do all this? Special cells known as **receptors** receive information from your surroundings. In this activity the receptors are located in your finger. Messages travel from these receptors to your spinal cord and brain through **sensory neurons.** Your spinal cord and brain contain **interneurons.** Interneurons connect sensory neurons to **motor neurons.** It is through motor neurons that the messages from your brain and spinal cord are sent to a muscle cell or gland cell in your body. The muscle cell or gland cell that is stimulated by the motor neuron is called an **effector.**

Figure 19–4 *One of the body's billions of neurons can be seen in this photograph. The axon is the ropelike structure at the bottom of the photograph. What is the function of the axon?*

Figure 19–5 *There are three types of neurons in the nervous system: sensory neurons, interneurons, and motor neurons. What is an effector? A receptor?*

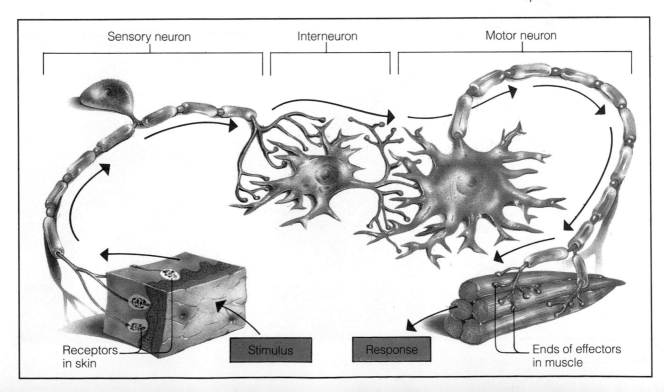

Sensory neuron Interneuron Motor neuron

Receptors in skin

Stimulus

Response

Ends of effectors in muscle

The Nerve Impulse

You have just read that the path of a message, which is more accurately known as a **nerve impulse,** is basically from sensory neuron to interneuron to motor neuron. But how exactly does a message travel along a neuron? And how does it get from one neuron to another neuron? **When a nerve impulse travels along a neuron or from one neuron to another neuron, it does so in the form of electrical and chemical signals.**

An electrical signal, which in simple terms is thought of as changing positive and negative charges, moves a nerve impulse along a neuron (or from one end of the neuron to the other). The nerve impulse enters the neuron through the dendrites and travels along the length of the axon. The speed at which a nerve impulse travels along a neuron can be as fast as 120 meters per second!

The way in which a nerve impulse travels from one neuron to another is a bit more complex. Do you know why? The reason is that the neurons do not touch one another. There is a tiny gap called a **synapse** (SIHN-aps) between the two neurons. Somehow, the nerve impulse must "jump" that gap. But how? Think of the synapse as a river that flows between a road on either bank. When a car gets to the

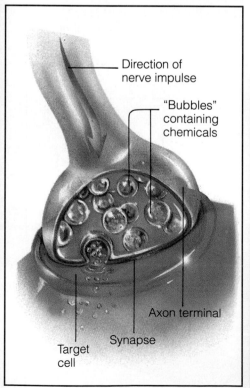

Figure 19–6 *The tiny gap between two neurons is called a synapse. The small reddish circles in the photograph are bubbles that contain chemicals which pour out of the axon terminal in one neuron, cross the synapse, and trigger a nerve impulse in the second neuron.*

Direction of nerve impulse

"Bubbles" containing chemicals

Axon terminal

Synapse

Target cell

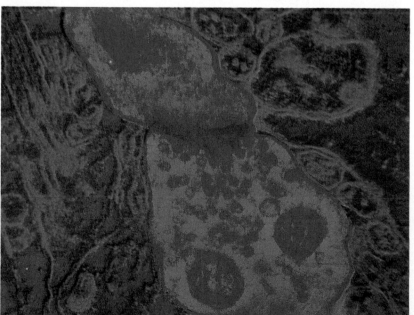

river, it crosses over by ferry. Then it drives right back onto the road and continues its journey.

Similarly, a nerve impulse is "ferried" across the synapse by a chemical signal. This chemical signal pours out of the ends of the neuron (axon terminals) as the nerve impulse nears the synapse. The electrical signal that brought the nerve impulse to this point shuts down, and the chemical signal takes the nerve impulse aboard, moving it across the synapse to the next neuron along its route. Then the chemical signal triggers the electrical signal again, and the whole process is repeated until the nerve impulse reaches its destination. You can appreciate how efficient this process is when you consider that for certain actions, this all happens in a matter of milliseconds!

19–1 Section Review

1. What are the functions of the nervous system?
2. What is a neuron? Describe its structure.
3. Identify the three types of neurons.
4. Describe a nerve impulse.

Critical Thinking—*Making Comparisons*
5. In the human nervous system, nerve impulses travel in only one direction along a neuron. How is this one-way traffic system better than a two-way traffic system along the same neuron?

ACTIVITY
DISCOVERING

A Reflex Action

1. Sit with your legs crossed so that one swings freely.

2. Using the side of your hand, gently strike your free-swinging leg just below your knee.

What happened when you struck that area? Describe in words or with a diagram the path the nerve impulse took as it traveled from your leg to the central nervous system and back to your leg.

■ What advantage does a reflex have over a response that involves a conscious choice?

19–2 Divisions of the Nervous System

In the previous section, you learned about the neuron as the basic unit of structure and function of the nervous system. You also gained some insight into the amazing job neurons do to keep you and your body in touch with the world inside and around you. Neurons, however, do not act alone. Instead, they are joined to form a complex communication network that makes up the human nervous

Guide for Reading

Focus on these questions as you read.

▶ *What are the two major parts of the human nervous system?*

▶ *What is the function and structure of each of the two major parts of the human nervous system?*

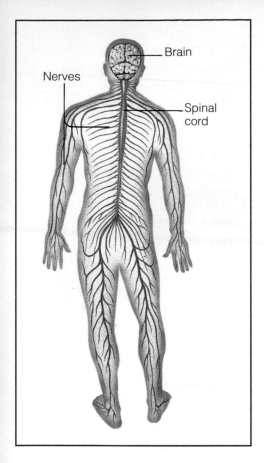

Figure 19–7 *The human nervous system is made up of the central nervous system and the peripheral nervous system. The central nervous system contains the brain and the spinal cord. The peripheral nervous system contains all the nerves that branch out from the central nervous system.*

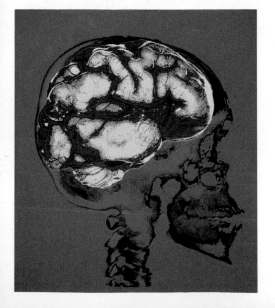

system. The human nervous system is divided into two parts: the central nervous system and the peripheral nervous system.

All information about what is happening in the world inside or outside your body is brought to the central nervous system. **The central nervous system, which contains the brain and the spinal cord, is the control center of the body**.

The other part of the human nervous system is the peripheral (puh-RIHF-uh-ruhl) nervous system. **The peripheral nervous system consists of a network of nerves that branch out from the central nervous system and connect it to the organs of the body.** Put another way, the peripheral nervous system is made up of all the nerves that are found outside the central nervous system. In fact, the word peripheral means outer part.

The Central Nervous System

If you were asked to write a list of your ten favorite rock stars and at the same time name all fifty states aloud, you would probably say you were being asked to do the impossible. And you would be quite correct. It is obvious that the nervous system is not able to control certain functions at the same time it is busy controlling other functions. What is less obvious, however, is just how many functions the brain can control at one time! For example, even an action as simple as sitting quietly in a movie theater requires several mental operations.

Many kinds of impulses travel between your central nervous system and other parts of your body as you watch a movie. Some nerve impulses control the focus of your eyes and the amount of light that enters them. Other nerve impulses control your understanding of what you see and hear. At the same time, still other nerve impulses regulate a variety of body activities such as breathing and blood circulation. And all these impulses may be related to one another. For example, if you are frightened by a scene in the movie, your breathing and heart rates

Figure 19–8 *This photograph is actually a combination of two photographs. One is an X-ray of a human skull. The other is of a human brain that has been properly positioned over the X-ray. What is the function of the skull?*

will likely increase. If, on the other hand, you are bored, these rates may decrease. In fact, you might even fall asleep!

The activities that occur within the central nervous system are very complex. Interpreting the information that pours in from all parts of your body and issuing the appropriate commands to these very same parts are the responsibility of the two parts of the central nervous system: the **brain** and the **spinal cord.** The brain is the main control center of the central nervous system. It transmits and receives messages through the spinal cord. The spinal cord provides the link between the brain and the rest of the body.

THE BRAIN If you are a fan of the English author Agatha Christie, you may remember the words uttered by her fictional detective Hercule Poirot as he attempted to solve a mystery: "These little gray cells! It is up to them." Indeed, much of the human brain does appear to be gray as a result of the presence of the cell bodies of billions of neurons. Underneath the gray material is white material, which is made of bundles of axons.

Despite the presence of billions of neurons, the mass of the brain is only about 1.4 kilograms. As you might expect of such an important organ, the brain is very well protected. A bony covering called the skull encases the brain. (You may recall from Chapter 15 that the skull is part of the skeletal system.) The brain is also wrapped by three layers of connective tissue, which nourish and protect it. The inner layer clings to the surface of the brain and follows its many folds. Between the inner layer and the middle layer is a watery fluid. The brain is bathed in this fluid and is thus cushioned against sudden impact, such as when you bump heads with another person while playing soccer or when you take a nasty fall. The outer layer, which makes contact with the inside of the bony skull, is thicker and tougher than the other two layers.

Looking like an oversized walnut without a shell, the **cerebrum** (SER-uh-bruhm) is the largest and most noticeable part of the brain. As you can see from Figure 19–11 on page 488, the cerebrum is lined with deep, wrinkled grooves. These grooves greatly increase the surface area of the cerebrum, thus allowing more

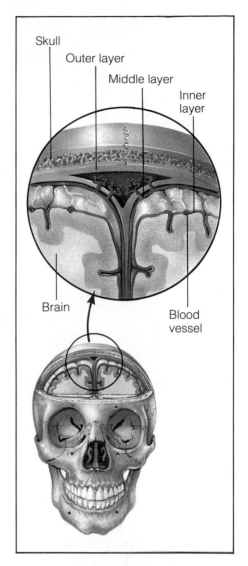

Figure 19–9 *The brain is wrapped by three layers of connective tissue, which nourish and protect it. Covering the brain and its three layers of connective tissue is a bony skull.*

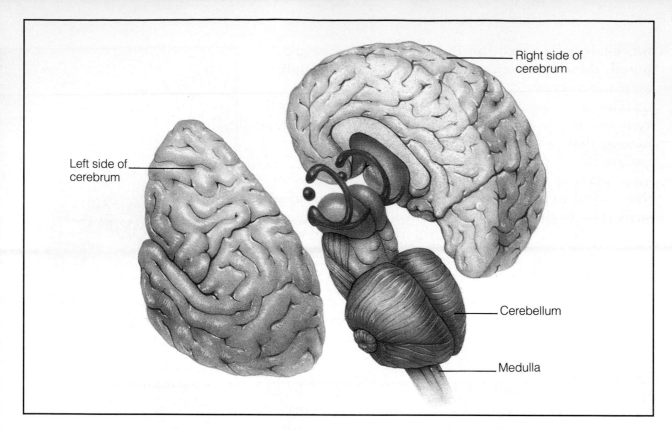

Right side of cerebrum

Left side of cerebrum

Cerebellum

Medulla

Figure 19–10 *The human brain consists of the cerebrum, cerebellum, and medulla. What is the function of each part?*

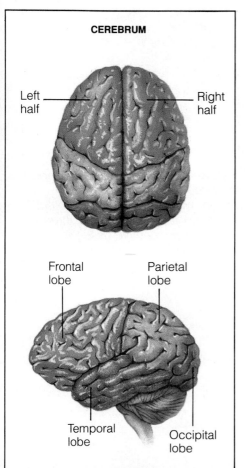

CEREBRUM

Left half

Right half

Frontal lobe

Parietal lobe

Temporal lobe

Occipital lobe

activities to occur there. You can appreciate how important this feature is when you consider that the cerebrum is the area where learning, intelligence, and judgment occur. Increased surface area means increased thinking ability. But this is not all the cerebrum does. It also controls all the voluntary (under your control) activities of the body. In addition, it shapes your attitudes, your emotions, and even your personality.

Another interesting feature of the cerebrum (which you may have noticed in Figure 19–11) is that it is divided into halves: a right half and a left half. Each half controls different kinds of mental activity. For example, the right half is associated with artistic ability and the left half is associated with mathematical ability. And each half controls the movement of and sends sensations to the side of the body opposite it. In other words, the right side of the brain

Figure 19–11 *The cerebrum is divided into two halves. Each half contains four lobes, or sections. What are the names of these lobes?*

controls the left side of the body; the left side of the brain controls the right side of the body.

Below and to the rear of the cerebrum is the **cerebellum** (ser-uh-BEHL-uhm), the second largest part of the brain. The cerebellum's job is to coordinate the actions of the muscles and to maintain balance. As a result, your body is able to move smoothly and skillfully.

Below the cerebellum is the **medulla** (mih-DUHL-uh), which connects the brain to the spinal cord. The medulla controls involuntary actions, such as heartbeat, breathing, and blood pressure. Can you name some other types of involuntary actions?

SPINAL CORD   If you bend forward slightly and run your thumb down the center of your back, you can feel the vertebrae that make up your spinal column. As you may recall from Chapter 15, the vertebrae are a series of bones that protect the spinal cord. The spinal cord runs the entire length of the neck and back. It connects the brain with the rest of the nervous system through a series of 31 pairs of

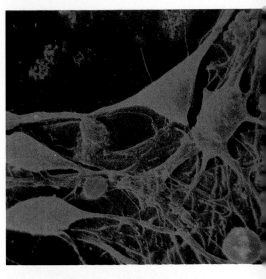

Figure 19–12 *Impulses are constantly traveling across neurons such as these located in the brain. To what part of the human nervous system does the brain belong?*

Figure 19–13 *The brain directs and coordinates all the body's activities. What is the function of the cerebellum?*

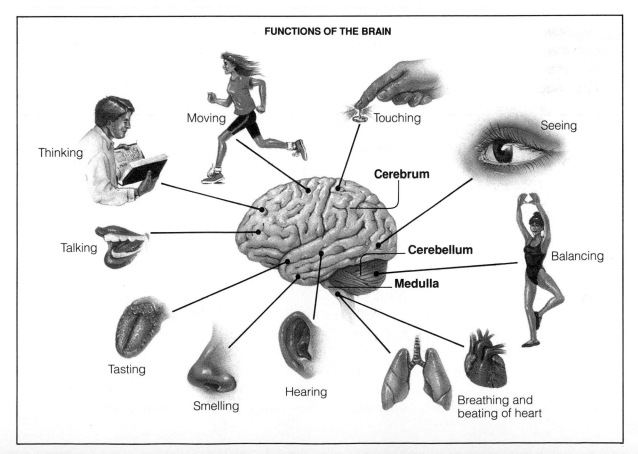

FUNCTIONS OF THE BRAIN

Thinking

Moving

Touching

Seeing

Talking

Cerebrum

Cerebellum

Balancing

Medulla

Tasting

Smelling

Hearing

Breathing and beating of heart

Figure 19–14 *The spinal cord, which provides the link between the brain and the rest of the body, is about 43 centimeters long and as flexible as a rubber hose. As the diagram shows, the spinal cord is protected by a series of bones called vertebrae that make up the vertebral column.*

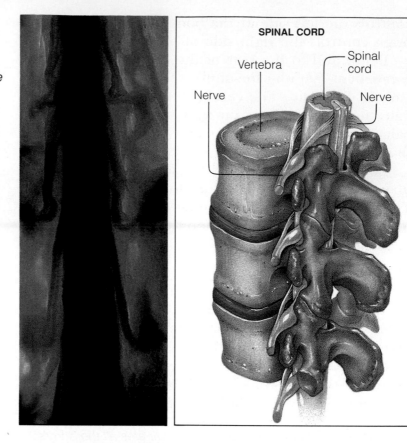

SPINAL CORD

Vertebra

Spinal cord

Nerve

Nerve

Figure 19–15 *If you touch a thumbtack, you will pull your finger away from it quickly. This reaction is an example of a reflex.*

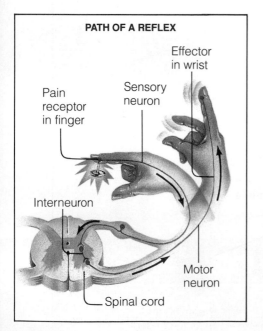

PATH OF A REFLEX

Effector in wrist

Pain receptor in finger

Sensory neuron

Interneuron

Motor neuron

Spinal cord

nerves. These nerves carry nerve impulses to and from the spinal cord.

Quite possibly, you are so interested in reading this chapter that you do not notice a fly circling in the air above your head. But if the fly happens to come close to your eyes, your eyes will automatically blink shut. Why?

A simple response to a stimulus (fly coming near your eyes) is called a **reflex.** In this example, the reflex begins as soon as the fly approaches your eyes. The fly's action sends a nerve impulse through the sensory neurons to the spinal cord. In the spinal cord, the nerve impulse is relayed to interneurons, which send the nerve impulse to motor neurons. The motor neurons stimulate the muscles (effectors) of the eyes, causing them to contract and so you blink.

Reflexes are not only lightning-fast reactions, they are also automatic. Their speed and automatic nature are possible because the nerve impulses travel only to the spinal cord, bypassing the brain. The brain does become aware of the event, however, but only after it has happened. So the instant after you blink, your brain knows that you blinked and why you blinked.

The Peripheral Nervous System

The peripheral nervous system is the link between the central nervous system (brain and spinal cord) and the rest of the body. The peripheral nervous system consists of pairs of nerves (43 to be exact) that arise from the brain and spinal cord and lead to organs throughout your body. Many of the nerves in the peripheral nervous system are under the direct control of your conscious mind. For example, when you "tell" your leg to move, a message travels from your brain to your spinal cord and through a peripheral nerve to your leg. There is one part of the peripheral nervous system, however, that is not under the direct control of your conscious mind. This part, called the autonomic (awt-uh-NAHM-ihk) nervous system, controls body activities that are involuntary—that is, body activities that happen automatically without your thinking about them. For example, contractions of the heart muscle and movement of smooth muscles surrounding the blood vessels and the organs of the digestive system are activities under the control of the autonomic nervous system.

The nerves of the autonomic nervous system can be divided into two groups that have opposite effects on the organs they control. One group of nerves triggers an action by an organ while the other group of nerves slows down or stops the action. Thus, the nerves of the autonomic nervous system work against each other to keep body activities in perfect balance.

ACTIVITY DISCOVERING

Fight or Flight?

1. Working with a partner, determine your pulse rate (heartbeats per minute) and breathing rate (breaths per minute) while you are at rest. Record your data.

2. Now do ten jumping jacks. **CAUTION:** *If you have any respiratory illnesses, do not perform steps 2 and 3.*

3. After exercising, measure your pulse rate and breathing rate. Your partner can measure your pulse while you are counting your breaths. Record this "after exercise" data.

Describe any changes in pulse rate and breathing rate after exercising.

■ How do these changes compare with those that occur when you are faced with an emergency situation? What other body changes occur when you react to an emergency?

Part of Body Affected	Autonomic Nervous System Nerve Group That Triggers Action	Autonomic Nervous System Nerve Group That Slows Down Action
Pupil of eye	Widened	Narrowed
Liver	Sugar released	None
Urinary bladder muscle	Relaxed	Shortened
Muscle of heart	Increased rate and force	Slowed rate
Bronchi of lungs	Widened	Narrowed

Figure 19–16 *The nerves of the autonomic nervous system can be divided into two groups that have opposite effects on the organs they control.*

491

If you truly enjoy a mystery, you may want to do some investigating on your own by reading some of Agatha Christie's books. The title of the book that was quoted on page 487 is *The Mysterious Affair at Styles.* If your local library does not have this particular work, ask your librarian for a list of some other Agatha Christie books.

For example, when you are frightened, nerves leading to organs such as the lungs and the heart are activated. This action causes your breathing rate and heartbeat to increase. Such an increase may be necessary if extra energy and strength are needed to deal with the frightening situation. But when the frightening situation is over, the other group of autonomic nerves bring your breathing rate and heartbeat back to normal.

19–2 Section Review

1. What are the two major parts of the human nervous system? What is the function of each?
2. Identify the three main parts of the brain and give their functions.
3. What is the function of the spinal cord?
4. Describe a reflex.

Critical Thinking—*Applying Concepts*
5. If a person's cerebellum is injured in an automobile accident, how might the person be affected?

Guide for Reading

Focus on these questions as you read.
▶ *What are the five sense organs?*
▶ *What are the functions of the five sense organs?*

Activity Bank

A Gentle Touch, p. 824

19–3 The Senses

You know what is going on inside your body and in the world around you because of neurons known as receptors (neurons that respond to stimuli). Many of these receptors are found in your sense organs. Sense organs are structures that carry messages about your surroundings to the central nervous system. **Sense organs respond to light, sound, heat, pressure, and chemicals and also detect changes in the position of your body.** The eyes, ears, nose, tongue, and skin are examples of sense organs.

Most sense organs respond to stimuli from your body's external environment. Others keep track of the environment inside your body. Although you are not aware of it, your sense organs send messages to the central nervous system about almost everything—from body temperature to carbon dioxide and oxygen levels in your blood to the amount of light entering your eyes.

Vision

Your eyes are one of your most wonderful possessions. They enable you to watch a beautiful sunset, pass a thread through the eye of a needle, and learn about a variety of topics by reading the printed word. They can focus on a speck of dust a few centimeters away or on a distant star many light-years away. Your eyes are your windows on the world.

Your eyes are designed to focus light rays (a form of energy you can see) to produce images of objects. But your eyes are useless without a brain to receive and interpret the messages that correspond to these images. What the brain does is receive the messages coming in through the eyes. These messages are then interpreted by the brain's visual center, located at the back of the brain. You will learn more about the brain's role in vision a little later in this section.

The eye is more correctly known as an eyeball—which is an appropriate name, as it is shaped like a ball. You may wish to refer to Figure 19–18 on page 494 as you read about the structures of the eyeball. The eyeball is slightly longer than it is wide. The eye is composed of three layers of tissue. The outer, protective layer is called the sclera (SKLEER-uh). The sclera is more commonly known as the "white" of the eye. In the center of the front of the eyeball, the sclera becomes transparent and colorless. This area of the sclera is called the **cornea.** The cornea is the part of the eye through which light enters. For this reason, the cornea is sometimes called "the window of the eye."

Figure 19–17 *Most sense organs respond to stimuli in the environment. But every now and then, sense organs can be fooled into sensing something that is not really as it should be. The optical illusion shown here, which is produced by mirrors, tricks the eyes into seeing many images of this young person.*

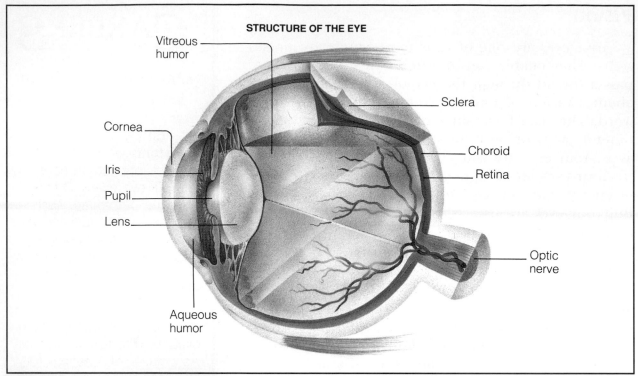

STRUCTURE OF THE EYE

Vitreous humor

Cornea

Iris

Pupil

Lens

Aqueous humor

Sclera

Choroid

Retina

Optic nerve

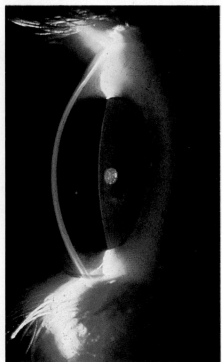

Figure 19–18 *What structures of the eye can you identify?*

Just inside the cornea is a small chamber filled with a fluid called aqueous (AY-kwee-uhs) humor. At the back of this chamber is the circular colored portion of the eye called the **iris.** The iris is the part of the eye people refer to when they say a person's eyes are blue, brown, black, or hazel. The iris is part of the choroid (KOR-oid), or middle layer of the eye. Unlike the sclera and the cornea, the choroid contains blood vessels.

In the middle of the iris is a small opening called the **pupil.** The pupil is not a structure but an actual opening through which light enters the eye. The amount of light entering the pupil is controlled by the size of the opening. And the size of the opening is controlled by tiny muscles in the iris, which relax or contract to make the pupil larger or smaller. By observing the pupils of your eyes in a mirror as you vary the amount of light in the room, you can actually see the opening change size. Your pupils get larger in dim light and smaller in bright light. Why? Pupils get smaller in bright light to prevent light damage to the inside of the eye. They get larger in dim light to let in more light.

Just behind the iris is the **lens.** The lens focuses the light rays coming into the eye. Small muscles attached to the lens cause its shape to change constantly, depending on whether objects are close by or far away. When the muscles relax, the lens flattens out, enabling you to see distant objects more clearly. When the muscles contract (shorten), the lens returns to its normal shape, enabling you to see objects that are close by more clearly. Behind the lens is a large chamber that contains a transparent, jellylike fluid called vitreous (VIH-tree-uhs) humor. This fluid gives the eyeball its roundish shape.

The light that passes through the lens is focused on the back surface of the eye, which is known as the **retina** (REHT-'n-uh). The retina is the eye's inner layer of tissue. It contains more than 130 million light-sensitive receptors called rods and cones. Rods react to dim light but not to colors. Cones are responsible for color vision, but they stop working in dim light. This is the reason why colors seem to disappear at night, when you are seeing with only your rods.

Both rods and cones produce nerve impulses that travel from the retina along the optic nerve to the visual center of the brain. There the nerve impulses are interpreted by the brain. Because of the way the lens bends light rays as they enter the eye, the image that appears on the retina is upside down. The brain must automatically turn the image right side up— and do so quickly! The brain must also combine the two slightly different images provided by each eye into one three-dimensional image. This is a complex task, indeed, but your brain does it quickly and automatically almost every second of your waking day. Just imagine what it would be like living in a world in which everything was upside down!

Figure 19-19 *This image of a cat was produced by a silicon chip developed to imitate the light-sensitive cells in the retina. What are these light-sensitive cells called?*

Figure 19-20 *The retina, which is the eye's inner layer of tissue, contains the light-sensitive cells called the rods and cones (right). The lens of the eye focuses light onto the retina. The upside-down image that you see in the photograph (left) was taken with a special camera that looked through the pupil of the eye.*

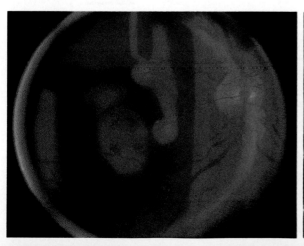

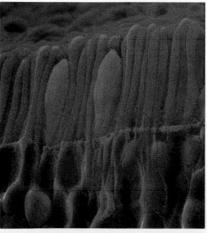

495

I Can See Clearly Now

Look around at the students in your classroom. You will notice that some of them are wearing eyeglasses. Why do some people need glasses whereas others do not? The answer to this question has to do with the structure of the eyeball. Look at the diagrams of the eyeball shown here. Notice that when the eyeball looks at an object, the light rays from that object enter the eyeball and come to a focus point on the retina.

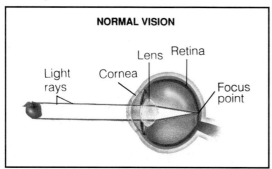

NORMAL VISION

Sometimes, however, the light rays do not come to a focus point on the retina. When the eyeball is too long from front to back, the light rays come together at a point in front of the retina. The result is a blurred image of distant objects. This disorder is called nearsightedness. When the eyeball is too short from front to back, the light rays come together at a point behind the retina. The result is a blurred image of nearby objects. This disorder is called farsightedness.

To fix these disorders, eyeglasses containing corrective lenses are worn. Examine the path of the light rays through each of the two lenses below—a biconcave (sunken in at both surfaces) lens and a biconvex (arched at both surfaces) lens.

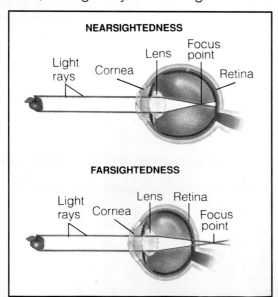

NEARSIGHTEDNESS

FARSIGHTEDNESS

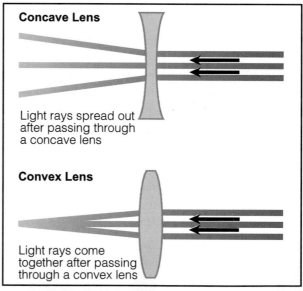

Concave Lens

Light rays spread out after passing through a concave lens

Convex Lens

Light rays come together after passing through a convex lens

Interpreting Diagrams

1. Which type of lens corrects nearsightedness?

2. Which type of lens corrects farsightedness?

3. Why is nearsightedness an appropriate name for this disorder?

4. Why is farsightedness an appropriate name for this disorder?

5. What are bifocals?

Hearing and Balance

When someone laughs or the telephone rings, the air around the source of the sound vibrates. These vibrations move through the air in waves. Hearing actually begins when some of the sound waves enter the external ear. If you look at Figure 19–21, you will see the external ear. This is the part of the ear with which you are probably most familiar. It is made mostly of cartilage covered with skin. You may recall from Chapter 15 that cartilage is strong enough to support weight, yet flexible enough to be bent and twisted. You can prove this to yourself by bending your external ear.

The funnellike shape of the external ear enables it to gather sound waves. These waves pass through the tubelike ear canal to the **eardrum.** The eardrum is a tightly stretched membrane that separates the ear canal from the middle ear. As sound waves

Figure 19–21 *Sound waves enter the ear and are changed into nerve impulses that are carried to the brain. The photograph of the middle ear shows the eardrum, which is colored yellow, and the three tiny bones known as the hammer, the anvil, and the stirrup.*

How Sensitive Are You?

1. Fill one cup with very warm water, a second with cold water, and a third with lukewarm water.

2. Place the index finger of your left hand in the very warm water. Then place the same finger of your right hand in the cold water. Allow your fingers to remain in the cups of water for 1 minute.

3. After 1 minute, remove your fingers from the water. Dip each finger alternately into and out of the lukewarm water.

How does the finger from the very warm water feel? The finger from the cold water? What does this activity show?

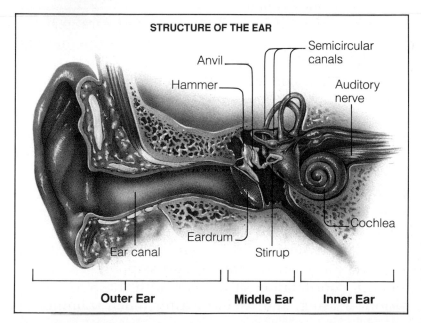

STRUCTURE OF THE EAR

Anvil

Hammer

Semicircular canals

Auditory nerve

Eardrum

Ear canal

Stirrup

Cochlea

Outer Ear   **Middle Ear**   **Inner Ear**

strike the eardrum, it vibrates in much the same
way that the surface of a drum vibrates when it
is struck.

Vibrations from the eardrum enter the middle
ear, which is composed of the three smallest bones
in the body—the hammer, anvil, and stirrup. The
hammer, the first of these bones, picks up the
vibrations from the eardrum and passes them along
to the anvil and then to the stirrup. The stirrup
vibrates against a thin membrane covering the opening into the fluid-filled inner ear.

Vibrations in the inner ear pass through the fluid
and are channeled into a snail-shaped tube called
the **cochlea** (KAHK-lee-uh). The cochlea contains
nerves that are stimulated by the vibrations from a
wide variety of sounds and range of loudness. The
stimulated nerves produce nerve impulses that
are carried from the cochlea to the brain by the
auditory nerve. Once in the brain, these nerve
impulses are interpreted, and you hear.

The ear not only enables you to hear, it also enables you to be aware of changes in movement and
to keep your balance. The structures in the ear that
are responsible for your sense of balance are the
semicircular canals and the two tiny sacs behind
them. The semicircular canals are three tiny canals
located within your inner ear just above the cochlea.
They are called semicircular because, as you can
see from Figure 19–22, each makes a half circle (the
prefix *semi-* means half).

The semicircular canals and the tiny sacs near
them are filled with fluid and lined with tiny hairlike
cells. These cells are embedded in a jellylike
substance that contains tiny grains called hearing
stones. When your head moves, the hearing stones
roll back and forth, bending the hairlike cells. The
hairlike cells respond by sending nerve impulses to
the cerebellum of your brain. If your brain
interprets these impulses to mean that your body is
losing its balance, it will automatically signal some
muscles to contract and others to relax until your
balance is restored.

Even the most ordinary actions—such as walking,
jogging, jumping, swimming, and skipping—require
smooth coordination of muscles with the senses of
vision, hearing, and balance. After much training

Figure 19–22 *The semicircular
canals are arranged at right angles
to one another so that they can
respond to up-and-down, side-to-
side, and bending motions (top).
Tiny grains commonly called
hearing stones also play a part in
maintaining balance (bottom). In
what part of the ear are the
semicircular canals located?*

and practice, your brain can learn to quickly coordinate balance with eye and hand movements so that you can walk a tightrope as easily as you can lift a spoon to your mouth!

Figure 19–23 *The role of the ears in maintaining balance makes all sorts of activities possible.*

Smell and Taste

Unlike the senses of vision and hearing, the senses of smell and taste do not respond to physical stimuli such as light and sound vibrations. To what stimuli, then, do these senses respond? The following story—perhaps similar to an experience in your own kitchen—may provide the answer.

You are standing near the oven. Suddenly you smell the wonderful aroma of a chocolate cake. You cannot see a cake, so what tells you that there is one baking in the oven? Your sense of smell tells you, of course. Sense receptors in your nose react to invisible stimuli carried by the air from the oven to your nose. The invisible stimuli are chemicals that affect the smell receptors in your nose. So your sense of smell is a chemical sense. In turn, the smell receptors produce nerve impulses that are carried to the brain, where they are interpreted. As a result, you are not only able to smell a cake, but you are able to identify the smell as a chocolate cake!

Your sense of taste is also a chemical sense. In the case of taste, the chemicals are not carried through the air but in liquids in your mouth (solid foods mix with saliva to form liquids). The receptors for taste are located in the taste buds on your tongue. Although there are only four basic kinds of tastes—sweet, sour, bitter, and salty—there are at least 80 basic odors. Taken together, tastes and odors produce flavors. Thus your sense of smell must work

Figure 19–24 *You have no trouble in identifying the wonderful aroma of a chocolate cake thanks to the sense receptors in the nose.*

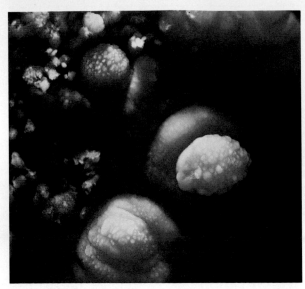

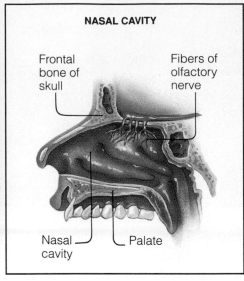

NASAL CAVITY

Frontal bone of skull

Fibers of olfactory nerve

Nasal cavity

Palate

Figure 19–25 *Smell receptors in your nose (right) and taste receptors on your tongue (left) are responsible for identifying the flavors of foods. What are taste receptors called?*

with your sense of taste in order for you to detect the flavors of foods. Perhaps you are already aware of this fact. Think back to the last time you had a stuffy nose due to a cold or an allergy. Were you able to taste the flavor of food? Probably not. Because the smell receptors in your nose were covered by extra mucus, only your sense of taste was working—not your sense of smell. Without a combined effort, the food you ate had little, if any, flavor.

Touch

The sense of touch is not found in any one place. The sense of touch is found in all areas of the skin. For this reason, you can think of the skin as your largest sense organ!

Near the surface of the skin are touch receptors that allow you to feel the textures of objects. You do not need much force to produce nerve impulses in these receptors. Prove this to yourself by gently running your fingertips across a piece of wood so that you can feel the grain. You have stimulated these touch receptors. Located deeper within the skin are the receptors that sense pressure. The sense of pressure differs as much from the sense of touch as pressing your hand firmly against a piece of wood differs from feeling it with your fingertips.

Notice in Figure 19–27 that there are other types of sense receptors. These receptors respond to heat, cold, and pain. The receptors that respond to heat and cold are scattered directly below the surface of

Figure 19–26 *The sense of touch, unlike the other senses, is not found in one particular place. All regions of the skin are sensitive to touch. For this reason, the sense of touch is one of the most important senses on which sightless people rely.*

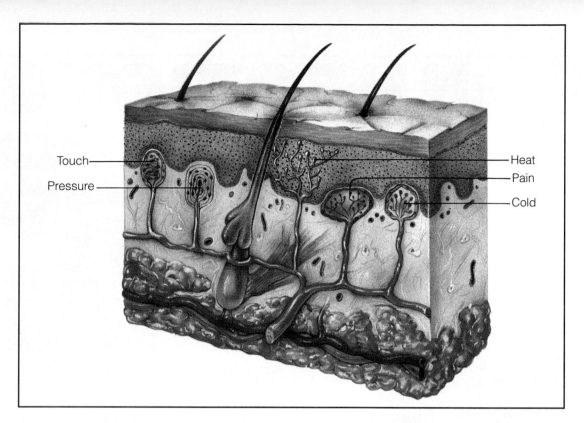

Figure 19–27 *Human skin contains five types of sense receptors: pressure, touch, pain, heat, and cold.*

the skin. Pain receptors are found all over the skin. It should not surprise you to learn that pain receptors are important to the survival of your body, no matter how uncomfortable they may seem at times. Pain, you see, often alerts your body to the fact that it might be in some type of danger.

19–3 Section Review

1. What are the five basic senses? What organs are responsible for these senses?
2. Describe the structure of the eye. Identify the functions of the major structures.
3. Trace the path of sound from the external ear to the auditory nerve.
4. Explain the role of the ear in maintaining balance.
5. What are the four basic tastes?

Connection—*You and Your World*
6. Design an experiment to show that your sense of smell is important in determining the flavor of food.

ACTIVITY
DISCOVERING

Keeping Your Balance

  1. Focus on an object in the room and close your eyes. Point to where you think it is.

  2. Open your eyes. How accurate were you?

  3. Now spin around twice and try to point to the same object again. Were you successful? Explain.

■ Why do you think ballet dancers can keep their balance while spinning?

501

With or Without Pepperoni?

Do not be too surprised if sometime soon you walk into a pizzeria and discover that the pizza you ordered is being whipped together by a voice-activated robot. As you may already know, robots are mechanical devices that do routine tasks. However, PizzaBot, as the pizza-making robot is called, is equipped with a little something extra—*artificial intelligence*. Artificial intelligence is a branch of *computer science* concerned with designing computer systems that perform tasks which seem to require intelligence. These tasks include reasoning, adapting to new situations, and learning new skills. When you recognize a face, learn a new language, or figure out the best way to arrive at a destination, you are performing such tasks.

Until recently, computers have only been able to follow instructions (a computer program). Now, however, scientists have developed computers that "think," or are able to perform complex

tasks such as diagnosing disease, locating minerals in the soil, and even making pizza! In order to "think," these computers need vast amounts of information. To make a pizza, a computer needs to recognize the sounds of a human voice as a pizza is ordered, to "decide" what possible pizza size and toppings it has just "heard," to repeat the order to confirm it (both aloud and on a screen), and then to follow the program for that pizza. The computer then processes these data one step at a time but extremely fast. (In contrast, your brain, with its billions of neurons, processes information along many pathways at the same time.)

As you can see, some of the applications of artificial intelligence are quite exciting, especially those in the field of *robotics*, or the study of robots. Just imagine the effects "thinking" robots such as PizzaBot could have on your life. The possibilities seem almost endless. In the not-too-distant future, you might even own a minirobot that would monitor your room, darting out every now and then to pick up the crumbs from your last snack! Seems impossible now, but who knows what will happen in the next few years. . . .

19–4 The Endocrine System

It is late at night, and your room is dark. As you feel your way toward the light switch in the pitch-black room, something warm brushes against your leg. You let out a piercing shriek, or perhaps only a gasp. It is not until you realize it is the cat you have encountered that you breathe a sigh of relief. As your pounding heart begins to slow down and your stiffened muscles relax, you begin to feel calmer. Have you ever wondered what causes your body to react this way? As you read on, you will find the answer to this question.

Endocrine Glands

The reactions you have just read about are set in motion not only by your nervous system, but also by another system called the endocrine (EHN-doh-krihn) system. **The endocrine system is made of glands that produce chemical messengers called hormones. Hormones help to regulate certain body activities.** By turning on and turning off or speeding up and slowing down the activities of different organs and tissues, **hormones** (HOR-mohnz) do their job. Together, the nervous system and the endocrine system function to keep all the parts of the body running smoothly.

The rush of fear that you felt as you brushed against an unknown object in the dark is an example of how the nervous system and the endocrine system work together. Your senses reported all the necessary information about the event to your brain. Because your brain interpreted the information as a threat, it quickly sent nerve impulses through selected nerves. These nerves triggered certain glands of the endocrine system. The selected glands produced hormones, which traveled through the blood to their specific destinations.

In this particular example, the hormones that were produced caused an increase in your heartbeat, made your lungs work harder, and prepared your muscles for immediate action. In such a state, you were ready to fight or to flee. Put another way, you were ready to defend yourself or to run. Your body

Guide for Reading

Focus on these questions as you read.

▶ *What is the function of the endocrine system?*

▶ *How does the endocrine system keep the internal environment of the body stable?*

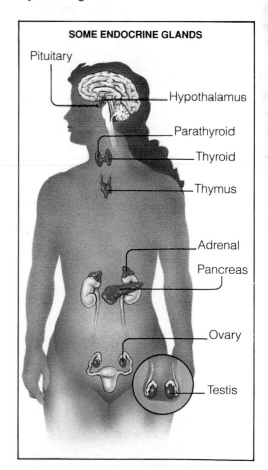

Figure 19–28 *The diagram shows some of the major glands of the endocrine system. What is the name of the chemicals produced by these glands?*

SOME ENDOCRINE GLANDS

Pituitary
Hypothalamus
Parathyroid
Thyroid
Thymus
Adrenal
Pancreas
Ovary
Testis

503

Bacterially Produced Hormones

Scientists have developed certain bacteria that produce large amounts of some human hormones. Using reference material in the library, find out more information about the bacterially produced hormones. Use the information in a written report. Be sure to provide answers for the following questions: Which hormones are produced by bacteria? What is the function of the hormone? How are these hormones produced? Include labeled diagrams that show how the bacteria are made to produce these hormones.

remained prepared for any further trouble until your brain stopped sending out danger signals. Then the endocrine glands responded in turn, and your body calmed down.

Endocrine glands are not the only type of glands found in your body. You have another set of glands called exocrine (EHKS-oh-krihn) glands. Exocrine glands give off their chemicals through ducts, or tubes, into nearby organs. Unlike endocrine glands, exocrine glands do not produce hormones. They produce tears, sweat, oil, and digestive juices to name a few examples. Common exocrine glands include the salivary glands in the mouth and sweat glands in the skin.

The hormones secreted (given off) by the endocrine glands are delivered to their destinations through the circulatory system. Thus, endocrine glands do not need to be near the organs they control. No matter where hormones enter the bloodstream, they always find their way through the nearly 100,000 kilometers of blood vessels (that's almost two and a half times around the Earth!) to their intended target area. How is this possible? Body tissues have the ability to "recognize" the hormones that are made for them. Tissue cells are programmed to accept certain hormones and reject others. Hormones not meant for a particular type of tissue or organ will pass on until they come to their target tissue or organ.

Each of your body's endocrine glands releases a different set of hormones and thus controls different body processes. In the next few pages, you will read about eight of these glands, their hormones, and the body activities they control. This information is summarized in Figure 19–29. How many of these glands and hormones sound familiar to you?

HYPOTHALAMUS The **hypothalamus** (high-poh-THAL-uh-muhs) produces hormones that help turn on and turn off the seven other endocrine glands in your body. The hypothalamus, which is a tiny gland located at the base of the brain, is the major link between the nervous system and the endocrine system. In fact, the hypothalamus is as much a part of one system as it is of the other. That is why the hypothalamus can be thought of as the way in which the brain and body "talk" to each other.

SOME ENDOCRINE GLANDS

Gland	Location	Hormone Produced	Functions
Hypothalamus	Base of brain	Regulatory factors	Regulates activities of other endocrine glands
Pituitary Front portion	Base of brain	Human growth hormone (HGH)	Stimulates body skeleton growth
		Gonadotropic hormone	Stimulates development of male and female sex organs
		Lactogenic hormone	Stimulates production of milk
		Thyrotropic hormone	Aids functioning of thyroid
		Adrenocorticotrophic hormone (ACTH)	Aids functioning of adrenals
Back portion		Oxytocin	Regulates blood pressure and stimulates smooth muscles; stimulates the birth process
		Vasopressin	Increases rate of water reabsorption in the kidneys
Thymus	Behind breastbone	Thymosin	Regulates development and function of immune system
Thyroid	Neck	Thyroxine	Increases rate of metabolism
		Calcitonin	Maintains the level of calcium and phosphorus in the blood
Parathyroids	Behind thyroid lobes	Parathyroid hormone	Regulates the level of calcium and phosphorus
Adrenals Inner tissue	Above kidneys	Adrenaline	Increases heart rate; elevates blood pressure; raises blood sugar; increases breathing rate; decreases digestive activity
Outer tissue		Mineralocorticoids	Maintains balance of salt and water in the kidneys
		Glucocorticoids— cortisone	Breaks down stored proteins to amino acids; aids in breakdown of fat tissue; promotes increase in blood sugar
		Sex hormones	Supplements sex hormones produced by sex glands; promotes development of sexual characteristics
Pancreas Islets of Langerhans	Abdomen, near stomach	Insulin	Enables liver to store sugar; regulates sugar breakdown in tissues; decreases blood sugar level
		Glucagon	Increases blood sugar level
Ovaries	Pelvic area	Estrogen	Produces female secondary sex characteristics
		Progesterone	Promotes growth of lining of uterus
Testes	Scrotum	Testosterone	Produces male secondary sex characteristics

Figure 19–29 *The location of some endocrine glands, the hormones they produce, and the functions they perform are shown in the chart. Where is thymosin produced? What is its function?*

505

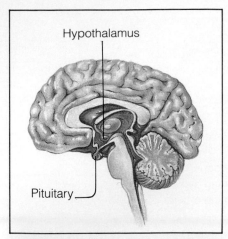

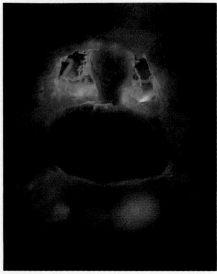

Figure 19–30 *The pituitary, which is found just under the hypothalamus, is located at the base of the brain in the center of the skull. The pea-shaped structure in the photograph is the pituitary, which is connected to the hypothalamus by a short stalk. What is the function of the pituitary?*

Messages that travel to and from the brain go through the hypothalamus. So the hypothalamus "knows about" sensations you are aware of—a lovely sunset, a painful bee sting, or a pleasant smell. It also controls things you are not aware of—the level of hormones in the blood, the amount of nutrients in the body, or the internal temperature of the body.

PITUITARY The hypothalamus depends on another endocrine gland for information about the body. This gland is the **pituitary** (pih-TOO-uh-tair-ee). The hypothalamus "talks to" the pituitary—sometimes by means of nerve impulses and sometimes by way of hormones. In response to these stimuli from the hypothalamus, the pituitary produces its own hormones.

The pituitary, which is no larger than a pea, is found in the center of the skull right behind the bridge of the nose. The pituitary controls blood pressure, growth, metabolism (all the chemical and physical activities that go on inside the body), sexual development, and reproduction. For many years, the pituitary was called the "master gland" of the body. This was because the hormones the pituitary produces control many of the activities of other endocrine glands. When it was discovered that the pituitary itself was controlled by its own master—the hypothalamus—the nickname "master gland" gradually dropped out of use.

THYMUS Just behind the breastbone is another endocrine gland—the **thymus** (THIGH-muhs). Large in infancy, the thymus begins to get smaller as you grow. By the time you reach adulthood, the thymus has shrunk to about the size of your thumb. The thymus is responsible for the development of the immune system, which you will learn in Chapter 21 is your main defense against disease-causing organisms. During infancy, the thymus produces white blood cells that protect the body's tissues, triggering an immune response against invaders. Later, other organs in the body take over the thymus's job of producing these white blood cells.

THYROID Before the mid-1800s, doctors actually thought that another endocrine gland, the **thyroid,** which is located in the neck, lubricated and protected the vocal cords. It was not until 1859 that the true function of the thyroid was discovered. That function is to control how quickly food is burned up in the body.

PARATHYROIDS Embedded in the thyroid are four tiny glands called the **parathyroids.** They release a hormone that controls the level of calcium in the blood. Calcium is a mineral that keeps your nerves and muscles working properly.

ADRENALS Of all the hormones in the body, adrenaline (uh-DREHN-uh-lihn) is perhaps one of the best understood by scientists. The effects of adrenaline are so dramatic and powerful that you can actually feel them as your heart rate increases and blood pulses through your blood vessels.

Adrenaline is part of the body's emergency action team. Whenever you are in a dangerous situation, such as the frightening dream you read about at the beginning of this section, your body reacts in a number of ways. Your first reaction is usually a nervous one—messages from your surroundings are sent to the brain, warning you of the danger. The brain shocks the body into action to avoid the threat. A rapid series of nerve impulses to the appropriate muscles makes you take whatever actions are necessary to ensure your safety. At the same time, the brain alerts the two **adrenals** to produce adrenaline. The word adrenal means above (*ad-*) the kidney (*-renal*). And that is exactly where each adrenal is located—atop each of the two kidneys.

PANCREAS Insulin, which is another hormone that scientists know a lot about, plays an important role in keeping the levels of sugar (glucose) in the bloodstream under control. It does this by helping body cells absorb the sugar and use it for energy. It also helps to change excess sugar into a substance called glycogen (GLIGH-kuh-juhn), which can be stored in the liver and the skeletal muscles until it is needed by the body. In this way, insulin prevents the level of sugar in the blood from rising too high. Without enough insulin, however, a person can develop diabetes mellitus (digh-uh-BEET-eez muh-LIGHT-uhs). Diabetes mellitus is a disorder in which the level of sugar in the blood is too high.

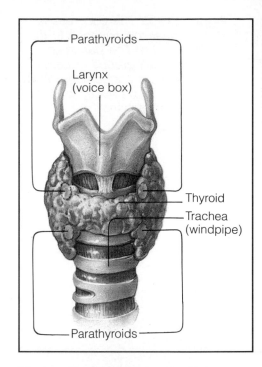

Figure 19–31 *The parathyroids are four tiny glands embedded in the thyroid, which is located in the neck. What hormone does the thyroid produce?*

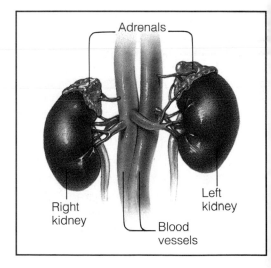

Figure 19–32 *Located atop each of the two kidneys is an adrenal gland. What is the function of the adrenal glands?*

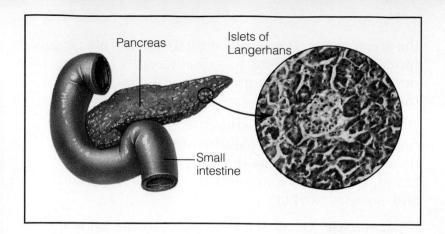

Figure 19–33 *The pancreas is located near the entrance to the small intestine. The pancreas contains small groups of cells called islets of Langerhans. What hormones are produced by the islets of Langerhans?*

Insulin is produced by a small group of cells called the **islets** (IGH-lihts) **of Langerhans** (LAHNG-er-hahns) within the pancreas. You may recall from Chapter 16 that the pancreas is also part of the digestive system, releasing enzymes into the small intestine. In addition to insulin, the islets of Langerhans produce another hormone called glucagon (GLOO-kuh-gahn). The effect of glucagon in the body is exactly opposite that of insulin. Glucagon increases the level of sugar in the blood by speeding up the conversion of glycogen to sugar in the liver.

Together, the effects of insulin and glucagon ensure that the level of sugar in the blood is always just right. If the level of sugar in the blood drops, the pancreas releases more glucagon to make up for the loss. If the level of sugar in the blood rises, the pancreas releases more insulin to get rid of the excess sugar.

OVARIES AND TESTES The **ovaries** (OH-vuh-reez) are the female reproductive glands, and the **testes** (tehs-teez; singular: testis, TEHS-tihs) are the male reproductive glands. The reproductive glands produce sex hormones that affect cells throughout the body. The ovaries and testes will be discussed in more detail in Chapter 20.

Negative-Feedback Mechanism

You can compare the way the endocrine system works to the way a thermostat in a heating and cooling system works. A thermostat is a device that controls the system in order to keep the temperature within certain limits. Suppose you set the thermostat in your classroom at 20°C. If the temperature of the room goes above 20°C, the thermostat turns on the

ACTIVITY

CALCULATING

How Much Is Enough?

The body cells are very sensitive to hormones. As little as 0.000001 milligram of a hormone per milliliter of blood can cause body cells to respond. How much of a hormone is needed to cause a response in 5000 mL of blood? In 10,000 mL?

air conditioner. The cooling effect produced by the air conditioner brings the temperature of your classroom back down to 20°C. At this point, the thermostat turns the air conditioner off. If, on the other hand, the temperature of the room falls below 20°C, the thermostat turns on the heater rather than the air conditioner. The heater, which has a warming effect, stays on until the temperature again returns to 20°C. In this way, the thermostat controls the internal environment of your classroom. In a similar way, a **negative-feedback mechanism** automatically controls the levels of hormones in your body. **In a negative-feedback mechanism, the production of a hormone is controlled by the amount of another hormone in the blood, thereby keeping the body's internal environment stable.**

The actions of the pituitary and the thyroid are probably the best examples of the negative-feedback mechanism. The pituitary is very sensitive to the amount of thyroxine (thigh-RAHKS-een) in the blood. Thyroxine is the name of the hormone that is released by the thyroid. When the level of thyroxine in the blood drops too low, the pituitary releases its hormone, a hormone called thyroid-stimulating hormone, or TSH. This action causes the thyroid to make more thyroxine, thus restoring the level of thyroxine in the blood. When the amount of thyroxine in the blood is just right, the pituitary stops releasing TSH, and the thyroid stops producing thyroxine. In this way, the negative-feedback mechanism helps to keep the internal environment of the body stable.

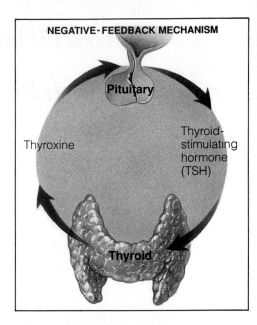

Figure 19–34 *The release of TSH into the bloodstream by the pituitary stimulates the production of thyroxine by the thyroid. When the level of thyroxine in the bloodstream increases, the pituitary reacts negatively by lowering the amount of TSH it releases. This is an example of a negative-feedback mechanism, which controls the levels of hormones in the blood.*

19–4 Section Review

1. What is the function of the endocrine system?
2. What is a hormone?
3. List eight endocrine glands in the body.
4. What is the negative-feedback mechanism?
5. Explain how the negative-feedback mechanism helps to maintain a state of balance within the body.

Critical Thinking—*Relating Facts*

6. If a person has diabetes mellitus, would his or her production of glucagon be increased or decreased? Explain your answer.

Laboratory Investigation

Locating Touch Receptors

Problem

Where are the touch receptors located on the body?

Materials *(per pair of students)*

scissors	9 straight pins
metric ruler	piece of card-
blindfold	board (6 cm x
	10 cm)

Procedure

1. Using the scissors, cut the piece of cardboard into five rectangles each measuring 6 cm x 2 cm.

2. Into one cardboard rectangle, insert two straight pins 5 mm apart. Into the second cardboard rectangle, insert two pins 1 cm apart. Insert two pins 2 cm apart into the third rectangle. Insert two pins 3 cm apart into the fourth rectangle. In the center of the remaining cardboard rectangle, insert one pin.

3. Construct a data table in which the pin positions on the cardboard appear across the top of the table.

4. Blindfold your partner.

5. Using the cardboard rectangle with the straight pins 5 mm apart, carefully touch the palm surface of your partner's fingertip, palm of the hand, back of the hand, back of the neck, and inside of the forearm. **CAUTION:** *Do not apply pressure when touching your partner's skin.* In the data table, list each of these body parts.

6. If your partner feels two points in any of the areas that you touch, place the number 2 in the appropriate place in the data table. If your partner feels only one point, place the number 1 in the data table.

7. Repeat steps 5 and 6 with the remaining cardboard rectangles.

8. Reverse roles with your partner and repeat the investigation.

Observations

On which part of the body did you feel the most sensation? The least?

Analysis and Conclusions

1. Which part of the body that you tested had the most touch receptors? The fewest? How do you know?

2. Rank the body parts in order from the most to the least sensitive.

3. What do the answers to questions 1 and 2 indicate about the distribution of touch receptors in the skin?

4. **On Your Own** Obtain a variety of objects. Blindfold your partner and hand one of the objects to your partner. Have your partner describe how the object feels. Your partner is not to name the object. Record the description along with the name of the object. Repeat the investigation for each object. Reverse roles and repeat the investigation. How well were you and your partner able to "observe" with the senses of touch?

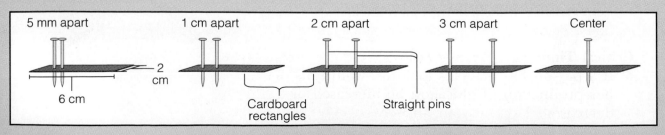

Summarizing Key Concepts

19-1 The Nervous System

▲ The nervous system receives and sends out information about activities within the body and monitors and responds to changes in the environment.

▲ The basic unit of structure and function of the nervous system is the neuron, which is made up of the cell body, dendrites, an axon, and axon terminals.

▲ A nerve impulse sends messages in the form of electrical and chemical signals. The gap between neurons is called a synapse.

19-2 Divisions of the Nervous System

▲ The central nervous system is composed of the brain and the spinal cord. The brain is divided into three parts: the cerebrum, the cerebellum, and the medulla.

▲ The peripheral nervous system consists of all the nerves that connect to the central nervous system.

▲ The autonomic nervous system consists of two sets of nerves that have opposite effects on the organs they control.

19-3 The Senses

▲ Light entering the eye passes through the cornea, aqueous humor, lens, and vitreous humor to the retina. The optic nerve carries the impulses to the brain.

▲ Sound enters the ear as vibrations and strikes the eardrum, causing the hammer, anvil, and stirrup to vibrate. These vibrations finally reach the cochlea. The auditory nerve carries the impulses to the brain.

▲ Smell and taste are chemical senses.

▲ The skin contains receptors for touch, pressure, pain, heat, and cold.

19-4 The Endocrine System

▲ The endocrine system includes the hypothalamus, pituitary, thymus, thyroid, parathyroids, adrenals, pancreas, and ovaries or testes.

▲ In the feedback mechanism, the production of a hormone is controlled by the amount of another hormone in the blood, thereby keeping the body's internal environment stable.

Reviewing Key Terms

Define each term in a complete sentence.

19-1 The Nervous System
stimulus
neuron
cell body
dendrite
axon
receptor
sensory neuron
interneuron
motor neuron
effector
nerve impulse
synapse

19-2 Divisions of the Nervous System
brain
spinal cord
cerebrum
cerebellum
medulla
reflex

19-3 The Senses
cornea
iris
pupil
lens
retina
eardrum
cochlea
semicircular canal

19-4 The Endocrine System
hormone
hypothalamus
pituitary
thymus
thyroid
parathyroid
adrenal
islet of Langerhans
ovary
testis
negative-feedback mechanism

Chapter Review

Content Review

Multiple Choice

Choose the letter of the answer that best completes each statement.

1. A change in the environment is a(an)
   a. effector.　　　c. reflex.
   b. stimulus.　　　d. hormone.
2. The short fibers that carry messages from neurons toward the cell body are the
   a. dendrites.　　　c.　synapses.
   b. axon terminals.　　d.　axons.
3. The gap between two neurons is called the
   a. dendrite.　　　c. synapse.
   b. cell body.　　　d. axon.
4. The part of the brain that controls balance is the
   a. spinal cord.　　c. cerebellum.
   b. cerebrum.　　　d. medulla.
5. Which endocrine gland provides a link between the nervous system and the endocrine system?
   a. pituitary　　　c. parathryoid
   b. adrenal　　　d. hypothalamus

6. The largest part of the brain is the
   a. spinal cord.　　c. cerebellum.
   b. cerebrum.　　　d. medulla.
7. Which of the following is part of the central nervous system?
   a. medulla
   b. semicircular canals
   c. retina
   d. auditory nerve
8. The pancreas produces the hormones insulin and
   a. thyroxine.
   b. glucagon.
   c. human growth hormone.
   d. adrenaline.
9. The layer of the eye onto which an image is focused is the
   a. retina.　　　c. choroid.
   b. sclera.　　　d. cornea.

True or False

If the statement is true, write "true." If it is false, change the underlined word or words to make the statement true.

1. The part of the neuron that contains the nucleus is the <u>axon</u>.
2. The <u>pituitary</u> produces adrenaline.
3. The brain and the spinal cord make up the <u>peripheral</u> nervous system.
4. The reproductive glands are the ovaries and the <u>testes</u>.
5. The <u>retina</u> is the watery fluid between the cornea and the lens of the eye.
6. The <u>auditory nerve</u> carries impulses from the ear to the brain.
7. The outer layer of the eye is the <u>choroid</u>.

Concept Mapping

Complete the following concept map for Section 19–1. Then construct a concept map for the entire chapter.

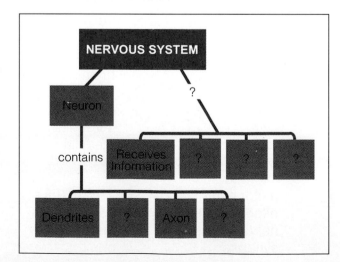

512

Concept Mastery

Discuss each of the following in a brief paragraph.

1. What is a stimulus? Give two examples.
2. What are the functions of the three types of neurons found in the nervous system?
3. Compare the functions of a receptor and an effector.
4. Explain how an impulse crosses a synapse.
5. Describe the role of the lens in vision.
6. Compare the effect of adrenaline and insulin on the body.
7. What is the function of the hypothalamus?
8. Explain what a negative-feedback mechanism is. Give an example.
9. Explain why it is an advantage to you that your reflexes respond quickly and automatically.
10. How does an endocrine gland differ from an exocrine gland?
11. How is the central nervous system protected?
12. Trace the path of light through the eye.
13. Trace the path of sound through the ear.

Critical Thinking and Problem Solving

Use the skills you have developed in this chapter to answer each of the following.

1. **Making comparisons** Compare the nervous system to a computer. How are they similar? Different?
2. **Applying concepts** Explain why many people become dizzy after spinning around for any length of time.
3. **Interpreting graphs** The accompanying graph shows the levels of sugar in the blood of two people during a five-hour period immediately after a typical meal. Which line represents an average person? Which line represents a person with diabetes mellitus? Explain your answers.

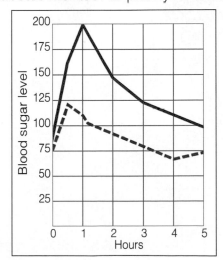

4. **Relating concepts** A routine examination by a doctor usually includes the knee-jerk test. What is the purpose of this test? What could the absence of a response indicate?
5. **Applying concepts** Explain why after entering a dark room, you are surprised to see how colorful the room is when the lights are turned on.
6. **Applying concepts** Sometimes as a result of a cold, the middle ear becomes filled with fluid. Why do you think this can cause a temporary loss of hearing?
7. **Making predictions** What might happen if the cornea becomes inflamed and as a result more fluid collects there?
8. **Using the writing process** Select a picture in a book or magazine. In a short essay, explain how what you see in the picture is influenced by your sense of touch, hearing, smell, or taste as well as your sense of vision.

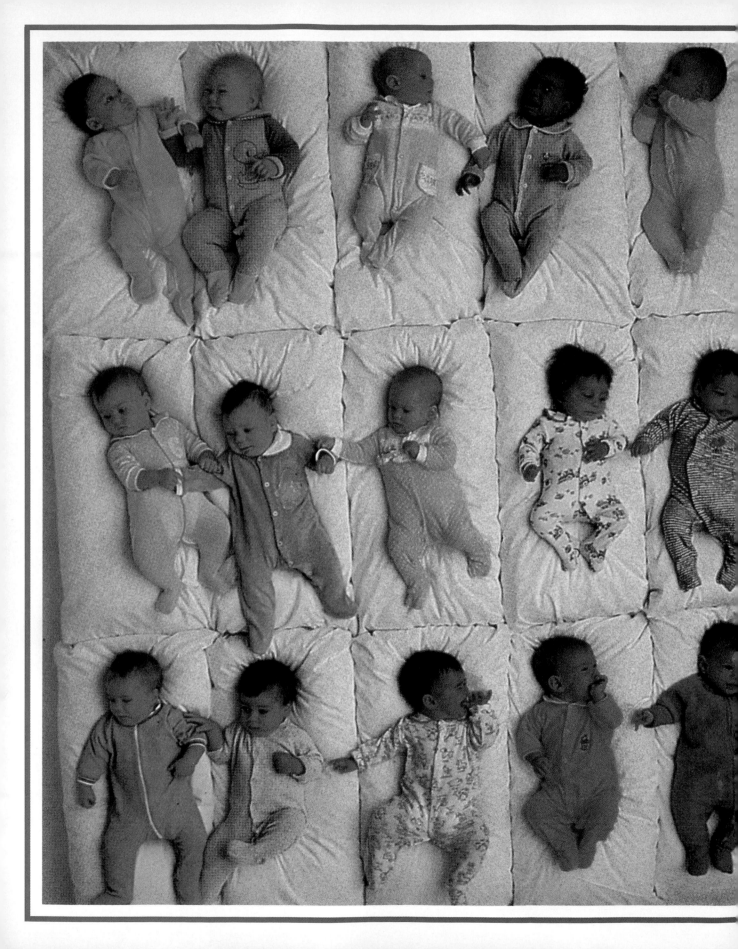

Reproduction and Development 20

20–1 The Reproductive System

- Identify the function and importance of the reproductive system.
- Define fertilization.
- Compare the functions and structures of the male and female reproductive systems.

20–2 Stages of Development

- Describe the changes that occur between fertilization and birth.
- Describe the process of birth.
- List and describe the stages of development after birth.

Almost everyone loves babies—all kinds of babies: animal babies (bunnies, kittens, and puppies, to name just a few) and human babies. Babies can be one of the funniest and most appealing subjects of photography. Just look at the photograph on the opposite page!

One of the many common characteristics of all newborn human babies is their total helplessness. They cannot sit up, move from one place to another, feed themselves, or talk in a language understood by other people. Their basic means of communicating hunger, discomfort, unhappiness, or pain is by crying. With proper care and training, however, babies gradually learn to do some things for themselves. And they eventually become children, adolescents, and then adults.

At this point, you may be asking yourself this question: What changes take place as a baby develops and grows into a full-sized adult? As you read this chapter you will find the answer to this question as well as the answers to others. And you will also discover that human development is an exciting, ongoing process.

Journal *Activity*

You and Your World Place photographs of yourself as an infant, toddler, or young child in your journal. Below each photograph, describe what you were doing when the photograph was taken and what you remember about it. What physical and social changes have you undergone since the photographs were taken?

◀ *These human babies—products of reproduction—guarantee the survival of the human species.*

Guide for Reading

*Focus on these questions as
you read.*

▶ *What is the importance of
reproduction?*

▶ *What are the structures of
the male and female
reproductive systems?*

20–1 The Reproductive System

In the previous chapters of this textbook, you learned about the human body systems that are vital to the survival of the individual. Without the proper functioning of these systems, humans would no doubt be unable to live healthy, normal lives. Yet there is one body system that is not essential to the survival of the individual. In fact, humans can survive quite well without the functioning of this system.

The body system is the reproductive system, which contains special structures that enable **reproduction** to take place. **Reproduction is the process through which living things produce new individuals of the same kind. Thus the reproductive system ensures the continuation of the species.**

You may find this unbelievable, but you began life as a single cell! This single cell was produced by the joining of two other cells. These other cells are the **sperm** and the **egg,** or ovum (OH-vuhm; plural: ova). The sperm is the male sex cell and the egg is the female sex cell. The joining of a sperm cell with an egg cell is called **fertilization.** Fertilization is an important part of reproduction. Sperm are produced in the male reproductive system and eggs are produced in the female reproductive system.

Figure 20–1 *The process of reproduction results in new individuals of the same kind. Without reproduction, humans and, for that matter, all species of living things would cease to exist.*

A sperm cell has a head, a middle part, and a tail. See Figure 20–2. Compared to the sperm, the egg is enormous. It is one of the largest cells in the body. Although the egg's shape and size differ from the sperm's, the cells share an important feature. Both cells contain thick, rodlike structures known as **chromosomes** (KROH-muh-sohmz). Chromosomes pass on inherited characteristics from one generation of cells to the next.

Each cell of the human body, except the sex cells, contains 46 chromosomes. Each sex cell contains half this number, or 23 chromosomes. After fertilization, the fertilized egg contains 46 chromosomes. So a fertilized egg gets 23 chromosomes from the sperm and 23 chromosomes from the egg. The fertilized egg contains all of the information needed to produce a complete new human being.

The Male Reproductive System

The male reproductive system has two **testes** (TEHS-teez; singular: testis). They are oval-shaped objects found inside an external sac called the scrotum (SKROHT-uhm). The testes are the organs that produce sperm. Sperm swim from each testis through

Figure 20–2 *The tadpole-shaped sperm, which consists of a head, a middle piece, and a tail, is the male sex cell. The ball-shaped egg is the female sex cell. What is the name of the process in which the nuclei of these two sex cells join?*

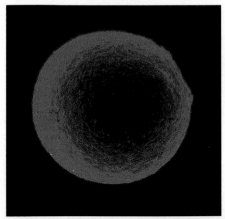

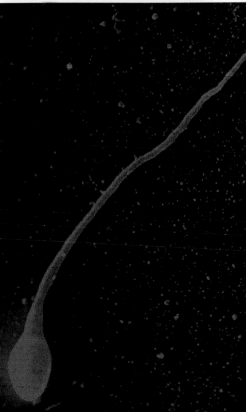

Figure 20–3 *Chromosomes are thick rodlike structures that are responsible for passing on inherited characteristics. The photograph shows the size, number, and pairs of chromosomes for a human body cell. How many chromosomes are in each human body cell?*

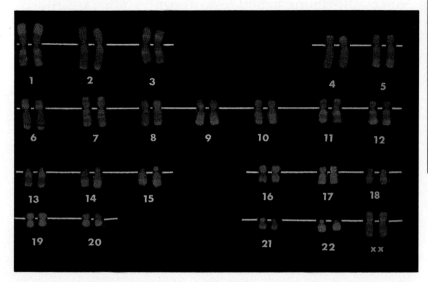

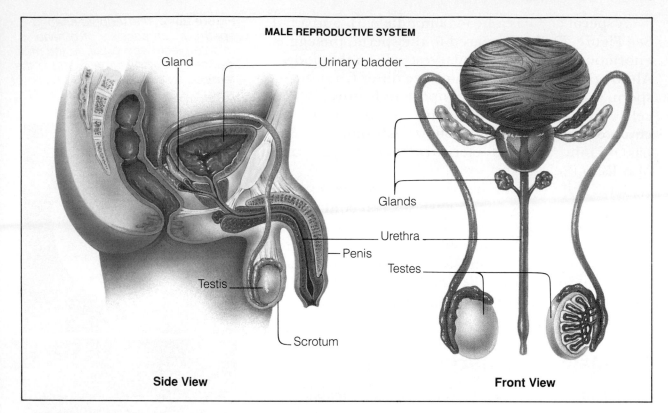

MALE REPRODUCTIVE SYSTEM

Gland

Urinary bladder

Glands

Urethra

Penis

Testes

Testis

Scrotum

Side View

Front View

Figure 20–4 *In the male reproductive system, sperm and the hormone testosterone are produced within two oval-shaped organs called the testes. Sperm travel from the testes through tubes to the urethra. What is the function of testosterone?*

many small tubes to a larger tube called the urethra (yoo-REE-thruh). As you learned in Chapter 18, the urethra is also the tube through which urine leaves the body. The urethra runs through an organ called the penis. Sperm is transferred to a female's body through the penis.

In addition to producing sperm, the testes produce a hormone called testosterone (tehs-TAHS-tuh-rohn). Testosterone is responsible for the growth of facial and body hair, broadening of the shoulders, and deepening of the voice in males.

The Female Reproductive System

Unlike the male reproductive system, all the parts of the female reproductive system are within the female's body. Two structures called **ovaries** (OH-vuh-reez) are located at about hip level, one on each side of a female's body. The almond-shaped ovaries produce the eggs. Like the testes, the ovaries produce hormones. One of these hormones, called estrogen, triggers the broadening of the hips in females. Estrogen also starts the maturation of egg cells in the ovaries.

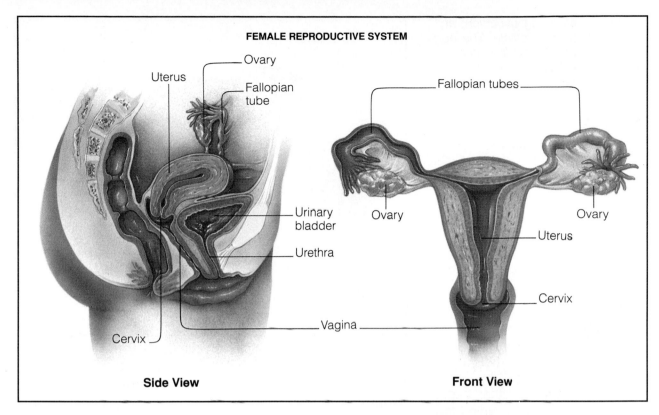

FEMALE REPRODUCTIVE SYSTEM

Uterus

Ovary

Fallopian tube

Urinary bladder

Urethra

Cervix

Vagina

Side View

Fallopian tubes

Ovary

Ovary

Uterus

Cervix

Front View

Figure 20–5 *In the female reproductive system, the ovaries produce eggs and hormones. From an ovary, an egg travels through a Fallopian tube to the uterus. What is another name for a Fallopian tube? For the uterus?*

Located near each ovary, but not directly connected to it, is a **Fallopian** (fuh-LOH-pee-uhn) **tube.** An egg travels through this tube from the ovary. Another name for a Fallopian tube is an oviduct.

At the end of the Fallopian tube, the egg reaches a hollow, muscular organ called the **uterus** (YOOT-uhr-uhs), or womb. The uterus is a pear-shaped structure in which the early development of a baby takes place. At the lower end of the uterus is a narrow section called the cervix (SER-vihks). The cervix opens into a wider channel called the vagina (vuh-JIGH-nuh), or birth canal. The vagina is the canal through which the baby passes during birth.

The Menstrual Cycle

The monthly cycle of change that occurs in the female reproductive system is called the **menstrual** (MEHN-struhl) **cycle.** The average length of this cycle for many females is about 28 days, or almost a month. In fact, the word *menstrual* comes from the Latin word for *month*. During the menstrual cycle, an egg develops in an ovary. The mature egg is released into a Fallopian tube. This process is called **ovulation.**

519

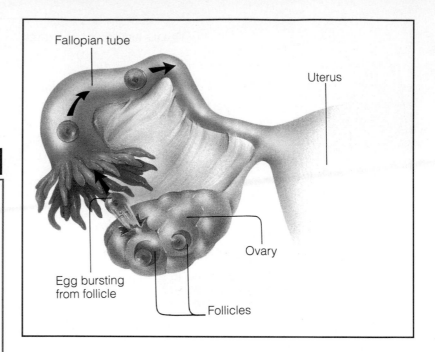

Figure 20–6 *During ovulation, an egg bursts from a follicle. The egg is then swept into the feathery tunnel-shaped opening of a Fallopian tube.*

Labels: Fallopian tube, Uterus, Ovary, Egg bursting from follicle, Follicles

ACTIVITY

Jelly-Bean Chromosomes

1. Obtain 5 paper cups and a package of jelly beans.

2. Put 2 different-colored pairs of jelly beans (a total of 4 different-colored jelly beans) in a paper cup.

3. Add 4 more identically colored jelly beans to the same cup.

4. Divide the 8 jelly beans evenly between 2 other cups, so that each cup contains the same number of each color jelly bean.

5. Divide the contents of the 2 cups evenly so that you have 4 cups that each contain 1 of each color jelly bean.

How do the number of jelly beans that were placed in the original cup relate to the number of jelly beans found in the last 4 cups?

■ What do you think each cup represents?

■ This process is sometimes called reduction division. Explain why.

An egg meets a sperm and is fertilized in the Fallopian tube. During this time, not only are changes occurring in the ovary, but also in the uterus. For example, during most of the menstrual cycle, the lining of the uterus thickens. The lining is being prepared for a fertilized egg. If a fertilized egg reaches this lining, the egg attaches to the lining. There the egg grows and develops into a baby.

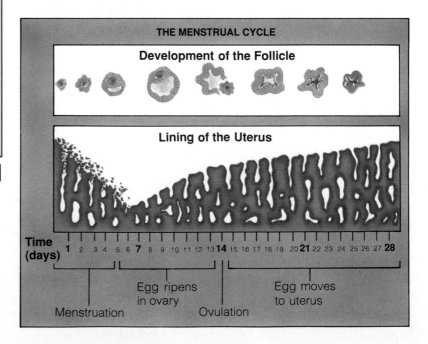

THE MENSTRUAL CYCLE

Development of the Follicle

Lining of the Uterus

Time (days) 1 2 3 4 5 6 **7** 8 9 10 11 12 13 **14** 15 16 17 18 19 20 **21** 22 23 24 25 26 27 **28**

Menstruation — Egg ripens in ovary — Ovulation — Egg moves to uterus

Figure 20–7 *The monthly cycle of change that occurs in the female reproductive system is called the menstrual cycle. It consists of a complex series of events that occur in a periodic fashion. What events take place during menstruation?*

If the egg is not fertilized, both the egg and the lining of the uterus break down. The blood and tissue from the thickened lining of the uterus pass out of the body through the vagina. This process is called **menstruation** (mehn-STRAY-shuhn). On the average, menstruation lasts for five days. At the same time that menstruation occurs, a new egg is maturing in the ovary and the cycle continues.

An egg can only be fertilized during the short time of ovulation. In many females, ovulation usually occurs about 14 days after the start of menstruation. After the egg is released into the Fallopian tube, the egg takes about one or two days to make its way along the tube to the uterus. Only if sperm are present at this time, can the egg be fertilized.

20–1 Section Review

1. What are the structures and functions of the male and female reproductive systems?
2. What is fertilization?
3. Describe the menstrual cycle.

Critical Thinking—*Relating Facts*
4. A Fallopian tube is lined with mucus. How does this contribute to the function of the tube?

CAREERS

School Social Worker

School social workers must be objective, sensitive, and emotionally mature in order to advise and counsel students. In many states it is necessary to become licensed, or registered. This certification requires work experience and an examination. If you are interested in a career in social work, write to the National Association of Social Workers, Inc., 7981 Eastern Avenue, Silver Spring, MD 20910.

20–2 Stages of Development

Almost immediately after a **zygote,** or fertilized egg, is formed, a new human being begins to develop. The zygote divides into two cells. Then each of these cells divides again and again, and so on. Change and growth continue for approximately nine months or 280 days until birth. This time between fertilization and birth is called pregnancy.

Human beings go through various stages of development before and after birth. **Before birth, a single human cell develops into an embryo and then a fetus. After birth, humans pass through the stages of infancy, childhood, and adolescence to adulthood.**

Guide for Reading

Focus on these questions as you read.

▶ *What are the stages of human development that occur before birth?*

▶ *What are the stages of human development that occur after birth?*

ACTIVITY

DISCOVERING

Multiple Births

A multiple birth occurs when two or more children are born at one time to one mother. Using reference materials in the library, look up information on twins. In a written report, describe how twins develop. Include diagrams in your explanation.

■ What is the difference in origin and appearance between identical and fraternal twins?

Figure 20–8 *The placenta provides a connection between the mother and the developing baby. Through blood vessels in the umbilical cord, food and oxygen from the mother and wastes from the developing baby are exchanged. What is the function of the amniotic sac?*

Development Before Birth

As the zygote first begins to divide, the cells remain close together and give the appearance of a bunch of berries. By the time this berry-shaped group of cells reaches the uterus, the cells have divided a few more times and look like a hollow ball of cells. During this early stage of development, and for the next eight weeks or so, the newly formed organism is called an **embryo** (EHM-bree-oh).

Once the embryo enters the uterus, it attaches itself to the wall of the uterus. In the uterus, several membranes form around the embryo. A clear membrane called the amnion forms a fluid-filled sac. This **amniotic sac** cushions and protects the developing baby. Another membrane forms the **placenta** (pluh-SEHN-tuh). The placenta is made partly from tissue that develops from the embryo and partly from tissue that makes up the wall of the uterus.

The placenta is a kind of transfer station between the embryo and its mother. Both mother and embryo have separate circulatory systems and separate blood supplies. However, oxygen obtained by the mother's lungs and food from her digestive system pass through the placenta to the embryo.

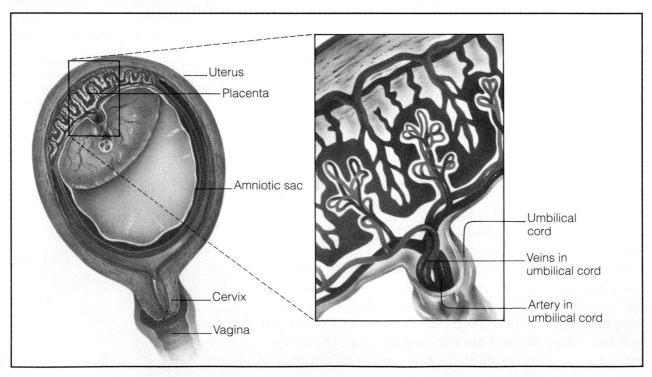

Uterus
Placenta
Amniotic sac
Cervix
Vagina

Umbilical cord
Veins in umbilical cord
Artery in umbilical cord

Wastes pass out of the embryo through the placenta and are eliminated by the mother. An embryo is connected to the placenta by a cord called an **umbilical** (uhm-BIHL-ih-kuhl) **cord.** The umbilical cord contains blood vessels that transport food, oxygen, and wastes back and forth between the embryo and the placenta.

After eight weeks, the embryo is called a **fetus** (FEET-uhs). A fetus has developed eyes, ears, cheeks, arms, and legs. After three months, it is easy to identify the fetus as a male or a female. During months six through nine, the fetus grows rapidly.

In recent years, methods have been developed that allow doctors to study and even treat fetuses before they are born. One of these methods consists of drawing off a small amount of the fluid in which the fetus floats. The fluid contains cells from the fetus that can be studied to determine its health, as well as many of its inherited characteristics. In another process, sound waves that produce an image on a television screen are sent through the uterus of the mother. This procedure gives a detailed, moving image of the fetus. See Figure 20–9. Sound pictures have been used to safely diagnose and treat fetuses with medical problems before they are born.

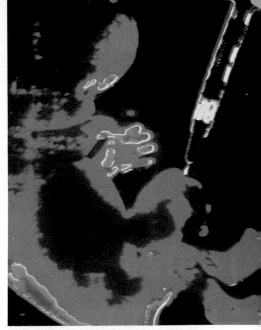

Figure 20–9 *In this photograph you can see a needle removing a small amount of fluid from the amniotic sac. This sac contains cells from the fetus that will be examined to determine the health of the fetus.*

Birth

After about nine months of development and growth inside the uterus, a baby is ready to be born. Strong muscular contractions of the uterus begin to push the baby out of the uterus into the vagina. This process is called labor. As labor progresses, the contractions of the uterus become stronger and occur more frequently. Eventually the baby, still connected to the placenta by the umbilical cord, is forced out of the mother.

Development After Birth

Within a few seconds after birth, a baby begins to cry. This action helps its lungs to expand and fill with air. The umbilical cord, which is still attached to the placenta, is cut close to the baby's body. This does not cause any pain to the baby. When the cut heals, it forms a scar. You know this scar as your navel. What is a common nickname for the navel?

Figure 20–10 *After about 9 months of growth and development inside the uterus, a baby is born. This baby is only minutes old. What are the names of the three stages in the birth process?*

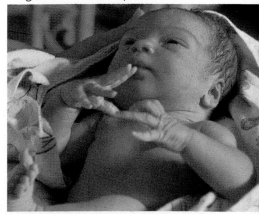

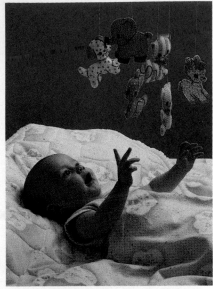

Figure 20–11 *During infancy, which extends from about 1 month to 2 years, mental and muscular skills begin to develop. What skills are illustrated by the 5-month-old (top) and the 1-year-old (bottom)?*

INFANCY Have you ever watched a six-month-old infant for a few minutes? Its actions, or responses, are very simple. An infant can suck its thumb, grasp objects, yawn, stretch, blink, and sneeze. When lying in bed, an infant often curls up in a position much like the one it had in the uterus.

One of the most obvious changes during **infancy,** which extends from 1 month to about 2 years of age, is a rapid increase in size. The heads of young babies are very large in proportion to their bodies. As the infant gets older, the head grows more slowly and the body, legs, and arms begin to catch up.

Mental and muscular skills begin to develop in a fairly predictable order. However, the exact ages at which they occur vary from baby to baby. A newborn infant cannot even lift its own head. After about three months, it can hold its head up and can also reach for objects. In about two more months, the infant can grasp objects. At about seven months, most infants are able to move around by crawling. Somewhere between 10 and 14 months, most infants begin to walk by themselves.

CHILDHOOD Infancy ends and **childhood** begins around the age of 2 years. Childhood continues until the age of 13 years. During childhood, mental abilities increase. Memory is strengthened. Muscular skills develop. With practice, a small child becomes better and better at walking, holding a knife and fork, writing with a pencil, or playing sports. Over a period of several years, baby teeth are lost and replaced by permanent teeth.

Little by little, young children develop language skills. All babies make basically the same babbling sounds. Then, as a child becomes aware of itself and others, these sounds are shaped into language. Language skills come from observing and imitating others. At first, a child uses only one word at a time, such as "ball." Soon the child uses an action word and produces a two-word sentence, for example, "hit ball." By the age of four or five, the child is able to hold an adultlike conversation.

Figure 20–12 *Childhood begins around the age of 2 years and continues until the age of 13 years. In addition to understanding and speaking a language, children can be taught to read before they attend school (top). Children also learn to interact socially with others, as these 8- to 11-year-olds are doing (bottom).*

In addition to understanding and speaking a language, children can be taught to read and solve problems even before they attend school. During childhood, children learn a great deal about their environment. They also learn to behave in socially appropriate ways.

ADOLESCENCE In many cultures, **adolescence** is thought of as a passage from childhood to adulthood. The word adolescence comes from a latin word that means "growing up." Adolescence begins after the thirteenth year and continues through the teenage years. The beginning of adolescence is called **puberty** (PYOO-buhr-tee). During puberty, the sex organs develop rapidly. Menstruation begins in girls and the production of sperm begins in boys.

In addition, a growth spurt also occurs during adolescence. A growth spurt is a sudden increase in height and weight. In females, this rapid growth occurs between the ages of 10 and 16. During these years, females may grow about 15 centimeters in

Figure 20–13 *In many cultures, adolescence is seen as a passage from childhood to adulthood. In this ceremony, a 14-year-old Apache girl is sprinkled with cattail pollen by members of her tribe to signify this passage. In Austin, Texas, teenagers socialize at a dance.*

Figure 20–14 *By the time people reach adulthood, all their body systems have become fully matured.*

ACTIVITY

DOING

Reaching for the Heights

1. To find out the range of heights for your age group, make a chart of as many of your friends' heights as you can.

2. Then construct a graph of your findings. Mark off the number of friends of each height on the vertical portion of the graph. On the horizontal portion of the graph, mark off the heights in centimeters.

What was the height of most of your friends?

Do you think that you would have similar results if you were to do a graph for your friends' shoe sizes?

height and gain about 16 kilograms or more. In males, the growth spurt occurs between the ages of 11 and 17. During this time, males may grow about 20 centimeters and gain 20 kilograms or more.

ADULTHOOD At about the age of 20, **adulthood** begins. All body systems, including the reproductive system, have become fully matured and full height has been reached. As a human being passes from infancy through adulthood, fat beneath the skin keeps moving farther and farther away from the surface. The round, padded, button-nosed face of the baby is slowly replaced by the leaner, more defined face of the adult. The nose and the ears continue to grow and take on a more individual shape.

After about 30 years, a process known as aging begins. This process becomes more noticeable between the ages of 40 and 65. At this time, the skin loses some of its elasticity, the hair sometimes loses its coloring, and muscle strength decreases. During this period, females go through a physical change known as menopause. After menopause, menstruation stops and ovulation no longer occurs. As men age, they may become bald. After age 65, the aging process continues, often leading to less efficient heart and lung action. But the effects of aging can be lessened if a person follows a good diet and exercise plan throughout life.

20–2 Section Review

1. What stages of development does a human go through before birth?
2. What stages of development does a human go through after birth?
3. What is a developing baby called during the first 8 weeks of development? After the first 8 weeks?
4. What is the function of the amniotic sac? The placenta?
5. What is puberty?

Connection—*Medicine*
6. Why is it important for pregnant women to have good health practices?

Electronic Reproduction

Have you ever wondered what it would be like to have several exact copies of yourself? One could go to class and do homework. One could do chores at home. One could spend the day playing—or perhaps you would let the real you do that. Well, dream on. By now, you know how complex the process of human reproduction really is and that there is only one "you" in the world. There will never be another.

Fortunately, the same is not true for photographs, illustrations, or the printed word. For today, modern photocopying machines can print out exact copies at the rate of hundreds per minute. Hundreds of copies per minute—now that's reproduction!

sheet of paper you want to copy on the machine, light shines onto it. The blank parts of the paper reflect the light and the light strikes the circular drum. Wherever the light strikes, the charge on the drum is removed. The dark parts of the paper (either words or visuals) do not reflect the light onto the drum. So the drum has parts that are charged and parts that have had the charge removed. When, in the next step, a liquid known as toner is introduced onto the drum, the toner is attracted to the charged parts only. The parts of the drum that are not charged do not attract toner. In seconds, the toner is laid down and an image is created on the photocopying machine paper.

You might be surprised to learn that photocopying machines do not use ink. They rely instead on *electricity,* or the flow of charged particles called electrons. Inside the photocopy machine is a circular drum. The drum is charged with static electricity and is coated with a material that conducts electricity when exposed to light.

Let's say you want to make a copy of a page of this textbook. When you place the

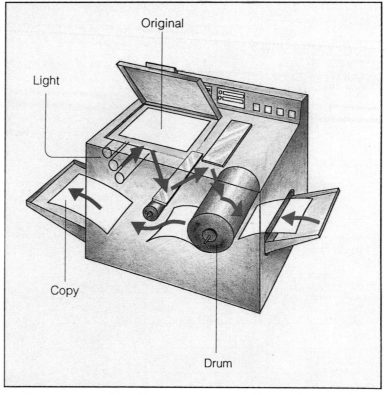

Original

Light

Copy

Drum

Laboratory Investigation

How Many Offspring?

Problem

How do the length of gestation, number of offspring per birth, age of puberty, and life span of various mammals compare?

Materials *(per group)*

graph paper
colored pencils

Procedure

1. Study the chart, which shows the length of gestation (pregnancy), the average number of offspring per birth, the average age of puberty, and the average life span of certain mammals.

2. Construct a bar graph that shows the length of gestation for each mammal.

3. Construct another bar graph that shows the average number of offspring of each mammal.

4. Construct a third bar graph that shows the life span of each mammal. Color the portion of the bar that shows the length of childhood, or time from birth to puberty.

Observations

1. Which of the mammals has the longest gestation period?

2. Which mammal has the largest number of offspring per birth?

3. Which of the mammals has the shortest life span?

4. Which mammal takes longer to reach puberty than Rhesus monkeys?

Analysis and Conclusions

1. What general conclusions can you draw after studying the graphs you have made?

2. If a mouse produces five litters per year, how many mice does the average female mouse produce in a lifetime?

3. Of all the mammals listed, which care for their young for the longest period of time after birth? Why do you think this is the case?

4. **On Your Own** Gather the same kinds of data for five additional mammals. Add these data to your existing graphs. How do the five new mammals compare with those provided in this investigation?

Mammal	Gestation Period (days)	Number of Offspring per Birth	Age at Puberty	Life Span (years)
Opossum	12	13	8 months	2
House mouse	20	6	2 months	3
Rabbit	30	4	4 months	5
Dog	61	7	7 months	15
Lion	108	3	2 years	23
Rhesus monkey	175	1	3 years	20
Human	280	1	13 years	74
Horse	330	1	1.5 years	25

Study Guide

Summarizing Key Concepts

20–1 The Reproductive System

▲ The joining of a sperm, or male sex cell, and an egg, or female sex cell, is known as fertilization.

▲ Each sperm and egg contains 23 chromosomes, which pass on inherited characteristics from one generation of cells to the next.

▲ The male reproductive system includes two testes, which produce sperm and a hormone called testosterone. The female reproductive system includes two ovaries, which produce eggs and hormones.

▲ Located near each ovary is a Fallopian tube that leads to a hollow, muscular uterus. At the lower end of the uterus is a narrow cervix, which opens into the vagina, or birth canal.

▲ The monthly cycle of change that occurs in the female reproductive system is called the menstrual cycle.

▲ During the menstrual cycle, ovulation, or the release of an egg from an ovary, occurs. The lining of the uterus also thickens in preparation for the attachment of a fertilized egg. If fertilization does not take place, the egg and thickened lining of the uterus break down and pass out of the body. This process is called menstruation. If sperm are present in the Fallopian tube at the time of ovulation, an egg may become fertilized.

20–2 Stages of Development

▲ A fertilized egg is called a zygote. A zygote undergoes a series of divisions, forming a ball-shaped structure of many cells.

▲ During the first 8 weeks of its development, the developing human is called an embryo. It is surrounded and protected by several membranes. One of these membranes, called the placenta, provides the embryo with food and oxygen and eliminates its wastes. Another membrane forms around the fluid-filled amniotic sac, which cushions and protects the embryo.

▲ The umbilical cord, which contains blood vessels, connects the fetus to the placenta.

▲ During the birth process, the baby and placenta pass out of the uterus through the cervix into the vagina.

▲ Humans pass through various stages of development during their lives. These stages are infancy, childhood, adolescence, and adulthood. Adolescence begins at puberty, when the sex organs develop rapidly.

Reviewing Key Terms

Define each term in a complete sentence.

20–1 The Reproductive System
reproduction
sperm
egg
fertilization
testis
ovary
Fallopian tube

uterus
menstrual cycle
ovulation
menstruation

20–2 Stages of Development
zygote
embryo

amniotic sac
placenta
umbilical cord
fetus
infancy
childhood
adolescence
puberty
adulthood

Chapter Review

Content Review

Multiple Choice

Choose the letter of the answer that best completes each statement.

1. What is the female sex cell called?
   a. testis   c. egg
   b. sperm   d. ovary
2. Sperm are produced in male sex organs called
   a. testes.   c. scrotums.
   b. ovaries.   d. urethras.
3. Sperm leave the male's body through the
   a. testes.   c. vagina.
   b. scrotum.   d. penis.
4. Eggs are produced in the
   a. scrotum.   c. cervix.
   b. ovaries.   d. Fallopian tubes.
5. A structure made up of tissues from both the embryo and the uterus is the
   a. ovum.   c. cervix.
   b. placenta.   d. fetus.

6. Another name for the womb is the
   a. Fallopian tube.   c. vagina.
   b. uterus.   d. scrotum.
7. The release of an egg from the ovary is known as
   a. ovulation.   c. menstruation.
   b. fertilization.   d. urination.
8. The structure in which a fertilized egg first divides is the
   a. ovary.   c. uterus.
   b. Fallopian tube.   d. vagina.
9. Sex organs develop rapidly during
   a. infancy.   c. puberty.
   b. childhood.   d. adulthood.
10. Adulthood begins at about the age of
    a. 13 years.   c. 20 years.
    b. 1 year.   d. 30 years.

True or False

If the statement is true, write "true." If it is false, change the underlined word or words to make the statement true.

1. The joining of a sperm and an egg is called <u>fertilization</u>.
2. The testes are found inside a sac called the <u>scrotum</u>.
3. To reach the uterus, an egg travels through the <u>cervix</u>.
4. An egg can be fertilized only while it is in a <u>Fallopian tube</u>.
5. If an egg is not fertilized, the lining of the uterus leaves the body through the <u>urethra</u>.
6. The structure that connects the embryo to the placenta is the <u>uterus</u>.
7. At 2 years of age, a person is considered to be an <u>infant</u>.

Concept Mapping

Complete the following concept map for Section 20–1. Then construct a concept map for the entire chapter.

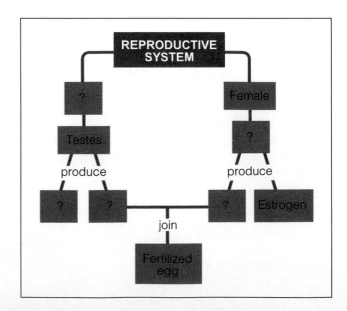

Concept Mastery

Discuss each of the following in a brief paragraph.

1. What changes occur in the female reproductive system during the menstrual cycle?
2. Describe how a fetus receives food and oxygen and how it gets rid of wastes.
3. How does a zygote form?
4. Describe the birth process.
5. Describe one method that is used by doctors to study babies while they are in the uterus.
6. Summarize the four stages of human development after birth.
7. Why is the process of reproduction so important?

Critical Thinking and Problem Solving

Use the skills you have developed in this chapter to answer each of the following.

1. **Making comparisons** In what way is development during adolescence similar to development before birth?
2. **Relating cause and effect** Why is it dangerous for pregnant women to smoke, drink, or use drugs not prescribed by a doctor?
3. **Relating facts** Why do you think the first stage in the birth process is called labor?
4. **Making inferences** The word adolescence means to grow up. Why is adolescence a good name for the teenage years of life?
5. **Applying concepts** Explain why a proper diet and an adequate amount of exercise can lessen the effects of aging.
6. **Drawing conclusions** Why do broken bones heal more rapidly in young children than in elderly people?
7. **Making comparisons** In what way is amniotic fluid similar to the shock absorbers of a car?
8. **Making predictions** Explain how a child's environment can affect its development.
9. **Relating facts** Explain how the shape of a sperm helps it function.
10. **Relating concepts** Why do you think a 1- to 2-year-old child is called a toddler?

11. **Making graphs** Use the information in the table to construct a graph. What conclusions can you draw from the graph?

Age Group in Years	Average Height in Centimeters	
	Female	*Male*
At birth	50	51
2	87	88
4	103	104
6	117	118
8	128	128
10	139	139
12	152	149
14	160	162
16	163	172
18	163	174

12. **Using the writing process** Develop an advertising campaign highlighting the dangers of alcohol and drug use during pregnancy.

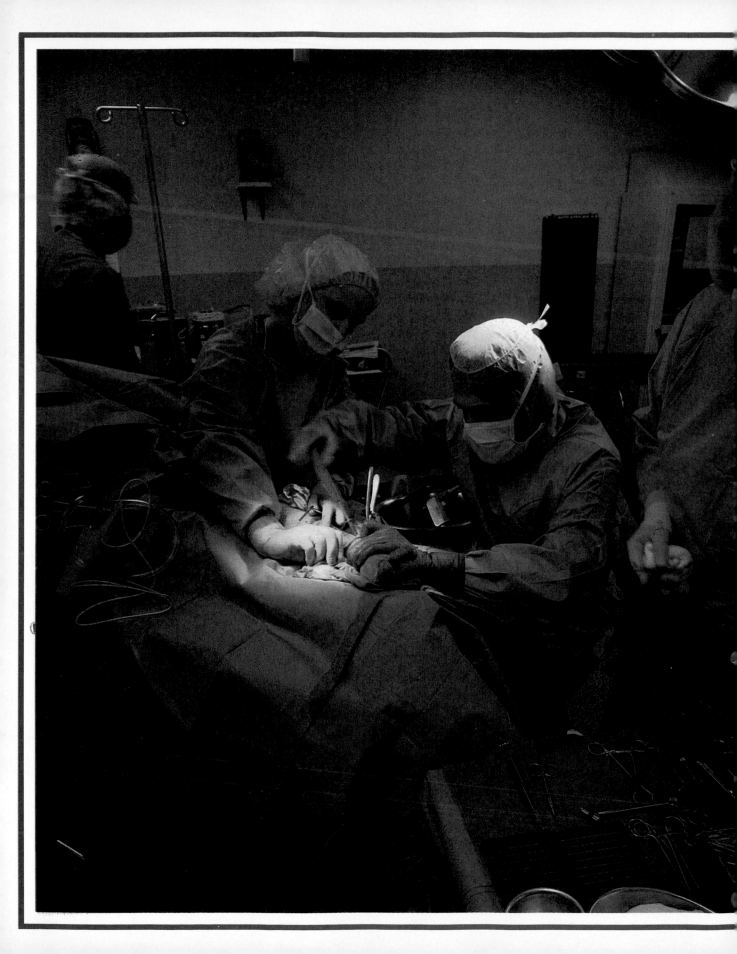

Immune System

21

Guide for Reading

After you read the following sections, you will be able to

21–1 Body Defenses

- Describe the function of the immune system.
- Describe the body's three lines of defense against invading organisms.
- Define antibody and antigen.

21–2 Immunity

- Define immunity.
- Compare active and passive immunity.
- Describe how vaccines work.

21–3 Diseases

- Describe how diseases spread.
- List some examples of infectious and noninfectious diseases.

The scene: a dimly lit room. Occupying the middle of the room is a rectangular table covered with large soiled cloths. A patient ready for surgery lies on the table. The operation is about to begin.

But wait! Why is the patient lying on dirty cloths? Why are the surgeons wiping their hands (and on soiled cloths!) instead of washing them? Is this a scene from a horror movie?

What you are reading about actually occurred in hospital operating rooms before the middle of the 1800s. Fortunately, such scenes no longer take place. And we have the work of the English surgeon Joseph Lister to thank for that! In 1865, Lister demonstrated that microorganisms were the cause of many deaths after surgery. Thus Lister reasoned that if the microorganisms could be kept away from surgical wounds many more patients would survive surgery.

Today, surgeons wash thoroughly before an operation and wear surgical gowns, masks, and gloves. And operating rooms are kept spotlessly clean and free of germs. As you read the pages that follow, you will learn some interesting things about microorganisms and disease. And you may even make a discovery as important as Lister's!

Journal *Activity*

You and Your World Have you ever had a sore throat? How about an upset stomach? A fever? How did you feel? What did you do? In your journal, explore your thoughts and feelings during these times.

◄ *Today, operations are performed in spotlessly clean operating rooms by surgical teams wearing gowns, gloves, and masks.*

ctivity Bank

It's No Skin Off Your Nose, p. 826

Figure 21–1 *Every minute of every day fierce battles are fought within your body. The invaders in these battles—such as influenza viruses (left) and the flatworm that causes the disease known as schistosomiasis (right)—are incredibly tiny. What body system defends against disease-causing organisms?*

21–1 Body Defenses

Considering the number of entries that invaders can successfully make into the body, it is amazing that a disease rarely occurs. Amazing, but no accident. Almost every human has a body system that works 24 hours a day all over the body to ensure its health. This body system is the immune system. **The immune system is the body's defense against disease-causing organisms.** The immune system not only repels disease-causing organisms, it also "keeps house" inside the body. It does this by removing dead or damaged cells and by looking for and destroying cells that do not function as they should.

The immune system has the remarkable ability to distinguish friend from foe. It identifies and destroys invaders and, at the same time, recognizes the body's own tissues. How does the immune system do all this? If you continue reading, you will find the answer.

The Body's First Line of Defense

Your body has certain important structures that help the immune system, although they are not actually part of it. Most invaders must first encounter these structures. These structures make up your body's first line of defense, forming a barrier between the body and its surroundings. The skin and the substances it produces, as well as protective reflexes such as sneezing and coughing, make up the first line of defense.

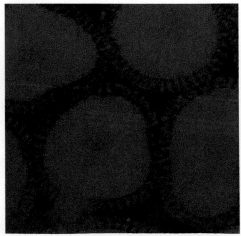
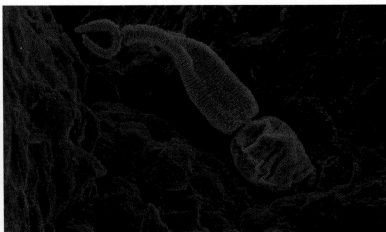

As you may recall from Chapter 18, the skin forms a protective covering over most of the body. This extraordinary organ has the ability to produce new cells and repair itself. Despite its daily dose of ripping, scratching, burning, and exposure to harsh chemicals and weather, the skin still performs admirably. It continues to produce new cells in its outer layer (epidermis) and repair tears in its inner layer (dermis). When cuts occur in the skin, however, they provide a means of entry for disease-causing organisms. What results is an infection, or a successful invasion into the body by disease-causing organisms.

Not all disease-causing organisms enter the body through the skin, however. Some are inhaled from the air. In much the same way as the skin defends the entire body against invaders, mucus (MYOO-kuhs) and cilia (SIHL-ee-uh) defend the respiratory system against airborne organisms. Mucus is a sticky substance that coats the membranes of the nose, trachea, and bronchi (parts of the respiratory system). As organisms enter these structures along with incoming air, they are trapped by the mucus and are thus prevented from traveling any farther into the body. In addition to mucus, the membranes are lined with tiny hairlike structures called cilia. The cilia, acting like brooms, sweep bacteria, dirt, and excess mucus out of the air passages at an amazing rate—about 2.5 centimeters a minute! These unwanted materials are carried to the throat, where they can be coughed out or swallowed.

Sometimes disease-causing organisms enter the body through the mouth, rather than through the skin or the nose. Here they mix with saliva, which is loaded with invader-killing chemicals. Most invaders do not survive the action of these chemicals. Those that do soon find themselves encountering a powerful acid in the stomach. This acid is so strong that it destroys the invaders. The dead invaders are eliminated from the body along with the body's other wastes.

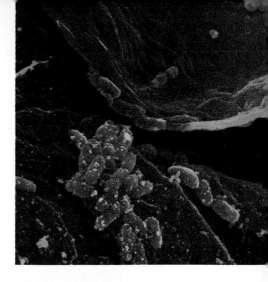

Figure 21–2 *The green objects in this photograph of the surface of the skin are bacteria. The skin is one of the body's first lines of defense against invading organisms.*

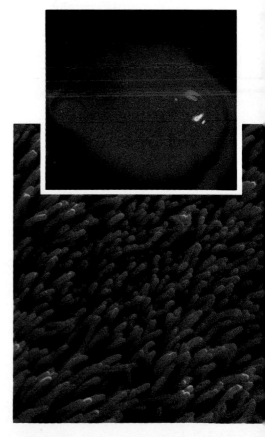

Figure 21–3 *As disease-causing organisms invade the body through the respiratory system, they are trapped by excess mucus that coats the membranes of the bronchus (top). The membranes are also lined with hairlike cilia that sweep the organisms out of the respiratory system (bottom).*

ACTIVITY
WRITING

*Antiseptics
and Disinfectants*

Find out the following information about antiseptics and disinfectants by using reference materials in the library. What is the function of these substances? How do they help to control disease? What are three examples of each substance? Arrange this information in the form of a written report. Include the work of Joseph Lister and any other scientists who contributed to the discovery of these substances.

The Body's Second Line of Defense

If the first line of defense fails and disease-causing organisms enter the body, the second line of defense goes into action. When disease-causing organisms such as bacteria enter through a cut in the skin, they immediately try to attack body cells. The body, however, is quick to respond by increasing the blood supply to the affected area. This action causes white blood cells, which constantly patrol the blood and defend the body against disease-causing organisms, to leave the blood vessels and move into nearby tissues. Once inside, some of the white blood cells—the tiny ones—attack the invading organisms and then gobble them up.

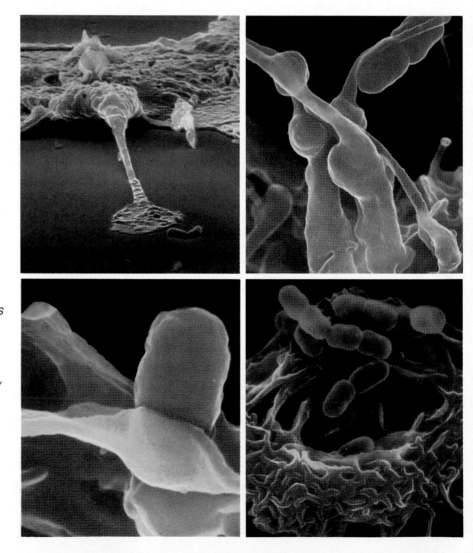

Figure 21–4 *White blood cells make up the body's second line of defense. This sequence of photographs shows what happens when a white blood cell encounters bacteria. The white blood cell first reaches out toward two bacterial cells (top left). Extensions from the white blood cell trap the bacteria (top right). Chemicals produced by the white blood cells begin to digest one of the bacterial cells (bottom left). Eventually, the bacteria will be digested and the material of which they are made will be absorbed by the white blood cells (bottom right).*

Soon after, the tiny white blood cells are joined by reinforcements—larger white blood cells. The larger white blood cells, which are similar to the heavy artillery used by an attacking army, destroy almost all bacteria they attack. In time, the area resembles a battlefield. Dead bacteria and the dead and wounded white blood cells are everywhere. Taken together, these events form the body's second line of defense—the **inflammatory** (ihn-FLAM-uh-tor-ee) **response.** Sometimes an infection (a successful invasion into the body by disease-causing organisms) causes a red, swollen area to develop just below the skin's surface. If you were to touch the infected area, you would discover that it is hotter than the surrounding skin area. For this reason, the area is said to be inflamed, which actually means "on fire."

In addition to the inflammatory response, the body has another second line of defense called **interferon.** Interferon is a substance produced by body cells when they are attacked by viruses. Interferon "interferes" with the reproduction of new viruses. As a result, the rate at which body cells are infected is slowed down. Other lines of defense have the time to move in and destroy the viruses.

Figure 21–5 *Although having a fever is no fun, there is a good reason for it. A fever, if mild and short-lived, helps the body fight disease-causing organisms.*

The Third Line of Defense

Although most disease-causing invaders are stopped by the body's first and second lines of defense, a few invaders are able to make it past them. If this happens, it is time for the body's third line of defense—the **antibodies**—to go to work. Antibodies are proteins produced by the immune system. Some antibodies are attached to certain kinds of white blood cells. Others are found floating freely in the blood. But regardless of their type, all antibodies are responsible for destroying harmful invaders.

Unlike the body's first two lines of defense, which you just read about, antibodies are very specific—they attack only a particular kind of invader. Thus, they can be thought of as the body's guided missiles, zeroing in on and destroying a particular target. The invading organism or substance that triggers the action of an antibody is called an **antigen**. The word antigen is derived from the term *anti*body *gen*erator, which means producer of antibodies.

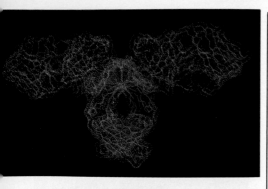

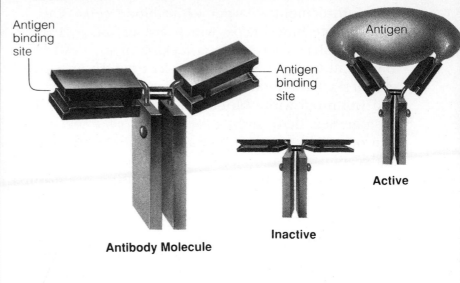

Antigen binding site

Antigen binding site

Antigen

Active

Inactive

Antibody Molecule

Figure 21–6 *Antibodies, such as the one in the computer-generated photograph, are proteins produced by the immune system. As the diagram illustrates, an antibody particle has two identical antigen-binding sites. What happens to the shape of an antibody particle when it encounters its specific antigen?*

What does an antibody look like? If you look at Figure 21–6, you can get a pretty good idea. Notice that the shape of an antibody is much like the letter T. When an antibody encounters its specific antigen, it changes shape—converting from a T shape to a Y shape. This action activates the antibody so that the two arms of the Y attach and bind to the antigen. In this way, an antibody prevents invaders such as viruses from attaching to cells.

When antibodies attach to surfaces of antigens such as bacteria, fungi, and protozoans, they slow down these organisms so that they can be gobbled up by white blood cells. Some antibodies may even destroy invaders by blasting a hole in the outer covering of the invaders' cells.

How does the immune system produce specific antibodies? How do the antibodies bind to antigens? The answers involve special white blood cells called T-cells and B-cells. (The T in T-cells stands for thymus, which is where T-cells originate; the B in B-cells refers to the bone marrow, which is where B-cells mature.) The function of T-cells is to alert B-cells to produce antibodies. If this is the first time the body is invaded by a particular antigen, it may take the B-cells a longer time to produce antibodies. During

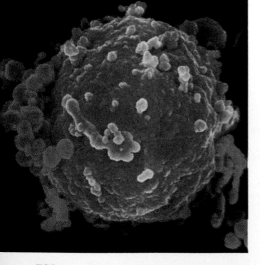

Figure 21–7 *This photograph shows a B-cell covered with bacteria. B-cells produce antibodies that attack particular kinds of invaders. What are these invaders called?*

this time, the person is experiencing the symptoms, or physical signs, of the disease. In other words, the person feels sick. Eventually, the B-cells begin to produce antibodies. The antibodies then join with the invading antigens much as the pieces of a jigsaw puzzle join together. Once joined to the invaders, the antibodies are able to destroy them. It is important to note that an antibody is specific for a certain antigen, and thus is not effective against any other antigens.

21–1 Section Review

1. What is the function of the immune system?
2. What are the body's three lines of defense against invading organisms?
3. What roles do B-cells and T-cells play in the immune system?

Critical Thinking—*Relating Concepts*
4. Explain why it is an advantage that the immune system produces antibodies specific for certain antigens rather than antibodies that work against any and all antigens.

21–2 Immunity

As you have just read, it takes time for your immune system to produce antibodies the first time a particular antigen enters your body. While your body is waiting for the immune system to make antibodies, you will, unfortunately, become ill. However, the next time the same antigen invades your body, your immune system may be ready for it. Your B-cells and T-cells, which are now familiar with the antigen, will be ready and waiting. In fact, they will produce antibodies so quickly that the disease will never even get a chance to develop. And what is more important, you will now have an **immunity** (ihm-MYOON-ih-tee) to that antigen. **Immunity is the resistance to a disease-causing organism or a harmful substance. There are two basic types of immunity: active immunity and passive immunity.**

ACTIVITY

WRITING

Vaccines

Using reference materials found in the library, make a list of five diseases that have been treated and controlled by the use of vaccines. What symptoms did these diseases produce? How and when was each vaccine developed?

Active Immunity

Suppose you come into contact with an antigen. Your immune system responds by producing antibodies against the invader. Because your own immune system is responding to the presence of an antigen, this type of immunity is called **active immunity**. The word active means you are doing the action. In this case, you are making the antibodies.

In order to gain active immunity, one of two things must occur—either you come down with the disease or you receive a **vaccination** (vak-sih-NAY-shuhn) for the disease. A vaccination is the process by which antigens are deliberately introduced into a person's body to stimulate the immune system. The antigens are usually developed from disease-causing organisms that have been killed or weakened in a laboratory. Now called a vaccine (vak-SEEN), the antigens alert the body's white blood cells to produce antibodies. Most vaccines are introduced into the body by an injection through the skin. You probably experienced this firsthand when you received your measles vaccination. Some other vaccines, such as the Sabin polio vaccine, are taken into the body through the mouth. In general, vaccines will not usually cause the symptoms of a disease to occur.

Figure 21–8 *There are two types of immunity: active and passive. This young boy is receiving a vaccine. Vaccines are made from disease-causing organisms that have been killed or weakened in a laboratory. Which type of immunity do you develop as a result of having a disease or receiving a vaccine?*

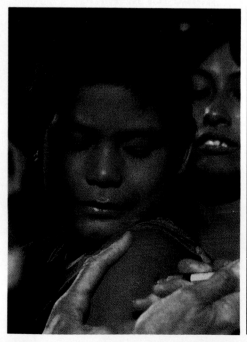

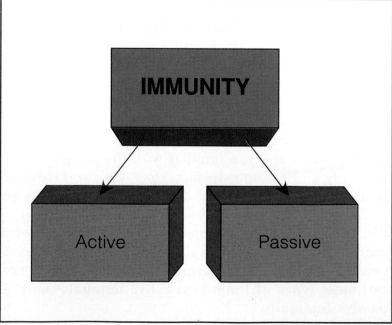

How long does active immunity last? There is no set answer to this question because the length of immunity to a disease (actually to the antigen that causes the disease) varies with the type of antigen. For example, an immunity to the common cold lasts only a few weeks, whereas an immunity to the chicken pox lasts for a person's lifetime. Even after receiving a vaccination, the body sometimes has to be reminded how to produce antibodies. In such a case, a booster shot has to be given. A booster shot, as its name implies, boosts (increases) the production of antibodies in the body. Diseases that require the use of booster shots include measles, German measles, poliomyelitis, mumps, whooping cough, diphtheria, and tetanus.

Passive Immunity

The way in which you receive **passive immunity**, the second type of immunity, is to get the antibodies from a source other than yourself. In other words, you are not actually producing the antibodies that protect you—another organism is. (You are not active; you are passive.) For example, passive immunity can be acquired by the transfer of antibodies from a mother to her unborn baby across the placenta. Following the baby's birth, the antibodies give protection to the baby during its first few months. Eventually, however, the mother's antibodies are eliminated by the baby, who must then rely on its own immune system to protect itself from disease.

A person can receive passive immunity in another way. If an animal such as a horse is vaccinated, its immune system will respond by producing antibodies. The antibodies can be removed from the animal and injected into a person's bloodstream. Unfortunately, this method gives the body only temporary immunity. Soon after these antibodies do their job (which is only about a few weeks), they are eliminated from the body.

Immune Disorders

As you have just read, the function of the immune system is to defend the body against invaders. Sometimes, however, the immune system

ACTIVITY
DISCOVERING

How Antibodies Work

1. On a sheet of white paper, trace two adjacent pieces of a jigsaw puzzle.

2. With scissors, cut out the drawings. **CAUTION:** *Be careful when using scissors.*

3. Repeat steps 1 and 2 using two other sets of adjacent pieces of the puzzle.

4. Mix up the six puzzle pieces. Place them on a flat surface. Label three pieces Antibody A, Antibody B, and Antibody C. Label the remaining puzzle pieces Antigen A, Antigen B, and Antigen C.

5. Now try to fit the matching pieces of the puzzle together.

Prepare a chart that shows which antibody fits together with which antigen. How are antibodies and antigens like the pieces of a puzzle?

■ Why do you think it is important that each antibody attaches to a specific antigen?

Figure 21–9 *Allergies result when the immune system is overly sensitive to certain substances called allergens. Examples of allergens are dust, which contains dust mites (top left); feathers (top right); pet hairs (bottom left); and pollen (bottom right).*

becomes overly sensitive to foreign substances or overdoes it by attacking its own tissues. In some instances, the immune system may be fooled by invaders that hide within its cells. Whatever the cause of the malfunction, the outcome is usually serious, as you will now discover.

ALLERGIES Achoo! Achoo! And so it begins. Another attack of hay fever. As you may already know, hay fever is neither a fever nor is it caused by hay. Hay fever is an **allergy** that is caused by ragweed pollen. An allergy results when the immune system is overly sensitive to certain substances called allergens (AL-er-jehnz). Allergens may be in the form of dust, feathers, animal hairs, pollens, or foods.

When an allergen such as pollen enters the body, the immune system reacts by producing antibodies. Unlike the antibodies that help to fight infection,

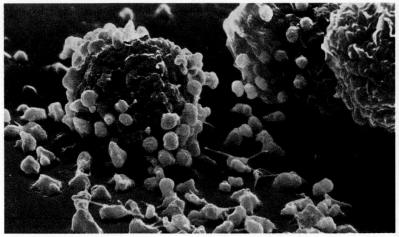

the antibodies that are produced by allergens release histamines (HIHS-tuh-meenz). Histamines are chemicals that are responsible for the symptoms of the allergy—that is, the itchy, watery eyes; the runny nose; the tickly throat; and the sneezing.

Although no complete cure for an allergy exists, people may be able to avoid allergy attacks by avoiding the allergen that causes them. This may involve removing from their diet the foods that contain the allergen or finding a new home for their pet. But if parting with a favorite food or a beloved pet is simply out of the question, then some relief may be obtained from antihistamines. As the name implies, antihistamines work against the effects of histamines.

AIDS *Acquired Immune Deficiency Syndrome,* or **AIDS,** is a very serious disease caused by a virus that hides out in healthy body cells. The virus, first discovered in 1983, is named *human immunodeficiency virus,* or HIV. When HIV enters the body, it attacks helper T-cells. This action prevents helper T-cells from carrying out their regular job—to activate the immune system when a threat arises. Once inside a helper T-cell, HIV reproduces and thereby destroys the T-cell. Although the body produces antibodies against HIV, the virus evades them by growing within the cells that make up the immune system. HIV slowly destroys most of the helper T-cells.

The destruction of helper T-cells leaves the body practically undefended. As a result, disease-causing invaders that would normally be destroyed by a healthy immune system grow and multiply. It is the

Figure 21–10 *The large round objects in this photograph are white blood cells that are found in the lining of the nose, eyes, and throat. When allergens attach themselves to white blood cells, the white blood cells explode, releasing tiny structures that contain histamines. For those who suffer from hayfever, a bubble helmet with hose and filter may be the last resort.*

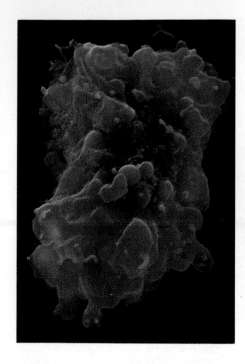

Figure 21–11 *The virus that causes AIDS—seen as tiny blue dots in this photograph—has infected a T-cell. What is the function of a T-cell?*

repeated attacks of disease that weaken and eventually kill people with AIDS.

How is AIDS spread? Contrary to popular belief, AIDS can be spread only if there is direct contact with the blood and/or body secretions of an infected person. Because HIV has been found in semen and vaginal secretions, it can be spread through sexual contact. In fact, recent data point to an alarming increase in AIDS among sexually active teenagers. Contaminated blood can also spread HIV from one person to another. Prior to 1985, this made blood transfusions a possible source of HIV transmission. Since 1985, however, mandatory screening of all blood donations for HIV has been in effect. AIDS can also be spread by the sharing of needles among intravenous (directly into a vein) drug users. Even unborn babies can be victims of AIDS, as HIV can also travel across the placenta from mother to unborn child.

Is there a cure for AIDS? Unfortunately, there is none at this time. However, there are several drugs that appear effective in slowing down the growth of the virus, thereby allowing AIDS patients to live longer. It is hoped that a drug to cure this terrible disease will be developed soon. In the meantime, there is only one way to prevent AIDS—avoid exposure to HIV, the virus that causes AIDS.

Figure 21–12 *Pamphlets such as these inform people about AIDS: what it is and how it is spread. What is the name of the virus that causes AIDS?*

21–2 Section Review

1. What is immunity? Compare active immunity and passive immunity.
2. How do vaccines work?
3. What is an allergy? An allergen?
4. What is AIDS? What causes it? How does AIDS affect the immune system?

Critical Thinking—*You and Your World*
5. After receiving a vaccine, you may develop mild symptoms of the disease. Explain why this might happen.

21–3 Diseases

You may not realize it, but few people go through life without getting some type of disease. Even the healthiest person has probably come down with the common cold at one time or another. Now that you have an understanding of how the body defends and protects itself, let's see just what it is up against. In the next few pages, you will read about the causes and symptoms of several diseases.

Infectious Disease

Many diseases are caused by tiny living things such as bacteria, viruses, protozoans, and fungi that invade the body. These living things are commonly called germs. Scientists, however, call them microorganisms. **Diseases that are transmitted among people by disease-causing microorganisms are called infectious** (ihn-FEHK-shuhs) **diseases.** There are three ways by which an **infectious disease** can be transmitted, or spread. They are by people, by animals, and by nonliving things. Sometimes, an infectious disease becomes very contagious (catching) and sweeps through an area. This condition is called an epidemic.

Many common infectious diseases are spread as a result of close contact with a sick person. Such contact often takes place through coughing or sneezing. A cough or a sneeze expels droplets of moisture that may contain disease-causing microorganisms. You

Guide for Reading

Focus on these questions as you read.

▶ *What are some examples of infectious diseases, and how are they spread?*

▶ *What are some examples of noninfectious diseases?*

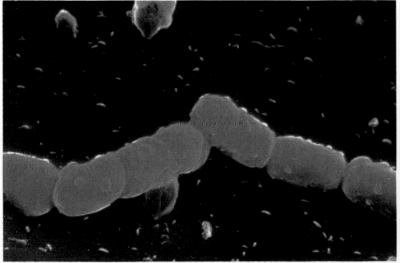 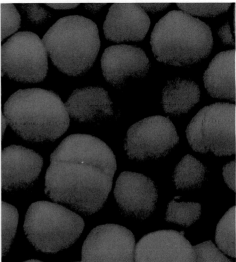

Figure 21–13 *Bacterial diseases can be caused by certain round bacteria called cocci (right) and by certain rod-shaped bacteria called bacilli (left).*

545

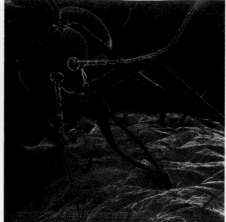

Figure 21–14 *Many infectious diseases are spread by the cough of a sick person (left), by infected animals such as mosquitoes (center), and by contaminated water (right).*

may be surprised to learn that a sneeze may contain as many as 5000 droplets and that these droplets may travel as far as 3.7 meters (almost the entire length of a small room)! If you are standing near a person who coughs or sneezes, you will probably breathe in these droplets—and the disease-causing microorganisms along with them. Diseases that are spread mainly through coughing and sneezing include colds, flu, measles, mumps, and tuberculosis.

Some infectious diseases are transmitted when a healthy person comes into direct contact with a person who has the disease. Such is the case for gonorrhea and syphilis, which are examples of sexually transmitted diseases, or STDs.

Animals can spread infectious diseases, too. Ticks, which are cousins of the spider, are responsible for spreading Lyme disease (named after the town in Connecticut where it was first observed) and Rocky Mountain spotted fever (named after the region in the United States where it was first discovered). Some other types of animals that are responsible for spreading disease are mammals and birds. Rabies, a serious disease that affects the nervous system, is transmitted by the bite of an infected mammal such as a raccoon or a squirrel.

Figure 21–15 *Animals are also responsible for the spread of disease. The female deer tick can carry the microorganism that causes Lyme disease. What is another disease that is spread by the bite of a tick?*

Living things are not the only transmitters of disease. Contaminated (dirty) food or water can also spread infectious diseases. Food contaminated with certain bacteria, for example, can cause food poisoning. And in areas that have poor sanitation, diseases such as hepatitis, cholera (KAHL-er-uh), and typhoid (TIGH-foid) fever are fairly common.

DISEASES CAUSED BY VIRUSES   Your head aches, your nose is runny, and your eyes are watery. You also have a slight cough. But do not be alarmed. More than likely, you are suffering from the common cold.

The common cold is caused by perhaps one of the smallest disease-causing organisms—a virus. A virus is a tiny particle that can invade living cells. When a virus invades the body, it quickly enters a body cell. Once inside the cell, the virus takes control of all the activities of the cell. Not only does the virus use up the cell's food supply, it also uses the cell's reproductive machinery to make more viruses. In time, the cell—now full of viruses—bursts open, releasing more viruses that are free to invade more body cells. Viruses cause many infectious diseases, including measles, chicken pox, influenza, and mononucleosis.

DISEASES CAUSED BY BACTERIA   If you are like most people, you probably think that all bacteria (one-celled microscopic organisms) are harmful and cause disease in humans. Then perhaps this fact will surprise you: Most bacteria are harmless to humans! Those bacteria that do produce diseases do so in a variety of ways. Some bacteria infect the tissues of the body directly. For example, the bacterium that causes tuberculosis grows in the tissues of the lungs. As the bacterium multiplies, it kills surrounding cells, causing difficulty and pain in breathing.

Other bacteria cause disease by producing toxins, or poisons. One such bacterium causes tetanus. The tetanus bacterium lives in dust and dirt and enters the body through breaks in the skin. Once inside the body, the tetanus bacterium begins to produce a toxin that affects muscles far from the wound. Because the toxin causes violent contractions of the jaw muscles, which make it hard for an infected person to open his or her mouth, tetanus is commonly called lockjaw.

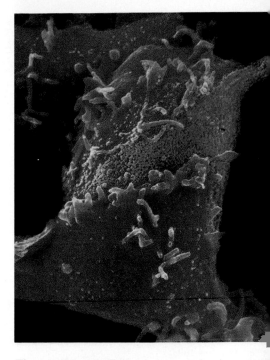

Figure 21–16 *This photograph shows how viruses—seen as tiny blue dots—are released by an infected human cell when it ruptures.*

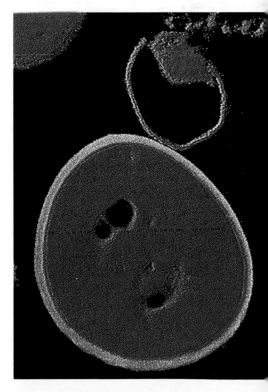

Figure 21–17 *The round objects in this photograph are bacterial cells. The bacterial cell at the top of the photograph has burst because of the addition of an antibiotic. An antibiotic is a substance produced by living organisms such as fungi that weakens or kills bacteria.*

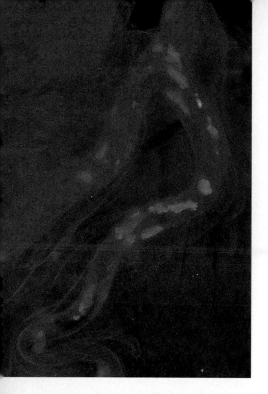

Figure 21–18 *The yellow-colored material in these arteries of the heart is a buildup of fatty substances. Such substances block the flow of blood to the heart muscle. What are the diseases that affect the heart and blood vessels called?*

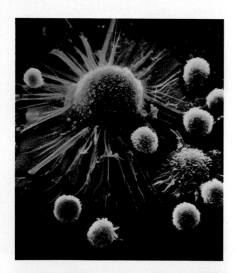

Figure 21–19 *Notice the crablike growth of the large cancer cell. The round objects are T-cells that have surrounded the cancer cell and are preparing to attack and destroy it.*

Noninfectious Diseases

Diseases that are not caused by microorganisms are called noninfectious diseases. There are many causes of **noninfectious diseases**. Some noninfectious diseases are caused by substances that harm or irritate the body. Others come from not eating a balanced diet. Still others are produced when the immune system fails to function properly. Worry and tension can also cause illness.

Because modern medicine has found more and more ways to combat many infectious diseases through the use of drugs and vaccines, people have begun to live longer. And as people's life spans have increased, so have the number of people who suffer from noninfectious diseases.

Some of the more serious noninfectious diseases are cancer, diabetes mellitus (digh-uh-BEET-eez muh-LIGHT-uhs), and cardiovascular diseases. You will now read about two noninfectious diseases—cancer and diabetes mellitus. Cardiovascular diseases, or diseases that affect the heart and blood vessels, were discussed in Chapter 17.

CANCER The noninfectious disease that is second only to cardiovascular diseases in causing death is **cancer**. Cancer is a disease in which cells multiply uncontrollably, destroying healthy tissue. Cancer is a unique disease because the cells that cause it are not foreign to the body. Rather, they are the body's own cells. This fact has made cancer difficult to understand and treat.

Cancer develops when something goes wrong with the controls that regulate cell growth. A single cell or a group of cells begin to grow and divide uncontrollably, often resulting in the formation of a tumor. A tumor is a mass of tissue. Some tumors are benign (bih-NIGHN), or not cancerous. A benign tumor does not spread to surrounding healthy tissue or to other parts of the body. Cancerous tumors, on the other hand, are malignant (muh-LIHG-nehnt). Malignant tumors invade and eventually destroy surrounding tissue. In some cases, cells from a malignant tumor break away and are carried by the blood to other parts of the body.

Although the basic cause of cancer is not known, scientists believe that it develops because of repeated and prolonged contact with carcinogens (kahr-SIHN-uh-juhnz), or cancer-causing substances. In a few cases, scientists have found certain cancer-causing hereditary material (genes) in viruses. The hereditary material in the viruses transforms normal, healthy cells into cancer cells. Scientists also suspect that people may inherit a tendency to develop certain types of cancer. This does not mean, however, that such people will get cancer.

The most important weapon in the fight against cancer is early detection. If a cancer is detected early on, the chances of successfully treating it are quite good. Doctors mainly use three methods to treat cancer: surgery, radiation therapy, and drug therapy. These methods may be used alone or in combination with one another.

Doctors tend to use surgery to remove malignant tumors that are localized, or are not capable of spreading. In radiation therapy, radiation (energy in the form of rays) is used to destroy cancer cells. Drug therapy, or chemotherapy, is the use of specific chemicals against cancer cells. Like radiation, these chemicals not only destroy cancer cells, but they also can injure normal cells. These injuries may account for undesirable side effects, such as nausea and high blood pressure, that often accompany such treatment.

Recently, scientists have been experimenting with drugs that can strengthen the body's immune system against cancer cells. These drugs, called monoclonal (mahn-oh-KLOH-nuhl) antibodies, are produced by joining cancer cells with antibody-producing white blood cells. Monoclonal antibodies have already

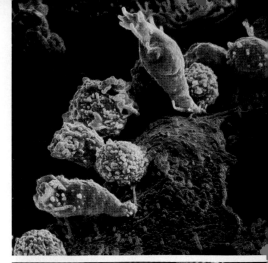

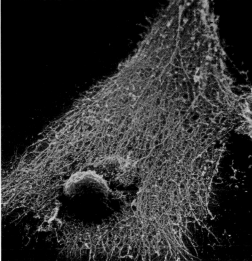

Figure 21–20 *Normally round killer T-cells become elongated when they are active, such as when they are destroying a cancer cell (top). All that remains of a cancer cell that has been attacked by a T-cell is its fibrous skeleton (bottom). What is cancer?*

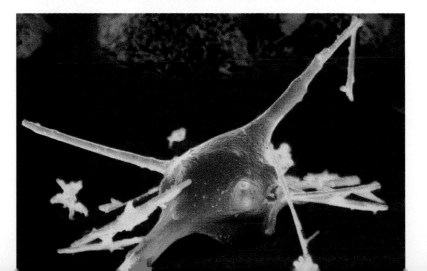

Figure 21–21 *Some chemicals, such as asbestos, are carcinogenic, or cancer-causing. The asbestos fibers visible in this photograph are being engulfed by a white blood cell.*

proven to be effective against certain types of flu virus and a type of hepatitis virus. It is hoped that monoclonal antibodies will play an important role in the fight against cancer.

DIABETES MELLITUS Loss of weight, excess urine production, weakness, and extreme hunger and thirst are all symptoms of a serious disease known as **diabetes mellitus.** Diabetes mellitus occurs because the body either secretes (releases) too little insulin or is not able to use the insulin that it does secrete.

As you may recall from Chapter 19, insulin is a hormone that is produced by the islets of Langerhans (clusters of cells in the pancreas). The job of insulin is to reduce the level of sugar (glucose) in the blood by helping the body cells absorb sugar and use it for energy. Without insulin, sugar cannot be absorbed into body cells and energy cannot be produced. This condition causes the body to look elsewhere for its energy. And, unfortunately, the body looks to its own tissues for "food." As a result, a person begins to show the symptoms of diabetes (weight loss, weakness, and extreme hunger).

There are two types of diabetes mellitus. Juvenile-onset diabetes, as its name implies, most commonly develops in people under the age of 25. In this type of diabetes, there is little or no secretion of insulin. The treatment for this type of diabetes includes daily insulin injections and strict diet control. Adult-onset diabetes, on the other hand, develops in people over the age of 25. Although most people with adult-onset diabetes produce normal amounts of insulin, for some unknown reason their body cells cannot use the insulin to absorb the much-needed sugar. Adult-onset diabetes can often be controlled by diet.

Figure 21–22 *With proper treatment and diet control, people who have diabetes can exercise and participate in sports. Wade Wilson of the Minnesota Vikings is a perfect example. What is diabetes mellitus?*

ACTIVITY
READING

A Fight Against Cancer

What happens when a teenager develops a cancerous brain tumor?

How does he cope with his disease?

What effects does his disease have on his family?

Read *Death Be Not Proud* by the teen's father, John Gunther.

21–3 Section Review

1. What is an infectious disease? A noninfectious disease? Give two examples of each.
2. How are infectious diseases spread?

Critical Thinking—*Applying Facts*

3. It's a fact: There is no single cure for the common cold. Why do you think this is so?

CONNECTIONS

A Cure for Us or Yews?

Recently, doctors announced the discovery of a new cancer drug capable of melting away tumors that have resisted all other treatment. Unfortunately, very few people will receive this drug, which is known as taxol. Why? The answer lies in its source—the Pacific yew tree.

When it became clear that taxol has great potential in the fight against cancer, certain people became alarmed about what effect this would have on the Pacific yew trees. They started asking how many Pacific yews there were and what was going to happen to them. These people are concerned about *ecology*. Ecology is the study of the relationships and interactions of living things with one another and with their environment. As one ecology activist said of the Pacific yews, "Our concern is that there will not be any left the way we are approaching this."

In the past, Pacific yews were seen as commercially unimportant. So they were treated as weeds and were cut down and burned. As a result, the population of Pacific yews, which are found in forests in the Pacific Northwest, dwindled. Of the remaining Pacific yews, most are far too small to be used for making taxol. The height at which a Pacific yew is harvested for taxol is about 9 meters (or the distance needed to make a first down in football). It takes 100 years for a yew to grow that tall! In addition, it takes six 100-year-old Pacific yews to treat one cancer patient!

To further complicate the situation, Pacific yews are found in areas where logging is prohibited in order to protect the habitat of the spotted owl. The spotted owl is an endangered species. But if the yews continue to be harvested for taxol, they, too, may become an endangered species. So what can be done? Does a decision have to be made as to which is more important—cancer treatment or ecology? Most ecology activists believe that if people are careful, the yew can be preserved even as the maximum number of trees are harvested for taxol. What do you think?

Laboratory Investigation

Observing the Action of Alcohol on Microorganisms

Problem

What effect does alcohol have on the growth of organisms?

Materials *(per group)*

glass-marking pencil	alcohol
2 paper clips	100-mL beaker
2 thumbtacks	transparent tape
2 pennies	graduated cylinder
	forceps
2 petri dishes with sterile nutrient agar	

Procedure 🧪 📷

1. Obtain two petri dishes containing sterile nutrient agar.

2. Using a glass-marking pencil, label the lid of the first dish Soaked in Alcohol. Label the lid of the second dish Not Soaked in Alcohol. Write your name and today's date on each lid. **Note:** *Be sure to keep the dishes covered while labeling them.*

3. Using a graduated cylinder, carefully pour 50 mL of alcohol into a beaker.

4. Place a paper clip, a thumbtack, and a penny into the alcohol in the beaker. Keep these objects in the alcohol for at least 10 minutes.

5. Slightly raise the cover of the dish marked Not Soaked in Alcohol. **Note:** *Do not completely remove the cover from the dish.* Using clean forceps, place the other paper clip, thumbtack, and penny into the dish. Cover the dish immediately.

6. Again using clean forceps, remove the paper clip, thumbtack, and penny from the alcohol in the beaker. Slightly raise the cover of the dish marked Soaked in Alcohol and place these objects into it.

7. Tape both dishes closed and put them in a place where they will remain undisturbed for 1 week.

8. After 1 week, examine the dishes. Make a sketch of what you see.

9. Follow your teacher's instructions for the proper disposal of all materials.

Observations

What did you observe in each dish after 1 week?

Analysis and Conclusions

1. What effect did alcohol have on the growth of organisms?

2. Why did you use forceps, rather than your fingers, to place the objects in the dishes?

3. Why did you have to close the petri dishes immediately after adding the objects?

4. Explain why doctors soak their instruments in alcohol.

552

Study Guide

Summarizing Key Concepts

21–1 Body Defenses

▲ The immune system is the body's defense against disease-causing organisms.

▲ The body's first line of defense consists of the skin, mucus, and cilia.

▲ The body's second line of defense is the inflammatory response.

▲ The body's third line of defense consists of antibodies. Antibodies are produced by special white blood cells called B-cells. B-cells are alerted to produce antibodies by T-cells when there is an antigen in the body.

21–2 Immunity

▲ Immunity is the resistance to a disease-causing organism or a harmful substance. There are two types of immunity: active and passive.

▲ Active immunity results when a person's own immune system responds to an antigen by producing antibodies. To have active immunity, a person must get the disease or receive a vaccination. Passive immmunity results when antibodies are produced from a source other than oneself.

▲ An allergy occurs when the immune system is overly sensitive to certain substances called allergens.

▲ AIDS is a disease caused by a virus called HIV. HIV destroys helper T-cells, which ordinarily activate the immune system when a threat arises.

21–3 Diseases

▲ Diseases that are transmitted among people by disease-causing microorganisms are called infectious diseases. Some infectious diseases are caused by viruses and bacteria.

▲ Diseases that are not caused by microorganisms are called noninfectious diseases. Cancer, diabetes mellitus, and cardiovascular diseases are examples of noninfectious diseases.

▲ Cancer is a disease in which cells multiply uncontrollably, destroying healthy tissue.

▲ In diabetes mellitus, the body either secretes too little insulin or is not able to use the insulin that it does secrete.

Reviewing Key Terms

Define each term in a complete sentence.

21–1 Body Defenses
inflammatory response
interferon
antibody
antigen

21–2 Immunity
immunity
active immunity
vaccination

passive immunity
allergy
AIDS

21–3 Diseases
infectious disease
noninfectious disease
cancer
diabetes mellitus

Chapter Review

Content Review

Multiple Choice

Choose the letter of the answer that best completes each statement.

1. What is the body's second line of defense?
   a. skin
   b. antibodies
   c. inflammatory response
   d. cilia
2. Proteins that are produced by the immune system in response to disease-causing invaders are called
   a. antibodies.
   b. antigens.
   c. allergens.
   d. vaccines.
3. The resistance to a disease-causing invader is called
   a. immunity.
   b. vaccination.
   c. interferon.
   d. antigen.
4. A vaccination produces
   a. active immunity.
   b. passive immunity.
   c. no immunity.
   d. both active and passive immunity.
5. An example of an allergy is
   a. rabies.
   b. diabetes mellitus.
   c. tetanus.
   d. hay fever.
6. Which disease is caused by HIV?
   a. rabies
   b. cancer
   c. hay fever
   d. AIDS
7. Which is an example of an infectious disease?
   a. cancer
   b. diabetes mellitus
   c. measles
   d. allergy
8. Tumors that are not cancerous are said to be
   a. benign.
   b. infectious.
   c. malignant.
   d. contagious.
9. Another name for a cancer-causing substance is a(an)
   a. carcinogen.
   b. allergen.
   c. interferon.
   d. vaccination.
10. Which disease results from the secretion of too little insulin?
    a. measles
    b. cancer
    c. AIDS
    d. diabetes mellitus

True or False

If the statement is true, write "true." If it is false, change the underlined word or words to make the statement true.

1. The body's first line of defense against invaders is the <u>inflammatory response</u>.
2. An <u>allergen</u> is a substance that is produced by body cells when they are attacked by viruses.
3. Antibodies are produced to fight <u>antigens</u>.
4. <u>T-cells</u> produce antibodies.
5. A vaccine usually contains dead or weakened <u>antigens</u>.
6. <u>Cancer</u> is a disease in which cells multiply uncontrollably
7. Cancer and diebetes mellitus are examples of <u>noninfectious diseases</u>.

Concept Mapping

Complete the following concept map for Section 21–1. Then construct a concept map for the entire chapter.

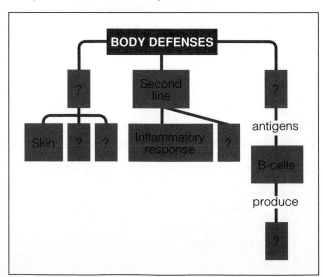

Concept Mastery

Discuss each of the following in a brief paragraph.

1. Explain how the skin functions as the body's first line of defense.
2. Explain how antibodies are produced.
3. Describe three methods by which infectious diseases are spread.
4. What is a benign tumor? A malignant tumor?
5. What are three methods that are used for treating cancer?
6. What are monoclonal antibodies? How are they produced?
7. Describe what happens in the body of a person who has an allergy to dust.
8. How do antibodies fight antigens in the body?
9. What effect does AIDS have on the body? How is AIDS prevented?

Critical Thinking and Problem Solving

Use the skills you have developed in this chapter to answer each of the following.

1. **Relating concepts** Why do you get mumps only once?
2. **Relating facts** Why should you clean and bandage all cuts?
3. **Applying concepts** Explain why you should not go to school with the flu.
4. **Interpreting diagrams** The chart shows the occurrence and survival rates of some cancers in the United States. Which type of cancer has the worst survival rate? The best? Why do you think the five-year survival rates increased between 1960–1963 and between 1977–1983?

FIVE-YEAR SURVIVAL RATES		
Site of Cancer	**1960–63**	**1977–83**
Digestive tract		
Stomach	9.5%	16.0%
Colon and rectum	36.0%	46.0%
Respiratory tract		
Lung and bronchus	6.5%	12.0%
Urinary tract		
Kidney and other		
urinary structures	37.5%	51.0%
Reproductive system		
Breast	54.0%	68.0%
Ovary	32.0%	38.0%
Testis	63.0%	74.5%
Prostate gland	42.5%	63.0%
Skin	60.0%	79.0%

5. **Applying concepts** Explain why it is important for you to know what vaccines you have been given and when they were given.
6. **Making predictions** Suppose your cilia were destroyed. How would this affect your body?
7. **Recognizing fact and opinion** Are colds caught by sitting in a draft? Explain your answer.
8. **Applying concepts** Suppose a person was born without a working immune system. What are some of the precautions that would have to be taken so that the person could survive?
9. **Relating concepts** The Black Death, or bubonic plague, swept through England in the seventeenth century killing thousands of people. This disease is spread by fleas infected with plague microorganisms. These fleas transmit the plague microorganisms to humans by biting them. Explain why the Black Death is not a problem today.
10. **Using the writing process** In the United States, the incidence of sexually transmitted diseases is on the rise. Prepare an advertising campaign in which you alert people to the serious medical problems of these diseases.

"Before I'll ride with a drunk, I'll drive myself." —Stevie Wonder

Driving after drinking, or riding with a driver who's been drinking, is a big mistake. Anyone can see that.

Alcohol, Tobacco, and Drugs

Guide for Reading

After you read the following sections, you will be able to

22–1 What Are Drugs?
- Define the word drug.
- Describe the effects of drug abuse.

22–2 Alcohol
- Describe the effects of alcohol abuse.

22–3 Tobacco
- Relate cigarette smoking to certain diseases.

22–4 Commonly Abused Drugs
- Describe the effects of smoking marijuana.
- Classify inhalants, depressants, stimulants, hallucinogens, and opiates.

Only one more kilometer to go and you will have reached your goal! You and your friends are running a marathon to raise money for SADD, or *S*tudents *A*gainst *D*runk *D*riving. You are running to gain support for your battle against a dangerous combination—alcohol and driving. Alcohol-related accidents are the greatest health hazard facing teenagers today.

What effect does alcohol have on the body? Why do people use alcohol? Why do they abuse it? What are the long-term effects of heavy drinking? Is alcoholism a disease? Is there a cure for it? As you read the pages that follow you will find the answers to these questions. And you will learn that alcohol is not the only substance that threatens the health and safety of teenagers and adults. Tobacco and other drugs have profound effects on the body. Read on and get wise!

Journal *Activity*

You and Your World   A friend of yours is thinking of smoking cigarettes. In your journal, write a letter to your friend explaining that tobacco use is harmful. Then, after you have completed the chapter, reread your letter.

◀ *Posters such as this alert people to the dangers of drunk driving.*

22–1 What Are Drugs?

Drugs! You probably hear and see that word a lot today—on radio, television, billboards, and in newspaper articles and advertisements. What is a drug, and why are drugs drawing so much attention? **A drug is any substance that has an effect on the body.** Many substances fit this definition—even aspirin, which is used to reduce pain. Drugs that are used to treat medical conditions are called medicines. Aspirin is a medicine. There are two groups of medicines: prescription drugs and over-the-counter drugs.

Figure 22–1 *Drugs come in many shapes and sizes. Some are legal; some are not. What is a drug?*

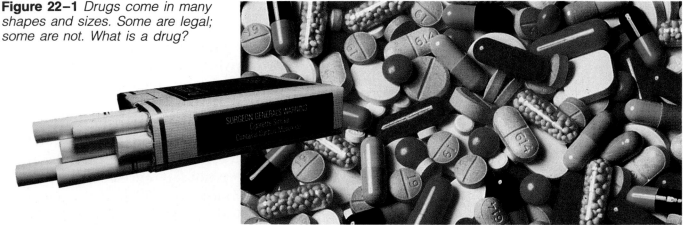

Prescription drugs usually are strong drugs that are safe to use only under the supervision of a doctor. Prescription drugs are used to treat diseases or to control conditions such as high blood pressure and pneumonia. Over-the-counter drugs, on the other hand, do not need a doctor's prescription and may be purchased by anyone. Aspirin and cold tablets are examples of over-the-counter drugs.

Drug Misuse and Drug Abuse

When you use a prescription drug exactly as it is prescribed or take an over-the-counter drug according to its directions, you are engaging in drug use. Some people, however, use prescription or over-the-counter drugs incorrectly. Usually these people do so because they are misinformed. The improper use of drugs is called drug misuse.

ACTIVITY
WRITING

What Are Generic Drugs?

Today there is a great deal of talk about generic drugs. Using reference books and materials in the library, find out what the term generic drug means. What are the advantages of generic drugs? What are the possible disadvantages?

Some people misuse drugs by taking more than the amount a doctor prescribes. They mistakenly believe that such action will speed their recovery from an illness. Other people take more of the drug because they have missed a dose. This action is particularly dangerous because it could cause an overdose. An overdose can cause a serious reaction to a drug, which can sometimes result in death.

When people deliberately misuse drugs for purposes other than medical ones, they are taking part in **drug abuse**. Some drugs prescribed by doctors are abused. Other drugs that are abused are illegal drugs. Drug abuse is extremely dangerous. Do you know why? As you have just read, drugs are substances that have an effect on the body. Drugs can produce powerful changes in your body.

Why do people use drugs? There are many answers to this question. Some seek to "escape" life's problems; others to intensify life's pleasures. Some take drugs because their friends do; others because their friends do not. Some people abuse drugs to feel grown up; others to feel young again. The list is as endless as the range of human emotions. Unfortunately, the desired effects are often followed by harmful and unpleasant side effects.

Dangers of Drug Abuse

People of all ages abuse drugs. Some know that they are abusing drugs; others do not. And still others deny their abuse. The 18- to 25-year-old age group has the highest percentage of drug abuse.

Drug abuse is dangerous for a number of reasons. When you take a drug, for example, the internal functioning of your body changes immediately. Over time, your body also changes its response to the drug. These responses can produce some serious side effects. Let's examine some of these serious and sometimes fatal side effects.

TOLERANCE When a drug is used or abused regularly, the body may develop a **tolerance** to it. Tolerance causes the body to need increasingly larger amounts of the drug to get the same effect that was originally produced. This is exactly what happens to people who abuse drugs. They soon discover that they must take more of the drug each time in order

Figure 22–2 *This clay tablet contains the world's oldest known prescriptions, dating back to about 2000 BC. The prescriptions show the medicinal use of plants.*

Figure 22–3 *Notice the expiration date on this container of pills. Using a medicine after its prescription has expired is an example of drug misuse. What is a prescription drug?*

ACTIVITY

DISCOVERING

Drugs and Daphnia

1. With your teacher's help, place a *Daphnia* (water flea) in the depression on a depression slide.

2. Cover the slide with a coverslip and place the slide under a microscope.

3. Use the low-power objective to observe the *Daphnia*. You should be able to clearly see the *Daphnia*'s heart beating.

4. Calculate the average heart rate per minute of the *Daphnia*.

5. Remove the coverslip and with a dropper, place one drop of cola in the depression. Replace the coverslip and observe the *Daphnia* again.

6. Calculate the average heart rate per minute again.

Was there a difference in heart rate after the cola was added? If there was a difference, what may have caused it?

■ What does this investigation tell you about cola?

to get the same feeling they did in the beginning. Tolerance can cause people to take too much of a drug—a problem that can lead to overdose and even death.

DEPENDENCE Some drugs produce a dependence, or a state in which a person becomes unable to control drug use. Dependence can be psychological (sigh-kuh-LAHJ-ih-kuhl), physical, or both. In all cases, dependence changes the way the body functions, and it can seriously damage a person's health.

Psychological dependence is a strong desire or need to continue using a drug. When people become psychologically dependent on a drug, they link the drug with specific feelings or moods. When the drug's effect wears off, so does the feeling.

Drug abusers who are psychologically dependent on a drug often believe they can stop using the drug if they want to. Unfortunately, stopping drug abuse once a person is psychologically dependent is not easy and may require a doctor's care.

Physical dependence occurs when the body becomes used to a drug and needs the drug to function normally. This type of dependence generally takes time to develop and usually occurs as tolerance builds. Physical dependence is sometimes referred to as an addiction.

WITHDRAWAL A person who is physically dependent on a drug such as heroin needs to take the drug at least three to four times a day. Miss a dose and the body begins to react: The nose runs, the eyes tear. Miss several doses and the body reacts more violently: chills, fever, vomiting, cramps, headaches, and body aches. In time, the muscles begin to jerk wildly, kicking out of control. This is the beginning of **withdrawal**, or stopping the use of a drug.

Figure 22–4 *In this anti-crack wall mural, an artist describes his attitude toward drug abuse. These children express their views during an anti-drug rally. What types of dependence can result from drug abuse?*

Although it takes a few days, the most painful symptoms of heroin withdrawal pass. However, heroin abusers are never entirely free of their need for the drug. In fact, far too many heroin abusers who have "kicked the habit" return to the drug again unless they receive medical, psychological, and social help.

Figure 22–5 *People take drugs for many reasons. They mistakenly think that drugs can solve their problems.*

22–1 Section Review

1. What is a drug? Compare prescription and over-the-counter drugs.
2. What is drug misuse? Drug abuse?
3. Compare psychological and physical dependence.

Critical Thinking—*You and Your World*
4. How might you convince someone not to use drugs?

22–2 Alcohol

Alcohol is a drug. In fact, alcohol is the oldest drug known to humans. Egyptian wall writings, which are among the oldest forms of written communication, show pictures of people drinking wine. It was not until the Egyptian writing symbols were decoded, however, that the meaning of some of the wall paintings was revealed. Their message warned of the dangers of alcohol abuse. **The abuse of alcohol can lead to the destruction of liver and brain cells, and it can cause both physical and psychological dependence.**

How Alcohol Affects the Body

Unlike food, alcohol does not have to be digested. Some alcohol, in fact, is absorbed directly through the wall of the stomach into the bloodstream. If the stomach is empty, the alcohol is absorbed quickly, causing its effects to be felt almost immediately. If the stomach contains food, the alcohol is absorbed more slowly. Upon leaving the

Figure 22–6 *This Egyptian wall painting, painted thousands of years ago, shows how grapes were gathered to make wine.*

ACTIVITY

Figure 22–7 *As this diagram illustrates, alcohol can cause harmful effects throughout the body. What effect does alcohol have on the brain?*

stomach, the alcohol enters the small intestine, where more of it is absorbed.

After the alcohol is absorbed, it travels through the blood to all parts of the body. As the alcohol in the blood passes through the liver, it is changed into carbon dioxide and water. Carbon dioxide and some water are released from the body by way of the lungs. Most of the water, however, passes out of the body as perspiration and urine.

Because the liver can convert only a small amount of alcohol at a time into carbon dioxide and water, much of the alcohol remains unchanged in the blood. When the alcohol reaches the brain, it acts as a **depressant**. A depressant is a substance that slows down the actions of the central nervous system (brain and spinal cord). Perhaps this seems confusing to you if you have noticed that people who drink do not seem to be depressed at all. Rather, they seem quite energetic.

The reason for this false sense of energy is that alcohol initially affects the part of the brain that controls judgment and self-control. At the same time, alcohol makes people become more relaxed and unafraid. The net result is that the controls people put on their emotions are reduced, causing them to behave in ways they would never normally consider. Thus, people may seem quite stimulated during this time.

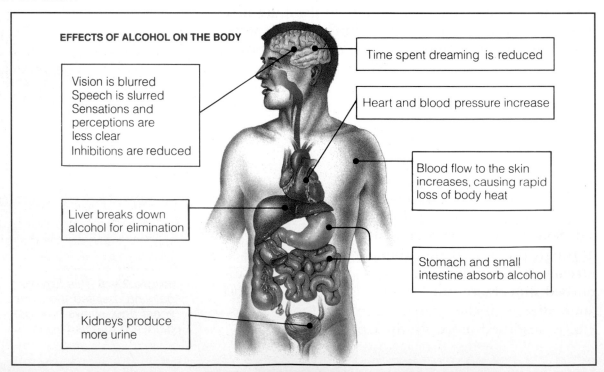

EFFECTS OF ALCOHOL ON THE BODY

Vision is blurred
Speech is slurred
Sensations and perceptions are less clear
Inhibitions are reduced

Liver breaks down alcohol for elimination

Kidneys produce more urine

Time spent dreaming is reduced

Heart and blood pressure increase

Blood flow to the skin increases, causing rapid loss of body heat

Stomach and small intestine absorb alcohol

Figure 22–8 *Blood alcohol concentration, or BAC, is a measure of the amount of alcohol in the bloodstream per 100 mL of blood. The BAC is expressed as a percentage. The higher the BAC, the more powerful the effect of alcohol on the brain. What type of behavior occurs if the BAC is 0.1 percent?*

ALCOHOL'S EFFECTS ON THE BRAIN

BAC	Part of Brain Affected	Behavior
0.05%		Lack of judgment; lack of inhibition
0.1%		Reduced reaction time; difficulty in walking and driving
0.2%		Saddened, weeping, abnormal behavior
0.3%		Double vision; inadequate hearing
0.45%		Unconscious
0.65%		Death

But if people continue to drink, the alcohol in their blood begins to affect other areas of the brain. Soon the areas that control speech and muscle coordination are affected. A person may slur words and have trouble walking. More alcohol can lead to a state of total confusion as more of the brain is affected. Often a person loses consciousness. Sometimes the areas of the brain controlling breathing and heartbeat are affected. Such an overdose of alcohol is life threatening.

Alcohol and Health

For most people, the moderate use of alcohol does not result in health problems. Drinking large amounts of alcohol on a daily basis, however, can cause health problems. Prolonged alcohol abuse may cause mental disturbances, such as blackouts and hallucinations (seeing or hearing things that are not really there). It can also damage the linings of the stomach and small intestine. The risk of cancer of the mouth, esophagus, throat, and larynx is increased among alcohol abusers. Continued use of alcohol also causes cirrhosis (suh-ROH-sihs) of the liver. Cirrhosis is a disease in which liver cells and the connective tissue that hold the cells together are damaged by the heavy intake of alcohol. The damaged liver cells and connective tissue form scar tissue, which interferes with the liver's ability to perform its normal functions. Figure 22–9 shows the difference in appearance between a normal liver and a liver with cirrhosis. Cirrhosis is responsible for about 13,000 deaths in America every year.

The abuse of alcohol can lead to **alcoholism**. Alcoholism is an incurable disease in which a person is physically and psychologically dependent on alcohol. A person who has the disease is called an alcoholic. An alcoholic needs both medical and psychological help. The aid of organizations such as Alcoholics Anonymous is also important in helping alcoholics

Figure 22–9 *Long-term alcohol use destroys liver cells. Notice the differences in appearance of a normal liver (left), one that has some fatty deposits due to alcohol abuse (center), and one that is consumed by cirrhosis (right).*

overcome their problems. There are even organizations for the relatives of the 10 million or more alcoholics in this country. One, called Alateen, is for the children of people who have an alcohol problem.

Knowing about the damage that alcohol does to the body and the brain, one would think alcohol abusers would stop drinking. Unfortunately, withdrawal from alcohol can be very difficult. Like other drug abusers, alcoholics may suffer from withdrawal symptoms when they try to stop drinking. About one fourth of the alcoholics in the United States experience hallucinations during withdrawal.

CONNECTIONS

"Bad Breath?"

You have probably seen television programs in which a person suspected of driving while intoxicated is stopped by police and asked to exhale into a breath analyzer. A breath analyzer is a device that determines the amount of alcohol in the body.

The first breath analyzer, which consisted of an inflatable balloon, was developed in the late 1930s by the American doctor Rolla N. Hager who called it a "Drunkometer." Today, most breath analyzers in use are electronic. That is, they are powered by *electric currents* (flow of charged particles). About the size of a television remote-control device, an electronic breath analyzer contains a fuel cell that works like a battery. A person exhales into the breath analyzer, and the air is pulled into the fuel cell through a valve. There the air comes in contact with a small strip of positively charged platinum. This strip is in contact with a disk containing sulfuric acid. The platinum changes any alcohol that might be present to acetic acid. When this happens, particles of platinum lose electrons and an electric current is set up in the disk. The electric current then flows from the positively charged platinum particles to the negatively charged particles on the other side of the disk.

The more alcohol the breath contains, the stronger the electric current. A weak electric current or no electric current produces a green light, indicating that a person's breath contains little or no alcohol. A stronger current produces an amber light, showing that a person's breath contains some alcohol. A very strong electric current produces a red light, meaning that a person's breath contains a lot of alcohol. In the case of either an amber light or a red light, a person has failed the breath test. The person needs to be tested further to determine exactly how much alcohol the body contains.

22-2 Section Review

1. How does alcohol affect the body?
2. What is alcoholism?

Critical Thinking—*You and Your World*
3. Why is driving after drinking dangerous?

22-3 Tobacco

In 1988, the Surgeon General (chief medical officer in the United States Public Health Service) warned that the nicotine in tobacco products is as addictive (habit-forming) as the illegal drugs heroin and cocaine. This report was the fifth on the effects of smoking tobacco to come from the Surgeon General's office. The first report, which was issued in 1964, declared that cigarette smoking causes lung cancer, heart disease, and respiratory illnesses. In 1972, the Surgeon General issued the first report to suggest that secondhand (passive) smoke is a danger to nonsmokers. A 1978 report warned pregnant women that smoking could affect the health of their unborn children. This report also stated that smoking could prevent the body from absorbing certain important nutrients. In 1982, cigarette smoking was named as the single most preventable cause of death in the United States. Four years later, another report published the results of studies linking secondhand smoke to lung cancer and respiratory diseases in nonsmokers. Despite all these warnings, our nation still has millions of tobacco smokers!

Guide for Reading

Focus on this question as you read.

▶ *What effects does tobacco have on the body?*

Some Harmful Chemicals In Tobacco Smoke
acetaldehyde
acetone
acetonitrile
acrolein
acrylonitrile
ammonia
aniline
benzene
benzopyrene
2,3 butadione
butylamine
carbon monoxide
dimethylamine
dimethylnitrosamine
ethylamine
formaldehyde
hydrocyanic acid
hydrogen cyanide
hydrogen sulfide
methacrolein
methyl alcohol
methylamine
methylfuran
methylnaphthalene
nicotine
nitric oxide
nitrogen dioxide
phenol
pyridine
toluene

Figure 22-10 *Smoking at any age is dangerous. In addition to the harmful substances listed in the chart, about 4000 other substances are inhaled when smoking cigarettes. Why do people smoke cigarettes?*

ACTIVITY

Up in Smoke

1. Place a few pieces of tobacco in a test tube. Using some cotton, loosely plug up the mouth of the test tube.

2. With your teacher's permission, use a Bunsen burner to heat the test tube until the tobacco burns completely. **CAUTION:** *Be very careful when working with a Bunsen burner.*

3. Allow the test tube to cool before removing the cotton plug.

Describe the appearance of the cotton plug before and after the investigation. Which substance in tobacco smoke was collected in the cotton?

■ Design an investigation in which you determine whether a brand of cigarettes that is advertised as low in tar really is.

Figure 22–11 *There is a significant difference between the walls of the bronchus of a nonsmoker (right) and those of a smoker (left). This difference can often be fatal. The large grayish-green objects are cancer cells.*

Effects of Tobacco

Why is smoking so dangerous? When a cigarette burns, about 4000 substances are produced. Many of these substances are harmful. Some of these substances are listed in Figure 22–10. Although 10 percent of cigarette smoke is water, 60 percent is made of poisonous substances such as nicotine and carbon monoxide. Nicotine, as you have just read, is an addictive drug. Once in the body, nicotine causes the heart to beat faster, skin temperature to drop, and blood pressure to rise. Carbon monoxide is a poisonous gas often found in polluted air. Yet even the most polluted air on the most polluted day in history does not contain anywhere near the concentration of carbon monoxide that cigarette smoke does!

The remaining 30 percent of cigarette smoke consists of tars. Tars are probably the most dangerous part of cigarette smoke. As smoke travels to the lungs, the tars irritate and damage the entire respiratory system. Unfortunately, this damage is particularly serious in the developing lungs of teenagers.

Tobacco and Disease

Cigarette smoking causes damage to both the respiratory system and the circulatory system. Long-term smoking can lead to lung diseases such as bronchitis (brahng-KIGH-tihs) and emphysema (ehm-fuh-SEE-muh). These diseases are often life threatening. In addition, a heavy smoker has a twenty-times-greater chance of getting lung cancer than a nonsmoker has.

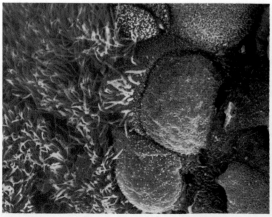

In addition to lung irritation, smoking also increases heartbeat, lowers skin temperature, and causes blood vessels to constrict, or narrow. Constriction of blood vessels increases blood pressure and makes the heart work harder. Heavy smokers are twice as likely to develop some forms of heart disease than are nonsmokers.

The Surgeon General's 1982 report not only named cigarette smoking as the single most preventable cause of death in the United States, it also contained a long list of cancers associated with smoking. In addition to lung cancer, the report named cancer of the bladder, mouth, esophagus, pancreas, and larynx. In fact, at least one third of all cancer deaths may be caused by smoking.

Not everyone who experiences the harmful effects of cigarette smoking has chosen to smoke. Many people are passive, or involuntary, smokers. A passive smoker is one who breathes in air containing the smoke from other people's cigars, pipes, or cigarettes. If one or both of your parents smoke, you probably have been a passive smoker all your life. As you may already know, passive smoking can be extremely unpleasant. It can cause your eyes to burn, itch, and water, and it can irritate your nose and throat.

What is even more important, however, is that passive smoking is harmful to your health. Recent research shows that nonsmokers who have worked closely with smokers for many years suffer a decrease in the functioning of the lungs. Other studies show that infants under the age of one year whose mothers smoke have twice as many lung infections as infants of nonsmoking mothers.

THIS IS A

SMOKE-FREE
BUILDING

Figure 22–12 *Because passive smoking is harmful, some companies have made their buildings totally smoke free.*

22–3 Section Review

1. What effects does tobacco smoking have on the body?
2. What is nicotine? Tar?

Critical Thinking—*You and Your World*

3. What factors do you think influence someone to use tobacco?

ACTIVITY

CALCULATING

Cigarette Smoking

   In 1980, there were 54 million smokers in the United States. If these people smoked 630 billion cigarettes each year, approximately how many cigarettes did each person smoke in a year? In a month?

22–4 Commonly Abused Drugs

As you have already learned, drugs are substances that have an effect on the body. The specific effects differ with the type of drug. Some drugs affect the circulatory system, whereas others affect the respiratory system. The most powerful drugs, however, are those that affect the nervous system and change the user's behavior.

For the most part, drugs that affect the nervous system are the drugs that are most commonly abused. **Some commonly abused drugs include inhalants, depressants, stimulants, hallucinogens** (huh-LOO-sih-nuh-jehnz)**, and opiates** (OH-pee-ihtz)**.** In this section you will learn about the effects these drugs have on the body.

Inhalants

Drugs that are inhaled to get a desired effect are called **inhalants**. Because inhalants are able to enter the bloodstream directly through the lungs, they affect the body quickly.

Typically, people abuse inhalants to get a brief feeling of excitement. One such example of inhalant abuse is glue sniffing. After the effects of inhaling the fumes have worn off, the abuser often has nausea, dizziness, loss of coordination, blurred vision, and a headache. Some inhalants do permanent damage to the brain, liver, kidneys, and lungs. Continued abuse can lead to unconsciousness and even death.

Other examples of inhalants include nitrous oxide, amyl nitrite (AM-ihl NIGH-tright), and butyl (BYOO-tihl) nitrite. Nitrous oxide, which is more commonly known as "laughing gas," is used by dentists as a painkiller because it causes the body to relax. Long-term abuse of nitrous oxide can cause psychological dependence and can damage the kidneys, liver, and bone marrow. Both amyl nitrite and butyl nitrite cause relaxation, light-headedness, and a burst of energy. As with nitrous oxide, abuse of these drugs can cause psychological dependence and certain circulatory problems.

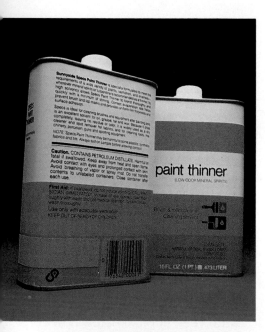

Figure 22–13 *Because products such as paint thinner give off dangerous fumes, their labels contain warnings for their use in well-ventilated rooms.*

COMMONLY ABUSED DRUGS

Type of Drug	Examples	Basic Action on Central Nervous System	Psychological Dependence	Physical Dependence	Withdrawal Symptoms	Development of Tolerance
Opiates and related drugs	Heroin Demerol Methadone	Depressant	Yes, strong	Yes, very fast development	Severe but rarely life-threatening	Yes
Barbiturates	Phenobarbital Nembutal Seconal	Depressant	Yes	Yes	Severe, life-threatening	Yes
Tranquilizers (minor)	Valium Miltown Librium	Depressant	Yes	Yes	Yes	Yes
Alcohol	Beer Wines Liquors Whiskey	Depressant	Yes	Yes	Severe, life-threatening	Yes, more in some people than in others
Cocaine	As a powder Crack	Stimulant	Yes, strong	Yes	Yes	Possible
Cannabis	Marijuana Hashish	Ordinarily a depressant	Yes, moderate	Probably not	Probably none	Possible
Amphetamines	Benzedrine Dexedrine Methedrine	Stimulant	Yes	Possible	Possible	Yes, strong
Hallucinogens	LSD Mescaline Psilocybin	Stimulant	Yes	No	None	Yes, fast
Nicotine	In tobacco of cigarettes, cigars; also in pipe tobacco, chewing tobacco	Stimulant	Yes, strong	Yes	Yes	Yes
Inhalants	Nitrous oxide Amyl nitrite Butyl nitrite	Depressant	Yes	No	None	No

Figure 22–14 *This chart lists some of the commonly abused drugs. What type of drug is nicotine?*

Depressants

Earlier you read that alcohol is a depressant. Depressants slow down or decrease the actions of the nervous system. Two other commonly abused depressants are the powerful barbiturates (bahr-BIHCH-er-ihts) and the weaker tranquilizers (TRAN-kwihl-ighz-erz). Usually, these drugs are taken in pill form.

Because depressants calm the body and can bring on sleep, doctors once prescribed them for people who had sleeping problems or suffered from

Figure 22–15 *When people take drugs such as barbiturates in combination with alcohol, the results are often fatal. Why?*

Figure 22–16 *Under the influence of amphetamines, an orb-weaver spider weaves an irregular web. What type of drug is an amphetamine?*

nervousness. But depressants, particularly barbiturates, cause both physical and psychological dependence. Withdrawal from barbiturate abuse is especially severe and can result in death if done without medical care. And because a tolerance to depressants builds up quickly, a person must continue to take more and more of the drug. This can lead to an overdose, which can lead to death. When barbiturates are used with alcohol, the results are often fatal because the nervous system can become so slowed down that even breathing stops.

Stimulants

While depressants decrease the activities of the nervous system, **stimulants** increase these activities. Caffeine, a drug in coffee, is a stimulant. However, caffeine is a mild stimulant. Far more powerful stimulants make up a class of drugs called amphetamines (am-FEHT-uh-meenz).

Today, the legal use of amphetamines is limited. Yet many people abuse amphetamines illegally. They seek the extra pep an amphetamine pill may bring. Long-term amphetamine abuse, however, can lead to serious psychological and physical problems. Perhaps no side effects are more dramatic than the feelings of dread and suspicion that go hand in hand with amphetamine abuse.

A stimulant that has been increasingly abused in recent years is cocaine. Cocaine comes from the leaves of coca plants that grow in South America. Cocaine may be injected by needle but is usually inhaled as a powder through the nose. In time, the lining of the nose becomes irritated from the powder. If abuse continues, it is not uncommon for cocaine to burn a hole through the walls of the nose.

Psychological dependence from cocaine abuse is so powerful that the drug is difficult to give up. Long-term cocaine abuse can lead to the same mental problems as those of amphetamine abuse.

Within the last 10 years, a very dangerous form of cocaine known as crack has become popular. Unlike cocaine, crack is smoked. Once in the body, crack travels quickly to the brain, where it produces an intense high. This high, however, wears off quickly, leaving the user in need of another dose. Crack is

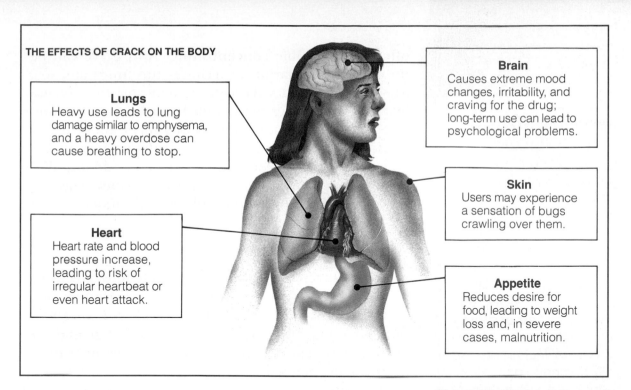

THE EFFECTS OF CRACK ON THE BODY

Lungs
Heavy use leads to lung damage similar to emphysema, and a heavy overdose can cause breathing to stop.

Brain
Causes extreme mood changes, irritability, and craving for the drug; long-term use can lead to psychological problems.

Heart
Heart rate and blood pressure increase, leading to risk of irregular heartbeat or even heart attack.

Skin
Users may experience a sensation of bugs crawling over them.

Appetite
Reduces desire for food, leading to weight loss and, in severe cases, malnutrition.

Figure 22–17 *Crack is an extremely powerful form of cocaine. What effects does crack have on the brain?*

among the most addictive drugs known. A crack user can become hooked on the drug in only a few weeks. Figure 22–17 shows some effects that crack has on the body.

Marijuana

Another drug that is usually smoked is **marijuana**. Marijuana is an illegal drug made from the flowers and leaves of the Indian hemp plant. The effects of marijuana are due mainly to a chemical in the plant known as THC. The THC in marijuana affects different people in different ways. And the effects are often hard to describe once they have passed.

Some users of marijuana report a sense of well-being, or a feeling of being able to think clearly. Others say that they become suspicious of people and cannot keep their thoughts from racing. For many, marijuana distorts the sense of time. A few seconds may seem like an hour, or several hours may race by like seconds.

Research findings now point to a variety of possible health problems caused by marijuana. Like alcohol, marijuana slows reaction time and is the direct cause of many highway accidents. Marijuana seems to have an effect on short-term memory. Heavy users

Figure 22–18 *Marijuana is an illegal drug made from the flowers and leaves of the Indian hemp plant. What chemical in marijuana is responsible for its effects?*

often have trouble concentrating. And there can be no doubt that marijuana irritates the lungs and leads to some respiratory damage. It may surprise you to learn that smoking marijuana harms the lungs more than smoking tobacco does. Long-term abuse of marijuana produces psychological dependence but does not seem to lead to physical dependence. Withdrawal symptoms usually do not occur, but heavy users may suffer sleep difficulties and anxiety.

Hallucinogens

All **hallucinogens** are illegal. Hallucinogens are drugs that alter a user's view of reality. Abusers of hallucinogens cannot tell what is real and what is not. They may also experience memory loss and personality changes, and they may not be able to perform normal activities.

The strongest hallucinogen is LSD. The effects of LSD are unpredictable—it can either stimulate or depress the body. Abusers commonly see colorful pictures. A person may report seeing sound and hearing color. Solid walls may move in waves. Not all hallucinations are pleasant, however. Some people experience nightmarelike "bad trips" in which all sense of reality is lost. Fears are heightened, and a feeling of dread overcomes the user. During this time, accidental deaths and even suicide are not uncommon. A small percentage of abusers do not recover from an LSD experience for months and have to be hospitalized.

The hallucinogen called PCP or "angel dust" was originally developed as an anesthetic (painkilling substance) for animals. PCP may be smoked, injected, sniffed, or eaten. PCP can act as a stimulant, depressant, or hallucinogen. PCP abusers often engage in violent acts and some have even committed suicide.

Opiates

Some of the most powerful drugs known are the **opiates**, or painkilling drugs. Opiates, which are produced from the liquid sap of the opium poppy plant, include opium, morphine, codeine, paregoric (par-uh-GOR-ihk), and heroin. With the exception of

Figure 22–19 *A close-up of a ripe poppy pod shows some of the opium-containing juice oozing out (left). The roundish yellow structure in the middle of the poppy flower is the pod (right).*

heroin and opium, all opiates can legally be used under a doctor's supervision.

In addition to causing a strong physical and psychological dependence, there are other dangers of opiate abuse. The most obvious to nonabusers is the antisocial behavior of people who have a strong need for the drug heroin but no money with which to buy it illegally. Such abusers become trapped in a world from which they cannot escape without help. And the longer they use heroin, the longer they are likely to suffer the dangers of its abuse. For example, most abusers risk an overdose. And overdoses often lead to death. In addition, life-threatening diseases such as AIDS and hepatitis can be transmitted by sharing needles. In their weakened condition, heroin abusers are no match for such serious diseases.

22–4 Section Review

1. Compare the effects a depressant and a stimulant have on the body.
2. Describe the effect hallucinogens have on the body.

Critical Thinking—*You and Your World*

3. You are at a party where drugs are being used. What should you do?

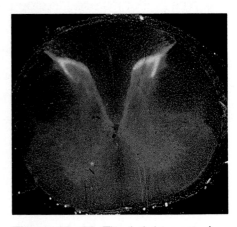

Figure 22–20 *The bright spots in this cross section of the spinal cord are opiate receptors. Opiate receptors are those areas where opiates attach to nerve cells.*

Laboratory Investigation

Analyzing Smoking Advertisements

Problem

How are advertisements used to convince people to smoke or not to smoke?

Materials   *(per group)*

magazines
paper

Procedure

1. Choose two or three different types of magazines. Glance through the magazines to find advertisements for and against cigarette smoking.

2. On a sheet of paper, make a chart like the one shown. Then, for each advertisement you found, fill in the information in the chart. In the last column, record the technique that the advertisement uses to attract the public to smoke or not to smoke. Examples of themes used to attract people to smoke are "Beautiful women smoke brand X"; "Successful people smoke brand Y"; "Brand Z tastes better." Examples of themes used to stop people from smoking are "Smoking is dangerous to your health"; "Smart people do not smoke"; "If you cared about yourself or your family, you would not smoke."

Observations

1. Were there more advertisements for or against smoking?

2. Which advertising themes were used most often? Least often?

Analysis and Conclusions

1. Which advertisements appealed to you personally? Why?

2. In general, how are the advertising themes that are used related to the type of magazine in which the advertisements appear?

3. **On Your Own** Repeat the procedure, but this time look for advertisements for and against drinking alcohol. Compare the way in which drinking alcohol is advertised to the way in which smoking cigarettes is advertised.

Magazine	Advertisements for Smoking (specify brand)	Advertisements Against Smoking (specify advertisement)	Theme

Study Guide

Summarizing Key Concepts

22-1 What Are Drugs?

▲ A drug is any substance that has an effect on the body.

▲ Tolerance, dependence, and withdrawal are serious dangers of drug abuse.

▲ Tolerance causes the body to need increasingly larger amounts of the drug to get the same effect originally produced.

▲ Psychological dependence is a strong desire or need to continue using a drug. Physical dependence, or addiction, occurs when the body becomes used to a drug and needs it to function normally.

▲ Withdrawal is stopping the use of a drug.

22-2 Alcohol

▲ The abuse of alcohol can lead to destruction of liver and brain cells and can cause both physical and psychological dependence.

▲ In the brain, alcohol acts as a depressant and slows down the actions of the central nervous system.

▲ Treatment for alcoholism includes medical and psychological help.

22-3 Tobacco

▲ Cigarette smoking causes damage to both the respiratory system and the circulatory system.

▲ Cigarette smoke contains poisonous substances such as nicotine, carbon dioxide, and tars.

▲ Cigarette smoking is the most important cause of lung cancer. Cigarette smoking irritates the lining of the nose, throat, and mouth; increases heartbeat; lowers skin temperature; and constricts blood vessels.

▲ Passive smokers are those people who breathe in air containing smoke from other people's cigars, cigarettes, and pipes.

22-4 Commonly Abused Drugs

▲ Some commonly abused drugs include inhalants, depressants, stimulants, hallucinogens, and opiates.

▲ Inhalants are drugs that are inhaled to get a desired effect.

▲ Depressants are drugs that decrease the actions of the nervous system.

▲ Stimulants speed up the actions of the nervous system.

▲ The effects of marijuana are due mainly to a chemical called THC. Like alcohol, marijuana slows down reaction time.

▲ Hallucinogens are drugs that produce hallucinations.

▲ Opiates, which are produced from the opium poppy, are used as painkillers.

Reviewing Key Terms

Define each term in a complete sentence.

22-1 What Are Drugs?
drug
drug abuse
tolerance
psychological
  dependence
physical dependence
withdrawal

22-2 Alcohol
depressant
alcoholism

22-4 Commonly Abused Drugs
inhalant
stimulant

marijuana
hallucinogen
opiate

Chapter Review

Content Review

Multiple Choice

Choose the letter of the answer that best completes each statement.

1. Which requires no prescription?
   a. barbiturate   c. amphetamine
   b. tranquilizer   d. aspirin
2. Which is not an example of drug misuse?
   a. buying an over-the-counter drug
   b. taking an illegal drug
   c. taking more of a drug than the amount prescribed by a doctor
   d. taking a drug prescribed for someone else
3. Alcohol acts as a(an)
   a. stimulant.   c. hallucinogen.
   b. opiate.   d. depressant.
4. Alcohol mainly affects the
   a. heart.   c. brain.
   b. muscles.   d. stomach.
5. Which system does bronchitis, a disorder aggravated by smoking, affect?
   a. respiratory   c. digestive
   b. circulatory   d. nervous

6. An addictive drug found in tobacco products is
   a. tar.   c. nicotine.
   b. THC.   d. heroin.
7. An example of an inhalant is
   a. THC.
   b. a barbiturate.
   c. codeine.
   d. nitrous oxide.
8. Barbiturates are
   a. opiates.
   b. hallucinogens.
   c. depressants.
   d. stimulants.
9. Crack is classified as a(an)
   a. stimulant.   c. depressant.
   b. opiate.   d. hallucinogen.
10. Heroin is a(an)
    a. stimulant.   c. depressant.
    b. opiate.   d. hallucinogen.

True or False

If the statement is true, write "true." If it is false, change the underlined word or words to make the statement true.

1. The deliberate misuse of drugs for uses other than medical ones is known as <u>drug abuse</u>.
2. <u>Physical dependence</u> is also known as addiction.
3. The abuse of alcohol can lead to <u>alcoholism</u>.
4. Cirrhosis affects the <u>lungs</u>.
5. The most dangerous part of cigarette smoke is <u>carbon dioxide</u>.
6. <u>Amphetamines</u> and barbiturates are examples of depressants.
7. LSD belongs to a group of drugs known as <u>opiates</u>.

Concept Mapping

Complete the following concept map for Section 22–1. Then construct a concept map for the entire chapter.

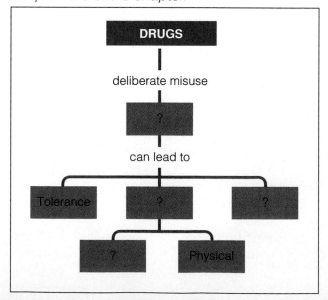

Concept Mastery

Discuss each of the following in a brief paragraph.

1. Explain how any drug can be abused.
2. It has been said that no one is ever cured of drug dependence. Explain why.
3. Why is alcohol considered a depressant?
4. What are dependence, withdrawal, and tolerance?
5. List the six commonly abused drugs. Describe the effect each has on the body.
6. How does an alcoholic differ from those who drink occasionally?
7. Describe the substances in cigarette smoke and their effects on the body.
8. List and describe some of the disorders that can result from smoking.
9. Compare psychological dependence and physical dependence.

Critical Thinking and Problem Solving

Use the skills you have developed in this chapter to answer each of the following.

1. **Applying facts** What precautions would you take when working with paint thinner?
2. **Applying concepts** Explain why heroin abusers need medical help while they are going through withdrawal.
3. **Relating facts** Almost 30 percent of the people in the United States smoke. Explain why people smoke even when they know the dangers.
4. **Making comparisons** Compare cocaine and crack.

5. **Relating cause and effect** How is cigarette smoke related to respiratory and circulatory problems?
6. **Relating concepts** Cigarette smoke is harmful to nonsmokers as well as to smokers. Explain this statement.
7. **Expressing an opinion** What are some ways in which people who abuse drugs can be discouraged from doing so?
8. **Applying concepts** Explain the meaning of this old Japanese proverb: "First the man takes a drink, then the drink takes a drink, then the drink takes the man!"
9. **Making inferences** In what ways are drug abuse and criminal acts related?
10. **Using the writing process** Imagine you are a parent. Write a letter to your child in which you try to discourage your child from experimenting with drugs.

G·A·Z·E·T·T·E

Stephen Hawking:

Meeting the Challenge

Scientists have long struggled to find the connection between two branches of physics. One of these branches deals with the forces that rule the world of atoms and subatomic particles. The other branch deals with gravity and its role in the universe of stars and galaxies. Physicist Stephen Hawking has set himself the task of discovering the connection. Leading theoretical physicists agree that if anyone can discover a unifying principle, it will certainly be this extraordinary scientist.

Dr. Hawking's goal, as he describes it, is simple. "It is complete understanding of the universe, why it is as it is and why it exists at all." In order to achieve such an understanding, Dr. Hawking seeks to "quantize gravity." Quantizing gravity means combining the laws of gravity and the laws of quantum mechanics into a single universal law.

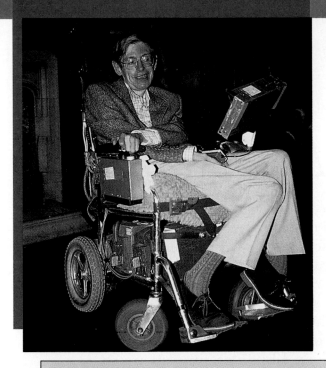

▲ **Stephen Hawking is Lucasian professor of mathematics at Cambridge University—a position once held by Isaac Newton. Hawking has received numerous prizes for his work.**

Dr. Hawking and other theoretical physicists believe that with such a law, the behavior of all matter in the universe, and the origin of the universe as well, could be explained.

Dr. Hawking's search for a unifying theory has led him to study one of science's greatest mysteries: black holes. A black hole is an incredibly dense region in space whose gravitational pull attracts all nearby objects, virtually "swallowing them up." A black hole is formed when a star uses up most of the nuclear fuel that has kept it burning. During most of its life as an ordinary star, its nuclear explosions exert enough outward force to balance the powerful inward force of gravity. But when the star's fuel is used up, the outward force ceases to exist. Gravity takes over and the star collapses into a tiny core of extremely dense material, possibly no bigger than the period at the end of this sentence.

Hawking has already proved that a black hole can emit a stream of electrons. Prior to this discovery, scientists believed that noth-ing, not even light, could escape from a black hole. So scientists have hailed Hawking's discovery as "one of the most beautiful in the history of physics."

Probing the mysteries of the universe is no ordinary feat. And Stephen Hawking is no ordinary man. Respected as one of the most brilliant physicists in the world, Hawking is considered one of the most remarkable. For Dr. Hawking suffers from a serious disease of the nervous system that has confined him to a wheelchair, and he is barely able to move or speak. Although Dr. Hawking gives numerous presentations and publishes countless articles and papers, his addresses must be translated and his essays written down by other hands.

Hawking became ill during his first years at Cambridge University in England. The disease progressed quickly and left the young scholar quite despondent. He even considered giving up his research, as he thought he would not live long enough to receive his Ph.D. But in 1965, Hawking's life changed. He married Jane Wilde, a fellow student and language scholar. Suddenly life took on new meaning. "That was the turning point," he says. "It made me determined to live, and it was about that time that I began making professional progress." Hawking's health and spirits improved. His studies continued and reached new heights of brilliance. Today, Dr. Hawking is a professor of mathematics at Cambridge University who leads a full and active life.

Dr. Hawking believes that his illness has benefited his work. It has given him more time to think about physics. So although his body is failing him, his mind is free to soar. Considered to be one of the most brilliant physicists of all times, Dr. Hawking has taken some of the small steps that lead science to discovery and understanding. With time to ponder the questions of the universe, it is quite likely that Stephen Hawking will be successful in uniting the world of the tiniest particles with the world of stars and galaxies.

UNIT FIVE

Heredity and Adaptation

A unicorn is a mythical animal with the body and head of a horse, the hind legs of a stag, the tail of a lion, and a single horn in the middle of its forehead. Unfortunately (or fortunately), the unicorn exists only in people's imaginations. However, some animals equally as unusual and fabulous as unicorns did exist millions of years ago. Do you know what these animals are called? If you said dinosaurs, you are correct.

◀ *The unicorn is a mythical animal that could not exist in real life. However, many other plants and animals almost as bizarre as the unicorn do live on Earth.*

▲ *Notice the family resemblance inherited by the children from their parents.*

Where are the dinosaurs now? What happened to these creatures? There are many theories that try to explain their disappearance, but no one knows for sure. However, the extinction of dinosaurs signaled the way for another group of animals to flourish—the mammals.

The descendants of mammals include whales, dogs, mice, and humans. Like all living things, mammals resemble their parents. Why? In this unit you will discover how living things pass their characteristics on to their offspring. You will also learn how scientists are beginning to use genetic engineering to produce organisms that will benefit humans in many ways. And finally, you will examine some of the evidence that shows that living things have evolved, or changed over time. Then you will understand the relationship between genetics and evolution. And who knows? Maybe you will develop your own ideas about the disappearance of the dinosaurs.

Dinosaurs such as the baby emerging from its shell roamed the Earth millions of years ago. ▶

Discovery *Activity*

Variations on a Theme

Think of a particular human trait, or characteristic—such as hair color, eye color, or skin color. Look around your classroom. How many different variations of this trait do you see among your classmates? For example, how many have red hair? How many have brown hair? Record your observations in a chart or table.

■ Based on your observations, which form of the trait is most common in your classroom? Least common? Do you think there is any reason for this?

Genetics

Guide for Reading

After you read the following sections, you will be able to

23–1 History of Genetics
- Describe how traits are passed from one generation to another.

23–2 Genetics and Probability
- Relate the law of probability to the study of genetics.

23–3 Chromosomes
- Describe the functions of genes and chromosomes.

23–4 DNA
- Describe the structure of DNA and how it replicates.

23–5 Human Genetics
- Explain how the basic principles of genetics can be applied to human heredity.

Do you have a cat, or do you have a friend who has a cat? You probably know that there are many different kinds of cats. Some cats have long, soft hair and fluffy tails. Others have short, curly hair and skinny tails. There is even one kind of cat that appears to have no hair at all! Despite these, and many other, variations, you can still recognize these animals as cats. Why is this so? What makes one cat different from another and yet still recognizable as a member of the cat family? The answer can be found in the science of genetics.

The study of genetics explains why one cat is different from all other cats and also why a cat is different from a human or a maple tree. All living things, including cats, resemble their parents. But each individual also has certain unique characteristics that make it different from every other living thing on Earth. As you will learn in this chapter, the history of genetics is a fascinating story of mystery and discovery. The story begins with one man in a garden more than 100 years ago. . . .

Journal *Activity*

You and Your World Have you ever seen a litter of kittens or puppies? Did all the kittens or puppies look exactly alike? In your journal, describe how they were alike and how they were different. Do you have any idea why they look as they do?

◄ *These kittens may have different colors and markings, but they all look like cats.*

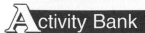

Activity Bank

Tulips Are Better Than One, p. 828

Figure 23–1 *Gregor Mendel is shown in his garden studying how traits are passed on from parents to offspring. What organisms did Mendel study?*

23–1 History of Genetics

During the 1860s, an Austrian monk and biologist named Gregor Mendel worked among hundreds of pea plants in the garden of a small monastery in what is now the Czech Republic. Mendel experimented with pea plants to see if he could find a pattern in the way certain characteristics are handed down from one generation to the next generation. Another word for the characteristics of an organism is **trait.** So Mendel actually studied the way certain traits are passed on from one generation of organisms to the next generation. Pea plant traits include how tall the plants grow, the color of their seeds, and the shape of their seeds.

Although Mendel did not realize it at the time, his experiments would come to be considered the beginning of **genetics.** For this reason, Mendel is called the Father of Genetics. **Genetics is the study of heredity, or the passing on of traits from an organism to its offspring.**

Mendel chose pea plants for his experiments because pea plants grow and reproduce quickly. So he knew that he could study many generations of pea plants in a short amount of time. Mendel also knew that pea plants had a variety of different traits that could be studied at the same time. That is, he could study plant height, plant seed color, plant seed shape, and other traits in the same experiment.

Mendel also chose pea plants because he could easily breed, or cross, them through pollination. Pollination is the transfer of pollen from the male reproductive part of the plant's flower to the female reproductive part. Usually, a pea plant pollinates itself in a process called self-pollination. But Mendel found that he could cross different pea plants by transferring pollen from the male part of one flower to the female part of another flower. This process is called cross-pollination.

The Work of Gregor Mendel

Mendel discovered that when he transferred pollen from the male part of pea plants with short stems to the female part of short-stemmed pea plants, only short-stemmed plants grew from their seeds. So the

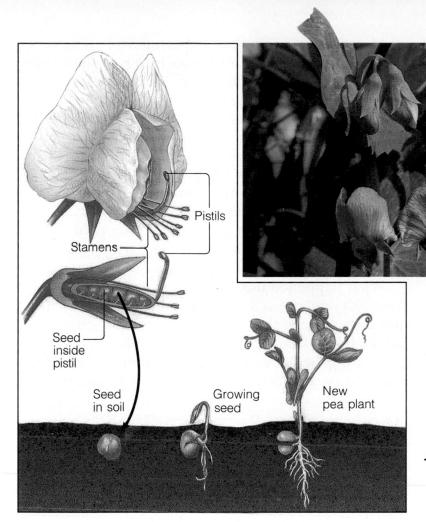

Pistils

Stamens

Seed inside pistil

Seed in soil

Growing seed

New pea plant

Figure 23–2 *Stamens produce pollen, which contains sperm cells. The pistil produces eggs. As a result of pollination, fertilized eggs develop into seeds. When planted, a seed grows into a new pea plant.*

ACTIVITY

WRITING

Genetic Scientists

You may be interested in finding out more about some of the people listed below. They are all scientists who have contributed to the study of genetics and heredity. The library has many resources to help you find out about these people and their work. Choose one of these people and find out what she or he discovered about heredity and genetics. Present your findings in a report.

Rosalind Franklin
James D. Watson
Martha Chase
Jacques Monod
Barbara McClintock

next generation of these short-stemmed plants was also short-stemmed. This result was what he, and everyone else at that time, expected. The plants always resembled the parent plants. Mendel called these short-stemmed plants true-breeding plants, by which he meant those plants that always produce offspring with the same traits as the parents.

Mendel then repeated his experiments by crossing tall-stemmed pea plants with other tall-stemmed pea plants. Naturally, he expected all of the offspring to be tall. But Mendel was in for a surprise. Some of the tall-stemmed pea plants produced only other tall-stemmed pea plants. These plants were true breeders for tall stems. However, some of the tall-stemmed pea plants produced both tall- and short-stemmed offspring. Mendel was not, as yet, able to explain how tall-stemmed plants could produce some short-stemmed offspring. But he realized quickly that not all tall-stemmed plants are true breeders. Why?

ACTIVITY

Dominant and Recessive Traits

1. Obtain two coins.

2. Cut four small, equal-sized pieces of masking tape to fit on the coins without overlapping the edges.

3. Place a piece of tape on each side of both coins.

4. Write a capital letter T on one side of each coin and a lowercase letter t on the other side.

5. Toss both coins together 100 times. Record the letters of the genetic makeup for each toss of the coins.

What are the possible gene combinations? What is the percentage of each?

Mendel knew that more experiments had to be performed before he could show how pea plants pass on their traits to their offspring. He began to wonder what would happen if he crossed true-breeding tall plants and true-breeding short plants. Mendel called these true-breeding parent plants the parental, P_1, generation. When Mendel crossed the P_1 generation, he discovered that all of the plants in the next generation were tall. It was as if the traits for shortness that had existed in some of the parent plants had simply disappeared in the next generation! He called the second generation of plants the filial (FIHL-ee-uhl), or the F_1 generation, plants. See Figure 23–3.

What happened next was even more of a mystery. When Mendel crossed the tall plants of the F_1 generation, he expected that they would produce only tall plants. Instead, some of the plants of the second filial, or F_2, generation, were tall and some were short. The trait for shortness seemed to have reappeared!

Dominant and Recessive Genes

By keeping careful records of his work, Mendel realized that the tall plants of the F_1 generation were not true breeders. This is because some of the tall plants in the F_1 generation produced both short and

Figure 23–3 *Mendel crossed tall and short pea plants. He discovered that the offspring in the first generation were all tall. What kind of plants were produced in the second generation?*

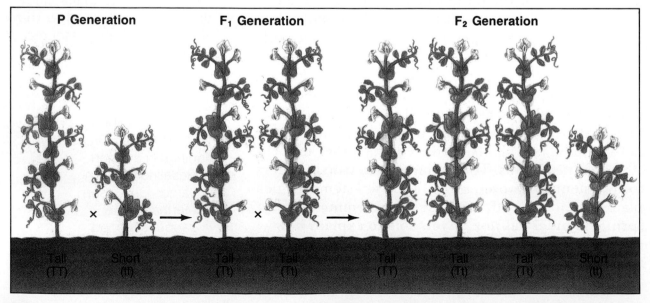

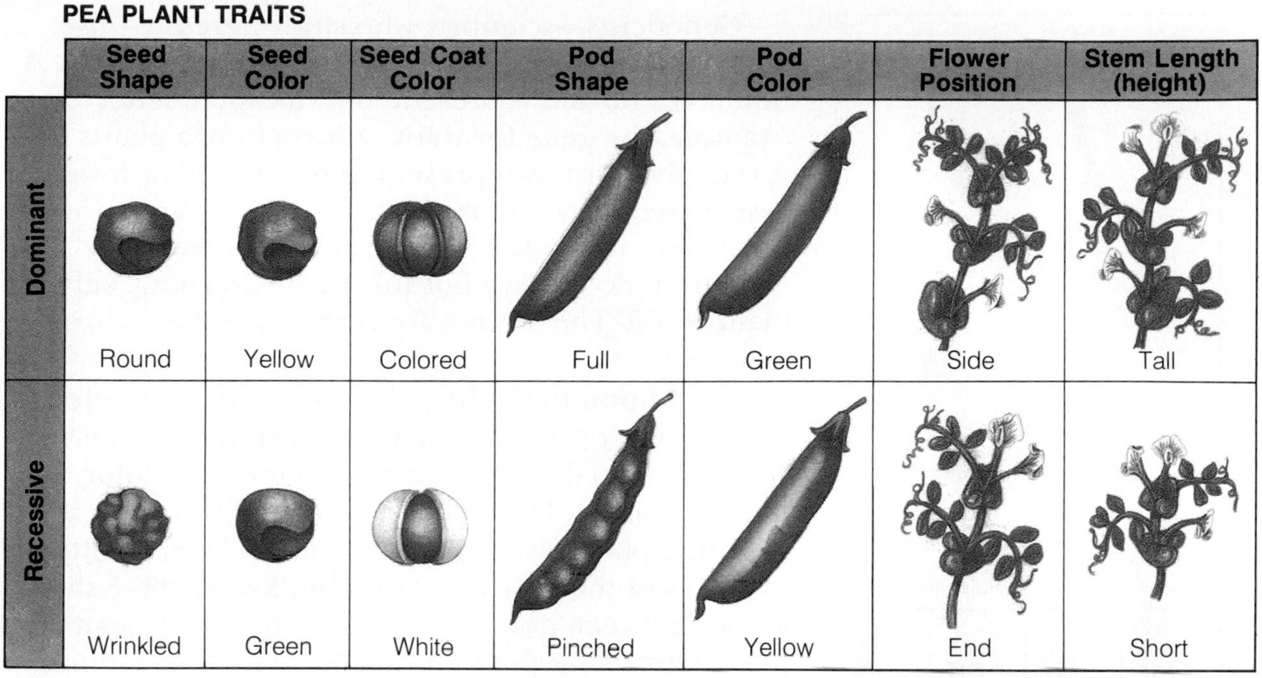

PEA PLANT TRAITS

	Seed Shape	Seed Color	Seed Coat Color	Pod Shape	Pod Color	Flower Position	Stem Length (height)
Dominant	Round	Yellow	Colored	Full	Green	Side	Tall
Recessive	Wrinkled	Green	White	Pinched	Yellow	End	Short

Figure 23–4 *The chart shows the seven characteristics that Mendel studied in pea plants. Each characteristic has a dominant gene and a recessive gene. Which seed color is dominant in pea plants?*

tall plants in the F₂ generation. But how could the shortness trait disappear in the F₁ generation and then mysteriously reappear in the F₂ generation? Obviously, the trait did not disappear—it was merely hidden, or masked, in some of the plants.

Mendel realized that each plant must contain two factors for a particular trait. In some plants, the two factors were both for the tallness trait. Plants with two tallness factors were true breeders and only produced other tall plants. In the same way, short plants contained two shortness factors and were true-breeding short plants. But some plants, Mendel reasoned, contained a tallness factor and a shortness factor. If a plant contained both tallness and shortness factors, the plant would grow tall. But it might still pass on its shortness factor to the next generation of plants. These factors, which Mendel called "characters," are now called **genes.** Genes are the units of heredity.

From his observations, Mendel also concluded that when he crossed two true-breeding plants with opposite traits (tallness and shortness, for example), the offspring plants showed only one of the traits (tallness). That trait seemed to be "stronger" than the other trait (shortness). The stronger trait is called the **dominant** trait. The "weaker" trait, or the trait that seemed to disappear, is called the **recessive** trait.

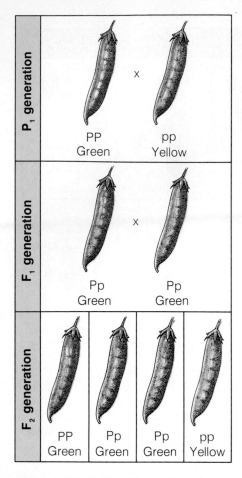

Figure 23–5 *The illustration shows a cross between two pea plants. Examine the first and second generations. Which pod color is recessive?*

Geneticists—scientists who study heredity—use symbols to represent the different forms of a gene. A dominant form is represented by a capital letter. For example, the gene form for tallness in pea plants is T. A recessive form is represented by a small, or lower-case, letter. Thus, shortness is t. Every organism has two forms, or **alleles** (uh-LEELZ), of the gene for each trait. So the symbol for a true-breeding tall plant is TT. The symbol for a true-breeding short plant is tt.

In addition to the height of pea plants, Mendel studied other traits. These traits were seed shape, seed color, seed coat color, pod shape, pod color, and flower position. In every case, crossing two true-breeding plants with opposite traits did not result in mixtures of the trait. For example, Figure 23–5 shows a cross between a plant with green pods (PP) and a plant with yellow pods (pp). The type of pods that are produced in the F_1 generation are all green. Why? The allele for green pods, P, is dominant. It masks, or hides, the allele for yellow pods, which is recessive. Therefore, all the pods are green. What happens when the F_1 generation pollinates itself? Most of the pods are green and some are yellow. The recessive trait for yellow pods reappears in the F_2 generation.

Scientists call organisms that have alleles that are alike for a particular trait, such as PP or pp, pure-bred. An organism that has alleles that are different for a trait (Pp) is called a **hybrid** (HIGH-brihd). Is a short-stemmed pea plant a purebred or a hybrid?

Inheriting Traits

By examining his observations and results, Mendel formed a hypothesis about how traits are inherited. A hypothesis is a suggested explanation for a scientific problem. Mendel's hypothesis was that each pea plant parent has a pair of factors. Mendel further reasoned that each parent could contribute only one of these factors to each pea plant in the next generation. In that way, the next generation also had two factors for each trait, one from each parent.

Now Mendel was finally able to account for the results of his pea plant experiments. You may recall that when he crossed true-breeding tall plants, all the generations that followed were tall. The reason for this was that all the tall plants were purebreds. That is, the alleles in each of the tall plants consisted of only tallness alleles. So the alleles for these plants were TT. Each of these plants could contribute one tallness allele (T) to its offspring. So each offspring received two tallness alleles (TT), one from each parent. And all the offspring were tall.

The same was true for Mendel's cross between two short plants. The alleles for each parent plant were tt. So each plant in the F_1 generation received a shortness allele (t) from each parent. The offspring all had two shortness alleles (tt) and all were short.

What happened when Mendel then crossed a purebred tall plant (TT) with a purebred short plant (tt) to produce the F_1 generation? Each parent could contribute one allele to its offspring. As a result, the offspring were hybrids (Tt) because they received a tallness allele (T) and a shortness allele (t). Because the dominant tallness allele masked the recessive shortness allele, all of the offspring were tall. Although the offspring had a shortness allele, it was masked by the tallness allele. The shortness trait seemed to disappear in the F_1 generation.

When Mendel crossed the hybrid plants of the F_1 generation to produce the F_2 generation, some of the plants were tall and some of them were short. The reason for this was that each parent in the F_1 generation had one tallness allele and one shortness allele (Tt). So each parent could contribute a tallness allele or a shortness allele to the next generation. Most of the time, one of the parents contributed a tallness

ACTIVITY

DISCOVERING

Observing Traits

Visit a garden center or greenhouse. Take a notebook and a pencil to record your observations.

1. Choose one type of flowering plant to observe, such as petunias, marigolds, or chrysanthemums.

2. To observe the genetic traits of the flowering plant you chose, you must observe 10 of these plants. Look closely at each of the plants.

3. Note common and uncommon traits among the plants, such as the shape of the leaves or the color of the flower petals.

What common traits did you observe on most of the plants?

What uncommon traits did you see on one or more of the plants but not on most of them?

■ How can you detemine which traits are dominant?

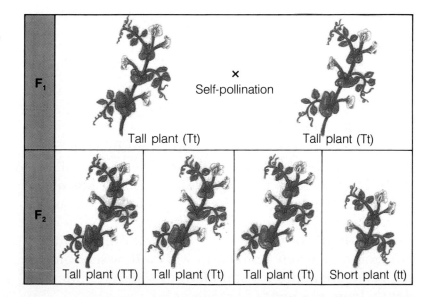

Figure 23–6 *To Mendel's surprise, when he crossed two tall pea plants from the F_1 generation, the trait of shortness reappeared in the F_2 generation. Why did the shortness trait reappear?*

589

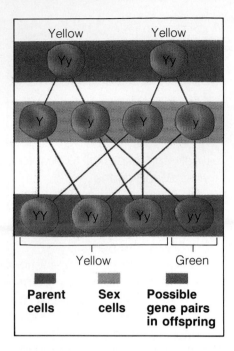

Yellow	Yellow	
Yy	Yy	
Y	y	Y	y
YY	Yy	Yy	yy
Yellow		Green

▬	▬	▬
Parent cells	**Sex cells**	**Possible gene pairs in offspring**

Figure 23–7 *Mendel discovered that a pea plant with green seeds can develop from a cross between parents with yellow seeds. How does this happen?*

Figure 23–8 *The diagram illustrates the law of segregation, describing how one of the parent's genes goes to each sex cell. Why do organisms resemble their parents?*

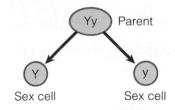

Yy Parent

Y y

Sex cell Sex cell

LAW OF SEGREGATION

allele to the F_2 generation. So most of the F_2 generation had at least one tallness allele. Therefore, most of the plants were tall. But some of the time both parents contributed a shortness allele to the F_2 generation. Those plants in the F_2 generation that received a shortness allele from both parents had the alleles tt. And all of these plants were short. The shortness trait that had mysteriously disappeared in the F_1 generation had reappeared in the F_2 generation.

Mendel applied his experimental results to the other traits he studied. For example, he could explain why a cross between parents with yellow seeds could produce some plants with green seeds. Why? The yellow seed allele is dominant. But the plants were not purebred. That is, the plants with yellow seed alleles also contained a recessive green seed allele. The allele for yellow seed can be written as Y. The allele for green seed can be written as y. A parent that has Yy alleles would have yellow seeds. But if plants with Yy alleles were crossed, some of the offspring would receive a recessive green seed allele (y) from both parents. Those offspring would have two green seed alleles (yy) and would have green seeds—even though both their parents had yellow seeds! See Figure 23–7.

When the parent plant forms sex cells (sperm or eggs), the parent's gene pairs segregate, or separate. This process is known as the **law of segregation.** According to the law of segregation, one allele from each pair goes to each sex cell. Half of the sex cells of a hybrid pea plant with the gene pair Yy have an allele for yellow seeds (Y). The other half of the sex cells carry an allele for green seeds (y). As a result of sexual reproduction, a male sex cell (sperm) and a female sex cell (egg) unite to form a fertilized egg. Each fertilized egg contains one allele for seed color from each parent, so the gene pair for seed color is formed again.

Mendel also crossed pea plants that differed from one another by two or more traits. The results of these crosses led to the development of the **law of independent assortment.** The law of independent assortment states that each gene pair for a trait is inherited independently of the gene pairs for all other traits. For example, when a tall plant with yellow seeds forms sex cells, the genes for stem length separate independently from the genes for seed color.

Incomplete Dominance

Mendel's ideas that genes are always dominant or recessive often hold true—but not always. In 1900, Karl Correns, a German botanist, made an important discovery. Correns discovered that in some gene pairs the genes are neither dominant nor recessive. These genes show **incomplete dominance.** In incomplete dominance, neither gene in a gene pair masks the other.

Working with four-o'clock flowers, Correns discovered that when he crossed purebred red four-o'clocks (RR) with purebred white four-o'clocks (WW), the result was all pink four-o'clock flowers (RW). See Figure 23–9. Notice that the symbols for the gene pairs for red, white, and pink are all capital letters. No one gene is dominant over the others.

Incomplete dominance also occurs in animals. One of the most famous examples of this is seen in the beautiful horses known as palominos. Palominos are pale golden-brown with a white mane and tail. If a purebred chestnut-brown horse (BB) is crossed with a purebred creamy-white horse (WW), their offspring will all be palominos (BW). If two palominos are crossed, what colors will their offspring be? Is it possible to have purebred palominos?

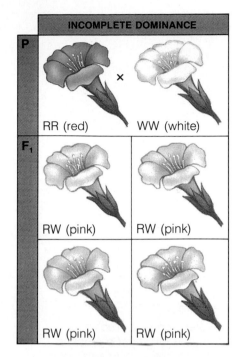

Figure 23–9 *In four-o'clock flowers, neither the red gene nor the white gene is dominant. When these two genes are present in the same plant, a pink flower results.*

Principles of Genetics

Through the work of scientists such as Mendel and Correns, certain basic principles of genetics have been established. These basic principles are

- **Traits, or characteristics, are passed on from one generation of organisms to the next generation.**
- **The traits of an organism are controlled by genes.**
- **Organisms inherit genes in pairs, one gene from each parent.**
- **Some genes are dominant, whereas other genes are recessive.**
- **Dominant genes hide recessive genes when both are inherited by an organism.**
- **Some genes are neither dominant nor recessive. These genes show incomplete dominance.**

Incomplete Dominance

1. Obtain two coins.

2. Cut four equal pieces of masking tape to fit on the coins without overlapping.

3. Place a piece of tape on each side of both coins.

4. Write the letter R on one side of each coin and the letter W on the other side.

5. Toss both coins 100 times. Record each toss.

What is the percentage of occurrence for each gene pair?

Guide for Reading

Focus on this question as you read.

▶ How can you predict the results of genetic crosses using probability and Punnett squares?

ctivity Bank

Flip Out!, p. 829

Figure 23–10 *According to the law of probability, a coin will land heads up 50 percent of the time and tails up 50 percent of the time.*

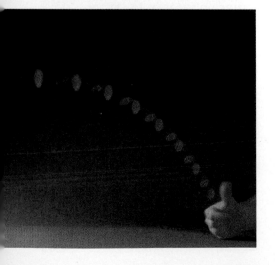

23–2 Genetics and Probability

In one of Mendel's experiments, he crossed two plants that were hybrid for yellow seeds (Yy). When he examined the plants that resulted, he discovered that about one seed out of every four was green. By applying the concept of **probability** to his work, Mendel was able to express his observations mathematically. He could say that the probability of such a cross producing green seeds was 1/4, or 25 percent. Probability is the possibility, or likelihood, that a particular event will take place. **Probability can be used to predict the results of genetic crosses.**

Probability

Suppose that you are about to toss a coin. What are the chances that the coin will land heads up? If you said a 50 percent chance, you are correct. What are the chances that the coin will land tails up? Again, the answer is 50 percent. Although you may not realize it, you, like Gregor Mendel, used the laws of probability to arrive at your answers. You figured out the chance, or likelihood, that the coin would come up heads (or tails) on one toss.

A probability is usually written as a fraction or as a percentage. For example, the chance that a sex cell will receive a Y gene from a parent with a Yy gene pair is 1/2, or 50 percent. In other words, you would expect one half, or 50 percent, of the sex cells to receive a Y gene.

generations of offspring very quickly. Third, their body cells have only four pairs of chromosomes (eight chromosomes), making them easy to study.

Morgan quickly discovered something strange about the fruit flies' four pairs of chromosomes. In female fruit flies, the chromosomes of each pair were the same shape. In males, however, the chromosomes of one pair were not the same shape. One chromosome of the pair was shaped like a rod, and the other chromosome was shaped like a hook. Morgan called the rod-shaped chromosome the X chromosome and the hook-shaped chromosome the Y chromosome.

After performing a number of experiments and analyzing his results, Morgan discovered that the X and Y chromosomes determine the sex of an organism. For this reason, the X and Y chromosomes are called **sex chromosomes.** In general, an organism (such as a fruit fly or a human) that has two X chromosomes (XX) is a female. An organism that has one X chromosome and one Y chromosome (XY) is a male. There are some exceptions to this general rule. Female birds, for example, have an X chromosome and a Y chromosome instead of two X chromosomes. Based on this information, can you predict what sex chromosomes are found in male birds?

Mutations

In 1886, while out on a walk, Hugo De Vries (duh-VREES), a Dutch botanist, made an accidental discovery that would go beyond Mendel's work. De Vries came across a group of flowers called American evening primroses. As with Mendel's pea plants, some

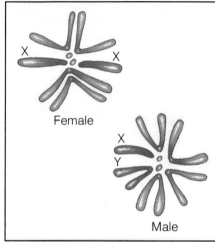

Figure 23–16 *A fruit fly, shown here magnified ten times, has four pairs of chromosomes. A female fruit fly has two X chromosomes. A male fruit fly has one X and one Y chromosome. What are the X and Y chromosomes called?*

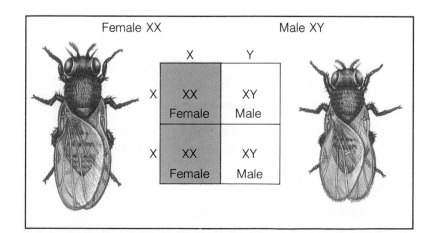

Activity Bank

Stalking the Wild Fruit Fly, p. 832

Figure 23–17 *You can see from the drawings of the male and female fruit flies that they have some physical differences. The Punnett square shows the probable sex of their offspring.*

597

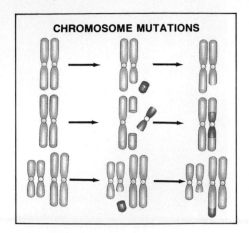

CHROMOSOME MUTATIONS

Figure 23–18 *In chromosome mutations, part of a chromosome may be lost (top), turned around (center), or become attached to a different chromosome (bottom). What may happen if one of these mutations occurs in a sex cell?*

Figure 23–19 *A mutation has left this frog with six legs. These sweet and juicy navel oranges are also the result of a mutation.*

primroses appeared very different from others. De Vries bred the primroses and got results similar to the results of Mendel's work with pea plants. But he also found that every once in a while, a new variety of primrose would grow—a variety that could not be accounted for by the laws of genetics at that time. De Vries called the sudden changes he observed in the characteristics of primroses **mutations.** A mutation is a change in a gene or chromosome.

If a mutation occurs in a body cell such as a skin cell, the mutation affects only the organism that carries it. But if a mutation occurs in a sex cell, then that mutation can be passed on to an offspring. The mutation may then cause a change in the characteristics of the next generation.

Many mutations reduce an organism's chances for survival or reproduction. For example, sickle cell anemia is a serious blood disease caused by a mutation in a gene. Sickle cell anemia results in blood cells that are shaped like a sickle or half circle. People who have sickle cell anemia have difficulty obtaining enough oxygen. This happens because the sickle-shaped cell cannot carry enough oxygen to all the cells in the body. The sickle-shaped cells may clump and clog tiny blood vessels.

Some mutations cause desirable traits in living things. For example, when mutations occur in crop plants, the crops may become more useful to people. A gene mutation in potatoes has produced a new variety of potato called the Katahdin potato. This potato is resistant to diseases that attack other potatoes and also looks and tastes better.

Many mutations are neutral and do not produce any obvious changes in an organism. Still others are lethal, or deadly, and result in the immediate death of an organism.

23–3 Section Review

1. What is the role of chromosomes in heredity?
2. Explain the chromosome theory of heredity.
3. What is meiosis?
4. What is a mutation?

Connection—*Environmental Science*
5. How can a particular mutation be helpful in preventing environmental pollution?

Incomplete Dominance

Mendel's ideas that genes are always dominant or recessive often hold true—but not always. In 1900, Karl Correns, a German botanist, made an important discovery. Correns discovered that in some gene pairs the genes are neither dominant nor recessive. These genes show **incomplete dominance.** In incomplete dominance, neither gene in a gene pair masks the other.

Working with four-o'clock flowers, Correns discovered that when he crossed purebred red four-o'clocks (RR) with purebred white four-o'clocks (WW), the result was all pink four-o'clock flowers (RW). See Figure 23–9. Notice that the symbols for the gene pairs for red, white, and pink are all capital letters. No one gene is dominant over the others.

Incomplete dominance also occurs in animals. One of the most famous examples of this is seen in the beautiful horses known as palominos. Palominos are pale golden-brown with a white mane and tail. If a purebred chestnut-brown horse (BB) is crossed with a purebred creamy-white horse (WW), their offspring will all be palominos (BW). If two palominos are crossed, what colors will their offspring be? Is it possible to have purebred palominos?

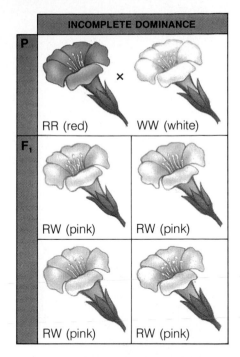

Figure 23–9 In four-o'clock flowers, neither the red gene nor the white gene is dominant. When these two genes are present in the same plant, a pink flower results.

Principles of Genetics

Through the work of scientists such as Mendel and Correns, certain basic principles of genetics have been established. These basic principles are

- **Traits, or characteristics, are passed on from one generation of organisms to the next generation.**
- **The traits of an organism are controlled by genes.**
- **Organisms inherit genes in pairs, one gene from each parent.**
- **Some genes are dominant, whereas other genes are recessive.**
- **Dominant genes hide recessive genes when both are inherited by an organism.**
- **Some genes are neither dominant nor recessive. These genes show incomplete dominance.**

Incomplete Dominance

1. Obtain two coins.

2. Cut four equal pieces of masking tape to fit on the coins without overlapping.

3. Place a piece of tape on each side of both coins.

4. Write the letter R on one side of each coin and the letter W on the other side.

5. Toss both coins 100 times. Record each toss.

What is the percentage of occurrence for each gene pair?

23–1 Section Review

1. What is genetics?
2. Compare dominant and recessive traits.
3. List six basic principles of genetics.
4. What is incomplete dominance?
5. What is a hybrid organism?

Critical Thinking—*Relating Concepts*

6. Can a short-stemmed pea plant ever be a hybrid? Explain why or why not.

Guide for Reading

Focus on this question as you read.

▶ *How can you predict the results of genetic crosses using probability and Punnett squares?*

ctivity Bank

Flip Out!, p. 829

Figure 23–10 *According to the law of probability, a coin will land heads up 50 percent of the time and tails up 50 percent of the time.*

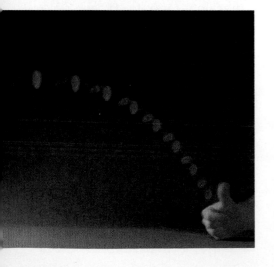

23–2 Genetics and Probability

In one of Mendel's experiments, he crossed two plants that were hybrid for yellow seeds (Yy). When he examined the plants that resulted, he discovered that about one seed out of every four was green. By applying the concept of **probability** to his work, Mendel was able to express his observations mathematically. He could say that the probability of such a cross producing green seeds was 1/4, or 25 percent. Probability is the possibility, or likelihood, that a particular event will take place. **Probability can be used to predict the results of genetic crosses.**

Probability

Suppose that you are about to toss a coin. What are the chances that the coin will land heads up? If you said a 50 percent chance, you are correct. What are the chances that the coin will land tails up? Again, the answer is 50 percent. Although you may not realize it, you, like Gregor Mendel, used the laws of probability to arrive at your answers. You figured out the chance, or likelihood, that the coin would come up heads (or tails) on one toss.

A probability is usually written as a fraction or as a percentage. For example, the chance that a sex cell will receive a Y gene from a parent with a Yy gene pair is 1/2, or 50 percent. In other words, you would expect one half, or 50 percent, of the sex cells to receive a Y gene.

23–4 DNA

"We wish to suggest a structure for the salt of deoxyribose nucleic acid." So began a letter from two scientists in 1953 to a scientific journal. What followed was a description of the structure that would help unlock the deepest secrets of genetics.

The structure written about in the letter was deoxyribonucleic (dee-AHK-sih-righ-boh-noo-KLAY-ihk) acid, or **DNA.** DNA is the basic substance of heredity. **DNA stores and passes on genetic information from one generation to the next.**

The two scientists who wrote the letter about DNA were James Watson, an American biologist, and Francis Crick, a British biologist. In 1962, they, along with Maurice Wilkins, were awarded the Nobel Prize for physiology or medicine for their work on the structure of DNA. Many scientists believe that the discovery of the structure of DNA was the most important biological event of this century.

Watson and Crick's discovery showed that chromosomes are made of molecules of DNA. And the DNA molecules in chromosomes contain the genes. So DNA is the hereditary material that carries the genes that control all traits passed on from parents to offspring.

The Structure of DNA

The structure of DNA looks like a twisted ladder, or spiral staircase, with steps made of nitrogen bases. See Figure 23–20. Notice that the steps, or rungs, of this twisted ladder are formed by pairs of substances called nitrogen bases. Nitrogen bases are substances that contain the element nitrogen. There are four different nitrogen bases in DNA. They are adenine (AD-uhn-een), guanine (GWAH-neen), cytosine (SIGHT-uh-seen), and thymine (THIGH-meen).

You can see in Figure 23–22 on page 600 that the two nitrogen bases that make up each rung of the DNA ladder combine in very specific ways. Scientists use the capital letters, A, G, C, and T to represent each of the four nitrogen bases. In the DNA ladder, adenine (A) always pairs with thymine (T). Guanine (G) always pairs with cytosine (C).

Guide for Reading

Focus on this question as you read.

▶ *What is the role of DNA in heredity?*

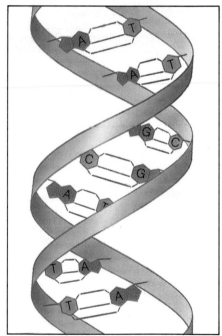

Figure 23–20 *This illustration shows the ladderlike structure of a DNA molecule (top). The DNA molecule is made up of smaller units consisting of a sugar, a phosphate group, and a nitrogen base (bottom).*

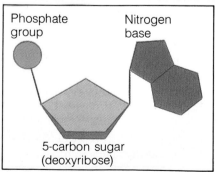

Phosphate group

Nitrogen base

5-carbon sugar (deoxyribose)

Figure 23–21 *James Watson and Francis Crick are shown in front of their model of a DNA molecule (left). Cytosine—one of the nitrogen bases found in DNA—has been synthetically produced in the laboratory (right).*

ACTIVITY

READING

Discovering the Discoverers

James Watson's book *The Double Helix* provides an inside look at the process of scientific discovery.

Figure 23–22 *In a DNA molecule, the nitrogen bases that make up the rungs of the ladder always combine in a specific way. Which nitrogen base always combines with thymine?*

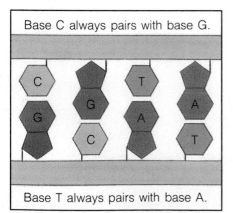

Base C always pairs with base G.

C — G
T — A
G — C
A — T

Base T always pairs with base A.

The DNA ladder may contain hundreds or even thousands of rungs. So a DNA molecule may contain hundreds or even thousands of pairs of nitrogen bases. In addition to discovering DNA's structure, Watson and Crick found out that the order of the nitrogen bases on a DNA molecule determines the particular genes on a chromosome. That is why DNA is said to carry the genetic code. The genetic code is actually the order of nitrogen bases on the DNA molecule.

Because a DNA molecule can have many hundreds of bases arranged in any order, the number of different genes is almost limitless. That is why living things on Earth can display such a wide variety of traits. Changing the order of only one pair of nitrogen bases in a DNA molecule can result in a new gene that determines a completely different trait.

DNA Replication

In Chapter 3, you read how body cells divide into two similar cells in a process called mitosis. Before a body cell can divide into two cells, the DNA in the nucleus must be duplicated, or copied, so that each new cell gets the same amount and kind of DNA as the original parent cell. Just how does this happen?

The process in which DNA molecules form exact duplicates is called **replication** (rehp-luh-KAY-shuhn). During replication, the DNA ladder separates, or unzips. See Figure 23–23. The separation, or unzipping, occurs between the two nitrogen bases that form each rung of the DNA molecule. So after the

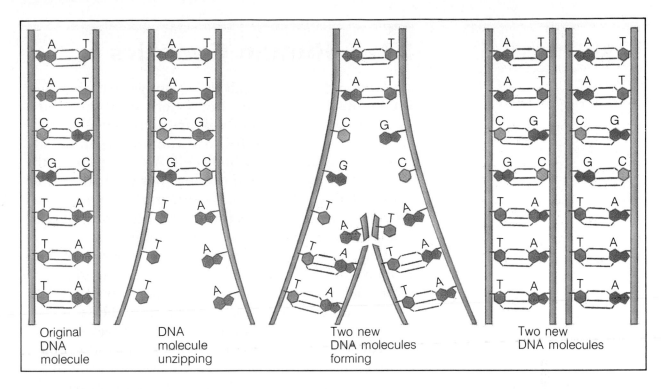

Original DNA molecule   DNA molecule unzipping   Two new DNA molecules forming   Two new DNA molecules

first step in replication, the DNA has split into two "halves of a ladder." Next, free nitrogen bases that are "floating" in the nucleus begin to pair up with the nitrogen bases on each half of DNA. Remember that adenine (A) attaches to thymine (T) and guanine (G) attaches to cytosine (C).

Once each new base has attached itself to a base on each half of the DNA molecule, two new DNA molecules form. And each molecule is an exact duplicate of the original DNA molecule. Look at Figure 23–23 again.

Figure 23–23 *In this illustration, you can see how a DNA molecule duplicates itself in the process of replication. What is the first step in the process of DNA replication?*

23–4 Section Review

1. What role does DNA play in heredity?
2. Describe the structure of DNA. What four nitrogen bases are found in DNA?
3. What is replication? List the steps in the process of replication.

Critical Thinking—*Making Inferences*

4. The nitrogen bases on one half of a DNA molecule are in the following order: AGTTCTCCAG. What is the order of the nitrogen bases on the other half of the molecule?

ACTIVITY

CALCULATING

Counting Bases

Suppose that a DNA molecule contains 2000 nitrogen base pairs. If 30 percent of the bases are thymines, how many adenines are there in this DNA molecule?

23–5 Human Genetics

Human beings, like all living things, are what they are because of the genes they inherit from their parents. These genes—and there are about 100,000 of them—are located on the 46 chromosomes in the nucleus of almost every body cell. An exception is the sex cells, which have half the number of chromosomes. The 46 chromosomes consist of 23 pairs. Each pair has matching genes for a particular trait such as eye color, hair color, and ear lobe shape.

Because a person gets one matching chromosome from each parent, the person gets matching genes from each parent. For example, you received genes for eye color from each of your parents. The way these genes combined determined your eye color.

As you can see, human genes seem to follow the same pattern of inheritance as the genes in the pea plants that Mendel studied more than a century ago. **Scientists can now apply some of the basic principles of genetics to the study of human heredity.** Read on to discover more about human traits.

Multiple Alleles

Earlier in this chapter, you learned that a trait, such as the color of a flower, is determined by how a pair of genes act. You learned that one gene in the pair may be dominant or recessive. And the same can be said of the other gene in the pair.

In humans, some traits are not so easily determined. Skin color, for example, is determined by several genes. Various combinations of these genes can produce all the skin colors of all people. Each form of a gene is called an **allele** (uh-LEEL). In many flowers, there are only two alleles for flower color. In human skin, there may be three or more alleles for a single skin-color gene. In other words, the gene has **multiple alleles,** or more than two alleles.

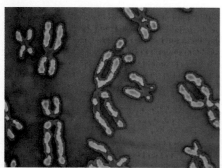
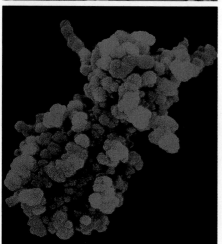

Figure 23–24 *In the photograph on the top you can see some of the 23 chromosome pairs found in human cells. One human chromosome, magnified about 20,000 times by an electron microscope, is shown in the photograph on the bottom. How many chromosomes does each human body cell contain?*

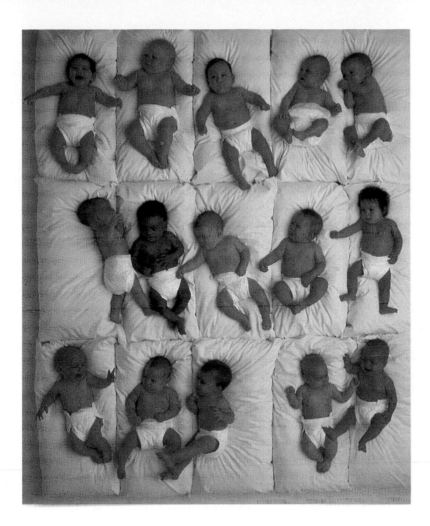

Figure 23–25 *Because eight alleles determine human skin color, humans come in a rainbow of skin colors. What is an allele?*

In addition to skin color, the four major human blood groups are also determined by multiple alleles. These groups are called A, B, AB, and O. Scientists know blood groups are determined by multiple alleles because there is no way a single pair of alleles can produce four different characteristics.

Both the allele for group A blood and that for group B blood are dominant. In other words, they are codominant. When two codominant alleles are inherited, both are expressed. For example, a person who inherits an allele for group A blood from one parent and an allele for group B blood from the other parent will have group AB blood. The O allele, however, is recessive. So a person who inherits an O allele and an A allele will have group A blood. A person who inherits an O allele and a B allele will have group B blood. What two alleles must a person inherit to have group O blood?

Figure 23–26 *According to the table, what two possible allele combinations might a person with group A blood have?*

BLOOD GROUP ALLELES	
Blood Groups	**Combination of Alleles**
A	AA or AO
B	BB or BO
AB	AB
O	OO

ACTIVITY

Discovery of Sickle Cell Anemia

Sickle cell anemia was discovered and named by James Herrick, an American doctor. Use library references to find out about Dr. Herrick and how he came to discover sickle cell anemia. Write a brief report of your findings.

Inherited Diseases

Sometimes the structure of an inherited gene contains an error. If the gene controls the production of an important protein such as hemoglobin, the hemoglobin will also have an error in its structure. Hemoglobin is the red pigment in blood. In such a case, the hemoglobin may not do its job well. This is an example of what scientists call an inherited disease.

People with sickle cell anemia have inherited two sickle cell genes, one from each parent. This is because the gene for normal hemoglobin is codominant with the sickle cell gene. (Remember that when two codominant genes are inherited, both are expressed.) When each gene is present, the person is said to be a carrier of the sickle cell trait. About half of a carrier's hemoglobin is normal. Carriers, therefore, show few of the harmful effects of sickle cell anemia. When both sickle cell genes are present, however, the person has sickle cell anemia and suffers all of the effects of the disorder.

In the United States, most carriers of sickle cell anemia are African Americans. In fact, about 10 percent of African Americans carry the sickle cell trait. As many as 40 percent of the population in some parts of Africa may be sickle cell carriers. The frequency of sickle cell anemia in certain areas has to do with the relationship between sickle cell anemia and

Figure 23–27 *As you can see, the shape of a red blood cell in a person who has sickle cell anemia (left) is quite different from the normal shape of a red blood cell (right). Can a person inherit sickle cell anemia from only one parent?*

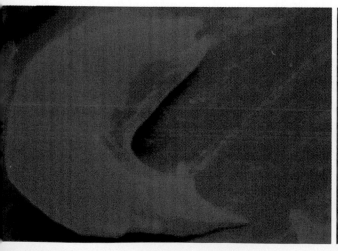
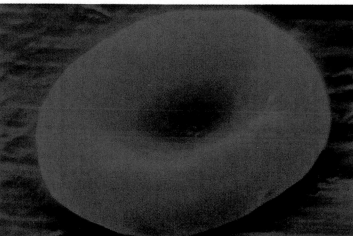

PROBLEM ??? Solving

Pedestrian Genetics

The inhabitants of the planet Pedestria (called Pedestrians) never invented the wheel, so they walk a lot. As a result of all this walking, they have very big feet. The feet of the Pedestrians may be either red, blue, purple, or green, depending on what combination of genes for foot color they inherit from their parents. The table shows the relationship between foot color (phenotype) and gene combinations (genotype).

How many alleles are there for Pedestrian foot color? Are any of the alleles dominant? Recessive? Codominant? Suppose a male Pedestrian with blue feet (BG) marries a female Pedestrian with purple feet (RB). Is it possible for them to have a child with green feet? Why or why not? What percentage of their offspring could have each possible phenotype? Genotype?

Phenotype	Genotype
Red	RR or RG
Blue	BB or BG
Purple	RB
Green	GG

malaria. Malaria is a disease that is common in Africa and other tropical parts of the world. Malaria (like sickle cell anemia) affects the red blood cells. Scientists have found that sickle cell carriers are partially resistant to malaria. Thus the sickle cell trait probably developed as a mutation that helped people who were carriers of the trait to resist malaria.

Sex-Linked Traits

You will remember from earlier in the chapter that X and Y chromosomes are sex chromosomes. The X and Y chromosomes are the only chromosome pairs that do not always match each other. All body cells of normal human males carry one X chromosome and one Y chromosome. Females have two matching X chromosomes, or XX.

Figure 23–28 *As shown in this illustration, there is a 25 percent chance that a female who carries a gene for hemophilia and a normal male will have a son with hemophilia. Why is hemophilia called a sex-linked trait?*

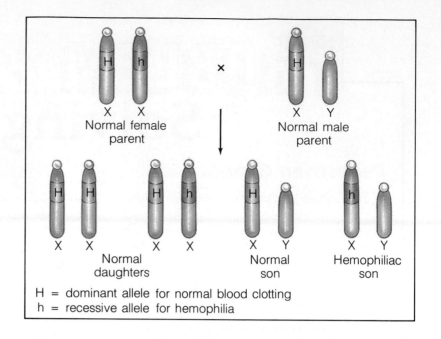

Figure 23–28 *As shown in this illustration, there is a 25 percent chance that a female who carries a gene for hemophilia and a normal male will have a son with hemophilia. Why is hemophilia called a sex-linked trait?*

Figure 23–29 *Colorblindness is a sex-linked trait. Why are very few females colorblind?*

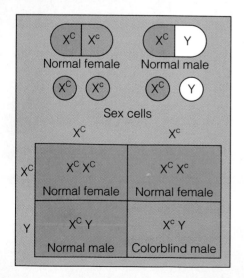

X chromosomes also carry genes for traits other than sex. However, Y chromosomes carry few, if any, genes other than those for maleness. Therefore, any gene—even a recessive gene—carried on an X chromosome will produce a trait in a male who inherits the gene. This is because there is no matching gene on the Y chromosome. Such traits are called **sex-linked traits** because they are passed from parent to child on a sex chromosome, the X chromosome. Because a female has two X chromosomes, a recessive gene on one X chromosome can be masked, or hidden, by a dominant gene on the other X chromosome.

An example of a disorder caused by a sex-linked trait is hemophilia (hee-moh-FIHL-ee-uh). Hemophilia is an inherited disease in which the blood clots very slowly or not at all. This disease was very common in the royal families of Europe. During the nineteenth century, Queen Victoria of England had a son and three grandsons with hemophilia. At least two of her daughters and four of her granddaughters carried the gene for hemophilia on one X chromosome. But they did not have the disease because they carried a gene for normal blood clotting on their other X chromosome. Hemophilia spread through the royal families in Europe as Victoria's descendants married other royalty and passed the hemophilia gene on.

Colorblindness is another sex-linked recessive trait. A person who is colorblind cannot see the difference between certain colors, such as red and green. Difficulty in distinguishing between the colors red and green is the most common type of colorblindness. More males than females are colorblind. A colorblind female must inherit two recessive genes for colorblindness, one from each parent. But a colorblind male needs to inherit only one recessive gene. Why is this so? Remember that males do not have a matching gene on the Y chromosome that could mask the recessive gene on the X chromosome.

Nondisjunction

During meiosis, or the process through which sex cells are formed, chromosome pairs usually separate. But in rare cases a pair may remain joined. This failure of chromosomes to separate from each other is known as **nondisjunction** (nahn-dihs-JUHNG-shuhn). When this happens, body cells inherit either extra or fewer chromosomes than normal.

Look carefully at Figure 23–30. This is an example of a human karyotype (KAR-ee-uh-tighp). A karyotype shows the size, number, and shape of chromosomes in an organism. Usually, people have 46 chromosomes, or 23 chromosome pairs. But now look again at Figure 23–30. How many chromosomes are there?

Figure 23–30 *Down syndrome is a genetic disorder in which all the body cells have an extra twenty-first chromosome. Although people with Down syndrome are mentally and physically challenged, many lead full, active, and productive lives.*

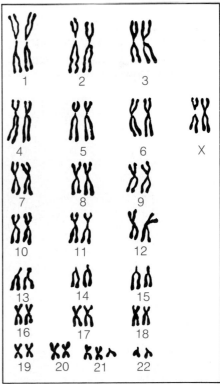

If you said 47, you are correct. The extra chromosome is found in what would normally be the twenty-first pair. When a person has an extra chromosome on the twenty-first pair, a condition called Down syndrome results. People with Down syndrome may have various physical problems and some degree of mental retardation. However, many people with Down syndrome hold jobs and make important contributions to society.

Is there a way of determining before a child is born whether he or she will have Down syndrome or another inherited problem? There are a number of ways. One way to determine before a child is born whether the child will have an inherited disease is called **amniocentesis** (am-nee-oh-sehn-TEE-sihs). Amniocentesis involves the removal of a small amount of fluid from the sac that surrounds a baby while it is still in its mother. This fluid contains some of the baby's cells. Using special techniques, doctors and scientists can examine the chromosomes in these cells. In this way, doctors can discover whether or not an unborn child has Down syndrome. Various other tests can reveal the presence of a variety of inherited disorders. Scientists hope that such tests will eventually lead to the treatment of some disorders before babies are born.

23–5 Section Review

1. What are multiple alleles?
2. If a woman with blood group O marries a man with blood group B, can they have a child with blood group A? Explain.
3. What are sex-linked traits?

Critical Thinking—*Applying Concepts*
4. A man and a woman each have a gene for sickle cell anemia. What is the probability that their child will inherit one gene or both genes for sickle cell anemia?

CONNECTIONS

Hemophilia in History

Queen Victoria of England had a son and three grandsons with hemophilia. Victoria and at least two of her daughters and four of her granddaughters were carriers of the disease. That is, they carried the gene for hemophilia on one X chromosome. They did not have the disease because they carried a normal gene on the other X chromosome. However, they could pass the disease on to their offspring. Hemophilia spread throughout the royal families of Europe as Victoria's descendants passed the hemophilia gene on to their offspring.

Princess Alexandra, one of Queen Victoria's granddaughters, married the Russian czar Nicholas II. Alexandra was a carrier of hemophilia. She passed the disease on to her son, the czarevitch Alexis, who was heir to the throne. Although Alexandra had no experience in ruling, she greatly influenced the actions of her husband, the czar. Unfortunately, she often made bad decisions based on her concern for her son. The monk Rasputin had convinced Alexandra that he could cure Alexis. As a result of his control over Alexandra, Rasputin was able to direct the czar's actions as well. The people's anger at Rasputin's evil influence over the royal family may have played some part in the Russian Revolution of 1917, in which the czar was overthrown.

Laboratory Investigation

Observing the Growth of Mutant Corn Seeds

Problem

What is the effect of a mutation on the growth of corn plants?

Materials *(per group)*

10 albino corn seeds	string
10 normal corn seeds	tape
flower box	marking pen
potting soil	

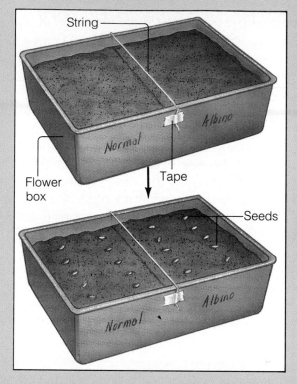

Procedure

1. Fill a flower box about three-fourths full of potting soil.

2. Use a piece of string to divide the flower box in half across the width of the box. Tape the ends of the string to the box to hold the string in place.

3. Label the right side of the box Albino. Label the left side of the box Normal.

4. On the right side of the box, plant each of the albino seeds about 1 cm below the surface of the soil. The seeds should be spaced about 1 cm apart. Water the soil.

5. On the left side of the box, plant each of the normal seeds as you did the albino seeds in step 4.

6. Place the flower box on a table near a window or on a windowsill where it will receive direct sunlight. Keep the soil moist. Observe the box every day for three weeks.

Observations

1. What was the total number of seeds that sprouted?

2. How many albino seeds sprouted? How many normal seeds?

3. What happened to the plants a week after they sprouted? Two weeks?

4. Describe the difference in appearance between the albino plants and the normal plants.

Analysis and Conclusions

1. Did the albino seeds grow as well as the normal seeds?

2. Which seeds, albino or normal, showed the mutation?

3. What effect did the mutation have on the growth of the corn plants?

4. **On Your Own** If you were a farmer, which corn plants—albino or normal—would you choose to grow for their desirable traits? Explain.

Study Guide

Summarizing Key Concepts

23-1 History of Genetics

▲ Genetics is the study of the passing on of traits from an organism to its offspring.

▲ A purebred trait has genes that are alike. A hybrid has genes that are different.

▲ "Stronger" traits are called dominant. "Weaker" traits are called recessive.

▲ According to the law of segregation, one allele from each gene pair goes to each sex cell.

▲ The law of independent assortment states that each gene pair is inherited independently of the gene pairs for all other traits.

▲ In some gene pairs, neither gene is dominant nor recessive. This is known as incomplete dominance.

23-2 Genetics and Probability

▲ Scientist use probability in predicting the results of genetic crosses.

▲ Punnett squares show possible results of a cross between two organisms.

▲ A phenotype is a visible characteristic, while a genotype is the gene makeup.

23-3 Chromosomes

▲ The chromosome theory states that chromosomes are the carriers of genes.

▲ The process of meiosis produces sex cells.

▲ A mutation is a change in the genes that cause the inheritance of a new trait.

23-4 DNA

▲ DNA is the basic substance of heredity.

▲ In DNA replication, two identical copies of the original DNA molecule are formed.

23-5 Human Genetics

▲ Many human traits are controlled by multiple alleles.

▲ In sickle cell anemia, a damaged gene is responsible for making abnormal hemoglobin.

▲ Sex-linked traits are passed from parent to child on the X chromosome.

Reviewing Key Terms

Define each term in a complete sentence.

23-1 History of Genetics
trait
genetics
gene
dominant
recessive
allele
hybrid
law of segregation
law of independent assortment
incomplete dominance

23-2 Genetics and Probability
probability
phenotype
genotype

23-3 Chromosomes
chromosome
chromosome theory
meiosis
sex chromosome
mutation

23-4 DNA
DNA
replication

23-5 Human Genetics
multiple allele
sex-linked trait
nondisjunction
amniocentesis

Chapter Review

Content Review

Multiple Choice

Choose the letter of the answer that best completes each statement.

1. The study of the passing on of characteristics from one organism to its offspring is
   a. microbiology.   c. genetics.
   b. ecology.   d. botany.
2. The factors, or units of heredity, that produce traits are
   a. genes.   c. hybrids.
   b. mutations.   d. triplets.
3. The process by which sex cells are formed is known as
   a. mitosis.   c. replication.
   b. incomplete   d. meiosis.
      dominance.
4. An organism that has genes that are different for a trait is known as a
   a. multiple allele.
   b. dominant.
   c. recessive.
   d. hybrid.
5. The gene makeup of an organism is called its
   a. genotype.   c. mutation.
   b. multiple allele.   d. phenotype.
6. Which states that chromosomes are the carriers of genes?
   a. replication
   b. nondisjunction
   c. chromosome theory
   d. incomplete dominance
7. The basic substance of heredity is
   a. guanine.   c. RNA.
   b. DNA.   d. cytosine.
8. If a girl inherits the allele for group B blood from her mother and the allele for group O blood from her father, she will have blood group
   a. A.   c. AB.
   b. B.   d. O.

True or False

If the statement is true, write "true." If it is false, change the underlined word or words to make the statement true.

1. <u>Thomas Hunt Morgan</u> is known as the Father of Genetics.
2. In the genotype Yy, y represents the <u>recessive</u> gene.
3. An organism that has genes that are different for a trait is called a <u>hybrid</u>.
4. The visible characteristic of an organism is called a <u>phenotype</u>.
5. X and Y are <u>body</u> chromosomes.
6. The process of making more DNA is called <u>meiosis</u>.
7. Colorblindness is a <u>sex-linked</u> trait.
8. The failure of chromosomes to separate is known as <u>nondisjunction</u>.

Concept Mapping

Complete the following concept map for Section 23–1. Then construct a concept map for the entire chapter.

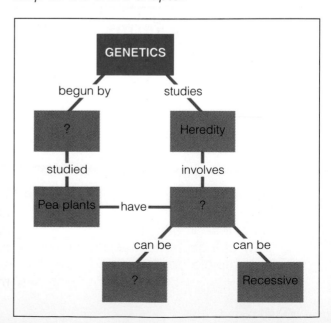

Concept Mastery

Discuss each of the following in a brief paragraph.

1. Explain why Gregor Mendel chose pea plants for his experiments.
2. In your own words, explain the law of segregation and the law of independent assortment, using specific examples.
3. Describe the process of DNA replication. Why is replication necessary?

4. Explain how chromosomes determine the sex of an organism.
5. Does colorblindness occur more frequently in men or in women? Explain.
6. What is nondisjunction? How can nondisjunction cause a genetic disorder?

Critical Thinking and Problem Solving

Use the skills you have developed in this chapter to answer each of the following.

1. **Making predictions** A family has four daughters. What is the probability that a fifth child will be a girl? Does the fact that there are already four daughters in the family increase the probability of having another girl? Explain.
2. **Applying concepts** If a woman developed skin cancer as a result of a gene mutation in the skin cells of her arm, could she pass the skin cancer on to her children? Explain.
3. **Relating concepts** Each body cell in a mouse contains 40 chromosomes. How many chromosomes did the mouse receive from each of its parents? How many chromosomes are present in the mouse's sex cells?
4. **Making calculations** Why are there only 64 possible three-letter code words that can be formed from the four nitrogen bases?
5. **Making inferences** A mutation caused one Bengal tiger in the photograph to be born white instead of orange like other

Bengal tigers. Do you think this mutation would be helpful, harmful, or have no effect on the tiger? Explain.
6. **Using the writing process** As the science reporter for your school newspaper, you have been assigned to interview a doctor who is doing research to try to find a cure for a genetic disorder. Write out a list of questions that you would like to ask the doctor.

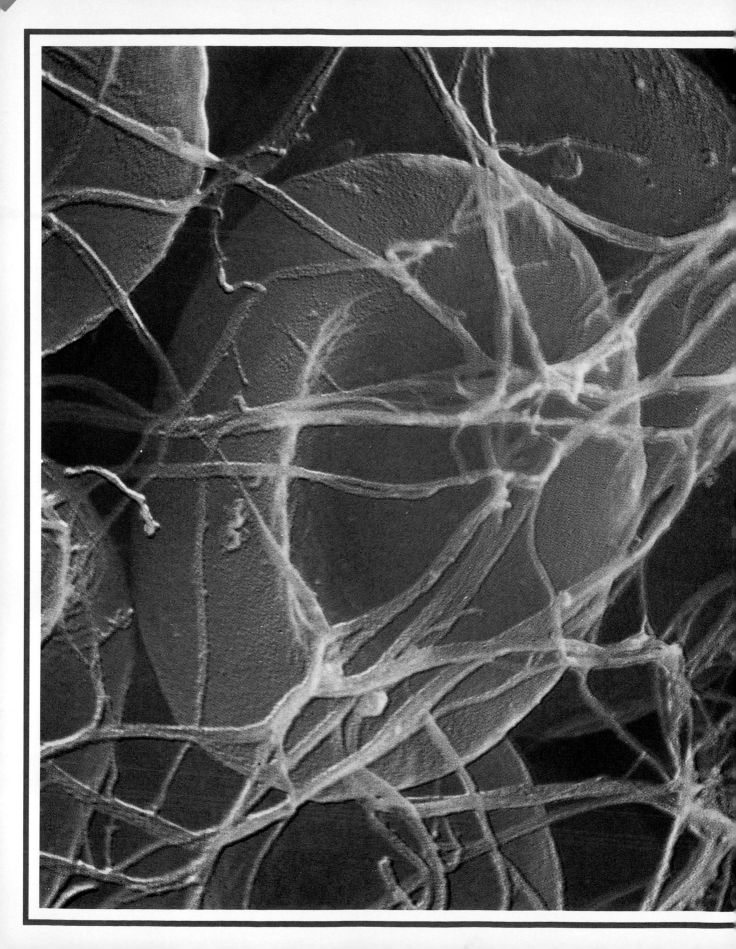

Applied Genetics

In 1990, a young boy named Ryan White died from complications of AIDS. Ryan had hemophilia, a disease caused by a defect in a gene that codes for an important blood-clotting factor. Like thousands of other people with hemophilia, Ryan was dependent on regular injections of this clotting factor to avoid bleeding to death. Usually, this factor is extracted from donated blood. Unfortunately, in Ryan's case the donated blood was contaminated with HIV, the virus that causes AIDS.

Today, donated blood is tested to be sure that it is free of HIV contamination. But people with hemophilia still depend on injections of the clotting factor. Now researchers in California are experimenting with human skin cells that have been genetically altered to produce the missing clotting factor. The researchers hope that implanting the genetically altered cells into the body of a person with hempohilia will enable the body to produce the clotting factor on its own.

In this chapter you will learn how humans have used genetics to produce more nutritious crop plants and stronger, healthier farm animals. You will also find out how scientists are learning to apply the principles of genetics in medicine and agriculture.

Journal *Activity*

You and Your World What do you know about the controversy over the use of genetic engineering in agriculture and medicine? In your journal, describe what you know about genetic engineering and explain why it is controversial.

◄ *This false-color scanning electron micrograph shows how strands of fibrin weave around red blood cells, forming a blood clot.*

24–1 Plant and Animal Breeding

More than 12,000 years ago, people living in the part of the world now called Iraq discovered that wild wheat could be used as food. Through a process of trial and error, these early farmers were able to select and grow wheat that had larger and more nutritious grains than the original wild wheat. People have been breeding plants and animals to produce certain desired traits ever since. This process is called **selective breeding.** Selective breeding is the crossing of plants or animals that have desirable characteristics to produce offspring with those desirable characteristics. Through selective breeding, modern plant and animal breeders are able to produce organisms that are larger in size, provide more food, or are resistant to certain diseases. For example, leaner cattle produce low-fat beef that is more healthful than the beef from fatter cattle. What other examples of selective breeding are you familiar with?

name="Activity Bank" /> **ctivity Bank**

How Can You Grow a Plant From a Cutting?, p. 833

Figure 24–1 *Selective plant and animal breeding has resulted in modern strains of nutritious wheat and disease-resistant cattle.*

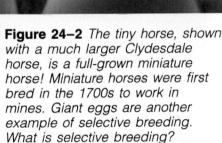

Figure 24–2 *The tiny horse, shown with a much larger Clydesdale horse, is a full-grown miniature horse! Miniature horses were first bred in the 1700s to work in mines. Giant eggs are another example of selective breeding. What is selective breeding?*

Hybridization

Sometimes breeders produce desired traits in the offspring by combining two or more different traits from the parents. To do this, breeders use a technique called **hybridization** (high-brihd-ih-ZAY-shuhn). **Hybridization is the crossing of two genetically different but related species of organisms.** When the organisms are crossed, a hybrid is produced. (Recall from Chapter 23 that a hybrid is an organism that has two different genes for a particular trait.) A hybrid organism is bred to have the best traits of both parents. For example, a mule is a hybrid that combines the traits of two different species, horses and donkeys. A mule is the offspring of a female horse and a male donkey.

Some hybrids are produced naturally. Ancient wild wheat, for example, was a hybrid that formed naturally from the crossing of one species of wild wheat with a species of wild goat grass. The result was a wheat plant with nutritious grains that could be made into bread. Early farmers were able to preserve this new hybrid wheat by selecting some of the best grains and planting them for the next harvest.

ACTIVITY

Luther Burbank

The American plant breeder Luther Burbank produced hundreds of new plant varieties through selective breeding. Read a biography of Burbank and write a report describing some of his contributions to selective plant breeding.

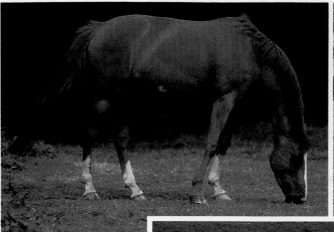

Figure 24–3 *A mule (bottom) combines the best traits of a horse (top left) and a donkey (top right). What is this selective-breeding technique called?*

ACTIVITY

DOING

Cloning

A clone is an organism that is genetically identical to its parent. Seedless grapes and navel oranges are examples of clones. Use library reference materials to learn more about cloning. What are some methods of cloning? What kinds of organisms can be produced by cloning? Make a poster or bulletin board display to illustrate your findings.

In some ways, hybrid offspring may have traits that are better than those of either parent. The hybrid offspring may be stronger or healthier than its parents. Such offspring are said to have hybrid vigor. The word vigor means strength or health. Mules, for example, have more endurance than horses and are stronger than donkeys. One disadvantage of hybridization, however, is that the hybrid offspring is usually sterile, or unable to reproduce.

Inbreeding

Another selective-breeding technique is called **inbreeding.** Inbreeding is the opposite of hybridization. **Inbreeding involves crossing plants or animals that have the same or similar sets of genes, rather than different genes.** Inbred plants or animals have genes that are very similar to their

Figure 24-4 *As a result of inbreeding, all cheetahs are closely related and are susceptible to the same diseases. Why might this be hazardous to the cheetahs' survival?*

parents' genes. One purpose of inbreeding is to keep various breeds of animals, such as horses, pure. Purebred animals tend to keep and pass on their desirable traits. For example, a purebred racehorse that has won many races may be able to pass on its speed and strength to its offspring.

Unfortunately, inbreeding reduces an offspring's chances of inheriting new gene combinations. In other words, inbreeding produces organisms that are genetically similar. This similarity, or lack of genetic difference, in inbred plants and animals may cause the organisms to be susceptible to certain diseases or changing environmental conditions. For example, almost all cheetahs are genetically identical. If all cheetahs have nearly the same genes, they are all susceptible to the same diseases. As a result, wild cheetahs might eventually become extinct, or die off.

24-1 Section Review

1. What is selective breeding?
2. How is inbreeding different from hybridization?
3. What is one advantage of inbreeding? What is one disadvantage?

Critical Thinking—*Making Inferences*
4. Why do you think animals that are produced through inbreeding look so much alike?

ACTIVITY DOING

Examining Different Fruits

In this activity, you will examine a tangelo, which is a cross between a grapefruit and a tangerine. You will also compare the characteristics of a tangelo with those of a grapefruit and those of a tangerine.

1. Obtain a tangelo, a grapefruit, and a tangerine. Place each fruit on a paper towel.

2. Construct a data table to record the following traits for each fruit: size, color, seed size, juiciness, taste, odor.

3. Use a knife to cut each fruit in half. **CAUTION:** *Be careful when using a knife or any sharp instrument.*

4. Examine the tangelo, grapefruit, and tangerine for each trait listed in the data table. Record your observations.

What were the desirable traits in each fruit?

What were the undesirable traits in each?

Why are fruits such as the tangelo developed by plant breeders?

24–2 Genetic Engineering

At one time, most hybrid plants and animals were produced through selective-breeding techniques. In the not-too-distant future, **genetic engineering** may be the primary method of producing hybrids. **Genetic engineering is the process in which genes, or pieces of DNA, from one organism are transferred into another organism.** The production of the supermouse you read about at the beginning of this chapter is an example of genetic engineering.

Recombinant DNA

In one form of genetic engineering, parts of an organism's DNA are joined to the DNA of another organism. The new piece of combined DNA is called **recombinant DNA.** Pieces of recombinant DNA contain DNA from two different organisms. Usually, DNA is transferred from a complex organism (such as a human) into a simpler one (such as a bacterium or a yeast cell). Bacteria and yeast cells are used because they reproduce quickly. As the bacteria or yeast cells reproduce, copies of the recombinant DNA are passed on from one generation to the next. In each generation, the human DNA causes the bacteria or yeast cells to produce human protein.

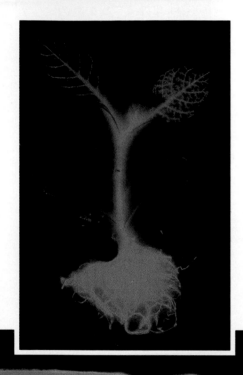

Figure 24–5 *The round structure in the center of this photograph is a developing mouse egg about to be injected with recombinant DNA. The strange-looking plant glows in the dark because it contains firefly genes. The transparent objects in the dish are synthetic celery seeds.*

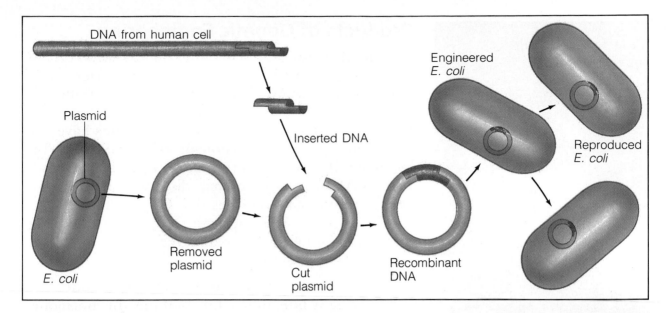

Figure 24–6 *To make recombinant DNA, a plasmid from a bacterium such as* E. coli *is snipped open. A short piece of DNA is then removed from a human cell. The human DNA is inserted into the cut plasmid. Then the plasmid is placed back into the bacterium. What happens next?*

Activity Bank

How Do Bacteria Grow?, p. 835

Making Recombinant DNA

Scientists use special techniques to make recombinant DNA. Figure 24–6 illustrates this process using bacterial and human DNA. Refer to this diagram as you read the description that follows.

Some of the DNA in the bacterium *E. coli* is in the form of a ring called a **plasmid.** You might think of a plasmid as a circle of string. Using special techniques, scientists first remove a plasmid from a bacterium and cut it open. Then they remove a piece of DNA from a human cell. Think of this human DNA as a short piece of string. The scientists then "tie" this piece of human DNA to the cut ends of the bacterial DNA. The bacterial DNA again forms a closed ring. But the bacterial DNA ring now contains a human gene that directs the production of a human protein!

Finally, the scientists put the recombinant DNA back into the bacterial cell. What do you think happens next? The bacterial cell and all its offspring now produce the human protein coded for by the gene in the human DNA. In this way, large amounts of human protein can be produced outside the human body.

Figure 24–7 *Color has been added to this photograph of a bacterial plasmid to highlight two genes (red and blue sections of the plasmid).*

621

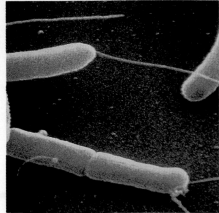

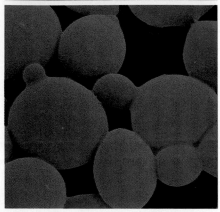

Figure 24–8 *Bacteria, such as E. coli (top), and yeast cells (bottom) are often used by scientists to make recombinant DNA. Why are bacteria and yeast useful for this purpose?*

ACTIVITY

READING

Return of the Dinosaurs

For a fictional account of how genetic engineering might help scientists recreate extinct dinosaurs, read *Jurassic Park* by Michael Crichton.

Products of Genetic Engineering

Scientists use genetic engineering to turn certain bacteria and yeast cells into protein "factories." Grown in huge containers, billions of genetically engineered bacteria and yeast cells produce enormous quantities of proteins. These proteins have important uses in both medicine and agriculture. In medicine, the proteins are used to test for diseases such as AIDS, to treat human disorders such as diabetes, and to make vaccines that help fight diseases such as hepatitis B. In agriculture, genetic engineering is used to help make plants resistant to cold, drought, and disease.

MEDICINE One important product of genetic engineering is human insulin. Without this hormone, the level of sugar in the blood rises, causing a disorder called diabetes mellitus. Some people with diabetes must receive one or more injections of insulin daily. In the past, the insulin used to treat diabetes came from animals such as pigs and cattle. However, many people with diabetes were allergic to this animal insulin. In addition, supplies of animal insulin were limited and expensive. Today, human insulin is produced by genetically engineered bacteria. This insulin does not cause allergies in humans. Supplies are plentiful, and the insulin is inexpensive as a result.

Another protein made by bacteria through genetic engineering is human growth hormone. This hormone, which is normally produced by a gland near the brain, controls growth. A lack of human growth hormone prevents children from growing to their full height. Children whose bodies do not produce enough human growth hormone can be given injections of the hormone. These children often grow 6 to 8 centimeters more each year than they would without the injections of growth hormone. Until 1981, however, there was only a limited supply of human growth hormone available. Many children could not be treated. Then in 1982, bacteria were genetically engineered to produce human growth hormone. Now an almost unlimited supply is available.

Vaccines can also be produced through genetic engineering. When introduced into a person's body, a vaccine triggers the production of antibodies.

Figure 24–9 *Children normally grow at different rates. If a child's body does not produce sufficient amounts of human growth hormone, however, genetically engineered human growth hormone may be administered.*

Antibodies protect a person from disease. Vaccines are made from disease-causing viruses or bacteria. At one time, making the vaccine for hepatitis B (a serious liver disease) was expensive. Now scientists can remove a gene from the hepatitis B virus and insert the gene into a yeast cell. The yeast cell multiplies rapidly and makes large amounts of viral protein. The viral protein is then used to make hepatitis B vaccine. Hepatitis B vaccine is now less expensive to make than it was before genetic engineering.

Another product of genetic engineering is interferon. Interferon, a protein normally produced by human body cells, helps the body fight viruses. One form of interferon may even be helpful in fighting the virus that causes AIDS. Scientists are not really sure how interferon fights viruses. But they do know that when a virus enters a cell, it produces interferon. The interferon then leaves the infected cell and prevents the virus from infecting other cells. Interferon was once very expensive to make. But now, as a result of genetic engineering, supplies of interferon are less expensive and more plentiful.

AGRICULTURE A wide variety of viruses infect important crop plants, including wheat, corn, potatoes, tomatoes, and tobacco. For example, a virus called tobacco mosaic virus attacks and damages tobacco and tomato plants. Scientists have now found a way to protect these plants from the disease-causing virus. Using genetic engineering, scientists can insert genes from the tobacco mosaic virus into plant cells. Although scientists do not yet know why, the viral genes make the plant resistant to tobacco mosaic disease.

Figure 24–10 *You can see the effects of tobacco mosaic virus on the leaves of the tobacco plant. How might genetic engineering help to protect plants from being infected with the tobacco mosaic virus (inset)?*

Figure 24–11 *Are these strawberries ruined? Genetically engineered ice-minus bacteria might have saved them.*

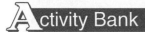

Activity Bank

Sub-Zero, p. 836.

Another interesting use of genetic engineering in agriculture is the development of "ice-minus" bacteria. These genetically engineered bacteria help slow the formation of frost on plants. To understand how ice-minus bacteria work, you must first know something about the bacteria that normally live on plants. These normal bacteria are referred to as ice-plus bacteria. An ice-forming gene in ice-plus bacteria controls the production of a protein that triggers freezing. When the temperature drops to the freezing point of water (0°C), the water in plant cells freezes and turns to ice. The formation of ice in plant cells causes the cells to rupture and die. Many commercially important crop plants are ruined every year by frost damage.

When the ice-forming gene is removed from ice-plus bacteria, the protein that triggers freezing is not produced. Without the protein, ice still forms in plant cells, but at a lower temperature (−5°C). The bacteria are now called ice-minus bacteria. Scientists hope that some day soon crop plants such as strawberries and oranges will be protected from frost damage by using genetically engineered ice-minus bacteria.

Many environmentalists oppose the use of ice-minus bacteria. They are concerned that if the genetically engineered bacteria are released into the environment, they might turn out to be harmful. Further tests will be necessary before ice-minus bacteria can be used by farmers.

24–2 Section Review

1. What is genetic engineering?
2. What is recombinant DNA? Describe the process of making recombinant DNA.
3. Why are bacteria and yeast cells used to make large amounts of human proteins?
4. Describe two ways in which genetic engineering has been useful in medicine. In agriculture.

Connection—*You and Your World*
5. How are ice-minus bacteria similar to the antifreeze used in an automobile radiator?

CONNECTIONS

Frankenstein Fishes

"We're going to have Frankenstein fish!" exclaims one geneticist. "We're going to feed the world," says another. What are they talking about? Both scientists are discussing new, genetically engineered fishes that are larger and grow faster than normal fishes.

In 1985, scientists in China announced the transfer of a gene for human growth hormone into goldfish eggs. As the goldfish developed, some of them grew two to four times their normal size! Three years later, scientists in the United States transferred a growth gene from rainbow trout into another type of fish called carp. These carp grew 20 to 40 percent larger than usual. "Not only did they grow bigger and faster," reported the leader of the team of scientists, "but their offspring grew faster too."

Since these experiments were performed, fishes have been genetically altered in a variety of ways. In addition to growing bigger fishes, scientists are also experimenting with alterations that would make fishes resistant to diseases and pollutants in the *environment*, and also able to withstand very cold temperatures. Because fishes are an important source of food, these experiments could be important to commercial aquaculture, or fish farming.

Although it will be several years before genetically engineered fishes are available commercially, environmentalists are concerned that these fishes could cause problems in aquatic ecosystems. As of now, genetically engineered fishes are kept in aquaculture ponds or laboratory tanks. But what might happen if these fishes were released into the wild? No one knows. However, scientists, environmentalists, and government agencies agree on the need for safety guidelines and regulations to control the research and release of genetically engineered fishes.

Laboratory Investigation

Recombinant DNA

Problem

How can you make models to represent recombinant DNA?

Materials *(per group)*

construction paper (different colors)
tracing paper
drawing compass
tape
scissors

Procedure

1. Use a drawing compass to draw a circle 6 cm in diameter on a piece of construction paper.

2. Inside the large circle, draw a smaller circle 2.5 cm in diameter. You should now have a strip about 1.8 cm wide between the inner circle and the outer circle.

3. Using scissors, carefully cut around the outer circle and cut away the inner circle. **CAUTION:** *Be careful when using scissors or any sharp instrument.* You should now have a closed ring of construction paper.

4. Repeat steps 1 through 3 to make two more construction paper rings.

5. Trace each of the DNA segments shown here on a piece of tracing paper. Label each segment as shown.

6. Carefully cut out each DNA segment from the tracing paper. Using each DNA segment as a pattern, cut three DNA segments from construction paper. Use a different-colored piece of construction paper for each DNA segment.

7. Use the scissors and tape to make three models of recombinant DNA from the three closed rings and DNA segments. Refer to the sequence of steps described in Section 24–2 and Figure 24–6 on page 621 as a guide.

Observations

1. What do the rings of construction paper represent in your models?

2. What do the DNA segments represent?

Analysis and Conclusions

1. What human protein would each of your recombinant DNA molecules produce in a living organism?

2. **On Your Own**   The technique of making recombinant DNA is sometimes called gene splicing. Do you think this is a good name? Why or why not? (*Hint:* Look up the word splice in a dictionary.)

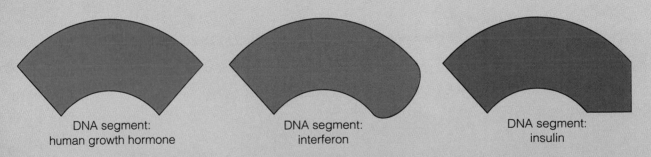

DNA segment:
human growth hormone

DNA segment:
interferon

DNA segment:
insulin

Summarizing Key Concepts

24-1 Plant and Animal Breeding

▲ Plant and animal breeders use selective breeding to produce offspring with desirable characteristics.

▲ Hybridization is a form of selective breeding in which two genetically different species are crossed.

▲ Hybrids are bred to have the best traits of both parents.

▲ Hybrids that are stronger or healthier than either parent are said to have hybrid vigor.

▲ Inbreeding is a form of selective breeding that involves crossing organisms with similar genes.

▲ Inbreeding produces organisms that are genetically similar.

▲ As a result of inbreeding, an offspring's chances of inheriting new genetic combinations is greatly reduced. This can make an entire inbred species susceptible to disease and could lead to extinction.

24-2 Genetic Engineering

▲ Through genetic engineering, genes, or pieces of DNA, are transferred from one organism to another organism.

▲ One form of genetic engineering involves the use of recombinant DNA, which contains pieces of DNA from two different organisms.

▲ Bacteria and yeast cells are commonly used in genetic engineering to produce human proteins.

▲ To make recombinant DNA, scientists remove a plasmid, or ring of DNA, from a bacterium and insert a piece of human DNA.

▲ As a result of genetic engineering, human proteins can be made outside the human body.

▲ Products of genetic engineering are used in medicine to produce hormones and vaccines and in agriculture to make plants resistant to disease and freezing.

Reviewing Key Terms

Define each term in a complete sentence.

24-1 Plant and Animal Breeding
    selective breeding
    hybridization
    inbreeding

24-2 Genetic Engineering
    genetic engineering
    recombinant DNA
    plasmid

Chapter Review

Content Review

Multiple Choice

Choose the letter of the answer that best completes each statement.

1. Crossing two genetically different plants or animals is called
   a. inbreeding.
   b. hybridization.
   c. genetic engineering.
   d. crossbreeding.
2. The word vigor in the term hybrid vigor means
   a. offspring.   c. strength.
   b. weakness.   d. trait.
3. Purebred plants and animals are produced through
   a. inbreeding.
   b. hybridization.
   c. genetic engineering.
   d. recombinant DNA.
4. Inserting genes from one organism into another is an example of
   a. hybridization.
   b. inbreeding.
   c. crossbreeding.
   d. genetic engineering.

5. To make recombinant DNA, human DNA is usually transferred into yeast cells or
   a. mouse cells.   c. viruses.
   b. bacteria.   d. plant cells.
6. Inbreeding produces organisms that are genetically
   a. different.   c. identical.
   b. similar.   d. opposite.
7. Genetic engineering can be used to produce
   a. insulin.
   b. human growth hormone.
   c. interferon.
   d. all of these.
8. The human protein needed to treat diabetes mellitus is
   a. human growth hormone.
   b. interferon.
   c. insulin.
   d. hemoglobin.

True or False

If the statement is true, write "true." If it is false, change the underlined word or words to make the statement true.

1. Hybridization is the process of crossing two genetically <u>similar</u> organisms.
2. A hybrid offspring combines the <u>worst</u> traits of both parents.
3. A method of selective breeding that is the opposite of hybridization is called <u>inbreeding</u>.
4. Inbreeding <u>increases</u> an offspring's chances of <u>inheriting</u> different gene combinations.
5. As a result of <u>hybridization</u>, some organisms might be in danger of becoming extinct.

Concept Mapping

Complete the following concept map for Section 24–1. Then construct a concept map for the entire chapter.

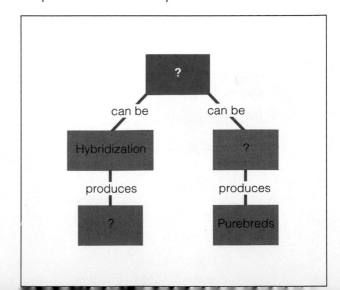

Concept Mastery

Discuss each of the following in a brief paragraph.

1. How do breeders produce organisms with desired characteristics?
2. What is genetic engineering? How has genetic engineering affected modern life?
3. Describe the steps involved in the production of recombinant DNA.
4. Explain how bacteria and yeast cells can be used as "factories" to make human proteins.
5. What is the advantage of developing ice-minus bacteria? Are there any disadvantages? Explain.
6. What is one disadvantage of inbreeding? Give an example.
7. Describe three applications of genetic engineering in medicine.
8. Describe how selective plant breeding was first used in agriculture.

Critical Thinking and Problem Solving

Use the skills you have developed in this chapter to answer each of the following.

1. **Sequencing events** The diagram below shows the steps involved in the process of making recombinant DNA. However, the steps are out of order. Place the steps in the proper sequence.

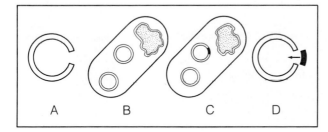

A   B   C   D

2. **Relating concepts** Do you think you would be able to predict the traits of the puppies resulting from a cross between two mixed-breed dogs? Why or why not?
3. **Applying concepts** Suppose you were asked to develop a wheat plant that can grow in a cold, dry environment and that is resistant to disease. How would you go about developing such a plant? What characteristics would you want your wheat plant to have? Why would these characteristics be important?
4. **Making inferences** Scientists working with ice-minus bacteria discovered that the ice-forming proteins produced by ice-plus bacteria could be used to help make snow at ski resorts. Ski resorts now use these proteins to make snow faster and in warmer weather. Do you think that releasing ice-forming proteins into the environment caused the same concerns as releasing ice-minus bacteria? Why or why not?
5. **Using the writing process** Many people are concerned about the introduction of new, genetically engineered organisms into the environment. These people think that genetically engineered organisms may be harmful to the environment or to other living things. What safety guidelines would you recommend concerning the possible development of genetically engineered plants and animals? Write an essay describing your guidelines and giving your reasons for including each guideline.

Changes in Living Things Over Time

Guide for Reading

After you read the following sections, you will be able to

25–1 Evolution: Change Over Time
- Describe the process of evolution.

25–2 Evidence of Evolution
- Describe evidence that supports evolution.

25–3 Charles Darwin and Natural Selection
- Define and describe natural selection.

25–4 Punctuated Equilibrium
- Describe punctuated equilibrium.

One of the great mysteries in the history of life on Earth is when animals first crawled out of the sea and began to live on land. The reconstructed fossil of a strange-looking animal called *Acanthostega* may provide a clue. Although *Acanthostega* had gills and other fish-like characteristics, it also had four legs. At 360 million years old, *Acanthostega* is thus the oldest known four-legged animal. What is most surprising about *Acanthostega*, however, is that its four legs appear to have evolved for life underwater. Scientists think that *Acanthostega* used its stubby legs to walk around in shallow water.

Before *Acanthostega*, scientists assumed that because four legs work well for walking on land, they must have evolved for that purpose. The story of *Acanthostega* points up an important lesson: Evolution does not follow a simple, straightforward path.

Even as you read this chapter, other fossils that provide clues to Earth's past are being sought. The Earth gives up its secrets grudgingly, one clue at a time. Do we have all the answers? Not by a long shot. But we do know a good deal about the changes that have occurred in living things over time—changes we call the evolution of living things.

Journal *Activity*

You and Your World Suppose you were lucky enough to discover the bones of a creature that walked the Earth millions of years ago. In your journal, describe your thoughts and feelings about finding an organism never before seen by people. If you wish, include a drawing of your find.

◀ *The impressive teeth in this fossilized skull of a sabertooth tiger provide a frightening clue about the eating habits of the living animal!*

25–1 Evolution: Change Over Time

The quagga vanished from its home in South Africa about 100 years ago. Descriptions of the animal create a strange picture. The quagga had stripes like a zebra. But the stripes covered only its head, neck, and the front part of its body. Was this animal closely related to the zebra? Or was it completely different?

Scientists often asked these similar questions about other animals and plants that appeared to be closely related. The scientists knew that in one way or another all living things are related to each other. But which are closely related and which are only distantly related?

Today scientists believe that the process known as **evolution** holds the key to these answers. **Evolution is a change in a species over time.** A species is a group of organisms that share similar characteristics and that can interbreed with one another to produce fertile offspring. But how do living things change? And why do some organisms survive while others die off? During the history of life on this planet, chance mutations of genes produce new or slightly modified

Figure 25–1 *This chart shows a history of the development of life on Earth. During which era did flowering plants first appear?*

HISTORY OF LIFE ON EARTH

Era	Years Before Present Time	Changes in Plant and Animal Life	
Precambrian	4,600,000,000	First life forms develop — bacteria, algae, jellyfish, corals, and clams. 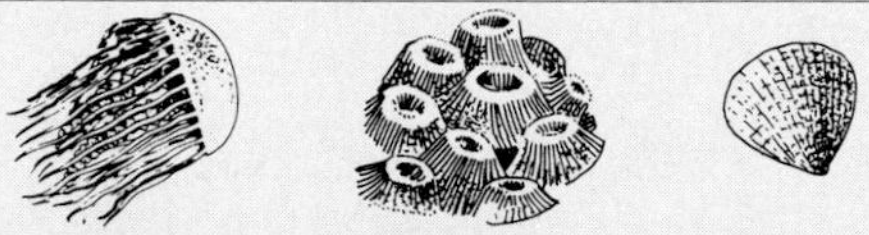	
Paleozoic	570,000,000	First land plants, fishes, insects, amphibians, and first reptiles develop. 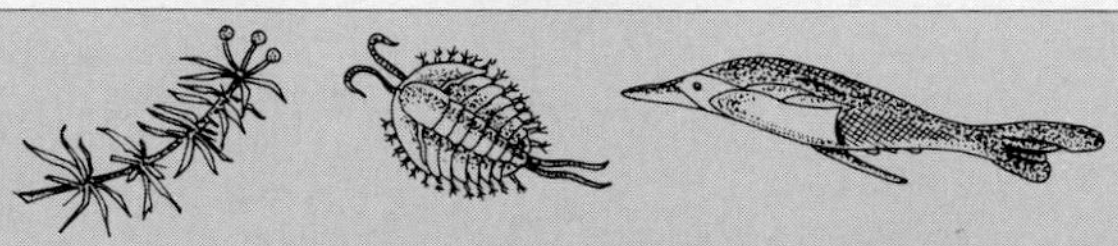	
Mesozoic	225,000,000	Cone-bearing and flowering plants, dinosaurs, and first birds and mammals appear. 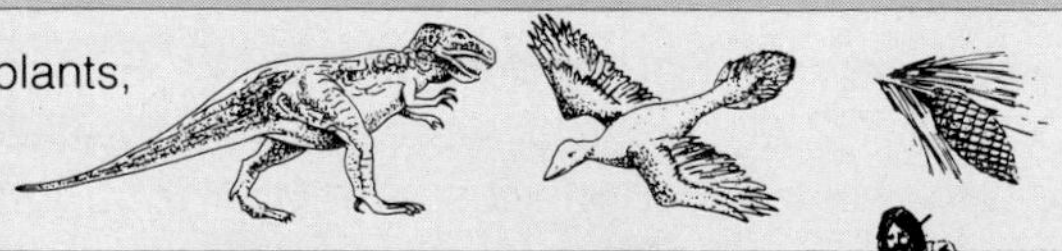	
Cenozoic	65,000,000	Modern plants and mammals develop; human beings appear. 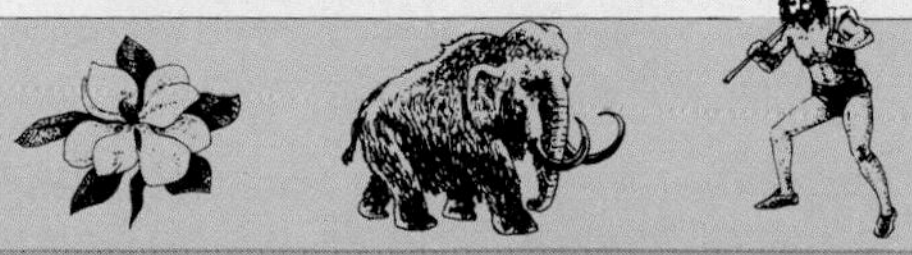	

living things. Most of these new living things cannot compete with other organisms and soon die off. But some new life forms do survive. They survive and reproduce because they just happen to meet the demands of their environment better than other organisms do. Because of this process, many living things that inhabit our planet today did not exist millions of years ago. Figure 25–1 shows the history of life on Earth. When did human beings appear?

25–1 Section Review

1. What is evolution?
Critical Thinking–Interpreting Diagrams
2. In which era did the first amphibians appear?

Extinct Species

Visit a museum of natural history. Find the exhibits of extinct animals such as dinosaurs, woolly mammoths, saber-toothed cats, and others. Find out when and where each of these animals lived. Also find out the reasons scientists believe these animals became extinct. Present your findings to the class.

25–2 Evidence of Evolution

There is a great deal of scientific evidence to support the theory of evolution. You will be able to examine this evidence for yourself in this chapter. This evidence has allowed scientists to develop the theory of evolution. A scientific theory is a very powerful and useful idea. It is an explanation of facts and observations. Moreover, it is an explanation that has been tested many times by many scientists. If a scientific theory fails a test, the theory is modified. Scientific theories also let scientists make predictions of future events. If these predictions come true, the theory passes a key test. **There are many different types of evidence that support the theory of evolution.**

Fossil Evidence of Change

When dinosaurs mysteriously disappeared from the Earth 65 million years ago, the soft parts of their bodies quickly decayed. Only the hard parts—the bones—were left. Many of these bones were buried under layers of mud and wet sand. Over millions of years, the bones turned to stone. The bones of the dinosaurs are known as **fossils.**

Guide for Reading

Focus on this question as you read.

▶ *What types of evidence support the theory of evolution?*

Figure 25–3 *Scientists can learn much about the Earth's past from alligatorlike fossils and fossil shark teeth. What characteristics of the shark's teeth indicate that it was a meat-eater?*

A fossil is the remains or evidence of a living thing. A fossil can be the bone of an organism or the print of a shell in a rock. A fossil can even be a burrow or tunnel left by an ancient worm. The most common fossils are bones, shells, pollen grains, and seeds.

Most fossils are not complete organisms. Fossils are generally incomplete because only the hard parts of dead plants or animals become fossils. The soft tissues either decay or are eaten before fossils can form. Decay is the breakdown of dead organisms into the substances from which they were made.

Radioactive Dating

A method used by scientists to measure the age of fossils or the age of the rocks in which fossils are found is called **radioactive dating.** Radioactive dating involves the use of radioactive elements. A radioactive element is one whose atoms give off radiation as it decays, or breaks down, into the atoms of a different element.

Some radioactive elements decay in a few seconds. Some take thousands, millions, or even billions of years to decay. But the rate of decay for each element is steady. Scientists measure the decay rate of a radioactive element by a unit called **half-life.** The half-life of an element is the time it takes for half of the radioactive element to decay.

For example, if you begin with 1 kilogram of a radioactive element, half of that kilogram will decay during one half-life. So at the end of one half-life, you will have 0.50 kilogram of the radioactive element and 0.50 kilogram of the decay element. Half of the remaining element (half of a half) will decay during another half-life. At this point one quarter of the radioactive element remains. How much of the decay element is there? This process continues until all the radioactive element has decayed. Figure 25–4 illustrates the decay of a radioactive element with a half-life of 1 billion years.

If certain radioactive elements are present in a rock or fossil, scientists can find the absolute age of the rock or fossil. For example, suppose a rock contains a radioactive element that has a half-life of 1 million years. If tests show that the rock contains equal amounts of the radioactive element and its decay element, the rock is about 1 million years old. Because the proportion of radioactive element to decay element is equal, the element has gone through only one half-life. Scientists use the proportion of radioactive element to decay element to determine how many half-lives have occurred. If the rock contains three times as much decay element as it does radioactive element, how many half-lives have occurred? How old is the rock?

Figure 25–4 *The rate of decay of a radioactive substance is measured by its half-life. How much of the radioactive element remains after 2 billion years?*

DECAY OF A RADIOACTIVE ELEMENT WITH A HALF-LIFE OF 1 BILLION YEARS		
Time	**Amount of Radioactive Element**	**Amount of Decay Element**
4 billion years ago, when rock became solid	1 kg (1)	0 kg (0)
3 billion years ago	0.5 kg (1/2)	0.5 kg (1/2)
2 billion years ago	0.25 kg (1/4)	0.75 kg (3/4)
1 billion years ago	0.125 kg (1/8)	0.875 kg (7/8)
Present	0.0625 kg (1/16)	0.9375 kg (15/16)

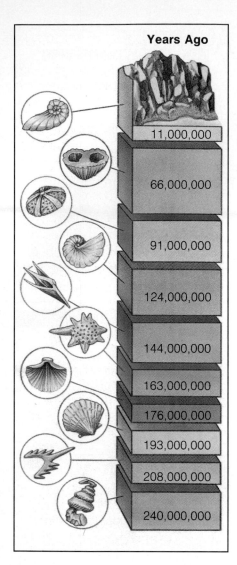

Years Ago

11,000,000
66,000,000
91,000,000
124,000,000
144,000,000
163,000,000
176,000,000
193,000,000
208,000,000
240,000,000

Figure 25–5 *Fossils are usually found in sedimentary rocks. If the sedimentary rock layers are in the same positions in which they formed, lower layers are older than upper ones. This principle is known as the law of superposition. How old are the fossils in the bottom layer of the diagram? The top layer?*

The Law of Superposition

Another way to date fossils is to examine the sedimentary rock layers in which most fossils are found. **Sedimentary rocks** are made of layers of sediments that have piled up one atop the other. Sediments are small pieces of rocks, shells, and other materials that were broken down over time. If the sediments have been left untouched, then clearly the layers of rocks at the bottom are older than those at the top. Put another way, the sedimentary layers are stacked in order of their age.

The **law of superposition** states that in a series of sedimentary rock layers, younger rocks normally lie on top of older rocks. The word superposition means one thing placed on top of another.

The law of superposition is based on the idea that sediments have been deposited in the same way throughout Earth's history. This idea was first proposed by the Scottish scientist James Hutton in the late eighteenth century. Hutton theorized that the processes acting on Earth's surface today are the same processes that have acted on Earth's surface in the past. These processes include weathering, erosion, and deposition. Weathering is the breaking down of rocks into sediments. Erosion is the carrying away of sediments. Deposition is the laying down of sediments.

Scientists use the law of superposition to determine whether a fossil or a layer of rock is older or younger than another fossil or layer of rock. Think of the layers of sedimentary rocks as the unnumbered pages of a "history book." The beginning pages hold stories of long ago, while the end pages hold more recent stories. Now think of the words on each page as being a fossil. The words (fossil) on an earlier page (layer of rock) are older than the words (fossil) on a later page (layer of rock).

Sediments are still being formed today. As you read these words, the fossils of tomorrow are being trapped in the sediments at the bottoms of rivers, lakes, and seas. For example, the Mississippi River deposits sediments at a rate of 80,000 tons an hour—day after day, year after year—at the point where the river flows into the Gulf of Mexico.

The Fossil Record

All the fossil evidence scientists have collected forms what is known as the **fossil record.** The fossil record is the most complete biological record of life on Earth.

Here is an example of how scientists read the fossil record. Some years ago in the Mississippi River valley scientists found the fossil bones of a leg and a foot of an unknown animal. The fossils were in a deposit of sedimentary rock. From the bones, scientists discovered that the animal had four toes on each of its front feet. Moreover, the toes were spread apart.

The discovery of other fossils in the same sedimentary layer helped scientists piece together what the entire animal probably looked like. It was about the size of a modern-day cat. But except for its small size, short teeth, and four toes, it looked a lot like a horse. Scientists named it *Eohippus*, meaning "dawn horse" or "early horse."

The scientists used radioactive dating to measure the age of the rock layer in which *Eohippus* was found. The rock layer was about 50 million years old and, therefore, so was *Eohippus*.

From the fossils of plants and animals found in the same layer of sedimentary rock as *Eohippus*, scientists also were able to tell what the Mississippi River valley may have been like when *Eohippus* lived. Most of the other fossils found in the *Eohippus* layer resemble plants and animals that live in warm, wet climates today. This is evidence that *Eohippus* probably lived in a tropical climate, surrounded by swamps and mud.

The structure of *Eohippus*'s foot was also well suited to the kind of surroundings in which the animal lived. Look at Figure 25–6 on page 638. Notice how the toes of *Eohippus* are spread apart. This arrangement allows its mass to be spread over a larger area, thus making it easier for *Eohippus* to walk on soft mud.

Unlike *Eohippus*, today's horse spends most of its life on dry, hard ground. Its single hard hoof lessens the shock of walking more than four spread toes could ever do. The modern horse also has larger teeth than *Eohippus*. As a result, modern horses can chew the tough, dry grasses of the prairie.

50 million years ago	35 million years ago	26 million years ago	3 million years ago
Eohippus	*Mesohippus*	*Merychippus*	*Equus*
38 cm	52 cm	100 cm	135 cm
Forefoot Skull	Forefoot Skull	Forefoot Skull	Forefoot Skull

Figure 25–6 *Living things have evolved, or changed over time. The diagram shows the fossil record of the past 50 million years in the evolution of the horse. How are modern horses similar to their ancestors? How are they different?*

Scientists conclude that the fossils of *Eohippus* and other plants and animals are evidence that generations of species go through changes. These chance changes in the genes of organisms have produced new or slightly modified living things. As you may recall from Chapter 23, a gene is a unit of heredity that is passed on from parent to offspring. A change in a gene will produce a change in the offspring of an organism. Changes in genes are called mutations. And mutations are one of the driving forces behind evolution.

Mutations: Agents of Change

Most of the time, a mutation in a gene produces an organism that cannot compete with other organisms. This new organism usually dies off quickly. Sometimes, however, the change in the organism is a positive one. The change makes the organism better suited to its environment. A change that increases an organism's chances of survival is called an **adaptation.**

Organisms that are better adapted to their environment do more than just survive. They are able to produce offspring, which produce more offspring, and so on. Over a long period of time, so many small adaptations may occur that a new species may evolve. The new species may no longer resemble its ancient

ancestors. In addition, the new species may be so successful in its environment that the species from which it evolved can no longer compete. The original species dies off. Thus the development of a new species can result in the extinction of another species.

Anatomical Evidence of Change

Fossil evidence is not the only piece of evidence of evolution. There are some other ways scientists explore the evolution of living things.

In the early 1800s, a French biologist named Jean-Baptiste de Lamarck came to the conclusion that living things had changed over time. In his book *Philosophie zoologique,* Lamarck suggested that all forms of life could be organized into one vast "family tree." Lamarck looked to anatomy, or the study of the structure of living things, for evidence of evolution. Look at the bones of a human's arm, a bat's wing, a whale's flipper, and a dog's leg in Figure 25–8. Can you see any similarities in the shape and arrangement of the bones of these animals? When ancestral body parts that are similar in structure evolve, they are called **homologous** (hoh-MAHL-uh-guhs) **structures.** A human's arm, a bat's wing, a whale's flipper, and a

Figure 25–7 *A hummingbird's beak is an example of an adaptation for feeding. What is an adaptation?*

Figure 25–8 *Human arms, bat wings, whale flippers, and dog legs are superbly adapted to performing different tasks. However, their internal structure is remarkably similar. What are such structures called? What do they indicate?*

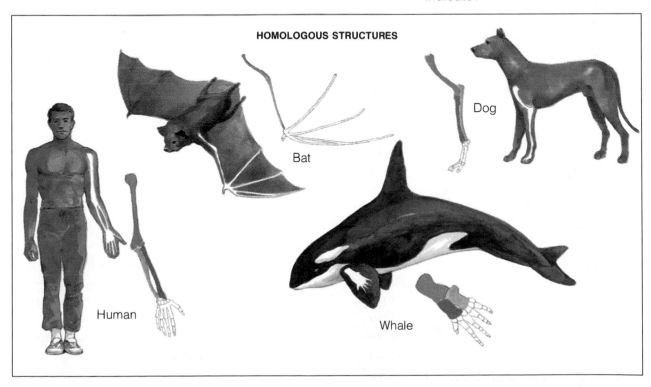

HOMOLOGOUS STRUCTURES

Bat

Dog

Human

Whale

639

Figure 25–9 *How would Lamarck have explained the evolution of the ostrich's strong legs for running? How would a modern scientist explain their evolution?*

Figure 25–10 *The embryos of vastly different animals look quite similar during the earliest stages of development, hinting at genes inherited from a common ancestor.*

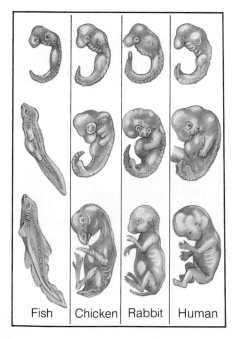

Fish | Chicken | Rabbit | Human

dog's leg are homologous structures. It was through the study of homologous structures that Lamarck concluded that living things had evolved and had become better adapted to their environment.

Despite his insight into the concept of evolution, Lamarck proved to be wrong about most of his theories concerning the process of evolution. Lamarck believed that organisms change because of an inborn will to change. He believed, for example, that the ancestors of birds had a desire to fly. Over many years, that desire enabled birds to acquire wings—and to be better adapted to their environment as well.

Lamarck also believed that organisms could change their body structure by using body parts in new ways. For example, because birds tried so hard to use their front limbs for flying, the limbs eventually changed into wings. In much the same way, Lamarck reasoned, a body part would eventually grow smaller or even disappear from disuse. For example, by slithering along the ground, a snake would eventually lose its limbs.

As you have read earlier, one of the driving forces behind evolution is mutations. And mutations are changes in genes. Lamarck's beliefs about how and why organisms change are incorrect. Wanting a new body part cannot cause a mutation. Using a body part in a different way—or not using it at all—cannot cause a mutation. Mutations happen; they are chance events. Mutations are independent of a desire to change and of a need to adapt to the environment.

Embryological Evidence of Change

Another type of evidence for evolution is based on embryology, or the study of developing organisms. Scientists can compare the embryos, or developing organisms, of different species to see how closely related they are.

The embryos of vertebrates, or animals with backbones, are very similar in the early stages of development. The more similar the structure of the embryos of different organisms, the more closely related those organisms are. Scientists think that the development of different organisms is similar because the organisms inherit their traits from a common ancestor. See Figure 25–10.

Chemical Evidence of Change

Think back for a moment to the quagga—the animal that resembles a zebra. One type of evidence that might show if the zebra evolved from the quagga is chemical similarities in their DNA. In Chapter 23, you learned that DNA is the basic substance of heredity.

Chemical similarities in DNA molecules are one kind of evidence of evolution. In fact, this kind of evidence was used to show the relationship between quaggas and zebras.

Among other things, the theory of evolution predicts that the more closely related two living things are, the more similar the structure of their DNA molecules will be. In 1985, Dr. Allen Wilson of the University of California at Berkeley analyzed DNA taken from the muscle tissue attached to the preserved skin of a quagga. The skin had been stored for more than a hundred years in a German museum. Dr. Wilson also analyzed DNA taken from a modern-day plains zebra. The structure of the DNA in the two samples was 95 percent identical!

Dr. Wilson concluded that the quagga and the plains zebra were, indeed, close relatives that shared a common ancestor about 3 million years ago. In other words, both the quagga and the plains zebra evolved from an animal that lived earlier. Scientists use this method of DNA comparison to show the relationship between many other types of organisms.

Figure 25–11 *The DNA in a living zebra is 95 percent identical to that of the extinct quagga. This indicates that zebras and quaggas belong to separate but closely related species.*

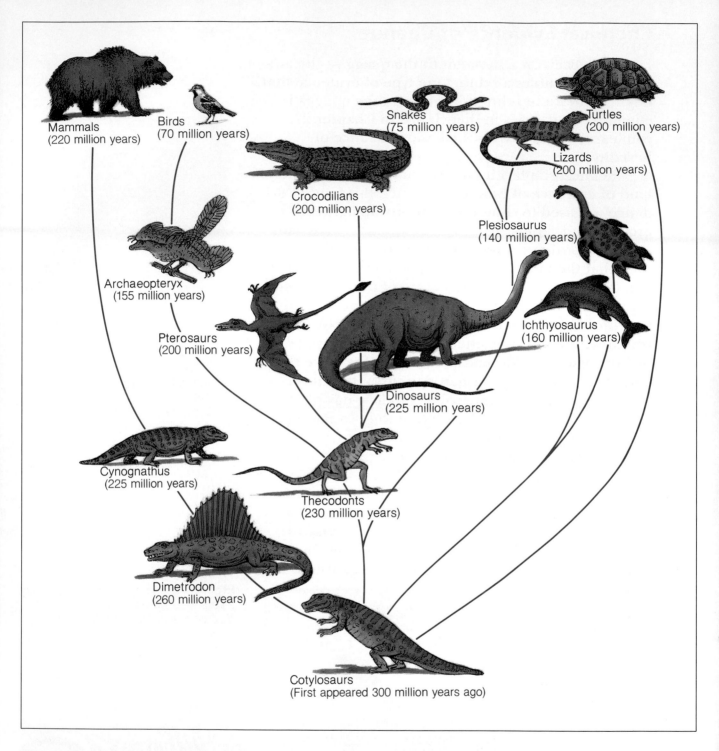

Mammals
(220 million years)

Birds
(70 million years)

Snakes
(75 million years)

Turtles
(200 million years)

Crocodilians
(200 million years)

Lizards
(200 million years)

Plesiosaurus
(140 million years)

Archaeopteryx
(155 million years)

Pterosaurs
(200 million years)

Ichthyosaurus
(160 million years)

Dinosaurs
(225 million years)

Cynognathus
(225 million years)

Thecodonts
(230 million years)

Dimetrodon
(260 million years)

Cotylosaurs
(First appeared 300 million years ago)

Figure 25–12 *All of the evidence of evolution that scientists have gathered indicates that many different species develop from a common ancestor. Notice that some descendants of the cotylosaur* do not resemble it at all.

Molecular Evidence of Change

You have just read how similarities in DNA structure can be used to show relationships between organisms. Similarities in other kinds of molecules can be used in an almost identical way. Proteins are molecules that are used to build and repair body parts. Scientists believe that the more similar the structure of protein molecules of different organisms, the more closely related the organisms are. Scientists further believe that the closer the similarity in protein structure of different organisms, the more recently their common ancestor existed.

Scientists have developed a method of measuring the difference between the proteins of different species. In addition, scientists have developed a scale that can be used to estimate the rate of change in proteins over time. This scale of protein change is called a **molecular clock.**

By comparing the similarities in protein structure of different organisms, scientists can determine if the organisms have a common ancestor. If they do, the molecular clock can be used to determine how long ago the organisms branched off from that ancestor.

What do all these various types of evidence (fossils, homologous structures, embryo comparisons, DNA similarities, and molecular clocks) tell us? The answer is clear. Living things have evolved through modification of earlier life forms. That is, living things have descended from a common ancestor.

The Path to Modern Humans

Various types of evidence for evolution support the theory that both humans and apes evolved from a common primate ancestor. Primates are an order of mammals that includes humans as well as apes, monkeys, and about 200 other species of living things. Scientists believe that humans developed from an apelike animal over millions of years. During that time the posture of humans became more upright, their jaws became shorter, their teeth became smaller, and their brains became larger.

The oldest humanlike fossil found to date was found in Africa in 1977. The fossil was named *Australopithecus afarensis* (aw-stray-loh-PIHTH-uh-kuhs af-uh-REHN-sihs) and nicknamed "Lucy." Lucy is believed to be about 3.5 million years old.

A more recent species of primate that was actually called "human" was *Homo erectus* (HOH-moh ih-REHKT-uhs), or upright human. Fossils of this species, which lived 1.6 to 0.5 million years ago, were first found on

Figure 25–13 *This skeleton of Australopithecus afarensis was nicknamed Lucy by its discoverers. Lucy is one of the oldest and most complete of the early hominids yet to be found.*

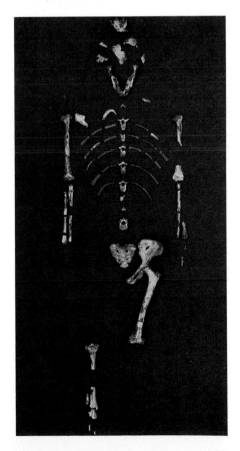

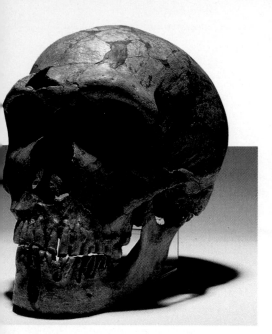

Figure 25–14 *This Neanderthal skull, which was found in France, is between 35,000 and 53,000 years old. The pattern of wear on the teeth indicates that the hominid probably used its teeth for more than eating—perhaps for softening hides.*

the island of Java in Indonesia. *H. erectus* had thicker bones than modern humans, a sloped forehead, and a very large jaw. *H. erectus* was able to use fire and make tools.

About 500,000 years ago, another species of human appeared. Because this species had a larger brain capacity than other humans, scientists named the species *Homo sapiens* (HOH-moh SAY-pee-uhnz), or wise human. Two early types of *Homo sapiens* were the Neanderthals (nee-AN-duhr-thahlz) and the Cro-Magnons (kroh MAG-nuhnz).

Neanderthals lived in Europe and Asia from about 150,000 to 35,000 years ago. Neanderthals were shorter than modern humans. Their average height was only about 150 centimeters. They were able to hunt, fish, cook, and make tools. Neanderthals buried their dead with tools or animal bones. Sometimes they arranged the bones in patterns that suggest religious rituals.

The first humans identical to modern humans began to appear on Earth about 40,000 years ago. These large-brained people were called Cro-Magnons, after the place in southwestern France where they were first discovered. The tool-making skills of these humans far surpassed those of earlier humans. Cro-Magnons are believed to have worked together to make tools, build shelters, and hunt. To do so they probably used language.

25–2 Section Review

1. What types of evidence are used to develop the theory of evolution?
2. Give an example of homologous structures.
3. What is a fossil?
4. What is the law of superposition?
5. How can scientists learn about evolution by studying embryology?
6. What are the differences and similarities between Neanderthals and Cro-Magnons?

Critical Thinking—*Applying Concepts*

7. Would you expect there to be more similarities in the DNA molecules of a cat and a lion or in those of a cat and a dog? Explain your answer.

25–3 Charles Darwin and Natural Selection

The Galapagos Islands rise out of the Pacific Ocean about 1000 kilometers from the west coast of South America. The islands received their name from the giant Galapagos tortoises that live there. The tortoises' long necks, wrinkled skin, and mud-caked shells make them look like prehistoric creatures. Sharing the islands with the tortoises are many other animals, including penguins, long-necked diving birds called cormorants, and large, crested lizards called iguanas.

The most striking thing about the animals of the Galapagos is the way in which they differ from related species on the mainland of South America. For example, the iguanas on the Galapagos have extra-large claws that allow them to keep their grip on slippery rocks, where they feed on seaweed. On the mainland, iguanas have smaller claws. Smaller claws allow the mainland iguanas to climb trees, where they feed on leaves.

In 1831, a young British student named Charles Darwin set sail for a five-year voyage on a ship called the *Beagle*. Serving as the ship's naturalist, Darwin studied animals and plants at every stop the ship made. When Darwin arrived at the Galapagos, he soon noticed many of the differences between island and mainland creatures. As he compared the animals

ACTIVITY

DISCOVERING

Survival of the Fittest

Scatter a box of red and green toothpicks in a grassy area. Then have a friend pick up in 10 minutes as many toothpicks as he or she can.

■ How can a variation such as color affect the process of natural selection?

Figure 25–15 *A giant tortoise from the Galapagos Islands (right) looks quite different from its much smaller cousin from the South American mainland (left). Observations of the tortoises and other creatures of the Galapagos helped to inspire Darwin's theory of evolution.*

Figure 25–16 *A green iguana's long toes, sharp claws, and green scales make it well suited for life in a tropical rain forest (top). Although they evolved from lizards similar to the green iguana, marine iguanas have webbed toes, thick claws, and brownish-gray scales. Their webbed toes and rounded snouts are adaptations for swimming (bottom).*

Activity Bank

Variety Is the
Spice of Life, p. 839

on the mainland to those on the islands, he realized something special. It appeared that each animal was perfectly adapted to survival in its particular environment.

Darwin took many notes and collected many specimens. For the next 20 years he tried to find an underlying theory that could explain his observations. In 1858, Darwin and another British biologist, Alfred Wallace, presented independently a new and exciting concept—the theory of evolution.

This theory was discussed by Darwin in a book entitled *On the Origin of Species*. In this book, Darwin presented an entirely new idea—the concept of **natural selection.** Darwin used this concept to explain how evolution occurs, or the mechanics of evolution. **Natural selection is the survival and reproduction of those organisms best adapted to their surroundings.** To better understand how natural selection works, you must first learn about the role of overproduction in nature.

Overproduction and Natural Selection

Biologists have long known that many species seem to produce more offspring than can be supported by the environment. Every year, for example, dandelions grow seeds with sails that form into a white puff on the stem. The wind blows the seeds through the air. Most seeds land in a place where conditions are unfavorable for new dandelion growth. Only a few seeds land in a place with the right soil, light, and water conditions. These seeds grow into new dandelion plants. Through overproduction, nature assures that at least some seeds will survive to continue the species.

Quite often, overproduction of offspring results in competition for food or shelter among the different members of a species. In the case of tadpoles, which hatch from frog eggs, competition can be fierce. The food supply in a pond often is not large enough for every tadpole to survive. Only those strong enough to obtain food and fast enough to avoid enemies will live. These animals will eventually reproduce. The others will die before producing offspring.

The process in which only the best-adapted members of a species survive is sometimes called survival

646

of the fittest. In a sense, the fittest animals are selected, or chosen, by their surroundings to survive. This is basically what Darwin meant by natural selection—nature selects the fittest.

Variation and Natural Selection

Although the members of a species are enough alike to mate, normally no two are exactly the same. In other words, even members of the same species have small variations. For example, some polar bears have thicker coats of fur than others do. This thicker fur gives them more protection against the cold. Such polar bears are fitter, and thus more likely to survive and pass on the characteristic. In this case, a variation in a species will cause some members to survive and reproduce. Over time, the variation will become the norm as those members of the species with the variation survive in greater numbers than do those members without the variation. Can you think of another example of variation in a species?

In the same way, members of the same plant species may show minor variations in the length and thickness of roots. Plants with deeper root systems can reach under ground more easily and thus will have a better chance for survival than do plants with shorter root systems. In this example, the plants with deeper roots are more likely to be "selected" by nature and to pass on their traits to generations that follow. The plants with shallow root systems are not quite as fortunate. These plants would have a better chance for survival in an area in which most water was close to the surface. As you can see, variations among members of a species are another reason natural selection can lead to changes in living things over time.

Minor variations in a species are common. Sometimes, however, mutations can cause a change in an organism's characteristics that is far from minor. For example, in White Sands National Monument in New Mexico, the sand dunes are white. White mice live on these dunes. The light color of the mice is a result of a helpful mutation. Because white mice blend in better with their environment than darker mice do, they are less likely to be eaten by predators. If a mutation occurred that darkened some of the mice, these

Figure 25–17 *Although these flamingoes may look alike, there are variations among them. The flamingoes best suited for their environment survive and reproduce, passing on their characteristics to the next generation.*

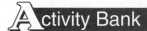

Activity Bank

Where Are They?, p. 837

Figure 25–18 *Natural selection may produce some amazing results. The markings and behavior of this caterpillar trick hungry birds into thinking that it is a bird-eating snake.*

Figure 25–19 *After the start of the Industrial Revolution, the light gray bark of trees was darkened by the soot from factories. In each photograph, which peppered moth would most likely be noticed by a hungry bird? How did pollution affect the way that natural selection acted upon peppered moths?*

darker mice would not be able to blend in with their surroundings. The mutation that caused the darker color would be considered a harmful mutation. In this case, natural selection would "weed out" the mice with the harmful mutation. As generations of mice reproduced, the darker mice, along with their harmful mutation, would be eliminated from the species. The white mice with the helpful mutation would survive and multiply.

Mirrors of Change

In some ways living things become a mirror of the changes in their surroundings. The British peppered moth is a recent example of this phenomenon. In the 1850s, most of the peppered moths near Manchester, England, were gray in color. Only a few black moths existed. Because the gray moths were almost the same color as the tree trunks on which they lived, they were nearly invisible to the birds that hunted them for food. Most of the black moths, however, were spotted by the birds and eaten. The species as a whole survived because of the gray moths. Then changes in environmental conditions had a drastic effect on the moths that lived in the area.

As more factories were built in the area, soot from the chimneys blackened the tree trunks. The gray moths could now be seen against the tree trunks. The few surviving black moths, however, now blended in with the tree trunks. As a result, they survived. These moths produced more black offspring. In time, practically all peppered moths were black. Again, the species as a whole survived.

25–3 Section Review

1. What is natural selection?
2. Describe how living things can become a mirror of the changes in their environment.

Connection—*Ecology*

3. There is evidence that Earth's climate is getting warmer. This phenomenon is called global warming. How might global warming affect the evolution of living things?

25–4 Punctuated Equilibrium

In the chapter opener you read about the dinosaurs. Dinosaurs dominated the Earth for more than 150 million years. Then, about 65 million years ago, all living species of dinosaurs became extinct. (Around the same time, about 95 percent of all other living things also became extinct.) Scientists call such extinctions mass extinctions.

Mass extinctions seem rather harsh. After all, suddenly a great many species disappear, never to be seen again. In evolutionary terms, however, mass extinctions play an important role in the development of new species. After a mass extinction, a wide variety of previously occupied niches become available to those species that still exist. A niche is the combination of a species's needs and its habitat (where it lives). The process in which one species evolves into several species, each of which fills a different niche, is called **adaptive radiation.** In adaptive radiation, organisms of a species "radiate," or move away, from other organisms in that species and occupy new niches. Keep in mind that in adaptive radiation, the new species all share a common ancestor. If you now go back to Figure 25–12 on page 642, you will be able to interpret that diagram as representing adaptive radiation.

As you might expect, many adaptive radiations occur after a mass extinction, as species move into new niches. In fact, after the mass extinction of the dinosaurs, a type of living thing that had existed for more than 50 million years in the shadow of the dinosaurs underwent a great adaptive radiation. This type of living thing began to fill unoccupied niches throughout the world. Do you know what this type of living thing is? You are correct if you said mammal. You are a mammal. So is a dog, a lion, a whale, and a skunk. Mammals are the dominant life form on Earth today primarily because the dinosaurs died off, leaving so many niches for mammals to fill.

In most cases, natural selection as described by Darwin is a long, slow process. Scientists do not doubt that natural selection occurs or that it leads to the evolution of living things. However, the fossil record

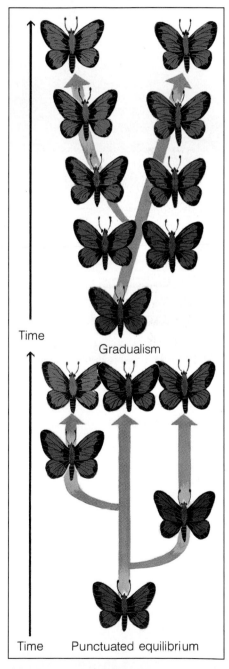

Figure 25–20 *Organisms may change slowly and gradually over time. Or they may remain the same for a long time, then change quickly and abruptly.*

Time

Gradualism

Time   Punctuated equilibrium

Figure 25–21 *Natural disasters such as forest fires create new niches and may open up old ones. How have large-scale natural disasters shaped the evolution of life on Earth?*

shows very little evidence of gradual change. (Remember, most organisms do not leave fossils. So this lack of fossil evidence is to be expected.) But the fossil record does seem to indicate that some species may not change at all for long periods of time. This period of stability, or equilibrium, may continue for millions of years. Then suddenly, a great adaptive radiation may occur and a species may evolve into many new species, filling new niches. The equilibrium is broken, or punctuated.

In 1972, scientists Stephen Jay Gould and Niles Eldridge developed a theory called **punctuated equilibrium.** As you read its definition, keep in mind that in evolutionary terms, "short" can mean thousands of years. **According to punctuated equilibrium, there may be periods in Earth's history in which many adaptive radiations occur in a relatively short period of time.**

When does punctuated equilibrium seem to occur? As you might expect, it is most common when many niches are opened. This occurs during a mass extinction. It can also occur as a result of isolation, such as the isolation of organisms in Australia.

Today scientists believe that evolution can occur gradually—as described by Darwin—as well as fairly rapidly—as described by Gould and Eldridge. Neither theory disputes the other, and both seem to be valid. Punctuated equilibrium does not mean that gradual change is incorrect. And Darwin's theory of gradual change does not mean that punctuated equilibrium is incorrect. Both forms of evolution seem to have occurred during Earth's 4.6-billion-year history.

25–4 Section Review

1. What is punctuated equilibrium? What is a mass extinction? How are they related?

Critical Thinking—*Making Inferences*
2. In what ways does the fossil record support punctuated equilibrium?

CONNECTIONS

Planetary Evolution

While we tend to think of evolution as a biological event, the term is relevant to other sciences as well. Astronomers, for example, talk of the evolution of our solar system. The current theory on the evolution of our solar system is called the *nebular theory.*

According to the nebular theory, our solar system evolved from a huge cloud of dust and gas called a nebula. Shock waves, probably from the explosion of a nearby star, disrupted the dust and gas in the nebula. In reaction to the shock waves, the gases in the nebula began to contract inward, causing the nebula to shrink. As it shrank, the dust and gases began to spin around the center of the nebula. In time, the spinning nebula flattened into a huge disk almost 10 billion kilometers in diameter.

Near the center of the disk a new sun or *protosun* began to form. Gases and other matter surrounding the newly formed sun continued to spin. Some of the gas and matter began to clump together. Small clumps became larger and larger clumps. The largest clumps became *protoplanets,* or the beginnings of planets.

Over time the protoplanets near the sun became so hot that most of their gases boiled away, leaving behind a rocky core. Today these planets are known as Mercury, Venus, Earth, and Mars. Planets farther from the sun did not lose their gases because they did not receive as much heat. These planets became the gas giants. Today these gas giants are known as Jupiter, Saturn, Uranus, and Neptune.

Now here's a question for you to try to answer: How do you think Pluto, the ninth planet, formed? *Hint:* Pluto is a cold, barren world much different from the outer gas giants.

Laboratory Investigation

Comparing Primates—From Gorillas to Humans

Problem

What changes occurred as humans evolved from earlier primates?

Materials   *(per student)*

scissors	metric ruler
clean paper	protractor

Procedure

1. Insert a 6 cm X 9 cm strip of paper lengthwise into your mouth. Place the paper over your tongue so that it covers all your teeth, including your back molars. Bite down hard enough to make an impression of your teeth on the paper. Remove the paper from your mouth.

2. Draw a line on the paper from the center of the impression of the left back molar to the center of the impression of the right back molar. Mark the midpoint of this line. Use the protractor to draw a perpendicular line from the midpoint of the line connecting the back molars to the front teeth.

3. Measure the width of the jaw by measuring the length of the line between the back molars. Measure the length of the jaw by measuring the line from the back of the mouth to the front teeth. Record your measurements in a data table.

4. Calculate the jaw index by multiplying the jaw width by 100 and then dividing by the length of the jaw. Record the jaw index.

5. Repeat steps 3 and 4 using the drawings of gorilla and *Australopithecus* jaws.

6. Find the indentation at the bottom of your palm near the ball of your thumb. Measure the length of your thumb from the indentation to its tip. Measure the length of

your index finger from the indentation to its tip. Record these measurements.

7. Calculate the thumb index by multiplying the thumb length by 100. Divide by the index-finger length. Record the thumb index.

8. Repeat steps 6 and 7 using the drawings of the thumb and index finger of both the gorilla and *Australopithecus*.

Observations

What trend did you observe regarding the relative length of the jaw? The relative length of the thumb and index finger?

Analysis and Conclusions

1. Was *Australopithecus* a mammal with characteristics somewhere in between those of gorillas and humans? Give evidence to support your answer.

2. Based on the thumb index, what adaptive change occurred in human evolution? What was the advantage of this change?

3. Based on your observations, what other change occurred as humans evolved?

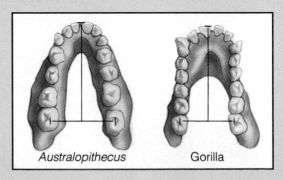

Australopithecus   Gorilla

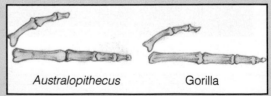

Australopithecus   Gorilla

Study Guide

Summarizing Key Concepts

25-1 Evolution: Change Over Time

▲ Evolution is defined as a change in a species over time.

25-2 Evidence of Evolution

▲ Fossils are the imprints or remains of once-living things. By measuring the decay of radioactive substances in fossils or rocks, scientists are able to date fossils.

▲ The half-life of a radioactive element is the amount of time it takes for half the atoms in a sample of that element to decay.

▲ The law of superposition states that in a series of sedimentary rock layers, younger rocks normally lie on top of older rocks.

▲ Through the fossil record, scientists can show that species have evolved.

▲ An adaptation is any change that increases an organism's chances of survival.

▲ Homologous structures demonstrate that living things share a common ancestor.

▲ A scale that scientists use to estimate the rate of change in proteins over time is called the molecular clock.

25-3 Charles Darwin and Natural Selection

▲ Natural selection is the survival and reproduction of those organisms best adapted to their surroundings.

▲ Overproduction in nature leads to competition within a species for food, water, and shelter. Only the best adapted members of that species will survive and reproduce.

25-4 Punctuated Equilibrium

▲ The process in which one species evolves into several species, each of which fills a different niche, is called adaptive radiation.

▲ According to the punctuated equilibrium theory, there may be periods in Earth's history in which many adaptive radiations occur in a relatively short period of time.

Reviewing Key Terms

Define each term in a complete sentence.

25-1 Evolution: Change Over Time
evolution

25-2 Evidence of Evolution
fossil
radioactive dating
half-life
sedimentary rock
law of superposition
fossil record
adaptation
homologous structure
molecular clock

25-3 Charles Darwin and Natural Selection
natural selection

25-4 Punctuated Equilibrium
adaptive radiation
punctuated equilibrium

Chapter Review

Content Review

Multiple Choice

Choose the letter of the answer that best completes each statement.

1. Which of these is not used as evidence of evolution?
   a. fossils
   b. similarities in DNA
   c. intelligence
   d. homologous structures

2. A bat's wing and a whale's flipper are examples of
   a. natural selection.
   b. homologous structures.
   c. variation.
   d. fossils.

3. A technique used to measure the age of fossils is
   a. anatomical dating.
   b. radioactive dating.
   c. homologous dating.
   d. natural selection.

4. A change that increases an organism's chances of survival is known as a(an)
   a. adaptation.   c. mutation.
   b. variation.   d. extinction.

5. The oldest humanlike fossil ever found was
   a. *Australopithecus afarensis.*
   b. *Homo sapiens.*
   c. *Homo erectus.*
   d. Neanderthal.

6. Another way to say "survival of the fittest" is
   a. competition.   c. natural selection.
   b. natural variation. d. overproduction.

7. Small differences between members of a species are called
   a. variations.
   b. homologous structures.
   c. punctuations.
   d. modifications.

8. The process in which one species evolves into several species is called
   a. mutation.
   b. adaptive radiation.
   c. punctuated equilibrium.
   d. variation.

True or False

If the statement is true, write "true." If it is false, change the underlined word or words to make the statement true.

1. <u>Natural selection</u> is a change in a species over time.
2. The idea of evolution is a <u>law</u>.
3. Homologous organs are organs that have similar <u>functions</u>.
4. Fossils in lower layers of rock are <u>younger</u> than fossils in upper layers.
5. Chemical similarities in DNA show that the quagga and the <u>zebra</u> are closely related.
6. <u>Cro-Magnons</u> probably used language.
7. Most species <u>underproduce</u> the number of young that the environment can support.

Concept Mapping

Complete the following concept map for Section 25–1. Then construct a concept map for the entire chapter.

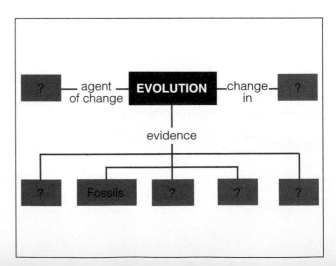

654

Concept Mastery

Discuss each of the following in a brief paragraph.

1. List two differences between *Eohippus* and the modern horse. Provide an explanation for each difference.
2. Discuss the changes that have occurred in the peppered moths near Manchester, England, over the last 150 years. Include in your discussion an explanation for the changes.
3. How are radioactive elements used to determine the age of rocks and fossils?
4. Explain how protein structures are used to measure differences between species.

Include a definition of molecular clock in your explanation.
5. Explain how Neanderthals and Cro-Magnons differ.
6. Discuss the role of overproduction in nature.
7. Use an example to explain the concept of natural selection.
8. Evolution is an ongoing process. It continues as it has for millions of years. Why are scientists usually unable to see evolution in action?

Critical Thinking and Problem Solving

Use the skills you have developed in this chapter to answer each of the following.

1. **Making inferences** Darwin was amazed at the diversity of life he observed on the Galapagos. How might this diversity have contributed to his ideas about evolution?
2. **Evaluating options** Is protecting an endangered species defying natural selection? Explain your answer.
3. **Applying concepts** Do you think evolution on Earth has stopped? If not, do you think evolution will ever stop? Explain your answers.
4. **Applying concepts** The giant panda occupies a very small niche by eating only one kind of food: bamboo. How can being adapted to such a small niche actually endanger this species?

5. **Relating concepts** People often say that evolution means that humans evolved from monkeys and apes. Explain why such a statement is not an accurate representation of human evolution.
6. **Making calculations** A radioactive element has a half-life of 500 million years. After 2 billion years, how many half-lives have passed? How many kilograms of a 10-kilogram sample would be left at this time? If the half-life were 4 billion years?
7. **Developing a theory** Explain why an animal species that reproduces every year would have a better chance of surviving a change in its environment than an animal species that reproduces only once or twice in ten years does.
8. **Using the writing process** You are a young reporter for a local newspaper near the home of Charles Darwin. You have been asked to interview Darwin about his theory of evolution. Develop a list of five questions you would like to have Darwin discuss. Then see whether you can answer them in the manner Darwin would.

GAZETTE

As he roamed his family's ranch in Argentina, listening to the songs of birds, the young Fernando Nottebohm felt the first stirrings of becoming a naturalist. The birds' songs intrigued him. As he walked, he would play the game of matching each song he heard to the type of bird that produced it. In this way, he created his own private hit parade—his own "Top Twenty." Any unfamiliar melody would arouse his curiosity even more, so that he would follow the sound until he discovered its source.

"That's how a naturalist develops, I think," says Nottebohm. "You just have this joy in poking around and spying on things, always hoping to find something novel." And many years later, that's exactly what Nottebohm is doing—poking around and discovering things. Only, it is birds' brains (not songs) that the naturalist-turned-zoologist is now researching. And you can be sure that plenty of novel situations have presented themselves over the course of this researcher's career.

Working at Rockefeller University in New York and directing the school's Field Research Center for Ecology and Ethology, Nottebohm has extended his bird studies into an area that is both intriguing and astonishing. In addition, his discoveries hold promise for applications which are nothing less than revolutionary.

The area of Nottebohm's study is neurogenesis, which is the birth of new neurons. Neurons are nerve cells in the brain. As far as anyone knows, nerve cells in the human brain that have been destroyed by injury or disease do not regenerate (grow back). Functions once carried out by these neurons can often be performed by other, healthy cells in the brain, but the dead cells themselves can never be replaced by new ones. All the neurons you will ever have were formed by the time you were six months old. But according to Nottebohm's research, an adult bird can generate as many as 20,000

FERNANDO NOTTEBOHM

FROM BIRD SONGS TO REBORN BRAINS

new neurons in a single day! If Nottebohm and his fellow researchers can figure out exactly what factors control neurogenesis in birds, they may be on their way to figuring out how to trigger this same process in humans.

Nottebohm's journey into the mysteries of the human brain has taken him far afield of his original ambitions. "I was mainly just interested in bird behavior and evolution at the beginning," he says. That interest in evolution was sparked at age 17, when Nottebohm first read Charles Darwin's *Voyage of the Beagle*. The content, vibrancy, and romanticism that Darwin brought to zoology convinced Nottebohm to try to make a career out of his love for nature. But the prospects for earning a living as a bird zoologist in Argentina were extremely poor. So with the encouragement of his father, Nottebohm decided to study agriculture, run the family ranch, and pursue his bird interests on the weekends.

After studying for a year at the University of Nebraska, Nottebohm transferred to the University of California at Berkeley. There he became captivated by the zoology lectures of Peter Marler, who would become internationally famous for his work on vocal communication in songbirds, monkeys, and apes. It was not long before Nottebohm, as a graduate student working with Marler, returned to his original fascination—bird songs. Only this time his approach was different: His research examined how a membrane in the bird's voice box, or syrinx, vibrates as the animal sings.

As is often the case in science, the search for an answer to one particular question generates new questions and new areas of research. And so Nottebohm soon found himself investigating more than just one membrane of a bird's syrinx. The link between the brain and the syrinx became the target of his research. Identifying the song-control areas of the brain and tracing the neural pathways between brain and syrinx was a project that took Nottebohm five years.

But the series of discoveries was not to end there. Along the way, Nottebohm and neurobiologist Arthur Arnold discovered that in canaries male and female brains are different. And in male canaries the size of the song-control areas changes dramatically with the seasons—increasing in size in the spring and shrinking at the end of the summer. Then finally, the most amazing discovery of all: Neurogenesis occurs in adult birds.

Today, a major aim of Nottebohm and his research team is to identify the genes that govern the birth of new neurons in bird brains and to determine the chemical signals that turn these genes on. As Nottebohm sees it, because evolution tends to be conservative, these genes should also be present in our own brains. Indeed, it is probably just these genes that control neurogenesis during the early development of humans. "The challenge," says Nottebohm, "is to figure out how to reawaken this genetic potential that may be lying dormant within certain brain cells in mammals, including ourselves."

> The tracings show the songs of two canaries recorded with a sound spectrograph. One canary suffered damage to the right side of its brain, which did not greatly affect its song (top). The other had damage to the left side of its brain, after which its song became distorted (bottom).

Ecology

The rat snake's tongue flickers in and out of its mouth, tasting the air. Food is nearby—warm, fat baby birds! The snake slithers up an old, diseased pine tree in search of its prey. But before it can reach the cavity in the tree trunk where the nest is hidden, the snake slithers into an unexpected patch of sticky pine sap. The sap gums up the snake's scales so that it loses its grip and falls off the tree.

A few minutes later, a red-cockaded woodpecker flies into the cavity in the old pine tree. After feeding its babies, the woodpecker does some housekeeping. Clinging to the trunk of the tree, the woodpecker pecks several holes

▼ *The red-cockaded woodpecker has an amazing way of protecting its young from the red rat snake.*

▼ *Many different kinds of places are home to Earth's living things. This forest of pink rhododendrons, Douglas firs, and redwoods is located in California's Redwoods State Park.*

into the bark surrounding the cavity. Sap runs out of the holes and oozes slowly down the tree. Then the woodpecker flies off to gather more food for its hungry babies.

The pine tree, snake, and woodpeckers you have just read about interact in an interesting way. In this textbook, you will first learn about the different kinds of interactions that occur among living things and between living things and their nonliving surroundings. Next, you will read about life cycles and other patterns of change in nature. You will then learn about the basic kinds of places that are home to Earth's living things. Finally, you will explore the reasons why organisms such as the red-cockaded woodpecker are in danger of disappearing forever from the Earth.

Living things interact in many different ways. Locking horns to establish who's the boss, these two bull moose are battling in Alaska's Denali National Park.

Discovery Activity

Seeds of Change

1. Collect as many different kinds of uncooked seeds as you can from the foods you eat.
   - What kinds of foods contain or are made up of seeds?
   - Where are these foods grown?

2. Obtain a paper towel and a small glass jar with a lid. Fold the paper towel so that it can line the sides of the jar. Moisten the paper towel with water. Then place some of the seeds in the jar so that they are sandwiched between the glass and the paper towel. Cover the jar.

3. Observe the seeds daily.
   - How do the seeds change over time?
   - How might new kinds of plants appear in an area?
   - What sorts of things might affect what happens to the seeds?

Interactions Among Living Things

26

Guide for Reading

After you read the following sections, you will be able to

26–1 Living Things and Their Environment
- Define ecosystem and identify the parts of an ecosystem.

26–2 Food and Energy in the Environment
- Discuss the interactions among producers, consumers, and decomposers.
- Describe how energy flows within an ecosystem.

26–3 Interaction and Evolution
- Discuss how interactions affect evolution.

26–4 Life in the Balance
- Explain why a disturbance in the balance in one part of an ecosystem can affect the entire ecosystem.

As sunlight falls on the leaves of a plant, substances in the leaves capture the sunlight's energy and use it to make food. But even as the leaves are making food, a tiny thief is stealing some of it. A small aphid (an insect) pokes its strawlike mouthparts into the leaf and begins to suck up food-rich sap.

Suddenly, a hungry ant scurries along the leaf toward the aphid. Is the aphid doomed to end up as the ant's lunch? No. Upon reaching the aphid, the ant begins to stroke the smaller insect with its feelers. The aphid responds by releasing a drop of a sugary substance called honeydew. The ant eagerly licks up the honeydew. Then the ant gently picks up the aphid in its jaws and carries it to another leaf. There the aphid is added to a "herd" being tended by ants. The ants take care of the aphids in exchange for meals of honeydew. The ants move the aphids to fresh leaves when the old ones wither. When it rains, the ants carry the aphids to more sheltered leaves. The ants also defend their herd from ladybugs and other aphid-devouring animals.

The interactions among aphids, ants, ladybugs, sunlight, and plants are just a few of the countless relationships that link living things to one another and to their surroundings. Read on to discover more about interactions among living things.

Journal *Activity*

You and Your World In your journal, explore the thoughts and feelings you have about environmental issues.

◀ *These orange-colored ants are busily tending a large "herd" of dark gray aphids.*

▶ Why do ecologists study both the living and the nonliving parts of an environment?

▶ What do the following terms mean: environment, ecosystem, community, population, and habitat?

26-1 Living Things and Their Environment

A thousand meters below the ocean's surface, the last traces of sunlight fade into nothingness. The water temperature is only a few degrees above freezing. There is very little food or oxygen. Yet the harsh, dark world of the deep sea is home to many organisms (living things). Nightmarish fishes with huge teeth and eyes glow with ghostly lights made by their own bodies. Octopuses and squids with webbed arms pulse through the water or float like falling parachutes. Strange spiky sea cucumbers sift through the muddy ocean floor for the bits of food that drift down from the sunlit world above.

On land, in a lush tropical rain forest, tall trees with clinging vines thrive in the warmth and sunlight. In the treetops, brightly colored parrots munch on seeds while monkeys chatter to one another. Snakes and lizards climb up and down the tree trunks in search of food. And piglike tapirs calmly make their way along the ground.

The deep sea and a rain forest are only two of the many different **environments** found on Earth. An

Figure 26-1 *The huge jaws and enormous teeth of this deep-sea fish enable it to catch and eat animals that are larger than itself. The eyelash viper and the* Heliconia *flowers on which it is coiled live in the same kind of environment as the blue-and-gold and scarlet macaws. What kind of environment is home to these organisms?*

environment consists of all the living and nonliving things with which an organism may interact.

Organisms obtain the food, water, and other resources they need to live and grow from their environment. Consider for a moment some of the things a parrot gets from its rain-forest environment. The parrot feeds on seeds and fruits from plants. It drinks water from puddles and streams. It has trees in which to perch and build its nest. It has air to breathe and to fly through. The parrot can live in a rain forest because this environment contains all the things a parrot needs to survive. Why wouldn't a parrot be able to live in an environment that is quite different from the rain forest, such as the deep sea or a desert? Can you explain why different environments contain different kinds of organisms?

Living things do not simply exist in their environment like photos in a frame. They constantly interact with their environment. Organisms can change in response to conditions in the environment. These changes can often be quite rapid. For example, within a few seconds, the fish known as a flounder can change its colors and spots to match the sand and pebbles on a new patch of ocean floor. Or the changes can be much slower. On windswept mountains, for example, trees grow so that they bend in the direction of the wind. Some slow changes involve entire groups of organisms, not just individual organisms. In Section 26–3, you will read about some of the ways organisms have evolved (changed over time) in response to their environment.

In addition to changing in response to their environment, living things also cause change in their environment. Earthworms and other burrowing animals dig tunnels in the soil. Woodpeckers drill holes in trees. Tree roots break up sidewalks. Beavers build dams that block flowing streams and thus create ponds. Can you identify some ways in which humans change their environment?

All of the living and nonliving things in an environment are interconnected. You can think of an environment as being like a giant spider web. However, the threads of this web are not spun from silk. The threads of an environment's web are the relationships among its plants, animals, soil, water, temperature, light, and other living and nonliving things.

Figure 26–2 *A few moments ago, the chameleon's environment was changed by the appearance of a juicy cricket. How does the chameleon respond to such short-term changes in its environment?*

Figure 26–3 *The relationships among the living and nonliving parts of the environment can be thought of as being like a giant spider web. But an environmental web is more complex—and perhaps more fragile—than the delicate web of a spider.*

Think for a moment about what happens when an insect gets caught in a spider's web. As one thread of the web is disturbed, the shaking motion is transferred to all the threads that are part of the web. In an environmental web, changes in one thread may also be transmitted to other threads and have an effect on them. For example, cutting down the trees in a forest may affect the rainfall in a distant city. And when a thread is broken, the entire web is weakened.

To understand the changes that can occur in an environment and how they can affect the environment, you can study the science called **ecology.** Ecology is the study of the relationships and interactions of living things with one another and with their environment. Scientists who study these interactions are called ecologists.

Ecosystems

Living things inhabit many environments on Earth. From the polar ice caps to the forests and plains of the equator, living things can be found under ground, in air, in water, and on land. Organisms have been found at the bottom of ocean trenches kilometers deep and floating in the air more than eight kilometers above the Earth's surface.

To make sense of the number and variety of interactions among Earth's living things and their environment, ecologists find it useful to divide the world up into separate units known as **ecosystems.** An ecosystem consists of all the living and nonliving things in a given area that interact with one another. A forest ecosystem, for example, includes birds and squirrels in the trees, foxes and rabbits in the bushes, the trees and bushes themselves, insects and spiders, shade-loving wildflowers, ferns, mushrooms and other fungi, microorganisms (microscopic organisms) such as bacteria and protists, dead leaves, chemicals in the soil, rocks, sunlight, rain water, and many other living and nonliving things. How do the trees in a forest ecosystem interact with squirrels? With the soil?

An ecosystem can be as tiny as a drop of pond water or a square meter of a garden. Or it can be as large as an ocean, a forest, or a planet. The size of

Figure 26–4 *A forest of broad-leaved trees is just one of the many kinds of ecosystems on Earth. What kinds of organisms would you find in this ecosystem?*

an ecosystem is defined by the ecologist who is studying it. What ecosystem would you expect an ecologist interested in the interactions of freshwater swimming microorganisms to study? Would an ecologist studying the wildlife in and around Lake Tahoe, California, use a similar ecosystem? Why or why not?

It is useful to talk about ecosystems as if they were separate, self-contained units. However, it is important to keep in mind that ecosystems are not isolated. Ecosystems overlap and affect one another. The grizzly bears of a forest ecosystem may feed on the salmon of a stream ecosystem. Chemicals from aerosol cans, air conditioners, and refrigerators in the United States and elsewhere are carried great distances by the wind and eventually break down the protective ozone layer in the air above the poles. The "holes" thus created in the ozone layer allow extra radiation from the sun to reach the ecosystems near the poles, damaging them. Damage to these ecosystems may, in turn, result in damage to other ecosystems—including ones in which you live! So it is important that you realize all the living and nonliving things on Earth are ultimately connected to one another.

Communities

The living part of any ecosystem—all the different organisms that live together in that area—is called a **community.** The community of a pond, for example, might include fishes, frogs, snails, microorganisms, and water lilies. The members of a community interact with one another in many different ways. Lily pads provide a resting place for frogs. Large fishes

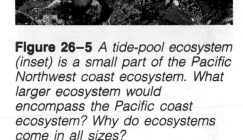

Figure 26–5 *A tide-pool ecosystem (inset) is a small part of the Pacific Northwest coast ecosystem. What larger ecosystem would encompass the Pacific coast ecosystem? Why do ecosystems come in all sizes?*

ACTIVITY

DOING

Identifying Interactions

Ecosystems are all around you. Choose one particular ecosystem—an aquarium, swamp, lake, park, or city block, for example—and study the interactions that occur among the living and nonliving parts of the ecosystem. Include drawings and diagrams in your observations.

Figure 26–6 *The plains of Africa are home to many different kinds of living things. What members of the African plains community can you identify here?*

Figure 26–7 *Some populations— such as that of the flamingoes in Botswana, Africa—are enormous. Others—such as that of the treehoppers on a twig in Costa Rica—are quite small.*

eat frogs. Microorganisms break down the bodies of dead organisms, producing products such as nitrogen compounds that can be used by plants. Can you think of some other ways in which the members of a pond community interact? In the next two sections, you will learn about some of the specific interactions that take place within communities.

Populations

You, like all other living things on Earth, belong to an ecological community. Your community probably contains many different kinds of living things: people, dogs, cats, birds, insects, grass, and trees, to name a few. What other kinds of organisms are found in your community?

Each kind of living thing makes up a **population** in the community. A population is a group of organisms of the same type, or species, living together in the same area. (A species is a group of similar organisms that can produce offspring. You and all other humans belong to the same species. But cats belong to another species.) For example, all the rainbow trout living in a lake are a population. All the redwood trees in a forest are a population.

But a group consisting of all the wildflowers in a meadow is not considered to be a population. Can you explain why?

Habitats

Where would you go to find a lion? How about a pigeon? Where in a forest would you look for a squirrel? A mushroom? An earthworm? Would you discover all these organisms in the same place? Probably not. Lions live on the grassy plains of Africa. Pigeons live in cities, among other places. In a forest, squirrels live in the trees, mushrooms grow on the forest floor, and earthworms burrow in the soil. Each of these organisms lives in a different place.

The place in which an organism lives is called its **habitat.** A habitat provides food, shelter, and the other resources an organism needs to survive. Living things such as lions, pigeons, and mushrooms live in different habitats because they have different requirements for survival. Organisms such as lions, zebras, and giraffes also have different requirements for survival. Yet these organisms live in the same habitat. Why? Because their requirements—such as for temperature, water, and open space—overlap in many ways. The size of an organism's habitat depends on the organism's habits and needs. The habitat of a humpback whale is the open ocean. The habitat of a certain tiny mite, on the other hand, is the ear of a moth.

26–1 Section Review

1. Why do ecologists study both the nonliving and living things in an environment?
2. What is an ecosystem? Give an example of an ecosystem.
3. What is the difference between a community and a population?

Connection—*Architecture*
4. Explain why an architect designing a new home for the cheetahs in a zoo must know something about the natural habitat of cheetahs.

Guide for Reading

*Focus on these questions as
you read.*

▶ *How do producers, con-
sumers, and decomposers
interact?*

▶ *What is the difference
between a food chain
and a food web?*

26–2 Food and Energy in the Environment

If you enjoy watching or playing team sports, you know that the members of a team usually play different positions. Basketball players may be centers, forwards, or guards. Baseball players may be pitchers, catchers, shortstops, center fielders, and so on. Each position has a particular role associated with it. For example, a pitcher throws the ball to the batters. A guard tries to prevent the members of the other team from scoring a basket. Similarly, organisms have special roles that they play in an ecosystem.

Energy Roles

Organisms may be **producers, consumers,** or **decomposers.** These three terms indicate how an organism obtains energy and how it interacts with the other living things in its community.

PRODUCERS Some organisms, such as green plants and certain microorganisms, have a very special ability that sets them apart from all other living things: They can make their own food. Such organisms are known as producers. Producers are able to use a source of energy (such as sunlight) to turn simple raw materials (such as water and carbon dioxide gas) into food (such as the sugar glucose). Organisms that cannot make their own food may eat the producers directly. Or they may eat other organisms that cannot make their own food. However, all organisms that cannot make their own food ultimately depend on producers. **Producers are the source of all the food in an ecosystem.**

Figure 26–8 *Towering redwood trees, indigo Texas bluebonnets, and bright pink phlox are examples of producers. Why are producers essential for life on Earth?*

CONSUMERS   Organisms that cannot make their own food depend on producers for food and energy. **An organism that feeds directly or indirectly on producers is called a consumer.**

There are many kinds of consumers. Some organisms, such as grasshoppers and rabbits, are plant eaters. Plant eaters are known as herbivores. The term herbivore comes from the Latin words *herba,* which means grass or herb, and *vorare,* which means to eat. Spiders, snakes, and wolves, which eat other animals, are known as carnivores. The Latin word *carnis* means of the flesh. Why is the term carnivore appropriate for organisms that eat meat?

Organisms that eat both plants and animals are known as omnivores. (The Latin word *omnis* means all.) Crows, bears, and humans are just a few examples of omnivores.

There are many other terms that are used to group consumers according to what they eat. One such term is scavenger. A scavenger is an animal that feeds on the bodies of dead animals. Jackals, hyenas, and vultures are examples of scavengers. So are certain crayfish and crabs, who "clean up" watery environments by eating dead organisms.

DECOMPOSERS   After living things die, organisms called decomposers use the dead matter as food. **Decomposers break down dead organisms into simpler substances.** In the process, they return important

Figure 26–9 *The caterpillars, shark, and hyena and vulture are all consumers.*

ACTIVITY DOING

Diet Delights

1. Use a dictionary to find out what these specialized feeders eat: piscivore, insectivore, detritovore, myrmecophage, frugivore, coprophage, necrophage, nectarivore, granivore, apivore, carpophage.

2. Invent a term to describe the feeding habits of Count Dracula (and other vampires).

Activity Bank

Garbage in the Garden, p. 841

669

Figure 26–10 *Nestled among the fallen leaves on the forest floor, these mushrooms are slowly breaking down a dead branch for food. Why are mushrooms considered to be decomposers?*

ACTIVITY

DOING

Your Place in Line

Every time you eat, you are assuming a particular place in a food chain. You can determine your place in a food chain through the following activity.

Make a list of all the foods you ate for breakfast, lunch, and dinner. For each food, figure out the probable links in the food chain that lead up to you. Be sure to answer the following questions:

1. Who are the producers?
2. Who are the consumers?

materials to the soil and water. You may be familiar with the term "decay," which is often used to describe this process. Molds, mushrooms, and many kinds of bacteria are examples of decomposers.

Decomposers are essential to the ecosystem because they rid the environment of the bodies of dead plants and animals. Even more importantly, decomposers return nutrients (compounds containing chemicals such as nitrogen, carbon, phosphorus, sulfur, and magnesium) to the environment. These nutrients are then used by plants to make food, and the cycle of nutrients through the environment continues. If the nutrients were not returned to the environment, organisms within that ecosystem could not survive for long.

Food Chains and Food Webs

In general, food and energy in an ecosystem flow from the producers to the consumers, and finally to the decomposers. The food and energy links among the producers and consumers in an ecosystem are represented by **food chains** and **food webs.**

A food chain represents a series of events in which food and energy are transferred from one organism in an ecosystem to another. The first link in a food chain is always a producer. The second link is a herbivore. The third link and all the links after that are almost always carnivores.

Let's take a look at an example of a food chain. In an Antarctic food chain, the producers are one-celled organisms known as diatoms. The diatoms capture energy from the sun and use it to make food. When a diatom is eaten by a shrimplike animal called a krill, the food energy and matter in the diatom are transferred to the krill. In the following links of the food chain, the krill is eaten by a squid, which is eaten by a penguin, which is eaten by a leopard seal, which is eaten by a killer whale. Both food energy and matter are transferred at each successive link of the food chain. Figure 26–11 illustrates another food chain.

The "end" of a food chain is connected to the "beginning" by decomposers. In the Antarctic food chain, decomposers break down the body of the killer whale when it dies. This makes matter in the

form of nutrients available to the producers. What do the producers do with these nutrients?

A food chain gives you a glimpse of the food and energy relationships in an ecosystem. But it does not give you the whole picture. There are many organisms in an ecosystem, and few of them eat only one kind of food. Thus there must be overlapping food chains in an ecosystem. Figure 26–12 on page 672 shows how a number of organisms in the Antarctic ecosystem are linked by food and energy relationships. This kind of diagram is known as a food web. Can you see why the name food web is an appropriate one? A food web consists of many overlapping food chains. One of the food chains in this food web was just described. Another food chain might be: a diatom is eaten by a tiny water animal that is eaten by a fish that is eaten by a penguin. Take a moment now to identify three of the many other food chains in this food web.

Feeding Levels and Energy

A feeding level is the location of an organism along a food chain. Producers form the first feeding level. Herbivores form the second feeding level. And carnivores form the third feeding level.

At each feeding level, organisms use the energy they obtain to digest their food, reproduce, move,

Figure 26–11 The links of this desert food chain include a flowering Saguaro cactus (left), an iguana (top right), and a roadrunner (bottom right). What role does each organism play in this food chain?

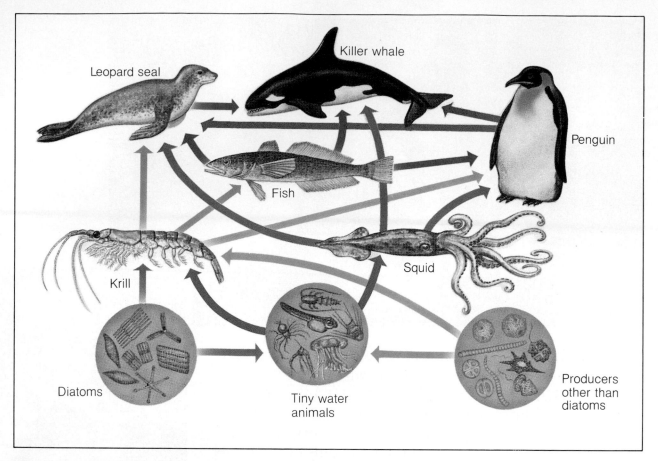

Figure 26–12 *Food webs can be quite complicated, even when they show only a few of the organisms in an ecosystem. What are the producers in this Antarctic food web? What are the herbivores and carnivores?*

grow, and carry out other life activities. What does this mean for living things at higher feeding levels? It means that there is less energy available to them. As you can see in Figure 26–13, the amount of energy at the second feeding level is much smaller than that at the first feeding level. The amount of energy at the third feeding level is smaller still. At each successive level, there is less energy than there was before. Because a diagram that shows the amount of energy at the different feeding levels looks like a pyramid—wide at the base and narrowing toward the top—it is called a pyramid of energy.

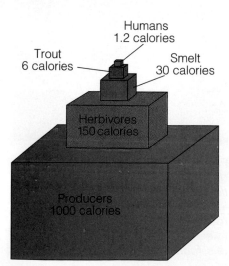

Figure 26–13 *With each successive feeding level, the amount of energy decreases greatly. How does the amount of energy in trout compare to that in smelt? Why can more people be fed if smelt is eaten instead of trout? Why do some experts think that a first step in solving the problem of world hunger might be to encourage people to eat lower on the food chain?*

26–2 Section Review

1. Explain how producers, consumers, and decomposers interact. For each energy role, give two examples of organisms that perform that role in their ecosystem.
2. What is a food chain? A food web?
3. What is the relationship between feeding levels and amount of available energy?
4. How does energy flow through an ecosystem?

Critical Thinking—*Evaluating Diagrams*

5. Why are decomposers left out of almost all diagrams of food chains and food webs? Do you think this is a good practice? Why or why not?

26–3 Interaction and Evolution

Guide for Reading

Focus on this question as you read.

▶ *What are competition, predation, and symbiosis?*

Each organism in a community has its own unique role to play. This role, or **niche** (NIHCH), consists of more than the organism's place in a food chain. It includes everything the organism does and everything the organism needs in its environment. In other words, an organism's niche includes the place in which it lives, the food it eats, the organisms that feed on it, the organisms that interact with it in other ways, the amount of light and humidity it needs, and the physical conditions in which it can survive.

As you learned in the previous section, two or more species (kinds of organisms) can share the same habitat, or place in which to live. For example, the coral reef habitat is home to corals that build stony skeletons, soft flowerlike sea anemones, flat ribbons and thin threads of seaweed, spiny sea urchins, scuttling crabs, fishes in a rainbow of colors, and many other organisms. Two species can also share similar habits and food requirements. For example, flying fox bats and toucans are both flying animals that live in trees and eat fruit. Sharks and

Eat or Be Eaten

Draw a food web that contains the following: bread crumbs, food scraps, pigeon, mouse, cockroach, cat, rat, bacteria, starling, spider, fly. Where would you be likely to find this food web? What feeding level is missing from this food web? Why is this feeding level missing?

Figure 26–14 *The flying fox bat of Australia and the Toco toucan of Brazil both enjoy feasting on fruit. How are their niches similar? How are they different?*

dolphins are fast-swimming ocean animals that both eat fish. Two or more species *cannot* share the same niche. If two species try to occupy the same niche for a long period of time, one of the species will become extinct, or die off. Why? The answer has to do with a special kind of relationship between organisms—a relationship you are now going to read about.

Competition

Ecosystems cannot satisfy the needs of all the living things in a particular habitat. There is only a limited amount of food, water, shelter, light, and other resources in an environment. Because there are not enough resources to go around, organisms must struggle with one another to get the things they need to survive. This type of interaction is known as **competition.**

One of the resources for which organisms compete is food. The shortage of other resources, such as water, light, and suitable places to live, also results in competition. Regardless of the specific causes, competition can have a powerful effect on the size and location of a population in an ecosystem.

Competition can occur within a species as well as between species. A male lion will fight with another male lion for control over a group of female lions. Pairs of penguins squabble with other pairs of penguins over the pebbles used in nest building. And if there is not enough space between two plants of the same species, they will compete with one another for

Figure 26–15 *Bighorn rams knock their horns together with a resounding crash as they compete to determine which one will gain control of a group of females.*

water, nutrients, and light. (This is why gardeners have to thin out seedlings in a flower bed or vegetable patch.)

In order to better understand how competition works in nature, it might be helpful for you to think about some more familiar kinds of competition. People who read for a play, audition for a musical group, or try out for a sports team compete with one another for limited resources: roles, chairs, and positions, respectively. Nonliving things can also be thought of as being in competition with one another. Have you ever walked down the aisle of a supermarket and gazed in amazement at the number of different kinds of breakfast cereal displayed? Like living things, products such as breakfast cereals, cars, shampoos, blue jeans, and even science textbooks compete with one another for a limited resource. In this case, the resource is a customer's purchase choice. The products that are most successful at obtaining this resource (the ones that are bought most often) continue to be sold. The products that are least successful soon cease to be manufactured.

Predation

Slowly and silently, the cat sneaks up on an unsuspecting mouse. The cat crouches down. The tip of its tail twitches and its muscles tense. Then the cat pounces!

For thousands of years, people have valued the cat's ability to kill rats and mice. Living things, such as cats, that catch, kill, and eat other living things

ACTIVITY READING

"Avenues of Delight and Discovery"

The works of Rachel Carson (1907–1964) prove that scientific writings can be as beautiful and poetic as any work of literature. Although she was a marine biologist by training, two of her most famous books are not about the sea and its creatures. Read *The Silent Spring* and *The Sense of Wonder*, by Rachel Carson. Explore the beauty and mystery of the natural world by simply making a trip to the library!

Figure 26–16 *How can you tell that the lioness (right), the great blue heron (top left), and the hawk (bottom left) are predators? What kinds of prey do these predators hunt? By the way, the attacking redwing blackbird is not trying to prey on the hawk. The hawk simply flew too close to the blackbird's nest, upsetting the smaller bird.*

are called **predators.** The organisms that are eaten by predators are called **prey.** Although people usually think of predators and their prey as being animals, ecologists consider just about all situations in which one organism kills and eats another as examples of predation.

Predation, like competition, plays an important part in shaping the structure of communities. In catching and eating prey, predators help to reduce the size of prey populations. By helping to control the size of prey populations, predators also help to maintain the diversity in an ecosystem. When predators are absent, prey species can become too numerous and crowd out other organisms.

This is exactly what happened with the rabbits that were introduced to Australia about 150 years ago by European settlers. The rabbits had few predators, so their population increased very quickly. These harmless-looking animals were soon stripping the grasslands bare of vegetation. Many of the native animals that also fed on this vegetation, such as kangaroos, starved. To save their herds, cattle ranchers put up special fences to keep the rabbits out of their pastures. This situation continued until the 1950s, when scientists introduced a rabbit-killing predator to Australia: a virus that caused a fatal rabbit disease. The disease killed off about 80 percent of the rabbits, making it possible to reclaim land for native Australian wildlife and livestock.

PROBLEM Solving

To Bee or Not to Bee

The honeybees in the United States are in trouble! Pests from distant lands have been accidentally introduced into this country. These pests now threaten the $150-million-a-year beekeeping industry. Agricultural researchers, bee specialists, and other experts are searching frantically for a way to fight these pests before it's too late. Can you help them find a solution to the problem of the pests?

For each of the following situations, (1) identify the type of interaction involved, (2) describe the problem you perceive and propose a solution, and (3) predict the effects that the situation may have on the further evolution of the honeybee.

Evaluating situations

1. Tracheal mites live inside a bee's breathing tubes. There they suck fluids from the bee's body and interfere with its breathing. American honeybees are descendants of European honeybees, which rarely have tracheal mites. However, tracheal mites have been a major problem for American honeybees since 1984.

2. *Varroa* mites, which were first discovered in the United States in September 1987, attach to the outside of adult bees and young bees. The mites weaken the bees by feeding on their body fluids. In addition, they may transmit diseases from one bee to another.

3. Although "killer bees" belong to the same species as American honeybees, they are much more aggressive. Killer bees were accidentally released in Brazil in 1957. Since then, they have been expanding their range northward. In October 1990, the first swarm of killer bees entered the United States.

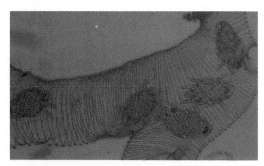

Figure 26–17 *The ratel loves honey, but cannot easily find beehives (top). The honeyguide can easily find beehives, but is too small, weak, and vulnerable to bee stings to get at the beeswax it likes to eat (bottom). Together, the ratel and honeyguide can obtain their favorite treats. What is this kind of partnership called?*

Symbiosis

In a tropical ocean, a remora fish uses a structure on top of its head to attach itself to the belly of a shark and get a free ride. Chirping and fluttering, a honeyguide bird in Africa leads a furry black-and-white ratel to a wild beehive. With its sharp claws, the ratel rips open the hive. The ratel then laps up the honey as the honeyguide bird dines on beeswax. In the United States, a dog sleeping on a rug suddenly sits up and begins to scratch an itchy flea bite.

What do these events have in common? They are all examples of **symbiosis** (sihm-bigh-OH-sihs; plural: symbioses). **Symbiosis is a close relationship between two organisms in which one organism lives near, on, or even inside another organism and in which at least one organism benefits.** Symbioses are placed into three categories: **commensalism, mutualism,** and **parasitism.** In commensalism, one of the organisms benefits and the other is not harmed by the association. In mutualism, both organisms benefit. And in parasitism, one organism benefits and the other is harmed. Is the relationship between a dog and a flea an example of commensalism, mutualism, or parasitism? What kind of symbiosis do you have with a pet animal?

As you read the following examples of commensalism, mutualism, and parasitism, keep in mind that science is a constantly changing body of knowledge. New observations may lead scientists to conclude that what was thought to be one kind of symbiosis is in fact another kind altogether. Try to think of additional ways in which the partners in a symbiosis may help—or harm—each other.

COMMENSALISM High in the branches of a tree, a large, fierce hawk called an osprey builds a big, flat nest for its eggs. Smaller birds, such as sparrows and wrens, set up their homes beneath the osprey's nest. Because the osprey eats mostly fish, these smaller birds are in no danger from the osprey. In fact, the little birds obtain protection from their enemies by living close to the fierce hawk.

Beautiful orchids and exotic bromeliads (relatives of pineapples) survive in dense, shadowy jungles by growing on tall trees. There among the tree branches, the plants get a great deal of sunlight. The roots

of these plants are exposed, so they can take water and nutrients right out of the air or off the surface of the tree's bark. Can you explain why the relationship between a bromeliad and a tree is an example of commensalism?

Like a giant tropical tree, you have smaller members of your community living on you. Dozens of tiny mites live at the base of the hairs that make up your eyebrows. Don't rush to the mirror to check—these mites can be seen only with a microscope. And don't worry about being a home to these mites. They are quite harmless, and everybody has them!

MUTUALISM   Remember the ants and aphids you read about at the beginning of this chapter? This relationship is one of the many examples of mutualism that exist among Earth's living things.

The goby fish and snapping shrimp shown on the following page live in a sandy burrow built by the shrimp. Because the shrimp is nearly blind, it keeps one of its long feelers on the goby. When danger approaches, the goby warns its partner with flicks of its fins, and both partners retreat to their burrow. Neither the goby nor the shrimp can survive on its own. Gobies without homes and shrimp without guides are soon eaten up by predators.

Some of the most important (if not the most interesting) examples of mutualism involve microorganisms that live inside the body of much larger partners. The microorganisms obtain a safe home

Figure 26–18 *Sea anemones use stinging tentacles to catch and stun small fishes and other prey. This clownfish, however, is immune to the anemone's sting and thus is safe in the anemone's deadly embrace (left). The bromeliads that grow on forest trees are in turn involved in commensalism with smaller creatures, such as this red-eyed tree frog, that make their home in the vaselike center of the plant (right).*

Figure 26–19 *In mutualism, both organisms benefit from the symbiosis. The small brown oxpeckers on the rhino's nose and belly feed on ticks and other parasites (right). (The white cattle egrets are involved in commensalism with the rhino—they eat insects flushed from hiding as the rhino walks through the grass.) The honeybee is extending a tubelike mouthpart to sip nectar (a sugary liquid) from a flower (top left). The yellow dust on the bee's head is pollen. Most flowers need to receive pollen from another flower in order for their seeds to develop. The goby and snapping shrimp depend on each other for survival (bottom left).*

inside their partner. In return, they help their partner in some way. Bacteria that live inside your digestive system help to produce certain vitamins that your body needs. Microorganisms in certain species of water animals (deep-sea tube worms, giant clams, corals, flatworms, and sea slugs, to name a few) produce food for their partners. Microorganisms in the intestines of cattle, horses, rabbits, termites, and other herbivores help these animals to digest the tough plant materials that they eat. Flashlight fish have structures beneath their eyes that contain symbiotic bacteria. These bacteria produce light, which the flashlight fish are able to turn on and off. The blinking lights of a school of flashlight fish are thought to confuse predators and perhaps enable the fish in the school to communicate.

PARASITISM Have you ever had a cold or been bitten by a mosquito or flea? If so, you have had firsthand experience with parasitism.

Parasites come in many shapes and sizes. Blood-drinking animals such as fleas, ticks, mosquitoes, leeches, and vampire bats are parasites. The fungi that cause athlete's foot and ringworm are also parasites. Some parasites live inside the body of another organism. Disease-causing bacteria and viruses are internal parasites. So are a number of worms, including the heartworm that affects pet dogs. Although they vary greatly in habit and appearance, all parasites have one trait in common: They are involved in a symbiotic relationship in which they harm their partner.

Ecologists often regard parasitism and predation as being different forms of the same basic kind of interaction. In predation and almost all examples of parasitism one organism eats another organism. In predation, the predator usually kills its prey before it eats it. In parasitism, the **parasite** usually lives on or in a much larger organism and feeds on it while it is still alive. The parasite's unlucky "partner" is called its **host.** Parasites usually do not kill their host, although many weaken it greatly. Why do you think it is an advantage to a parasite not to kill its host?

A few parasites do kill their host. For example, certain wasps lay their eggs on caterpillars. The eggs hatch into wormlike young wasps that burrow into the body of the caterpillar. The young wasps feed on the caterpillar's tissues, avoiding the caterpillar's major organs so that it stays alive. After about 30 or 40 days, the young wasps chew their way out of their dying host's body and spin cocoons. Inside the cocoons, the young wasps develop into adult wasps.

Some organisms are considered parasites even though they do not feed on their host. Cuckoos (and a few other types of birds) lay their eggs in other birds' nests. When the baby cuckoo hatches, it pushes the eggs and young of its foster parents out of the nest. The foster parents are tricked into feeding and caring for the intruder as if it were their own offspring. How does the cuckoo's behavior harm other birds? Why are cuckoos considered to be parasites?

Figure 26–20 *The vampire bat bites host animals with its razor-sharp fangs, then drinks their blood (bottom right). The white ovals on this caterpillar are the eggs of a wasp (top right). When the young wasps hatch, they will slowly eat the caterpillar. The cuckoo continues to trick its unlucky foster parents into caring for it—even after it has grown much larger than they are (top left). Why are these animals considered to be parasites?*

Adapting to the Environment

Have you ever heard the phrase "survival of the fittest"? Hiding behind this simple phrase is a complicated process. In response to the challenges of their environment, species evolve, or change over time. The evolutionary changes that make organisms better suited for their environment occur by means of a process known as natural selection. Natural selection works like this: Only the individuals that are best suited for their environment survive and produce offspring. These offspring inherit the characteristics that made their parents well suited for the environment. Over the course of a number of generations, these well-suited individuals continue to thrive and reproduce. At the same time, the characteristics that make individuals poorly suited for the environment disappear. This is because the individuals that have these characteristics are less likely to survive. Such individuals have few, if any, offspring to inherit their characteristics. The net result of natural selection are changes in the behavior and physical characteristics of species that make them better suited for their environment. This process is called adaptation.

Organisms cannot choose how they change. They also cannot invent new characteristics. Even with these limitations, living things have been changed in many strange and marvelous ways through natural selection to meet the challenges of their environment. Some of the most interesting adaptations have their origin in the way organisms interact with other living things in their community.

ADAPTING TO PREDATORS Organisms have evolved many adaptations to defend themselves against predators. Animals, such as deer and rabbits, are able to escape from predators by running very fast. Turtles, snails, and coconuts have hard shells that shield them from attackers. Skunks, stinkbugs, and mustard plants produce odors that repel predators. Fawns (baby deer) and many insects have colors and shapes that allow them to blend into their backgrounds. So do the flounder fish you read about earlier. Wasps, sea anemones, and nettle plants can sting. Roses, porcupine fish, hedgehogs, and sea urchins have long sharp thorns or spines. Toads,

Figure 26–21 *One adaptation to the environment involves the size of an animal's ears. Small ears, such as those of the arctic fox, help to conserve body heat (top). Large ears, such as those of the desert fox, help to get rid of excess heat (bottom). How else are these foxes adapted to their physical environment?*

puffer fish, certain mushrooms, and many plants contain poisonous chemicals. And seventeen-year cicadas and the seeds of century bamboo plants show up so rarely that predators are not used to eating them. (Imagine waiting a hundred years—or even seventeen years—for your next meal!)

But predators are not so easily discouraged! They have evolved in ways that help them get around their prey's defenses. Cheetahs, for example, can achieve bursts of speed that allow them to catch swiftly running gazelles.

Some types of animals—prairie dogs, musk oxen, bees, and ants, to name a few—live in large groups. Individuals in these groups can take turns looking out for enemies. They can also band together to fight off predators. Can you think of other ways in which living in groups helps organisms to survive? Why can living in groups be considered an adaptation?

ADAPTING TO COMPETITORS Organisms have evolved many adaptations for dealing with competition. One strategy is for competing species to divide up the habitat. Take a look at the Central and South American hummingbirds in the photographs on the next page. What do you notice about them?

Although these birds are similar in form, it is obvious that they have very different beaks. Each different (specialized) beak limits a particular

Figure 26–22 *Some organisms defend themselves by looking like something they're not. This caterpillar looks like a bird-eating viper (right). What do the spiny bugs (left) and the praying mantis (center) resemble?*

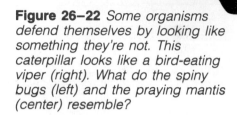

Figure 26–23 *Brilliant colors warn predators that the sea slug is too dangerous to eat. The orange projections on the sea slug's back are loaded with stinging structures from the sea anemones it eats (top). What adaptations has the cactus evolved that protect it from predators?*

Figure 26–24 *The long-tailed hermit (left), sicklebill (center), and green violet-ear (right), Central and South American hummingbirds, feed on the nectar of flowers. What is the most obvious way in which these birds have evolved to avoid competition?*

hummingbird to drinking nectar from only certain flowers. Can you explain how this makes it possible for several species of these small, brightly colored birds to share the same habitat?

A different sort of strategy is used by plants such as sunflowers, mesquite, and purple sage. Instead of sharing their habitat, these plants reduce competition by killing off their competitors. They release chemicals into their surroundings that discourage the growth of other plants.

The bacterium *Streptomyces* and the fungus *Penicillium* also produce chemicals that discourage the growth of competitors. You may be familiar with these chemicals in a more common form—that of antibiotics. Antibiotics help humans cure diseases by killing the microorganisms that cause them. The drug streptomycin is obtained from *Streptomyces*. Penicillin is obtained from *Penicillium*.

ADAPTING IN SYMBIOSIS The partners in many symbioses are extremely well-adapted to each other. For example, certain acacia trees in Latin America and Africa have huge hollow thorns or hollow swellings the size of Ping-Pong balls on their branches. These structures are inhabited by ants. The acacias also have other types of structures on or near their leaves that produce food for the ants. Thus the acacias feed the ants as well as provide them with a home. In return, the ants catch and eat small herbivores, such as grasshoppers, that land on their tree. If a large herbivore tries to nibble on the acacia's leaves (or if a curious person touches the acacia), the ants swarm onto the intruder, biting and stinging. The ants that live on the Latin American acacias also help their partner deal with competitors. They chew off any tree branches that come into contact with their acacia. This enables the tree to get plenty of light even though it lives in a dense tropical forest. Imagine the series of evolutionary adjustments that were necessary to make the ants and acacias so well suited to living together!

26–3 Section Review

1. Describe the three basic types of symbiosis. Give two examples of each.
2. What is competition? Why does it occur?

Critical Thinking—*Making Generalizations*
3. The myxomatosis virus is spread by mosquitoes. When the virus was first introduced to Australia, it killed many rabbits very quickly. Now, the virus is slower and less deadly. Explain how and why the rabbits and virus have changed. What impact might this have on the Australian ecosystem?

Figure 26–25 *The round structures on the whistling thorn acacia provide a home for symbiotic ants.*

26–4 Life in the Balance

Earlier in this chapter you learned that all of the living and nonliving things in an environment are interconnected, like the strands of a spider's web. Touching a single strand can cause the entire web to tremble. If too many threads are broken, the web collapses and must be built anew.

An ecosystem, however, is not an unchanging structure like a spider web. Changes are constantly occurring in an ecosystem. Populations increase and decrease. Trees fall and animals die. The weather changes with the seasons. Birds fly to warmer places for the winter. Each time a change occurs, an adjustment in the balance of an ecosystem is required.

Sometimes ecosystems are thrown completely out of balance by a natural disaster, such as a hurricane, landslide, forest fire, or volcanic eruption. Perhaps

Guide for Reading

Focus on this question as you read.

▶ *What are some ways in which humans can affect the balance of an ecosystem?*

Figure 26-26 *In May 1980, the lush green forests of Mount St. Helens were destroyed by a volcanic eruption. The blast knocked over trees and covered the surrounding area in volcanic ash. But eventually life began to return to the area. The ecosystem of Mount St. Helens is slowly regaining its balance.*

you have read about or possibly even experienced the explosive eruption of Mount St. Helens in 1980, the forest fires in Yellowstone National Park in 1988, or Hurricane Hugo in 1989. What effects did these disasters have on the ecosystems in the area? In certain cases, however, events that seem like natural disasters are not really disasters at all. Instead, they are events that may actually help to maintain the balance in certain ecosystems. For example, naturally occurring forest and brush fires may clear away shrubs and dead wood, creating room for new plants to grow. Burning also breaks down dead plant materials and thus returns nutrients to the soil. Some organisms in fire-prone areas have evolved in ways that enable them to cope with periodic fires. A few even need fires. The seeds of the jack pine tree, for example, require the temperatures of a forest fire in order to be released from their protective pine cones.

Ecosystems are also put out of balance by human activities. **The damaging effects of activities such as chopping down forests or putting poisonous chemicals into rivers are quite obvious. Apparently harmless human actions may also cause widespread damage.** One of the more dramatic examples of the unexpected ways in which human activities can damage ecosystems involves Mono Lake, in eastern California.

Mono Lake is a beautiful saltwater lake fed by streams of melting snow from the Sierra Nevada Mountains. Two small islands within Mono Lake attract thousands of birds, especially seagulls. More than 80 species of birds nest on these islands and feed on the lake's shrimp, flies, and algae. That is, they did until 1981. During the summer of that year, many baby seagulls were found dead. How strange this seemed to be for an ecosystem that had long provided food, water, and shelter for seagulls! As people investigated the situation, they discovered that the ecosystem had been disturbed by actions taken far away from the lake many years before.

About 40 years ago, the city of Los Angeles began to use water from the major streams that feed into Mono Lake. As less and less water emptied into Mono Lake, the lake began to dry up. Thousands of acres of dust formed where there was once water.

As the amount of water in the lake decreased, the concentration of salt dissolved in the water increased. The shrimp that seagulls fed on could not survive in water so salty. As the shrimp died, less food was available for the seagulls. Baby seagulls starved to death.

To make matters worse, as the water level in Mono Lake dropped, a land bridge that connected the shore to the nesting islands formed. Coyotes crossed this bridge, killed many seagulls, and invaded the gulls' nests.

Figure 26–27 *In January 1991, the Iraqi army occupying Kuwait dumped millions of liters of oil into the Persian Gulf, causing one of the world's worst environmental disasters. What effect did this oil spill have on wildlife?*

Figure 26–28 *Mono Lake has the potential to be home to thousands of birds (left). But when too much of its water supply is taken away, the lake dries up and becomes virtually lifeless (right).*

Many people want to save Mono Lake. But it will not be easy. In order to conserve water and save the lake, some profitable farmland must be allowed to turn back into desert. In addition, people must change their lifestyles and give up nice things like green lawns, swimming pools, decorative fountains, and weekly car washes. As you can imagine, the government of California is going to have a hard time getting people to cooperate with water-saving measures. To complicate the situation, the area around Los Angeles received less rainfall in the late 1980s and early 1990s than it usually does. This has made the water shortage even more severe.

Without a water conservation plan, Mono Lake will continue to dry up. And the delicate balance between living and nonliving things in this ecosystem may be altered beyond all hope for recovery.

The story of Mono Lake is only one example of the effects humans have on the balance in ecosystems. There are thousands and thousands of other stories. Some end sadly with something beautiful or strange lost forever. A few have happy endings. And many are unfolding even as you read these words. With careful planning, people can help these stories end happily. By understanding the interactions within the environment, people can both use the resources around them and preserve the beauty, diversity, and balance within ecosystems.

ACTIVITY

WRITING

Who Missed the Moose?

Isle Royale is a long, narrow island in Lake Superior, 25 kilometers from the shore of Canada. In the early 1900s, a few moose swam to the island. Within 20 years, the population had increased to more than 2000!

During the next 40 years, the moose population underwent several changes. Using books and other materials in the library, find out what changes occurred on Isle Royale and what caused the changes. Include answers to the following questions in your report.

1. What are limiting factors and in what ways do they affect a population?

2. How do birth and death rates affect a population?

3. What is a population cycle?

26–4 Section Review

1. How can human activities affect the balance of ecosystems?
2. How did humans change the balance in the Mono Lake ecosystem?

Connection—*You and Your World*

3. A picture-perfect lawn or golf course is usually a lush green expanse of just one kind of grass. Its appearance is kept up by a program of constant mowing, fertilizing, watering, and applying pesticides and weedkillers. Using what you have learned about interactions and balances in an ecosystem, explain why "perfect" lawns and golf courses are so difficult to maintain.

CONNECTIONS

Down for the Count

You might recall watching one of the adults in your household filling out a *census* form in 1990. Every 10 years, the government conducts a census of the people of the United States. Special forms are mailed out to every household in the country. People report the number of people in their household, the sex and age of each person, their income, the number of rooms in their dwelling, and many other facts. Then they mail back the forms.

Occasionally, there are problems. Some people give silly answers. Others fail to return their forms. And a few people may be overlooked by the census takers.

These problems seem minor compared to those faced by biologists performing a wildlife census. For one thing, wild animals do not have a mailing address! And even if they did, they could not fill out a census form! So the biologists must travel to the places where the animals live and put up with insect bites, awful weather, and other discomforts.

Some large, conspicuous organisms—such as caribou, elephants, and wildebeests—are simply counted from aerial photographs. The sizes of the populations of most other organisms are determined indirectly: Biologists count or estimate the size of part of a population, then use this figure to calculate the probable size of the entire population. For example, a biologist studying wolves may let out a howl, then count the number of answering howls from real wolves. Suppose the biologist knows that about a quarter of the wolves in the area will respond to the fake howl. If the biologist hears eight responding howls, how many wolves are probably in the area?

Some wildlife census methods involve catching animals. As you can imagine, this can be more hazardous than ringing doorbells in a city or town for the Census Bureau! While counting animals, biologists have been bitten, scratched, pecked, sprayed by skunks, menaced by bears, and even chased up a tree by a moose that recovered too soon from a dose of tranquilizer delivered by a dart gun.

Faced with all these difficulties, why do biologists conduct a census of wildlife? Because knowing the size of populations and how populations have changed over time gives people some of the information they need for deciding how to manage wildlife and the environment.

Laboratory Investigation

A Little Off Balance

Problem

How does adding lawn fertilizer affect the balance of an aquatic (water) ecosystem?

Materials *(per group)*

2 2-L wide-mouthed jars
pond water
8 *Elodea* (or other aquatic plant)
lawn fertilizer (or house plant food)
teaspoon

Procedure 🧪

1. Label the jars A and B.
2. Fill each jar about three-fourths full with pond water.
3. Place four *Elodea* in each jar.
4. Add one-half teaspoon of lawn fertilizer to jar B.
5. Place the jars next to each other in a lighted area.
6. Predict what will happen to the jars over the course of three weeks. Record your predictions.
7. Observe the jars daily for three weeks. Record your observations.

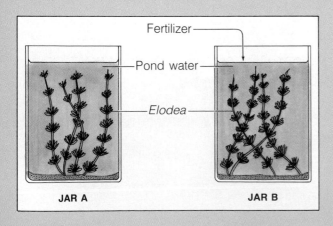

Fertilizer

Pond water

Elodea

JAR A   **JAR B**

Observations

1. Were there any differences between jars A and B? If so, what were the differences? When did you observe them?
2. How did your results compare to your predictions?

Analysis and Conclusions

1. What was the control in this experiment? The variable?
2. Why did you place the jars next to each other? Why did you place them in the light?
3. What effect did the fertilizer have on the *Elodea*?
4. Lawn fertilizer contains nitrogen, phosphorus, and potassium. These nutrients are often present in sewage as well. Predict the effects of dumping untreated sewage into ponds and lakes.
5. **On Your Own** Design an experiment to test the effects of different amounts of lawn fertilizer on the balance of an aquatic ecosystem. Predict the results of your experiment. If you receive the proper permission, you may perform your experiment and find out if your predictions are correct.

Study Guide

Summarizing Key Concepts

26–1 Living Things and Their Environment

▲ All of the living and nonliving things in an environment are interconnected.

▲ An ecosystem consists of all the living and nonliving things in a given area that interact with one another.

26–2 Food and Energy in the Environment

▲ Producers are the source of all the food in an ecosystem.

▲ Consumers cannot make their own food. They feed directly or indirectly on producers.

▲ Decomposers break down dead organisms into simpler substances. In the process, they return important materials to the soil and water.

▲ A food chain represents a series of events in which food and energy are transferred from one organism in a ecosystem to another.

▲ A food web consists of many overlapping food chains.

▲ The amount of energy at each feeding level in an ecosystem can be diagrammed as a pyramid of energy.

26–3 Interaction and Evolution

▲ An organism's niche consists of everything the organism does and everything the organism needs in its environment.

▲ Two or more species cannot share the same niche.

▲ Interactions such as predation, competition, and symbiosis have had a powerful effect on the course of evolution.

26–4 Life in the Balance

▲ Ecosystems are sometimes thrown completely out of balance by natural disasters or by human activities.

Reviewing Key Terms

Define each term in a complete sentence.

26–1 Living Things and Their Environment
environment
ecology
ecosystem
community
population
habitat

26–2 Food and Energy in the Environment
producer
consumer
decomposer
food chain
food web

26–3 Interaction and Evolution
niche
competition
predator
prey
symbiosis
commensalism
mutualism
parasitism
parasite
host

Chapter Review

Content Review

Multiple Choice

Choose the letter of the answer that best completes each statement.

1. The study of the interactions between living things and their environment is called
   a. commensalism.   c. ecology.
   b. parasitism.   d. botany.
2. Evolutionary changes usually occur by means of a process called
   a. mutualism.   c. predation.
   b. natural selection.   d. competition.
3. A desert is an example of a(an)
   a. ecosystem.   c. food chain.
   b. population.   d. niche.
4. A group of organisms of the same species living together in the same area is called a(an)
   a. population.   c. community.
   b. ecosystem.   d. niche.

5. Which term best describes the relationship between a honeybee and a flower?
   a. commensalism   c. competition
   b. predation   d. mutualism
6. An organism that eats plants is best described as a(an)
   a. omnivore.   c. scavenger.
   b. herbivore.   d. carnivore.
7. Everything an organism does and needs in its environment is known as its
   a. feeding level.   c. habitat.
   b. niche.   d. adaptation.
8. Which term best describes the relationship between a fox and a wolf?
   a. competition   c. predation
   b. symbiosis   d. mutualism

True or False

If the statement is true, write "true." If it is false, change the underlined word or words to make the statement true.

1. Producers break down dead organisms.
2. Any close relationship between two organisms in which one organism lives near, on, or even inside another organism and in which at least one organism benefits is known as mutualism.
3. The living part of an ecosystem is called a community.
4. The organisms on which a predator feeds are known as its hosts.
5. An animal that feeds on the bodies of dead animals is known as a scavenger.
6. The relationship between a dog and a flea is an example of commensalism.
7. Consumers, such as green plants, are the first link in a food chain.
8. Within a food chain, there is more energy available at each higher feeding level.

Concept Mapping

Complete the following concept map for Section 26–1. Then construct a concept map for the entire chapter.

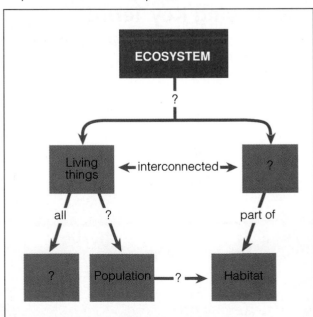

692

Concept Mastery

Discuss each of the following in a brief paragraph.

1. Explain how the terms environment and ecosystem differ in meaning.
2. Name and briefly describe the three basic energy roles in an ecosystem. For each role, give an example of an organism that plays that role.
3. Explain how the following terms are related to one another: community, ecosystem, feeding level, habitat, niche, population, species.
4. How are a food chain, a food web, and a pyramid of energy different from one another? Describe the relationship among the three.
5. Using specific examples, explain how predation, competition, and symbiosis can affect evolution.
6. Explain this statement. "In the environment, change is a two-way street."

Critical Thinking and Problem Solving

Use the skills you have developed in this chapter to answer each of the following.

1. **Applying concepts** African tickbirds can often be found perching on large animals such as Cape buffalo and rhinoceroses. The tickbirds eat bloodsucking ticks found on the skin of the large animals. What type of symbiosis is this? Explain.
2. **Making diagrams** Draw a food web that includes the following organisms: cat, caterpillar, corn, cow, crow, deer, hawk, human, lettuce, mouse, fox, grass, grasshopper, rabbit. Identify each organism as a producer or a consumer.

3. **Making predictions** How could the spraying of an insecticide interfere with the balance in an ecosystem?
4. **Relating concepts** Explain why the sun is considered to be the ultimate source of energy for almost all ecosystems.
5. **Identifying relationships** Take a look at the pyramid of energy in Figure 26–13 on page 672. What trend would you expect to see in the number of organisms at each level as you move from the bottom of the pyramid toward the top? Why?
6. **Assessing concepts** "If an ecosystem is properly selected, it contains four basic parts: the physical environment, the living things, energy, and the nutrients that circulate between its living and nonliving elements." Examine the accompanying photograph of a deer licking a block of salt. Explain whether you can identify each of these elements in the photograph. Then explain whether you think this description of an ecosystem is a useful one.
7. **Using the writing process** Write a short story or poem about a change in the balance of an ecosystem that you yourself have observed.

Cycles in Nature

Guide for Reading

On a cool spring night in southern California, the ocean waves surge up onto the beach. As each wave retreats, small silver fish known as grunion (GROON-yuhn) appear. The wet sand near the top of the high tidemark glitters with grunion.

The female grunion squirm into the sand tail first. They then deposit their pale orange eggs below the surface of the sand. The male grunion curve their bodies around their mates and fertilize the eggs. Then the next wave washes over the beach and sweeps the grunion back to sea.

Grunion deposit their eggs at places on the beach reached only once every two weeks by the highest tides. Hidden beneath the sand, the eggs are safe from the waves—and egg-eating predators in the ocean. By the time the tides are at their highest point again and the waves reach the eggs, the young grunion are ready to hatch. As the waves swirl the eggs from the sand, the tiny grunion pop out and are carried to the ocean. The process repeats itself year after year, generation after generation. It is an age-old cycle that ties the survival of a tiny fish to the movements of the sea, the Earth, and the moon. It is one of the many cycles in nature. Turn the page, and learn about more.

Journal *Activity*

You and Your World What is your favorite season? Why? What observations have you made about nature as the seasons change? Explore your thoughts and feelings in your journal.

◀ *On spring and summer nights with a full moon or a new moon, grunion ride the ocean waves onto the beaches where they mate and lay their eggs.*

Guide for Reading

Focus on these questions as you read.

▶ What controls the rhythms of life?

▶ What are some examples of daily, lunar, and annual rhythms?

27–1 Cycles in Time: Rhythms of Life

What do you think of when you hear the word rhythm? A musician might think of the beat of a song or a dance. A soldier might think of the pace of marching in a parade. A biologist might think of the way a heart beats, a seagull flaps its wings, or a cricket chirps. Or a biologist might think of slower rhythms than these—for example, the way fiddler crabs change their color from light gray to dark gray and back again to light gray during the course of a day. Or the way whales travel from cold polar waters to warmer regions closer to the equator during the course of a year. A rhythm is any pattern that occurs over and over again.

Slower biological rhythms are often in harmony with certain natural cycles, such as the passage of day into night, the rise and fall of the tides, and the changing seasons. As summer changes to autumn, for example, the leaves of maple trees become red, yellow, and orange in color.

One of the most interesting things about many of the slower rhythms of life is that they continue even if an organism is removed from its natural environment. Once a year, ground squirrels will go into their winter sleep and starlings (small black birds) will breed as if it were spring—even when they live in a cage in the unchanging, seasonless world of a laboratory. Human volunteers living in a sunless cave

Figure 27–1 *The elegant flowers of the night-blooming cereus open in the evening and close in the morning. In certain areas, the leaves of many kinds of trees change color during the autumn. Once a year, albatrosses woo a mate by strutting about and bobbing their heads. Why are these events considered to be examples of biological rhythms?*

without any way to tell time still experience daily changes in blood pressure, body temperature, wakefulness, and other biological functions. Evidence from experiments such as these indicate that many of life's rhythms are not simply responses to changes in the environment. Something inside humans, squirrels, birds, and other living things keeps track of the passage of time. But what exactly is this something that monitors the passage of time?

Internal timers known as **biological clocks** may be responsible for keeping track of many different cycles of time. These cycles may range in length from a few minutes to many years. When the time is right, biological clocks "tell" organisms to change their appearance, behavior, or body functions in some way. For example, biological clocks tell grunion when to ride the waves onto a beach. **Biological clocks help living things stay in step with rhythmic cycles of change in their environment.**

To better understand why biological clocks are so important to living things, it might help you to think about the way alarm clocks help people stay in step with their daily activities. Have you ever used an alarm clock to help you get up in the morning? If you have, you know that it would be silly to set your alarm clock for the time that you want to leave for school. You need time to get out of bed, get dressed, eat breakfast, and so on. So if you need to be at school at 8:00, you might set your alarm clock for 6:45. This gives you time to get ready for your day. Biological clocks are important to living things for the same reason—although they may measure

Figure 27–2 Biological clocks help living things stay in step with their environment. Biological clocks let snow geese know when it is time to fly south for the winter and tell morning glories to open their flowers during the day.

time periods other than 24-hour days! How might having biological clocks be better for organisms than simply responding to changes in the environment as they happen?

In nature, biological clocks are extraordinarily accurate. However, under unchanging conditions (in a laboratory, for example), biological clocks usually run a little too slow or a little too fast. For example, in a laboratory setting where light, temperature, and all other factors remain the same, a fiddler crab's cycle of color changes might take 23 hours rather than 24. Each day, the crab would change color an hour earlier than crabs in their natural environment. After a while, the crab's internal cycle would be completely out of step with its natural environment.

Why don't organisms get out of step in nature? The answer is simple: Biological clocks are set and reset by environmental cues such as dawn or dusk, day length, moisture, and temperature. But because biological clocks are influenced by the environment, it is not always easy to tell which changes in organisms are caused by a biological clock and which are caused by environmental cues. It is easy to see, however, that the rhythms of life are linked to natural cycles in time. In the next few pages, you will read about some of the ways the rhythms of life are in step with daily, lunar (of the moon), and annual (yearly) cycles.

Daily Rhythms

As night falls, the creatures of the day prepare to sleep. A flock of birds circles high above some trees, then suddenly drops into the branches. Colorful flowers close. A dog turns around several times before curling up on its bed with a sigh. Meanwhile, the creatures of the night are becoming active. A swarm of bats bursts from a cave. Mushrooms emerge and grow among the dead leaves on a forest floor. Certain microorganisms in the ocean begin to glow with an eerie bluish light.

Organisms that are active during the day are said to be **diurnal** (digh-ER-nuhl). Those that are active at night are said to be **nocturnal** (nahk-TER-nuhl). Are humans diurnal or nocturnal?

Evolution has shaped the characteristics of organisms in such a way that diurnal organisms are well suited for the warm, dry, brightly lit day and nocturnal organisms are well suited for the cool, moist, dimly lit night. Take a look at the nocturnal night monkey and the diurnal emperor tamarin in Figure 27–3. What is the most obvious difference in the facial features of these two monkeys (other than the emperor tamarin's moustache)? That's right—the "eyes" have it! Like many nocturnal animals, night monkeys have much larger eyes than their diurnal relatives. Larger eyes gather a larger amount of the available light and allow the nocturnal animals to find their way in the darkness of the night.

Not all nocturnal animals have oversized eyes. Many rely on other senses to guide them in the dark. For example, owls and bats rely a great deal on their sense of hearing. And many noctural insects have extremely long feelers that allow them to explore the nighttime world through their senses of touch, taste, and smell.

Figure 27–3 *The nocturnal owl monkey (bottom) and the diurnal emperor tamarin (top right) both live in the forests of Latin America. Some organisms are neither nocturnal nor diurnal. The vole (top left) is most active at dawn and at dusk.*

Lunar Rhythms

Have you ever spent an entire day at the beach? If so, you might have noticed that each successive wave seemed to reach a little less far up the beach. After a while, you might have realized that the level of the ocean had dropped, revealing once-hidden rocks, seaweed, barnacles, and mussels.

Figure 27–4 *Organisms that live at the edge of the ocean—such as the giant green sea anemone (bottom right), fiddler crab (top right), ringed top snail (top left), and red East African starfish (bottom left)—show patterns of activity that match the rise and fall of the tides.*

An examination of the rocks, wet sand, and tide pools at the water's edge might have revealed some interesting creatures becoming active at the low tide. Certain crabs pop out of their burrows and scurry around on the wet sand. Small starfish push their stomachs out of their mouths and absorb bits of food from the surface of the sand. Microscopic one-celled diatoms and small green worms rise to the surface of the sand, creating small, faint patches of brown and green.

Other organisms become inactive at low tide. Mussels and barnacles shut their shells tightly. Snails and other small animals hide beneath seaweed or within cracks in rocks. Sea anemones pull in their tentacles and contract into sand-covered blobs.

If you stayed at the beach long enough, you might have seen the waves come in once more, slowly washing away sand castles and gradually hiding the things that you had seen at low tide. With the return of the water at high tide, the crabs retreat to their burrows and block the entrances with sand. The diatoms and worms sink back under the sand to avoid being washed away by the waves. Snails begin to creep around. Mussels and barnacles open their

shells and filter food from the water. And sea anemones open up in flowerlike splendor.

The rise and fall of the tides are controlled by the moon (and to a lesser degree, the sun). As a result, tidal rhythms are considered to be lunar rhythms. (The word lunar means of the moon.) There are two kinds of tidal rhythms. You have just read about the high- and low-tide cycle, which occurs twice a day (every 12.4 hours, to be exact). The other type of tidal rhythm is roughly a two-week cycle (14.8 days) during which the high tides gradually become higher, peak, and then decrease.

Biological clocks in a number of organisms are in harmony with the two-week cycle of the tides. The grunion you read about at the beginning of the chapter are an example. They lay their eggs on the nights of the highest high tide. On a small island west of Australia, female red crabs release their eggs into the ocean during the lowest high tide. In tropical oceans, strange worms break in two at night during the lowest high tide. One half remains in its burrow at the bottom of the sea. The other half swims to the surface. There it joins millions of other half-worms. Many of these swimming half-worms are eaten by fishes, birds, and humans (who consider the worms a treat!). The remaining half-worms burst open at sunrise, releasing huge numbers of eggs and sperm.

As you might expect, 12-hour and 2-week tidal rhythms occur mostly in organisms that live near and in the ocean. However, some land organisms have rhythms that are in harmony with the lunar cycle. For example, the average length of a human pregnancy is almost ten lunar months from the time the egg cell is released to the time the baby is born.

Annual Rhythms

Some of life's rhythms are closely associated with the seasons of the year. In the spring, for example, songbirds build their nests. Bears awaken from their winter sleep. Trees that were bare throughout the winter begin to grow a new cover of leaves. Daffodils, tulips, and primroses bloom. And many animals give birth to their young. Can you think of some other events that occur in the spring? How

ACTIVITY READING

But What Will You Do When It Grows Up?

This is a question often asked of someone who is raising a wild animal. It is also a question people must ask themselves as their "pet" progresses in its life cycle. Some books that deal with this question are: *Rascal*, by Sterling North; *The Yearling*, by Marjorie Rawlings; *The Story of Elsa*, by Joy Adamson; and *Ring of Bright Water*, by Gavin Maxwell.

Figure 27–5 *Chrysanthemums normally bloom in the autumn in response to lengthening nights. How do florists cause chrysanthemums to produce flowers for Mother's Day?*

ACTIVITY

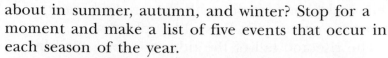
All the Right Moves

Write a report on the annual migrations of the animal of your choice. Some migratory animals include: springbok, monarch butterflies, ruby-throated hummingbirds, storks, certain eels, sea turtles, and certain bats. In your report, include a map that shows the route of the animal's migration.

Figure 27–6 *Caribou migrate between their summer home in the far north and their winter home in the forests hundreds of kilometers to the south. During their annual migration on Christmas Island, red crabs appear everywhere!*

about in summer, autumn, and winter? Stop for a moment and make a list of five events that occur in each season of the year.

As you look over your list, you will probably discover that many of the events occur once a year, every year. Such events are examples of yearly, or annual, rhythms.

There are many examples of annual rhythms in nature. Many animals—such as grunion, deer, and red crabs—reproduce only during certain times of the year, when conditions are best for the young to survive. Can you explain why most animals bear their young in the spring, rather than in the winter?

In response to seasonal variations in temperature, food supply, light, and other factors, some organisms migrate. This means they journey from one place to another. For example, many birds in the northern hemisphere migrate south for the winter. In the spring, the birds migrate back to northern regions to breed and raise their young. Birds are not the only organisms that migrate, however. Wildebeest, whales, bats, salmon, and red crabs are just a few of the other living things that migrate.

For the most part, **migrations** are annual rhythms in which organisms travel from the place where they breed to the place where they feed. In general, organisms migrate to more beneficial environments as seasonal changes make their old environment less favorable.

Some organisms have a different way of escaping unfavorable seasonal changes. They simply "sleep" through the bad periods of the year. These organisms are active only when conditions are favorable. For example, as winter approaches, the body functions of toads, bears, and certain other animals slow down. This enables these animals to wait out the cold winter months in sheltered hiding places. In their slowed-down state, the animals can survive without food or water until the coming of spring. This winter resting state is known as **hibernation.** (The Latin word *hibernus* means winter.)

In places where the summer months are extremely harsh, hot, and dry, organisms may enter a resting state known as **estivation.** (The Latin word *aestivus* means summer.) For example, as the shallow lakes in which African lungfish live begin to dry up, the lungfish may bury themselves in the mud at the bottom of the lake. They can survive for up to four years in their shell of dried mud.

A few organisms, such as certain plants and insects, simply do not live through the harsh seasons in their environment. But before they die, these organisms produce weather-resistant eggs, spores, or seeds. The eggs, spores, or seeds are able to grow and develop when the seasons change and conditions become favorable once more. The life cycle of such organisms is usually an annual (yearly) cycle. For example, the plants known as annuals—such as marigolds, petunias, and sweet peas—start from seeds in spring, mature and bear seeds by autumn, and die in winter. The next spring, new plants sprout from the seeds and the cycle continues.

Figure 27–7 *A chipmunk escapes the cold, hungry days of winter by hibernating. A spadefoot toad avoids the harshest conditions of its desert home by estivating in an underground burrow.*

Figure 27–8 *Annual organisms, such as California poppies, simply do not live through the most unfavorable seasons. How do annual organisms ensure that their species continue from year to year?*

703

27-1 Section Review

1. What is a biological clock? How do biological clocks affect organisms? Give three examples of events controlled by a biological clock.
2. How are hibernation and estivation similar? How are they different?
3. What is migration? How does migration help organisms survive?

Critical Thinking—*Applying Concepts*

4. A person who has just traveled a long distance by airplane (for example, from New York to Hawaii) might start to fall asleep during dinner and be wide awake at three in the morning. This condition is sometimes known as "jet lag." Explain why jet lag occurs.

Guide for Reading

Focus on this question as you read.

▶ *How do water, oxygen, carbon, and nitrogen flow through the environment?*

27-2 Cycles of Matter

There are many types of cycles in nature. The changing seasons form a cycle, as do the rising and falling tides and the passage of day into night. Organisms have life cycles in which they are born, grow, reproduce to create the next generation, and eventually die. Stars also undergo a series of changes from the time they are "born" as hot spinning clouds of gases to the time they "die" explosively. Rocks are worn down into sand, which may then be transformed by heat and pressure back into rock. Circular series of chemical reactions, or chemical cycles, turn carbon dioxide gas into food and break down food to release energy and carbon dioxide.

In Chapter 26, you learned about the way energy flows through an ecosystem. As you may recall, energy is used up at each feeding level. But ecosystems constantly receive a new supply of energy—usually in the form of sunlight.

Figure 27–9 *Cycles in nature do not always involve living things. New stars may be formed from the matter that remains after a star explodes.*

Figure 27–10 In the rock cycle, sand may be transformed into rock, which may then be worn down to sand. The slow wearing-down of sandstone may produce arches and other amazing rock formations.

Activity Bank

A Saucepan Simulation of a Cycle, p. 844

The supply of matter in an ecosystem, however, is not renewed. But matter, unlike energy, can be recycled, or reused. **Matter, in the form of chemicals, flows in cycles from the nonliving part of the environment to living things and back again.**

There are many cycles of matter, and most of them are quite complex. Fortunately, you do not need to know every detail of every cycle. In this section, you will learn about the basic steps (and only the basic steps!) of four of the most important cycles of matter: the **water cycle,** the **oxygen cycle,** the **carbon cycle,** and the **nitrogen cycle.**

The Water Cycle

For many of the world's cultures, water has long symbolized life. Countries with water usually prospered—and those that lacked water often faced disaster. Knowing where water was and where it would be was a key to success. Many thousands of years ago, people became aware that there is a natural cycle to the flow of water on this planet—a cycle people still rely on today.

"Earth" is not a particularly appropriate name for our planet. "Water" would actually be more fitting, for three fourths of the planet Earth is covered by lakes, streams, rivers, and oceans. Water circulates continuously between the Earth's surface and the atmosphere (the envelope of air surrounding the Earth). Water on the Earth's surface is heated by the sun and evaporates. In other words, it changes from a liquid into a gas, or vapor. The water vapor then

Figure 27–11 From a distance, the Earth is blue with large bodies of water and white with clouds. In Chinese mythology, dragons were in charge of the Earth's rivers, bodies of water, and rain. Why is this dragon surrounded by tiny clouds?

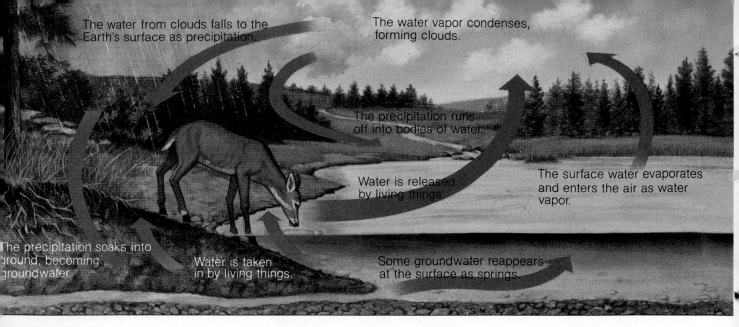

The water from clouds falls to the Earth's surface as precipitation.

The water vapor condenses, forming clouds.

The precipitation runs off into bodies of water.

Water is released by living things.

The surface water evaporates and enters the air as water vapor.

The precipitation soaks into ground, becoming groundwater.

Water is taken in by living things.

Some groundwater reappears at the surface as springs.

Figure 27–12 *Water cycles through both the living and the nonliving part of the environment. What happens to water that falls as precipitation?*

rises up into the air. In the upper atmosphere, water vapor cools and condenses into liquid droplets. It is these droplets that form clouds. Eventually, the droplets fall back to the surface of the Earth as precipitation—rain, snow, sleet, or hail.

Most precipitation falls directly back into the oceans, lakes, rivers, and streams. Some of the rest falls on the surface of the land and then runs off into these bodies of water. In either case, water that evaporates into the air returns to the surface of the Earth, and the cycle repeats itself.

Not all water, of course, goes directly back into the Earth's bodies of water. Some is taken in by living things and later returned to the nonliving part of the environment. For example, plants take in liquid water through their roots and release some water vapor through their leaves. Animals drink water, but they also give water back to the environment when they breathe and in their wastes.

The Oxygen and Carbon Cycles

Like most living things, you need oxygen to survive. The atmosphere, which is 20 percent oxygen, supplies you and other air-breathing organisms with this vital gas. Oxygen from the atmosphere that has dissolved in water is breathed by fish and other aquatic organisms. Clearly, living things would have used up the available oxygen supply in the atmosphere millions of years ago if something did not return the oxygen to the air. But what could that something be?

Consider this: When you inhale, you take in oxygen. When you exhale, you release the waste gas carbon dioxide. If something used carbon dioxide and released oxygen, it would balance your use of oxygen. That something, as you may already know, are producers such as green plants and certain microorganisms. These producers use carbon dioxide gas, water, and the energy of sunlight to make carbon-containing compounds that are often referred to as "food." During the food-making process, the producers also produce oxygen, which is released into the environment. Through this process, known as the oxygen cycle, there is always a plentiful supply of oxygen available for air-breathing organisms.

But what happens to the carbon in food? How is it transformed back into carbon dioxide? In order to extract energy from food, organisms must digest the food, or break it down into simpler substances. This process ultimately produces water and carbon dioxide, which are released back into the environment. Figure 27–14 illustrates the oxygen and carbon cycles. Can you explain why these two cycles are usually discussed together?

The Nitrogen Cycle

About 78 percent of the atmosphere is made up of "free" nitrogen, or nitrogen that is not combined with other elements. All living things need nitrogen to build proteins and certain other body chemicals. However, most organisms—including plants, animals, and fungi—cannot get the nitrogen they need from the free nitrogen in the air. They can use only nitrogen that is combined with other elements in compounds. But how are these nitrogen-containing compounds made?

Certain kinds of bacteria are able to use the free nitrogen in the air to make nitrogen compounds through a process known as nitrogen fixation. Most of the nitrogen fixation on Earth occurs as a result of the activity of bacteria. Some of these bacteria live

Figure 27–13 *The water in this tiger's breath is visible as white droplets condensing in the cold winter air. What other substances does the tiger exhale?*

① Carbon dioxide is used by producers such as green plants.

② Oxygen is released by producers such as green plants.

③ Oxygen is used by air-breathing organisms.

④ Carbon dioxide is released by air-breathing organisms.

Figure 27–14 *Carbon and oxygen cycle between producers and other living things, including elephants. How does the carbon in carbon dioxide become the carbon in food?*

707

ACTIVITY
THINKING

Miniature Worlds

Certain companies make sealed glass globes that contain air, water, some small water plants, a few tiny shrimp, and certain microorganisms. If kept in a sunny place, the living things in the glass globe can survive indefinitely. How do the nitrogen, oxygen, and carbon cycles work in these miniature ecosystems?

in the soil. Others live in the water. Still others grow inside structures on the roots of certain plants, including beans, clover, alfalfa, peas, and peanuts.

One family of nitrogen compounds produced by nitrogen-fixing bacteria consists of substances called nitrates. Nitrates can be taken from the soil by plants. Inside the plants, the nitrogen in the nitrates is used to make compounds such as proteins. The compounds made by the plants can be used by animals, fungi, and other organisms that cannot use nitrates directly. Take a moment now to look at Figure 27–15. Trace the steps of the nitrogen cycle from the free nitrogen in the air to the nitrogen in the bodies of animals.

You have just read about the part of the nitrogen cycle in which nitrogen is transferred from the nonliving portion of the environment into living things. Now let's look at the part of the nitrogen cycle that returns nitrogen to nonliving things.

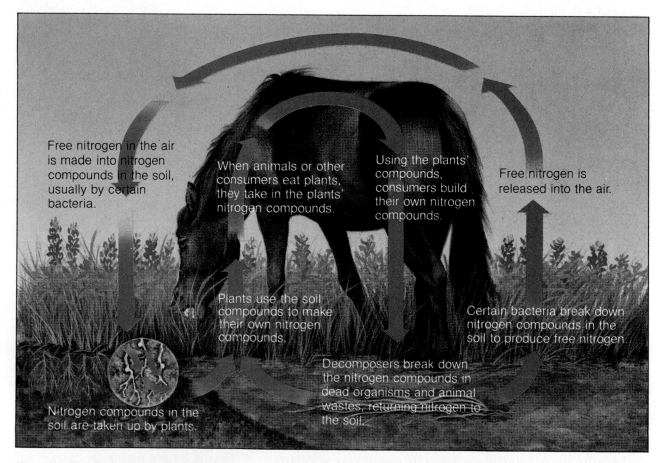

Free nitrogen in the air is made into nitrogen compounds in the soil, usually by certain bacteria.

When animals or other consumers eat plants, they take in the plants' nitrogen compounds.

Using the plants' compounds, consumers build their own nitrogen compounds.

Free nitrogen is released into the air.

Plants use the soil compounds to make their own nitrogen compounds.

Certain bacteria break down nitrogen compounds in the soil to produce free nitrogen.

Nitrogen compounds in the soil are taken up by plants.

Decomposers break down the nitrogen compounds in dead organisms and animal wastes, returning nitrogen to the soil.

Figure 27–15 *Nitrogen flows through the air, the soil, and living things. What would happen to the nitrogen cycle if all bacteria suddenly vanished from the Earth?*

708

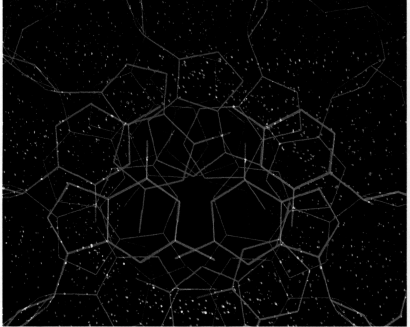

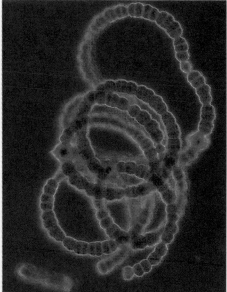

Decomposers, such as certain bacteria, break down the complex nitrogen compounds in dead organisms and animal wastes. This returns simple nitrogen compounds to the soil. These simple compounds may be used by bacteria to make nitrates.

Nitrogen can go back and forth between the soil and plants and animals many times. Eventually, however, certain kinds of bacteria break down nitrogen compounds to produce free nitrogen. The free nitrogen is released into the air, completing the cycle.

Figure 27–16 *Lightning may cause chemical reactions that change free nitrogen into nitrogen compounds. Most nitrogen fixation on Earth, however, is performed by bacteria (top right). The fixed nitrogen can then be used to produce proteins and other important compounds, including DNA (top left).*

27–2 Section Review

1. Show the basic steps of the nitrogen, water, oxygen, and carbon cycles by drawing a simple diagram for each cycle. (Do not copy the diagrams in your textbook!)
2. Why is it important for matter to be recycled in ecosystems?

Connection—*Ecology*
3. Every fourth year, a farmer plants alfalfa or clover on a field instead of wheat. Explain this practice.

27–3 Cycles of Change: Ecological Succession

Imagine that you have built a time machine in a secret clearing in a forest. The big day has arrived—you are finally ready to test your invention! Your hands shake with excitement as you set the controls. You are about to travel hundreds of years back in time. You start the machine, and . . .

Splash! You find yourself in the middle of a pond. What's going on here? You started in a forest and now you're in a pond. Can a forest have once been a pond? You decide to use your time machine to discover an answer to this question. (Fortunately, your time machine is waterproof!) On your way back to the future, you will make a few stops so you can look around and see if your surroundings change over time.

At first, the pond is quite deep. No plants grow at the very bottom of its center. Not enough light can penetrate through the deep water for plants to survive. The pond is inhabited by fishes, the young of insects such as dragonflies, and a huge number of small aquatic animals and microorganisms.

As time passes, particles of dirt, fallen leaves, and the remains of dead water organisms begin to accumulate at the edges and bottom of the pond. As the pond becomes more shallow, new organisms can get a foothold. Underwater plants line the bottom of the pond. Eventually, water plants that poke out of the water—such as water lilies, reeds, and cattails—start growing around the edges of the pond.

Figure 27–17 *The process of succession is considered to begin with bare rock, such as that resulting from a lava flow, or with a newly formed pond. Succession then gradually changes the area. How did succession affect this pond up to now? How will it probably change the pond in the future?*

As the pond continues to fill in, the fish begin to die off. They are replaced by air-breathing animals such as frogs and turtles. The water lilies, reeds, and other plants grow all across the pond. Materials from the dead plants further fill in the pond.

Eventually only a few patches of open water are left. The pond has become a marsh. Like the pond, the marsh keeps filling in. In time, it becomes dry land. Rabbits and deer roam where fish and frogs once lived. Bushes and then trees take root. What began as a pond has become a forest.

Over time, one ecological community succeeds, or follows, another. **The process in which the community in a particular place is gradually replaced by another community is called ecological succession.** And, as your time-machine adventure has shown you, the process of **ecological succession** can completely change what a place looks like.

If the community in a particular place is left alone, it may in time consist of a group of species that are not replaced by new arrivals. This stable collection of plants, animals, and other organisms is known as a **climax community.** The climax community varies from place to place. In the northeastern United States, for example, a climax community may be characterized by oak and hickory trees. In certain areas of northern California, the climax community may be dominated by huge redwood trees.

The process of succession does not have to start with a pond or other body of water. It can begin with the bare rock formed by a lava flow or landslide. It can also occur on soil that has been cleared of vegetation by a disaster or in areas where some sort of ecological disturbance such as logging or farming has been stopped.

Succession usually takes a long time. To go from a tiny pond to a forest can take more than a hundred years. Outside forces, however, can affect the rate of succession. For example, certain pollutants, such as sewage and phosphate-containing detergents, can cause the plants in a body of water to grow extremely quickly. How would this affect succession?

Figure 27–18 *Succession resumes when an area, such as a corn field, is left alone. The first year, a few weeds and grasses take root. After two years, the field is covered with grass. After ten years, there are shrubs and young trees. After twenty years, the field has become a young forest.*

Figure 27–19 *In 1988, terrible fires destroyed much of the forest in Yellowstone National Park. How did this affect succession?*

Some events can slow down succession or set it back a few steps. Plowing a field prevents bushes and trees from gaining a foothold. Fire can burn a developing forest and set it back. Floods can fill a dying pond with water again. Because of these kinds of changes in the environment, succession usually moves in cycles rather than in a straight line.

When making decisions about how natural resources should be used, it is important to keep this in mind: Succession can take many different paths and can lead to different climax communities. The end result of succession is due in a large part to chance. A particular pond, for example, may end up as a forest of willow and alder trees or a treeless peat bog. Because of this, people cannot assume that an ecosystem will recover and return to the way it was after it has been disturbed. It is possible that succession will restore an ecosystem after trees are cut down, land is dug up for mining, oil is spilled, or any other kind of environmental damage occurs. But it is also possible that succession will take a different path and the ecosystem will never be the same again. Because of this, people must be very careful in deciding which resources should be used. Succession will occur—but no one can accurately predict the course it will take.

ACTIVITY

DISCOVERING

Backyard Succession

1. Locate a backyard, field, or park lawn that is usually mowed.

2. After obtaining the proper permission, measure an area that is 1 meter on each side.

3. Do not mow or disturb that area for six weeks or longer.

4. After six weeks, carefully explore your area to see what organisms are living in it.

■ Compare the organisms you find in your area with the ones that are growing in the mowed area. What conclusion can you reach?

27–3 Section Review

1. What is ecological succession? How do ecosystems change as a result of succession?

2. What is a climax community?

Critical Thinking—*Appraising Conclusions*

3. Logging companies often plant pine seedlings in places where they have cut down all the trees. They argue that there is nothing wrong with harvesting trees from any forest, as long as measures such as replanting are taken. Many ecologists argue that forests that have not yet been affected by logging should be left alone. Using what you have learned about succession, explain why the ecologists take this position. Do you think this is reasonable?

CONNECTIONS

Cycles and Stories

Why are there seasons? What causes day to turn into night? Why does the moon seem to grow and then shrink during the course of a month?

Today we know that these never-ending cycles of change are caused by the movement of the Earth and the moon. But long ago, people did not know about the way the Earth and moon spin through space. As they looked in wonder at the world around them, people created stories, or *myths* (MIHTHS), to explain what they saw. Here is one such myth from Nigeria, a country in Africa.

Why the Moon Grows and Shrinks

The bush baby (a small monkeylike animal) was very poor. His friend the mouse-deer felt sorry for him, and wanted to help. So the mouse-deer, who had two pairs of eyes, gave one pair to the bush baby.

The mouse-deer's eyes were large, round precious stones that shone with a light of their own. But no one could afford to buy such fine gems. So the bush baby broke the eyes into tiny pieces.

Unfortunately, when the bush baby went to sell the tiny sparkling gems, the wind blew them all over the town. It took the children of the town a month to gather up the tiny gems and put them in a box. But as soon as they had finished, the wind began to blow them out of the box once more.

Every month, the wind scatters the bush-baby's tiny gems across the town of the sky, where they glitter as stars. And each month, the children gather up the stars and put them into the box of the moon. But as soon as the moon is full, the wind begins to blow away the gathered gems.

■ What are some myths about nature that belong to your own cultural heritage? Discover the myths of your ancestors by talking to the older members of your family or by going to the library.

Laboratory Investigation

Going in Cycles

Problem

What are the steps in the life cycle of a housefly?

Materials *(per group)*

magnifying glass
rubber band
cotton ball
glass jar
piece of gauze cloth large enough to
    cover the top of the glass jar
20 mL bran flakes
10 mL diluted canned milk
paper towel
houseflies
metal bottle cap

Procedure 🧪 🐭

1. To make a fly cage, place a paper towel in the bottom of a glass jar. Put 20 mL of bran flakes and 10 mL of diluted canned milk on the towel.

2. Wet a cotton ball with water and put it in the metal bottle cap. Put the bottle cap, with the cotton ball facing up, into the glass jar.

3. Put the flies your teacher gives you into the cage. Stretch the gauze cloth over the mouth of the jar and hold it in place with the rubber band.

4. Using the magnifying glass, check to be sure there is at least one female fly. Female flies have pointed tails and small eyes. Males have rounded tails and large eyes.

5. When eggs appear, release your adult flies outdoors. Fly eggs are small, white, and shaped like sausages.

Observations

1. Each day, check the jar and write a description of what you see.

2. For how many days do you see eggs?

3. Larvae (wormlike young flies) come from the eggs. Draw a larva. For how many days do you see larvae?

4. A larva becomes a pupa. Draw a pupa. For how many days do you see pupae?

5. What does a pupa become?

Analysis and Conclusions

1. Using your drawings and other data from your investigation, prepare a diagram showing the life cycle of a housefly.

2. **On Your Own** Design an investigation to examine the life cycle of another kind of organism—a bean plant, fruit fly, guppy (a fish), or frog, for example. If you receive the proper permission, you may perform the investigation you have designed.

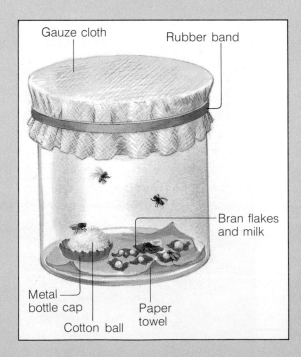

Gauze cloth

Rubber band

Bran flakes and milk

Metal bottle cap

Cotton ball

Paper towel

Summarizing Key Concepts

27–1 Cycles in Time: Rhythms of Life

▲ Biological clocks help living things stay in step with rhythmic cycles of change in their environment.

▲ Biological clocks are set and reset by environmental cues such as dawn or dusk, day length, moisture, and temperature.

▲ The rhythms of life are linked to daily, lunar, and annual cycles in time.

▲ Organisms that are active during the day are said to be diurnal. Those that are active at night are said to be nocturnal.

▲ Tidal rhythms are one type of lunar rhythm. There are two kinds of tidal rhythms: a roughly two-week cycle and a roughly 12-hour cycle.

▲ Events that occur once a year, every year are examples of annual rhythms.

▲ Migration is the movement of organisms from one place to another. Many animals have annual migrations.

▲ In winter, some organisms enter a resting state known as hibernation.

▲ In summer, some organisms enter a resting state known as estivation.

27–2 Cycles of Matter

▲ Unlike energy, matter can be recycled. Matter flows in cycles from the nonliving part of the environment to living things and back again.

▲ There are many cycles of matter in ecosystems. Four of the most important are the water, oxygen, carbon, and nitrogen cycles.

27–3 Cycles of Change: Ecological Succession

▲ The process in which the set of living things in a particular place is gradually replaced by another set of living things is called ecological succession.

▲ In time, a particular place may possess a stable collection of plants, animals, and other organisms known as a climax community. The climax community varies from place to place.

▲ Succession usually takes a long time. Outside forces, however, can affect the rate of succession and may even reset the cycles of succession.

Reviewing Key Terms

Define each term in a complete sentence.

27–1 Cycles in Time: Rhythms of Life
biological clock
diurnal
nocturnal
migration
hibernation
estivation

27–2 Cycles of Matter
water cycle
oxygen cycle
carbon cycle
nitrogen cycle

27–3 Cycles of Change: Ecological Succession
ecological succession
climax community

Chapter Review

Content Review

Multiple Choice

Choose the letter of the answer that best completes each statement.

1. Organisms that are active during the day are said to be
   a. nocturnal.
   b. diurnal.
   c. lunar.
   d. annual.
2. In the winter, frogs and ground squirrels enter a resting state known as
   a. succession.
   b. estivation.
   c. hibernation.
   d. migration.
3. Fiddler crabs are most active at low tide. What kind of rhythm are the fiddler crabs showing?
   a. annual
   b. diurnal
   c. daily
   d. lunar
4. The act of traveling to a new environment when seasonal changes make the old environment less favorable is known as
   a. succession.
   b. estivation.
   c. hibernation.
   d. migration.

5. Clouds are formed from water vapor by
   a. condensation.
   b. evaporation.
   c. precipitation.
   d. denitrification.
6. Organisms that are active at night are said to be
   a. nocturnal.
   b. diurnal.
   c. lunar.
   d. annual.
7. Succession may result in a stable set of organisms known as a(an)
   a. ecosystem.
   b. climax community.
   c. transitional community.
   d. migration.
8. Most nitrogen fixation on Earth occurs through the activity of
   a. plants.
   b. bacteria.
   c. animals.
   d. fungi.

True or False

If the statement is true, write "true." If it is false, change the underlined word or words to make the statement true.

1. Biological clocks are inner timers that help organisms stay in step with natural cycles in time.
2. Unlike energy, matter cannot be recycled.
3. The movement of organisms from the place where they feed to the place where they breed is known as estivation.
4. The approximate 12-hour cycle of the tides is an example of a daily rhythm.
5. Liquid water changes into water vapor through precipitation.
6. Succession can be speeded up, slowed down, or reset by outside forces.
7. Air-breathing organisms exhale carbon dioxide, which can then be used by producers such as green plants.

Concept Mapping

Complete the following concept map for Section 27–1. Then construct a concept map for the entire chapter.

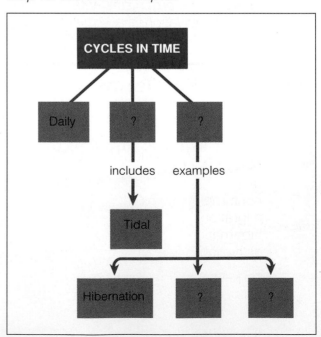

Concept Mastery

Discuss each of the following in a brief paragraph.

1. Using specific examples, describe four different strategies for dealing with seasonal changes in the environment.
2. How is reproduction in grunion tied to daily, lunar, and annual cycles of time?
3. Do you live in a climax community? What observations lead you to this conclusion?
4. Why are cycles of matter important to living things?
5. How do the oxygen and carbon cycles link you to green plants?
6. Describe the basic steps of the nitrogen cycle.
7. What is succession? Explain how succession can change a marsh into a forest.

Critical Thinking and Problem Solving

Use the skills you have developed in this chapter to answer each of the following.

1. **Relating cause and effect** There is much evidence to support the theory of the "greenhouse effect." According to this theory, excess amounts of carbon dioxide in the atmosphere can cause temperatures all over the world to rise. Explain how destruction of the world's forests may contribute to the greenhouse effect.
2. **Making predictions** A volcano is forming a new island in the ocean southeast of the island of Hawaii. This island will emerge from the sea in a thousand years or so. How might succession change this island over time? How might further volcanic eruptions on the island affect succession?
3. **Relating cause and effect** The accompanying photograph shows one use of fossil fuels—to power cars, buses, and trucks. As they burn, fossil fuels (coal, oil, natural gas, and gasoline, to name a few) release energy and carbon dioxide. For about two hundred years, people have been burning huge amounts of fossil fuels for energy. How does this affect the oxygen and carbon cycles?
4. **Making diagrams** Nitrogen in your food today may have once been part of a dinosaur. Draw a diagram that shows how the nitrogen might have gotten from the dinosaur to you.
5. **Assessing concepts** Is it better to think of succession as a one-way street or as a series of cycles? Explain your answer.
6. **Using the writing process** Imagine that you are a drop of water. Describe your journey through the water cycle. What changes do you undergo along the way? What living and nonliving things do you meet? What do you think about them? Is going through the water cycle fun or is it an unpleasant chore?

Exploring Earth's Biomes

Guide for Reading

After you read the following sections, you will be able to

28–1 Biogeography
- Explain how plants and animals move from one area to another.

28–2 Tundra Biomes
- Describe the characteristics of tundra biomes.

28–3 Forest Biomes
- Compare the characteristics of three forest biomes.

28–4 Grassland Biomes
- Describe the characteristics of grassland biomes.

28–5 Desert Biomes
- Describe the characteristics of desert biomes.

28–6 Water Biomes
- Identify and describe the characteristics of the major water biomes.

Night falls quickly on the vast Serengeti Plain of East Africa, as if a black velvet curtain has suddenly been drawn over the land. The scattered acacia trees and the great herds of zebras, wildebeests, and gazelles that graze on the Plain during the day disappear in the sudden darkness.

Safe in camp, you sit in your tent and listen to the mysterious sounds of the night. Nearby, a family of zebras snorts and stomps, startled perhaps by the rumble of distant thunder. The wildebeests, or gnus, stir and shuffle as they settle down for the night. And then the lions begin to roar. The wild music of the lions sends chills down your spine.

Lions, zebras, wildebeests, and gazelles do not live everywhere in Africa. They inhabit only the open plains, or savannas, with few or no trees and plenty of grass. Different animals live in the steamy jungles, which have many trees but not much grass. As you will discover in the pages that follow, animal and plant populations are not the same from place to place. They vary because different areas of the Earth have different climates. Climate conditions play a large role in determining where organisms make their homes.

Journal *Activity*

You and Your World Perhaps you have camped in a state or national park, spent the night in a tent in your own backyard, or imagined what it would be like to camp out. In your journal, describe your experiences, whether they are actual or imagined.

◀ *Alert and watchful, a group of lionesses scan the grassy African plain for their prey.*

28-1 Biogeography

You are an explorer. In this chapter, you are going on a trip around the world. Your trip will take you from the cold, barren lands surrounding the North Pole to the dense jungles near the equator—and even into the depths of the oceans. As you travel, you will discover many strange and wonderful plants and animals. You will find that the kinds of plants and animals change as you move from place to place on your journey around the world.

The study of where plants and animals live throughout the world (their distribution) is called **biogeography.** Biogeographers, then, are interested in ecology, or the study of the relationships among plants, animals, and their environment.

The kinds of animals that live in an area depend largely on the kinds of plants that grow there. Do you know why? Animals rely on plants as one source of food. For example, zebras eat mostly grass. They would have a difficult time finding enough food in a jungle, where grass is scarce. But grassy plains are a good habitat, or living place, for zebras. Plains are also a good habitat for lions. Why? Lions are meat eaters (carnivores) that hunt plant eaters (herbivores), such as zebras, for food.

Figure 28-1 *The gray-headed albatross makes its nest out of mud and grass on small wind-swept islands in the Southern Hemisphere (bottom left). Meerkats live in Africa's Kalahari desert (top). In what kind of African habitat would you expect to find a lowland gorilla (bottom right)?*

In turn, the plant life in an area is determined mainly by climate. Climate describes the average conditions of temperature and precipitation (rain, snow, sleet, hail) in an area over a long period of time. Trees grow tall and dense in warm, rainy climates, especially if the days are long and there is plenty of sunlight throughout the year. Fewer trees grow in cold, dry climates, where the short days of winter arrive early and stay late.

Dispersal of Plants and Animals

In addition to studying where plants and animals live, biogeographers also study why plants and animals spread into different areas of the world. The movement of living things from one place to another is called **dispersal.** Plants and animals disperse in many ways. For example, about 50 million years ago, horses evolved in North America. During prehistoric times, the sea level dropped and a land bridge formed between Alaska and Siberia, which is in Asia. Horses soon moved westward across this natural land bridge into Asia. Over many thousands of years, horses dispersed all across northern Asia and into Europe.

Sometimes plants and animals disperse with help—from water, wind, and even people. Certain lizards, for example, have spread from island to island on floating branches. Some seeds, such as coconuts, also reach new places by floating on water. Certain microorganisms, the spores of fungi, dandelion seeds, baby spiders, and many other small, light organisms may be carried by the wind to new places.

Figure 28–2 *Some organisms disperse with the help of water, wind, and other living things. The dispersal of coconuts (top) and lizards (bottom right) may be assisted by water. What helps the dispersal of dandelion seeds (bottom left)?*

Often animals are brought to new homes by other animals. Fish eggs may be carried on the feet of ducks and other water birds. Insects may hitch a ride in the fur of mammals. You may be familiar with this form of dispersal if your pet dog or cat brings fleas into your home!

People have also been responsible for the dispersal of plants and animals. About one hundred years ago, a bird lover released some European birds called starlings in New York City. From New York, the starlings quickly spread across the country. Today, starlings are so common that some people consider them pests.

During the 1800s, ships bound for the Hawaiian Islands carried water for their crews in large barrels. Before the ships left their home ports, mosquitoes laid eggs in the water. The eggs hatched during the voyage. When the ships landed in Hawaii, they introduced mosquitoes to the islands. Unfortunately, the mosquitoes carried an organism that causes a serious bird disease called avian malaria. When the mosquitoes bit the Hawaiian birds, they transmitted the organism, causing the death of many birds.

Not all plants and animals carried to new homes by people are harmful. When European explorers came to the Americas they found the Native Americans growing corn, tomatoes, and squash. These plants were taken by the explorers to many parts of the world, where they are now important crops. Water buffaloes from southern Asia were brought to Europe and South America, where they became useful work animals.

Barriers

After the prehistoric horses traveled from North America to Asia, the sea level rose again and covered the land bridge they had crossed. The sea became a natural fence, or barrier, that kept the horses from moving back and forth between the two continents. Eventually, horses became extinct (died out) in North America. Horses were unknown to Native Americans until European explorers arrived with them about 500 years ago.

Water is one of many natural barriers that can prevent plants and animals from dispersing. However, what may be a barrier for one kind of animal may not be for others. For example, water is a highway for fishes. Other natural barriers include deep valleys and high mountains.

Objects built by people may also be barriers. For example, suppose that a dam on a river acts as a barrier to salmon. Adult salmon cannot swim up the river to reach the places where they lay their eggs. Young salmon cannot reach the ocean, the place where they grow into adults. How do you think the dam will affect the salmon's ability to survive and reproduce? What will eventually happen to the salmon?

Natural barriers can also be ecological. This means that they have to do with an organism's relationship to its environment—both the living and the nonliving parts. When a habitat (living place) does not meet the needs of certain plants and animals, it is an ecological barrier. The Virginia opossum has spread from the South into the northeastern United States. During cold winters, opossums in northern states suffer from frostbite on their hairless ears and tails. It is a sign that they have met an ecological barrier—a cold climate—that probably will keep them from moving much farther north.

Biomes of the World

The climate and the organisms living in an area give that area its special character. A grassland environment, for example, is quite different from a forest environment. Of course, sometimes it is a bit difficult to tell where one environment ends and another begins. In East Africa many grasslands are savannas—flat plains dotted with trees. When are there enough trees on a savanna to make it a forest and not a grassland? Settling such questions is a task for biogeographers.

To bring some order to the variety of environments on our planet, scientists have grouped environments with similar climates and ecological communities into divisions called **biomes.** Biome divisions are merely a classification system to help scientists describe the natural world. As you might expect, not all scientists divide the world into the same numbers and kinds of biomes. However, as a

Figure 28–3 *During their annual migration, salmon are able to swim and jump up small, natural waterfalls (bottom). But they cannot jump over artificial dams many meters high. Fish ladders— which look like large, low staircases covered by water—help the salmon get over dams (top).*

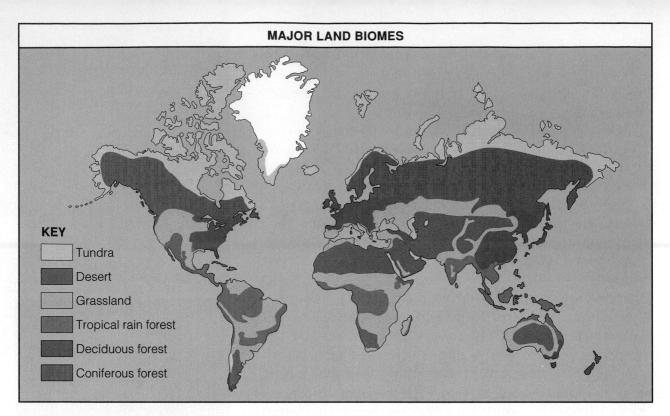

MAJOR LAND BIOMES

KEY
- Tundra
- Desert
- Grassland
- Tropical rain forest
- Deciduous forest
- Coniferous forest

Figure 28-4 *This map shows the distribution of biomes throughout the world. The white area on Greenland is an ice desert. In which biome do you live?*

rule, at least six land biomes are accepted by most scientists. **The six major land biomes are tundras, coniferous forests, deciduous forests, tropical rain forests, grasslands, and deserts.** In your exploration of the Earth's biomes, you will visit each one of these areas and discover something about the plants and animals that live there.

28–1 Section Review

1. Describe three ways in which plants and animals may disperse from one place to another. How do barriers prevent plants and animals from dispersing? Give two examples.
2. What are the six major land biomes?
3. How do scientists classify biomes?
4. What is biogeography?

Critical Thinking—*Relating Concepts*
5. In some places where there are dams on a river, people have built structures called "fish ladders." How do you think a fish ladder helps the fishes get over a dam?

28–2 Tundra Biomes

The first stop on your journey through the Earth's biomes is the tundra. A tundra biome circles the Arctic Ocean all around the North Pole. You set up camp near the ocean in Canada's Northwest Territories. It is winter, and despite your heavy clothing, the wind cuts to the bone. **The climate of a tundra biome is very cold and dry.** A tundra is, in fact, like a cold desert. The yearly temperatures are less than -5°C. And during most years, less than 25 centimeters of rain and snow fall on the tundra.

Most water on the tundra is locked in ice within the soil. Even in spring and summer (which last a total of only three months!) the soil stays permanently frozen up to about a finger's length of the surface. The permanently frozen soil is called **permafrost.** Permafrost, along with the fierce tundra winds, prevents large trees from rooting. The few trees that do grow on the tundra are dwarf willows and birches less than knee high.

In the Antarctic tundra, lichens are the dominant plants. Actually, lichens consist of fungi and algae growing together. Lichens cover the rocks and bare ground like a carpet. They are the main food of caribou, a type of reindeer. During winter, the caribou search out places where the snow is thinnest so they can find lichens easily. By the time the snow is

Figure 28–5 *For part of the year, the tundra is dotted with shallow pools of water. The water cannot sink into the soil because of the permafrost layer. The permafrost is one reason tundra plants, such as the dwarf willow, do not grow very large. The thick, shaggy coats of musk oxen help them survive the long, cold tundra winters.*

Figure 28–6 *The tundra birds called ptarmigans have white feathers in the winter. In the spring, the white feathers fall out and brownish feathers grow in. How does this change of feathers help ptarmigans survive?*

very deep, the caribou herds travel toward the forests south of the tundra. Wolves often follow close behind the herds, picking off the old and weak caribou.

As you leave your camp, you see great shaggy beasts with drooping horns pawing through the snow looking for dwarf willows to eat. They are musk oxen. Under their long outer coat is another coat of fine hair, which insulates them from the cold.

Many small animals inhabit the tundra too. Among the most common are lemmings, small rodents that look like field mice. When winter approaches, the claws of some kinds of lemmings grow thick and broad, helping them burrow in the snow, ice, and frozen soil. Lemmings spend the winter under the snow, feeding on green shoots and grasses.

You stay on the tundra until spring. As the surface soil melts, pools of water appear. Clouds of mosquitoes swarm around these pools. Unless you wear netting over your face, they make you miserable. With spring, the tough grasses and tiny flowers of the tundra burst into life. The sky is filled with birds. Vast flocks of ducks, geese, and shore birds, such as sandpipers, migrate from the south to nest on the tundra. Weasels and arctic foxes hunt the young birds in their nests. Ground squirrels, which hibernate in burrows during the cold winter months, awaken. The days are long and sunny, but some of the nights are frosty. The hint of frost warns you that on the tundra, winter is never very far off. It is time to continue your journey.

28–2 Section Review

1. Describe the tundra climate.
2. What is permafrost? What effect does permafrost have on the plant life of the tundra?
3. Unlike ground squirrels, lemmings do not hibernate during the winter. How do lemmings survive winter on the tundra?

Critical Thinking—*Making Comparisons*
4. Why can a tundra biome be compared to a cold desert?

28–3 Forest Biomes

After leaving the tundra, you head south toward the Earth's forest biomes. **The three major forest biomes are coniferous forests, deciduous forests, and tropical rain forests.** Traveling south, you reach the coniferous forests first.

Coniferous Forests

The northernmost forest biome, the coniferous forests, stretches in a belt across Canada, Alaska, northern Asia, and northern Europe. Fingers of these forests reach south along the high slopes of mountains such as the Rockies, where the climate is colder than in the lands below. Coniferous forests are made up of trees called **conifers.** Conifers, or evergreens, produce their seeds in cones.

Sometimes called "the great north woods," the coniferous forests have fewer types of trees than forests in warmer climates. Not many kinds of trees can stand the cold northern winters as well as firs, spruces, pines, and other conifers can. When you look closely at a conifer, you discover that its needles have a waxy covering. What purpose do you think this covering serves? You are right if you said it protects the needles from freezing. Because of the cold, fallen branches, needles, and dead animals do not decay as fast in coniferous forests as they do in warmer regions. Because the decay of plant and animal remains is one of the main factors in producing fertile soil, the soil of the coniferous forests is not particularly rich. Poor soil is another reason why many kinds of trees are unable to grow in coniferous forests.

Shade from the thick conifer branches, together with the poor soil, keeps many plants from growing on the forest floor. You find that as you hike through the north woods, you hardly ever have to hack through underbrush. Instead, the ground is usually covered with a thick, springy layer of fallen needles.

It happens to be late spring, however, so the going is not all that easy. The ground is spongy and soggy, and pools of water dot the forest floor. Unlike

Figure 28–7 *Most of the trees in coniferous forests produce their seeds in cones.*

ACTIVITY
DOING

Forest Food Webs

On a piece of posterboard, construct a food web for each of the three forest biomes. Use string to show the connections between organisms. Label each organism. Identify the food chains in each biome.

Figure 28–8 *Animals that live in the coniferous forests of North America include moose, lynx, and beaver.*

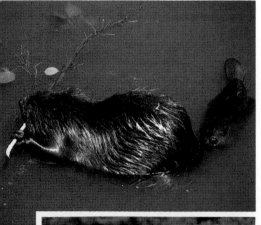

permafrost, soil in a coniferous forest thaws completely in spring, making some parts of the forest like a swamp. Indeed, these areas are often called **taiga,** a Russian word meaning "swamp forest." The taiga includes not only these swampy areas but also the entire northernmost region of the forests.

Approaching a lake, you see a huge moose, shoulder deep in water. It dips its head and comes up with a mouthful of juicy water plants from the lake bottom. The lake, you discover, has been formed behind a dam of sticks and branches built by beavers across a stream. As you walk along the lake, you might just spot a Canadian lynx stalking a snow-shoe hare. Or you might see one of the many members of the weasel family—perhaps a marten—hunting red squirrels. Some of the same kinds of animals you saw on the tundra also inhabit the coniferous forests—a fact you discover when you hear the howling of a wolf pack as you slip into your tent for the night.

Bird songs awaken you in the morning. Warblers, which leave for the south in autumn, twitter. Gray jays, which stay all year round, scold. A reddish bird with a crisscrossed bill lands on a pine tree branch just above your tent. It is a crossbill, a bird adapted to feeding on pine cones. In a moment, you see exactly how. The crossbill pries the scales of a pine cone apart with its bill and removes a seed with its tongue. Meanwhile, on the forest floor, another bird called a spruce grouse feeds on the needles and buds of spruce and other conifers. Packing your gear, you prepare to move on.

Figure 28–9 *The great gray owl (left), crossbill (center), and spruce grouse (right) are just a few of the many birds that make their home in coniferous forests.*

Deciduous Forests

Heading south from the coniferous forest, you reach a deciduous forest. Deciduous forests start around the border between the northeastern United States and Canada. They cover the eastern United States. Other deciduous forests grow throughout most of Europe and eastern Asia. Deciduous trees, such as oaks and maples, shed their leaves in autumn. New leaves grow back in the spring.

Deciduous forests grow where there is at least 75 centimeters of rain a year. Summers are warm and winters are cold, but not as cold as in the northern coniferous forests. You wander among oaks, maples, beeches, and hickories. A thick carpet of dead leaves rustles underfoot. The decaying leaves help make the soil of a deciduous forest richer than that of a coniferous forest. Hordes of insects, spiders, snails, and worms live on the forest floor. In early spring, when the new leaves still are not fully grown, large patches of sunlight brighten the forest floor. Wildflowers and ferns grow almost everywhere.

An occasional mouse scurries across your path. Many more small mammals are out of sight under the leaves. A gray squirrel watches you pass and then disappears in the branches. Suddenly, up ahead, you hear a stirring in the underbrush and see a flash of white. A white-tailed deer has spotted you and has dashed away, showing the snowy underside of its tail.

Figure 28–10 *In the spring and summer, the trees and shrubs in a deciduous forest are green. In autumn, however, the leaves of deciduous plants change color and are then shed.*

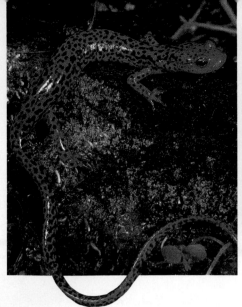

Figure 28–11 *The red fox makes its home in deciduous forests. Salamanders, such as this long-tailed salamander, are also residents of deciduous forests.*

By the side of a rushing stream, you spy a print in the mud. It looks almost like the print of a small human hand. But you know the print was made by a raccoon searching for frogs during the night. Thrushes, woodpeckers, and blue jays flit back and forth between the trees. The ruffled grouse, a relative of the spruce grouse, rests in a tangle of bushes and watches cautiously as you walk by. Under a rotting log, you find a spotted salamander—jet black with big yellow spots. A black snake slithers away as it senses your approach.

By winter, many of the birds have migrated south. (Do you know why?) Snakes and frogs hibernate through the winter. Raccoons, grown fat in autumn, spend the coldest months sleeping in their dens, from which they may emerge during warm spells. The trees in winter are bare, and their branches rattle in the wind. With the coming of spring, however, the leaves will bud and the birds will return. The deciduous forests will come to life once again. But now you are ready to continue your journey.

Tropical Rain Forests

Your travels now bring you farther south—all the way to the Amazon River of South America. You camp there in a tropical rain forest. Tropical rain forest biomes are also found in central Africa, southern Asia, Hawaii, and even a bit of Australia.

Setting up your tent beneath the dripping trees, you discover that the rain forest is rightly named. In fact, it rains almost every day. Tropical rain forests get at least 200 centimeters of rain yearly. The climate is like summer year round, so plants can grow for all 12 months of the year.

After only a few minutes, your clothes are soaked with dampness and perspiration. The air is muggy and still, although not as hot as you expected. The temperature in the tropical rain forest, or jungle, is hardly ever higher than the temperature on a scorching summer day in Chicago or New York City. Why? The answer is overhead, where the tops of the trees meet to form a green roof, or **canopy,** 30 to 50 meters above the ground. According to explorer and zoologist Ivan Sanderson, the light below the canopy "is strange, dim, and green." Only along river banks and in places where people or fires have made clearings in the trees does enough sunlight get through the canopy to allow plants to grow on the forest floor.

Most plant life in a rain forest grows in the trees. Woody vines called lianas—some thicker than your leg and more than 30 to 50 meters long—snake along the branches. You can see orchids and ferns perched on the branches and in the hollows of trees. Tropical rain forests have more varied plant life than any other land biome. The forest you are exploring has more than 40,000 plant species!

Animal life in the rain forest is also marvelously varied. However, many of the jungle's creatures are out of your sight. High atop the tallest trees, poking here and there above the canopy, sit harpy eagles. Their keen eyes search the canopy below for monkeys and other prey. The canopy is full of parrots, toucans, and hundreds of other colorful birds. At night, bats flit among the trees.

Wild cats called ocelots and 3-meter-long snakes called boa constrictors hunt birds and monkeys in the shorter trees that grow just below the canopy. Standing quietly, you are careful not to startle the tapirs feeding on the ground among the trees. You cannot see the Amazon's big cat, the jaguar, which is very secretive. But as you continue to explore, you think you hear one roaring far off in the jungle. Underfoot, the soil is full of small creatures—centipedes, spiders, ants, and beetles.

Figure 28–12 *Tropical rain forests are home to more types of living things than all other biomes combined. The large, unusual flowers of a* Heliconia *plant are just one of the strange and beautiful things you might see in a tropical rain forest.*

Figure 28-13 *The rain forest is home to many animals. The enormous claws of the tamandua help it climb trees and tear open the nests of ants and termites on which it feeds (left). The velvet worm lives among the fallen leaves on the forest floor (right).*

As you make your way back to camp, you hear a strange sound that you cannot identify at first. Then you realize what it is: the ugly noise of a chain saw ripping through the trunk of a giant tree. The most dangerous animal in the jungle is at work! A few seconds later you hear a dull thud as the tree—which has been home to so many birds, monkeys, insects, and frogs—comes crashing to the ground. And you remember that every day an area of tropical rain forest bigger than the city of Chicago is cut down. At that rate, all the rain forests will be gone by the year 2081. Sadly, you prepare to leave the Amazon rain forest, wondering how much of it will be left when you return.

Figure 28-14 *Tropical rain forests are being destroyed at an alarmingly rapid rate. What happens to the other residents of the forest when the trees are cut down and burned?*

28-3 Section Review

1. What are the three forest biomes? How are they different from one another?
2. What are conifers? What are deciduous trees? Give an example of each.
3. What keeps sunlight from reaching the floor of a tropical rain forest?

Connection—*You and Your World*
4. You probably know that many people in the United States, as well as in other countries, are trying to find ways to save the rain forests. Why do you think the rain forests are being cut down? Why do you think people feel it is important to stop the destruction of the rain forests? Do you think that the rain forests should be saved? Why or why not?

28-4 Grassland Biomes

From the Amazon rain forest, you travel across the Atlantic Ocean until you reach the grasslands of East Africa. **In a grassland biome, between 25 and 75 centimeters of rain fall yearly.** As you might expect from its name, grasses are the main group of plants in a grassland biome. Africa has the largest grasslands in the world, although other large grasslands are found in North America, central Asia, South America, and near the coasts of Australia. Grasslands with a few scattered trees, such as those in Africa, are known as savannas.

Your camp is in a field of grass occasionally dotted with thorny trees called acacias. There are few trees in the grasslands because of the low rainfall. Wildfires, which often rage over the grasslands, also prevent widespread tree growth. And people often set fire to the grasslands on purpose to control the spread of trees.

The animals that roam the grasslands also keep trees from spreading by eating new shoots before they grow too large. As you watch a herd of elephants tearing up acacia trees and feeding on

Guide for Reading

Focus on this question as you read.

▶ What is the climate of a grassland biome?

Activity Bank

Grandeur in the Grass, p. 846

733

their leaves, you realize that even large trees are not safe.

Grasses, however, can survive trampling and low rainfall, and still grow thickly. That is why grasslands can feed the vast herds of large herbivores, such as the zebras and antelope you see grazing around you. These animals, in turn, are food for lions, African wild dogs, and cheetahs.

Many mice, rats, and other small animals also inhabit the grasslands, eating seeds, sprouts, and insects. Snakes prowl among the grasses, hunting these creatures. As you walk about your camp in the evening, you take care not to step on a puff adder or other poisonous snake as it searches for prey.

The smaller animals, including snakes, are the prey of the sharp-eyed hawks and eagles that continually sail over the savannas or perch in the acacias. In the distance, vultures circle in the sky, ready to feed on the remains of a zebra killed by lions.

Like the grasslands of North America and many other parts of the world, much of the African savannas has been turned into farms and ranches. And here, as in other parts of the world, overgrazing and overplanting may eventually destroy the grasslands. As you begin the last stage of your journey through the Earth's biomes, you reflect that your next stop—the Sahara Desert—was once a grassland!

Figure 28–15 *The grasslands of Africa are home to many different kinds of organisms, including acacia trees, giraffes, grasses, antelope, zebras, and ostriches. What other organisms would you expect to see in an African grasslands biome?*

28–4 Section Review

1. How much rain does a grassland biome receive each year?
2. Where is the largest grassland biome found?
3. What three factors prevent trees from overrunning grasslands?

Critical Thinking—*Making Predictions*
4. If all the savannas in Africa are turned into farms and ranches, what effect will this have on the large herbivores that now live on the savannas? How will this affect the carnivores that prey on them?

28–5 Desert Biomes

North of the savannas, the grasslands of Africa become increasingly dry. Eventually you come to the Sahara Desert, which covers almost all of North Africa. In fact, the Sahara is about as big as the entire United States! And it is getting bigger, expanding into the grasslands to the south. **A desert biome is an area that receives less than 25 centimeters of rainfall a year.** Other desert biomes are found in western North America, western Asia, the center of Australia, and along the west coast of South America.

Guide for Reading

Focus on these questions as you read.

▶ *What is the climate of a desert biome?*
▶ *What is the difference between a hot desert and a cold desert?*

Figure 28–16 *The Sahara, in northern Africa, is a hot desert (left). Its average annual temperature is about 20° C. The Atacama Desert in South America is a cold desert (right). Its average annual temperature is about 17° C.*

ACTIVITY

DISCOVERING

A Desert Terrarium

Use a wide-mouthed jar to build a small desert terrarium. Add 2 to 5 cm of sand to the bottom of the jar. Plant a few small cacti and other desert plants in the sand. **Note:** *Do not put any animals in your terrarium because it is too small for them.* Cover the mouth of the jar with a piece of screening such as that used in screen doors. Place the jar where it will get plenty of sunlight and heat. Water your desert terrarium no more than once a month.

■ What do you think would happen to the plants in your terrarium if you watered them every day?

Although most people think of a desert as always being hot, a desert can actually be hot or cold. The Sahara is a hot desert—scorching by day, chilly at night. In a cold desert, such as the Gobi Desert in northern China or the Atacama Desert along the west coast of South America, there is also a great difference between daytime and nighttime temperatures. But in a cold desert, daytime temperatures during the winter may be below freezing (0°C)!

Freezing is the last thing you need to worry about as you walk through the burning sands of the Sahara Desert. You cannot help but notice that the plants in the desert are adapted to the lack of rainfall. Many have widespread roots that are close to the surface. This enables the roots to absorb water quickly, before it evaporates. Like the cactus plants of the North American deserts, the aloe plants of the African deserts have thick, fleshy stems that help them store water. After a rainfall, the stem of an aloe plant swells to almost 3 meters in diameter. You may be familiar with aloe as an ingredient in many soaps and hand lotions. Aloe is extremely useful in soothing skin irritations and minor burns (including sunburn).

Even though you look hard, you see few animals in the Sahara. But they are there. By day, lizards and small rodents often escape the heat in underground burrows. Here the temperature may be as much as

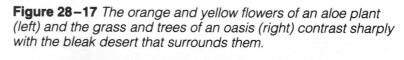

Figure 28–17 *The orange and yellow flowers of an aloe plant (left) and the grass and trees of an oasis (right) contrast sharply with the bleak desert that surrounds them.*

30°C cooler than at the surface. Night brings the animals to the surface searching for food.

Like the plants, desert animals must live on as little water as possible. Most of the water used by desert animals comes from the seeds and stems of plants, which are about 50 percent water. The most famous desert animals—camels—can live without water if there are enough plants available for them to eat. In fact, camels can get along without water for up to 10 days! During this time, they live off the water stored in the body fat in their humps. And like other desert animals, camels lose almost no water in their wastes. Only in these ways can they survive in a world where rain hardly ever falls.

As your trek across the dry Sahara comes to an end, you realize you have completed your journey through the Earth's major land biomes. That means you are now ready to explore the largest biome on Earth—the oceans.

Figure 28–18 *Certain animals have evolved in ways that help them to survive in the harsh conditions of desert biomes. The chameleon holds its body as far from the ground as possible as it tiptoes along (top left). The sidewinding movement of the adder is also an adaptation that minimizes contact with the hot sand (top right). What are some of the adaptations camels have for surviving in the desert (bottom)?*

28–5 Section Review

1. Describe the main characteristics of a desert biome.
2. What is the difference between a hot desert and a cold desert?
3. In what ways are desert plants and animals adapted to the lack of rainfall? Give two examples of each.

Critical Thinking—*Making Inferences*
4. Why do you think there are no tall trees in the desert?

28–6 Water Biomes

Your trip around the world would not be complete without a visit to the water biomes. After all, most of the Earth's surface is covered with water. **The two major water biomes are the marine biome and the freshwater biome.**

The Marine Biome

The **marine biome,** or ocean biome, covers about 70 percent of the Earth. Organisms that live in this biome have adaptations that allow them to survive in salt water. Other factors that affect ocean organisms are sunlight, temperature, water pressure, and water movement. The oceans can be divided into different zones, or areas, based on these factors. Each of these zones contains organisms that are adapted to conditions in that zone.

You begin your exploration of the ocean near the shore. Most marine organisms live near the surface or near the shore. Animals that live near the shore are alternately covered and uncovered by the tides. Many of the animals burrow into the sand while others attach themselves to rocks to keep from being washed out to sea. Strolling along the shore you find clams, barnacles, and sea stars in shallow tidepools.

Past the low-tide line, algae and microscopic plants called **phytoplankton** live near the surface of the ocean where they can receive the most sunlight. They use the sunlight to produce food. Almost all the animals in the ocean depend either directly or

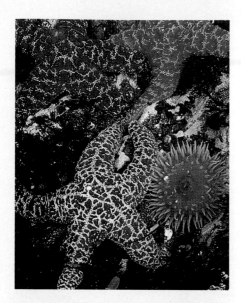

Figure 28–19 *Starfish, flowerlike sea anemones, and seaweed are some of the marine organisms that live at the edge of the sea.*

Figure 28–20 *The enormous seaweed known as kelp forms vast marine "forests," which are often home to the playful sea otter.*

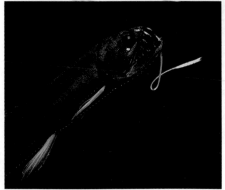

indirectly on these plants for food. In shallow water, you find lobsters and crabs crawling along the bottom. In deeper water, marine animals in a variety of shapes and sizes swim through the open ocean. These animals include many types of fishes, such as tuna and swordfish, as well as dolphins, whales, and other marine mammals. (Yes, dolphins and whales are mammals like you. They are not fishes!) Large sea birds, such as albatrosses, spend most of their lives in the skies above the open ocean.

At one time, scientists thought that the deepest parts of the ocean had no life at all. The deep ocean is an area of cold temperatures, high pressures, and complete darkness. Now, however, scientists have discovered that some of the strangest marine organisms live in the deep ocean. Many of them have unusual adaptations for survival in this dark environment. For example, some deep-sea fishes and squid actually have organs that are capable of producing light. In 1974, scientists discovered previously unknown organisms—giant tube worms, blind crabs, and huge clams—clustered around hot-water vents on the ocean floor. These strange creatures do not rely on energy from the sun to survive. Instead, they use chemicals from deep inside the Earth.

Figure 28–21 *Many marine animals are creatures of the open sea. The albatross spends most of its life soaring above the waves (center). The sailfish may use its long bill to kill or injure prey (top right). Dolphins are not fish, but mammals (left). Some deep-sea fishes are monstrous in appearance, but not really in size (bottom).*

Figure 28-22 *The young mayfly lives in fast-moving freshwater streams. Although young mayflies live in aquatic habitats, adult mayflies are winged creatures of the air.*

The Freshwater Biome

From the depths of the oceans, you move on to the Earth's other water biome. The **freshwater biome** includes both still water and running water. Lakes and ponds are still water. Streams and rivers are running water.

As in the marine biome, there are a number of factors that affect freshwater life. These factors are temperature, sunlight, the amount of oxygen and food available, and the speed at which the water moves. These factors determine which organisms live in a freshwater environment.

Walking along a fast-moving stream, you find that the organisms in the stream have special structures that keep them from being swept away. Many plants have strong roots that anchor them to the stream bottom. Others have stems that bend easily with the moving water. Mosses cling to rocks in the stream. And the young of some insects have suckerlike structures on their bodies that help them to attach themselves to rocks or other objects in the stream. Fishes such as trout have streamlined bodies for swimming in the fast-moving water.

Leaving the stream, you next visit a small lake. Here such common freshwater plants as waterlilies and cattails grow around the shore of the lake, while

Figure 28-23 *Frogs (bottom right) and grebes (top) live in still freshwater habitats (bottom left). Although excellent swimmers, grebes can barely walk on land. How does building a floating nest of reeds, such as the one shown here, help grebes survive?*

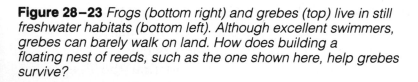

algae and duckweed float on the surface. In the middle of the lake, a fish—perhaps a yellow perch or a bluegill—breaks the surface. A water snake glides silently by. You notice the bulging eyes of a frog staring out at you from among the duckweed. You cannot see the microscopic plants and animals that are a part of any freshwater biome. You do catch a glimpse of a family of ducks and a shy raccoon, however. These animals visit freshwater biomes to feed or nest. What other animals might you see in a freshwater biome?

Estuaries

After leaving the lake, you move on to the last stop on your journey, the Chesapeake Bay on the eastern coast of the United States. Now you are at an **estuary** (EHS-tyoo-air-ee)—the boundary between a freshwater biome and a marine biome. The Chesapeake Bay is the largest estuary in the United States. Estuaries include salt marshes, lagoons, mangrove swamps, and the mouths of rivers that empty into an ocean. Estuaries are areas that contain a mixture of fresh water and salt water. Some scientists think that estuaries make up a separate biome, while others consider them as ecosystems.

Because estuaries are usually shallow, sunlight can reach all levels of the water. Marsh grasses, algae, and other kinds of plants live in estuaries and provide food for a variety of fishes, crabs, oysters, and

ACTIVITY READING

Life Near a Trout Stream

Many writers have been influenced by nature. Sean O'Faolain (1900–1991) was born in Ireland and often wrote stories about life in the Irish countryside. You might enjoy reading his short story "The Trout."

Figure 28–24 *Estuaries include salt marshes (left) and mangrove swamps (right). The spreading roots of the mangrove tree help to keep the plant from falling over.*

shrimp. Estuaries are especially important as "nurseries" for many different types of young fishes and other animals before they head out to the open ocean. Many sea birds also nest in estuaries.

An estuary such as the Chesapeake Bay is very fertile. Because the Bay produces so many crabs, oysters, and fishes, it is an important part of the economy in Virginia and Maryland. Many people also find the Bay a pleasant area in which to live or spend their leisure time.

As you look back on your trip through the Earth's biomes, you wonder what will become of estuaries—and of forests, deserts, and grasslands—in the future. Can people enjoy the Earth's wild places without destroying them? What can you do to help protect the Earth's biomes?

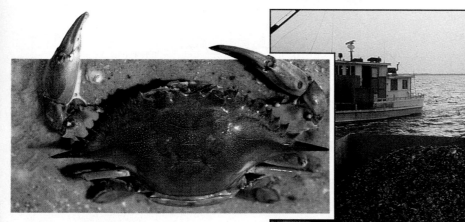

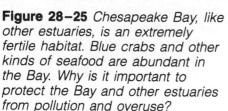

Figure 28–25 *Chesapeake Bay, like other estuaries, is an extremely fertile habitat. Blue crabs and other kinds of seafood are abundant in the Bay. Why is it important to protect the Bay and other estuaries from pollution and overuse?*

28–6 Section Review

1. Describe the two major water biomes.
2. Compare the factors that affect marine life with the factors that affect freshwater life.
3. Why are there no green plants on the bottom of the ocean?
4. Why are estuaries important?

Connection—*You and Your World*
5. What effect might population growth in the area around the Chesapeake Bay have on the ecology of the Bay? How might this affect the area's economy? What do you think can be done to protect the Bay?

CONNECTIONS

Fish Farming

What do you think of when you hear the word farm? You may think of neat rows of corn, chickens scratching in a barnyard, or cows grazing in a meadow. But do you ever think of fishes?

Fish farming, or aquaculture, has become a booming business in the United States. Americans are increasingly concerned about their *health* and are eating more fish and less meat. Today, about one fourth of all the fish and other kinds of seafood served in restaurants or sold in supermarkets has been farmed rather than caught in a lake or stream.

The most popular fish being farmed in the United States is catfish. Part of the appeal of catfish is the popularity of Cajun food from Louisiana—blackened catfish is a favorite dish in this culture. The second most popular fish is trout, which was the first fish to be widely farmed in the United States. Trout farmers have combined aquaculture with new breeding techniques to create "efficient" fishes that mature in 10 months rather than in the natural 18. Trout farmers hope to soon breed fishes that mature even faster.

Fish farming is done both outdoors and indoors. Outdoor farming may be done in special ponds or in portions of the ocean that have been sectioned into pens. Indoor fish farming takes place in large tanks that look like giant aquariums. Indoor fish farmers are even able to raise tilapia, a popular tropical fish that is native to the Nile River in Egypt.

Other kinds of seafood farmed in the United States include shrimp and salmon. Salmon are farmed mainly in Washington State and Maine, where they are raised in floating pens in saltwater bays. Shrimp are farmed mostly in Texas, in ponds in the Rio Grande Valley. Fish farming may become even more widespread as more people realize that fish is a healthful and tasty alternative to red meat.

Laboratory Investigation

Building a Biome

Problem

How do different plants grow in different biomes?

Materials *(per group)*

2-L cardboard milk carton	scissors
sandy soil or potting soil	lamp
5 lima bean seeds	index card
30 rye grass seeds	tape
10 impatiens seeds	stapler
clear plastic wrap	

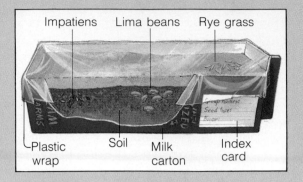

Procedure

1. Your teacher will assign your group one of the following biomes: desert, grassland, deciduous forest, rain forest.

2. Cut away one side of a milk carton. Poke a few small holes in the opposite side for drainage. Staple the spout closed.

3. Fill the carton with soil to within 3 cm of the top. **Note:** *If your group has been assigned the desert biome, use sandy soil.*

4. At one end of the carton, plant impatiens seeds. In the middle of the carton, plant lima bean seeds. Scatter rye grass seeds on the soil at the other end of the carton.

5. On an index card, identify your group, the seeds planted, and the type of biome. Tape the card to the carton.

6. Water the seeds well. Cover the open part of the carton with plastic wrap.

7. Put the carton in a warm place where it will remain undisturbed. Observe daily.

8. After the seeds have sprouted, follow the instructions for your group's biome:
   Desert: Let the soil dry to a depth of 2.5 cm; 5 to 6 hours of light per day.
   Grassland: Let the surface dry, then add water; 5 to 6 hours of light per day.
   Deciduous forest: Let the surface dry, then add water; 1 to 2 hours of light per day.
   Rain forest: Keep the soil surface wet; no direct light.

9. Observe the development of the plants in the biomes of all the groups.

Observations

1. After the seeds have grown for a week, describe the growth in each biome.

2. In which biome did most of the seeds grow best?

3. Where did the rye grass seeds grow best? The lima beans? The impatiens?

4. Which plants grew well in more than one biome?

5. How do lima beans react to little light?

Analysis and Conclusions

1. Explain why the plants grew differently in each biome.

2. Why did the seeds need water when they were planted?

3. What was the variable in this experiment?

4. **On Your Own** Predict how the impatiens, lima bean, and rye grass seeds would grow in tundra and coniferous forest biomes. Design an experiment to test your prediction.

Summarizing Key Concepts

28–1 Biogeography

▲ Biogeography is the study of where plants and animals live throughout the world.

▲ Biomes are divisions based on similar climate, plants, and animals.

▲ The major land biomes are tundras, coniferous forests, deciduous forests, tropical rain forests, grasslands, and deserts.

28–2 Tundra Biomes

▲ Tundra biomes are very cold and dry.

▲ Most of the water on the tundra is permanently frozen in the soil as permafrost.

28–3 Forest Biomes

▲ The three major forest biomes are coniferous forests, deciduous forests, and tropical rain forests.

▲ Trees in a coniferous forest are conifers, which produce seeds in cones.

▲ Deciduous trees shed their leaves in the autumn and grow new leaves in the spring.

▲ Tropical rain forests have more varieties of plants and animals than any other land biome.

28–4 Grassland Biomes

▲ Grassland biomes receive between 25 and 75 centimeters of rain yearly.

▲ Low rainfall, fires, and grazing animals prevent the widespread growth of trees on grasslands.

28–5 Desert Biomes

▲ Deserts receive less than 25 centimeters of rain yearly.

▲ Deserts can be either hot or cold.

▲ Plants and animals in a desert are adapted to the lack of rainfall.

28–6 Water Biomes

▲ The two major water biomes are the marine biome and the freshwater biome.

▲ The marine, or ocean, biome covers about 70 percent of the Earth.

▲ The freshwater biome includes both still water (lakes and ponds) and running water (streams and rivers).

▲ An estuary is an area that contains a mixture of fresh water and salt water.

Reviewing Key Terms

Define each term in a complete sentence.

28–1 Biogeography
biogeography
dispersal
biome

28–2 Tundra Biomes
permafrost

28–3 Forest Biomes
conifer
taiga
canopy

28–6 Water Biomes
marine biome
phytoplankton
freshwater biome
estuary

Chapter Review

Content Review

Multiple Choice

Choose the letter of the answer that best completes each statement.

1. The freshwater biome includes all of the following except
   a. lakes.
   b. streams.
   c. ponds.
   d. oceans.

2. The forest biome that reaches farthest north is the
   a. rain forest.
   b. coniferous forest.
   c. deciduous forest.
   d. savanna.

3. You would probably expect to find caribou living in a
   a. rain forest biome.
   b. grassland biome.
   c. desert biome.
   d. tundra biome.

4. All of the following are examples of estuaries except
   a. mangrove swamps.
   b. rivers.
   c. salt marshes.
   d. lagoons.

5. Anything that prevents plants and animals from moving from place to place is called a
   a. biome.
   b. habitat.
   c. barrier.
   d. community.

6. Most living things in the marine biome are found near the shore or
   a. in fast-moving streams.
   b. in the deep ocean.
   c. near the ocean surface.
   d. in small ponds.

7. Not many trees grow in a grassland biome because of low rainfall, fires, and
   a. animals.
   b. freezing temperatures.
   c. high winds.
   d. floods.

8. The greatest variety of plant and animal species is found in a(an)
   a. desert.
   b. estuary.
   c. rain forest.
   d. taiga.

True or False

If the statement is true, write "true." If it is false, change the underlined word or words to make the statement true.

1. Horses dispersed from North America into Asia by crossing a <u>mountain range</u> between Alaska and Siberia.
2. Lakes and ponds are part of the <u>marine</u> biome.
3. A climate that is too cold for an organism to survive is an example of an <u>ecological barrier</u>.
4. Trees that shed their leaves in autumn are called <u>conifers</u>.
5. Most of the plant life in a tropical rain forest can be found growing <u>on the forest floor</u>.

Concept Mapping

Complete the following concept map for Section 28–1. Then construct a concept map for the entire chapter.

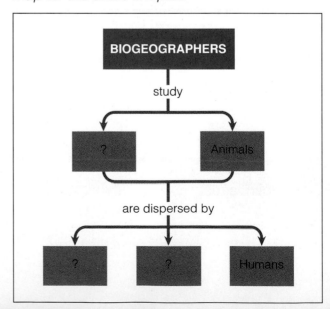

Concept Mastery

Discuss each of the following in a brief paragraph.

1. How do barriers prevent plants and animals from spreading into new areas? Give three examples.
2. Why is climate an important factor in dividing the Earth into biomes?
3. Why do you think it is difficult for scientists to agree on the number and kinds of biomes?
4. Briefly describe each of the six major land biomes.
5. Why are most organisms that live in a marine biome unable to survive in a freshwater biome?
6. What kinds of adaptations are needed by organisms living in the deepest parts of the ocean?

Critical Thinking and Problem Solving

Use the skills you have developed in this chapter to answer each of the following.

1. **Making generalizations** Why is it difficult to tell exactly where one biome ends and another begins?
2. **Relating cause and effect** In which biome would you expect to find the animals shown below? What effect do they have on their environment?

3. **Relating facts** A tropical rain forest has a greater variety of species than any other biome. What characteristics of a tropical rain forest could account for this?
4. **Making predictions** What do you think would happen to the lions and other carnivores on the African savannas if a disease killed all the herbivores, such as zebras and wildebeests?
5. **Making inferences** What characteristics would you expect animals that remain on the tundra all year instead of moving south for the winter to have?
6. **Relating concepts** An estuary is an area where fresh water and salt water meet. Explain why it is difficult for scientists to classify estuaries as either freshwater or marine biomes.
7. **Using the writing process** Imagine that you are a reporter for your local newspaper. You have been assigned to interview a rancher in South America who wants to clear an area of tropical rain forest in order to provide grazing land for cattle. Write out a list of questions that you will ask the rancher in your interview.

747

Conservation of Living Things

29

Guide for Reading

After you read the following sections, you will be able to

29–1 Identifying Problems

- Discuss the reasons for the extinction of organisms.
- Explain why people should try to save endangered species.

29–2 Seeking Solutions

- Describe some conservation measures aimed at saving wildlife.

As the noisy truck approaches, the rhinoceros begins to run away. But it is not fast enough. One of the people in the truck picks up a rifle, aims, and fires. The rhino stumbles and falls to the dusty ground of the African plain. The people drive up to the fallen rhino. One of them takes out a saw and begins to cut off the rhino's horns.

Rhino horns are nothing more than large curved cones made of the same substance as your fingernails. But in some parts of the world, people believe that rhino horns have magical properties. So the horns are worth more than their weight in gold.

Fortunately for this one rhinoceros, things are not always what they seem. The rhino was shot by a tranquilizer dart and is fast asleep. Its horns are being removed by skilled game wardens. Without its horns, the rhino looks rather strange—but it is now safe from illegal hunters. It is also still safe from other predators, because it is the rhino's size and not its horns that deters attacks.

Removing rhino horns is one of the more unusual ways of protecting wildlife. What are some other things that people do to help save rare organisms? Why do organisms become rare in the first place? Read on to find out the answers to these questions.

Journal *Activity*

You and Your World   Explore your thoughts and feelings about dinosaurs and other organisms that have vanished from the Earth.

The black rhinoceros peers nearsightedly at an uncertain future. In the past 20 years, over 90 percent of Africa's black rhinoceroses have been killed for their horns.

Guide for Reading

Focus on these questions as you read.

▶ *What is extinction? How do organisms become endangered or extinct?*

▶ *Why should people care about endangered species?*

Figure 29–1 *A 1990 reconstruction shows the dodo as a sleek bird with a small, dignified tail. This is quite a change from the obese, stupid bird with a silly feather-duster tail in John Tenniel's illustration for Lewis Carroll's* Alice in Wonderland.

29–1 Identifying Problems

About 1190 kilometers east of Africa, in the warm tropical waters of the Indian Ocean, lies the small island of Mauritius. This island is best known for the dodo—a large, fat, flightless bird that once lived there. You may know about the dodo from jokes or expressions such as "dumb as a dodo." But the real story of the dodo is not funny at all.

After Mauritius was discovered by Europeans in the early sixteenth century, ships began stopping there regularly to pick up fresh supplies of food and water. Huge numbers of dodos were killed by sailors for food and for sport. (A twentieth-century person might not think it sporting to walk up to a practically tame bird and hit it over the head!) Amazingly, the dodo was able to survive a hundred years of assault by sailors armed with clubs. But it was not able to survive thirty years of the first permanent human settlement on Mauritius.

The people who settled on Mauritius brought with them dogs, pigs, cats, monkeys, and rats. (The settlers probably did not intend to bring rats, but rats manage to accompany humans almost everywhere.) The pigs, cats, monkeys, and rats killed and ate the dodos' eggs and chicks. The dogs killed the adult birds. The settlers themselves killed all the dodos they could find, even though the birds were quite harmless and not worth eating. By 1681, dodos had become **extinct.** In other words, their species no longer existed.

The process by which a species passes out of existence is known as extinction. Extinction is a natural part of our planet's history. In fact, about 90-99 percent of all the living things that have ever existed on Earth are now extinct. Since life began on Earth more than 3.5 billion years ago, countless species of microorganisms (microscopic organisms), fungi, plants, and animals have appeared, survived for a time, and then passed out of existence. For the last 600 million years, species have become extinct at the average rate of about one per year. But in the past three hundred years or so, human activities—such as hunting, farming, building cities, and cutting down forests—have greatly increased the rate of extinction.

Experts estimate that the extinction rate is now 40-100 species per day. And unless current trends are stopped, the extinction rate could be up to many species per hour by the end of the century!

Human activities increase the rate of extinction because they change the environment too quickly for organisms to adapt. Adaptation occurs through the slow process of evolution. And in evolutionary terms, something that takes place over a period of hundreds—even thousands—of years occurs quickly. (Although humans are not responsible for all the quick changes that occur, natural events that cause sudden changes are few and far between.)

Let's return for a moment to the example of the dodo. Like organisms the world over, the dodo evolved in response to the challenges of its environment. These challenges did not include predators such as humans, dogs, cats, pigs, monkeys, and rats. When humans settled on Mauritius, they made a major change in the island's environment—in the blink of an evolutionary eye, humans added fierce predators to the island's ecosystems. Unable to change quickly enough to survive the challenge of the predators, the dodo became extinct. So did giant tortoises, owls, and many other native organisms.

When their environment changes for the worse, organisms become rarer and rarer. Organisms that are so rare that they are in danger of becoming extinct are said to be **endangered.** About 880 kinds of animals and 320 kinds of plants are endangered. In addition, hundreds of species are not known well enough to be formally classified as endangered.

Figure 29–2 *Dinosaurs, such as* Triceratops, *became extinct millions of years ago. Bones that have turned to stone are all that remain (right). An artist's reconstruction shows what* Triceratops *might have looked like when it was alive (left).*

Figure 29-3 *The Texas blind salamander (top right), sifaka (bottom right), aye-aye (top left), and Knowlton cactus (bottom left) are all endangered species. The aye-aye is in particular trouble because people consider it to be bad luck and kill it on sight. What does it mean to say a species is endangered?*

The human activities that cause species to become endangered or extinct are many. They also are the results of a variety of motives. In this textbook, we have chosen to divide the human activities that threaten wildlife into two broad categories based on their main purpose. The first category includes human activities whose main purpose is to kill specific kinds of wildlife. We have called this category "intentional killing." The second category includes activities that are not specifically directed at killing wildlife. These activities may kill as many or more living things as purposeful killing, but their main purpose is not the death of organisms. Such activities include cutting down forests, introducing foreign species, and running over animals in boat or car accidents.

Intentional Killing

The rhinoceros you read about in the chapter opener belongs to a species that numbered about 65,000 in 1970 and about 3000 in 1991. Almost all of the rhinos that died during that 21-year period were killed by poachers (illegal hunters). A poacher is able to sell a rhino horn for about $200. This may not seem like a lot of money. But in the poorest countries of Africa, the average person makes only about $200 a year—which may not be enough to obtain necessities such as food and shelter. Can you see why it is not always easy to stop overhunting of wild animals?

Rhinos have been overhunted for their horns, which are used to make dagger handles in Yemen and folk remedies in Asia. Other animals have been overhunted for other reasons. Some—such as wolves and bald eagles—were shot, poisoned, and trapped because they were believed to prey on humans and livestock. Others—sun bears, fruit bats, whales, and sea turtles, to name a few—are killed for gourmet food. Still others are killed to fulfill the demands of fashion. Elephants are shot for their tusks, which are used to make ivory jewelry and trinkets. The endangered hawksbill turtle is hunted for its shell, which is used to make jewelry, and for its meat. Snow leopards, sea otters, and wild chinchillas are among the many animals that became endangered because their beautiful skins were in great demand for coats, hats, and other fur products. A fad for shoes, handbags, and other leather goods made from the tough, bumpy skins of American alligators came very close to killing off the species. Snowy egrets were nearly hunted into extinction for their lovely feathers, which were used to decorate hats.

Figure 29–4 *The sun bear gets its common and scientific names from the sun-colored crescent on its chest. It is endangered due to habitat destruction, the fur and pet trades, and its grilled paws being regarded as a delicacy. The snow leopard has been hunted to the brink of extinction for its fur. The passenger pigeon, once numerous, was slaughtered by the millions. The last passenger pigeon died in a zoo in 1914.*

Figure 29–5 *The beautiful golden-brown wood of the Hawaiian koa tree was once used extensively. Now the vast koa forests are gone.*

Figure 29–6 *This tropical forest was drowned by the construction of a dam in Brazil. Although quite useful to humans, dams destroy habitats up river, down river, and within the river itself.*

Up to this point, you have been reading about ways in which uncontrolled killing can lead to animal species becoming endangered. Uncontrolled killing can also cause the downfall of plant species. In Australia, for example, there were once huge forests of red cedar trees. The largest red cedar trees were cut down for their wood, which was used to make furniture. Soon there were no trees large enough to harvest for their wood. But the destruction did not stop there. Because cattle cannot eat red cedar trees, ranchers made a special effort to destroy all the red cedar trees they could find as they cleared away forests to make room for pastures. Now only a few trees remain.

Destroying Habitats

The examples you just read about involve living things that became endangered because they were (or are) being killed on purpose. However, far more species are in trouble because of the destruction of their habitats. (Recall from Chapter 26 that a habitat is the place where an organism lives and obtains the resources it needs to survive.) As you now read about habitat destruction, keep in mind that these are but a few of the many examples. Habitats have been damaged or destroyed, and continue to be damaged or destroyed, in every one of the biomes you learned about in Chapter 28.

DEFORESTATION People cut down forests to obtain wood or to clear land for farms, factories, shopping malls, office buildings, and homes. The removal of forests is known as **deforestation.** History shows that deforestation has been going on for a long time and has occurred in most of the countries of the world.

When Europeans first arrived in the New World, forests covered most of the eastern half of the United States. Almost all the original forest was cleared to make room for farms and towns and to harvest timber. When the old forests were destroyed, the plants and animals that had evolved to live in those environments had no place to go. Some, such as the ivory-billed woodpecker and eastern bison, became extinct. Others, such as the Oconee bells shown in

Figure 29–8 on the next page, are found in only a few places and are rare or endangered.

Today, forests in the western part of the United States are being cut. Many people are concerned that some of the rare species of the Pacific Northwest and Alaska—such as the spotted owl, Pacific yew, and American marten—will become extinct as their habitat shrinks.

The deforestation of greatest concern to people around the world is occurring in the tropical rain forests of Latin America, Africa, and Asia. Each year, an area of tropical rain forest the size of the state of Kansas disappears. About 50 percent of the Earth's tropical rain forests are already gone, and the rate of deforestation is increasing. Some tropical forest is destroyed as hardwood trees—such as teak and mahogany—are harvested. Much more is cut and burned to make room for farms and cattle pastures. The newly cleared land is productive at first. But most of the land stops producing enough food or grass within one to three years. New areas of forest must be cut in order to feed people and livestock. And as the forest shrinks, the plants, animals, and other organisms that live in, on, or among the trees disappear.

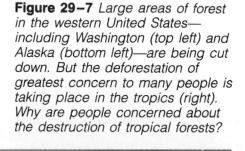

Figure 29–7 *Large areas of forest in the western United States—including Washington (top left) and Alaska (bottom left)—are being cut down. But the deforestation of greatest concern to many people is taking place in the tropics (right). Why are people concerned about the destruction of tropical forests?*

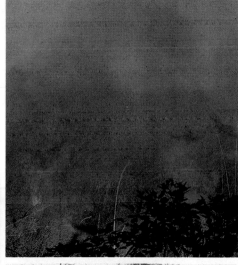

Figure 29–8 *Deforestation affects more than trees. What will happen to the two-toed sloth (top right), margay (bottom right), toad and black orchid (top left), cottontop tamarin (center left), and Oconee bells (bottom left) if their forest homes are destroyed?*

In Chapter 26, you learned that all ecosystems are interconnected. As you might expect, deforestation causes a great deal of damage to nearby ecosystems. For example, the burning of one area of forest in West Africa causes acid rain that damages other areas of the forest. Deforestation also hurts more distant ecosystems. When hills are stripped of their covering of trees, dirt that is usually held in place by plant roots can be washed into lakes and rivers, damaging freshwater biomes. Eventually, muddy rivers carry their load of dirt to the ocean. The excess dirt can then harm marine biomes. Ultimately, deforestation affects ecosystems all over the world. For example, when forests are cleared by burning, carbon dioxide is released into the air. This increases the amount of carbon dioxide in the air. Can you predict how deforestation affects the carbon and oxygen cycles all over the Earth?

DESERTIFICATION What do you think of when you hear the word desert? You may think of cactus plants and roadrunners. Or you may think of camels and shifting sand dunes. You probably do not think of grassy fields and grazing herds of goats, sheep, and cattle. Yet when too many animals graze in an area, grassland may be transformed into a desert. The process in which desertlike conditions are created where there had been none in the recent past is known as **desertification** (dih-zert-uh-fih-KAY-shuhn).

A little desertification occurs naturally at the places where deserts meet other biomes. If rainfall is plentiful for several years, the desert may shrink a bit; if rainfall is scarce, the desert may expand a bit. In recent years, however, more and more desertification has occurred as the result of human actions such as growing crops, raising livestock, and cutting down forests.

Unlike the natural deserts that you learned about in Chapter 28, deserts made by human actions are barren and lifeless. Sometimes, desert organisms move into a new desert and make it their home. Once in a while, the area may gradually return to its former state if there is enough rain and if the grazing animals are kept away. Too often, however, the newly made desert remains an empty wasteland.

Figure 29–9 *Overgrazing is one of the factors that transformed green pastures into barren desert in northeast Africa. What is the process of making a desert called?*

Figure 29–10 *Wetlands, such as this marsh in the Louisiana bayous, are home to many creatures. The survival of organisms such as the roseate spoonbill (left), whooping crane (center), and Everglades kite (right) is made uncertain by continued wetlands destruction.*

WETLANDS DESTRUCTION Wetlands are exactly what their name suggests—wet lands, such as swamps, marshes, and bogs. At one time, wetlands were considered nothing more than ugly breeding grounds for mosquitoes. Now people realize that wetlands are extremely valuable ecosystems. They are temporary homes for migrating waterbirds, and permanent homes for minks, alligators, mangroves, Venus' flytraps, frogs, turtles, and many other organisms. Wetlands are also the source of nutrients for many ocean biomes near the shore.

Unfortunately, about half the Earth's wetlands have been drained, filled in, or destroyed by pollution. The effects of wetlands destruction are far reaching. For example, farmers in southern Florida are draining marshes to grow more crops. The marshes contain snails eaten by small hawklike birds known as Everglades kites. As the marshes vanish, so does the kites' food supply. The rest of the story should be familiar to you by now. Yes, the Everglades kite is close to extinction. What are some other possible effects of continued wetlands destruction on the organisms that live there? How might this destruction affect fishing and duck hunting?

POLLUTION As you can see in Figure 29–11, pollution can be a threat to living things. Pollution comes in all shapes and sizes. Birds and useful insects may be poisoned when crops are sprayed with chemicals meant to kill pests. Acid rain can kill water plants, deform fish, and prevent fish eggs from developing. Birds, sea turtles, fishes, and other animals can become hopelessly tangled in bits of discarded plastic fishing lines and fishing nets. Can you think of other ways in which pollution harms wildlife?

Changing Communities

The sad story of the dodo illustrates what can happen when foreign species are introduced to an organism's environment. Species that are released into a place where they had not previously existed are known as **exotic species.** Don't be confused by this use of the word exotic—exotic species may not be strangely beautiful or different in a way that makes them striking or fascinating. Many exotic species are quite ordinary—the pigeon that you might see pecking at crumbs in a city park is an exotic species.

Exotic species may directly interact with the native species. This interaction may take the form of competition or predation—some examples of which you shall now read about.

If you are from the South, you are probably familiar with the kudzu vine. This vine, imported from Japan to feed sheep and goats, grows extremely rapidly all over everything in sight, including other plants. Kudzu competes with native plants for light, water, and nutrients. Eventually, the kudzu vine causes the death of the plants it has grown over by preventing them from getting enough light.

Exotic predators have been the downfall of many species, including the dodo. Pigs, rats, mongooses, cats, and dogs have each at some time been the main cause of extinction of at least two species of birds. Herbivores, which can be thought of as predators of plants, can also bring about the extinction of their prey. In Hawaii, goats and cattle have eaten several types of plants into extinction.

Figure 29–11 *Because synthetic substances such as plastics break down extremely slowly, they can be dangerous to wildlife for a long time. This seal tangled in nylon net survived its ordeal. Most entangled organisms are not so lucky.*

ACTIVITY

Once, a Once-ler . . .

What happens when careless greed has its way?

Why couldn't the Bar-baloots stay?

Why did the Swomee-Swans fly away?

How does the Once-ler cook his own goose?

Read *The Lorax*, by Dr. Seuss.

Figure 29–12 *Exotic species can be the downfall of other organisms. Kudzu vines have completely covered these trees in North Carolina (top left). The brown tree snake has killed off most of the birds of Guam (top right). The Indian mongoose, brought to Hawaii and the Caribbean islands to kill rats, found that native birds were more to its taste (bottom).*

Have you ever arranged dominoes in a long line and then tapped the first one? If so, you might have observed that as the first domino fell, it knocked over the second domino, which knocked over the third, and so on. In a similar way, when one species is killed, other species may be brought down with it. By interfering with the normal interactions in a community, exotic species can act like a finger tapping the first domino in a line. Thus exotic species can cause native organisms to become endangered or extinct even if the exotic species do not interact directly with them. When the goats and cattle ate the Hawaiian plants into extinction, they indirectly caused the extinction of certain native birds that fed on the plants. The extinction of the birds in turn caused the extinction of other kinds of plants, which depended on the birds to pollinate them.

Accidental Killing

Imagine an enormous gray animal with the round, fat body and front flippers of a porpoise, a paddlelike tail, beady eyes, and a rather "cute" face. This creature is the manatee, an endangered aquatic animal that lives in lakes and lagoons in Florida. It is a peaceful, slow-moving animal that spends its time near the surface of the water, grazing on floating plants. Unfortunately for the manatee, people have discovered that its habitat is ideal for whizzing around in motorboats. A collision with a motorboat's sharp, whirling propeller can badly injure or even kill a manatee. In the first six months

Figure 29-13 Government agents confiscated these parrots before the smuggler had a chance to sell the survivors. Trained whales and dolphins have helped to make people concerned about wild whales and dolphins. However, this benefit is not without its price. Most dolphins do not survive more than two years in captivity.

of 1990, more than 10 percent of Florida's manatees died. About one third of these deaths are known to have been caused by collisions with motorboats.

Very young children sometimes have to be warned not to hug the family pet too tightly, least they "love it to death." Strange as it may seem, some apparently harmless activities meant to increase people's appreciation for nature may pose a threat to the Earth's living things. People are loving wildlife to death!

Many people enjoy growing strange and beautiful plants in their gardens and homes. But some plants—certain kinds of cactuses, orchids, and tulips, for example—are collected from the wild. Overcollection has made a number of species rare or endangered in their natural habitat.

Owning unusual pets—such as parrots, monkeys, and saltwater fish—may help people feel closer to nature. But potential owners should be aware that some "pet" animals are taken from the wild. This unwise and selfish practice can also be extremely cruel and wasteful. For example, baby parrots can be captured by cutting down the trees that contain their nests. As you can imagine, very few baby birds survive the crash to the forest floor. For every 100 parrots taken from the wild, only about 10 survive long enough to be sold.

Figure 29-14 Recently, two new laws were put into effect. One limits the number of tourists who can visit the Galapagos Islands each year (bottom). The other prohibits whale-watching tours from getting close to the whales (top). Why were these laws enacted?

What Does This Mean to Me?

You have just learned about the many ways in which wildlife is threatened by human activities. And perhaps you're thinking "So what? What does all this mean to me? How can it possibly affect my life—today, tomorrow, in the years to come?"

Well, we could start off by giving you the least selfish reason for caring about the fate of wildlife: Wildlife is important because it is beautiful, worthwhile, and has just as much right to be in the world as humans do. But many people are unwilling to accept this as the only reason. So let's take a look at some of the practical reasons for saving wildlife.

ECONOMIC AND SCIENTIFIC VALUE Many products that we use every day and would probably not want to do without are harvested from wild sources. Such valuable products include latex (a rubbery substance used to make balloons, surgical gloves, paint, and other items), wood, and most kinds of seafood.

Many medicines are derived from chemicals extracted from wildlife. Some unusual sources of modern medicines include molds, snake venom, catfish slime, and sponges. Plants too are sources for medicine. In fact, about one fourth of the medicines used today come from plants. One plant that is particularly valuable for its medicinal uses is the rosy periwinkle. Medicines made from this plant are used to treat childhood leukemia (a type of cancer). At one time, only about 1 out of 5 patients with childhood leukemia survived. Now patients are treated with medicines made from the rosy periwinkle and about 19 out of 20 survive. Interestingly, the rosy periwinkle was nearly wiped out when its habitat in the rain forests of Madagascar was destroyed. Can you now explain why medical professionals should be concerned about deforestation?

Wild plants and animals are not only sources of useful products, they are also living banks of information. By studying them, humans can learn about the process of evolution, about the way the body works, and about the nature of behavior. And that's just the beginning!

GENETIC DIVERSITY One of the most important scientific reasons wildlife is valuable to humans is that it possesses most of the "library" of genetic

Figure 29–15 *Some modern medicines come from unusual wildlife sources, including snake venom and the rosy periwinkle plant.*

information that exists on Earth. This library is made up of units of heredity known as genes. You can think of genes as being extremely short, simple directions. The thousands upon thousands of genes that an organism has work together to determine the characteristics of that organism—what it is, what it looks like, how its body works, and so on.

There are many species of wild animals and plants and the individuals in each species are usually quite different from one another. Thus wild animals and plants have an enormous diversity of genes. This is not the case with domesticated animals and crop plants. Each species of these organisms is made up of a number of varieties, or breeds. Each individual in a particular variety is practically the same as any other individual. For example, a Holstein cow has pretty much the same genes as any other Holstein cow, and a corn plant is almost identical to all the other corn plants in a field. While this sameness has many advantages, it also means that the organisms react to diseases in exactly the same way. What, you might wonder, is the danger in that?

Suppose a terrible plant disease strikes a corn field. All the corn plants respond to the disease in the same way—they all die. Can you guess what happens when the disease is transmitted to a neighboring field that is planted with the same kind of corn? And what happens when the disease spreads to all the other corn farms in the area, which are also planted with the same kind of corn? That's right— all the corn dies. And the people who were depending on that corn to feed themselves and their livestock are in big trouble.

Now suppose the same plant disease spreads to a grassy hillside in which some wild relatives of corn are growing. Some of these wild relatives will die from the disease, just as all the corn plants did. But some may have genes that help them to resist the disease. These surviving plants can pass on their genes, including ones for disease resistance, to their offspring. And if scientists know about the genes for disease resistance, they can use techniques of plant breeding or genetic engineering to transfer the genes to domesticated corn plants. The result is the production of corn plants that are resistant to the disease.

Figure 29–16 *One Holstein cow looks very much like any other Holstein cow. How does this fact relate to the concept of genetic diversity?*

Figure 29–17 *In the past, scientists tried to convince South American villagers to "modernize" their agricultural practices. Now, scientists are encouraging them to grow their traditional crops, thus maintaining precious genetic diversity and preserving the villagers' culture.*

Figure 29–18 *The veterinarians (animal doctors) are doing a checkup on a young whooping crane. This is just one way people can help to preserve the web of life. What are some other ways?*

Finally, imagine the following situation. Long before the outbreak of the corn disease, the hillside is completely cleared of its wild plants and then planted with crops or grass good for livestock. Because of the destruction of their habitat, the wild relatives of corn become extinct. Their genes are lost forever. What do you think will happen when the corn disease strikes? Will scientists be able to develop a disease-resistant variety of corn? Perhaps they will; perhaps they won't. But certainly, their job has become a good deal harder.

PRESERVING THE WEB   The most selfish reason for caring about the fate of wildlife is also possibly the most compelling. Wildlife is necessary for the continued survival of the human species. In a previous chapter, you learned that Earth's environment can be thought of as a giant spider web. Each thread of the web represents an interaction between a living thing and its living and nonliving surroundings. What happens if too many strands of a spider's web are broken? As Chief Seattle (leader of the American Indian tribes of the Puget Sound area and the person for whom the city of Seattle, Washington is named) noted over a hundred years ago, "Man did not weave the web of life, he is merely a strand in it. Whatever he does to the web he does to himself."

29–1 Section Review

1. What is extinction? How do organisms become extinct?
2. What are some human activities that cause organisms to become endangered or extinct?
3. How do human activities affect the rate of extinction?
4. What are deforestation and desertification?
5. Why should people be concerned about wildlife?

Critical Thinking—*Making Generalizations*
6. Think about the extinct and endangered organisms you have learned about in this section and elsewhere. What sort of characteristics make it more likely for an organism to become extinct or endangered?

Oh, Dear. Deer!

"They ate my prize-winning roses!"

"They ate *my* vegetable garden."

"Did you try planting onions?"

"They ate those, too."

"They killed all the apple trees at the farm down the road last winter. Chewed off the bark."

"I heard one attacked a pickup truck a ways down the road."

"I wouldn't doubt it. The males go crazy in the autumn. Too many hormones or something."

"So much for Bambi."

Many towns in the northeastern United States are under attack—and by of all things, deer! The wolves and mountain lions that preyed on deer and thereby kept their number in check have long been gone from the area, killed off by previous generations of humans. As farms are turned into wooded suburbs, the deer population has skyrocketed.

The imaginary town of Deerfield is desperately searching for a solution to its deer problem. At the moment, the most popular proposal involves importing dingoes, which are wild dogs native to Australia. It is hoped that the dingoes will bring the deer population down.

Discovering Points of VIew

How do you think each of the following townspeople feels about this solution? What alternative solutions might each person propose? Why?

    an ecologist
    a hunter
    a sheep farmer
    an animal control officer (dog catcher)
    a veterinarian (animal doctor)
    an animal-rights activist
    a parent with small children
    a chemical manufacturer
    an apple farmer
    an electrician

29–2 Seeking Solutions

As you have learned in the previous section, human actions can harm Earth's living things. But fortunately for all of us, human actions can also protect them. **The methods used to preserve and protect endangered species, manage populations of wild organisms, and ensure the wise use of living resources are forms of wildlife conservation.** Conservation is the intelligent handling of resources (living

Guide for Reading

Focus on these questions as you read.

▶ *What is wildlife conservation?*

▶ *What are some methods of wildlife conservation?*

and nonliving) so that they provide the greatest possible benefit for the longest possible time. Conservation allows us to use part of a resource now and at the same time preserve a sufficient supply of the resource for the future. The conservation of Earth's plants, animals, and other living things is known as **wildlife conservation.**

Setting Limits

The fate of the dodo and other extinct species has taught us a sad lesson: People cannot be allowed to kill as many living things as they wish. Enough individuals must be left so that a species can maintain its numbers through reproduction. But how can this be achieved? One way of setting limits on the numbers of living things killed is by enacting hunting and fishing laws. Such laws specify how many animals a hunter or fisher is allowed to take from the wild. They may also place restrictions on the species, size, and sex of the animals captured. In addition, hunting and fishing laws specify at which times the animals can be hunted. For example, it is illegal to hunt ducks in the spring and summer, when they are breeding and raising their young.

Unfortunately, these kinds of limits are sometimes not enough. Louisiana's population of American alligators continued to decline rapidly even after the state enacted a law limiting the hunting season to sixty days and allowing each hunter to take only six alligators of a certain size. It was not long before the alligator was in danger of extinction throughout its habitat in the swamps of the southern United States. By 1967, it was necessary to ban alligator hunting in the United States.

Of course, laws need to be enforced if they are to work. And enforcement is often a difficult and dangerous task. Game wardens in the United States, Kenya, Brazil, and elsewhere have been killed in the line of duty. But when the laws are allowed to work, species can be brought back from the edge of extinction. One success story involves the American alligator you just read about. Under protection, the alligators have increased significantly in number. In many areas, they are no longer considered endangered and so they can once again be hunted for

their hides. As long as hunters continue to obey the laws, alligators will never again become endangered from overhunting.

Preserving Habitats

You have just arrived at the most important exhibit in the zoo—a parking meter. You cannot believe your eyes. A parking meter? Parking meters belong on streets and in parking lots, not in zoos! What's going on here?

A sign on the parking meter explains it all. The money that people put into the parking meter will be used to purchase land in the tropics. As you hunt through your pockets for change, you recall that habitat destruction has caused more species to become extinct or endangered than overhunting has. Thus, preserving habitats is the most important method of conserving wildlife. Now you agree: It makes sense for the parking meter to be considered the most important exhibit in the zoo.

Have you ever been to Yosemite or any other national park in the United States? If you have, you are probably aware of how hard the National Park Service works to keep the parks as close to their natural state as possible. This helps to preserve wildlife habitats. A few rare or endangered organisms—such as silversword plants, Attwater's greater prairie chicken, and American crocodiles—are found almost entirely in national parks or wildlife refuges. Many

Figure 29–19 *National and international laws protect rare and endangered species. Laws limit the number of American alligators and colobus monkeys that can be killed. Laws also protect the endangered* Rafflesia arnoldi *plant, which has the world's largest flower—more than 90 cm across and 6.8 kg in mass. Unfortunately, the flower smells like rotting meat.*

Figure 29–20 *The parking meter exhibit in the San Francisco Zoo collects donations of spare change. The donations are used to buy and protect wildlife habitats.*

other countries also have set up parks and preserves that cannot be developed by industry. In 1976, for instance, Costa Rican officials set aside over 500 square kilometers of rain forest as a preserve. Here many rare plants and animals live and thrive.

Habitats also need to be preserved in places other than national parks and wildlife refuges. The zoo's parking meter is one way of raising funds for habitat preservation outside of government reserves. By buying land, conservation organizations ensure that the land will remain in its natural state. After all, the people who own the land are the ones who make the decisions about what will happen to it.

Raising Reproductive Rates

Sometimes preserving habitats is not enough. To save highly endangered species from extinction, it may be necessary to raise their reproductive rate, or get individuals to produce more offspring. How can this be done?

Reproductive rates are sometimes raised through **captive breeding,** or causing animals in zoos to have offspring. For some species that have vanished from the wild, such as the California condor, captive breeding is the only way of saving the species.

Recently, advanced techniques originally invented for use in humans and cattle have been applied to captive breeding programs. As you can see in Figure 29–22, the results of these techniques are often a bit startling. A "test-tube baby" animal may look quite different from its host mother. But the host mother is usually quite content to care for "her" baby. Test-tube baby techniques allow an endangered-species

Figure 29–21 *National parks preserve places of natural beauty and wonder. They also protect the wildlife that lives in these places. Yosemite National Park in California is a temperate forest habitat (top). What kind of habitats are found in Everglades National Park in Florida (bottom left) and in Zion National Park in Utah (bottom right)?*

Figure 29–22 *Because California condors are nearly extinct, it is too risky to allow the real parents to bring up baby. To avoid confusing the condor chick, its keepers use a realistic hand puppet to feed and groom it. Although the test-tube baby bongo does not look much like its eland host mother, the eland takes good care of "her" baby.*

female to produce many more offspring during her lifetime than would otherwise be possible.

Other advanced techniques in reproductive biology allow individuals to produce offspring long after their lifetimes are completed. Scientists are currently developing ways of storing plant seeds and freezing animal sperm, eggs, and embryos so that they can survive in "suspended animation" for many years.

In some cases, captive breeding has been so successful that it has become possible to return animals to their natural habitats. Captive lion tamarin monkeys have been trained to live in the wild, then released into the rain forests of Brazil. In time, the offspring of these monkeys will breed with wild monkeys, thus adding some much-needed genetic diversity to the population. The Arabian oryx, a graceful antelope with long horns, became extinct in the wild in 1972. But because of captive breeding programs started 10 years before in the United States, the oryx was not lost forever to the deserts of the Arabian Peninsula. In the early 1980s, a small herd of formerly captive oryx were released in the country of Oman. Guarded day and night by rangers, the oryxes have thrived. Now, 10 years after their return, there are more than 100 oryx, over three fourths of which have known no home except the deserts of Oman.

ACTIVITY

WRITING

It's the Law

The legal protection of living things goes above the state level. One of the most important federal laws (laws that affect the entire United States) is the Endangered Species Act. One of the most important international laws is CITES (Convention on International Trade in Endangered Species of Fauna and Flora).

Using references available in the library, prepare a report on one of these laws.

CONNECTIONS

Computer Dating for Wildlife

In spite of many cartoons to the contrary, computer dating does not involve machines having a romantic candlelit dinner for two. Computer dating is actually a way of using *computers* to match up potentially compatible people so they can get together socially. For humans, computer dating is a way of meeting people with similar interests. With luck, a person will make new friends and establish new relationships.

For wildlife, computer dating is not a matter of matching up individuals with similar hobbies and outlooks on life. Its purpose is to match up individuals that are as dissimilar as possible in terms of their genes. This helps maintain the genetic diversity of the species. And genetic diversity helps to ensure the continued survival of species, both in zoos and in the wild.

Here's an example of computer dating for wildlife in action. In 1986, 68 European zoos agreed to participate in an international captive breeding program for Siberian tigers. The zoos sent a list of ancestors—parents, grandparents, great-grandparents, and so on—for each of their tigers to an organization that coordinates captive breeding programs. There, information on the zoos' 207 tigers was entered into a computer. The scientists managing the captive breeding program used the computer to analyze the information. The computer's analysis helped the scientists decide which tigers should be bred, when they should be bred, and to which other tigers they should be bred. The scientists also came up with a plan for moving the tigers from one zoo to another in order to meet their computer-assigned dates. So thanks to computer dating, tigers are now off on busy—but romantic—journeys around Europe.

Using People Power

Conserving the Earth's living resources is an awesome task. There are many complex social, political, and ethical issues that affect conservation measures—far too many to be discussed here. But achieving a balance between the needs of humans and the needs of wildlife is not impossible. Indeed, such a balance can ultimately benefit both humans and their fellow passengers on "Spaceship Earth."

In any conservation effort, it is important to keep human needs, attitudes, and desires in mind. When people understand environmental issues and realize how wildlife conservation benefits them, they become some of the best friends wildlife has.

The first step in getting people to support wildlife conservation is to make them aware that there is a problem. Sometimes this is done in spectacular ways: a concert or television special, perhaps. Or an environmental group may host a fair, a fundraising walk or race, or other event. But the process of making people aware goes on constantly in quieter, less obvious ways. The next time you visit a zoo or wildlife conservation park, read an article about endangered species, or hear an interview with a celebrity who supports conservation efforts, pay

Figure 29–23 *Captive-bred animals—such as lion tamarins (top left), Arabian oryx (top right), and red wolves (bottom)—have been trained to live in the wild, and then released. In some cases, the animals' release has inspired governments to increase the size of the wildlife preserve in which the animals live.*

771

Figure 29–24 *Making people aware of conservation issues is sometimes done in spectacular ways. The 1990 Earth Day festival in New York City's Central Park drew thousands of spectators and participants. By placing their bodies and their small boat between whaler's harpoons and whales, Greenpeace activists prevent the killing of whales.*

attention. You may be surprised at how many lessons about the environment are being taught.

In many cases, the interests of wildlife and those of the majority of people are not in conflict. Thus people do not have to be coaxed into liking conservation measures. They may already be aware of the problems and anxious to help. But what can ordinary people do?

Quite a lot, once they realize that their opinions matter and they can make a difference. In India, villagers have saved the forests near their homes by hugging the trees and getting in the way of loggers who want to cut the trees down. In Africa, farmers are learning new methods of growing their crops among the trees of the forest. In South America, many Amazon Indian tribes have united to form a powerful political group for rain forest preservation. And there are many, many other examples.

Every person, young or old, rich or poor, can help in the struggle to save Planet Earth. Even little things matter—the little efforts of a lot of people can make a big difference.

Here are a few simple things you can do to help save the Earth and its inhabitants.

• Recycle substances such as paper, steel, glass, and aluminum. This reduces the need for raw materials and helps save habitats from deforestation and mining.

- Write to companies to make them aware of environmental issues. This inspires them to find ways to do less harm to the environment—and even to help it!
- Support companies that are environmentally aware. This encourages them to continue their good work. It may also motivate companies that are less aware to improve their ways.
- Refuse to buy exotic pets, tortoise shell, ivory, furs, and other products made from rare and endangered animals. Ultimately, this makes it less desirable for people to obtain or sell such things.
- Make an effort to think about the ways your actions affect the web of life. This may help you find alternatives that are just as useful to you and more beneficial to the Earth.
- Can you think of other ways to help wildlife and the environment?

Perhaps the most important things you can do to help the Earth and its living things are to learn as much as you can about wildlife and the environment and to share your knowledge with others. Like the Lorax in the famous book by Dr. Seuss, you can "speak for the trees" and the other wild things that "have no tongues" and cannot speak for themselves. You and other people can make your voice the voice of the Earth and its voiceless wildlife. With a good understanding of the past and the present, people can work together to make a better future.

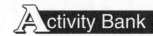
Activity Bank

Paper Route, p. 848

ACTIVITY
WRITING

Taking Action

There are many organizations that are dedicated to preserving planet Earth and its inhabitants. Here are just a few of the larger organizations.

Audubon Society
Greenpeace
World Conservation Union (WCU), formerly International Union for the Conservation of Nature (IUCN)
National/International Wildlife Federation
Nature Conservancy
Sierra Club
Wilderness Society
World Wildlife Fund

Prepare a report on one of these groups. Your report should explain the purpose of the group and describe its activities.

29–2 Section Review

1. What is considered to be the most important method of conserving wildlife? Why?

Connection—*You and Your World*
2. Design a conservation program for the rare or endangered organism of your choice. Explain how your plan takes into consideration the different conservation methods and issues that you read about in this section.

Laboratory Investigation

A Miniature World

Problem

How do human activities affect the environment?

Materials (per group)

large jar with cover	4 aquatic plants
table lamp	8 small pond snails
2 guppies	clean gravel

Procedure 🔺 🐁

1. Place gravel 3 cm deep on the bottom of the jar.

2. Fill the jar with tap water to about 6 cm from the top.

3. Let the jar stand uncovered for at least 48 hours.

4. Using the accompanying diagram as a guide, place plants in the jar.

5. Place the snails and guppies in the jar.

6. Close the jar tightly.

7. Place the jar in a location away from windows and other areas in which temperature and light change greatly.

8. Place the table lamp next to the jar so that the light shines on the jar. The light bulb should be about 15 to 20 cm from the jar.

9. Within 4 to 5 days, the water in the jar should be slightly green in color. If the water does not have any color in it, move the lamp closer to the jar. **Note:** *The light bulb should not touch the jar.* If the water is bright green, move the lamp away from the jar. Adjust the position of the lamp as needed until the water stays a pale green in color.

10. Observe the jar every 2 to 3 days.

Observations

How did the jar change over time?

Analysis and Conclusions

1. Why is the lamp necessary?

2. How do the plants and animals in the jar interact?

3. What would happen to the miniature world inside the jar if people killed all the snails and fish?

4. Imagine that an exotic plant disease which killed all the plants was accidentally introduced to your jar. How would this affect the miniature world in the jar?

5. You could have found the answers to questions 3 and 4 by doing something to simulate these forms of environmental damage. Explain why you were not asked to do this.

6. **On Your Own** Design an experiment to test the effects of deforestation on your miniature world. What results would you expect to obtain from your experiment?

Study Guide

Summarizing Key Concepts

29-1 Identifying Problems

▲ A species that no longer exists is said to be extinct. The process by which a species passes out of existence is known as extinction.

▲ Extinction is a natural part of Earth's history.

▲ In the past few hundred years, human activities have greatly increased the rate at which organisms become extinct.

▲ Organisms that are so rare that they are in danger of becoming extinct are said to be endangered.

▲ Some species become rare, endangered, or extinct because they are killed deliberately.

▲ Many species are threatened by the destruction of their habitats.

▲ The destruction of forests is known as deforestation. Deforestation harms both nearby and distant ecosystems.

▲ Although some desertification occurs naturally, most is caused by human activities.

▲ Pollution damages habitats and poses a threat to living things.

▲ Exotic, or non-native, species can upset the balance of interactions in an ecological community and cause native species to become endangered or extinct.

▲ Some activities meant to increase people's appreciation for the natural world may pose a threat to wildlife.

▲ Wildlife has economic and scientific value.

▲ The genetic diversity of wildlife provides keys for solving current and future problems.

▲ Because all living things are interdependent, wildlife is necessary for the continued survival of the human species.

29-2 Seeking Solutions

▲ Wildlife conservation is the wise management of Earth's living resources so that they can supply present and future needs.

▲ Preserving habitats is the most important method for conserving wildlife.

▲ In any conservation effort, it is important to keep human needs, attitudes, and desires in mind.

▲ Education is the first step in getting people to help with wildlife conservation.

▲ Captive breeding helps to raise reproductive rates and maintain genetic diversity.

▲ Wildlife conservation is not easy because it is closely linked to many complex social, political, and ethical issues.

▲ If everyone does a little bit to help conserve resources, wildlife and the environment will be helped a lot.

Reviewing Key Terms

Define each term in a complete sentence.

29-1 Identifying Problems
extinct
endangered
deforestation
desertification
exotic species

29-2 Seeking Solutions
wildlife conservation
captive breeding

Chapter Review

Content Review

Multiple Choice

Choose the letter of the answer that best completes each statement.

1. Which of the following is extinct?
   a. rhinoceros   c. snowy egret
   b. dodo   d. lion tamarin
2. The intelligent management of resources is known as
   a. desertification.   c. habitat restoration.
   b. recycling.   d. conservation.
3. Organisms can become endangered because of
   a. habitat destruction.
   b. interactions with exotic species.
   c. overhunting.
   d. all of these.
4. Wildlife is important because it is
   a. a source of valuable products.
   b. a source of genetic diversity.
   c. necessary for environmental balance.
   d. all of these.
5. The process by which a species passes out of existence is known as
   a. endangerment.
   b. extinction.
   c. deforestation.
   d. genetic diversification.
6. A species that is not native to an area is said to be
   a. exotic.   c. extinct.
   b. endangered.   d. endemic.
7. A species that is so rare that it is in danger of disappearing is said to be
   a. exotic.   c. extinct.
   b. endangered.   d. endemic.
8. The destruction of forests is known as
   a. desertification.   c. deforestation.
   b. timber harvesting. d. defoliation.

True or False

If the statement is true, write "true." If it is false, change the underlined word or words to make the statement true.

1. Extinction is a natural part of Earth's history.
2. The dodo is a(an) endangered species.
3. Enforcing hunting laws is the most important method of wildlife conservation.
4. Elephants have become endangered because of the demand for their meat.
5. Most desertification occurs as the result of natural processes.
6. Wetlands are considered to be extremely valuable ecosystems.
7. The deforestation of greatest concern to people worldwide is occurring in the coniferous forests of the United States.
8. Education does not play an important part in wildlife conservation.

Concept Mapping

Complete the following concept map for Section 29–1. Then construct a concept map for the entire chapter.

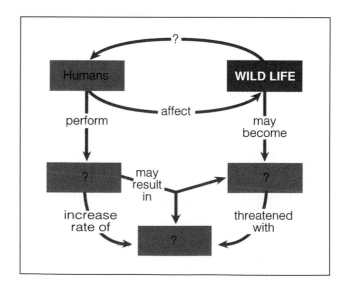

Concept Mastery

Discuss each of the following in a brief paragraph.

1. Explain why it is important to preserve genetic diversity.
2. Discuss five ways in which habitats are damaged or destroyed.
3. What is the difference between the terms extinct and endangered?
4. Giving specific examples, explain how the demands of fashion have caused organisms to become endangered.
5. How do human activities affect the rate of extinction? Why do they have this effect?
6. How does captive breeding help animals in the wild?
7. What does the phrase "loving it to death" mean? How does this apply to the relationship between people and wildlife?
8. List four useful products that come from wildlife.

Critical Thinking and Problem Solving

Use the skills you have developed in this chapter to answer each of the following.

1. **Applying concepts** Suppose one of your friends wanted to buy a pet parrot. What sort of things do you think your friend should know before the parrot is purchased? Do you think buying a pet parrot is a good idea? Why or why not?
2. **Making predictions** In June 1990, Florida passed a law that requires motorboats to go at very slow speeds in certain waterways. In addition, motorboats have been completely banned from a few waterways. How do you think these new restrictions on motorboats will affect manatees?
3. **Relating cause and effect** About 200 years ago, Hawaii's forests were inhabited by 58 species of birds that were not found in any other place in the world. Of these 58 species, 22 are extinct and 20 are endangered. How might each of the following factors have contributed to the disappearance of these birds?
   a. Destruction of three fourths of Hawaii's forests
   b. Exotic species such as sheep, cattle, and rabbits
   c. Exotic species such as cats, rats, and mongooses
   d. Exotic species such as pigeons, sparrows, and doves
   e. Hunting
4. **Using the writing process** Write a short book for first-graders on one of the following topics: endangered species; species that became extinct because of human activities; a method of wildlife conservation. Illustrate your book with your own drawings and/or with pictures from magazines. (Remember to get permission before you cut up the magazines!)

GAZETTE

There are few animals as impressive as a rhinoceros. Roughly 4 meters long from head to tail and about 2300 kilograms in mass, a large rhino is approximately the size of a small car. A rhino's enormous size, beady eyes, armored skin, curving horn (or horns), and stocky legs remind some people of the dinosaurs that roamed the Earth long ago.

Recently, it became apparent that rhinos were in great danger of sharing yet another characteristic with dinosaurs: being extinct. (The word extinct is used to describe a type of living thing that has died out completely and vanished forever.) Why? Because in the past 20 years, more than 90 percent of the world's rhinos have been killed for their horns.

African rhinos have two horns: a long one on the tip of their snout and a smaller one behind it. Asian rhinos have only one horn. In both types of rhinos, the horns are nothing more than large curved cones made of the same substance as your fingernails. But in some parts of the world, people believe that rhino horns have magical properties. In Yemen, for example, rhino horns are used to make the handles of special daggers. And in China, ground-up rhino horns are used in "medicines" for fevers and other ailments.

What can be done to stop the slaughter of the rhinos before it's too late? Groups of nations have agreed to prohibit trade in rhino horns. Individual countries have made rhino hunting illegal, set up protected wildlife parks, and supplied park rangers with better equipment for stopping illegal hunters. Zoos have developed ways of raising and breeding rhinos in captivity. And Michael Werikhe (WAIR-ree-kee), a young man from Kenya, has walked more than 7800 kilometers to make people aware of the threat to rhinos and to raise money for rhino conservation programs.

Michael Werikhe is not a politician, scientist, or professional fundraiser. He is a

MICHAEL WERIKHE
Saving the Rhino—One Step at a Time

security officer at an auto factory, and he doesn't particularly like to walk. But he is determined to do all he can to save rhinos from extinction.

As a boy, Werikhe played in the mangrove forests and explored the seashore near his home city of Mombasa. These childhood activities filled him with a deep appreciation for the living world. After high school, he took a government job that he thought might be related to his interest in wildlife. But it was not quite what he expected. He worked in a government warehouse that stored elephant tusks and rhinoceros horns confiscated from illegal hunters or collected from animals that had to be killed by game wardens. Werikhe's job was to sort these grisly trophies so that the government could sell them at auctions. Although Werikhe soon quit, the memory of the tusks, horns, and wasted wildlife they represented remained with him.

When Werikhe quit his job at the government warehouse, there were about 20,000 black rhinos in Kenya. Ten years later, there were about 500. To Werikhe, the rhinos became a symbol of all the threatened wildlife he loved. He had to do something. So he walked from Mombasa to Nairobi, a journey of about 480 kilometers. On his way, he stopped at many small villages and talked to people about the dangers rhinos faced.

"Too often, wildlife professionals assume that the average African cares little about preserving his natural heritage," Werikhe notes. "In my walks I've found that people *do* care, but feel left out."

In 1985, with the support of his employer and his fellow workers, Werikhe left his job and set off on a nearly 2100-kilometer trek across Africa. Three years later, he was off on another transcontinental hike. This time the continent was Europe. The walk raised $1 million for rhino conservation.

From April through September 1991, Werikhe, then 34 years old, undertook his third marathon walk. This walk took him to Washington, DC, Dallas, Toronto, San Diego, and many other major cities in North America. Three fourths of the approximately $2 million that he raised was for rhino programs in Africa; the rest was for rhino programs in North American zoos.

Werikhe has been honored for his work with a number of prestigious environmental

▲▼ In some parts of the world, people believe that rhino horns possess magical properties. As a result, African rhinos (top) and Indian rhinos (bottom) are in danger of becoming extinct.

awards, including the United Nations Environment Program's Global 500 Award. He has shown the world that the efforts of one ordinary person (with extraordinary determination) can go a long way toward solving global problems. But the accomplishment that might mean the most to Michael Werikhe is this: Thanks in large part to his efforts, the African rhino population seems to be back on the road to recovery.

For Further Reading

> If you have been intrigued by the concepts examined in this textbook, you may also be interested in the ways fellow thinkers—novelists, poets, essayists, as well as scientists—have imaginatively explored the same ideas.

Chapter 1: Exploring Life Science

Adamson, Joy. *Born Free, a Lioness of Two Worlds*. New York: Pantheon.

Clarke, Arthur C. *2001: A Space Odyssey*. New York: New American Library.

Freeman, Ira, and Mae Freeman. *Your Wonderful World of Science*. New York: Random House.

Kohn, Bernice. *The Scientific Method*. Englewood Cliffs, NJ: Prentice Hall.

Merle, Robert. *The Day of the Dolphin*. New York: Simon & Schuster.

Merrill, Jean. *The Toothpaste Millionaire*. Boston: Houghton Mifflin.

Chapter 2: The Nature of Life

L'Engle, Madeleine. *A Ring of Endless Light*. New York: Farrar, Straus & Giroux.

Ryder, Donald G. *The Inside Story: Living and Learning Through Life's Storms*. Pleasant Hill, CA: Ryder.

Watson, James D. *The DNA Story*. San Francisco: W.H. Freeman.

Chapter 3: Cells, Tissues, and Organ Systems

Davis, Natalie. *The Space Twin*. Nashville, TN: Winston-Derek.

Gonick, Larry, and Mark Wheelis. *Cartoon Guide to Genetics*. Fort Ann, NY: Barnes & Noble Books.

Hackman, Martha. *The Lost Forest*. San Marcos, CA: Green Tiger Press.

Llewellyn, Richard. *How Green Was My Valley*. New York: Dell.

Rowe, H. Edward. *Microscopic Monster: The Tricky, Devastating AIDS Virus*. Culpepper, VA: National AIDS Prevention Institute.

Whelan, Gloria. *The Pathless Woods*. Philadelphia: Lippincott.

Chapter 4: Classification of Living Things

Jarrell, Randall. *The Animal Family*. New York: Pantheon.

Paterson, Katherine. *Jacob Have I Loved*. New York: Thomas Y. Crowell.

Chapter 5: Viruses and Monerans

Christopher, John. *No Blade of Grass*. New York: Simon & Schuster.

De Kruif, Paul. *Microbe Hunters*. New York: Harcourt, Brace & World, Inc.

Chapter 6: Protists

Foster, Alan Dean. *The Thing*. New York: Bantam.

Perez, Norah A. *The Passage*. Philadelphia: Lippincott.

Chapter 7: Fungi

Cameron, Eleanor. *The Wonderful Flight to the Mushroom Planet*. Boston: Little, Brown and Co.

Hughes, William Howard. *Alexander Fleming and Penicillin*. Hove, U.K.: Wayland, Ltd.

Jones, Judith, and Evan Jones. *Knead It, Punch It, Bake It! Make Your Own Bread*. New York: Thomas Y. Crowell.

Chapter 8: Plants Without Seeds

Abels, Harriette E. *Future Food*. Mankato, MN: Crestwood House.

Kavaler, Lucy. *The Wonders of Algae*. New York: The John Day Co.

Sterling, Dorothy. *The Story of Mosses, Ferns, and Mushrooms*. Garden City, NY: Doubleday & Co.

(continued)

Chapter 20: Reproduction and Development

Eyerly, Jeanette. *He's My Baby Now.* New York: J.B. Lippincott Co.

Zindel, Paul. *The Girl Who Wanted a Boy.* New York: Bantam Books.

Chapter 21: Immune System

Crichton, Michael. *Five Patients: The Hospital Explained.* New York: Avon Books.

Hoffman, Alice. *At Risk.* London: Macmillan.

Lipsyte, Robert. *The Contender.* New York: Harper.

Chapter 22: Alcohol, Tobacco, and Drugs

Anonymous. *Go Ask Alice.* Englewood Cliffs, NJ: Prentice Hall.

Newman, Susan. *It Won't Happen to Me: True Stories of Teen Alcohol & Drug Abuse.* New York: Putnam.

Scott, Sharon. *How to Say No and Keep Your Friends: Peer Pressure Reversal.* Amherst, MA: Human Resource Development Press.

Chapter 23: Genetics

Arkin, Alan. *The Lemming Condition.* New York: Harper & Row.

Chetwin, Grace. *Gom on Windy Mountain.* New York: Lothrop, Lee & Shepard.

Greenfield, Eloise, and Lessie Jones Little. *Childtimes.* New York: Thomas Y. Crowell.

Sleator, William. *Singularity.* New York: E.P. Dutton.

Slepian, Jan. *The Alfred Summer.* New York: Macmillan Co.

Chapter 24: Applied Genetics

Ames, Mildred. *Anna to the Infinite Power.* New York: Scribner.

Babbitt, Natalie. *Tuck Everlasting.* New York: Farrar, Straus and Giroux.

Hilton, James. *Lost Horizon.* New York: Morrow.

Chapter 25: Changes in Living Things Over Time

Boulle, Pierre. *Planet of the Apes.* New York: Vanguard.

Denzel, Justin. *Boy of the Painted Cave.* New York: Philomel Books.

Kelleher, Victor. *Baily's Bones.* New York: Dial Press.

Lord, Bette Bao. *In the Year of the Boar and Jackie Robinson.* New York: Harper & Row.

Millstead, Thomas. *Cave of the Moving Shadows.* New York: Dial Press.

Chapter 26: Interactions Among Living Things

Attenborough, David. *The Trials of Life.* Boston, MA: Little, Brown.

Defoe, Daniel. *Robinson Crusoe.* New York: Penguin.

London, Jack. *Call of the Wild.* New York: Macmillan.

Chapter 27: Cycles in Nature

Adams, Richard. *Watership Down.* New York: Avon.

Burton, Jane, and Kim Taylor. *Nightwatch.* New York: Facts on File.

Kipling, Rudyard. *The Jungle Book.* New York: Penguin.

Chapter 28: Exploring Earth's Biomes

Carson, Rachel. *The Edge of the Sea.* New York: Signet.

George, Jean C. *My Side of the Mountain.* New York: Dutton.

Lopez, Barry. *Arctic Dreams: Imagination and Desire in a Northern Landscape.* New York: Scribner.

Perry, Donald. *Life Above the Jungle Floor: A Biologist Explores a Strange and Hidden Treetop World.* New York: Simon & Schuster.

Chapter 29: Conservation of Living Things

Henry, Marguerite. *Mustang, Wild Spirit of the West.* New York: Macmillan.

Lasky, Kathryn. *Home Free.* New York: Macmillan.

Mowat, Farley. *Never Cry Wolf.* New York: Bantam Books.

Activity Bank

Welcome to the Activity Bank! This is an exciting and enjoyable part of your science textbook. By using the Activity Bank you will have the chance to make a variety of interesting and different observations about science. The best thing about the Activity Bank is that you and your classmates will become the detectives, and as with any investigation you will have to sort through information to find the truth. There will be many twists and turns along the way, some surprises and disappointments too. So always remember to keep an open mind, ask lots of questions, and have fun learning about science.

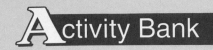

CALCULATING DENSITY

Calculating the density of a regular solid such as a cube is easy. Measure the sides of the object with a metric ruler and calculate the volume. Place the object on a balance to determine its mass. Then use the formula D = M/V to calculate the object's density. But can you determine the density of an object that has an irregular shape and is not easy to measure? A rock, for example. It's easy when you know how. Follow along and you can become the density calculator for your class.

Materials

graduated cylinder
rock
small piece of metal pipe
large nut or bolt
triple-beam balance
metric ruler
string

Procedure and Observations

1. Select one of the objects whose density you wish to calculate. Place the object on a balance and determine its mass. Enter the mass in a data table similar to the one shown on the next page.

2. Place some water in the graduated cylinder. Look at the water in the cylinder from the side. The water's surface will be shaped like a saucer. Notice that the water level dips slightly in the center. Add water carefully until the lowest part of the water's surface (the bottom of the dip) is at one of the main division lines on the side of the graduated cylinder. Enter the water-level reading in your data table.

3. You are going to determine the volume of your irregularly shaped object by water displacement. To do this, first tie a piece of string around the object you are going to use. Make sure the string is well tied.

4. Hold the end of the string and carefully lower the object into the water in the graduated cylinder. Read the new water level. Enter this reading in your data table. Subtract the first water-level reading from the second to determine the volume of the object. Enter this volume in your data table.

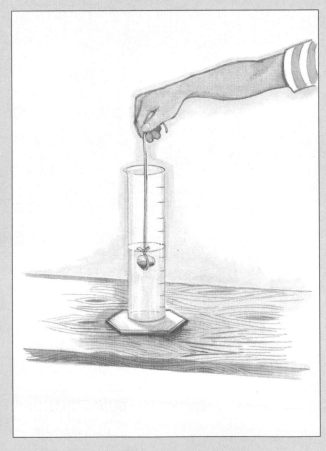

5. Repeat this procedure for each remaining object.

6. Use the formula D = M/V to calculate the density of each object you selected.

DATA TABLE

Object	Mass	First Water Level	Second Water Level	Water Displaced (mL)

Analysis and Conclusions

1. What is the volume of an object whose dimensions are 1.0 cm × 6.0 cm × 2.0 cm? Remember to include the proper units.
2. If the mass of this object is 60 g, what is its density?
3. What are the densities of the objects you measured?
4. Which object is made of the densest material?

Think About This

1. If an object with a density of 10 g/cm^3 is cut into two equal pieces, what is the density of each piece? Why?
2. Could the water displacement method be used to determine the volume of a rectangular object as well as an irregularly shaped object?
3. Why is the density of a substance important?

LIFE IN A DROP OF WATER

Just as good building tools can help a carpenter produce a fine home, so can good scientific tools aid a scientist in a variety of endeavors.

In this activity you will use one of the basic tools of life science: a microscope, a tool that lets scientists study worlds too small to be seen with the unaided eye.

You Will Use

microscope
glass slide
coverslip
water from your aquarium or pond water
medicine dropper

CAUTION: *Before you begin, make sure that you understand how to use a microscope.* Follow your teacher's instructions exactly. Examine the illustration of a microscope in Appendix B. A microscope is an expensive and valuable tool. Exercise care when using it and when using the slide and coverslip as well.

Now You Can Begin 🧪

1. Make sure that your microscope is in the correct position before you use it. Have your teacher check your setup before you begin. Use the illustration on page 852 in your textbook to familiarize yourself with the parts of your microscope.

2. There are several lenses on a microscope. The lens nearest the eye is called the ocular. The lenses closest to the slide are called the objectives. Note that each lens has a number etched on it. The number tells you how many times a particular lens magnifies the image that is viewed through it. Note the number on the ocular and the num-

ber on the smallest objective lens. Multiply one number by the other. This will tell the total magnification when these two lenses are used together. Enter the magnification near any drawing you make of what you observe.

3. Pick up a glass slide from your supply table. You will make a slide of a drop of water from your aquarium. (If you do not have an aquarium you can examine pond water that your teacher will supply. **CAUTION:** *Do not try to collect pond water without the help of an adult.*) Place one drop of aquarium water in the center of your slide.

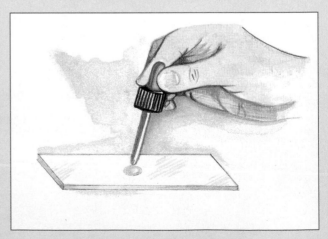

4. Pick up one of the coverslips and hold it as shown in the illustration. Carefully lower the coverslip onto the drop of water.

5. Place the slide on the microscope. Make sure the smallest, or low-power, lens is in position. Look through the ocular. Carefully turn the coarse adjustment knob until the image is in focus. Use the fine adjustment knob to get a clear image. Move the slide slowly back and forth. Draw what you observe.

6. Repeat the procedure with a drop of tap water.

7. When you are finished, follow your teacher's instructions for cleaning up.

Observations

1. What kinds of things did you observe in the drop of water from the aquarium?

2. Did these organisms move around or remain in one place?

3. What did you observe in the drop of tap water?

Analysis and Conclusions

1. How has the microscope helped scientists to study the natural world?

2. How can you explain the differences you observed in the aquarium water and the tap water?

Going Further

You can examine some other substances. Make a plan of study and check with your teacher before you proceed.

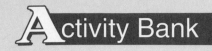

HYDRA DOING?

Hydras are members of the phylum *Cnidaria*. Like all cnidarians, hydras have soft bodies made up of two layers of cells. They also have stinging tentacles arranged in circles around their mouth. Do hydras have the characteristics that all forms of life share? To answer this question, you will need a medicine dropper, a culture of hydras, a depression slide, a microscope, a toothpick, and some fish food.

Procedure

1. Using a medicine dropper, remove a drop of the hydra culture from the bottom of the culture jar.

2. Place the drop on a depression slide.

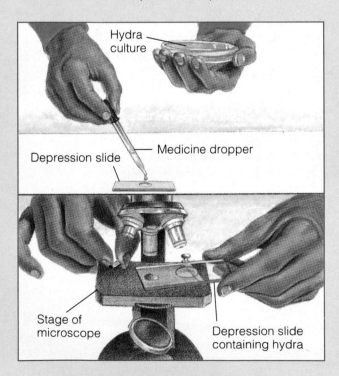

Hydra culture

Depression slide — Medicine dropper

Stage of microscope

Depression slide containing hydra

3. Put the slide on the stage of a microscope. Using the low-power objective, locate a hydra. Draw and label what you observe.

4. Carefully touch the hydra's tentacles with a toothpick. Observe what happens.

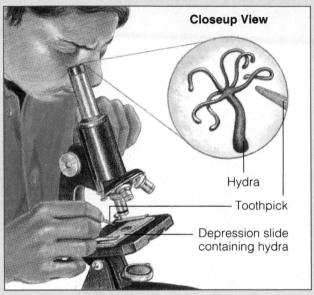

Closeup View

Hydra

Toothpick

Depression slide containing hydra

5. Place a tiny amount of fish food near the hydra and see what happens.

Observations

1. What happened to the hydra when you touched it with the toothpick?

2. How does the hydra move?

3. Describe how the hydra eats.

Analysis and Conclusions

1. What characteristics of living things does the hydra exhibit?

2. Does the hydra react as a whole organism or does just part of the hydra react? Explain.

Going Further

Place a drop of vinegar (weak acid) near a hydra. Observe what happens.

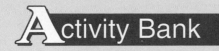

Activity Bank

One of the most important processes that occurs in a cell is diffusion. Diffusion regulates what enters and leaves the cell. To see how diffusion actually occurs, try this activity.

Materials

50 mL household ammonia
wide-mouthed jar
piece of cheese-cloth (15 cm × 15 cm)

rubber band
spatula
gelatin "cell"
clock with second indicator

Procedure 🧪 ⚗️ 👁

1. Select one member of the group to act as a Principal Investigator, a second member to act as a Timer, and a third member to act as a Recorder. The remaining members of the group will be the Observers. Be sure you understand your role in the activity before you continue.

2. Carefully pour 50 mL of ammonia in a wide-mouthed jar. **CAUTION:** *Keep the ammonia away from your skin and do not inhale its vapors. Keep the room well ventilated.*

3. Place the cheesecloth over the mouth of the jar. Hold it in place by putting a rubber band around the jar and the cheesecloth.

4. Using a spatula, place a gelatin "cell" on top of the cheesecloth as shown in the diagram. The gelatin "cell" contains a chemical called phenolphthalein. Phenolphthalein indicates the presence of bases such as ammonia. If a base is present, phenolphthalein will turn pink. **Note:** *Do not allow any ammonia to come into direct contact with the gelatin "cell."*

Household ammonia

Wide-mouthed jar

Cheesecloth

Rubber band

50 mL of household ammonia

Gelatin "cell"

5. Note the color of the gelatin "cell" immediately after placing it on the cheesecloth. Record its color in a data table similar to the one shown.

6. Observe the gelatin "cell" every 2 minutes for a total of 10 minutes. Record your observations in your data table.

Observations

DATA TABLE

Time (min)	Color Change
0	
2	
4	
6	
8	
10	

Analysis and Conclusions

1. Does the ammonia diffuse into the gelatin "cell" or does the material in the gelatin "cell" diffuse into the ammonia in the jar? How do you know?

2. What causes the gelatin "cell" to undergo changes without coming into direct contact with the ammonia?

3. Compare your results with those of your classmates. Are they similar? Different? If they are different, explain why.

Activity Bank

A KEY TO THE PUZZLE

One way of showing how objects are classified is a taxonomic key. A taxonomic key consists of many pairs of opposing descriptions. Only one of the descriptions in a pair is correct for a given object. Following the correct description is an instruction that directs you to another pair of descriptions. By following each successive description and instruction in a taxonomic key, you will eventually arrive at an object's correct classification group.

Don't worry—this sounds more complicated than it actually is. Let's take a look at a simple taxonomic key for the five kingdoms.

1a Made up of cells that contain a nucleus. Go to 2.

1b Made up of one cell that does not contain a nucleus. *Monera.*

2a Is unicellular. Go to 3.

2b Is multicellular. Go to 4.

3a Belongs to the green, red, or brown algae phylum. *Plantae.*

3b Does not belong to the green, red, or brown algae phylum. Go to 7.

4a Is an autotroph. *Plantae.*

4b Is a heterotroph. Go to 5.

5a Evolved from autotrophs. *Plantae.*

5b Did not evolve from autotrophs. Go to 6.

6a Has a cell wall. *Fungi.*

6b Does not have a cell wall. *Animalia.*

7a Is a yeast. *Fungi.*

7b Is not a yeast. *Protista.*

1. Using the taxonomic key for the five kingdoms, determine the kingdom to which each of the organisms described in the following stories belongs.

a. While looking at a sample of pond water through a microscope, you notice a rod-shaped unicellular heterotroph that has a cell wall and no nucleus.

b. In the same sample, you see a unicellular heterotroph that has a nucleus and moves by means of whiplike "tails." Because yeasts don't have "tails," you know it is not a yeast.

c. While walking through the woods one day, you notice some white, candy-cane-shaped multicellular heterotrophs growing on a dead log. The cells contain a nucleus and have a cell wall. Chemical study of the hereditary material reveals that they are descended from autotrophs.

d. In a tide pool, you see an autotroph that looks like sheets of green cellophane. It is made up of many cells that contain a nucleus. It looks exactly like the photograph in your field guide of the green alga known as sea lettuce.

e. Further examination of the organisms in the tide pool reveals a small, nonmoving, multicellular blob. At first, you think it's some kind of seaweed, but you later find out that it is a heterotroph whose cells lack cell walls.

2. According to the taxonomic key, how are animals and fungi similar? Different?

3. Invent a taxonomic key for pets. Test your key by using it to determine the kind of pet a friend or classmate is thinking of.

YUCK! WHAT ARE THOSE BACTERIA DOING IN MY YOGURT?

Introduction

Even newly opened, fresh-from-the-refrigerator yogurt is loaded with bacteria. But don't throw your yogurt away in disgust. Bacteria are supposed to be in yogurt. Why? Find out in this activity.

Materials

50 mL milk
10 mL diluted
   chocolate syrup
10 mL lemon juice
10 mL tea
10 mL vinegar

10 mL water
pH paper
5 paper cups
graduated cylinder
5 spoons

If you don't have a graduated cylinder, use a measuring spoon. One teaspoon equals 5 mL.

Procedure

1. Assign roles to each member of the group. Possible roles include: Recorder (the person who records observations and coordinates the group's presentation of results), Materials Manager (the person who makes sure that the group has all the materials it needs), Maintenance Director (the person who coordinates cleanup), Principal Investigator (the person who reads instructions to the group, makes sure that the proper procedure is being followed, and asks questions of the teacher on behalf of the group), and Specialists (people who perform specific tasks such as preparing the cups of liquids to be tested or testing the pH of the liquids). Your group may divide up the tasks differently, and individuals may have more than one role, depending on the size of your group.

2. On a separate sheet of paper, prepare a data table similar to the one shown in the Observations section.

3. Label the paper cups Chocolate, Lemon, Tea, Vinegar, and Water. Pour the appropriate liquid into each cup.

4. Dip a pH strip into each liquid. Compare the color of the strip to the key on the pH paper box. Record the pH in the appropriate place in your data table.

pH strip

5. Pour 10 mL of milk into each of the five cups. Use a different spoon to mix the milk with each of the other liquids. Record your observations in your data table.

Spoon
10 mL milk
Cup containing liquid

6. Measure the pH of the mixture in each cup. Record the pH in the appropriate place in your data table.

Observations

DATA TABLE

Liquid	pH Before	Observations	pH After
Chocolate			
Lemon			
Tea			
Vinegar			
Water			

Analysis and Conclusions

1. Describe what happened to the milk when it was added to the vinegar. Look at the substances formed when the milk reacted with the vinegar. How might these substances relate to the production of yogurt?

2. Did any other liquids cause the milk to change in the same way as the vinegar?

3. Relate the pH of the liquid to the way it reacts with milk.

4. Using what you have observed in this activity, explain why yogurt is thick and almost solid whereas milk is a thin liquid.

5. The essential ingredients of yogurt are milk and bacteria. (The bacteria are called "active cultures" on the ingredients label on a container of yogurt.) Without the bacteria, most yogurt would simply be fruit-flavored milk. What is the purpose of the bacteria in yogurt?

PUTTING THE SQUEEZE ON

Amebas are not the only protists with contractile vacuoles. In fact, most freshwater protists have contractile vacuoles. In this activity you will observe how this tiny structure works under different conditions.

Materials

3 *Paramecium caudatum* cultures at room temperature (25°C): fresh water, 0.5 percent table salt solution, 1.0 percent table salt solution

refrigerated (2°C) *Paramecium caudatum* culture in fresh water

medicine dropper

4 glass microscope slides

4 coverslips

microscope

cotton ball

Procedure 🧪

1. Using a medicine dropper, put a drop of water containing *Paramecium caudatum* in the center of a clean microscope slide.

2. Pull apart a small piece of cotton and put a few threads in the drop of water.

3. Cover the drop with a coverslip.

4. Locate and focus on a paramecium. Notice the alternating contractions of the two contractile vacuoles. How long does it take for a contractile vacuole to contract, refill, and contract once again? Record this information in the appropriate place in a data table similar to the one shown in Observations.

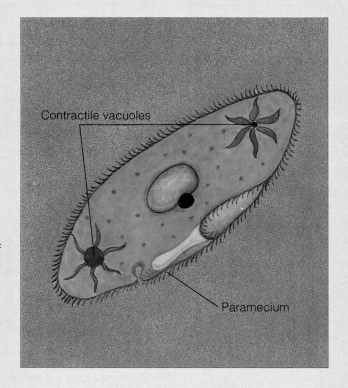

Contractile vacuoles

Paramecium

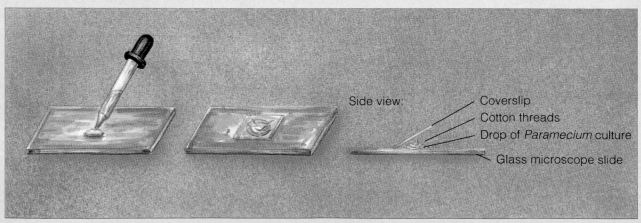

Side view:
Coverslip
Cotton threads
Drop of *Paramecium* culture
Glass microscope slide

5. Repeat steps 1 through 4 for a paramecium in a 0.5 percent table salt solution, a 1.0 percent table salt solution, and very cold water. Record your data.

6. Observe a paramecium in the very cold water. What happens as the water warms up?

Observations

DATA TABLE

Percent Table Salt	Temperature	Time Between Contractions
0	25°C	
0.5	25°C	
1	25°C	
0	2°C	

Analysis and Conclusions

1. What is the purpose of contractile vacuoles?

2. How does an increase in the concentration of salt in its environment affect a paramecium's contractile vacuoles?

3. What can you infer about the rate at which water enters the paramecium in salt solutions? Explain.

4. How is the rate at which a paramecium performs life functions, such as pumping out excess water, affected by very cold temperatures? What evidence do you have for this?

5. Compare your results with those obtained by your classmates. Did you obtain the same results? Why or why not?

SHEDDING A LITTLE LIGHT ON EUGLENA

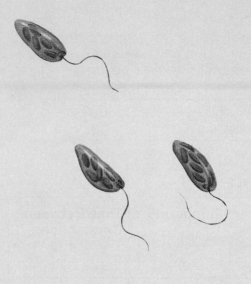

The plantlike protists known as euglenas are quite popular in scientific research—they are small, relatively easy to take care of, and fairly simple in structure. In Section 6–3, you read about the structure of euglenas. In this activity you will discover how the euglenas' structure enables them to function in a particular situation.

Procedure and Observations

1. Pour a concentrated culture of *Euglena* into a petri dish. What color is the concentrated culture? Why is the culture this color?

2. Cover half the dish with aluminum foil or a small piece of cardboard.

3. After 10 minutes, uncover the dish. What do you observe?

Analysis and Conclusions

1. How do euglenas respond to light?

2. Why do you think this occurs?

3. What structures in euglenas make this possible?

SPREADING SPORES

Have you ever opened a bag of bread and found fuzzy black mold growing on the slices you had planned to use? Or discovered spots of mildew that seemed to appear overnight in a clean bathroom? You may wonder how fungi manage to get just about everyplace. In this activity you will discover the secret of fungi's success.

What Do I Do?

1. Obtain a round balloon, cotton balls, tape, a stick or ruler about 30 cm long, modeling clay, and a pin.

2. Stretch the balloon so that it inflates easily. Do not tie off the end of the balloon!

3. Pull a cotton ball into five pieces about the same size. Roll the pieces into little balls no more than 1 cm in diameter.

4. Insert the little cotton balls through the opening in the neck of the balloon.

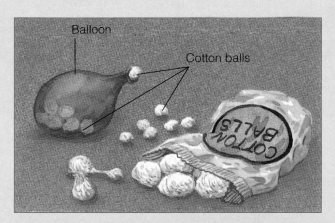

5. Continue making little cotton balls and putting them into the balloon until the balloon is almost full.

6. Inflate the balloon and tie a knot in its neck to keep the air inside.

7. Tape the knotted end of the balloon to the top of the stick.

8. Put the bottom of the stick into the modeling clay. Shape the modeling clay so that the stick stands upright.

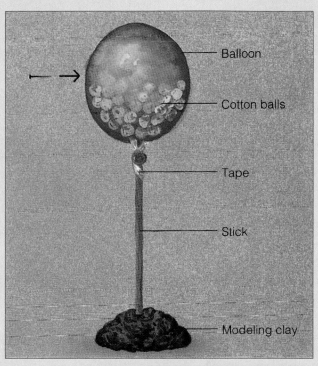

9. You have now made a model of the fruiting body of a bread mold. The balloon represents the spore case, the cotton balls represent spores, and the stick represents the stalk (a hypha) that supports the spore case. Make a drawing of your model. Label the spores, spore case, and stalk.

10. After you have finished admiring your model, jab the balloon with the pin.

What Did I Learn?

1. What happened when you jabbed the balloon with the pin?

2. Relate what you observed to reproduction in fungi. Why are fungi found just about everywhere?

SEAWEED SWEETS

How do people use seaweed? You can experience how seaweed is used as a food by using this old family recipe to make a traditional Chinese dessert. The name of this dessert is based on the Chinese dialect called Cantonese. *Popo* means maternal grandmother. *Kanten* means agar in general and this dessert in particular. Kanten is sold in Asian grocery stores. It comes in long, thin blocks.

Popo Thom's Kanten

2 blocks of kanten (one 0.5 oz package)

1 cup sugar

4 cups liquid (Popo Thom uses guava juice. You can use any kind of fruit juice you like.)

food coloring (optional)

Recipe Directions

1. Rinse kanten under running water.
2. Break kanten into cubes and put the cubes into a saucepan.
3. Add the liquid and sugar to the saucepan. Bring the mixture to a boil.

Kanten

1 cup sugar dissolved in 4 cups liquid

Then turn down the heat and cook, stirring, until the kanten dissolves.

4. Remove the saucepan from the heat. If you wish, stir in a few drops of food coloring to make the mixture a pretty color.
5. Pour the mixture into a shallow rectangular pan.
6. Let cool; then refrigerate until set.
7. Cut kanten into blocks and serve. Do you like the dessert, or do you think it's an acquired taste?

Another Chinese dessert, almond float, is made in a similar way. In step 3, use 2 cups of water and 2 tablespoons of almond extract as the liquid. In step 4, stir in 2 cups of evaporated milk. Almond float cubes are usually served with canned fruits in their syrup (canned lichee, or litchi nuts, are traditional; fruit cocktail is also good).

Things to Think About

1. The ingredients in a recipe often serve a particular function. For example, cornstarch thickens sauces, mustard helps the oil and vinegar in a salad dressing to mix, and egg helps to "glue" other ingredients together. What purpose does the kanten serve in this recipe? What purposes do the sugar and juice serve?
2. Share the kanten you have made with your family and/or classmates. What do they think of this dessert?
3. Working with some friends, brainstorm some other ways in which you might use kanten blocks.

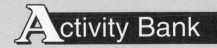
THE INS AND OUTS OF PHOTOSYNTHESIS

Introduction

Blue-green bacteria, plantlike protists, and green plants perform a special process known as photosynthesis (foh-toh-SIHN-thuh-sihs). In photosynthesis, light energy is used to combine carbon dioxide and water to form food and oxygen. As you read on pages 205–206 in the textbook, oxygen is very important to humans and many other living things. Oxygen, which we humans take in when we breathe in, is used to break down food to release energy—energy that powers all life processes. The breakdown of food also produces carbon dioxide, which is removed from the body when we breathe out. What do organisms that can perform photosynthesis do with carbon dioxide?

In this activity you will observe the "ins and outs" of photosynthesis and the complementary process of food breakdown, or respiration.

Materials

3 125-mL flasks
3 #5 rubber stoppers
100 mL graduated cylinder
bromthymol blue solution
2 sprigs of *Elodea*, about the same size
light source
drinking straw

Procedure 🧪 🧰

1. Using the graduated cylinder, measure out 100 mL of bromthymol blue solution for each of the three flasks. **CAUTION**: *Bromthymol blue is a dye and can stain your hands and clothing.* What color is the bromthymol blue solution?

2. Put the straw into one of the flasks. Gently blow bubbles into the solution until there is a change in its appearance. How does the solution change? Repeat this procedure with the other two flasks.

3. Place one sprig of *Elodea* in each of two of the flasks. Stopper all three flasks.

4. Put one flask containing *Elodea* in the dark for 24 hours. Put the other two flasks on a sunny windowsill for the same amount of time.

5. After 24 hours, examine each flask. What do you observe?

(continued)

On a Sunny Windowsill

Stopper

Elodea

In the Dark

Analysis and Conclusions

1. What substance did you add to the bromthymol blue solution when you blew bubbles into it? Where did this substance come from? What effect did this substance have on the solution?

2. What happened in the flask that was kept in the dark? Explain why this occurred.

3. What happened in the flask containing *Elodea* that was kept in a sunny spot? Why?

4. What was the purpose of the flask that did not contain *Elodea*?

5. How are the "ins," or raw materials, for photosynthesis related to the "outs," or products, of respiration?

6. How are the "outs" of photosynthesis related to the "ins" of respiration?

7. How is photosynthesis related to respiration?

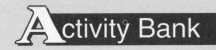

Activity Bank

LEAN TO THE LIGHT

Living things respond to their environment. Pet dogs and cats come running when they hear the can opener or the rustle of the pet-food bag. People put up umbrellas and hurry toward shelter when it starts to rain. In this activity you will discover one way in which plants respond to their environment.

What Do I Need?

2 half-gallon milk cartons with the tops cut off, old newspapers, old artist's smock or apron, black tempera (poster) paint, paintbrush, 2 plastic cups, soil, scissors, and 10 popcorn kernels.

What Do I Do?

1. Spread some old newspapers on a work surface. Wear old clothes on which it is okay to get paint, or wear an artist's smock or apron to protect your clothes. Paint the inside of the milk cartons black. Put the cartons on a sheet of old newspaper someplace where they can dry, and then clean up your work area.

2. Fill the cups about three-fourths full with soil. Water the soil so that it is moist but not soaking wet. Plant five popcorn kernels in each cup. The kernels should be just under the surface of the soil.

3. Cut a small hole about 1 cm across in the side of one of the dry milk cartons.

4. Set the cups in a well-lighted place. Cover each cup with a milk carton. Make sure to position the carton with the hole in it so that light can enter through the hole.

5. Examine your seedlings after several days. If the soil is dry, add a little water. Replace the cartons so that they are in exactly the same position they were originally.

What Did I Find Out?

1. Describe how your seedlings appear after they have been growing for a week. How are the two groups of seedlings different?

2. Why do you think this happens?

3. Why might your results be important to someone who has houseplants?

4. Draw a picture that show your results. Using the picture, share your findings with your classmates.

803

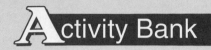
FRIENDS OR FOES?

Do animals and plants need each other? Can they survive without one another? Try this activity to find out the answers to these questions.

What Will You Need?

small plastic bag with a twist tie
distilled water
medicine dropper
bromthymol blue solution
pond snail
Elodea sprig

What Will You Do?

1. Fill a plastic bag two-thirds full with distilled water.

2. Put a few drops of bromthymol blue solution into the plastic bag to make the water blue.

3. Put a pond snail into the plastic bag. Seal the bag with a twist tie and put it in a place where it will remain undisturbed for 20 minutes.

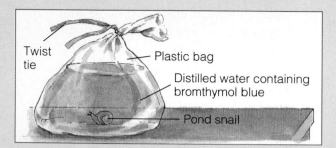

Twist tie
Plastic bag
Distilled water containing bromthymol blue
Pond snail

4. After 20 minutes, observe the color of the water. Bromthymol blue solution will turn yellow in the presence of carbon dioxide.

5. Unseal the plastic bag and add an *Elodea* sprig. Reseal the plastic bag and place it in an area that receives light (not direct sunlight) for 20 minutes.

Elodea sprig
Plastic bag
Distilled water containing bromthymol blue
Twist tie
Pond snail
Elodea sprig

6. After 20 minutes, observe any changes in the color of the water.

What Did You See?

1. What was the color of the water containing the pond snail after 20 minutes?

2. What was the color of the water containing the pond snail and *Elodea* sprig after 20 minutes?

What Did You Discover?

1. What happened to the carbon dioxide gas that was produced by the snail?

2. Do animals and plants need each other? Explain.

3. Many trees in the Amazon rain forest are being destroyed to clear the land for farming and ranching. Explain how the disappearance of the rain forest would affect the gases in the environment.

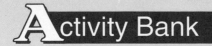

TO CLASSIFY OR NOT TO CLASSIFY?

Have you ever tried to organize the clothes in your room? If so, perhaps you put all your sweaters into one group, your socks into another group, and your jeans into still another group. In other words, you classified your clothes into specific groups based on their common characteristics. Why is it useful to classify objects? Try this activity and find out.

Part A. You will need 26 index cards and a pencil for this activity.

What Do You Need to Do?

1. Write each letter of the alphabet on an index card. Use only capital letters.

2. Choose any trait that will enable you to classify the letters. Arrange the letters in their appropriate groups.

3. After you have classified the letters according to one trait, choose another trait and again classify the letters into groups.

Index cards

What Did You Find Out?

1. What traits did you use to classify the letters of the alphabet?

2. How were the letters arranged in each group?

Part B. Now try your hand at classifying living things. You will need 20 photographs of plants for this activity.

What Do You Need to Do?

1. Collect 20 photographs of plants.

2. Classify the plants according to color.

3. Then classify the plants according to whether they live in water or on land.

4. Examine the photographs of the plants again. Determine whether another trait will help you classify the plants. Arrange the plants in their appropriate groups.

5. After you have classified the plants into their specific groups, name each group based on the trait that best describes it.

6. Give your photographs of the plants to a classmate and tell your classmate the names you have given each group. Have your classmate use your group names to classify the photographs. Then switch roles and try to do the same with your classmate's group names.

What Did You Find Out?

1. Is color a good way to classify plants? Explain your answer.

2. Is where a plant lives a good trait to use in classifying plants?

3. Did you and your classmate match each other's photographs with the appropriate group names?

4. Did either of you have any difficulty in doing so? If either of you did, what changes could be made in order to match the group name with the appropriate photograph?

5. Can you think of other traits that may be better for classifying plants?

6. Why do you think it is helpful to classify objects?

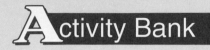
MOVING AT A SNAIL'S PACE

After insects, mollusks are the most varied group of animals on the Earth. Most mollusks have bodies that are covered by a shell. This activity will help you become more familiar with one small member of this group—a pond snail.

Materials

large dish	forceps
pond water	paper towel
pond snail	microscope slide
scissors	clock with second
metric ruler	indicator
lettuce and	2 cm x 6 cm piece
spinach leaves	of sandpaper

Procedure 🧪 🐌

1. Half fill the large dish with pond water and place the pond snail in the dish.

2. With the scissors, cut a 1-cm^2 section from the lettuce leaf and from the spinach leaf. Put the leaf squares in the dish with the pond snail.

3. Place the dish containing the pond snail and leaf squares in a place where they will remain undisturbed for 24 hours.

4. After 24 hours, remove the leaf squares from the dish and place them on the paper towel to remove excess water. Note how much of each square has been eaten.

5. Arrange the microscope slide in the dish so that the slide leans at a 45° angle against the side of the dish.

6. Place the snail at the top of the slide.

7. Measure the time it takes the snail to travel down and then up the microscope slide. Record the time for each.

8. Cover the microscope slide with the piece of sandpaper and repeat steps 5 through 7.

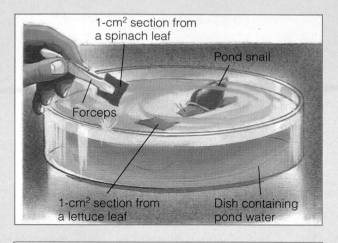

1-cm^2 section from a spinach leaf
Pond snail
Forceps
1-cm^2 section from a lettuce leaf
Dish containing pond water

Spinach leaf section
Pond snail
Forceps
Dish containing pond water
Lettuce leaf section
Paper towel

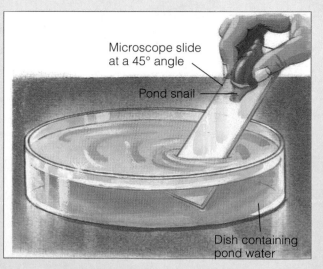

Microscope slide at a 45° angle
Pond snail
Dish containing pond water

Observations

1. How much of each food was eaten? Is the snail a carnivore or a herbivore?

2. How long did it take the pond snail to travel down the microscope slide? To travel up the slide?

3. How long did it take the pond snail to travel down the microscope slide covered with sandpaper? To travel up the slide?

Analysis and Conclusions

1. What is the pond snail's favorite food? How were you able to determine this?

2. Do snails travel up and down at the same rate? If not, what do you think accounts for the difference?

3. Share your results with your classmates. Were the results similar? Were they different? If they were different, explain why.

4. How does the texture of a surface affect the pond snail's speed?

Going Further

You may wish to repeat steps 5 through 7 in the activity using other materials to cover the microscope slide. Determine how fast the snail can travel over the surfaces of these materials.

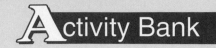

OFF AND RUNNING

Sow bugs are also called pill bugs because when disturbed they curl up into a tight, round pill shape. Pill bugs, which are really crustaceans and not insects, hibernate in the winter. However, they can be found under rocks or under piles of dead leaves close to the foundation of a house. To find out more about pill bugs, hold a pill bug derby. All you will need is a pencil, a sheet of unlined white paper, a pill bug, a clock with a second indicator, and a metric ruler.

What Do You Need to Do?

Have each member of the class use a pencil to mark an X in the middle of a sheet of unlined white paper. One member of your class should act as the official timer. When the timer shouts "Go!" each person should place their pill bug on the X and let it go. The timer should clock one minute while you track your racer with a pencil line. When the minute is up, measure the distance of your racer's trail. The pill bug that travels the farthest is the winner. On your mark, get ready, go!

What Did You Discover?

1. How many legs do pill bugs have?
2. Describe the other characteristics of pill bugs.
3. Based on the above information, to what group of animals do pill bugs belong?
4. Share with your classmates the distance your pill bug traveled. What was the greatest distance a pill bug traveled? The least distance?

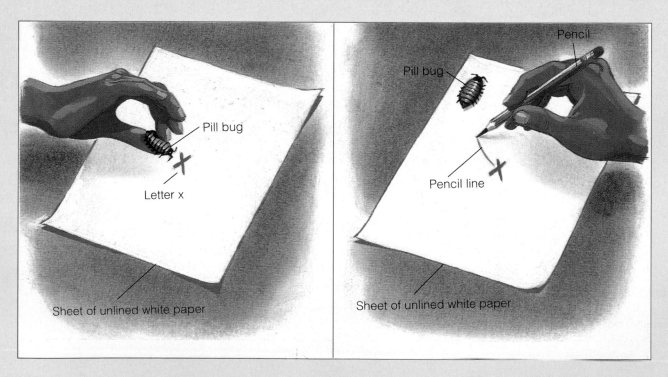

Pill bug

Letter x

Sheet of unlined white paper

Pencil

Pill bug

Pencil line

Sheet of unlined white paper

SPINNING WEBS

Do all spiders produce silk? Yes, they do. Some spiders, however, do not use the silk to build webs. Those spiders that do use silk to build webs weave intricate patterns. To see how a spider goes about spinning its web, or nest, perform this activity.

What You Will Need

wire coat hanger
wood block (10 cm x 40 cm x 1 cm)
large, clear plastic bag with twist tie
black-and-yellow garden spider

What You Will Do

1. Remove the hooked part of a wire coat hanger by bending it back and forth a few times.

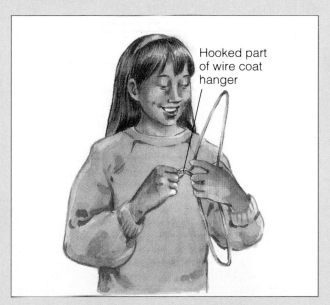

2. Bend the coat hanger into the shape of a square. Then insert the hanger, sharp side down, into a wood block so that it is supported by the wood block as shown in the drawing. This is called a net frame.

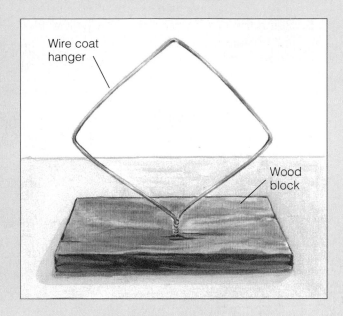

3. Blow up a large plastic bag and put the net frame inside.

4. Quickly place a black-and-yellow garden spider on the wood block and seal the plastic bag with the twist tie.

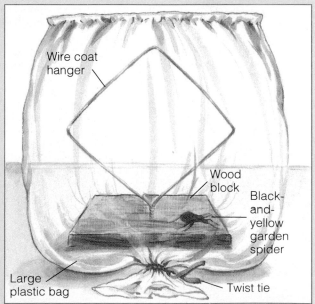

(continued)

5. Place the net frame in a place where it will remain undisturbed for two days. Record your daily observations in a data table similar to the one shown.

What You Will See

DATA TABLE

Day	Observations
1	
2	

What You Will Discover

1. Did your spider weave a web?
2. What time of day did your spider start to weave its web?
3. Did your spider build just one web?
4. Did your spider rebuild its web or did it build a new web?
5. If your spider built a new web, how often did it do so?
6. Share your results with your classmates. Were their results similiar? Different? Can you explain why?

Going Further

Release flying insects such as fruit flies and regular flies into the plastic bag with your spider. What happens to the insects? How does your spider react?

TO FLOAT OR NOT TO FLOAT?

How are most fishes able to swim at various depths in water? Bony fishes can raise or lower themselves in the water by adding gases to or removing them from their swim bladders. A swim bladder is a gas-filled chamber that adjusts the buoyancy of the fish to the water pressure at various depths. Water pressure is the force that water exerts over a certain area due to its weight and motion. To see firsthand how a swim bladder works, try this activity.

Materials

medicine dropper
2-L clear plastic soft drink bottle with cap

Procedure

1. Select one member of your group to act as the Principal Investigator and another to act as the Recorder. The other members of the group will be the Observers.

2. Fill the plastic soft drink bottle to the very top with water.

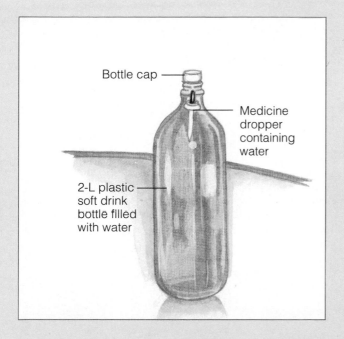

Bottle cap

Medicine dropper containing water

2-L plastic soft drink bottle filled with water

3. Place the medicine dropper in the bottle of water. The water should overflow. You may have to draw in or squeeze out more water from the medicine dropper so that it barely floats.

4. Screw the cap tightly on the plastic bottle. No water or air should leak out when the bottle is squeezed.

Squeezing the Bottle

Releasing the Bottle

5. Squeeze the sides of the bottle. Notice what happens.

6. Release the sides of the bottle. Notice what happens.

7. Have the Investigator and the Recorder reverse roles and repeat steps 5 and 6.

(continued)

Observations

1. What happens to the medicine dropper when the sides of the bottle are squeezed?

2. What happens to the medicine dropper when the sides of the bottle are released?

Analysis and Conclusions

1. What happens to the pressure of the water when you squeeze the sides of the plastic bottle?

2. Why is some of the water pushed up into the medicine dropper when you squeeze the bottle?

3. Why does the medicine dropper sink when you squeeze the sides of the bottle?

4. Why does the medicine dropper rise when you release the sides of the plastic bottle?

5. Two fishes are very similar in size to each other. However, one has more mass than the other. Which fish has more buoyancy?

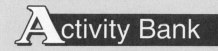
DO OIL AND WATER MIX?

An oil spill is an environmental disaster. Not only can an oil spill be fatal to ocean life but it can also endanger sea birds by damaging their feathers. To find out the effect of water and oil on the feathers of birds, try this activity.

Materials

hand lens
natural bird feather
small container of water
medicine dropper
small container of cooking oil

Procedure 🔬

1. Select one member of your group to be the Principal Investigator and another member to act as the Timer. The remaining members of the group will be the Observers.

2. With the hand lens, examine a natural bird feather.

3. Dip the feather into water for 1 minute. Take the feather out of the water and examine it with the hand lens.

4. Dip the feather into the cooking oil for 1 minute. Take it out and examine it with the hand lens.

5. Now dip the oil-covered feather back into the water for 1 minute. Take it out and examine it with the hand lens.

Observations

Describe the appearance of the feather in steps 2 through 5.

Analysis and Conclusions

1. What are the major changes in the feather after being placed in water? After being placed in oil?

2. What happened to the oil-covered feather when it was dipped in water?

3. How does exposure to oil affect normal bird activities?

4. What are some other examples of human-caused pollutants that can have harmful effects on wildlife?

Hand lens

Natural bird feather

Natural bird feather

Hand lens

AN EGGS-AGGERATION

Can you remove the shell from a hard-boiled egg without cracking it? The shell of an egg is made of a substance called calcium carbonate. Calcium carbonate will dissolve in vinegar (acetic acid) to form a solution. Why not try your hand at this activity and see if you can remove the shell without cracking it. You will need a cold hard-boiled egg, a wide-mouthed jar, some vinegar, safety goggles, and tongs.

What You Will Do

1. Place a cold hard-boiled egg in a wide-mouthed jar.

2. Add enough vinegar to cover the egg.

3. Put the jar in a place where it will remain undisturbed overnight.

4. The next morning remove the egg with tongs. Observe the egg.

What You Will See

Describe what happened to the egg.

What You Will Discover

1. What happened to the shell? Did it disappear completely?

2. What do you think happened to the shell?

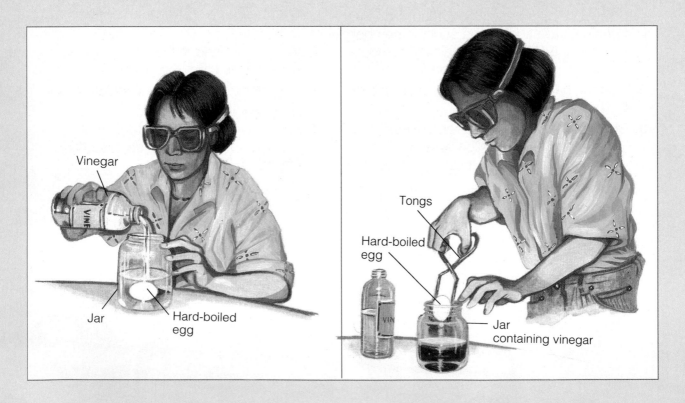

Vinegar

Jar

Hard-boiled egg

Tongs

Hard-boiled egg

Jar containing vinegar

A HUMAN CELL VS. AN AMEBA

What do you and a single-celled ameba have in common? Perhaps, you may think nothing. But if you were to look a little closer, you would see that you and an ameba have a lot more in common than you thought. Why not try this activity and find out for yourself.

Materials

flat toothpick
2 microscope slides
2 medicine droppers
2 coverslips

methylene blue
paper towel
microscope
ameba culture
pencil

Procedure 🧪 🧰

1. Put a drop of water in the center of a microscope slide.

2. Using the end of the toothpick, gently scrape the inside of your cheek. Even though you cannot see them, there will be cheek cells sticking to the toothpick.

3. Stir the scrapings into the drop of water on the slide.

4. To make a wet-mount slide, use the tip of the pencil to gently lower the coverslip over the cheek cells.

5. With a medicine dropper, put one drop of methylene blue at the edge of the coverslip. **CAUTION:** *Be careful when using methylene blue because it may stain the skin and clothing.*

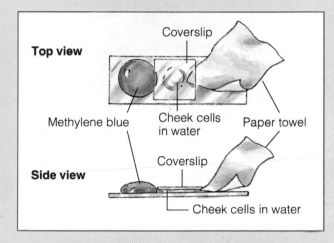

6. Place a small piece of paper towel near the edge of the coverslip and allow the paper towel to absorb the excess methylene blue.

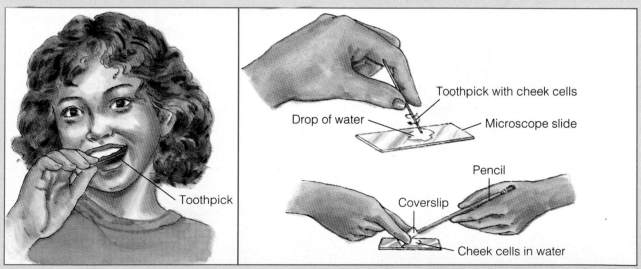

(continued)

7. With a medicine dropper, have your partner place a drop of the ameba culture on the other microscope slide.

8. Your partner should make a wet-mount slide of the ameba culture.

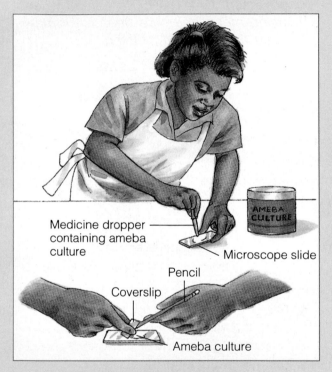

Medicine dropper containing ameba culture

Microscope slide

Pencil

Coverslip

Ameba culture

9. To remove any excess liquid, your partner should repeat step 6.

10. Place the slide of your cheek cells on the stage of the microscope and locate a cheek cell under low power. Then switch to the high-power objective lens.

11. Observe a cheek cell and sketch what you see. Label the cell parts that you see.

12. Have your partner repeat steps 10 and 11 using the slide of the ameba culture.

13. Reverse roles with your partner and repeat steps 1 through 12.

14. Construct a data table similar to the one shown here. If the cheek cell or the ameba contains any of the structures listed in the data table, write the word *present* in the appropriate place. If the cheek cell or the ameba does not have the structure, write the word *absent*.

Observations

DATA TABLE

Cell	Cell Membrane	Nucleus	Other
Human cheek			
Ameba			

Analysis and Conclusions

1. How are a human cheek cell and an ameba similar?

2. How are they different?

3. How many cells are you made of? An ameba?

4. Share your results with those of your classmates. Did the findings of any of your classmates differ from yours? Can you explain why there was a difference?

UNDER TENSION

Muscles are the only body tissues that are able to contract, or tighten up. You coordinate the movements of muscles without thinking by relaxing one muscle while you tighten another. Some movements, such as holding your hand out in front of you, are so slight that they go unnoticed. However, you can make these movements visible by doing this activity. All you will need is a table knife and a hairpin.

What You Will Do

1. Have your partner hold the knife out in front of him or her parallel to the top of a table or level desk. **Note:** *Your partner should not touch the table with his or her hand or arm.*

2. Place the hairpin on the knife as shown in the diagram.

Table knife

Desk

Hairpin

3. Have your partner raise the knife just high enough off the table for the "legs" of the hairpin to touch the table and the "head" of the hairpin to rest on the edge of the knife.

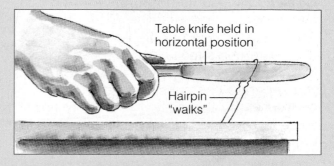

Table knife held in horizontal position

Hairpin "walks"

4. Have your partner hold the knife as steady as he or she can for 20 seconds. Observe what happens to the hairpin.

5. Repeat step 4, having your partner tighten his or her hold on the knife. Observe what happens.

6. Reverse roles with your partner and repeat steps 1 through 5. Share your results with your classmates.

What You Will Discover

1. What happened to the hairpin in step 4? What does this action show?

2. What happened to the hairpin when the hold on it was tightened? How do you explain this action?

3. Did your classmates have similar results?

Going Further

Repeat the activity but this time increase the time given in steps 4 and 5 to 1 minute. Observe what happens to the hairpin. How can you relate this activity to what happens when you have to stand in the same place for a long time?

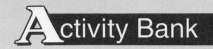
GETTING THE IRON OUT

Have you ever read the list of ingredients on the side panel of your box of breakfast cereal? Perhaps you should. The list of ingredients contains some important information about the nutrients your body needs. Nutrients include carbohydrates, proteins, fats, minerals, and vitamins. Sometimes nutrients are added to breakfast cereals, forming mixtures (combinations of substances that are not chemically combined). How can you separate one substance from another in a mixture? Try this activity to find out how you can separate the mineral iron from a breakfast cereal.

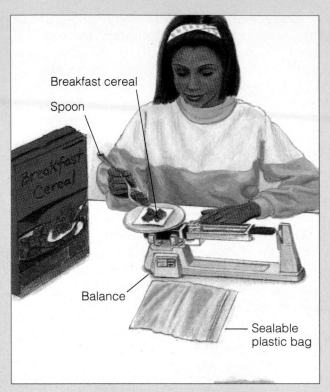

Materials

balance
breakfast cereal with 100 percent of the
    recommended Daily Value for iron
sealable plastic bag
large plastic container
bar magnet
clock or timer
white tissue paper
hand lens
spoon

Procedure

1. Measure out 50 g of a breakfast cereal. Place the cereal into a sealable plastic bag, pressing down on it to remove most of the air inside. **CAUTION:** *Do not eat any foods or drink any liquids during this activity.*

2. With your hands, crush the cereal into a fine powder and pour it into the plastic container. Add enough water to completely cover the cereal.

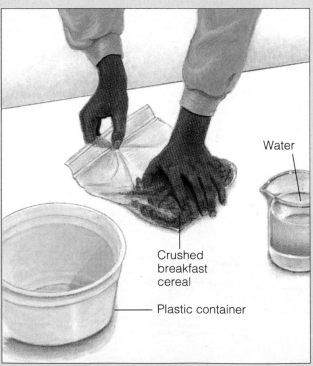

3. Use a bar magnet to stir the cereal-and-water mixture for at least 10 minutes.

Bar magnet

Plastic container

Cereal-and-water mixture

4. Remove the bar magnet from the mixture. Allow any liquid on the magnet to drain off.

5. Use a piece of tissue paper to scrape off any particles that are attached to the bar magnet. Observe the particles with a hand lens.

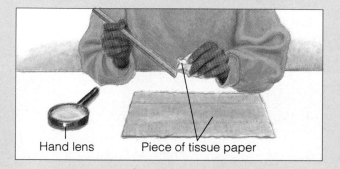

Hand lens

Piece of tissue paper

Observations

What did you observe when you looked at the particles scraped from the sides of the bar magnet?

Analysis and Conclusions

1. How do you know that the breakfast cereal is a mixture?

2. What do you think the particles scraped from the bar magnet are?

3. Why do you think it was possible to separate the particles from the rest of the cereal?

4. Do you think the cereal is a mixture made up of different materials unevenly spread out or a mixture of materials uniformly spread out? Explain.

Going Further

Repeat the procedure with 50 g of another cereal that contains less than 100 percent of the Daily Value for iron. Can you separate the iron from this cereal?

YOU'VE GOT TO HAVE HEART

Just as the mechanical pump in the water system in your home provides a constant pressure to force fluids along the pipes when you open the tap, so too does your heart provide pumping pressure. The job of any pump is to produce pressure and move a certain amount of fluid in a specific direction at an acceptable speed. Fluids, like blood, travel from an area of high pressure to an area of lower pressure.

Try to simulate the pumping action of your heart by doing this activity. You will need two plastic bottles of the same size, two one-hole rubber stoppers, and two 15-cm plastic tubes.

What You Will Do

1. Fill the two plastic bottles with water.
2. Insert the plastic tubes into the one-hole rubber stoppers. Then insert the rubber stoppers containing the plastic tubes into each bottle.
3. Have your partner squeeze one bottle with one hand, while you squeeze the other bottle with two hands. Observe what happens.

Squeezing plastic bottle with one hand

Squeezing plastic bottle with two hands

What You Will Discover

1. Which action squirted water further? Explain.
2. Which action better simulated the pumping action of the heart?
3. What general statement can you make about pressure and the distance water travels?
4. When blood is pumped out of the heart, where does it go?
5. How do your results and your partner's results compare with the class's results? Are they similar? Are they different? Explain why.

Plastic bottle   Water

Plastic tube

One-hole rubber stopper

Plastic bottle filled with water

THE SQUEEZE IS ON

If you could look inside an artery and a vein, you would discover that the wall of the artery is thicker and more muscular than the wall of the vein. Might this characteristic make the blood pressure in arteries higher than the blood pressure in veins? Let's see.

What Do You Need?

plastic squeeze bottle

15-cm plastic tube

two-hole rubber stopper

15-cm glass tube

2 large desk blotters

meterstick

scissors

transparent tape

What Do You Do?

1. Fill a plastic squeeze bottle with water.

2. Place a plastic tube into one of the holes in a two-hole rubber stopper. Place a glass tube of the same length into the second hole of the stopper.

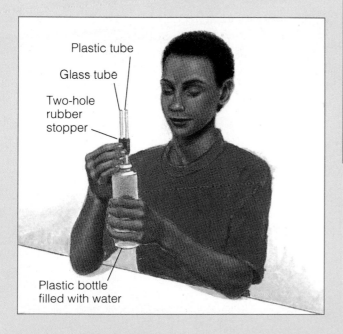

Plastic tube

Glass tube

Two-hole rubber stopper

Plastic bottle filled with water

3. Insert the rubber stopper into the plastic bottle.

4. Cut two large desk blotters into 30-cm strips. Tape several strips together to form three 120-cm strips.

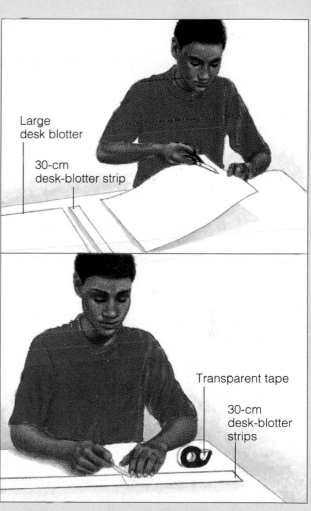

Large desk blotter

30-cm desk-blotter strip

Transparent tape

30-cm desk-blotter strips

5. Place one of the blotter strips on the floor. Kneel on the floor with your knees touching one end of the blotter strip.

6. Hold the plastic bottle so that the glass tube is on the left and the plastic tube is on the right. Firmly squeeze the plastic bottle once.

(continued)

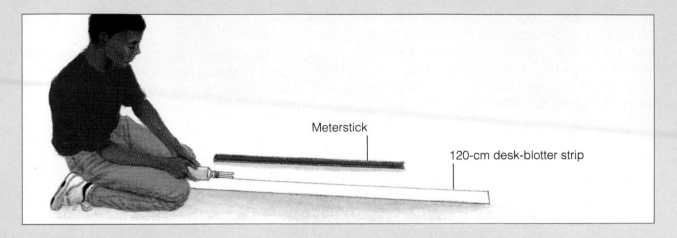

Meterstick

120-cm desk-blotter strip

7. With a meterstick, measure the distance from the edge of the blotter to where the wet spot for each tube first appears on the blotter. This is the distance water travels from each tube. Record this information in a data table similar to the one shown.

8. Repeat steps 5 through 7 two more times using the remaining blotter strips.

9. Calculate the average distance the water travels from each tube. Record the average distance for each tube.

What Did You See?

Which tube squirted water further?

DATA TABLE

Trial	Distance Water Traveled (cm)	
	Glass Tube	Plastic Tube
1		
2		
3		
Average		

What Did You Discover?

1. Which tube represents an artery? A vein?

2. What does the water in the tubes represent?

3. What does this activity tell you about blood pressure in arteries and veins?

4. What is the name of the body structure that forces the blood through the blood vessels?

5. How do your results compare with those of your classmates? If there were any differences, can you explain why?

HOW FAST DO YOUR NAILS GROW?

Your nails are rough and are made of a protein called keratin that gives them their characteristic strength. The visible part of the nail is called the body, or nail plate. It grows out of the root, which is hidden beneath the nail at its base. Also at the base, there is a whitish half-moon shape called the lunula (lunula is Latin for little moon). The area under the nail is called the nail bed. To find out how long it takes for your nail to grow from its base to its top, try this activity.

What You Will Need

thin paintbrush
acrylic paint
metric ruler

What You Will Do

1. Using a thin paintbrush, place a tiny dot of acrylic paint above the cuticle (area of hardened skin) at the base of one of your fingernails and one of your toenails. Let the paint dry. Allow the acrylic paint to remain there undisturbed for three weeks.

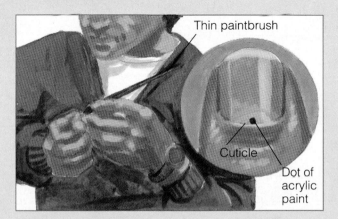

Thin paintbrush

Cuticle

Dot of acrylic paint

2. Observe the acrylic-paint dots each day. If they begin to wear away, put another dot of paint on. Be sure to place the new acrylic-paint dot exactly on top of the old acrylic-paint dot.

3. At the end of each week, use a metric ruler to measure the distance from the cuticle to the acrylic-paint dot on each nail. Record this measurement in a data table similar to the one shown. Continue to do this until the dot grows to the point that you cut it off when you clip your nails.

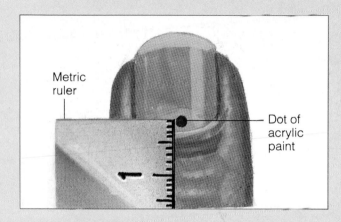

Metric ruler

Dot of acrylic paint

What Did You Find Out?

DATA TABLE

Day	Distance From Cuticle	
	Fingernail	**Toenail**
1		

1. What was the average weekly growth of your fingernail? Your toenail?

2. Which nail grew faster—fingernail or toenail? Suggest a possible explanation for your observation.

3. Compare your results with those of your classmates.

4. What functions do your nails serve?

A GENTLE TOUCH

If a large insect crawls on you, you can usually tell where it is, even with your eyes closed. The reason is that whenever something touches you, or you touch something, your sense of touch goes into action. To discover the remarkable things your sense of touch is capable of, try this activity.

Things You Will Need

nickel
dime
penny
quarter

small shoe box
   with cover
blindfold

Directions

1. Place the nickel, dime, penny, and quarter in the shoe box and cover the box.

2. Blindfold your partner and have your partner reach into the shoe box and remove one coin.

3. Have your partner identify the coin by holding it in his or her hand and touching it.

4. After your partner has identified the coin, have your partner remove the blindfold to see if he or she was correct.

5. Repeat steps 2 through 4 three more times. Record your observations in a data table similar to the one shown on the next page.

6. Remove the coins from the shoe box and set them flat on a table.

Tip of index finger

7. Put the blindfold on your partner again and this time have your partner touch the top of each coin with only the tip of his or her index finger. **Note:** *Do not allow your partner to pick up the coins.*

8. Have your partner identify each coin.

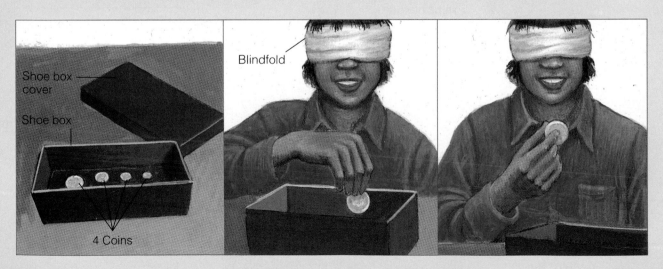

Shoe box cover

Shoe box

4 Coins

Blindfold

9. Repeat steps 7 and 8 three more times. Record your observations in your data table.

10. Reverse roles with your partner and repeat steps 1 through 9.

Things to Look For

DATA TABLE

Trial	Holding Coin in Hand		Touching Coin With Fingertip	
	What I Think Coin Is	What Coin Actually Is	What I Think Coin Is	What Coin Actually Is
1				
2				
3				
4				

Conclusions to Draw

1. Was it easier to identify the coins by picking them up and touching them or by touching their tops with your index finger? Give a reason for your answer.

2. In which case were you actually using only touch receptors to identify the coins?

3. In addition to touch receptors, what other receptors might you be using?

4. Compare your results with those of your classmates.

IT'S NO SKIN OFF YOUR NOSE

The skin is the body's largest organ. Its tough outer covering protects the body from invading microorganisms. As long as the skin remains uninjured, the invading microorganisms are kept outside the body. But what happens when the skin is injured? Find out by doing this activity.

Materials

4 sheets of
   unlined white
   paper
pencil
soap

4 apples
straight pin
cotton swab
rubbing alcohol

Procedure 🧰

1. Place four sheets of paper on a flat surface. Label the papers A, B, C, and D. Carefully wash your hands with soap and water. Dry them thoroughly.

2. Wash four apples and place one apple on each sheet of paper. Do not touch apple D for the remainder of this activity.

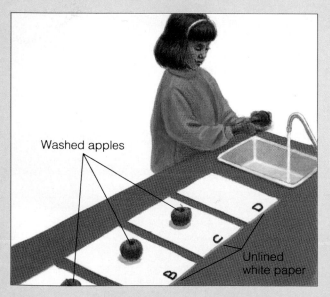

Washed apples

Unlined white paper

3. Using a straight pin, puncture four holes in apple B and four holes in apple C.

Washed apple with pinholes

Washed apple

Washed apple

4. Have your partner who has not washed his or her hands hold and rub apple A, apple B, and apple C.

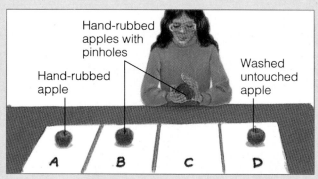

Hand-rubbed apples with pinholes

Hand-rubbed apple

Washed untouched apple

5. Dip a cotton swab in rubbing alcohol. Thoroughly swab each of the holes and their surrounding area in Apple B.

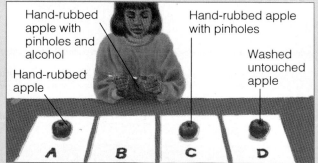

Hand-rubbed apple with pinholes and alcohol

Hand-rubbed apple with pinholes

Hand-rubbed apple

Washed untouched apple

6. Place the four apples in an area where they will remain undisturbed for one week. Examine each apple every day. **Note:** *Do not touch the apples while examining them.* Arrange your observations in a data table similar to the one shown.

7. After one week, compare the apples.

8. Share your results with the class.

Observations

DATA TABLE

Day	Observations
1	
2	
3	

Analysis and Conclusions

1. How did the apples compare?

2. What was the purpose of apple D?

3. What is the relationship between the apples and your skin?

4. How did your results compare with those of your classmates? Were they similar? Different? Explain any differences.

TULIPS ARE BETTER THAN ONE

Gregor Mendel was able to cross pea plants with different traits through the process of cross-pollination. In cross-pollination, pollen from the stamen of one flower is transferred to the pistil of another flower. In addition to stamens and pistils, what are the other parts of a flower? This activity will help you to find out. You will need a tulip flower and a hand lens. Now follow these steps.

1. Compare your tulip flower with the drawing of a typical flower shown here.

2. Identify the sepals on the underside of the flower. Record their number, color, and shape. Break off a sepal and examine it with a hand lens.

3. Examine the flower's petals, the colored parts just above the sepals. Record their number, color, and shape. Remove a petal and examine it with a hand lens. Does your flower petal have a fragrance?

4. Identify the stamens. Record their number, color, and shape. Remove a stamen and examine it with a hand lens. Identify the filament, which is the stalklike structure, and the anther, the structure at the tip of the filament. Where is the pollen located? Shake some pollen onto a sheet of paper and examine the pollen with a hand lens. Draw what you see.

5. Locate the pistil at the center of the flower. Refer to the drawing of a typical flower to help you identify the stigma, style, and ovary. Where do the seeds develop?

Do It Yourself

Did you know that some plants have both male and female flowers? The male flowers contain only stamens and the female flowers contain only pistils. Go to the library and find out the names of several plants that have male and female flowers. If possible, obtain a specimen of such a flower and show it to the class.

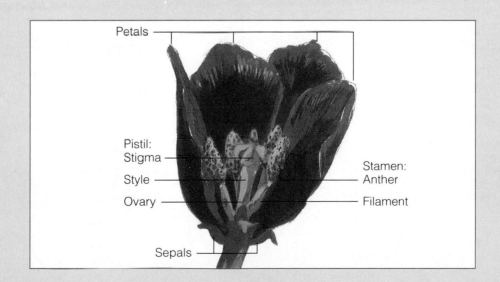

FLIP OUT!

Like Gregor Mendel, geneticists use the laws of probability to predict the results of genetic crosses. Do you ever use probability in your daily life?

Imagine that your school soccer team is about to play its first home game. The stands are filled to capacity. As team captain, you are about to take part in the coin toss. Nervously, you watch as the referee flips the coin into the air. "Heads!" you shout. Did you win the toss?

Probability is the likelihood that a coin will come up heads or tails on any one toss. What is the likelihood that the coin would land heads up and you would win the toss? You can perform a simple activity to find out. All you need is a coin.

First answer these questions. What are the possible ways the coin could have landed after it was tossed? What are the

chances that the coin would have landed heads up? Tails up?

Suppose you were to toss a coin 20 times. How many times do you predict the coin would land heads up? Tails up? What percentage of the time do you predict the coin would land heads up? Tails up?

Now test your predictions. Flip the coin 20 times. Record the number of times it lands heads up and the number of times it lands tails up. Find the percentages by dividing the number of times the coin landed heads up or tails up by 20 and then multiplying by 100. What percentage of the time did the coin land heads up? Tails up? Were your predictions correct? Explain.

Combine the results of the coin toss for the entire class. Are the combined results closer to your predictions? Explain.

A MODEL OF MEIOSIS

Meiosis is the process in which an organism's sex cells are produced. The process of meiosis ensures that each sex cell has half the normal number of chromosomes for that particular organism. In this activity you will construct a model of meiosis for an organism with four chromosomes in its body cells.

Materials

3 sheets of paper
drawing compass
4 red pipe cleaners
4 white pipe cleaners

Procedure

1. On a sheet of paper, draw a circle about 15 cm in diameter. This circle represents a parent cell about to undergo meiosis.

2. Arrange four pipe cleaners, two white and two red, randomly inside the circle. The pipe cleaners represent two pairs of chromosomes.

Pipe — cleaner

3. Place another white pipe cleaner next to each of the white "chromosomes." Place another red pipe cleaner next to each red "chromosome." These pipe cleaners represent the doubled chromosomes in the first step of meiosis.

4. Draw two circles side by side on a second sheet of paper. These circles represent the two new cells produced during the first cell division of meiosis. Divide the doubled "chromosomes" equally between the two new cells. How many white "chromosomes" are present in each new cell? How many red?

5. Draw four circles side by side on a third sheet of paper. These circles represent the sex cells that are the product of the second cell division of meiosis. Divide the pipe cleaners equally to represent the "chromosomes" present in the sex cells. How many white "chromosomes" are there in each sex cell? How many red?

Think for Yourself

1. Why is it important that each sex cell have only half the normal number of chromosomes found in body cells?

2. The process of meiosis is sometimes called reduction division. Do you think this term accurately describes the process? Why or why not?

Going Further

Make a model of meiosis for an organism with six chromosomes. How many more pipe cleaners will you need? Will you need to use a third color in addition to white and red? Why or why not?

STALKING THE WILD FRUIT FLY

Ever since the days of Thomas Hunt Morgan, fruit flies have been used for genetic experiments. These tiny flies are commonly seen on and around displays of fresh (and overripe) fruits and vegetables. In this activity you will collect fruit flies and observe the stages in their life cycle.

Materials

paper towel	ripe banana
2 glass jars, 1	cotton
with cover	hand lens

Procedure

1. Place a small piece of paper towel on the bottom of each jar.

2. Put a piece of ripe banana on the paper towel in each jar. Cover one jar tightly. Leave the second jar open.

3. Place both jars outdoors where they will not be disturbed for 24 hours.

4. After 24 hours observe the jars. Were fruit flies present in either jar? If so, which one?

5. Plug the mouth of the open jar with cotton. Use the hand lens to observe the adult fruit flies in the plugged jar. Can you see a difference between male and female fruit flies? Describe any differences you see.

6. Look for eggs that may have been deposited on the bottom of the jar. Describe the color and size of the eggs.

7. A few days after the eggs appear, look for tiny wiggly "worms" to emerge. These are fruit fly larvae, the second stage in their life cycle.

8. After a few days, watch for the larvae to crawl onto the paper and enter the pupa stage. The adult fruit flies will emerge from the pupae. How long did it take for the fruit flies to develop from eggs to adults?

Analysis and Conclusions

1. Describe the life cycle of fruit flies from egg to adult.

2. According to the old theory of spontaneous generation, fruit flies developed from rotting fruit. How does this activity disprove the theory of spontaneous generation?

HOW CAN YOU GROW A PLANT FROM A CUTTING?

Once plant breeders have developed plants with desirable traits, it is important that they be able to produce more of the plants. One way they do this is to take a cutting from the original plant and let the cutting grow into a new plant. The new plant will be identical to the parent plant. Like plant breeders, you too can grow a plant from a cutting.

Materials

houseplant	knife
small pot	pencil
peat moss	plastic bag
coarse sand	rubber band

Procedure 🔪

1. Mix equal amounts of peat moss and coarse sand. Fill a small pot with this mixture to just below the rim of the pot.

2. Using a sharp knife, cut off the top 7 to 10 cm of the stem or side shoot of a houseplant. **CAUTION:** *Be careful when using a knife or other sharp instrument.*

3. Pull off the lower leaves and make a clean cut across the stem just below a leaf node.

4. With a pencil, make a hole about 3 cm deep in the potting mixture. Make the hole near the edge of the pot.

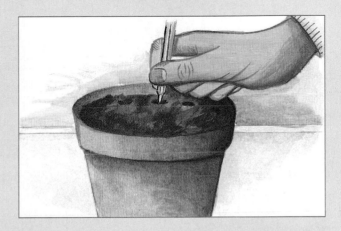

5. Insert the cutting so that the stem is supported by the edge of the pot. Gently firm the mixture around the cutting. **Note:** *You may want to make holes for several cuttings in the same pot.*

6. Water the cuttings thoroughly and let the pot drain.

(continued)

7. Cover the pot with a plastic bag. Hold the bag in place with a rubber band.

them in individual pots. Water your new plants and watch them grow!

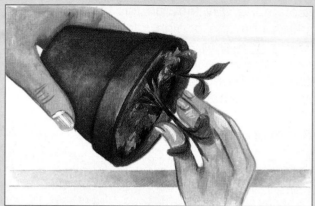

8. Put the pot in a warm, shaded spot. Keep the mixture moist.

9. After three to four weeks, you should see new growth at the tips of your cuttings. Remove the plastic bag and carefully tilt the pot to remove the cuttings. Separate the cuttings and plant

Do It Yourself

Growing a new plant from a cutting, as you did in this activity, is called vegetative propagation. Using reference materials, look up the meaning of this term. What are some other methods of vegetative propagation? Report on your findings to the class.

HOW DO BACTERIA GROW?

Bacteria are useful in genetic engineering because they reproduce quickly. Bacteria are single-celled organisms. They reproduce by splitting in two. This method of reproduction is called binary fission. ("Binary" means two and "fission" means to split.) In this activity you will observe how bacteria can be grown on agar, which is a substance made from seaweed.

Materials

2 sterile petri
   dishes with agar
glass-marking
   pencil

cotton swab
tape
hand lens

Procedure

1. Obtain two sterile petri dishes with agar. Why is it important that the petri dishes and agar be sterilized?

2. With a glass-marking pencil, label one petri dish A and the other dish B.

3. Draw a cotton swab across your desk, the back of your hand, a windowsill, or any other spot where you think bacteria might be present.

4. Raise one side of the lid of petri dish A. Move the cotton swab in a zigzag motion across the surface of the agar. Immediately close the lid of the petri dish. Why is it important that you raise only one side of the lid and then close it immediately?

5. Do not open petri dish B. Tape both petri dishes closed. What is the function of petri dish B?

6. Place both petri dishes in a warm, dark place where they will not be disturbed.

7. Observe each dish with a hand lens every day for four days. **CAUTION:** *Do not open the petri dishes.* Record your observations in a data table similar to the one shown here.

8. After four days, draw what you see in petri dish A and in petri dish B. In which petri dish did you see more bacteria growing?

Observations

DATA TABLE

Petri Dish	Day 1	Day 2	Day 3	Day 4
A				
B				

Analysis and Conclusions

1. Based on the results of this activity, what conditions are necessary for the growth of bacteria?

2. What are some things you could do to slow down the growth of bacteria?

3. Share your results with the class. In what locations were bacteria found to be present?

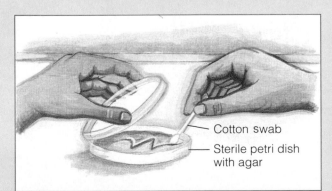

Cotton swab
Sterile petri dish with agar

SUB-ZERO

The freezing point of water is 0°C. This is the temperature at which liquid water freezes and becomes solid ice. In the presence of genetically engineered ice-minus bacteria, the freezing point of water can be lowered to -5°C. Is there any other way to lower the freezing point of water? Try this activity to find out.

Materials

ice cubes   plastic spoon
water   Celsius
Styrofoam™ cup   thermometer
salt

Procedure

1. Put some ice cubes into a Styrofoam™ cup and fill the cup with water.
2. Place a Celsius thermometer in the ice-water mixture. Wait a few minutes and

then read the temperature on the thermometer. What is the temperature of the ice-water mixture?

3. Remove the thermometer. Add one or two spoonfuls of salt to the ice-water mixture and stir to dissolve. Replace the thermometer.

4. Wait a few minutes and then read the temperature. What is the temperature of the ice-water mixture plus the dissolved salt? What effect did adding salt to the mixture have on the temperature?

Think for Yourself

Based on your observations, why do you think people often sprinkle rock salt on icy sidewalks?

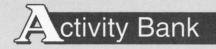

WHERE ARE THEY?

Natural selection is the survival and reproduction of those living things best adapted to their surroundings. To better understand how natural selection works, why not try this activity on camouflage, or the ability of living things to blend in with their background.

What Will You Need?

hole punch

colored construction paper (1 sheet of each of the following colors: black, blue, brown, green, orange, purple, red, white, yellow)

9 sealable plastic bags

80 cm × 80 cm piece of floral paper or cloth

transparent tape

What Will You Do?

1. Punch 10 dots of each color from the sheets of colored construction paper. Put the dots for each color in a different plastic bag.

2. Spread a piece of floral paper or cloth on a flat surface. Use transparent tape to attach each corner of the paper or cloth to the flat surface.

3. Choose one member of your group to be the recorder and another to be the predator. The other members of the group will be the prey.

4. Have the predator look away while the prey randomly spread the dots of each color over the paper.

Hole punch

Sealable plastic bags

Construction paper

Piece of floral paper

Transparent tape

(continued)

5. Have the predator turn back to the paper and immediately pick up the first dot he or she sees.

Spreading the Dots

Picking up the Dots

6. Repeat steps 4 and 5 until a total of 10 dots have been picked up. Make sure that the predator looks away before a selection is made each time.

7. In a data table similar to the one shown, have the recorder write the total number of dots selected by the predator next to the appropriate color.

8. Have the recorder and the predator reverse roles. Repeat steps 4 through 7.

9. On posterboard, construct a data table similar to yours. Have your classmates record their results in this data table.

What Will You See?

DATA TABLE

Color of Dots	Number of Dots Selected
Black	
Blue	
Brown	
Green	
Orange	
Purple	
Red	
White	
Yellow	

What Will You Discover?

1. Which colored dots were picked up from the floral background?

2. Which colored dots, if any, were not picked up? Explain.

3. How did your results compare with your classmates' results?

4. If the colored dots represent food to a predator, what is the advantage of camouflage?

5. If the colored dots (prey) were to pass through several generations, what trends in survival of prey would you observe?

VARIETY IS THE SPICE OF LIFE

The fossil record shows that living things have evolved, or changed over time. How do these changes produce complex living things from simple ones? How can one group of living things evolve into many different groups? How can you show these changes in the form of an evolutionary tree (diagram that shows the evolutionary relationships among different groups of living things)? To find out the answers to these questions, try this activity. You will need the following materials: sheets of construction paper (red, blue, green, and black), metric ruler, scissors, posterboard, glue, pencil, compass.

What You Will Do

1. With the scissors, cut out 12 4-cm squares from a sheet of green construction paper.

2. Cut out one 4-cm square from a sheet of black construction paper. Then cut the square in half diagonally so that you

Construction paper

have two black triangles. Put one triangle aside for now and discard the other.

3. Repeat step 2 using a sheet of red construction paper.

4. With a compass, draw a circle that has a diameter of 4 cm on a sheet of blue construction paper. Cut out the blue circle and put it aside for now.

5. Place the posterboard vertically on a flat surface. Draw a very faint line down the center of the posterboard.

6. Place one green square in the middle of the left side of the posterboard, about 5 cm from the bottom. Glue the green square in place.

7. Arrange 10 of the remaining green squares on the posterboard exactly as shown in the diagram on the left on the next page. You should have five rows of green squares: 1 square in the first row, 2 squares in the second and third rows, 3 squares in the fourth and fifth rows. Glue the squares in place.

8. Draw the arrows in as shown.

9. Go to the fifth row of green squares. Place the blue circle on top of the first green square so that it covers the square. Glue the blue circle in place.

10. On top of the middle green square in the fifth row, place the red triangle as shown in the diagram on the right on the next page. Glue the red triangle in place.

11. Above the third green square in the fifth row, place the last remaining green square so that you form a rectangle 8 cm × 4 cm. Then place the black triangle on top of the newly added fourth square. Glue the black triangle in place.

(continued)

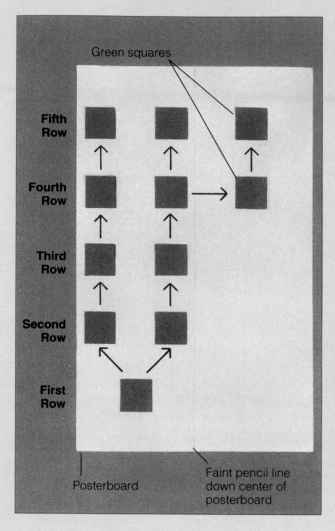

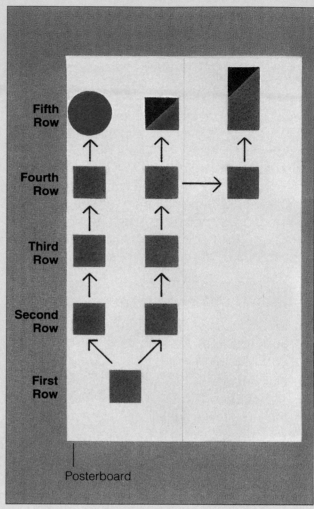

12. Observe the first row and the last row. Using the remaining sheets of colored construction paper, cut out the shapes that you think are needed to show the gradual change in shapes between the first row and the last row.

What You Will Discover

1. How does each row in your evolutionary tree compare with the row below it? With the row above it?

2. What relationship does this activity have with evolution?

3. Compare your evolutionary tree with those of your classmates. Are they the same? Are they different? Explain your answer.

Going Further

Replace the shapes in this activity with drawings of living things.

GARBAGE IN THE GARDEN

More and more people are starting to put garbage in their gardens. You might think this practice would endanger health, smell bad, and damage the garden. But if it is done properly, it is safe, free of unpleasant odors, and beneficial to plant growth. Thanks to the action of helpful bacteria (which are often assisted by burrowing creatures such as worms), the garbage breaks down to form a dark-colored, nutrient-rich substance called compost.

In this activity you will explore the process of making compost.

Materials

2-L clear plastic soda bottle	weeds and leaves
small nail or push pin	uncooked vegetables and fruit scraps
scissors	china marker
topsoil	cheesecloth
150 mL beaker	rubber band
scraps of paper	plastic fork
grass clippings	foam meat tray

Procedure

1. Carefully poke holes in the sides and bottom of the soda bottle with the nail. Use the accompanying diagram as a

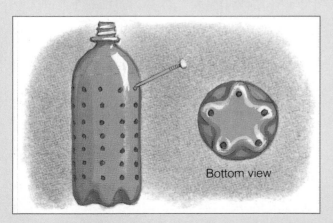

Bottom view

guide. **CAUTION:** *Be very careful and take your time.* Take turns making the holes—there are many to make.

2. Using the nail, poke a large hole near the top of the bottle at the point where the sides become vertical and the plastic thins out. Starting at this hole, carefully cut off the top of the bottle with the scissors. **CAUTION:** *Be careful when working with sharp objects.*

3. Label your bottle with the names of the people in your group and the date. Then put the bottle on the meat tray.

4. Fill the bottle about one-third full with grass clippings. Add 100 mL of soil, then 20 mL of water. The contents of the bottle should be moist but not soaking wet. If the contents are still dry, add a little more water.

5. With the scissors, cut the paper, leaves, weeds, and vegetable and fruit scraps into pieces no larger than 1 cm across. Fill the bottle about one-half full with the cut-up materials.

(continued)

6. Use the plastic fork to mix the contents of the bottle well. If any materials fall onto the meat tray, lift the bottle, remove the tray, and dump the tray's contents into the bottle. Then put the tray back under the bottle.

7. Make a mark on the outside of the bottle to indicate the height of the contents. Cover the bottle with a piece of cheesecloth. Secure the cheesecloth with the rubber band. Then place the bottle in a warm location.

8. Twice a week, observe the contents of the bottle. Touch the sides of the bottle and note whether the bottle feels warm or cool to the touch. **CAUTION:** *If the bottle feels hot, notify your teacher immediately.*

9. After you have made your observations, add some water if the contents are dry. Once a week, mix the contents with the fork and mark their height on the side of the bottle. Write the date next to the new mark. Make sure you replace the cheesecloth when you have finished making your observations. **Note:** *If the contents start to smell bad, like rotten eggs or vinegar, mix the contents every time you make your observations.*

Observations

1. How did the contents of the bottle change over time?

2. What kind of fruit and vegetable scraps did you add to the bottle? Which kinds of scraps decomposed the fastest? The slowest?

3. How did the level of the bottle's contents change over time?

4. How long did it take for the contents of the bottle to finish decomposing?

5. What does your "finished" compost look like?

Analysis and Conclusions

1. Why did the materials in the bottle change?

2. Why do you think you had to put holes in the bottle and cover the bottle with cheesecloth?

3. Some decomposer bacteria use oxygen, a substance that makes up about 21 percent of the air you breathe. Others do not use oxygen, but are not harmed by it. Still others are slowed down or even killed by oxygen. What can you infer about decomposer bacteria and making compost?

4. If the materials in a compost heap are not mixed regularly, it may start to smell bad. Explain why this might occur.

5. Predict what would have happened if the bottle and the materials in it had been sterilized. Would your results have been the same?

6. Compost improves the texture of garden soil, making it easier for plants to grow in it. It also acts like fertilizer. Explain why compost adds nutrients to the soil.

7. Landfills—commonly known as garbage dumps—are running out of space. In some parts of the country, little space is available for making new landfills. And people desperately need landfill space to dispose of garbage. How might making compost solve part of the landfill crisis?

8. Imagine that you and the members of your group have just been selected as part of a special task force. Your job is to devise a plan that will reduce by 90 percent the amount of yard waste that is ending up in the local landfill. Keep in mind the needs, attitudes, and abilities of the different kinds of people in your community as you work on the plan.

Going Further

Design an experiment to test how the formation of compost is affected by one of the following factors: light, heat, moisture, air.

A SAUCEPAN SIMULATION OF A CYCLE

The processes in the water cycle continuously move water between the Earth's surface and the atmosphere. In this activity you will observe the basic processes that form the water cycle: condensation, evaporation, and precipitation.

Materials

2 same-sized jars (such as those used for baby food), one of which has a lid

2 same-sized flat containers such as pie pans

measuring cup or 250-mL beaker

medium-sized saucepan (about 2.5 L, or 2 qt)

hot plate or stove

small saucepan with long heat-proof handle (about 1.5 L, or 1 qt)

ice

oven mitt or heat-proof glove

Procedure 🔥 👉

1. Measure 100 mL of water into each jar and each flat container. Securely cover the appropriate jar with its lid. Put the jars and one of the flat containers in a sunny place. Put the other flat container in a dark closet.

2. Let the jars and the containers stand for about a day, then examine them. Use the measuring cup to measure the amount of water in the jars and containers. Record your observations.

3. Fill the large saucepan about one-fourth full with water. Put the pan on the hot plate. Turn on the hot plate and bring the water in the pan to a boil. **CAUTION:** *Be careful when working with a heat source.* Record your observations.

4. Fill the small saucepan with ice cubes. Put on the oven mitt. Grasp the handle of the small saucepan with your covered hand. Hold the small saucepan so that the main part of the pan, but not the handle, is over the boiling water in the large saucepan. **CAUTION:** *Do not put your hand or any other part of your body directly above boiling water. Steam can cause bad burns.*

5. Watch what happens to the bottom of the small saucepan. Record your observations.

6. Turn off the hot plate and clean up after your equipment has cooled off.

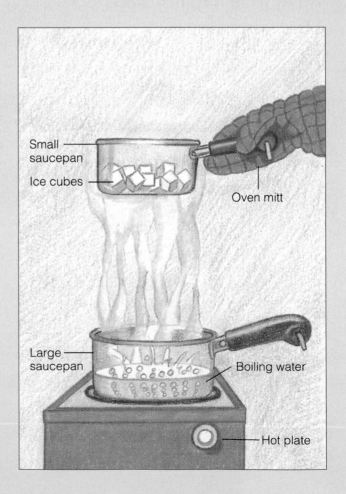

Small saucepan

Ice cubes

Oven mitt

Large saucepan

Boiling water

Hot plate

Observations

1. What happened to the water in the jars and flat containers?

2. Describe what you observed about the boiling water.

3. What happened to the bottom of the small saucepan?

Analysis and Conclusions

1. What water-cycle process caused the results in step 2?

2. Using the results from step 2, compare the amount of water in the two jars, in the two flat containers, and in the open jar and the flat container that were in the sunny place. What can you conclude about evaporation from these results?

3. Identify the water-cycle processes that you observed in step 5. Explain your answer.

4. Compare your results with those of your classmates. Are they similar or different? Explain why.

5. On a hot, sticky summer day, you notice water collecting on the outside of your glass of ice water. One of your friends says that the hot weather has caused the pores in the glass to open up so that the water leaks out. You suspect that the water got on the outside of the glass another way. What is your hypothesis? How might you go about testing your hypothesis?

6. Cold air can hold less water than warm air. The loss of enough heat energy causes water vapor to condense into liquid water. Use this information to explain the following events.

   a. Steam condenses on a pan that contains ice.

   b. Dew forms on grass during the night.

   c. Morning fog disappears as the day gets warmer.

   How do these events relate to the water cycle?

Activity Bank

GRANDEUR IN THE GRASS

The most noticeable grasslands animals are undoubtedly the large grass-eaters, such as the bison of the North American prairie, kangaroos of the Australian outback, zebras of the African savanna, saiga antelope of the Asian steppe, and rhea (an ostrichlike bird) of the South American pampas. However, grasslands teem with smaller, less noticeable organisms. Take a closer look at grasslands by doing this activity.

Materials

terrarium case or aquarium with a tightly-fitting fine screen cover

coarse gravel

activated charcoal

sand

potting soil

notebook and pencil

plastic bags and jars with covers for collecting organisms

plants and animals collected from a grassy field

Procedure

1. Put a layer of gravel 3 cm deep in the terrarium. Add some more gravel to the back of the terrarium to make one or two low hills. Sprinkle a little activated charcoal on the gravel.

2. Mix three parts of potting soil to one part of sand. Spread the sandy soil about 7 cm deep over the gravel, following the hills and valleys in the gravel.

3. Obtain the proper permission to collect organisms from a grassy field. Before you start collecting, look around. What kinds of plants do you see? What kinds of animals? Record your observations in your notebook in the form of drawings and written notes.

4. Collect grasses and a few other small plants from a grassy field. Be sure to include the roots and some of the soil around the roots. Put the plants in a plastic bag to protect them from drying out.

5. Catch a few small animals, such as insects, earthworms, and one or two spiders. Use the jars to hold your animals. **Note:** *Earthworms must be kept cool and moist, so make sure you put damp soil or moist paper towels in the jar with the earthworms.* Make sure that there are air holes in the covers of the jars and that the jars are covered securely.

6. Plant the plants you have collected in the terrarium. Water the plants. Then carefully transfer your animals from the jars into the terrarium.

7. Keep the terrarium in a sunny place. Water the plants every few days with a fine stream of water. Make sure that spiders and other insect-eaters have enough to eat. Observe the terrarium daily and record your observations in your notebook. Remember to record any changes you make in the terrarium, such as watering or adding new insects.

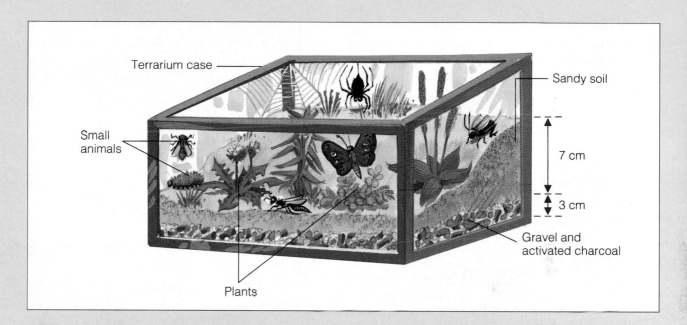

Terrarium case

Small animals

Plants

Sandy soil

7 cm

3 cm

Gravel and activated charcoal

Observations and Conclusions

1. Make a labeled drawing of your terrarium that shows what kinds of plants and animals it contains.

2. How does your terrarium change over time? Why do you think these changes occur?

3. How do the living and nonliving things in the terrarium interact with one another? How are they dependent on one another?

4. Compare your terrarium with those prepared by other groups in your class. How are they similar? How are they different? How can these similarities and differences be explained?

5. Prepare a poster to share what you have learned about smaller grasslands organisms.

PAPER ROUTE

A simple, yet effective conservation measure is recycling. In recycling, wastes such as scrap paper, old cans, empty plastic soda bottles, and broken glass jars are used as the raw materials for making new items. For example, old aluminum beverage cans are melted down to produce metal that is used for foil wrap, new beverage cans, and other useful products. In this activity you will try your hand at recycling old newspapers, junk mail, scraps of cloth and thread, and other odds and ends.

Materials

scrap paper (from sources such as newspapers, magazines, junk mail, notebook paper, and construction paper)
small amount of scraps of fabric and thread (optional)
scissors (optional)
1000-mL (1-L) beaker
hot water
laundry starch
dishpan, about 30 × 34 × 13 cm
egg beater
wood frame, about 25 × 30 cm
4 push pins
piece of window screen, about 25 × 30 cm
rolling pin
blotting paper

Procedure

1. Tear the paper into pieces less than 5 cm across. If you have fabric, rip or cut it into pieces less than 1 cm across. If you have thread, cut it into pieces less than 5 cm long. Put the pieces in the beaker. When the beaker is full, dump the pieces into the dishpan. Prepare about 1500 mL of pieces.

2. Add 6 L hot water and 360 mL starch to the dishpan.

3. Taking turns, use the eggbeater to beat the mixture in the dishpan until it is about the consistency of pancake batter or white glue. The beaten mixture is called pulp.

4. Attach the screen to the frame with the push pins, as shown in the illustration on the next page.

5. Slide the frame, screen-side up, into the pulp. Wriggle the frame a little so that bits of pulp are distributed evenly across the screen. Lift the screen straight up from the pan and let the water drip into the pan. Repeat this procedure two or three more times, or until the screen is completely covered by a layer of pulp several millimeters thick.

6. Unpin the screen. Carefully put the screen and the wet sheet of pulp on a piece of blotting paper. Cover the screen and sheet of pulp with another piece of blotting paper.

7. Firmly roll the rolling pin over the blotting paper to press the excess water from the pulp sheet.

8. Flip the "sandwich" of blotting paper over. Carefully remove the top piece of blotting paper and the piece of screen to reveal the piece of recycled paper that you have made.

9. Allow the recycled paper to dry. Then peel it off the bottom piece of blotting paper.

Observations and Conclusions

1. Describe the paper you made. Why is the paper said to be recycled?

2. Compare your sheet of paper to those made by your classmates. How do they differ? What do you think caused these differences?

3. How is your paper different from commercially made recycled paper? What do you think causes these differences?

4. What are some possible uses for the paper you made?

5. In your own words, explain why recycling is important.

Appendix A

The metric system of measurement is used by scientists throughout the world. It is based on units of ten. Each unit is ten times larger or ten times smaller than the next unit. The most commonly used units of the metric system are given below. After you have finished reading about the metric system, try to put it to use. How tall are you in metrics? What is your mass? What is your normal body temperature in degrees Celsius?

Commonly Used Metric Units

Length   The distance from one point to another

meter (m)   A meter is slightly longer than a yard.
1 meter = 1000 millimeters (mm)
1 meter = 100 centimeters (cm)
1000 meters = 1 kilometer (km)

Volume   The amount of space an object takes up

liter (L)   A liter is slightly more than a quart.
1 liter = 1000 milliliters (mL)

Mass   The amount of matter in an object

gram (g)   A gram has a mass equal to about one paper clip.

1000 grams = 1 kilogram (kg)

Temperature   The measure of hotness or coldness

degrees
Celsius (°C)   0°C = freezing point of water
100°C = boiling point of water

Metric–English Equivalents

2.54 centimeters (cm) = 1 inch (in.)
1 meter (m) = 39.37 inches (in.)
1 kilometer (km) = 0.62 miles (mi)
1 liter (L) = 1.06 quarts (qt)
250 milliliters (mL) = 1 cup (c)
1 kilogram (kg) = 2.2 pounds (lb)
28.3 grams (g) = 1 ounce (oz)
°C = 5/9 × (°F − 32)

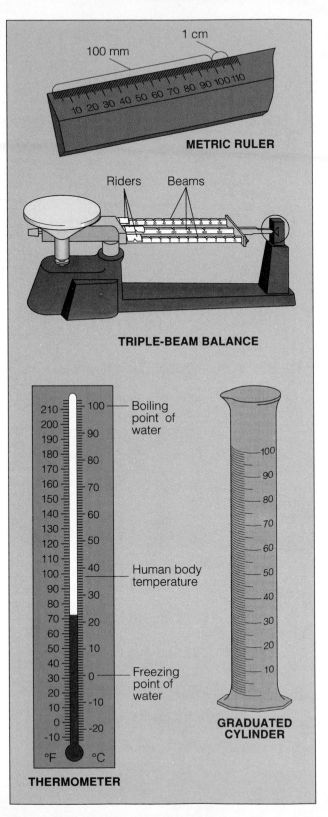

METRIC RULER

TRIPLE-BEAM BALANCE

THERMOMETER

GRADUATED CYLINDER

Appendix B

The microscope is an essential tool in the study of life science. It enables you to see things that are too small to be seen with the unaided eye. It also allows you to look more closely at the fine details of larger things.

The microscope you will use in your science class is probably similar to the one illustrated on the following page. This is a compound microscope. It is called compound because it has more than one lens. A simple microscope would contain only one lens. The lenses of the compound microscope are the parts that magnify the object being viewed.

Typically, a compound microscope has one lens in the eyepiece, the part you look through. The eyepiece lens usually has a magnification power of 10X. That is, if you were to look through the eyepiece alone, the object you were viewing would appear 10 times larger than it is.

The compound microscope may contain one or two other lenses. These two lenses are called the low- and high-power objective lenses. The low-power objective lens usually has a magnification of 10X. The high-power objective lens usually has a magnification of 40X. To figure out what the total magnification of your microscope is when using the eyepiece and an objective lens, multiply the powers of the lenses you are using. For example, eyepiece magnification (10X) multiplied by low-power objective lens magnification (10X) = 100X total magnification. What is the total magnification of your microscope using the eyepiece and the high-power objective lens?

To use the microscope properly, it is important to learn the name of each part, its function, and its location on your microscope. Keep the following procedures in mind when using the microscope:

1. Always carry the microscope with both hands. One hand should grasp the arm, and the other should support the base.

2. Place the microscope on the table with the arm toward you. The stage should be facing a light source.

3. Raise the body tube by turning the coarse adjustment knob.

4. Revolve the nosepiece so that the low-power objective lens (10X) is directly in line with the body tube. Click it into place. The low-power lens should be directly over the opening in the stage.

5. While looking through the eyepiece, adjust the diaphragm and the mirror so that the greatest amount of light is coming through the opening in the stage.

6. Place the slide to be viewed on the stage. Center the specimen to be viewed over the hole in the stage. Use the stage clips to hold the slide in position.

7. Look at the microscope from the side rather than through the eyepiece. In this way, you can watch as you use the coarse adjustment knob to lower the body tube until the low-power objective almost touches the slide. Do this slowly so you do not break the slide or damage the lens.

8. Now, looking through the eyepiece, observe the specimen. Use the coarse adjustment knob to raise the body tube, thus raising the low-power objective away from the slide. Continue to raise the body tube until the specimen comes into focus.

9. When viewing a specimen, be sure to keep both eyes open. Though this may seem strange at first, it is really much easier on your eyes. Keeping one eye closed may create a strain, and you might get a headache. Also, if you keep both eyes open, it is easier to draw diagrams of what you are observing. In this way, you do not have to turn your head away from the microscope as you draw.

10. To switch to the high-power objective lens (40X), look at the microscope from the side. Now, revolve the nosepiece so that the high-power objective lens clicks into place. Make sure the lens does not hit the slide.

11. Looking through the eyepiece, use only the fine adjustment knob to bring the specimen into focus. Why should you not use the coarse adjustment knob with the high-power objective?

12. Clean the microscope stage and lens when you are finished. To clean the lenses, use lens paper only. Other types of paper may scratch the lenses.

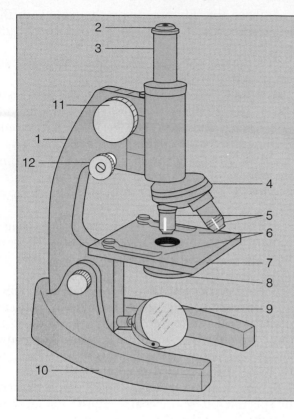

Microscope Parts and Their Functions

1. **Arm** Supports the body tube
2. **Eyepiece** Contains the magnifying lens you look through
3. **Body tube** Maintains the proper distance between the eyepiece and the objective lenses
4. **Nosepiece** Holds the high- and the low-power objective lenses and can be rotated to change magnification
5. **Objective lenses** A low-power lens, which usually provides 10X magnification, and a high-power lens, which usually provides 40X magnification
6. **Stage clips** Hold the slide in place
7. **Stage** Supports the slide being viewed
8. **Diaphragm** Regulates the amount of light let into the body tube
9. **Mirror** Reflects the light upward through the diaphragm, the specimen, and the lenses
10. **Base** Supports the microscope
11. **Coarse adjustment knob** Moves the body tube up and down for focusing
12. **Fine adjustment knob** Moves the body tube slightly to sharpen the image

Appendix C

One of the first things a scientist learns is that working in the laboratory can be an exciting experience. But the laboratory can also be quite dangerous if proper safety rules are not followed at all times. To prepare yourself for a safe year in the laboratory, read over the following safety rules. Then read them a second time. Make sure you understand each rule. If you do not, ask your teacher to explain any rules you are unsure of.

Dress Code

1. Many materials in the laboratory can cause eye injury. To protect yourself from possible injury, wear safety goggles whenever you are working with chemicals, burners, or any substance that might get into your eyes. Never wear contact lenses in the laboratory.

2. Wear a laboratory apron or coat whenever you are working with chemicals or heated substances.

3. Tie back long hair to keep it away from any chemicals, burners and candles, or other laboratory equipment.

4. Remove or tie back any article of clothing or jewelry that can hang down and touch chemicals and flames.

General Safety Rules

5. Read all directions for an experiment several times. Follow the directions exactly as they are written. If you are in doubt about any part of the experiment, ask your teacher for assistance.

6. Never perform activities that are not authorized by your teacher. Obtain permission before "experimenting" on your own.

7. Never handle any equipment unless you have specific permission.

8. Take extreme care not to spill any material in the laboratory. If a spill occurs, immediately ask your teacher about the proper cleanup procedure. Never simply pour chemicals or other substances into the sink or trash container.

9. Never eat in the laboratory.

10. Wash your hands before and after each experiment.

First Aid

11. Immediately report all accidents, no matter how minor, to your teacher.

12. Learn what to do in case of specific accidents, such as getting acid in your eyes or on your skin. (Rinse acids from your body with lots of water.)

13. Become aware of the location of the first-aid kit. But your teacher should administer any required first aid due to injury. Or your teacher may send you to the school nurse or call a physician.

14. Know where and how to report an accident or fire. Find out the location of the fire extinguisher, phone, and fire alarm. Keep a list of important phone numbers—such as the fire department and the school nurse—near the phone. Immediately report any fires to your teacher.

Heating and Fire Safety

15. Again, never use a heat source, such as a candle or burner, without wearing safety goggles.

16. Never heat a chemical you are not instructed to heat. A chemical that is harmless when cool may be dangerous when heated.

17. Maintain a clean work area and keep all materials away from flames.

18. Never reach across a flame.

19. Make sure you know how to light a Bunsen burner. (Your teacher will demonstrate the proper procedure for lighting a burner.) If the flame leaps out of a burner toward you, immediately turn off the gas. Do not touch the burner. It may be hot. And never leave a lighted burner unattended!

20. When heating a test tube or bottle, always point it away from you and others. Chemicals can splash or boil out of a heated test tube.

21. Never heat a liquid in a closed container. The expanding gases produced may blow the container apart, injuring you or others.

22. Before picking up a container that has been heated, first hold the back of your hand near it. If you can feel the heat on the back of your hand, the container may be too hot to handle. Use a clamp or tongs when handling hot containers.

Using Chemicals Safely

23. Never mix chemicals for the "fun of it." You might produce a dangerous, possibly explosive substance.

24. Never touch, taste, or smell a chemical unless you are instructed by your teacher to do so. Many chemicals are poisonous. If you are instructed to note the fumes in an experiment, gently wave your hand over the opening of a container and direct the fumes toward your nose. Do not inhale the fumes directly from the container.

25. Use only those chemicals needed in the activity. Keep all lids closed when a chemical is not being used. Notify your teacher whenever chemicals are spilled.

26. Dispose of all chemicals as instructed by your teacher. To avoid contamination, never return chemicals to their original containers.

27. Be extra careful when working with acids or bases. Pour such chemicals over the sink, not over your workbench.

28. When diluting an acid, pour the acid into water. Never pour water into an acid.

29. Immediately rinse with water any acids that get on your skin or clothing. Then notify your teacher of any acid spill.

Using Glassware Safely

30. Never force glass tubing into a rubber stopper. A turning motion and lubricant will be helpful when inserting glass tubing into rubber stoppers or rubber tubing. Your teacher will demonstrate the proper way to insert glass tubing.

31. Never heat glassware that is not thoroughly dry. Use a wire screen to protect glassware from any flame.

32. Keep in mind that hot glassware will not appear hot. Never pick up glassware without first checking to see if it is hot. See #22.

33. If you are instructed to cut glass tubing, fire-polish the ends immediately to remove sharp edges.

34. Never use broken or chipped glassware. If glassware breaks, notify your teacher and dispose of the glassware in the proper trash container.

35. Never eat or drink from laboratory glassware. Thoroughly clean glassware before putting it away.

Using Sharp Instruments

36. Handle scalpels or razor blades with extreme care. Never cut material toward you; cut away from you.

37. Immediately notify your teacher if you cut your skin when working in the laboratory.

Animal Safety

38. No experiments that will cause pain, discomfort, or harm to mammals, birds, reptiles, fishes, and amphibians should be done in the classroom or at home.

39. Animals should be handled only if necessary. If an animal is excited or frightened, pregnant, feeding, or with its young, special handling is required.

40. Your teacher will instruct you as to how to handle each animal species that may be brought into the classroom.

41. Clean your hands thoroughly after handling animals or the cage containing animals.

End-of-Experiment Rules

42. After an experiment has been completed, clean up your work area and return all equipment to its proper place.

43. Wash your hands after every experiment.

44. Turn off all burners before leaving the laboratory. Check that the gas line leading to the burner is off as well.

The laboratory balance is an important tool in scientific investigations. You can use the balance to determine the mass of materials that you study or experiment with in the laboratory.

Different kinds of balances are used in the laboratory. One kind of balance is the double-pan balance. Another kind of balance is the triple-beam balance. The balance that you may use in your science class is probably similar to one of the balances illustrated in this Appendix. To use the balance properly, you should learn the name, function, and location of each part of the balance you are using. What kind of balance do you have in your science class?

The Double-Pan Balance

The double-pan balance shown in this Appendix has two beams. Some double-pan balances have only one beam. The beams are calibrated, or marked, in grams. The upper beam is divided into ten major units of 1 gram each. Each of these units is further divided into units of 1/10 of a gram. The lower beam is divided into twenty units, and each unit is equal to 10 grams. The lower beam can be used to find the masses of objects up to 200 grams. Each beam has a rider that is moved to the right along the beam. The rider indicates the number of grams needed to balance the object in the left pan. What is the total mass the balance can measure?

Before using the balance, you should be sure that the pans are empty and both riders are pointing to zero. The balance should be on a flat, level surface. The pointer should be at the zero point. If your pointer does not read zero, slowly turn the adjustment knob so that the pointer does read zero.

The following procedure can be used to find the mass of an object with a double-pan balance:

1. Place the object whose mass is to be determined on the left pan.

2. Move the rider on the lower beam to the 10-gram notch.

3. If the pointer moves to the right of the zero point on the scale, the object has a mass less than

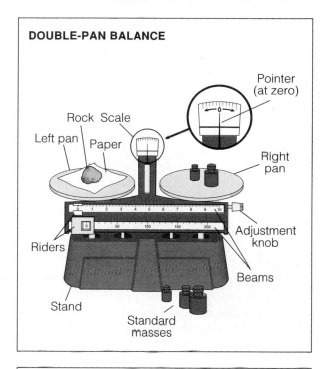

DOUBLE-PAN BALANCE

Rock · Scale · Pointer (at zero) · Left pan · Paper · Right pan · Riders · Adjustment knob · Beams · Stand · Standard masses

Parts of a Double-Pan Balance and Their Functions

Pointer Indicator used to determine when the mass being measured is balanced by the riders or masses of the balance

Scale Series of marks along which the pointer moves

Zero Point Center line of the scale to which the pointer moves when the mass being measured is balanced by the riders or masses of the balance

Adjustment Knob Knob used to set the balance at the zero point when the riders are all on zero and no masses are on either pan

Left Pan Platform on which an object whose mass is to be determined is placed

Right Pan Platform on which standard masses are placed

Beams Horizontal strips of metal on which marks, or graduations, appear that indicate grams or parts of grams

Riders Devices that are moved along the beams and used to balance the object being measured and to determine its mass

Stand Support for the balance

10 grams. Return the rider on the lower beam to zero. Slowly move the rider on the upper beam until the pointer is at zero. The reading on the beam is the mass of the object.

4. If the pointer did not move to the right of the zero, move the rider on the lower beam notch by notch until the pointer does move to the right. Move the rider back one notch. Then move the rider on the upper beam until the pointer is at zero. The sum of the readings on both beams is the mass of the object.

5. If the two riders are moved completely to the right side of the beams and the pointer remains to the left of the zero point, the object has a mass greater than the total mass that the balance can measure.

The total mass that most double-pan balances can measure is 210 grams. If an object has a mass greater than 210 grams, return the riders to the zero point.

The following procedure can be used to find the mass of an object greater than 210 grams:

1. Place the standard masses on the right pan one at a time, starting with the largest, until the pointer remains to the right of the zero point.

2. Remove one of the large standard masses and replace it with a smaller one. Continue replacing the standard masses with smaller ones until the pointer remains to the left of the zero point. When the pointer remains to the left of the zero point, the mass of the object on the left pan is greater than the total mass of the standard masses on the right pan.

3. Move the rider on the lower beam and then the rider on the upper beam until the pointer stops at the zero point on the scale. The mass of the object is equal to the sum of the readings on the beams plus the mass of the standard masses.

The Triple-Beam Balance

The triple-beam balance is a single-pan balance with three beams calibrated in grams. The back, or 100-gram, beam is divided into ten units of 10 grams each. The middle, or 500-gram, beam is divided into five units of 100 grams each. The front, or 10-gram, beam is divided into ten major units of 1 gram each. Each of these units is further divided into units of 1/10 of a gram. What is the largest mass you could find with a triple-beam balance?

The following procedure can be used to find the mass of an object with a triple-beam balance:

1. Place the object on the pan.

2. Move the rider on the middle beam notch by notch until the horizontal pointer drops below zero. Move the rider back one notch.

3. Move the rider on the back beam notch by notch until the pointer again drops below zero. Move the rider back one notch.

4. Slowly slide the rider along the front beam until the pointer stops at the zero point.

5. The mass of the object is equal to the sum of the readings on the three beams.

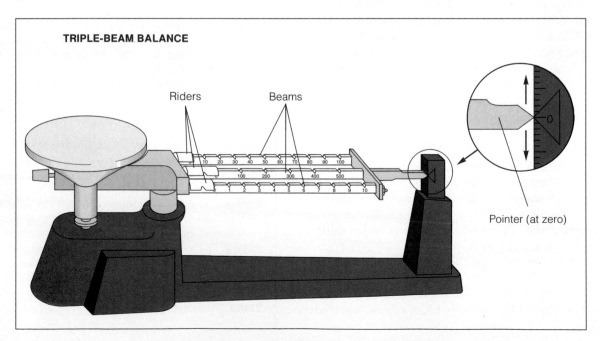

TRIPLE-BEAM BALANCE

Riders   Beams

Pointer (at zero)

Glossary

Pronunciation Key

When difficult names or terms first appear in the text, they are respelled to aid pronunciation. A syllable in SMALL CAPITAL LETTERS receives the most stress. The key below lists the letters used for respelling. It includes examples of words using each sound and shows how the words would be respelled.

Symbol	Example	Respelling
a	hat	(hat)
ay	pay, late	(pay), (layt)
ah	star, hot	(stahr), (haht)
ai	air, dare	(air), (dair)
aw	law, all	(law), (awl)
eh	met	(meht)
ee	bee, eat	(bee), (eet)
er	learn, sir, fur	(lern), (ser), (fer)
lh	fit	(fiht)
igh	mile, sigh	(mighl), (sigh)
oh	no	(noh)
oi	soil, boy	(soil), (boi)
oo	root, rule	(root), (rool)
or	born, door	(born), (dor)
ow	plow, out	(plow), (owt)

Symbol	Example	Respelling
u	put, book	(put), (buk)
uh	fun	(fuhn)
yoo	few, use	(fyoo), (yooz)
ch	chill, reach	(chihl), (reech)
g	go, dig	(goh), (dihg)
j	jet, gently, bridge	(jeht), (JEHNT-lee), (brihj)
k	kite, cup	(kight), (kuhp)
ks	mix	(mihks)
kw	quick	(kwihk)
ng	bring	(brihng)
s	say, cent	(say), (sehnt)
sh	she, crash	(shee), (krash)
th	three	(three)
y	yet, onion	(yeht), (UHN-yuhn)
z	zip, always	(zihp), (AWL-wayz)
zh	treasure	(TREH-zher)

active immunity: immunity in which a person's own immune system responds to the presence of an antigen

active transport: energy-requiring process that can "carry" a substance into the cell

adaptation: change that increases an organism's chances of survival

adolescence: stage of development that begins at age 13 and ends at age 20

adrenal (uh-DREE-nuhl): endocrine gland on top of each kidney that produces the hormone adrenaline

adulthood: stage of development that begins at age 20 and lasts the rest of a person's life

AIDS: Acquired Immune Deficiency Syndrome; disease in which certain cells of the immune system are killed by a virus called HIV

alcoholism: disease caused by drinking large amounts of alcohol daily

alga (AL-guh; plural: algae): nonvascular plant-like autotroph that uses sunlight to produce food

allele (uh-LEEL): each form of a gene

allergy: reaction that occurs when the body is especially sensitive to certain substances called allergens

alveolus (al-VEE-uh-luhs; plural: alveoli): grapelike cluster of tiny balloons in the lungs

ameba: sarcodine, a type of protist that lives in fresh water and moves by means of pseudopods

amino (uh-MEE-noh) **acid:** building block of protein

amniocentesis (am-nee-oh-sehn-TEE-sihs): process of removing fluid from the sac surrounding a developing baby

amniotic sac: fluid-filled sac that cushions and protects the developing baby in the uterus

anaphase: fourth stage of cell division during which the chromosomes split apart

anatomy: study of the structure of organisms

angiosperm (AN-jee-uh-sperm): type of seed plant whose seeds are covered by a protective wall

annual: plant that completes its life cycle in one growing season

antibiotic: chemical that destroys or weakens disease-causing bacteria

antibody: protein produced by certain kinds of white blood cells in response to an invasion by a particular organism or substance

antigen: invading organism or substance

aorta: largest blood vessel in the body

artery: blood vessel that carries blood away from the heart

arthropod (AHR-thruh-pahd): invertebrate that has jointed legs and an exoskeleton

asexual reproduction: reproduction requiring only one parent

atherosclerosis (ath-uhr-oh-skluh-ROH-sihs): disease caused by thickening of the inner lining of the arteries

ATP: energy-rich molecule

atom: smallest part of any element that keeps the properties of that element

atrium (plural: atria): upper heart chamber

autonomic nervous system: division of the peripheral nervous system that controls all involuntary body processes

autotroph (AWT-uh-trohf): organism that can make its own food from simple substances

axon: fiber that carries messages away from a body cell

bacterium (plural: bacteria): unicellular microorganism that does not have a nucleus

benign: harmless

biennial: plant that completes its life cycle in two years

bile: substance produced by the liver that aids in digestion

binomial nomenclature (bigh-NOH-mee-uhl NOH-muhn-klay-cher): naming system in which organisms are given two names: a genus and a species

biogeography: study of where plants and animals live throughout the world

biological clock: internal timer responsible for keeping track of many different time cycles

biome: division of area with similar climate, plants, and animals

bone: structure that makes up the body's skeleton

botany: study of plants

brain: main control center of the central nervous system

bronchus (BRAHNG-kuhs; plural: bronchi): tube that branches off from the trachea

brown alga: multicellular alga that contains a brown pigment

Calorie: amount of heat energy needed to raise the temperature of 1 kilogram of water 1°C

cancer: abnormal and uncontrolled cell reproduction

canine (KAY-nighn): sharp pointed tooth used for tearing and shredding meat

canopy (KAN-uh-pee): roof formed by tall trees in the forest

capillary: tiny, thin-walled blood vessel

capsule: cup-shaped part of the nephron

captive breeding: causing zoo animals to have offspring

carbohydrate: energy-rich substance found in foods such as vegetables, cereal grains, and breads

carbon cycle: recycling of carbon dioxide and oxygen in the environment

carcinogen (kahr-SIHN-uh-juhn): cancer-causing substance

cardiac muscle: muscle found only in the heart

cardiovasular (kahr-dee-oh-VAS-kyoo-luhr) **disease:** disease that affects the heart and blood vessels

carnivore (KAHR-nuh-vor): flesh-eating mammal

cartilage (KAHRT-'l-ihj): flexible tissue that gives support and shape to body parts

cell: basic unit of structure and function of a living thing

cell body: largest part of the neuron, which contains the nucleus

cell division: process in which one cell divides into two cells

cell membrane: thin, flexible envelope that surrounds a cell

cell theory: theory that states that all living things are made of cells; cells are the basic units of structure and function in living things; and living cells come only from other living cells

cell wall: outermost boundary of plant and bacterial cells that is made of cellulose

Celsius: temperature scale used in the metric system in which water freezes at 0° and boils at 100°

central nervous system: part of the nervous system made up of the brain and spinal cord

cerebellum (sair-uh-BEHL-uhm): part of the brain that controls balance and posture

cerebrum (SAIR-uh-bruhm): part of the brain that controls the senses, thought, and conscious activities

chemical digestion: breaking down of food by enzymes

childhood: stage of development that begins at about 2 years of age and continues until the age of 13

chlorophyll: green substance, needed for photosynthesis, found in green plant cells

chloroplast: large, irregularly shaped structure that contains the green pigment chlorophyll; food-making site in green plants

cholesterol: fattylike substance found in animal fats, meats, and dairy products

chromatin: threadlike coils of chromosomes

chromosome: rod-shaped cell structure that directs the activities of a cell and passes on the traits of a cell to new cells

chromosome theory: theory that states that genes are found on chromosomes and that genes are carried from the parental generation to the next generation on chromosomes

ciliate (SIHL-ee-iht): animallike protist that moves by means of cilia

cilium (SIHL-ee-uhm; plural: cilia): small, hairlike projection on the outside of a ciliate that acts like a tiny oar and helps the organism move

class: classification grouping between phylum and order

climax community: stable collection of plants, animals, and other organisms in a particular place

cochlea (KAHK-lee-uh): spiraling tube in the inner ear from which nerve impulses are carried to the brain

coldblooded: having a body temperature that can change somewhat with changes in the temperature of the environment

commensalism: symbiotic relationship in which only one partner in the relationship benefits

community: living part of any ecosystem

competition: struggle among living things to get the proper amount of food, water, and energy

compound: two or more elements chemically combined

compound light microscope: microscope having more than one lens and that uses a beam of light to magnify objects

cone: reproductive structure of a seed plant

conifer: evergreen that produces its seeds in cones

coniferous forest: northernmost forest biome, which contains conifers

connective tissue: type of tissue that provides support for the body and unites its parts

consumer: organism that feeds directly or indirectly on producers

contour feather: large feather used for flight that is found on a bird's wing and on most of the bird's body

control experiment: experiment done in exactly the same way as another experiment, but without the variable

conversion factor: fraction that always equals one

cornea: transparent protective covering of the eye

cytoplasm: all the protoplasm, or living material, outside the nucleus of a cell

data: recorded observations and measurements

deciduous forest: forest biome that contains decidious trees, which shed their leaves in autumn

decomposer: organism that feeds on dead organic matter and breaks it down into simpler substances

deforestation: removal of trees

dendrite: fiber that carries messages from a neuron toward the cell body

density: measure of how much mass is contained in a given volume of an object

depressant: drug that slows down the actions of the nervous system

dermis: inner layer of the skin

desert: biome that receives less than 25 centimeters of rainfall a year

desertification (dih-zert-uh-fih-KAY-shun): process in which desertlike conditions are created where there had been none

diabetes mellitus (digh-uh-BEET-eez muh-LIGHT-uhs): noninfectious disease in which the body either secretes too little insulin or is not able to use the insulin that it does secrete

diaphragm (DIGH-uh-fram): muscle at the bottom of the chest that aids in breathing

diatom (DIGH-uh-tahm): plantlike protist that is made of a tough glasslike material

diffusion: process by which food molecules, oxygen, water, and other materials enter and leave a cell through the cell membrane

digest: break down

digestion: process by which food is broken down into simpler substances

dimensional analysis: skill of converting one unit to another

dinoflagellate (digh-nuh-FLAJ-uh-liht): plantlike protist that has two flagella and armorlike cell walls

dispersal: movement of living things from one place to another

diurnal (digh-ER-nuhl): active during the day

DNA (deoxyribonucleic acid): nucleic acid that stores the information needed to build proteins and carries genetic information about an organism

dominant: stronger trait in genetics

down feather: short, fuzzy type of feather used for insulation

drug: substance that has an effect on the body

drug abuse: using too much of a drug or using a drug in a way doctors would not approve

eardrum: membrane in the ear that vibrates when struck by sound waves

echinoderm (ih-KEE-nuh-derm): invertebrate with rough, spiny skin

ecological succession: process of gradual change within a community

ecology: study of relationships and interactions of living things with one another and with their environment

ecosystem: group of organisms in an area that interact with one another, together with their nonliving environment

effector: part of the body that carries out the instructions of the nervous system

egg: female sex cell; ovum

egg-laying mammal: monotreme

electron: negatively charged particle of an atom

electron microscope: microscope that uses a beam of electrons to magnify objects

element: pure substance that cannot be separated into simpler substances by ordinary chemical processes

embryo (EHM-bree-oh): newly formed organism that is the product of fertilization

embryology: study of developing organisms

endangered: in danger of becoming extinct

endoplasmic reticulum (ehn-duh-PLAZ-mihk rih-TIHK-yuh-luhm): clear tubular passageway leading out from the nuclear membrane that is involved in the transport of proteins

endoskeleton: internal skeleton

environment: all the living and nonliving things with which an organism interacts

enzyme: chemical substance that helps control chemical reactions

epidermis (ehp-uh-DER-muhs): outer, protective layer of a leaf; outermost layer of the skin

epiglottis (ehp-uh-GLAHT-ihs): small flap of tissue that closes over the windpipe

epithelial (ehp-ih-THEE-lee-uhl) **tissue:** type of tissue that forms a protective surface for the body and lines the cavities and other body parts

esophagus (ih-SAHF-uh-guhs): pipe-shaped tube that transports food to the stomach

estivation: summer resting state of an organism

estrogen: hormone that triggers the broadening of the hips in females and starts the maturation of egg cells in the ovaries

estuary: boundary between a freshwater biome and a marine biome

euglena: plantlike protist that contains chloroplasts

evaporation: process in which radiant heat from the sun turns liquid water into a gas

evolution: change in a species over time

excretion: process of getting rid of waste materials

exoskeleton: rigid, outer covering of an organism

exotic species: species released into a place where they had never been before

external fertilization: fertilization that occurs outside the body of the female

extinct: having died out

extinction: process by which a species passes out of existence

Fallopian (fuh-LOH-pee-uhn) **tube:** oviduct; tube through which an egg travels from the ovary

family: classification grouping between order and genus

fat: substance that supplies the body with energy and also helps support and cushion the vital organs in the body

feather: important characteristic of a bird

fermentation: energy-releasing process in which sugars and starches are changed into alcohol and carbon dioxide; process by which yeasts obtain their energy

fertilization: joining of the egg and the sperm nuclei

fetus (FEET-uhs): developing baby from the eighth week until birth

fibrin: substance that helps to form a clot

flagellate (FLAJ-uh-layt): animallike protist that moves by means of flagella

flagellum (fluh-JEHL-uhm; plural: flagella): long, thin whiplike structure that propels an organism

flower: structure containing the reproductive organs of an angiosperm

food chain: food and energy links between the different plants and animals in an ecosystem

food web: all the food chains in an ecosystem that are connected

fossil: imprint or remains of plants or animals that existed in the past

fossil record: most complete biological record of life on earth

freshwater biome: biome that contains freshwater lakes, ponds, swamps, streams, and rivers

fruit: ripened ovary of an angiosperm

fruiting body: spore-containing structure in a fungus

fungus (FUHNG-uhs; plural: fungi): nonvascular plantlike organism that has no chlorophyll

gallbladder: organ that stores bile

gene: basic unit of heredity

genetic engineering: process in which genes, or parts of DNA, are transferred from one organism into another organism

genetics: study of heredity

genotype (JEE-nuh-tighp): genetic makeup of an organism

genus (plural: genera): group of organisms that are closely related; classification group between family and species

germination: early growth stage, or the "sprouting," of a young plant

gestation period: time the young spends inside the mother

gill: spore-producing structure in a mushroom; structure through which water-dwelling animals obtain their oxygen

grassland: biome made up mainly of grasses that receives between 25 and 75 centimeters of rainfall yearly

gravity: force of attraction

green alga: multicellular alga that contains a green pigment

gymnosperm (JIHM-nuh-sperm): type of seed plant whose seeds are not covered by a protective wall

habitat: place in which an organism lives

half-life: time it takes for half of a radioactive element to decay

hallucinogen (huh-LOO-suh-nuh-jehn): drug that produces powerful hallucinations

hemoglobin (hee-muh-GLOH-bihn): iron-containing protein in red blood cells

herbivore (HER-buh-vor): organism that eats only plants

heterotroph (HEHT-uh-roh-trohf): organism unable to make its own food

hibernation: winter sleep during which all body activities slow down

homeostasis (hoh-mee-oh-STAY-sihs): ability of an organism to keep conditions inside its body the same even though conditions in its external environment change

homologous (hoh-MAHL-uh-guhs) **structure:** structure that evolved from similar body parts

hormone: chemical messenger that travels through the blood

hornwort: tiny seedless plant that lives in moist places

host: organism in which another organism lives

hybrid: organism produced through hybridization; organism with two different genes for a particular trait

hybridization (high-bruh-duh-ZAY-shuhn): crossing of two genetically different but related species of an organism

hypertension: high blood pressure

hypha (HIGH-fuh; plural: hyphae: HIGH-fee): threadlike structure in fungi that produces enzymes to break down living or dead organisms

hypothalamus (high-puh-THAL-uh-muhs): endocrine gland at the base of the brain that controls body temperature, water balance, appetite, and sleep

hypothesis: suggested solution to a problem

immunity (ih-MYOON-uh-tee): body's ability to fight off disease without becoming sick

inbreeding: breeding that involves crossing plants or animals that have the same or very similar sets of genes

incisor (ihn-SIGH-zuhr): front tooth used for biting

incomplete dominance: condition that occurs when a gene is neither dominant nor recessive

infancy: stage of development that lasts from 1 month to about 2 years of age

infectious disease: disease that is transmitted among people by harmful organisms such as viruses and bacteria; communicable disease

inflammatory (inh-FLAM-uh-tor-ee) **response:** body's second line of defense against invading organisms, in which fluid and white blood cells leak from blood vessels into tissues

ingestion: taking in of food

inhalant: drug that is inhaled

interferon: substance produced by a body cell when invaded by a virus

internal fertilization: fertilization that takes place inside the body of the female

interneuron: type of neuron that connects sensory and motor neurons

interphase: first phase of cell division

invertebrate: animal without a backbone

iris: circular, colored portion of the eye that regulates the amount of light entering the eye

islet of Langerhans: small group of cells in the pancreas that produces the hormones insulin and glucagon

joint: place where two bones meet

kidney: major excretory organ

kilogram (kg)**:** basic unit of mass in the metric system

kingdom: largest classification grouping

large intestine: organ in the digestive system in which water is absorbed and undigested food is stored

larva: stage of insect that develops from an egg

larynx (LAR-ihngks): voice box

law: summarizing statement of observed experimental facts that has been tested many times and is generally accepted as true

law of independent assortment: law that states that each gene pair for a trait is inherited independently of the gene pairs for all other traits

law of segregation: law that states that gene pairs separate during the sex cell formation

law of superposition: law that states that in a series of sedimentary rock layers, younger rocks normally lie on top of older rocks

leaf: plant structure where photosynthesis occurs

lens: curved piece of glass that bends light rays as they pass through it; part of the eye that focuses the light ray coming into the eye

lichen (LIGH-kuhn): organism made up of a fungus and an alga that live together in a symbiotic relationship

life span: maximum length of time an organism can be expected to live

ligament: stringy connective tissue that holds the bones together

liter (L): basic unit of volume in the metric system

liver: organ that produces bile and breaks down excess amino acids

liverwort: tiny seedless plant that lives in moist places

lung: main respiratory organ

lymph: plasma that leaks out of the blood and surrounds and bathes body cells

lysosome (LIGH-suh-sohm): small, round structure involved in the digestive activities of a cell

macronucleus: large nucleus in a paramecium that controls all life functions except reproduction

mammary gland: structure in a female mammal that produces milk

marijuana: illegal drug that is made from the leaves and flowers of the Indian hemp plant

marine biome: ocean biome

marrow: soft material inside a bone

marsupial (mahr-SOO-pee-uhl): pouched mammal

mass: measure of the amount of matter in an object

matter: anything that takes up space and has mass

mechanical digestion: physical action of breaking down food into smaller pieces

medulla (mih-DUHL-uh): part of the brain located at the base of the brain stem that controls involuntary body processes

meiosis (migh-OH-sihs): process that results in cells with only half the normal number of chromosomes

menopause: physical change in females after which menstruation and ovulation stop

menstrual (MEHN-struhl) **cycle:** monthly cycle of change that occurs in the female reproductive system

menstruation (mehn-STRAY-shuhn): process in which the blood and tissue from the thickened lining of the uterus pass out of a female's body through the vagina

metabolism (muh-TAB-uh-lihz-uhm): all chemical activities that occur in an organism

metamorphosis (meht-uh-MOR-fuh-sihs): change in appearance due to development

metaphase: third stage of cell division

meter (m): basic unit of length in the metric system

metric system: universal system of measurement

microbiology: study of microorganisms

micronucleus: small nucleus that controls reproduction in a paramecium

microorganism: microscopic organism

microscope: instrument that produces an enlarged image of an object

migrate: move to a new environment during the course of a year

migration: annual rhythm in which organisms travel from breeding areas to feeding areas

mineral: simple substance found in nature that helps maintain the normal functioning of the body

mitochondrion (might-uh-KAHN-dree-uhn; plural: mitochondria): rod-shaped structure that is referred to as the powerhouse of a cell

mitosis (migh-TOH-sihs): duplication and division of the nucleus of a cell and the formation of two new daughter cells

molar: back tooth that grinds and crushes food

mold: fuzzy, shapeless fungus that grows on the surface of an object

molecular clock: scale used to estimate the rate of change in proteins over time

molecule (MAHL-uh-kyool): smallest particle of a compound having all the properties of that compound

mollusk (MAHL-uhsk): invertebrate with a soft, fleshy body that is often covered by a hard shell

molting: process by which arthropods shed their exoskeleton as they grow

moneran: member of the Monera kingdom

motor neuron: type of neuron that carries messages from the central nervous system to effectors

multicellular: having many cells

multiple allele: more than two alleles that combine to determine a certain characteristic

muscle tissue: type of tissue that has the ability to contract and make the body move

mushroom: fungus that has a cap on top of a stalk

mutation: change in genes or chromosomes that causes a new trait to be inherited

mutualism: symbiotic relationship that is helpful to both organisms

natural selection: survival and reproduction of those organisms best adapted to their surroundings

negative-feedback mechanism: mechanism by which the production of a hormone is controlled by the amount of another hormone

nematocyst (NEHM-uh-toh-sihst): special stinging structure in a cnidarian

nephron (NEHF-rahn): microscopic chemical-filtering factory in the kidneys

nerve impulse: message carried throughout the body by nerves

nerve tissue: type of tissue that carries messages back and forth between the brain and spinal cord and to every part of the body

neuron: nerve cell

neutron: neutral partide in the nucleus of an atom

newton: (N): basic unit of weight in the metric system

niche: role of an organism in its community or environment

nitrogen base: substance in DNA that contains the element nitrogen

nitrogen cycle: recycling of nitrogen in the environment

nocturnal (nahk-TER-nuhl): active at night

noninfectious disease: disease not caused by disease-causing microorganisms

nonvascular (nahn-VA-skyuh-luhr) **plant:** plant lacking transportation tubes that carry water and food throughout the plant

nuclear membrane: thin membrane that separates the nucleus from the rest of a cell

nucleic (noo-KLEE-ihk) **acid:** large organic compound that stores information that helps the body make the proteins it needs

nucleolus (noo-KLEE-oh-luhs): cell structure located in the nucleus and made up of RNA and protein

nucleus (NOO-klee-uhs): cell structure that directs all the activities of the cell

nutrient: usable portion of food

oil: energy-rich substance

omnivore (AHM-nuh-vor): organism that eats both plants and animals

opiate: pain-killing drug produced from the opium poppy

order: classification grouping between class and family

organ: group of different tissues working together; third level of organization in an organism

organelle (or-guh-NEHL): tiny cell structure

organic compound: compound in living things that contains carbon, which usually combines with hydrogen and oxygen

organism: entire living thing that carries out all the basic life functions; fifth level of organization

organ system: group of organs that work together to perform certain functions; fourth level of organization in an organism

osmosis: special type of diffusion by which water passes into and out of the cell

ovary (OH-vuhr-ee): hollow structure that contains the egg cells of a flower; female sex gland; endocrine gland that produces female hormones

ovulation: process in which an egg is released from the ovary into the Fallopian tube

ovule (OH-vyool): structure that contains the female sex cells of a seed plant

oxygen cycle: recycling of oxygen and carbon dioxide in the environment

pancreas (PAN-kree-uhs): organ that produces pancreatic juice and insulin

paramecium (par-uh-MEE-see-uhm; plural: paramecia): type of protist that moves by means of cilia

parasite (PAR-uh-sight): organism that feeds on other living organisms

parasitism: symbiotic relationship in which one organism is harmed by the other organism

parathyroid: endocrine gland producing a hormone that controls the level of calcium in the blood

passive immunity: immunity that is gotten from another source

pepsin: enzyme produced by the stomach that digests protein

perennial: plant that lives for many years

periosteum (pehr-ih-AHS-tee-uhm): tough membrane containing bone-forming cells and blood vessels that surrounds the solid bone

peripheral (puh-RIHF-uh-ruhl) **nervous system:** part of the nervous system that branches out from the central nervous system and includes a network of nerves and sense organs

peristalsis (per-uh-STAHL-sihs): powerful wave of muscle contractions that pushes food through the digestive system

permafrost: permanently frozen tundra soil

petal: colorful leaflike structure that surrounds the male and female reproductive organs in a flower

phenotype (FEE-nuh-tighp): visible characteristic of an organism

pheromone (FAIR-uh-mohn): chemical substance given off by insects and other animals to attract a mate

phloem (FLOH-uhm): tubelike plant tissue that carries food down the plant

photosynthesis (foht-oh-SIHN-thuh-sihs): process by which organisms use energy from sunlight to make their own food

phylum (FIGH-luhm; plural: phyla): second largest classification grouping

physical dependence: effect of drug abuse in which the body cannot function properly without the drug

phytoplankton: microscopic plants that live on the surface of the ocean

pigment: colored chemical

pistil: female reproductive organ of a flower

pituitary (pih-TOO-uh-tair-ee): endocrine gland located below the hypothalamus that produces hormones that control many body processes

placenta (pluh-SEHN-tuh): structure through which developing mammals receive food and oxygen while in the mother

placental mammal: mammal whose young develop within the female

plankton: small organisms that float or swim near the surface of water

plasma: yellowish liquid portion of blood

plasmid: bacterial DNA in the form of a ring

platelet (PLAYT-liht): blood cell fragment that aids in blood clotting

pollen: contains the male sex cells of a seed plant

pollination: transfer of pollen from the male part to the female part of a flower

pollution: introduction of harmful or unwanted substances into the environment

population: group of the same type of organism living together in the same area

poriferan (po-RIHF-uhr-uhn): member of the phylum porifera

pouched mammal: marsupial

predation: relationship that exists between a predator and its prey

predator: animal that kills and eats other animals

prey: organism that is killed and eaten by a predator

primate: order of mammals that includes humans, apes, and monkeys

probability: possibility that an event may or may not take place

producer: organism that can make its own food

prophase: first stage of cell division

protein: substance used to build and repair cells; made up of amino acids

protist: unicellular organism belonging to the kingdom Protista

pseudopod (SOO-doh-pahd): extension of the cytoplasm of a sarcodine that is used in moving and getting food

psychological dependence: emotional need for a drug

ptyalin (TIGH-uh-lihn): enzyme in saliva that breaks down some starches into sugars

puberty (PYOO-ber-tee): beginning of adolescence

punctuated equilibrium (PUHNGK-choo-wayt-uhd ee-kwuh-LIHB-ree-uhm): theory that evolution occurs in rapid and sudden changes in a species after a long period of little or no change

pupa (PYOO-puh): stage in an insect's life that follows the larva stage

pupil: circular opening at the center of the iris

radioactive dating: method based on radioactive elements used by scientists to measure the age of fossils or the age of the rocks in which fossils are found

receptor: part of the nervous system that responds to stimuli

recessive: weaker trait in genetics

recombinant DNA: new piece of DNA produced by combining parts of separate DNA strands

red alga: multicellular alga that contains a red pigment

red blood cell: cell that carries oxygen throughout the body

reflex: automatic reaction to a stimulus

regeneration: ability of an organism to regrow lost parts

replication (rehp-luh-KAY-shuhn): process in which DNA molecules form exact duplicates

reproduction: process by which living things give rise to the same type of living thing

respiration: process by which living organisms take in oxygen and use it to produce energy

response: some action or movement of an organism brought on by a stimulus

retina (REHT-uhn-uh): inner eye layer on which an image is focused

ribosome: grainlike body made up of RNA and attached to the inner surface of an endoplasmic passageway; a protein-making site of the cell

RNA (ribonucleic acid): nucleic acid that "reads" the genetic information carried by DNA and guides the protein-making process

root: structure that anchors a plant in the ground and absorbs water and minerals from the soil

sarcodine (SAHR-koh-dighn): animallike protist that moves by means of pseudopods

scavenger: organism that feeds on dead animals

scientific method: systematic approach to problem solving

scrotum (SKROHT-uhm): external sac in males that contains the testes

sedimentary rock: type of rock formed from layers of mud and sand that harden slowly over time

seed: structure from which a plant grows; contains a young plant, stored food, and a seed coat

selective breeding: crossing of animals or plants that have desirable characteristics to produce offspring with desirable characteristics

semicircular canal: curved tube in the inner ear that is responsible for balance

sensory neuron: type of neuron that carries messages from special receptors to the central nervous system

sepal (SEE-puhl): leaflike structure enclosing a flower when it is still a bud

septum: thick wall of tissue that separates the heart into right and left sides

sex chromosome: chromosome that determines the sex of an organism

sex-linked trait: characteristic passed from parent to child on a sex chromosome

sexual reproduction: reproduction usually requiring two parents

skeletal muscle: muscle that is attached to bone and moves the skeleton

skin: outer covering of the body

slime mold: funguslike protist that is flat and shapeless

small intestine: organ in the digestive system in which most digestion takes place

smooth muscle: muscle responsible for involuntary movement

species (SPEE-sheez): group of organisms that are able to interbreed and produce young

sperm: male sex cell

spicule: thin, spiny structure that forms the skeleton of many sponges

spinal cord: part of the nervous system that connects the brain with the rest of the nervous system

spontaneous generation: theory that states that life can spring from nonliving matter

spore: tiny reproductive cell

sporozoan (spohr-oh-ZOH-uhn): animallike protist that has no means of movement

stalk: stemlike structure in a mushroom that supports the cap

stamen (STAY-muhn): male reproductive organ of a flower

stem: structure that provides means by which materials are transported between roots and leaves of a plant

stigma (STIHG-muh): structure located at the top of the pistil

stimulant: drug that speeds up the activities of the nervous system

stimulus (plural: stimuli): signal to which an organism reacts; change in the environment

stomach: J-shaped, muscular organ connected to the end of the esophagus in which foods are physically and chemically digested

style: slender tube that connects the ovary to the stigma

swim bladder: sac filled with air that enables bony fish to rise or sink in water

symbiosis (sihm-bigh-OH-sihs): relationship in which an organism lives on, near, or in another organism

symptom: sign of disease

synapse (SIHN-aphs): tiny gap between an axon and a dendrite

taiga (TIGH-guh): northernmost area of a coniferous forest biome

telophase: fifth stage of cell division

tendon: connective tissue that connects muscle to bone

territory: area where an animal lives

testis (TEHS-tihs; plural: testes): male sex gland; endocrine gland that produces male hormones

testosterone (tehs-TAHS-tuh-rohn): hormone responsible for the growth of facial and body hair, broadening of the shoulders, and deepening of the voice in males

theory: most logical explanation for events that happen in nature

thymus (THIGH-muhs): endocrine gland that is responsible for the development of the immune system

thyroid (THIGH-roid): endocrine gland that produces a hormone that controls metabolism

tissue: group of cells that are similar in structure and perform a special function; second level of organization in an organism

tolerance: effect of drug abuse in which a person must take more and more of a drug each time to get the same effect

trachea (TRAY-kee-uh): windpipe; tube that carries air to lungs

trait: characteristic of an organism

transfusion: process of transferring blood from one body to another

transpiration: process for regulating water loss through the leaves of a plant

tropical rain forest: forest biome that receives at least 152-355 centimeters of rain yearly.

tropism (TROH-pihz-uhm): movement of a plant toward or away from a stimulus

tube foot: cuplike structure for suction, that helps echinoderms "walk"

tuber: underground stem of a plant

tumor: swelling of tissue that develops separately from the tissue surrounding it

tundra: biome that rims the Arctic Ocean around the North Pole and has a cold, dry climate

umbilical (uhm-BIHL-ih-kuhl) **cord:** structure that connects an embryo to its mother and transports food, oxygen, and wastes

unicellular: one celled

urea (yoo-REE-uh): nitrogen waste formed by the liver

ureter (yoo-REET-er): tube that conducts urine to the urinary bladder

urethra (yoo-REE-thruh): tube through which urine passes out of the body

urinary bladder: sac that stores urine

uterus (YOOT-er-uhs): pear-shaped structure in which the early development of a baby takes place

vaccination: process by which an antigen is deliberately introduced to stimulate the immune system

vacuole (VA-kyoo-wohl): large, round sac in the cytoplasm of a cell that stores water, food, enzymes, and other materials

variable: factor being tested in an experiment

variation: difference in members of the same species

vascular plant: plant that contains transporting tubes that carry materials throughout the plant

vein: blood vessel that carries blood to the heart

ventricle: lower chamber of the heart

vertebra (VER-tuh-bruh; plural: vertebrae): bone that makes up a vertebrate's backbone

vertebrate (VER-tuh-briht): animal with a backbone

villus (VIHL-uhs; plural: villi): hairlike projection in the small intestine through which food is absorbed into the bloodstream

virus: tiny particle that contains hereditary material

vitamin: nutrient that helps regulate growth and normal body functioning

vocal cord: tissue in the larynx that vibrates with the passage of air to form sounds

warmblooded: having a constant body temperature

water cycle: flow of water through the environment

water vascular system: system of fluid-filled internal tubes that carry food, oxygen, and wastes in an echinoderm

weight: measure of the attraction between objects due to gravity

white blood cell: blood cell that acts as a defense system against disease

wildlife conservation: conservation of Earth's living things

withdrawal: effect of drug abuse that occurs when a person who is physically dependent on a drug is taken off that drug

xylem (ZIGH-luhm): tubelike plant tissue that carries water and minerals through the plant

yeast: unicellular fungus

zooflagellate (zoh-oh-FLAJ-ehl-int): animallike protist that moves by means of whiplike flagella

zoology: study of animals

zygote: fertilized egg

Index

HIV transmission by, 544
Transpiration, 234
Tree ferns, 214
Tree rings, 228–229
Triceps, 405, 406
Triceratops, 751
Trichinella, 271
Trichinosis, 271
Trichocysts, 161
Tropical rain forests, 662, 730–732, 755
Tropisms, 248–249
Trout, aquaculture of, 743
True-breeding plants, 585
Truffles (fungi), 178, 179
Trunk-nosed mammals, 376–377
Trypsin, 426
Tube feet, 298, 299
Tuberculosis, 547
Tube worms, 254–255
Tumor, 548–549
Tundra biome, 725–726
Turtles, 334, 343–344
Tusks, 374–375
Two-shelled mollusks, 276

Ultrasonic sounds, 381
Umbilical cord, 522, 523
Unicellular organisms, 43, 48, 120–121, 392. *See also* Bacteria (monerans); Protists
fungi, 182, 186–187
green algae, early forms of, 206
Urea, 365, 469, 470, 471
Ureter, 470
Urethra, 470, 518
Urinary bladder, 470
Urine, 470
Uterus, 519, 520, 521, 523

Vaccination, 540, 541
Vaccine, 540, 622–623
Vacuoles, 79, 85, 158, 159, 160–161
Vagina, 519, 523
Valleys as natural barrier, 723
Valve, heart, 441–442, 445
Van Leeuwenhoek, Anton, 70, 71
Variable, 14, 16
Variation, natural selection and, 647–648

Vascular cambium, 228, 229
Vascular plants, 213–216. *See also* Seed plants
Vascular tissue, 213, 224
Veins, 444–445
Ventricles, 441, 442
Vertebrae, 397
Vertebral column, 308, 396, 397
Vertebrates, 257, 260, 261, 308–310. *See also* Amphibians; Birds; Fishes; Mammals; Reptiles
characteristics of chordates, 308
coldblooded vs. warmblooded, 58, 59, 310
embryos of, 640
phylogenetic tree of, 309
Villus(i), 428
Virchow, Rudolph, 70, 71
Viruses, 128, 129, 130–136
computer, 136
defining, 131–132
diseases caused by, 547
humans and, 134–135
interferon and, 537
reproduction of, 133–134
structure of, 130, 132–133
warts caused by, 327
Vision, 493–496
color, 366, 495
Vitamins, 415, 417–418, 428
Vitreous humor, 495
Vocal cords, 465
Volcanic eruptions, 36, 37
Volume, 18, 19, 21
Voluntary muscles. *See* Skeletal muscle
Voyage of the Beagle (Darwin), 657

Wallace, Alfred, 646
Walruses, 374
Warmblooded animals, 58, 59, 310. *See also* Mammals
Wastes, removal of, 468–472
Water, 56, 84–85, 145, 234, 415, 419, 562, 722–723
Water biome, 738–742
estuaries, 741–742
freshwater biome, 740–741
marine biome, 738–739
Water cycle, 705–706
Water-dwelling mammals, 379

Waterfowl, 355, 356
Water-soluble vitamins, 418
Water vapor, 463, 705–706
Water vascular system, 298
Watson, James, 599, 600
Weathering, 636
Web of life, preserving, 764
Webs, spider, 289
Weight, measuring, 20–21
Weight control, 430
Weiner, Alexander S., 450
Wetlands destruction, 758
Whales, 379
White blood cells, 68, 69, 447–448, 506, 536–537, 538
Wildlife, protection of. *See* Conservation of living things
Wildlife census, 689
Wildlife conservation, 765–773
habitat preservation, 767–768
raising reproductive rates, 768–770
setting limits, 766–767
using people power, 771–773
Wilkins, Maurice, 599
Willow Creek Anticline, fossils in, 386, 387
Wilson, Allen, 641
Windpipe, 423, 464
Withdrawal from drugs, 560–561, 564
Womb (uterus), 519
Wood, 228, 229–230
Woody plants, 228–230, 248
Worms, 269–274
flatworms, 270–271
roundworms, 271–272
segmented, 272–273
X chromosome, 597, 605–607
X-ray, 27
Xylem, 224–29

Y chromosome, 597, 605–607
Yeasts, 83, 184, 185, 186–187, 622
Yellow marrow, 399

Zooflagellates, 162–163
Zoology, 9
Zygote, 521

Credits

ers, Inc.; (right) Pictor/Uniphoto **312** (top to bottom) Jeffrey L. Rotman/Peter Arnold, Inc.; Tom McHugh/Steinhart Aqaurium/Photo Researchers, Inc.; Norbert Wu/Peter Arnold, Inc. **313** (left) Ken Lucas/Planet Earth Pictures; (right) Zig Leszczynski/Animals Animals/ Earth Scenes **314** (left) Marty Snyderman; (top right) Tom McHugh/Photo Researchers, Inc.; (bottom right) Robert Maier/Animals Animals/Earth Scenes **315** (top) Breck P. Kent; (bottom) Ken Lucas/Planet Earth Pictures **316** (left) Marty Snyderman; (top right) Tom McHugh/Sea World/Photo Researchers, Inc.; (bottom right) Charles Seaborn/Odyssey Productions **317** (top to bottom) Lynn Funkhouser/Peter Arnold, Inc.; Carl Roessler/Planet Earth Pictures; Jeff Rotman/Peter Arnold, Inc. **318** (top left) Zig Leszczynski/Animals Animals/Earth Scenes; (top right and bottom left) Marty Snyderman; (bottom right) Dr. J. Metzner/Peter Arnold, Inc. **319** (left) Tom McHugh/Steinhart Aquarium/ Photo Researchers, Inc.; (top right) Fred McConnaughey/Photo Researchers, Inc.; (bottom right) Tom McHugh/Photo Researchers, Inc. **320** (left) Dr. Paul A. Zahl/Photo Researchers, Inc.; (right) Tom McHugh/Steinhart Aquarium/Photo Researchers, Inc. **321** (left) R. Andrew Odum/Peter Arnold, Inc.; (top right) Phil A. Dotson/Photo Researchers, Inc.; (bottom right) Jany Sauvanet/Photo Researchers, Inc. **324** (top) David M. Dennis/Tom Stack & Associates; (center left) Hans Pfletschinger/Peter Arnold, Inc.; (center right) Nuridsany et Perennou/Photo Researchers, Inc.; (bottom left) Oxford Scientific Films/Animals Animals/Earth Scenes; (bottom right) David M. Dennis/Tom Stack & Associates **325** (top left) Stephen Dalton/Animals Animals/Earth Scenes; (bottom left) Zig Leszczynski/Animals Animals/Earth Scenes; (right) Suzanne L. Collins and Joseph T. Collins/Photo Researchers, Inc. **326** (left) Dr. E. R. Degginger/Animals Animals/Earth Scenes; (right) and **327** Breck P. Kent/Animals Animals/Earth Scenes **331** Tom McHugh/Steinhart Aquarium/ Photo Researchers, Inc. **334** (top left) Michael Fogden/Animals Animals/Earth Scenes; (top right) Cris Crowley/Tom Stack & Associates; (bottom left) Tom Ulrich/Tony Stone Worldwide/Chicago, Ltd.; (bottom right) Stan Osolinski/Tony Stone Worldwide/Chicago, Ltd. **336** (left to right) Joe B. Blossom/Photo Researchers, Inc.; Nancy Adams/Tom Stack & Associates; Zig Leszczynski/Animals Animals/Earth Scenes **337** Zig Leszczynski/Animals Animals/Earth Scenes **338** (top) Dr. E. R. Degginger/Animals Animals/Earth Scenes; (bottom) Leonard Lee Rue/Tony Stone Worldwide/Chicago, Ltd. **339** (left) L.L.T. Rhodes/Animals Animals/Earth Scenes; (top right) J. Zerschling/Photo Researchers, Inc.; (bottom right) Zig Leszczynski/Animals Animals/ Earth Scenes **340** (left) Zig Leszczynski/Animals Animals/Earth Scenes; (top right) W. H. Muller/Peter Arnold, Inc.; (bottom right) Stephen Dalton/Animals Animals/Earth Scenes **341** (top left) Stephen Dalton/Animals Animals/Earth Scenes; (top right) Bob McKeever/Tom Stack & Associates; (bottom) Jim Brandenburg/Minden Pictures, Inc. **342** (top left) Mike Severns/Tom Stack & Associates; (right) Tom McHugh/Photo Researchers, Inc.; (bottom left) Tom McHugh/Photo Researchers, Inc. **343** (top left) John Mitchell/Photo Researchers, Inc.; (top right) John Cancalosi/Tom Stack & Associates; (bottom left) Tom McHugh/Photo Researchers, Inc.; (bottom right) Jany Sauvanet/Photo Researchers, Inc. **344** (top left) Nicholas Parfitt/Tony Stone Worldwide/Chicago, Ltd.; (top right) Jany Sauvanet/Photo Researchers, Inc.; (center left) Jerry L. Ferrara/Photo Researchers, Inc.; (center right) Tom McHugh/Steinhart Aquarium/Photo Researchers, Inc.; (left top) Brian Parker/Tom Stack & Associates; (left bottom) Fred Whitehead/Animals Animals/Earth Scenes **345** (top) Jonathon Blair/Woodfin Camp & Associates; (center) Nancy Adams/Tom Stack & Associates; (bottom left) Joel Greenstein/ Omni-Photo Communications, Inc.; (bottom right) Tom McHugh/Photo Researchers, Inc. **346** David G. Barker/Tom Stack & Associates **347** Breck P. Kent/Animals Animals/Earth Scenes **348** (left to right) Dr. E. R. Degginger/Animals Animals/Earth Scenes; Stouffer Productions/Animals Animals/Earth Scenes; Fritz Prenzel/Tony Stone Worldwide/ Chicago, Ltd. **349** (top) Kevin Schafer/Martha Hill/Tom Stack & Associates; (inset, top) Jerome Wexler/Photo Researchers, Inc.; (inset, bottom) Tom and Pat Leeson/Photo Researchers, Inc.; (center left) Chip and Jill Isenhart/Tom Stack & Associates; (center right) Bud Lehnhausen/Photo Researchers, Inc.; (bottom) Calvin Larsen/Photo Researchers, Inc. **350** (top) David C. Fritts/Animals Animals/Earth Scenes; (bottom) H. A. Thornhill, National Audubon Society/Photo Researchers, Inc. **351** (top) Anna Zuckerman/Tom Stack & Associates; (center) Dan Guravich/Photo Researchers, Inc.; (bottom left) Scott Camazine/Photo Researchers, Inc.; (bottom right) Charles Palek/Animals Animals/Earth Scenes **352** (top left) Richard Kolar/Animals Animals/Earth Scenes; (top right) John Garrett/Tony Stone Worldwide/Chicago, Ltd.; (center) Bruce Davidson/Animals Animals/Earth Scenes; (bottom) Ron Austing/Photo Researchers, Inc. **353** (left to right) John Gerlach/Animals Animals/Earth Scenes; Jeffrey L. Rotman; Hans and Judy Beste/Animals Animals/Earth Scenes **354** (top left) Arthur Gloor/Animals Animals/Earth Scenes; (bottom left) Hans Reinhard/Tony Stone Worldwide/ Chicago, Ltd.; (right) Alan G. Nelson/Animals Animals/Earth Scenes **355** (top right) Harold E. Wilson/Animals Animals/Earth Scenes; (left) Jany Sauvanet/Photo Researchers, Inc.; (bottom right) John Chellman/Animals Animals/Earth Scenes **356** (top left) Manfred Danneger/Tony Stone Worldwide/Chicago, Ltd.; (top right) Jean-Luc Cherville/Tony Stone Worldwide/Chicago, Ltd.; (center) Tom McHugh/Photo Researchers, Inc.; (bottom left) Frans Lanting/Minden Pictures, Inc.; (bottom right) R. D. Estes/Photo Researchers, Inc. **357** (left) Frans Lanting/Minden Pictures, Inc.; (right) Jack Vartoogian **361** Tom Evans/Photo Researchers, Inc. **362, 363** Jeff Foott Productions **364** (top) Warren and Genny Garst/Tom Stack & Associates; (bottom left) Jeff Lepore/Photo Researchers, Inc.; (bottom right) Stephen J. Kraseman/DRK Photo **365** (left) Phil Dotson/Uniphoto; (right) Dominique Braud/Tom Stack & Associates **366** Jerry L. Ferrara/Photo Researchers, Inc. **368** (top) Taronga Zoo, Sydney/Tom McHugh/Photo Researchers, Inc.; (bottom) Tom McHugh/Photo Researchers, Inc. **369** (top) Dave Watts/Tom Stack & Associates; (bottom left) Dave Watts/Tom Stack & Associates; (bottom right) John Cancalosi/Tom Stack & Associates **370** (top) Tony Stone Images; (bottom left) Brian Parker/Tom Stack & Associates; (bottom right) Dr. E. R. Degginger/Animals Animals/Earth Scenes **372** (top left) Joe McDonald/Animals Animals/Earth Scenes; (top right) Rod Planck/Tom Stack & Associates; (bottom left) C. O. Harris/Photo Researchers, Inc.; (bottom right) Leonard Lee Rue III/Tom Stack & Associates **373** (top) Stephen Dalton/Animals Animals/Earth Scenes; (bottom) Oxford Scientific Films/Animals Animals/Earth Scenes **374** (top left) Gerard Lacz/Peter Arnold, Inc.; (top right) Pat and Tom Leeson/Photo Researchers, Inc.; (bottom left) Tim Davis/Photo Researchers, Inc.; (bottom right) Leonard Lee Rue III/Photo Researchers, Inc. **375** Ira Block/Image Bank **376** (top left) John Cancalosi/Peter Arnold, Inc.; (top right) Frederick J. Dodd/Peter Arnold, Inc.; (center) Warren Garst/Tom Stack & Associates; (bottom) Nicholas Parfitt/Tony Stone Images **377** (left) Thomas Kitchin/Tom Stack & Associates; (right) Frans Lanting/Minden Pictures, Inc. **378** (top to bottom) Karl Maslowski/Photo Researchers, Inc.; Leonard Lee Rue III/Uniphoto; John Cancalosi/Tom Stack & Associates **379** (top) Thomas Kitchin/Tom Stack & Associates; (center) Robert J. Herko/Image Bank; (left) D. Holden Bailey/Tom Stack & Associates; (right) James D. Watt/Animals Animals/Earth Scenes **380** (top to bottom) Michael Dick/Animals Animals/Earth Scenes; Charlie Palek/Animals Animals/Earth Scenes; Evelyn Gallardo/Peter Arnold, Inc. **381** (left) Tony Stone Images; (right) Stephen Dalton/Oxford Scientific Films/Animals Animals/Earth Scenes **385** C. C. Lockwood/Animals Animals/Earth Scenes **386** Phil Schofield **387** Copyright Douglas Henderson **388** (top) David Madison Photography; (bottom) Chris Jones/The Stock Market **389** David Madison/Duomo Photography, Inc. **390, 391** Leonard Kamsler **392** (left) M. P. Kahl/DRK Photo; (right) David M. Phillips/Visuals Unlimited **394** (top left) Bruce Iverson/Visuals Unlimited; (top right) Cabsioo/Visuals Unlimited; (center) Robert E. Daemmrich/Tony Stone Images; (bottom left) Dwight Kuhn Photography; (bottom right) Don W. Fawcett/Visuals Unlimited **396** Seltzer/OSU/Dan McCoy/Rainbow **398** Biophotos Associates/Photo Researchers, Inc. **399** From *Tissues And Organs: A Text-Atlas of Soanning Electron Microscopy* by Richard G. Kessel and Randy H. Kardon, Copyright © 1979 by W. H. Freeman and Company, Reprinted by permission **400** (top) Prof. Aaron Polllack/Science Photo Library/Photo Researchers, Inc.; (bottom) Tim Davis/David Madison Photography **401** (top) © Lennart Nilsson, *Behold Man*, Little Brown and Company; (bottom) © Lennart Nilsson, *The Incredible Machine*, National Geographic Society, Boehringer Ingelheim Internationl GmbH. **403** Brooks Dodge/Sports File **404** (left to right) Eric Grave/Photo Researchers, Inc.; Triach/Visuals Unlimited; Michael Abbey/Photo Researchers, Inc. **411** Biophoto Associates/Science Source/Photo Researchers, Inc. **412, 413** NASA **414** (right) United States Department of Agriculture; (left) Gary Buss/FPG International **416** (left) Myrleen Ferguson/Photoedit; (right) Don & Pat Valenti/F/Stop Pictures, Inc. **419** Guido Alberto Rossi/The Image Bank **422** Howard Sochurek, Inc. **423** (left) Omikron/Science Source/ Photo Re-searchers, Inc.; (right) © Lennart Nilsson, *Behold Man*, Little Brown and Company **424** L. V. Bergman & Associates **425** © Lennart Nilsson, *The Incredible Machine*, National Geographic Society, Boehringer Ingelheim International GmbH **428** © Lennart Nilsson, *Behold Man*, Little Brown and Company; (bottom) © Lennart Nilsson, *The Incredible Machine*, National Geographic Society, Boehringer Ingelheim Internationl GmbH. (bottom) and **429** L. V. Bergman & Associates **430** (top) Tony Duffy/Allsport; (bottom) Robert Rathe/Folio, Inc. **431** Derik Murray/Image Bank **435** Nancy Coplon **436, 437** David Wagner/Phototake **438** CNRI/Science Photo Library/ Photo Researchers, Inc. **440** © Lennart Nilsson, *The Incredible Machine*, National Geographic Society, Boehringer Ingelheim Internationl GmbH **442** (top) Phillippe Plailly/Science Photo Library/Photo Researchers, Inc.; (bottom) VU/SIU/Visuals Unlimited **444** © Lennart Nilsson, *The Incredible Machine*, National Geographic Society, Boehringer Ingelheim Internationl GmbH **447** (top to bottom) Bill Longcore/Photo Researchers, Inc.; CNRI/Science Photo Library/Photo Researchers, Inc.; © Lennart Nilsson, *The Incredible Machine*, National Geographic Society, Boehringer Ingelheim Internationl GmbH **448, 450, 451, 452** © Lennart Nilsson, *The Incredible Machine*, National Geographic Society, Boehringer Ingelheim Internationl GmbH **453** Alexander Tsiaras/Science Source/Photo Researchers, Inc. **454** Simon Fraser/Hexam General/Science Photo Library/ Photo Researchers, Inc. **456** Ken Karp **459** Dan McCoy/Rainbow **460, 461** Tim Davis/Duomo Photography, Inc. **462** (left) Michael Fogden/DRK Photo; (right) Peter Veit/DRK Photo **464** (top) © Lennart Nilsson, *The Incredible Machine*, National Geographic Society, Boehringer Ingelheim Internationl GmbH; (bottom) Chet Childs/Tony Stone Images **465** Art Siegel **466** © Lennart Nilsson, *The Incredible Machine*, National Geographic Society, Boehringer Ingelheim Internationl GmbH **467** David York/Medichrome/The Stock Shop **469** L. V. Bergman & Associates **470** CNRI/Science Photo Library/Photo Researchers, Inc. **472** (top) Eric Reynolds/Adventure Photo; (bottom) © Lennart Nilsson, *Behold Man*, Little Brown and Company **478, 479** Ed Bock/The Stock Market **480** (top) David Madison/Dùomo Photography, Inc.; (bottom left) Mary Kate Denny/Photoedit; (bottom right) Bob Daemmrich Photography **481** (left) Johnny Johnson/DRK Photo; (right) Bob Daemmrich/The Image Works **482** Michael Abbey/ Photo Researchers, Inc. **483** © Lennart Nilsson, *The Incredible Machine*, National Geographic Society, Boehringer Ingelheim Internationl GmbH. **484** CNRI/Science Photo Library/Photo Researchers, Inc. **486** Bill Longcore/ Photo Researchers, Inc. **489** CNRI/Science Photo Library/Photo Researchers, Inc. **490** © Lennart Nilsson, *The Incredible Machine*, National Geographic Society, Boehringer Ingelheim Internationl GmbH. **493** (left) Randy Trine/DRK Photo; (right) Andrew McClenaghan/Science Photo Library/Photo Researchers, Inc. **494** © Lennart Nilsson, *Behold Man*, Little, Brown and Company **495** (top) Jesse Simmons Photo; (bottom left) © Lennart Nilsson, *Behold Man*, Little, Brown and Company; (bottom right) © Lennart Nilsson, *The Incredible Machine*, National Geographic Society, Boehringer Ingelheim Internationl GmbH. **497** © Lennart Nilsson, *Behold Man*, Little, Brown and Company **498** (top) © Lennart Nilsson, *Behold Man*, Little, Brown and Company; (bottom) © Lennart Nilsson, *The Incredible Machine*, National Geographic Society, Boehringer Ingelheim Internationl GmbH. **499** (top left) John Zoiner/Stock Boston, Inc.; (top right) Hank Morgan/Rainbow; (bottom) Garry Gay/Image Bank **500** (top) © Lennart Nilsson, *Behold Man*, Little, Brown and Company; (bottom) Nathan Benn/Woodfin Camp & Associates **502** (top) Synaptek Scientific Products, Inc./Science Photo Library/Photo Researchers, Inc.; (bottom) Bill Redic **506** © Lennart Nilsson, *The Incredible Machine*, National Geographic Society, Boehringer Ingelheim Internationl GmbH. **508** Martin M. Rotker **514, 515** Michael Tcherevkoff/Image Bank **516** David W. Hamilton/Image Bank **517** (left) Dr. Ram Verna/Phototake; (top) John Giannicchi/Science Source/Photo Researchers, Inc.; (bottom) Dr. G. Schatten/Science Photo Library/Photo Researchers, Inc. **521** Bob Daemmrich/The Image Works **523** (top) Howard Sochurek, Inc.; (bottom) Mickey Pfleger **524** (top) Niki Mareschal/Image Bank; (bottom) Edward Lettau/FPG International **525** (top and bottom right) Bob Daemmrich Photography; (center) W. Rosin Malecki/Photoedit; (bottom left) Bill Hess/Running Dog Publications **526** Don Hamerman/Folio, Inc. **527** Karen Leeds/The Stock Market **532, 533** Larry Mulvehill/Photo Researchers, Inc. **534** (left) K. G. Murti/Visuals Unlimited; (right) © Lennart Nilsson, National Geographic Society **535, 536** © Lennart Nilsson, *The Incredible Machine*, National Geographic Society, Boehringer Ingelheim International GmbH **537** Gabe Palmer/The Stock Market **538** (top) E. D Getzoff, J. A. Tainer, A. J. Olson of the Scripps Research Institute; (bottom) Lennart Nilsson, National Geographic Society, © Boehringer Ingelheim International GmbH **540** Bob Daemmrich/The Image Works **542** (top left) Manfred Kage/Peter Arnold, Inc.; (top right) Robert Dudzic/F/Stop Pictures, Inc.; (bottom left) Dick Canby/DRK Photo; (bottom right) Dr. Jeremy Burgess/Science Photo Library/Photo Researchers, Inc. **543** (left) Lennart Nilsson, National Geographic Society, © Boehringer Ingelheim International GmbH; (right) Stuart Franklin/Sygma **544** (top) Lennart Nilsson, National Geographic Society, © Boehringer Ingelheim International GmbH; (bottom) Susan Van Etten/Photoedit **545** CNRI/Science Photo Library/Photo Researchers, Inc. **546** (top, left to right) Don Smetzer/Tony Stone Images; © Lennart Nilsson, *The Incredible Machine*, National Geographic Society; G. I. Bernard/Animals Animals/Earth Scenes; (bottom) Dr. Willy Burgdorfer/National Institutes of Health, Rocky Mountain Lab **547** (top) Lennart Nilsson, National Geographic Society, © Boehringer Ingelheim International GmbH; (bottom) CNRI/Science Photo Library/Photo Researchers, Inc. **548** (top) © Lou Lainey/1984 Discover Publications; (bottom) and **549** Lennart Nilsson, National Geographic Society, © Boehringer Ingelheim International GmbH **550** Lee Wardle/Sports File **551** Tom & Pat Leeson/Photo Researchers, Inc. **556, 557** Bobby Holland/Reader's Digest Foundation **558** (left) Michael P. Gadomski/Photo Researchers, Inc.; (right) Benn Mitchell/Image Bank **559** (top) The University Museum, University of Pennsylvania; (bottom) Ken Karp Photography **560** (left) Tony Savino/Sipa Press; (right) Bruce Delis/Gamma-Liaison, Inc. **561** (top) Richard Hutchings/Photo Researchers, Inc.; (bottom) Granger Collection **563** A. Glauberman/Science Source/Photo Researchers, Inc. **564** Stacy Pick/Stock Boston, Inc. **565** Richard Hutchings/Photo Researchers, Inc. **566** © Lennart Nilsson, *The Incredible Machine*, National Geographic Society, Boehringer Ingelheim International GmbH **567** Calvin Larsen/Photo Researchers, Inc. **568, 570** (top) Ken Karp; (center) Edward S. Ross/Phototake; (bottom) Howard Sochurek, Inc. **571** Fred Lombardi/Photo Researchers, Inc. **572** David Alan Harvey/Woodfin Camp & Associates **573** (top left) Walter H. Hodge/Peter Arnold, Inc.; (top right) Michael Hardy/Woodfin Camp & Associates; (bottom) National Institutes of Health **577** Wesley Bocxe/Photo Researchers, Inc. **578** Homer Sykes/Woodfin Camp & Associates **579** D. Gaywood/Gamma-Liaison, Inc. **580** Ronnie Kaufman/The Stock Market **581** Dr. E. R. Degginger **582, 583** Ron Kimball Studios **584** The Bettmann Archive **585** Jane Grushow/Grant Heilman Photography **592** Barry L. Runk/Grant Heilman Photography **595** (top) David M. Phillips/Visuals Unlimited; (bottom) Dr. Tony Brain/Science Photo Library/Photo Researchers, Inc. **597** Dr. E. R. Degginger/Animals Animals/Earth Scenes **598** (top) Barry L. Runk/Grant Heilman Photography; (bottom) Runk/Schoenberger/Grant Heilman Photography **600** (left) Cold Spring Harbor Laboratory Archives; (right) Erich Hartmann/Magnum Photos, Inc. **602** (top) Dan McCoy/Rainbow; (bottom) © Lennart Nilsson, *The Incredible Machine*, National Geographic Society, Boehringer Ingelheim Internationl GmbH. **603** Michel Tcherevkoff/The Image Bank **604** Stanley Fleger/Visuals Unlimited **607** William McCoy/Rainbow **608** Charles West/The Stock Market **609** The Bettmann Archive **613** Ron Kimball Studios **614, 615** NIBSC/Science Photo Library/Photo Researchers, Inc. **616** (left) David W. Hamilton/Image Bank; (right) John Colwell/ Grant Heilman Photography **617** (left) R. Van Nostrand/Photo Researchers, Inc.; (right) George D. Lepp/Bio-Tec Images **618** (left) Steven Dahlgren/ The Stock Market; (right) Wayne Lankinen/Bruce Coleman, Inc.; (bottom) Jeff Lepore/Photo Re-searchers, Inc. **619** Ron Kimball Studios **620** (top to bottom) Keith V. Wood/University of California at San Diego; Jon Gordon/Phototake; Ted Spiegel/ Black Star **621** P. A. McTurk, University of Leicester & D. Parker/Science Photo Library/Photo Researchers, Inc. **622** (top) David M. Phillips/Visuals Unlimited; (bottom) Dr. Jeremy Burgess/Science Photo Library/Photo Researchers, Inc. **623** (top to bottom) Myrleen Ferguson/Photoedit; Omikron/Science Source/ Photo Researchers, Inc.; Norm Thomas/Photo Researchers, Inc. **624** Jim Tuten/Black Star **625** Alabama Agricultural Experiment Station/Auburn University **630, 631** Tom McHugh/Photo Researchers, Inc. **634** (top to bottom) Jonathan Blair/Woodfin Camp & Associates; T. A. Wiewandt/DRK Photo; Norman Tomalin/Bruce Coleman, Inc. **637** Ken Karp **639** Michael Fogden/ DRK Photo **640** Robert & Linda Mitchell Photography **641** Frans Lanting/Minden Pictures, Inc. **643** Cleveland Museum of Natural History **644** © Margo Crabtree/Courtesy Musee de l'Homme **645** (left) Dr. E. R. Degginger/Animals Animals/ Earth Scenes; (right) Frans Lanting/Minden Pictures, Inc. **646** (top) Zig Leszczynski/Animals Animals/Earth Scenes; (bottom) Wolfgang Kaehler **647** Stephen J. Krasemann/DRK Photo **648** Breck P. Kent **650** Joe McDonald/Animals Animals/Earth Scenes **655** Frank Fournier/Woodfin Camp & Associates **656** Kimberly Butler **657** (left) © Tony Bucci/1990 Discover Magazine; (right) Journal of Comparative Neurology, F. Nottebohm, T. M. Stokes, C. M. Leonard, Copyright © 1976 reprinted by permission of Wiley-Liss, a division of John Wiley and Sons, Inc. **658** (top left) J. H. Robinson/Animals Animals/Earth Scenes; (bottom left) Julia Sims/Peter Arnold, Inc.; (right) Larry Ulrich/DRK Photo **659** Tom Bledsoe/DRK Photo **660, 661** Milton Rand/Tom Stack & Associates **661** Milton Rand/Tom Stack & Associates **662** (top left) P. David/Planet Earth Pictures; (bottom left) Michael Fogden/Animals Animals/Earth Scenes; (right) Kjell B. Sandved **663** (top) Zig Leszczynski/Animals Animals/Earth Scenes; (bottom) Kjell B. Sandved **664** D. Cavagnaro/DRK Photo **665** (top) Scott Blackman/Tom Stack & Associates; (bottom) Breck P. Kent **666** (top to bottom) Frans Lanting/Minden Pictures, Inc.; John Cancalosi/DRK Photo; Frans Lanting/Minden Pictures, Inc. **668** (top) Breck P. Kent; (bottom) John Shaw/Tom Stack & Associates **669** (top left) Terry Domico/Earth Images; (top right) Tim Davis/Photo Researchers, Inc.; (bottom) Jeffrey L. Rotman **670** S. Nielsen/Imagery **671** (top and center) T. A. Wiewandt/DRK Photo; (bottom) John Cancalosi/DRK Photo **674** (left) Hans and Judy Beste/Animals Animals/Earth Scenes; (right) F. Gohier/Photo Researchers, Inc. **675** Stouffer Productions/ Animals Animals/Earth Scenes **676** (top to bottom) Frans Lanting/Minden Pictures, Inc.; S. Nielsen/ DRK Photo; Wilbur Samuel Tripp **677** (background) Scott Camazine/Photo Researchers, Inc.; (silhouette) Timothy Eagan/Woodfin Camp & Associates; (left center) Timothy Eagan/Woodfin Camp & Associates; (right center) Scott Camazine/Photo Researchers, Inc.; (bottom right) Lilia I. DeGuzman/USDA **678** (top) Lee Lyon/Survival Anglia; (bottom) Peter Ward/Bruce Coleman, Inc. **679** (left) Charles Seaborn/Woodfin Camp & Associates; (right) Stephen J. Krasemann/DRK Photo **680** (top left) Dwight Kuhn Photography; (bottom left) Ashod Francis/Animals Animals/Earth Scenes; (right) Stephen J. Krasemann/DRK Photo **681** (left) Stephen Dalton/Natural History Photographic Agency; (top right) Michael Fogden/DRK Photo; (bottom right) Gary Milburn/Tom Stack & Associates **682** (top) Jim Brandenburg/Minden Pictures, Inc.; (bottom) Wayne Lynch/DRK Photo **683** (top left and center) Michael Fogden/DRK Photo; (top right) Stephen J. Krasemann/DRK Photo; (center right) David Denning/Earth Images; (bottom right) T. A. Wiewandt/DRK Photo **684** (left) Patti Murray/Animals Animals/Earth Scenes; (center and right) Michael Fogden/DRK Photo **685** (top) M. P. Kahl/DRK Photo; (bottom) Stephen J. Krasemann/DRK Photo **686** (top left) Superstock; (top right) Kevin Schafer/Tom Stack & Associates; (center) James Mason/Black Star; (bottom) Wolfgang Kaehler **687** (top) J. Langevin/Sygma; (bottom left) Craig Aurness/Woodfin Camp & Associates; (bottom right) John Gerlach/Animals Animals/Earth Scenes **689** Dwight Kuhn Photography **690** Ken Karp **693** Gary W. Griffen/Animals Animals/Earth Scenes **694, 695** Jeff Foott/DRK Photo **696** (top and right) Thomas A. Wiewandt, Ph.D.; (bottom left) Frans Lanting/Minden Pictures, Inc. **697** (left) Dr. E. R. Degginger/Picture Perfect; (right) Kjell B. Sandved **698** Paul Fusco/Magnum Photos, Inc. **699** (left) Dwight Kuhn Photography; (right) Gary Milburn/Tom Stack & Associates **700** (top left) F. Stuart Westmorland/Tom Stack & Associates; (bottom left) Zig Leszczynski/Breck P. Kent; (top right) Joe McDonald/Animals Animals/Earth Scenes; (bottom right) Robert & Linda Mitchell Photography **701** Dr. E. R. Degginger/Animals Animals/Earth Scenes **702** (left) Roger Garwood/Colorific; (right) Johnny Johnson/DRK Photo **703** (left) Frans Lanting/Minden Pictures, Inc.; (top right) Breck P. Kent; (bottom right) Thomas A. Wiewandt, Ph.D. **704** Lick Observatory, University of California **705** (left) Breck P. Kent; (top right) NASA; (bottom right) Robert & Linda Mitchell Photography **707** Pat Crowe/Animals Animals/Earth Scenes; **709** (top left) Dan McCoy/R. Langridge/Rainbow; (top right) Dwight Kuhn Photography; (bottom) Uniphoto **710** (left) Doug Wechsler/Animals Animals/Earth Scenes; (right) Dwight Kuhn Photography **711** Breck P. Kent **712** Jeff Foott Productions **713** Gary Milburn/Tom Stack & Associates **717** Vince Streano/The Stock Market **718, 719** Wolfgang Kaehler **720** (top) David Macdonald/Oxford Scienctific Films/Animals Animals/Earth Scenes; (bottom left) Frans Lanting/Minden Pictures, Inc.; (bottom right) Nancy Adams **721** (top) Jack Swenson/Tom Stack & Associates; (bottom left) Ed Degginger/Animals Animals/Earth Scenes; (bottom right) Zig Leszczynski/Animals Animals/Earth Scenes **722** Frans Lanting/Minden Pictures, Inc. **723** (top) Breck P. Kent; (bottom) Jeff Foott Productions **725** (top and bottom left) Stephen J. Krasemann/DRK Photo; (bottom right) Wolfgang Kaehler **726** (top) Chase Swift/Tom Stack & Associates; (bottom) Stephen J.Krasemann/DRK Photo **727** (top) Wolfgang Kaehler; (bottom) S. Nielsen/DRK Photo **728** (top) Leonard Lee Rue III/Uniphoto; (bottom left) Joseph R. Pearce/DRK Photo; (bottom right) Stephen J. Krasemann/DRK Photo **729** (top, left to right) Jeff

Foott/DRK Photo; Wayne Lankinen/DRK Photo; Stephen J. Krasemann/DRK Photo; (center) Robert Frerck/Odyssey Productions; (bottom) Stephen J. Krasemann/DRK Photo **730** (left) Zig Leszczynski/Animals Animals/Earth Scenes; (right) Stephen J. Krasemann/DRK Photo **731** (top) Michael Fogden/DRK Photo; (bottom) Breck P. Kent **732** (top) Michael Fogden/DRK Photo; (bottom) Wolfgang Kaehler **734** (top left) Frans Lanting/Minden Pictures, Inc.; (top right) Thomas A. Wiewandt, Ph.D.; (center) Kjell B. Sandved; (bottom) Wolfgang Kaehler **735** (left) Wolfgang Kaehler; (right) Breck P. Kent **736** (left) Patti Murray/Animals Animals/Earth Scenes; (right) Robert Freck/Odyssey Productions **737** (left) Frans Lanting/Minden Pictures, Inc.; (right) Anthony Bannister/Animals Animals/Earth Scenes; (bottom) Wolfgang Kaehler **738** (top) Breck P. Kent; (bottom left) Lewis Trusty/Animals Animals/Earth Scenes; (bottom right) Jeff Foott Productions **739** (top left) Paul Humann/Jeffrey L. Rotman; (top right) Doug Perrine/DRK Photo; (center) Frans Lanting/Minden Pictures, Inc.; (bottom) Peter David/Planet Earth Pictures **740** (top) Dwight Kuhn Photography; (center) Johnny Johnson/DRK Photo;

(bottom left) Robert P. Comport/Animals Animals/Earth Scenes; (bottom right) Zig Leszczynski/Animals Animals/Earth Scenes **741** (left) Breck P. Kent; (right) Dan McCoy/Rainbow **742** (left) Fred Whitehead/Animals Animals/Earth Scenes; (right) Timothy A. Murphy/Image Bank **743** (left) Thomas A. Wiewandt, Ph.D.; (right) Ed Degginger/Animals Animals/Earth Scenes **747** Breck P. Kent **748, 749** Stephen J. Krasemann/DRK Photo **750** (top) The dodo reconstructed (1990) - Based on research work by Dr. Andrew Kitchener, National Museums of Scotland, © National Museums of Scotland; (bottom) Illustration by John Tenniel from *Alice in Wonderland and Through the Looking Glass* by Lewis Carroll **751** Stephen J. Krasemann/DRK Photo **752** (top left and bottom right) Frans Lanting/Minden Pictures, Inc.; (top right) Robert & Linda Mitchell Photography; (bottom left) Stephen J. Krasemann/DRK Photo **753** (left) Don & Pat Valenti/DRK Photo; (top right) John Stern/Animals Animals/Earth Scenes; (bottom right) Ron Kimball Studios **754** (top) Doug Wechsler/Animals Animals/Earth Scenes; (bottom) Dr. Nigel Smith/Animals Animals/Earth Scenes **755** (top left) Dan McCoy/Rainbow; (top

right) Wolfgang Kaehler; (bottom left) Tom Bean/DRK Photo; (bottom right) Frans Lanting/Minden Pictures, Inc. **756** (top left) Kevin Schafer/Tom Stack & Associates; (top right) Michael Fogden/DRK Photo; (center left) Gary Milburn/Tom Stack & Associates; (bottom right) Kevin Schafer/Tom Stack & Associates; (bottom left) Richard Kolar/Animals Animals/Earth Scenes **757** (top) Alain Keller/Sygma; (bottom) Richard Hoffmann/Sygma **758** (center) Dan McCoy/Rainbow; (left) Stephen J. Krasemann/DRK Photo; (top) Tom Bean; (right) Patricia Caulfield/Animals Animals/Earth Scenes **759** Frans Lanting/Minden Pictures, Inc. **760** (top left) Fred Whitehead/Animals Animals/Earth Scenes; (top right) Gordon Rodda/Photo Resource Hawaii; (bottom) Johnny Johnson/Animals Animals/Earth Scenes **761** (top left) Zigy Kaluzny; (top right) Frans Lanting/Minden Pictures, Inc.; (center) Jeff Foott Productions; (bottom) Wolfgang Kaehler **762** (top) John Cancalosi/DRK Photo; (bottom) Frans Lanting/Minden Pictures, Inc. **763** (top) Larry Lefever/Grant Heilman Photography; (bottom) Robert Frerck/Odyssey Productions **764** Annie Griffiths/DRK Photo **765** Chase Swift/Tom Stack & Associates

766 Lowell Georgia/Photo Researchers, Inc. **767** (top left) Tom & Pat Leeson/DRK Photo; (top right) Kjell B. Sandved; (center) Mark Boulton/Photo Researchers, Inc.; (bottom) San Francisco Zoological Society **768** (top and right) David Muench Photography, Inc.; (left) Robert C. Simpson/Tom Stack & Associates **769** (left) Cincinnati Zoo; (right) and **770** (top) Ron Garrison/Zoological Society of San Diego; (center) Belinda Wright/DRK Photo; (bottom) John Chellman/Animals Animals/Earth Scenes **771** (top left) Gary Milburn/Tom Stack & Associates; (top right) Robert & Linda Mitchell Photography; (bottom) J. Robinson/Animals Animals/Earth Scenes **772** (left) Baker/Greenpeace; (right) Rick Falco/Sipa Press **777** P. La Tourrette/VIREO/The Academy of Natural Sciences of Philadelphia **778** Duncan Willets/Camerapix **779** (top) Frans Lanting/Minden Pictures, Inc.; (bottom) Belinda Wright/DRK Photo **780** Brian Parker/Tom Stack & Associates **781** Pat and Tom Leeson/Photo Researchers, Inc. **857** Zig Leszczynski/Animals Animals/Earth Scenes